FROMMER'S

DOLLARWISE GUIDE TO CRUISES

Including Alaska, Canada, the Caribbean, Hawaii, Mexico, Panama, and the U.S.

By Marylyn Springer and Don A. Schultz

1985-86 Edition

Published by Frommer/Pasmantier Publishers
A Division of Simon & Schuster, Inc.
1230 Avenue of the Americas
New York, NY 10020

ISBN 0-671-49904-1

Manufactured in the United States of America

CONTENTS

MAPS & ILLUSTRATIONS

A DISCLAIMER: Although every effort was made to ensure the accuracy of the prices and travel information appearing in this book, it should be kept in mind that prices do fluctuate in the course of time, and that information does change under the impact of the varied and volatile factors that affect the travel industry.

Introduction

DOLLARWISE GUIDE TO CRUISES

BLACK VELVET NIGHTS that slide as smoothly off the memory as vintage cognac. . . . Diamond days, bright and brilliant and everlasting.

Ah, cruises. Instant imagery, of . . . flashbulbs and champagne corks popping . . . of confetti in your hair and stars in your eyes . . . of chandeliers glittering, brass shining, and teak deck gleaming . . . of white-gloved stewards pouring tea . . . of organdy dresses fluttering in the sea breeze and dancing in the starlight.

Across the water comes the deep, unmistakable bellow of the ship's great whistle, signaling departure to the silvery beaches of the Caribbean Sea, the icy-blue depths of massive Alaskan glaciers, the pastel loveliness of the Mexican Riviera.

Can all this be yours?

Can it be you dining on seven-course dinners, leaning on the rail as emerald isles slip by and a silver wake streams out behind you slashing through sapphire waters like a river of shooting stars?

Can it be you dancing, dining, and dreaming the shimmering days away?

Of course it can be you, and to prove it, hear this: last year 1.6 million other dreamers just like you found their dream boat—and sailed away on it.

These days, thanks to the power of competition, this heady world, once the milieu of the powerful and full-pocketed, is available to the slimmest of wallets.

Now travelers everywhere are discovering the magic of multicourse meals followed by block-long midnight buffets, of 24-hour room service, high tea, mornings by the pool, afternoon naps, saunas and spas, rum punch at sunset, skeet shooting and deck tennis, dancing until dawn, glaciers by moonlight and beaches glittering in the sun.

The cruise vacation has become so popular that it has spawned an explosion of new cruise ships, which in the next few years will have added 10,000 berths to the present fleet! Never in recent history have the shipbuilders of Europe and America been so busy, and never have so many fleets grown so fast.

So popular has the cruise vacation become, in fact, that cruise lines themselves are calling it the "Cruise Revolution."

1. The Reason Why

"So what's all the fuss about?" you ask. Why are people taking to the sea in unprecedented numbers, dropping out of land vacations like human lemmings to sign up for floating resorts?

Why? Well, because it's entertaining, amusing, casual, formal, simple, complex, energetic, lazy, and most of all because it's rich in experience and cheaper in bankbook than ever.

In fact, in a recent poll of some happy cruisers the reasons they cited for taking to the high seas were:

- It's lazy and relaxing.
- There are no travel frustrations.
- It's an escape from the telephone and stress.
- It makes you feel like a millionaire.
- The sea is beautiful and fascinating.
- There's a feeling of shared adventure.
- It's fun for couples.
- It's comfortable for singles.
- You get good value for your money, whether you pay a lot—or a little—for your cabin.
- There's something to do every minute.
- There's lots of evening entertainment.
- Kids like cruises.
- You meet new friends.
- It's romantic and "alone" for honeymooners.
- Everyone's in a good mood.
- There's an activity to suit everyone.
- You discover new places.

There's a revolt afoot, all right, but in this cruise revolution the guerrillas are shooting mai-tais, lobbing nothing more lethal than a volleyball, and killing only ennui.

And why not? Don't you deserve it?

Surely, you know what we mean. You've been living, or should I say, surviving, in the age of the nouveau poor, the decade of no decadence.

Year after drab and dreary year you've togged out in crummy cutoffs and shoveled down Quickdraw hamburgers. You've endured airplanes packed so tightly that you once drank the cola of the guy next to you. You've made do with resorts that selected their employees from Surly Anonymous and their decor from Pink Plastic Inc.

Ah, but in your soul . . . in your *soul,* life was elegant. In your imagination the tuna casserole was filet of sole Véronique. In your dreams that week's vacation you spent painting the house was seven days on deck with a cold daiquiri and a warm companion.

Yes, we've all survived these last couple of years, decades maybe, telling ourselves that when the time was right, we'd certainly owe it to ourselves.

Well . . . the time is right.

2. Return with Us to the Days of Yesteryear

For those of us born *sans* silver spoon the time could not be righter. Supply and demand are for once making something less expensive than ever before—and that something is a cruise.

Less expensive they may be, but less expansive they most certainly are not. On one of today's floating resorts you can live every bit as royally as merchant princes of old, reliving in lovely formal evenings (or lovely informal ones) all the glitz and glamor that has for so long been associated with sea voyages.

Ah, the history of it all.

Beautiful women with glittering diamonds and fluttering fans, dashing gentlemen in tuxedos and wing collars . . . wealth and power, posturing and pampering and posh . . . a month or so of bracing sea air, physician-prescribed, of course . . . royalty and the regal, coquettes and crowned heads, Hollywood and the highborn, mixing ever-so-elegantly on ships designed to provide a suitably glittering backdrop for the glitterati.

Those were the days, my friend—days of fine wine and daily roses, days in which transoceanic cruises elevated travel from mere mundane movement to an art form, posh and elegant days that offered the fortunate few an opportunity to change scenery without sacrificing servitude—a truly moveable feast.

POSH IS BORN: Indeed that very word "posh" is a seaborn creation: **P**ort **O**ut **S**tarboard **H**ome, P & O Cruise Lines' designation for the choicest cabins on months-long voyages that were once a required course in the University of Life Above-Stairs.

Elegant cruising got its start for the most mundane of reasons: money. Shipping magnates looking for a way to make money from transoceanic cargo liners during slow winter seasons dreamed up a plan to send *people* on the ship. One of the first such voyages occurred as long ago as 1891, although P & O, the world's oldest line, had begun excursions from England as far back as 1844 in wooden paddle-steamers.

Back then, more than a century ago when ships were the only way to cross the vast expanses of water that separate continents, it took weeks and weeks to get across the Atlantic.

Communication has inspired many a tumultuous change in the history of mankind and communication played a vital part in the cruise industry too. Among the first goads to creation of speedy sailing ships was, of all things, mail.

An early entrepreneur by the name of Samuel Cunard (sound familiar?) took the first steps toward a fortune—and an enduring name—when he talked the British government into letting him carry mail to the U.S. abroad a small but quick (for those days) ship called the *Britannia,* an 1800-ton wooden paddlesteamer that crossed the Atlantic in just 14 days and eight hours!

SEA SPAS: Britons and Americans have always had a strong competitive streak, no less evident on the high seas where speed soon became the goal of every ship operator. So important were these sea races, in fact, that an award, the Blue Riband, was awarded for 80 years (from the 1880s to 1960) to the fastest ship afloat.

Emigrants and adventurers began to join the mail aboard these early mail boats, and soon the passenger race was on. Edward Collins, an American entrepreneur with five ships in his fleet, won over some of Cunard's business with amenities like steam heat, bathrooms, even (for goodness sakes!) a barbershop.

At the end of the 1800s people were beginning to be almost as infatuated with fitness as we are today, and spas of all kinds appeared. Floating spas called cruise ships became, for some, the solution to everything from gout to a broken heart. Many were the tears shed by a heartbroken lass as her parents dragged her aboard a sailing ship to remove her from the attentions of an ineligible suitor.

Sea cure enthusiasts were followed by adventurers and the socially alert in search of the status-broadening experiences of a European Grand Tour.

Ships architects met the demands of those early travelers with huge ballrooms lighted by equally huge chandeliers filled with candles and trimmed with fireplaces. Cabin stewards attended both passengers and their servants as they sailed with considerable fanfare on month-long voyages across the oceans.

Among the showiest vessels of those days was a black 1881 luxury liner named the *City of Rome.* It sported a massive bust of the emperor Hadrian as a figurehead, and boasted rooms trimmed in ebony and gold!

It was inevitable, of course, that we hoi-polloi would follow in their footsteps, anxious to share what was fast becoming the status symbol of the century: the transoceanic cruise. It is just as inevitable that this swirling of the socially pure waters would lead to the creation of proper places for all, a/k/a first class, second class, tourist class, and sometimes even third class.

Class hardly mattered to adventuresome students and Europa-philes who were intent on viewing the life Paris-style and didn't much care how they got there.

EVERYBODY INTO THE POOL: In the late 1800s many nationalities got into the shipping act, each replicating much of their national ambience on board their flagships.

By the early 1900s French, German, British, Scandinavian, Italian, and Dutch shipping magnates had launched such famous vessels as the *Deutschland,* Holland America's *Nieuw Amsterdam* and *Rotterdam,* Cunard's *Caronia* and *Carmania.* Britain also produced the *Lusitania* and the *Mauretania,* which surprised the cruising world with such goodies as private (!) bathrooms and some of the most elegant furnishings afloat.

Competition often breeds imitation, and it certainly did so aboard cruise ships, which set about to outdo each other until ships began to look like extravagant floating mansions: columned swimming pools, goldleaf moldings in the dining room, silk hangings, jewel-like colors verging on the gaudy, repeating at sea the fine china, the elegant silver service, the baroque and show-biz glitziness that characterized those times.

When war broke out in 1914, the New York–Europe waters were awash with transatlantic liners from many nations. War is not particularly conducive to high-flying good times. It certainly didn't do much for the shipping industry, except reduce the competition. A number of liners were damaged or destroyed by mines or U-boats in the North Sea, a circumstance that dampened voyagers' enthusiasm for ocean travel.

After the war, many lines returned to the passenger business. Ships that were to become legendary included the *Aquitania,* the *Mauretania,* Italy's *Conte di Savoia,* the *Île de France,* Germany's *Bremen* and *Europa,* the *Normandie* (with a regulation-size tennis court), and later the most famous of them all, the *Queen Mary* and *Queen Elizabeth,* constructed in the 1930s.

WET MARTINIS: During the 1920s transatlantic service flagged for a while, but regained some spirit, shall we say, from a strange source: Prohibition.

Ships flying foreign flags could still carry liquor, and did so happily. Passengers in search of a snort poured onto ships which by now were becoming quite egalitarian, aiming their appeal at many income brackets.

These voyages, dubbed "booze cruises," had quite a leveling influence on the formerly upper-crust world of cruises. Soon shipping companies were sending their vessels out for quickie cruises on which swingers of all ages and incomes mingled reasonably happily together for a few days at sea.

Cunard's *Berengaria,* a 50,000-ton ship, became known as the "Bargain Area" for its cheap gin-soused cruises on which fares began at $50.

It was not long before the barriers fell. First class, second class, tourist class, and all the other classes became one class—and that is the way they remain today on almost all cruising ships. (Cunard's massive *QE2* remains a haughty exception to that rule.

Historians agree that never before or since the 1930s have cruises and cruise ships been as grandly elegant as they were in those outdo-each-other days. Cole Porter took his piano on a 1935 cruise to Fiji where he wrote "Begin the Beguine," and the 83,000-ton *Normandie* of the French Line sailed to Rio (*sans* air conditioning), the largest ship ever to cross the equator. Some of her passengers had grand pianos in their suites too!

Where, you may be wondering, were the Americans in all this? In a word, nowhere. Rimmed as we are by water, you'd think Americans would take to the seas like dolphins, but it was not to be so.

As the years rolled by, Americans made many an attempt to run successful shipping operations and did create a massive vessel called the *United States,* but that ship along with the U.S.-flagged *Constitution, Independence, Brasil,* and *Argentina,* hit rocky financial waters. Two of those, the *Constitution* and *Independence,* have been restored and are now sailing Hawaiian waters, while the *United States* remains in Virginia, her restoration a dream as yet unfulfilled.

Time is the leveler of all things, including cruise ships, many of which have gone to junkyards or watery graves. Some, like the *Queen Mary,* have been salvaged. You can still see her, majestic as ever, permanently docked in Long Beach, California, where she serves as a floating hotel. Her sister, the first *Queen Elizabeth,* sank in Hong Kong harbor where she was to have become a floating university.

Some craft still afloat today were built in the 1940s as troop carriers, or in the 1950s when cruising experienced another resurgence of interest. Carnival Lines has refurbished some 1950s vessels, as has Costa Lines,

Eastern/Western Cruise Lines, Paquet Ulysses Line, Bahamas Line, and American Hawaii Lines. It's quite amazing how much difference a thorough restoration can make too, so don't reject a line or liner on age alone. Older ships are often more spacious, and retain nostalgic design elements that will give you a wonderful insight into the way we were in long-gone sailing days.

AIRING TROUBLES: Then, of course, was born that pedestrian, and altogether common, creation known as the aeroplane.

Suddenly, all was sacrificed for haste. One must mingle with the masses, survive coffee, tea, and mediocrity, and endure while the posh of pomp was eroded by the need for speed.

When Orville and Wilbur Wright appeared on the scene, little did anyone expect their creation to have an impact on anything, let alone on the world of sailing ships. That was exactly what was to happen, however, as Americans took to the air and abandoned ships. Fascination with jets and rapid transoceanic travel dealt the cruise industry a mighty blow.

But there is backlash in many things, helped along in this case by some clever marketing. In the 1970s that tidal wave of change from sea to air was to ebb, and for the strangest of reasons: television. In some fertile mind was born a program called "The Love Boat." Fantasy sailed on that craft. Romance reigned supreme and endings were inevitably happy. "Love Boat's" simplicity, its aura of glamor and entertainment, captured first the American imagination and then the American travel dollar. Space on popular ships was suddenly booked months in advance and the world's major shipyards were booming.

3. A Cruise Revolution

Of course, it wasn't a television show alone that fanned the spark that was to become a four-alarm blaze of interest in cruises. Something more mundane but infinitely more persuasive provided the final dénouement: money.

As the economy has shrunk in recent years and the cruise industry has burst its seams, competition for travel dollars spawned price wars and marketing maneuvers that made previous revolutions look like a tea party.

To lure travelers of all vacation beliefs and bank accounts to try this floating life of fun, sun, good food, and good times, cruise lines began offering all the inducements a group of very creative minds could dream up: free air fare from practically anywhere . . . third and fourth travelers at a laughable (or at least affordable) rate, sometimes even free . . . saunas fancier than a condominium, gymnasiums better equipped than the Y, fitness programs, walkathons, and jogging tracks . . . entertainment showy as a Broadway chorus line and variable as Las Vegas . . . stops in the most famous of world ports and intriguing lesser known destinations.

Meanwhile, air travel to many destinations was becoming increasingly expensive, and resort vacations that looked like bargains turned out to be something less than thrifty when service charges, restaurant bills, bar tabs, and often even energy add-ons were added to the accounting.

It wasn't long before those who watched their vacation pennies discovered that cruises offer something few land resorts can boast: transportation, accommodations, meals, and entertainment of all kinds—and all for a single prepaid price: no more surprises at check-out time; no more trying to figure taxi bills and car rentals, cover charges and tips, city tours and lunches; no more frantic calls to the credit-card company asking for please, just another $200. On cruises, the world discovered that you can leave home without it!

That alone was a feature irresistible to many travelers—but there was more. Now you could go from place to place in the comfort of a floating home staffed with plenty of smiling help: no more airport battles, no more luggage-wrestling, no more lines at the check-out desk. No longer was the fun limited to being there: now the fun was getting there too!

There you were, goggle-eyed in exotic ports, places you'd always dreamed of seeing, and you did nothing more strenuous on your way there than lift another martini.

All that—and competitive bargains tossed in for wonderful measure—have the cruise business booming. Some people discover they love this so much that they return over and over again, often to the same cruise ship which has become an old friend. We once met a really ship-lovesick lady who had sailed 25 times on the same ship and got stars in her eyes at the very mention of the vessel. On upper-crust lines like Royal Viking, as many as 50% of the travelers are repeat passengers!

Don't be the late-comers to a trend. Toss out all your doubts and go now before the world discovers what a bargain is out there waiting for them. That won't take long, either, if the cruise executives' predictions are to be believed.

On a visit to the Port of Miami any Saturday, you may very well think the world has already discovered the wonder of a cruise. It isn't true, however—only about 3% of the population has ever sailed away into the sunset—but cruise lines are running hard after that other 97%! Get there before the crowd.

4. Cruise Information Sources

As alluring as the world of cruise ships may seem to you, deep in your psyche there lurks a little voice crying, "But how will I pick a ship? How will I book a ticket? For goodness sakes, I don't know anything about all this."

Well, rest easy. There is someone near you who does know all about this: a travel agent. Never before in history has this career group been so important to the traveler.

TRAVEL AGENTS: When every airline charged the same amount and went to the same places at the same time, and there were only a few cruise lines to choose among, well, who really needed a travel agent? Just call up, order your ticket, and *voilà*! finished.

No more. As everything in our world grows, you have more and more choices—but also more and more decisions.

Travel agents can help you narrow those decisions down to manageable limits, and at least can stock you up with brochures so you can read and dream at home until you're convinced.

CLIA: Another source of information is **Cruise Lines International Association,** a cruise industry group to which most major lines belong. CLIA, as it is called, markets the idea of cruising in general rather than any specific line. It produces an interesting brochure called "Answers to the Most Asked Questions About Cruising," which you can get by writing CLIA, Pier 35, Suite 200, San Francisco, CA 94133.

SAFETY AT SEA: If you're concerned about safety at sea, you can perhaps rest easier knowing that your bureaucracy is at work. Since the mid-1960s all passenger ships calling at U.S. ports must meet stringent safety requirements outlined by the Safety of Life at Sea Act.

Frequent inspections by U.S. Coast Guard officials make sure that ships don't slip in their attention to safety factors. They take a very careful look at electrical connections, safety equipment, fire doors, fire equipment.

Those safety factors include such things as the boat drills in which you will participate soon after you board the ship. As silly as you may feel when you're messing about with a clumsy Mae West, you are learning survival methods, so pay attention.

Crew members have regular fire drills too, and fire-safety regulations aboard ships are stringent and carefully enforced by the captain and crew as well as by Coast Guard inspectors. (If a ship doesn't meet the approval of Coast Guard inspectors, it can be prohibited from sailing until the problems are corrected. This has happened in several highly publicized cases in recent years.)

Modern cruise ships are considered as near to fireproof as anything can be. Special inflammable materials are used in construction of the ships, and elaborate safety equipment is on board.

Ships also are required to meet standards set by the U.S. Public Health Service, whose inspections have been known to terrorize cruise-ship cooks. When health inspectors come on board (as they do regulary), they grade the ship on its regard for basic sanitation methods, most of them in the kitchens. If a ship does not get 85 of 100 points, it fails the inspection and can be prohibited from sailing.

You can get a copy of a Public Health Service report on cruise-ship inspections by writing to the U.S. Public Health Service, Center for Disease Control, Atlanta, GA 30333. Ask for the "Weekly Summary of Health Information for International Travel." That pamphlet will also keep you updated on the outbreak of diseases in various parts of the world.

Ships' officers claim that health inspections are so rigid and so strangely scored that the tiniest infraction can cause a ship to fail inspection. They even claim that inspections are so rigorous few mainland restaurants could pass the test.

Their claims seem rather well founded, as many of the ships afloat have failed an inspection at one time or another. It is still comforting to know, however, that someone is watching over sanitation aboard. Some lines are so concerned about the possibility of negative inspections—and the negative publicity that follows—that they have employed on-board sanitation experts to ensure that the most sanitary conditions are maintained.

SHIP REGISTRATION: Some novice cruisers worry a great deal about the country in which a ship is registered.

These days, that is not one of the things that should concern you, although you would do well to book a ship whose crew's primary nationality you appreciate, for whatever the reason.

You do not get to be a shipping entrepreneur by paying the highest taxes and the highest wages, as some early American ship owners learned to their dismay. That's why you will find most ships registered under flags known as "flags of convenience," which means that they are registered in countries that offer tax and wage breaks. Among the favorites are Panama, Liberia, Cyprus, and Singapore.

Meanwhile, the U.S. priced itself right out of the market for major cruise ships. Taxes reached such a level that vessels were paying up to half their income in taxes, *plus* union wages about twice what foreign crews are paid.

CRUISE BROCHURES / DECK PLANS: Brochures from the cruise lines you are contemplating sailing are not only the loveliest wish-books in town but they're also quite useful in helping you decide which love boat you will sail on.

Write or call a travel agent or the cruise line (many of them have toll-free numbers) and ask them to send you brochures outlining their ships and upcoming cruises. Be sure to tell them you want to see a deck plan of the ship (not every cruise line has deck plans in every cruise brochure, although most do).

When you get the plan, read it carefully, especially the back page where all the details of booking and sailing are outlined.

Just as you've become inured to beautiful travel brochures of all kinds, learn to overlook some of the more Madison Avenue aspects of the brochures. If a brochure doesn't show a typical cabin or pictures only lovely scenes of the ports it visits, perhaps you should wonder why and ask some careful questions about accommodations and on-board facilities.

If you're traveling with children, look carefully to see if there are any special facilities for the youngsters. Much as you love them, it's nice to have the little darlings busy somewhere *else* part of the day, at least. There's also the possibility that you don't want to travel on a ship that happily caters to the little ones.

You will of course not be surprised to discover that the most elegant and luxurious ships have matching brochures. Class will tell. If you look carefully and judge with your now-jaundiced eye, you will see plenty in even the glossiest of paper productions.

If you like sports, you will want to see what kinds of facilities there are on board. If you are interested in the finest dining, note how the line discusses its dining possibilites. They'll give all the selections fancy names of course, but if it boils down to some pretty simple culinary options and you're a gourmet (self-styled at least), you may want to search until you've found some really special kitchens.

As you're mulling over the cabins and price selections, keep an eye on where the cabin is located and be sure to look at the decks above and below it, as well as nearby public rooms. Right down the hall from the disco is great if you're a nightowl but horrible if you're not.

Port calls are important to most cruise passengers, so when you're looking at the brochure, take special note of the length of time in each port. Subtract a couple of hours from the length of time the ship appears to be in port to allow for docking and casting-off procedures. Brief port calls—say, less than five hours—can be very unsatisfactory. You'll find yourself spending much of your time looking at your watch and calculating how soon you ought to head back to the ship.

Some people care nothing at all about port calls and don't even bother to get off the ship. If you're one of those passengers, perhaps you should think about finding a cruise ship that spends most of its time at sea with port calls kept to a minimum.

If you like lots of service, you'll do well to take a look at the ratio of crew to passengers. If you like lots of space, deck or interior, you'll want to take a close look at the number of public rooms.

If a ship carries about 1000 passengers, as many do, but has only one dining room and one main lounge, you can expect to find yourself lining up to share the facilties with others. Ships are good at spreading passengers out so you don't feel crowded, but if you're determined to have lots of roaming rooms, pick a ship with plenty of lounges, nightclubs, bars, and sitting rooms (and high tonnage and low passenger figures).

Deck plans will also tell you some things about the size of your cabin, although not as much as you might like. Adjust to the possibility that unless you spend a great deal of money, your cabin will not be much bigger than about half the size of an average bedroom. You'll have rooom to change your clothes, sit around, and read, but you won't be dancing and throwing a party for half a dozen friends in there, unless they've *very* good friends.

If the cabins all seem to be the same size but some are higher priced than others, believe your eyes. Many modern ships have cabins that resemble each other more closely than peas in a pod so that all you are buying in the upper price brackets is proximity to public rooms. On those, book early and book cheap.

If you see some sizes or shapes you find interesting, call the line and ask for approximate cabin sizes. Subtract from that the size of the bathroom and figure in how much space the beds will take. Then you'll have an idea how much walking space you'll find. If you can afford it, a separate sitting area, even if it's only a couple of chairs and a table, is nice. (Rooms with beds that fold up out of the way give you moving-around space too.)

You can't tell much about ambience from a cruise brochure, but you can tell something. If more mention is made of informality than of formality, you'll find fewer formal evenings and a more devil-may-care attitude among the passengers aboard.

Price is an indicator, as it always is. Certainly there are good bargains, but you get what you pay for on cruise ships too. High-priced ships will treat you to the best of food, service, ambience, ports, and entertainment, while lower-priced craft will cut back on some or all of those features.

BOOKS TO READ: If you're sailing the Panama Canal, David McCullough's *Path Between the Seas* will give you a deeper appreciation of the wonder of that journey.

A difficult book to find, but one that beautifully describes man's love of and life with the sea, is Robert Wilder's *Wind From the Carolinas.* It details the story of early American Tory settlers who emigrated to the Bahamas rather than abandon their loyalty to the British king. Once there, their interplay with Bahamian residents makes an intriguing tale, made even more interesting by descriptions of the beautiful seas you too will meet in the Caribbean.

Peter Freuchen's *Book of the Seven Seas* will tell you absolutely everything you could want to know about the watery wonderland around you. You can spend fascinating hours out on deck or curled up in the ship's library with this one, reading about tides, winds, waves, great voyages like the *Kon Tiki,* sea battles, food from the sea, jewels plucked from the oceans, famous sea people, navigation—you name it, it's in there.

Joshua Slocum, a famous, famous seaman who once sailed around the world on a small boat, wrote about his experiences in *Sailing Around the World* and *The Voyage of the Liverdale.*

Ernest Hemingway spent much of his time living on or around the sea, penning one of his most famous novels, *The Old Man and the Sea,* while living and fishing, one of his favorite pastimes, in Florida.

A strange tale of the sea comes to us from Samuel Taylor Coleridge, who wrote a haunting poem called "The Rime of the Ancient Mariner."

Innocents Abroad is typically Mark Twain-ian with some interesting observations on his ship's passage across the sea. Anything Twain wrote makes wonderful pre-Mississippi River cruise reading too.

Other books that will give you a wonderful look at the fascinating history of the great cruise liners include: *Beau Voyage: Life Aboard the Last Great Ships,* by John M. Brinnin; *The Sway of the Grand Saloon: A Social History of the North Atlantic,* by John M. Brinnin; and *The Liners: A History of the North Atlantic Crossing,* by Terry Coleman.

A book called *The Great Luxury Liners, 1927–1954: A Photographic Record* (Dover Publications) offers some interesting photographs of famous cruise liners as does Melvin Maddock's *The Great Liners.*

Sail, Steam and Selendour: A Picture History of Life Aboard the Trans-Atlantic Lines (Times Books) gives you still another fascinating look at luxury afloat.

For more extensive information on ports, you might pick up copies of Frommer's guides to the region you'll be visiting. Among those Frommer titles available are *Dollarwise Guide to the Caribbean; Dollarwise Guide to Canada; Dollarwise Guide to Florida; Dollarwise Guide to California; Mexico on $25 a Day; Dollarwise Guide to the Southeast & New Orleans;* and Frommer's *South America on $25 a Day.*

If you're planning a cruise along the coastal or inland waterways of the eastern seaboard, state tourism offices and chambers of commerce in the states you'll be visiting can provide you with scads of reading material on the history and culture of those states. State tourism offices are a branch of that state government and can usually be reached at the state capital. Your local chamber of commerce will be able to provide you with an address and telephone number.

CRUISE ENTHUSIASTS: **Cruise Passengers Club International** produces an annual "Rating Report" that can be helpful in selecting a ship. The address of the group is Box 9, Cynwyd, PA 19004, and the report costs $10.

Cruise Travel magazine is a publication based in, of all places, Evanston, Illinois, proving once again that cruise enthusiasts come from all parts of the nation. Their inland-midland location doesn't stop editor Robert Meyers and publisher Norman Jacobs from producing a glossy and intriguing monthly magazine featuring a cruise, ship, and port of the month, plus some interesting looks at a wide variety of cruise topics ranging from paintings of the great liners to no-smoking policies on ships. Subscriptions are $12 a year. Write to Cruise Travel Magazine, P.O. Box 10139, Des Moines, IA 50340.

A club of cruise history buffs exists too. It's called Steamship Historical Society of America, 414 Pelton Ave., Staten Island, NY 10310 (tel. 212 727-9583).

PORT VISITS: If you live anywhere near a major port or are visiting a city with a port, check to see when and where cruise ships will be docked. Then stop by and see ships that interest you. That's particularly easy to do in Miami, where each weekend you can visit a dozen or so ships before they sail.

Most ships will give you a boarding pass to go aboard and roam around. Just give the line a call or ask your travel agent to arrange a visit for you.

REPEAT CRUISERS: Every cruise line likes to encourage repeat business and some of them do it with special clubs for their repeat passengers. These clubs publish newsletters, keeping members up to date on what's new at the line, and sometimes offer special bargains to previous passengers. Among the lines that have past-passenger clubs are Delta Queen Steamboat Co., Norwegian American Cruises, Norwegian Caribbean Lines, Princess Cruises, Royal Cruise Line, Royal Viking Line, Sitmar, and Sun Line. On Sun Line's Christmas cruise one year, members of the line's repeaters' club, called Odyssey Club, were each given 25 gifts to celebrate the line's 25th anniversary!

OTHER SAILORS: Some of the best insider information on cruise ships come from insiders! Those who have sailed on a vessel can—and will gladly—tell you a great deal about food, service, decor, and ambience aboard. During a recent plane journey, we casually mentioned the word "cruise" to a lovely lady nearby and were treated all the way to Houston to some interesting observations about ships and cruises, including this one:

"I always check the *Farmer's Almanac* before we go on a cruise," she said.

"For the weather?" we asked innocently.

"No, to see when there's a full moon," she replied. "You haven't lived until you've sat on the deck of a cruise ship with the breeze blowing gently and a huge, pale full moon rising on the horizon. It's . . . well, you'll see."

5. The $25-a-Day Travel Club—How to Save Money on All Your Travels

In this book we'll be looking at how to discover your value-for-money dream cruise, but there is a "device" for saving money and determining value on *all* your trips. It's the popular, international $25-a-Day Travel Club, now in its 22nd successful year of operation. The Club was formed at the urging of numerous readers of the $$$-a-Day and Dollarwise Guides, who felt that such an organization could provide continuing travel information and a sense of community to value-minded travelers in all parts of the world. And so it does!

In keeping with the budget concept, the annual membership fee is low and is immediately exceeded by the value of your benefits. Upon receipt of $15 (U.S. residents) or $18 U.S. by check drawn on a U.S. bank or via international postal money order in U.S. funds (Canadian, Mexican and other foreign residents) in U.S. currency to cover one year's membership, we will send all new members the following items:

(1) Any two of the Following Books

Please designate in your letter which two you wish to receive:

Europe on $25 a Day
Australia on $25 a Day
England and Scotland on $25 a Day
Greece on $25 a Day
Hawaii on $35 a Day
India on $15 and $25 a Day
Ireland on $25 a Day
Israel on $30 and $35 a Day
Mexico on $20 a Day
New York on $35 a Day
New Zealand on $20 and $25 a Day
Scandinavia on $25 a Day
South America on $25 a Day
Spain and Morocco (plus the Canary Is.) on $25 a Day
Washington, D.C. on $35 a Day

Dollarwise Guide to Austria and Hungary
Dollarwise Guide to Canada
Dollarwise Guide to the Caribbean (including Bermuda and The Bahamas)
Dollarwise Guide to Egypt
Dollarwise Guide to England and Scotland
Dollarwise Guide to France
Dollarwise Guide to Germany
Dollarwise Guide to Italy
Dollarwise Guide to Portugal (plus Madeira and the Azores)
Dollarwise Guide to Switzerland
Dollarwise Guide to California and Las Vegas
Dollarwise Guide to Florida
Dollarwise Guide to New England
Dollarwise Guide to the Northwest
Dollarwise Guide to the Southeast and New Orleans
Dollarwise Guide to the Southwest
(Dollarwise Guides discuss accommodations and facilities in all price ranges, with emphasis on the medium-priced.)

Dollarwise Guide to Cruises
(A comprehensive guide to cruises, in all price ranges, to Mexico, the Caribbean, Alaska, Canada, and U.S. coastal ports.)

How to Beat the High Cost of Travel
(This practical guide details how to save money on absolutely all travel

items—accommodations, transportation, dining, sightseeing, shopping, taxes, and more. Includes special budget information for seniors, students, singles, and families.)

The New York Urban Athlete
(The ultimate guide to all the sports facilities in New York City for jocks and novices.)

Museums in New York
(A complete guide to all the museums, historic houses, gardens, zoos, and more in the five boroughs. Illustrated with over 200 photographs.)

The Fast 'n' Easy Phrase Book
(The four most useful languages—French, German, Spanish, and Italian—all in one convenient, easy-to-use phrase guide.)

Where to Stay USA
(By the Council on International Educational Exchange, this extraordinary guide is the first to list accommodations in all 50 states that cost anywhere from $3 to $25 per night.)

A Guide for the Disabled Traveler
(A guide to the best destinations for wheelchair travelers and other disabled vacationers in Europe, the United States, and Canada by an experienced wheelchair traveler. Includes detailed information about accommodations, restaurants, sights, transportation, and their accessibility.)

Marilyn Wood's Wonderful Weekends
(This very selective guide covers the best mini-vacation destinations within a 200-mile-radius of New York City. It describes special country inns and other accommodations, restaurants, picnic spots, sights, and activities—all the information needed for a two- or three-day stay.)

Bed & Breakfast—North America
(A directory of all the major organizations—over 150—of bed & breakfast homes and referral agencies in the United States and Canada.)

(2) A one-year subscription to *The Wonderful World of Budget Travel*

This quarterly eight-page tabloid newspaper keeps you up to date on fast-breaking developments in low-cost travel in all parts of the world, bringing you the latest money-saving information—the kind of information you'd have to pay $25 a year to obtain elsewhere. This consumer-conscious publication also features columns of special interest to readers: **The Traveler's Directory** (a list of members all over the world who are willing to provide hospitality to other members as they pass through their home cities); **Share-a-Trip** (offers and requests from members for travel companions who can share costs and help avoid the burdensome single supplement); and **Readers Ask . . . Readers Reply** (travel questions from members to which other members reply with authentic firsthand information).

(3) A copy of *Arthur Frommer's Guide to New York*

This is a pocket-size guide to hotels, restaurants, nightspots, and sightseeing attractions in all price ranges throughout the New York area.

(4) Your personal membership card

This entitles you to purchase through the Club all Arthur Frommer publications, for a third to a half off their regular retail prices during the term of your membership.

So why not join this hardy band of international budgeteers and participate in its exchange of travel information and hospitality? Simply send your name and address, together with your annual membership fee of $15 (U.S. residents) or $18 U.S. (Canadian, Mexican, and other foreign residents), in U.S. currency to: $25-a-Day Travel Club, Inc., Frommer/Pasmantier Publishers, 1230 Avenue of the Americas, New York, NY 10020. And please remember to specify which *two* of the books in section (1) above you wish to receive in your initial package of members' benefits. Or, if you prefer, use the last page of this book, simply checking off the two books you select and enclosing $15 or $18 in U.S. currency

6. Some Final Thoughts

Ah, yes, weary travelers of the world, there is good news tonight. Speed's fascination has palled, permitting luxury, decadence and pure sloth to return to their rightful place in the scheme of things.

With Puritanism well out of the way, the luxuries of the luxury liners, with their long, lazy days and liquid star-filled nights, once again sing a siren's song to the hedonist in us all.

It's all out there waiting for you, the brass ring of glamor travel that will take you from here to anywhere in more comfort than home could ever offer and at a pace that pampers.

Ah, yes, black velvet nights . . . diamond days . . . you deserve it, of course.

Bon voyage!

Chapter I

WHICH WAY TO THE GLACIER?/BEACH?: PORTS OF CALL

1. Alaska/Northwest Passage
2. Caribbean Islands
3. Mexican Riviera / Yucatán Peninsula
4. Mississippi and Ohio Rivers
5. Bermuda / Northeast Passage / Inland Waterways
6. Panama Canal
7. South America

OH, THE GLORIES of the seaborne life; moonlight and roses, violins and vichyssoise, balmy breezes, salt air, saunas and white-glove service. . . .

Piffle, says one cruise executive, none of that is what sells cruises. What sells cruises, the man insists, are ports, ports, and ports.

And who can deny the seductive lure of a silvery beach trimmed with fluttering palms swaying in the trade winds? Or of a blue-white glacier rising from a sapphire sea? Or of pink pastel architecture, smoking volcanoes, exotic perfumes, lilting accents, and sloe-eyed beauties?

Who among us hasn't dreamed of being whisked away to a tiny secluded cove where warm waters lap across your toes and the only sound around is a bee buzzing about its business?

As intriguing as is the idea of lazy days and action-packed nights, one still dreams of finally getting somewhere, of setting foot on strange, exotic foreign lands that look nothing at all like home.

That change of scenery is what travel is all about, and why ship lines are in business, to take you somewhere, offering you as much fun in the getting there as in the being there.

Once you do get there, you can explore in two ways: on your own or on a group tour called a shore excursion. A day or so before you are due to arrive in a port, the cruise director or shore excursion director will deliver a little—or a long—spiel outlining points of interest in the upcoming port. That talk is certain to include a detailed description of the ship's shore excursions. These shore tours are arranged by the cruise line which buys tours from local tour operators. An office on board, usually called the shore excursion office or tour desk, then sells the land tour to you. You can also buy and pay for these tours when you book your ticket.

After the cruise director describes the upcoming port, what there is to see and do there, the planned shore excursions and how much they cost, you can trot over to the shore excursion office on the ship and buy your tickets. Port tours often are also outlined in the daily activity sheet "newspaper" delivered to your room or in brochures you'll find in your cabin.

Naturally you do not *have* to go on a shore excursion. After you've heard the cruise director's port description, you may decide you're not particularly interested in spending two or three hours driving around in a bus or visiting ruins or snorkeling or any of the other amusements the shore excursions offer.

You dream instead of staking a claim to a piece of beach, buying yourself an emerald or scrimshaw creation, or just roaming through historic streets and "discovering" this lovely spot on your own.

If that's the way you feel, do it. Nowhere is it written you must take a shore excursion or even that you must visit a port just because the ship and most of the other passengers are doing so. You can stay right on the ship if you like.

If you are one of those who decides to see the port on your own (and/or those who don't like organized activities) you can just get up in the morning (or afternoon), eat breakfast and walk off the ship any time you like.

You may, however, decide a shore excursion is worth it, and these tours often do give you a good overall view of the port, usually with knowledgeable commentary that provides a good introduction to the area.

If you decide to take a port tour, you will gather at an appointed hour at a designated spot and off you all will go on your tour. Most tours are only two or three hours long with several sipping stops included. Since you are usually in port for about eight hours, these tours leave you several hours to shop and roam about on your own.

Opinions on the value of shore excursions vary greatly. For our money, any archeological or historic site is much better (and more easily) visited on a shore excursion. Unless you are an historian or archeologist, you won't understand what you're seeing without the commentary of a knowledgeable guide.

On the other hand, some Caribbean island tours offer *such* an overview that you'd do just as well to hire a taxi driver to point out the sights (which sometimes are few indeed). Often you can team up with a couple of other passengers so the taxi tour costs you the same or less than a shore excursion.

Taxi hours have this added advantage: you can call it quits whenever you get bored or tired and you can stop for as long as you like anywhere you like.

You can also rent a car or motorscooter almost anywhere these days. Motorscooters are particularly popular in the Bahamas and in some Caribbean islands where the land is flat and easily negotiated on these putt-putts. Like taxis, rental vehicles offer you freedom to come and go as you please, to find a secluded beach or to drive up into the mountains for a crow's nest look at the ship and the city.

On the negative side, rental cars often take time to rent, unless (sometimes even if) you've ordered and paid for the car in advance. You have to find the office, fill out papers, and budget time to return the car and get back to the ship.

If you're going to be in port for a day or more (Acapulco, for instance), you may enjoy the freedom of a rental car, but if you're only visiting for six or eight hours, you may end up spending two of them at the car rental agency. That's particularly true in the Caribbean where absolutely nothing moves fast.

Ideally, you will have made those rental plans in advance with the advice and smoothing influence of a travel agent. If you haven't, you can just ask a taxi driver to take you to the nearest rental car company, where you will plunk down your money or your credit card and drive off into the noonday sun.

So, here you are, standing at the gangplank ready to set your sights ashore.

Once you walk down the gangplank or clamber out of the tender and hit terra firma, you will usually find yourself facing a horde of taxi drivers, all beaming happily—and hopefully. They will offer to take you on a private tour of the island/port/city/country/whatever and are happy to bargain over the price. If you don't want to go on *any* kind of tour, just say no thanks and keep on walking.

Walk where? you ask. Well, before you leave the ship, ask at the shore excursion office or the information desk for a map showing the port you're visiting. Most lines include a map of the day's port on the back of your daily activities sheet.

In many ports you will dock right in the middle of town so you can just set off the ship and follow the crowd to begin shopping or exploring. Or you can hire a cab to take you to the nearest (or best) beach. Most ports are pretty small places in which you soon will know your way around as well as any island native.

You shoppers might also remember that if you're planning to purchase liquor or other weighty items, many stores will deliver your purchases to the ship. Cruise lines have such faith in the delivery system, they will guarantee you replacement of any delivery that doesn't show up as expected. That very rarely happens. It is certainly worth the risk not to be carrying five pounds of liquor bottles in the heat of the Caribbean sun. You will need to order and pay for your liquor early, however, so the store has time to see to the delivery. Make that your first stop. All this liquor-carrying discussion, by the way, refers primarily to St. Thomas, the Caribbean's number one liquor port.

See, now wasn't that easy? Here you are aboard your floating resort visiting every corner of the world from the souks of Morocco to the sands of Hawaii, the icebergs of Alaska or the bathtub-warm waters of the Caribbean, the dramatic cliffs of Acapulco or the tranquil shores of the Mississippi.

Have you got the picture?

You, dipping a tentative toe into sea water so clear you can spot fish swimming by. . . .

You, sipping something tall and cool in the shadow of a gazebo under a spray of scarlet blossoms spread across the sky like floral fireworks. . . .

You, gazing in awe at a huge moon rising over a diamond-studded glacier. . . .

What are we waiting for? Hear that haunting foghorn booming out across the water, calling for all aboard who are coming aboard?

Quick, let's go! Let's see what there is to sea.

1. Alaska/Northwest Passage

Waterfalls crashing over soaring cliffs . . . snow-capped peaks misty in the moonlight . . . pine-clad slopes, stark white glaciers.

Alaska—an Arctic Circle wonderland at the top of the world, the kingdom, and the subject, of nature.

To sail past this dropjaw-awesome scenery is the dream of many a cruise enthusiast. An understandable dream it is too, for here you will see mammoth, eons-old glaciers soaring in great white peaks—and hear them too, as they crack with a great thunderous roar into pieces called pups.

On Alaska cruises, passengers spend every possible second up on deck just staring at the magnificence nature has created here in the farthest reaches of the globe. It's no wonder either, for this is humbling scenery, overpowering in grandeur.

Alaska looks so foreign a port and is so powerful an experience people often forget it's now an American state, the 49th, and has been since January 3, 1959.

It wouldn't have been were it not for the oft-maligned William Seward, secretary of state in the cabinets of Abraham Lincoln and Andrew Johnson. Seward negotiated the purchase of this mammoth slab of land and islands from Russia in 1867, and won himself a place in history—but not before his contemporaries derisively labeled the land "Seward's Icebox."

Named for the Aleut word for "great land," Alaska is about one-fifth the size of the rest of the United States put together. This massive state stretches over 586,400 square miles, yet has a population of only about 300,000. That's almost two square miles for every person (no crowding here)!

So vast is this land that, like the continental states, it stretches across four time zones. Juneau and most of the Yukon Territory are on Pacific Standard Time (the same as California, and three hours behind the East Coast). Anchorage (and most of the rest of the state) is on Alaska Standard Time (two hours behind California, and five hours behind the East Coast). And the Aleutian Islands project out so far into the ocean that they cause a major zigzag in the International Date Line.

As far northwest in the U.S. as you can go, Alaska includes the Aleutian Islands and the Alexander Archipelago, and cuddles up to the Bering Sea, the Pacific Ocean, and the Arctic Ocean. Its coastline is longer than the coastlines of the 48 continental states put together, 33,000 miles long.

Inside its boundaries you will find ten major rivers and 3,000,000 (!) lakes, plus 19 mountains higher than 14,000 feet and half the world's glaciers.

Similar in dramatic scenery to the fjords of Scandinavia, Alaska also shares that midnight sun and the starry wonder of the northern lights glowing on the horizon.

There might still be practically no one here were it not for the gold rush, all those cunning little mink and ermine running around waiting to drape a lucky shoulder, and the Alaskan Pipeline, which still employs

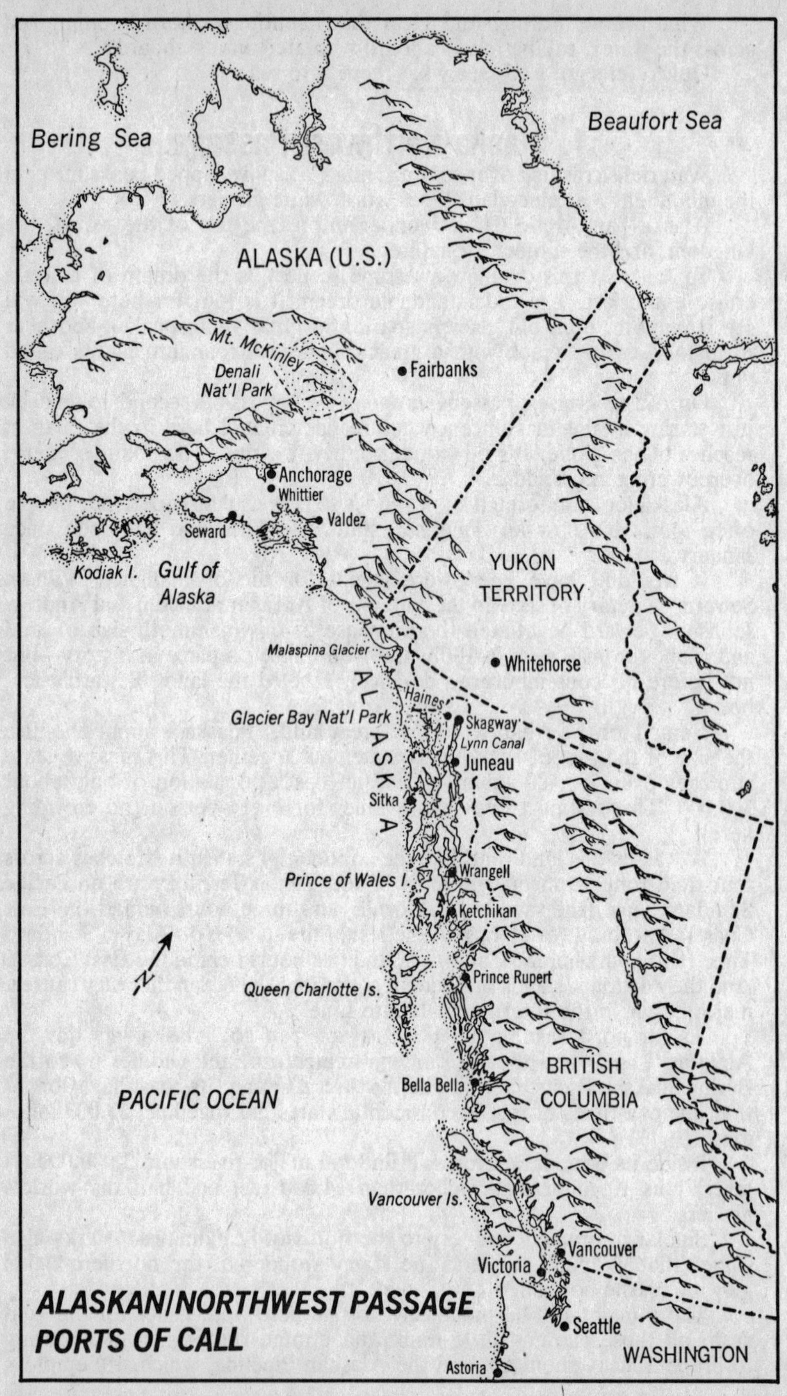

ALASKAN/NORTHWEST PASSAGE PORTS OF CALL

many at high salaries in which cold-blooded types would find warm comfort.

Summer months are Alaska's high season, but even at that time of year weather can be tricky, so take your rainhat and sweaters on this cruise (but don't bother packing suntan oil).

Alaskans speak English, of course, although many still speak native languages, including Tlingit, Tsimshian, Haida, Aleut, and several Eskimo and Athabascan dialects. Most natives are bilingual but older folks tend to stick to their native language.

Tlingit (prounced *Klink*-it) is a tribe you will hear much about in the favorite Alaska cruising region stretching from Ketchikan through Misty Fjords to Wrangell, Sitka, Juneau, and into Glacier Bay. Tlingit means "from-place-of-tidal-waters-people," and refers to the tribe that inhabited this long, narrow island section Alaskans call their "panhandle."

Rustic as it may be, Alaska is sometimes pricey. Expect to pay top dollar for what you eat, drink, and buy. Car rentals are not low either: you'll pay $200 a week for a subcompact up to $330 for a full-size car.

Crafts are beautiful and most unusual, stemming as they do from the handiwork of the native Indian tribes. Ivory, totem pole souvenirs, jade, hematite (often callled Alaska black diamonds), Russian dolls (one doll nested inside another), and Russian enameling crafts are good, although not cheap, buys. Everything you buy is duty free of course—this is the U.S.

Some other good buys here: woven cedar baskets, fur parkas, mukluks, caps and gloves, Alaska gold nugget jewelry, soapstone carvings, and rare Chickat blankets.

If you're an art collector, you'll see some very unusual artwork and crafts in this region. Bone up a bit with a book or two on Alaska and northern Indian artwork before you go so you'll have an idea what you're looking at and where to look for what.

The capital of Alaska is Juneau, a city of about 6,050, in the southeastern part of the state.

Don't expect to find slick discos and feathered dancing girls up in these parts. Entertainment here runs more toward get-together bars, tall-story telling, historic reenactments, and on really ripping occasions, perhaps the flash of a can-can girl's garter. Nightlife tends to end about 10 p.m.

Through Alaska runs the Alaska Highway, a road stretching from Dawson Creek in Canada's British Columbia, through the Yukon of gold rush fame, to Fairbanks, Alaska. Built in 1942, the road is 1527 miles long and is better known as the Alcan Highway.

Alaska's best known landmark is Mount McKinley, which rises to 20,270 feet and is the highest peak in the Alaska Range and the highest point in North America as well.

Southwest Alaska is a big peninsula that stretches between the Bering Sea and the Pacific, while the southeastern part of the state, the most popular cruise region, runs right alongside Canada's British Columbia and is a conglomerate of dozens of small and large islands, and misty fjords.

Despite its frigid image, the parts of Alaska you'll be touring on a cruise ship are quite pleasant in summer, ranging from an average high of 41° to 47° Fahrenheit in April to average temperatures of 63° to 72° in July,

53° to 55° in September. Juneau and the southern coast, warmed by the Japan Current, has winters like New York and summers like San Francisco.

Let's take a look at some of the ports you may be visiting on a cruise from San Francisco, Los Angeles, or Vancouver to Alaska.

Vancouver, British Columbia

Population: 1.2 million.

Climate: mild.

Currency: Canadian dollar; $1.00 U.S. = $1.25 Canadian.

Tourist Information: Greater Vancouver Convention and Visitors Bureau, 650 Burrard St. (tel. 604/682-2222).

Public Transportation: bus, taxi.

Car Rentals: Tilden, 1058 Alberni St. (tel. 685-6111); Budget, 450 W. Georgia St. (tel. 588-0261); Avis, 757 Hornby St. (tel. 682-1621); Hertz, 898 Burrard St. (tel. 688-2411).

Shopping Specialties: Northwest Indian crafts, jade carvings, Eskimo handiwork. Try Images (779 Burrard St.) or Tempo (1107 Robson St.) for Cowichan sweaters, fur gloves, moccasins, and toques featuring native designs; and Nikka Traders (643 Howe St; tel. 684-5374) for frozen, canned, or smoked salmon (if you're flying from here, they'll deliver it to the airport).

Restaurants: Schnitzel House, 1060 Robson St. (tel. 682-1210); Pyrogy Inn, 1536 Robson St. (tel. 684-2816); in Gastown, try Brother Jon's, 1 Water St. (tel. 685-3285) or Leo's Seafood, 170 Water St. (tel. 682-1235).

Many cruises depart from this lovely Canadian seaside city. Its proximity to the beauties of the glaciers means that you can see much of the most beautiful parts of the Alaskan coastline on a less-expensive seven-day cruise. Cruises from San Francisco or Los Angeles take longer, 10 to 12 days generally, and spend several days of that time getting to this area. Vancouver is usually a stop on these longer tours.

Founded in the mid-1800s, Vancouver offers you beautiful vistas everywhere you look—mountains, sea, gardens, harbor, tiny inlets.

Just 25 miles from the U.S. border, Vancouver is the third-largest city in Canada, after Montréal and Toronto. You'll find another ranking here too: the biggest Chinatown in America, after San Francisco. And there are lots of European influences here as well, as you can see from some of those restaurant selections.

The hit of the town and one of its most interesting sights is an area known as **Gastown.** Once a crumbling slum, Gastown was put back together again by concerned residents who restored its crooked alleys, cleaned it all up, and presented it to the world as an intriguing conglomeration of boutiques, galleries, and dining spots.

Named after Capt. George Vancouver, who took a small settlement here from the Spanish in 1790, the city was nothing more than a tiny way station until a character named John Deighton arrived with dog, Indian mistress, and whiskey in tow. Egged on by promises of the whiskey, local workers helped him build a saloon to dispense still more of the stuff. Others followed and, *voilà*! Vancouver. Deighton's loquaciousness earned him the name "Gassy Jack" and his area of town was later to become known as Gastown.

Misty Fjords

On your way up the coastline you'll cruise Misty Fjords National Monument, a place as beautiful as its name suggests. It is often misty too, but the mists lift early, burned away by the sunlight, and you see before you a stirring sight: deep blue waters and glistening white glaciers. Wildlife abounds here, so keep an eye out for a moose.

Ketchikan

Population: 10,000.

Tourist Information: Ketchikan Visitors Bureau, 131 Front St. (tel. 907/225-6166).

Car Rentals: Avis, Garina Island (tel. 907/225-4515).

Shopping Specialties: totem souvenirs.

Restaurants: Gilmore Hotel, 326 Front St. (tel. 907/225-9423).

Ketchikan likes to call itself the "Salmon Capital of the World" and proves it by offering you a look at salmon hatcheries—or at a grilled salmon platter.

Located on Revillagigedo Island in the Alexander Archipelago, Ketchkian was a supply point for miners in the 1890s gold rush and hasn't changed a great deal since those days. It is in fact still a distribution center for lumbering, fur farming, and mining, as well as a major center for the salmon industry.

This waterfront city is famous for its totems too, and at **Totem Bight Park** you can explore an excellent replica of a Tlingit community house and an intriguing display of totem poles. You can even learn to "read" them! **Totem Heritage Cultural Center** features Alaska's largest collection of original totems and an exhibit of rare Tlingit and Haida Indian artifacts. (In case you're wondering what totems are all about, you're not alone. No one knows the origin of totemism, an ancient religion in which people consider themselves direct descendants of an animal or bird. Clans may also consider themselves related to a clan totem and take their name from that totem.)

Water plays a very important role in this city whose name meant "salmon creek" in an Indian dialect. At the picturesque waterfront are three harbors, boats of all sizes and descriptions, docks, a seaplane base, and a ferry terminal. All the activity there makes for some intriguing photographs.

While you're here, don't miss **Creek Street.** Certainly none of the early gold bugs did! Once the red-light district of the city, it featured no fewer than 20 houses of . . . well, you know. Today the rainbow-hued dwellings built on pilings over a meandering stream contain an interesting Dolly's House Museum, plus galleries and shops.

Metlakatla

You may cruise by this island village, the only Indian reservation in Alaska and once the site of a religious colony. Today Metlakatla is a fishing village inhabited by Tsmishian Indians.

Sitka

Population: 4000.

Tourist Information: Greater Sitka Chamber of Commerce, Centennial Building, Harbor Drive (tel. 907/747-8604).

Car Rentals: Avis, Potlatch Motel, 713 Katliam St. (tel. 747-8611).

Shopping Specialties: totems, Tlingit crafts.

Restaurants: Sheffield Sitka Hotel, Katlin (tel. 907/747-6166).

Alaskan history lives on in this small town that has seen many a tourist from early Indian tribes to Russian settlers and today's cruise passengers. Much of the state's earliest history centered on this village which was for a time the capital of Alaska. In 1741 the Russians recorded their discovery of Alaska here, and it was here that proprietorship of Alaska was transferred from Russia to the United States in 1867.

Founded in 1799 by adventurer Alexander Baranov (who called it New Archangel), the town was destroyed by Indians in 1802, but intrepid settlers rebuilt. Ages ago the Tlingit Indians called this lovely mountain-ringed village home, and one of their clans, the Kiksadi, made it their ancestral home.

On a roam about the village, you'll find a picturesque harbor packed with small boats and colorful people—downright photographically inspirational. A landmark of Sitka is **St. Michael's Cathedral,** a handsome Russian Orthodox church containing glittering goldleaf adorning ornate chandeliers and carved moldings. This landmark church houses an extensive collection of icons and priceless religious artifacts carefully preserved, gleaming reminders of Sitka's past as a Russian colony when the city was known as the "Paris of the Pacific."

There are more reminders of this city's Russian heritage in the winsome forms of lovely, lively dancers called the **New Archangel Russian Dancers.** Dressed in floral babushkas, bright boots, and swirling skirts, these energetic lasses perform folk dances from various regions. You can sometimes see them at the docks, but usually at the Centennial Building where admission is $2 per person.

In the first three weeks of June each year Sitka celebrates a **summer music festival,** highly acclaimed by critics. Classical soloists perform in the Centennial Building, where they perform before a backdrop of glass that offers a spectacular view of the mountain and ocean scenery outside. Concerts are usually scheduled for Tuesday, Friday, and Saturday, and rehearsals are open.

The **Sheldon Jackson Museum** was built in 1895 by the noted Alaskan traveler Dr. Sheldon Jackson to house his collection of native art, artifacts, and historical items. Even way back then he figured out a way to make it as fireproof as possible, and today the museum is listed in the National Register of Historic Places.

If you're lucky enough to be in town in the last days of June, you can watch some of the nation's fanciest footwork rolling up a storm in the **All-Alaska Logging Championships,** which come complete with 17 events including the world championships in the Hooktender's Race and Team Splicing.

Sitka Historical National Park was the site of a fierce fight by the Tlingit tribes against the Russians, but is now home to Indian craftsmen who will show you how they carve wood into both tiny and monumental treasures.

Juneau

Population: 7000.

Tourist Information: Juneau Information Center, Davis Log Cabin, 3rd Street at Seward (tel. 907/586-2284).

Car Rentals: Avis, Juneau Municipal Airport, RR5 (tel. 907/789-9450); Hertz, Juneau Municipal Airport (tel. 907/789-9494).

Restaurants: Alaskan Hotel & Bar (featuring a turn-of-the-century oak bar), S. Franklin (tel. 907/586-1000); Cape Fox Sheffield Hotel, S. Franklin (tel. 907/586-6900); Red Dog Saloon, S. Franklin (tel. 907/586-6303).

This interesting city is the capital of Alaska, created lock, stock, and barrel during the 1880s rush for gold and named after Joe Juneau, the happy-go-spending prospector who first discovered gold in the state. If there is an unlovely view in Juneau, I certainly haven't seen it. Mountains, glaciers, and the sea are everywhere you look, providing views at once tranquilizing and stimulating.

Narrow streets and quiet, contemplative walkways give parts of this city a European flavor much loved by visitors and residents alike.

Mendenhall Glacier is a top Juneau sight, just a short ride from downtown Juneau. (Now what other state capital do you know that can boast a glacier just a stone's throw away?) A river of ice a mile long and a mile and a half wide, the huge Mendenhall Glacier is part of the Juneau Icefield. Mendenhall is backing off at the rate of about 50 feet a year, so in another couple of eons you'll have to go farther out of town to see it. Gray Line of Juneau (tel. 907/586-3773) has package tours of the city and the glacier.

At the **Alaska State Museum** you can see a life-size diorama and some fascinating exhibits of the history, native cultures, wildlife, and wilderness of Alaska, giving you some background on the Eskimo, Aleut, Athapascan, and Tlingit cultures about which you'll be hearing much in this part of the world.

Two interesting religious sites here are the **Shrine of St. Therese** and **Chapel-by-the-Lake.** Juneau's **St. Nicholas Russian Orthodox Church** offers another interesting look at the Russian influence that survives in Alaska.

If you like ski resorts, you can take a look at **Eaglecrest,** and if you like to look at animals in the wild, you can journey from Juneau by air or boat to **Admiralty Island,** a national Monument Wilderness where brown bears pad happily about and eagles soar. Tlingit and Haida Indians perform some of their intriguing tribal dances here.

Alaska tourists perform tribal rituals of a sort at the famed **Red Dog Saloon,** a must-stop spot of rusticity and whoop-it-up rib-tickling good times. Don't miss it.

Highrollers can take a seaplane at the waterfront and fly off to **Taku Lodge,** where you'll dine in a log cabin on grilled fresh salmon, biscuits, baked beans, and beer that doesn't need a refrigerator—they just stick it in a glacier.

A popular treat in Juneau is now celebrating nearly 15 years of open fire and sourdough. Called the **Gold Creek Salmon Bake,** the event is an evening activity departing at 6 p.m. from the Baranof Hotel and offering (at $14 for adults, $7 for children) all you can eat of Alaska salmon barbecued over an open fire, salads, and sourdough bread, plus exploration of an abandoned gold mine and a chance to pan for some of your own.

To get a 180-degree look at Alaska, stop in at the **Alaska Adventure Theatre and Gift Shop,** 145 Marine Way (tel. 907/586-2419), where you can see this vast state on a 180-degree wrap-around screen. Price is $5.75 for adults, $3 for children; it's open from 10 a.m. to 9 p.m. daily with shows on the hour.

Skagway

Population: 2000.

Tourist Information: Skagway Convention and Visitors Bureau, (tel. 907/983-2297).

Shopping Specialties: gold rush souvenirs, gold nuggets.

Restaurants: Golden North Hotel (tel. 907/983-2294); Klondike Hotel (tel. 907/983-2291).

You may not be able to buy happiness with gold, but you can certainly get a good start on it with a couple of sizable nuggets. At least that's the way they figured it in Skagway's good old days when, without the pursuit of shiny yellow, there wouldn't have been a Skagway.

Located at the foot of White Pass, Skagway was the gateway to the Klondike, so in 1897 you stood out of the way or the roaring tide of gold seekers would run you down. In those days, thousands of gold bugs tore into this tiny town, turning it into a booming metropolis with a population of 20,000—19,900 or so of them acquired in two years of the gold boom.

Tents went up, then cabins, then all the accoutrements of life: hotels, gambling houses and other houses, dance halls, saloons.

You can still see many of those rugged-but-ready structures today, carefully preserved by residents proud of their rough-and-tumble heritage. In fact, most of the downtown section of Skagway has been designated a **National Historic Park.**

Buildings with false fronts and boardwalks line the street. Over at City Hall you can roam through the **Trail of '98 Museum** and get an idea what it must have been like to be one of those early pioneers (admission is $2; open from 8 a.m. to 8 p.m.).

Just outside of town, the **Gold Rush Cemetery,** about a two-mile flat walk from the ferry terminal, was the end of the line for many a brawling, claim-contesting gold enthusiast, including two local legends, gangster Frank Reid and gambler Soapy Smith, who were victims of each other in an 1898 gunfight.

In summer the city recreates its past with a historical comic drama that's as hysterical as it is historical.

A simple walking tour is the best way to see this town—just don't forget your camera.

You can also take a conducted motorcoach sightseeing tour of **Klondike Gold Rush National Park** and the historical district of Skagway from Klondike Hotel. Alaska Hyway Tours, P.O. Box 536-DT, Skagway, AK 99840 (tel. 907/983-2241), has details.

Skagway city limits include part of Klondike Gold Rush National Historical Park, which commemorates the gold rush trail of '98. Roads from both Skagway and nearby Haines join the Alaska Highway.

Cruising Glacier Bay

Highlight of every Alaska cruise is the trip through a small part of the 11,400 square miles of **Glacier Bay National Monument,** where 16 towering ice mountains spill into the bay and its inlets. This is fjord country at its finest, with downright spectacular scenery that cannot be done justice by mere words.

As you sip a mid-morning mulled wine, your ship sails back 4000 years into the Ice Age as towering walls of ice glitter around you and icebergs bob in the water.

Great masses of ice break from the glaciers occasionally, accompanied by deep rumblings and thunderous cracks. It's called "calving," and the broken-off bits of ice that surge into the sea are called "pups." Two hundred years ago the land here was covered by ice that has receded to leave behind slopes covered in thick forests of spruce, alder, willow, and mosses.

In the 50 miles of sea here you may spot humpback and killer whales, porpoises, sunning seals, black and brown bear, and on the slopes, mountain goats and the bald eagle, one of some 200 species of birds. Under the water, trout, salmon, and halibut thrive, many of them likely to end up on your plate at dinner.

Glaciers are formed by heavy snowfall that accumulates, packs, and fuses into ice masses. Advance or retreat of glaciers is measured at the terminus of a glacier where the ice is melting and accumulating at the same time. Two hundred years ago ice 4000 feet deep and 20 miles wide walled the entrance to Glacier Bay, but by about a hundred years ago it had retreated nearly 50 miles to be replaced by the huge forests you see today. Glacier Bay's ice sheet is in fact shrinking at a pace so rapid that scientists are mired in controversy over the future of this glacial region.

By prearrangement, a naturalist comes on board every cruise ship cruising Glacier Bay and tells you a little about the evolutionary processes you see going on here. You'll get a good overview of the natural phenomenon you are witnessing from these naturalists, who love and respect the land they serve. Their talks are a highlight of the cruise.

Anchorage

Population: 48,000

Tourist Information: Anchorage Convention and Visitors Bureau, 201 East Third Ave. (tel. 907/276-4114).

Public Transportation: bus, train, ferry, taxi.

Car Rentals: Avis, 5th and B Streets (tel. 907/277-4567); Hertz, International Airport (tel. 907/243-3308).

Shopping Specialties: hand-knit garments made by Eskimos from wools combed from the Arctic musk ox at Oomingmak Musk Ox Producers' Co-op, 604 H St. (tel. 272-9225).

Restaurants: Sheraton Anchorage Hotel, Calista Square, 401 E. Sixth Ave. (tel. 907/276-8700); Hotel Captain Cook, 5th and K Sts. (tel. 276-6000); and Samovar Inn, 720 Gambell St. (tel. 277-1511).

If you think you've been down at sea level long enough, get up in the world on a chair-lift ride 2000 feet up to the **Skyride Restaurant** at Alyeska Resort. Located about 40 miles southeast of Anchorage, the resort features nightskiing in winter, hotel and condominium accommodations, a ski school, the works. In summer you can ride up to the restaurant in 45 minutes as a view of eight surrounding glaciers spreads out beneath your feet.

The largest city in Alaska, Anchorage is reached by train on a three-hour ride from the port at Whittier. Once there, you'll find quite a cosmopolitan city with all the restaurants, hotels, nightlife, and beautiful homes you'd expect to see in a major metropolis.

Founded in 1915 as the headquarters of the Alaska Railroad, the city is an important defense city for the U.S. and also is a center for commerce and communications in Alaska. About 48,000 people live here, many of them employed by fisheries, sawmills, and highway- or pipeline-related activities.

On the last Saturday in June the city welcomes summer with music, songs, dance, games, food, and plenty of fun at the annual **Alaska Fest** in Palmer State Fairgrounds.

An interesting springtime excursion from Anchorage takes you to a **gold mining area** older than the Klondike, where you can pan for gold. It's 3½ miles up Crow Creek Road.

At the **Alaska Zoo** Mile 2 O'Malley Rd. (tel. 344-8012) you can see orphaned native animals.

You can have a good time at an Alaska **show and sourdough buffet,** now in its tenth season here. Alaska's "ambassador," Larry Beck, recites poetry, sings songs, tells stories, and offers you a look at things Alaskana at a dinner and show. Phone 907/278-9225 for reservation.

Anchorage also sports a civic operation and concert association, a historical and fine arts museum featuring a rundown of man in Alaska from prehistory to the present (free), a Scottish pipe band, a Bach festival, and a dinner theater. You can even go up above the glaciers in a hot air balloon!

If you didn't pan for gold at Juneau or Skagway, here's your chance: **Crow Creek Mine,** 123 Hightower Rd., Girdwood (tel. 783-2915), harks back to 1898 and is in the National Register of Historic Places. It's open to visitors who come here to pan ore or, for those lacking panning enthusiasm, to purchase it in the mine's shop. All the panning equipment is furnished free, so why not give it a try? Finders keepers. . . .

Not far from Anchorage is the best known of the many national parks in the state: **Denali National Park and Preserve,** one of the most dramatic national parks in North America is 5.6 million acres of wilderness surrounding Mt. McKinley, the tallest mountain in the world (the Himalayas start at higher elevations). You can reach the park from Anchorage by train, plane, bus or car and stay right in the park at a hotel operated by the park service. Most people visit the region on a guided tour and one of the top Alaska tour operators is Westours (which also owns Holland America Cruise Lines). To see what the company has to offer, contact them at 800/426-0327.

If you're planning to stay in Anchorage for a few days, major hotels there include the **Sheraton Anchorage,** Calista Square, 401 E. Sixth Ave., Anchorage 99501 (tel. 907/276-8700); toll-free 800/325-3535) where rates are $119 to $132 double; **Best Western Golden Lion,** 1000 E. 36th Ave., Anchorage 99504 (tel. 907/278-4561 or toll-free 800/528-1234) where rates are $82 double; or **Hotel Captain Cook,** a 600-room hotel with swimming pool at 5th and K Streets, Anchorage 99501 (tel. 907/276-6000; toll-free 800/323-7500) where rates are $115 double. A budget choice is **Arctic Inn Motel,** 842 W. International Airport Rd., Anchorage AK 99502 (tel. 907/561-1328) where rates are $35 double/daily, $200 a week.

2. Caribbean Islands

Welcome to perpetual summer. In the frosty throes of February and the miserable days of March, these islands, stretching more than 2000 miles southward, are dressed in toasty golden sand and bathed in warm waters. Trade winds stream across the islands maintaining eternal June, as seasons pass with nary a whimper of falling leaves or changing temperatures.

Here in these islands are what many call the world's most beautiful seas, clear as a teardrop, sluicing over beaches described in equivalent superlatives. Tiny bays hugged by craggy cliffs . . . great sweeps of silver, pink, gold, or black sand . . . secluded coves meant for lovers of beaches and of each other—all those are the rule here, no exceptions.

Just as each new beach you happen upon is surprisingly different from the last strip of silica you roamed, these islands are as culturally diverse as a history of imperialistic battling can make them. On some islands, Trinidad and Tobago, for instance, you'll find a dozen or more nationalities ranging from Indian to Chinese, Venezuelan, French, Spanish, English, and Lebanese.

On each island are the remnants, or the still-strong presence, of France, Holland, Denmark, England, Sweden, Spain, and sometimes a combination of several or all of the above. St. Maarten / St. Martin is so culturally divided it has two names! Settled by Dutch and French crewmen left behind by a Spanish ship, the island's first colonists couldn't reach the folks back home to find out which nation should rule, so they just split it up themselves, your half and my half.

Descendents of the thousands of slaves imported here from Africa to become the lowliest of citizens, working vast sugar, tobacco, and banana plantations, are now prime ministers and governors, bureaucrats, businesswomen, and bar owners.

Not all of these islands are the somnolent sands they were when Columbus first visited here 500 years ago. Jet-plane-loads of tourists and an era of rapid communication have turned sandy spots like Puerto Rico into sophisticated centers sporting the latest in couture, cosmopolitan and chic.

Others have remained virtually untouched by the tides of time, their colonial architecture lovingly restored or crumbling softly, slowly into sandy oblivion.

When you visit here you'll be traveling in the wake of Columbus, Ponce de Leon, Balboa, DeSoto, Admiral Lord Nelson, plus humble sailors and marauding pirates—not all of them men either!

All came here seeking treasure, but many returned disappointed not to have found it. Little did they dream that in centuries to come their descendants would find that treasure, not in gold nuggets and shining jewels, but in golden sands and sapphire seas.

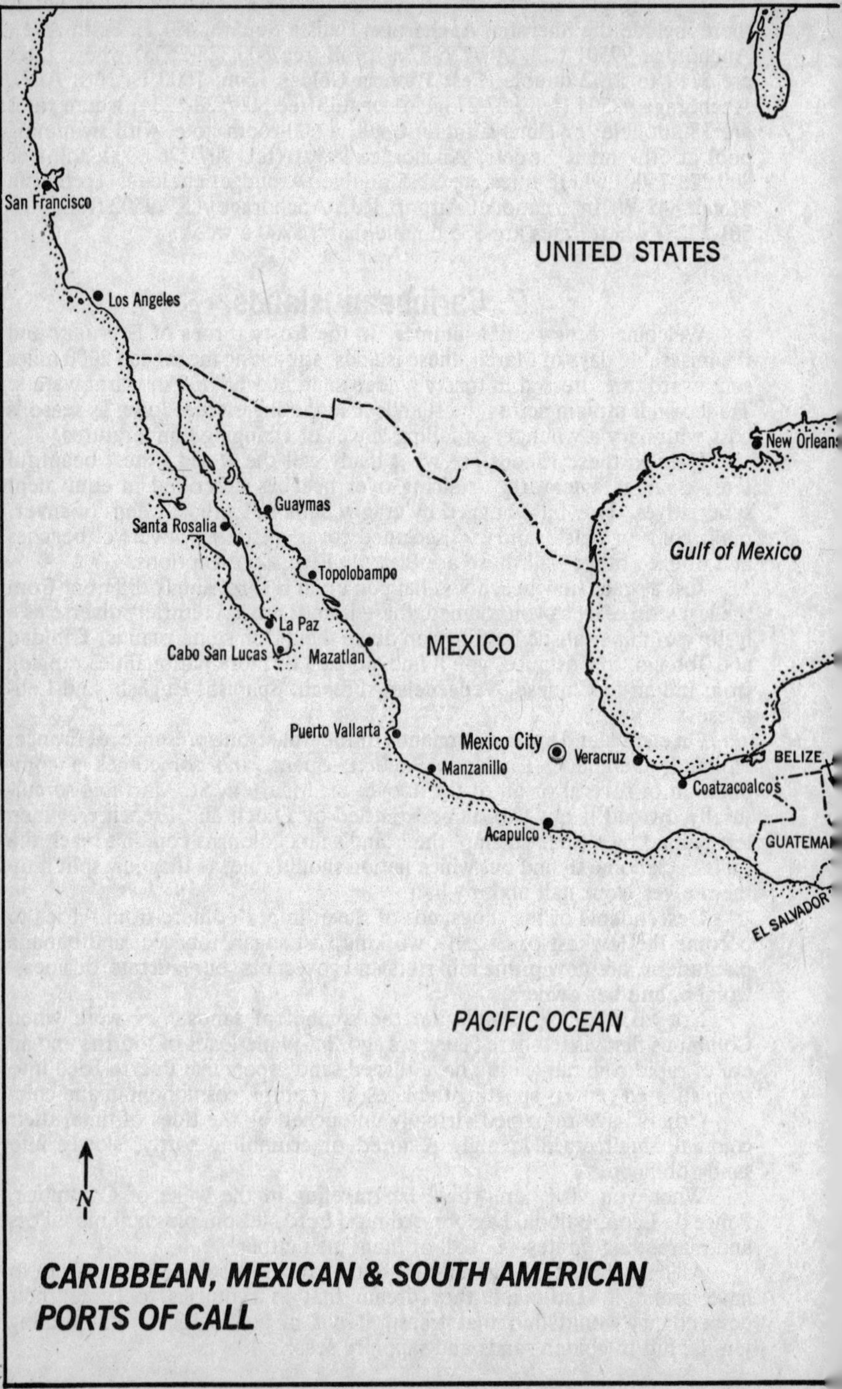

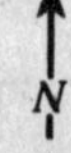

CARIBBEAN, MEXICAN & SOUTH AMERICAN PORTS OF CALL

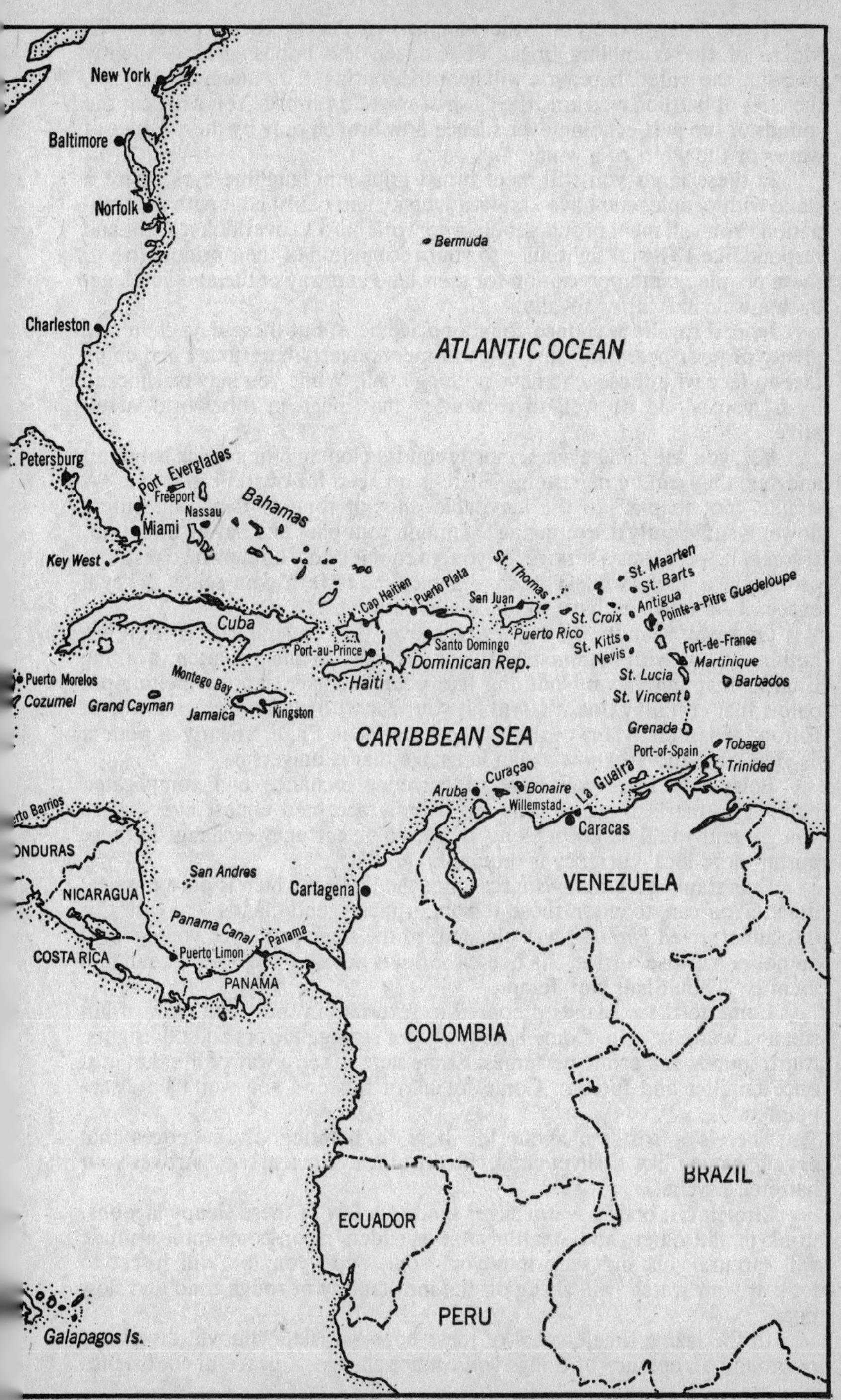
New York
Baltimore
Norfolk
Bermuda
Charleston
ATLANTIC OCEAN
Petersburg
Port Everglades
Freeport
Nassau
Bahamas
Miami
Key West
St. Thomas
St. Maarten
St. Barts
Antigua
Pointe-a-Pitre Guadeloupe
Cap Haitien
Puerto Plata
San Juan
Cuba
St. Croix
Puerto Rico
Santo Domingo
St. Kitts
Nevis
Fort-de-France
Port-au-Prince
Dominican Rep.
Martinique
Haiti
St. Lucia
Barbados
Puerto Morelos
Montego Bay
St. Vincent
Cozumel
Grand Cayman
Jamaica
Kingston
Grenada
CARIBBEAN SEA
Tobago
Port-of-Spain
Trinided
Curaçao
Aruba
Bonaire
La Guaira
Willemstad
Caracas
HONDURAS
San Andres
Cartagena
VENEZUELA
NICARAGUA
Panama Canal
Panama
COSTA RICA
Puerto Limon
PANAMA
COLOMBIA
BRAZIL
ECUADOR
PERU
Galapagos Is.

If you listen closely, on the ramparts of Puerto Rico's towering El Morro or the crumbling bricks of a dozen less imposing forts silently guarding the waters here, you will hear the roaring, fiery boom of cannons, the cries of battling warriors, the clash of sword on sword. You will hear the sounds of the past echoing over silence now broken only by the whisper of waves or the whirr of a wing.

In these lands you will meet broad grins and laughing eyes, share a smile with people who have known adversity and banished it with determination. You will meet proud people who work hard to overlook a slight and respond like 100-watt lightbulbs to your recognition of their pride. Give to these people quiet appreciation for their land and way of life and you'll get back a welcome fit for royalty.

Indeed royalty was once commonplace here, but these days there are plenty of poor peasants. Yes, you will meet poverty here today and come face-to-face with those who have nothing at all. While you may be shocked by it, you would do well to remember that much in this world is relative.

Yes, you will find beggars, mostly children looking for a quick handout, and yes, they can be persistent. There is no need for overkill, however. A simple "no, thanks" to the inevitable offer of song or dance or wilting flower is sufficiently discouraging. Maintain your pace and pay no attention. If someone performs a service for you, even if it's only holding a goat still or proffering a smile while you snap a picture, have a coin ready. They'll expect it—and we all have to make a living, right?

On many islands you will also discover that understanding often has nothing to do with common language. French, Spanish, Dutch, a lilting English that may sound nothing like your language, and a melting-pot patois that certainly doesn't, will hit your ear with all the foreign flavor of Europe. Fear not. Many of the local people speak English nearly as perfect as your own and all know a sign language that is universal.

Belay any fears you have of currency exchange and complicated banking. American greenbacks are happily accepted almost everywhere you go, and you'll be given plenty of advice on currency exchange in those ports where local currency is required.

Fear stems from many sources, not the least of which is pure physical dread. You can abandon those terrors in these gentle lands . . . with this disclaimer: even Paradise was plagued, so the same prudence you'd use at home seems wise advice. As one close to us advises: the 11th Commandment is "Thou Shalt Not Tempt."

Come to these islands prepared to luxuriate in the warm glow of hot sun and warm people. Come here ready for strange flavors and odd sights, weird sounds and exotic perfumes. Come here to see a way of life that is at once familiar and foreign. Come for all of this and you won't be disappointed.

There's a softness about life here, a blunting of the edges that envelopes you like a velvet cloak, that soothes your fears and strokes your battered psyche.

Stretch out on the warm silver sand of a few of these sleepy lagoons, drink in the quiet, and stealthily the islanders' soon-come-mon attitude will capture you and seep into your soul. Soon you too will forget to look at your watch, will shrug off the inevitability of rough road and slow boat.

In the lazing timelessness of these eons-old islets you will discover a newfound acceptance of things you cannot change, a peaceful coexistence with unseen forces that have shaped all this, and surely must have a masterplan for you too.

Antigua (and Barbuda)

Size: 108 square miles.

Capital and Port City: St. John's (pop. 30,000).

Population: 73,000 (1200 of these on Barbuda).

Language: English.

Average Temperatures: 78°F in winter, 83°F in summer.

Currency: Eastern Caribbean ("bee wee") dollar (E.C.$): $1.00 U.S. = E.C.$2.60.

Public Transportation: taxis (buses not recommended).

Tourist Information: Antigua & Barbuda Department of Tourism, High Street and Corn Alley, St. John's (tel. 462-0029).

Car Rentals: Antigua Car Rentals, Barrymore Hotel, Fort Rd., near St. John's (tel. 2-1055). Note that you must have a valid U.S. driver's license, but also must purchase an Antigua driver's license (price: E.C.$10) at the police station, High St., St. John's; the Inland Revenue Office, High St., St. John's, over the post office; or the car-rental agent.

Shopping Specialties: The main duty-free shops are on Redcliffe and Long Streets. Best buys are island fashions, shell jewelry, local crafts (polished stone jewelry, black coral), sea island cotton. A favorite gift is a Warri Board, a seed game (brought from Africa) played on a board with 14 holes.

Restaurants: The Spanish Main Inn, East Street (tel. 2-0660); Darcy's in Kensington Court, St. Mary's Street (tel. 2-6460); Golden Peanut, High Street (tel. 2-1415).

Long before Columbus trained a glass on Antigua in 1493 and named it after the Santa Maria la Antigua Church in Seville, Spain, Carib and Arawak Indians had found its shores hospitable. They left calling cards of shell tools and stone artifacts that you can still see today.

Antigua is the largest of the Leeward Islands. From its shores shallow hills rise to a height of 1330 feet at Boggy Peak. The few interior roads twist and turn among the hills, defying estimated driving times. But it's the beaches that lure travelers to Antigua's shores—365 separate coral beaches, one for each day of the year. And those are just on the Caribbean side (there are more on the Atlantic)!

Barbuda's circle of reefs harbors a rainbow of fish and lobster, many of which end their days as the main course in local restaurants.

The British first settled Antigua in 1632, and by 1704, huge, protected English Harbour, proclaimed one of the safest in the world, had become home port to the British fleet. When the American Revolution loomed, English ships fanned out through the Caribbean to engage potential predators to British colonies—the French, Dutch, and Spanish. From the Dockyard here Admiral Nelson set off to court and marry Fanny Nisbet, who lived on nearby Nevis. In more recent times Princess Margaret and Anthony Armstrong-Jones honeymooned at Clarence House, and in 1977 Queen Elizabeth and Prince Philip visited.

Not many years after America won its independence, activity at English Harbour began to decline. Antigua's importance as a naval center plummeted when, in 1789, copper sheathing was discovered to deter worms and barnacles from ship's bottoms. Careening and cleaning hulls at naval outposts was greatly reduced. The Industrial Revolution and the arrival of steamships in the 19th century issued the coup de grâce. English Harbour and the doors of Nelson's Dockyard formally closed in 1889, but in 1951 restoration of this historic harbor began.

In St. John's you'll see the cobblestone sidewalks and weather-beaten wooden houses that characterize this large, neatly laid-out town. Your ship will tie up on the right side of Deep-water Pier, less than a mile from the two towers of St. John's Cathedral. Drift down to the lower end of Market Street to the **open-air market.** Nowhere on Antigua can you drink in more of the local color that so typifies this exotic land. Fruits, vegetables, livestock, and colorful West Indian dresses battle for attention. It's a photographer's dream.

Seek out the landmark that has guided ships into St. John's for 300 years: **St. John's Cathedral,** at Church Lane between Long and Newgate Streets, the capital's most spectacular and famous structure, built in 1683. At the south entrance gates, erected in 1789, take a look at the figures of St. John the Baptist and St. John the Divine. Legend has it that these figures were redeemed from a Napoleonic ship and brought to Antigua by a British man-of-war.

Tours of the **Antigua Rum Distillery** at the Harbour can be arranged by the Tourist Office.

Take an excursion bus across the island to explore **English Harbour** and **Nelson's Dockyard.** Its docks and warehouses were built at great cost in human life. In the 18th century, 175,000 British soldiers are thought to have died fighting pirates, the French, the Dutch, and the Spanish, and from fatigue and disease contracted while erecting fortifications and docking facilities in the Caribbean.

Restoration of the Dockyard's port and historic buildings began in the 1950s. Accuracy of architectural detail has been a guiding principle, but now, in place of vast stores needed to supply a naval fleet, the warehouses and storehouses shelter shops, restaurants, and even an inn. To "do" the Dockyard, plan the better part of a day, so you can prowl Fort Berkeley and nearby Clarence House.

Clarence House, built in 1787, is filled with lovely furnishings and is the governor's weekend home, but open to the public at other times. A gatekeeper will guide you through the mansion.

General Shirley, governor of the Leewards in 1781, fortified the hills guarding English Harbour and the remnants of those fortifications remain, although they're now largely in ruins. Completed in 1731, **Fort Berkley** is at the entrance to English Harbour. Walk the footpath from the Dockyard gate to get a good look at it.

Aruba

Capital and Port City: Orangestad.

Size: 20 miles long by 6 miles wide.

Population: 66,000.

Climate: median temperature 83°F.

Language: Dutch, English.

Currency: Netherlands Antillean guilder; NA 1 = 56¢ U.S.

Tourist Information: Aruba Tourist Bureau, 2 A. Shuttestraat, Oranjestad (tel. 23777).

Public Transportation: bus, unmetered taxi (prices posted).

Shopping Specialties: The duty-free shops for quality imports, no sales tax. The main shopping street is Nassaustraat: New Amsterdam Store for general and gift items, Spritzer & Fuhrmann for great luxury items. Best buys: perfume, liquor, linens, jewelry, watches, cameras, designer clothes, crystal, china.

Restaurants: Italian, French, Indonesian, American, and Chinese cuisines available. Try Papiamento, 7 Wihelminastraat, for continental food; Bali, a floating houseboat docked at Schooner Harbor off Lloyd Smith Blvd. (tel. 2131), for Indonesian food.

Trade wind–sculptured divi-divi trees lean to the winds, their upper branches trailing like a mermaid's hair. Below the cliffs, thundering waves beat against a coral rock shore sending magnificent plumes of spray skyward. This is Aruba, where the pounding, turbulent Atlantic has pierced the coral cliffs, carving out the Caribbean's highest, most dramatic natural bridge.

So violent is this constant oceanic rage, so unsettling in its effect, so erie in its mood, that one forgets this is quiet Aruba, a sleepy land whose other shore sports acres of white sands and gently lapping waves.

Located just 15 miles from Venezuela's coast, this long, skinny island is dry and sunny year round. On the low hills a variety of cacti, set among odd and sometimes wild rock formations, play extravagant contrast to island houses painted in soft pastels and rising demurely from flower gardens whose splashes of color peek from behind cactus fences.

Away to the south this desert-like island rises to its highest point, Mount Yamanota, a 617-foot cone-shaped hill. On the coast a few miles away is Aruba's second city, St. Nicholaas, that sprang to life when Standard Oil of New Jersey built a refinery here in 1929.

Although Aruba's 66,000 people trace roots to 40 nationalities, about half count Arawak Indian among their ancestry. These gentle, smiling people were slender and distinctive in appearance, and Arubans have retained these traits. Unlike the fierce Carib Indians, the Arawaks were a peaceful people living in small settlements and in the many caves on the island's north and east shores.

Here, where the desolate land drops sharply into a turbulent sea, excavations are unearthing ancient clay pottery of fine craftsmanship and artistic design. Hieroglyphs painted on cave walls and ceilings, and on great granite rocks that dot the near-moonscape scenery, remain a mystery.

Spanish Capt. Alonso de Ojeda first saw Aruba in the last year of the 15th century. The 16th century, however, was not a good time for the Spanish. Wars with the Dutch and the British defeat of the Spanish Armada in 1588 weakened Spain, permitting the determined, adventurous Dutch to take possession of Aruba in 1636.

A highlight of Aruban history: Gold was discovered in 1824 and mined for 89 years. Occasionally a fat nugget is still found and gold fever again rages over the island. Riches also came to the island when in 1925 Standard Oil built a refinery near St. Nicholaas. But as the company turned to automation, even the "black gold" failed Arubans.

It wasn't until the 1970s that Aruba discovered its newest industry, tourism. Sun and sand worshipers worldwide found Aruba, and modern hotels and casinos have risen to meet the demand of steadily increasing numbers of visitors.

In Oranjestad, wander along an unusual marketplace: **Schooner Har-**

bor is an open boatman's market where sloops and ships of all kinds sell their wares from decks and stalls. This is the place to feel the throb of inter-island commercial life, and it doesn't take much to imagine what life must have been like here 200 years ago.

On the edge of town, explore **Fort Zoutman,** an 18th-century fort named after a Dutch rear admiral of the same name.

Then stroll over to **William III Tower:** the lighthouse lamp was first lit in 1867 on the king's birthday. Industrialists may want to pop over to Ranchostraat to see the gigantic lime kiln, reputedly the largest in the Caribbean.

To get a lasting impression of the real Oranjestad, keep looking up. Storefronts and shops along the streets have changed over the years, but the second stories still reflect **Dutch architecture.**

If you've always wanted to see an archeological excavation, the **Arawak hieroglyphs** in the cave at Fontein make a fascinating expedition. Combine your excursion with a swing up to the natural **coral bridge** before heading back through the middle of the island to see the strange natural rock formations at Ayo and Casibari. Some of these diorite boulders are the size of buildings and are a puzzle to geologists.

Should a stroll along the powdery sand beaches and a view of swanky hotels be more your style, catch a bus from downtown Oranjestad across from the Tourist Office and ride out to **Eagle** and **Palm Beaches.**

Sizable gold nugget finds around Bushiribana on the east coast and Balashi on the south Caribbean coast still generate rashes of **gold fever** periodically. If you're going to drive over to see these smelters, check with the Tourist Office in town for directions. Look around. Who knows?

The Tourist Office will also arrange for a tour of Standard Oil subsidiary, Lago Oil & Transport Company, Ltd., an **oil refinery** to the south near St. Nicholaas. Now largely automated, it's an overwhelming sight with a wild array of pipes and flues outside, slick automation inside.

No golf here but tennis players will find courts, and horses are available for equestrians.

Barbados

Capital and Port City: Bridgetown (pop. 97,000).

Size: 166 square miles.

Island Population: 247,000.

Climate: 75° to 85°F year round.

Language: English.

Currency: Barbados dollar $1.00 = 50¢ U.S.

Tourist Information: Barbados Board of Tourism, Prescod Blvd. and Harbour Rd., Bridgetown (tel. 986-6516).

Public Transportation: bus, taxi.

Car Rentals: Note that your U.S. driver's license must be validated at the police desk at the airport; fee: $10 U.S.

Dress: shorts for beach wear only.

Shopping Specialties: jewelry, china, crystal, rum (Mount Gay Rum has been produced since 1809), cashmere, Thai silks, French and Italian handbags. The duty-free shops are on Broad and Swan Streets. The three largest retailers—Harrison's, Da Costa & Musson, and Cave Shepherd Ltd.—are located on Broad Street. Try Pelican Village at Deep Water Harbour for straw goods and local handicrafts.

Food Specialties: flying fish, squid, lobster, crane chub, sea eggs (sea urchin roe), pepper-pot, suckling pig, and such fruits as soursop and pawpaws.

Restaurants: Le Bistro, near the Careenage (tel. 75161); Flying Fish, at Fairchild and Bay Streets (tel. 64537).

Only 100 miles east of the Lesser Antilles, Barbados floats like a green cloud on the horizon of an azure sea. It is as east as you can get in the Caribbean: waves born off Africa 7000 miles away surge across the Atlantic to crash on Barbados's eastern shores, while on the island's other coast serene beaches bake in the sun and the blue Caribbean laps the palm-lined shores like a lazy river.

Over eons these tropical seas, rich in marine life, built the island layer upon coral layer, ringed its shores with wide beaches, and in time laid down the soil that was to bring abundance to the land. From the shores, rolling hills climb to the interior of this tiny island to reach Barbados's highest point, Mt. Hillaby, 1105 feet above the sea.

Exotic tropical vegetation clothes the land: tamarinds and breadfruit and palm trees. Scarlet bougainvilleas, fragrant frangipani, flaming poinsettias, and starry stephanotis splash rainbow colors across the landscape. Such exquisite natural beauty is mirrored in pastel houses and cottages perched high on the rolling hillsides, flaunting colors as striking as the flowers.

Britannia ruled the waves and guided the destiny of this tiny island, only 14 miles wide and 21 miles long, for more than 300 years, until 1966 when the island gained independence. Three centuries of that influence has left an indelible imprint of British formality and courtesy. Yet the warm, hospitable nature of the island and its people remains distinctively Barbadian—they call it a Bajan welcome. Literacy rates here are the highest in the Caribbean.

When the British first landed in 1625, Barbados was already old. Arawak Indians, the first known Caribbean island-hoppers, had long before followed the stars up from South America, sailing here in canoes. There is evidence that Barbados was a regular port of call until the end of the 16th century, when for reasons lost in time, no more was seen of this tribe.

No one knows the origin of the name Barbados, but 16th-century Portuguese maps refer to Los Barbados, the beards. Legend says that when the Portuguese landed in 1536, a species of fig trees growing on the island reminded them of *barbas,* or beards.

British colonists introduced and tended a wide variety of crops, but sugarcane offered the greatest profits. By 1645 large plantations had sprung up around the island. You can still see them today, restored and refurbished. One of the more famous is Drax Hall, built by Sir William Drax, one of the earliest sugar barons.

That cane still grows green on rolling hills and sways in the trade winds. An economy based on it flouishes. Sugar—and time—has been sweet to Barbados.

The famed, the fortunate, and the infamous have left their footprints in Barbados's golden sands. George Washington not only slept here, he stayed here for many months of his 20th year in 1751. On the corner of Bay Street and Chelsea Road is a house known as the George Washington House.

Queen Elizabeth II and Prince Philip visited in 1966 at Villa Nova, a gracious stone house built in 1834 as a sugar plantation house, later owned by British Prime Minister Anthony Eden. Beautiful gardens sweep out from the house toward valleys and the sea beyond.

One of Barbados's swashbuckling visitors was Captain Bligh of the good ship *Bounty*. The harsh captain, a regular Johnny Appleseed of the Caribbean, is said to have planted the first breadfruit tree here, but several other islands make the same claim.

To get the most from your Barbados visit, first savor some Barbados flavor. At the **Careenage** look for the Barbadian Harbour Patrol, who wear starched middy blouses reminiscent of Lord Nelson's jacktars. In sailing days ships like Nelson's came into Barbados to scrape their hulls. This meant laying the ship over on its side—careened—in shallow water. When the tide went out, the exposed side of the hull bottom was scraped to remove barnacles built up in months of sailing.

Today you'll see inter-island schooners and motor vessles unloading cargoes of bananas, plantains and mangoes onto waiting carts and baskets —a photogenic sight.

Nearby is **Trafalgar Square** and **Chamberlain Bridge.** The square dates from 1874, but Admiral Lord Nelson's statue here was erected in 1815, about 25 years before London's famed monument to the victor of Trafalgar. Nelson and his fleet visited here on June 4, 1805, a few months before the battle and his death. On the north side of the square, public buildings, like the **House of Assembly,** are architecturally fascinating. The east wing has intriguing window paintings of British monarchs from James I to Elizabeth I.

In Bridgetown's Queen's Park you'll see oddity: a **boabab tree** more than 61 feet in circumference reputed to be 1000 years old. The boabab is native only to Africa and no one knows how this one got to Barbados.

Government House, at the corner of Belmont and Pine Roads, is a stately house built in 1680 of coral stone, the official residence of the queen's representative. Visitors are welcome to view this beautiful example of New World architecture and its gardens.

Barbados Museum, about 1½ miles down Highway 7, is housed in the old Military Detention Barracks, erected in 1853. Cells and warders' quarters have been made into galleries. The museum is a microcosm of Barbados past and present. A fine collection of archeological finds, including conch-shell tools used by the Arawak and Carib Indians, are on display and you can see silver, china, glass, and furniture typical of plantation days. Open Monday through Saturday from 9 a.m. to 6 p.m.

To get a glimpse of Barbados's plantation life and natural phenomena, drive out on the island. Although distances are small, the island speed limit is 30 miles per hour. All driving times given below are approximate, and assume a starting point of Trafalgar Square.

Harrison's Cave, in St. Thomas Parish, is about a 45-minute drive. You can tour this subterranean cavern by tram on an hour-long trip that visits the 150-foot-long Great Hall; two cascades, called Twin Falls, which plunge to the cave's floor and disappear; Mirror Lake; and the Rotunda Room, a stunning chamber 250 feet long and 100 feet high composed of cream and white formations that glitter like crystal.

Drax Hall, in St. George Parish, about an hour from town, is one of the oldest recorded buildings and operating sugar plantations on the island, and is still in the possession of the Drax family. Of particular interest is a Jacobean-designed archway carved of mastic wood no longer found here. Remember, too, as you drive around the island, and see its old plantations, that transporting sugar to the docks in the 17th century was a problem. Camels were the Bajun solution! They were imported here to carry bagged sugar to ships waiting in the harbor.

St. Nicholas Abbey, in St. Peter Parish, is about a 90-minute drive. Built about 1650, the abbey, although never an "abbey," is one of the oldest sugar plantation Great Houses still standing in the Caribbean. It is also one of only three Jacobean houses remaining in the Americas. The house contains antique English and Barbadian furniture, some early porcelain, and a fine collection of Wedgwood portrait medallions. Still a working sugar plantation, it's open Monday through Friday from 10 a.m. to 3:30 p.m.

Mullins Mill, in St. Peter Parish, about 90 minutes from town, is shown on a 1717 map of the island. The house itself is one of the most fascinating on the island as it's built around the plantation's old mill wall. The house was rebuilt and restored in 1964.

The Bahamas (Nassau and Freeport)

Capital and Port Cities: Nassau, New Providence; Freeport/Lucaya, Grand Bahama.

Size: New Providence—21 miles long by 7 miles wide (pop. 130,000); Grand Bahama—73 miles long by 4 to 8 miles wide (pop. 30,000).

Country Population: 230,000.

Language: English.

Currency: Bahamian dollar $1 = $1.00 U.S.; U.S. dollar is accepted everywhere.

Tourist Information: Nassau—Bahamas Tourist Office, Nassau Court on the east side of Rawson Square (tel. 322-7500); Freeport/Lucaya—in the International Bazaar (tel. 352-8044).

Public Transportation: Nassau—horse-drawn surreys, jitney bus, taxi; Freeport/Lucaya—taxi, jitney bus.

Car Rentals: Hertz, Sheraton British Colonial, Bay St. (tel. 53716); Avis, same as above (tel. 22889); motor scooters at Nassau Bicycle Co., West Bay Street (tel. 22787).

Shopping Specialties: Nassau—the straw market for all conceivable straw goods, woodcarvings, seashell jewelry, and other native crafts (expect to bargain); in other shops, a variety of imported goods from English crystal to coral jewelry, silver, china, cameras, cashmeres, and wools. Freeport/Lucaya—try the International Bazaar with dozens of shops with the architecture and culture of more than 25 countries.

Food Specialties: conch chowder, conch fritters, and turtle pie.

Restaurants: Nassau—Green Shutters Restaurant, 48 Parliament St. (tel 55702), and the Parliament Terrace Café, 20 Parliament St. (tel. 22836); Freeport/Lucaya—Sir Winston Churchill Pub, on the Mall at the International Bazaar (tel. 352-8866); Pub on the Mall, Ranfurly Circus (tel. 352-5110); the Stoned Crab, Taino Beach, Lucaya (tel. 373-1442); Britannia Pub, King's Rd. on Bell Channel (tel. 373-5919).

Nightlife: Nassau—casinos: at Paradise Island, and at Cable Beach Hotel and Casino at Cable Beach; for clubs: Ronnie's Rebel Room, W. Bay St. (tel. 34481), for the native show, and the Peanuts Taylor Drumbeat Club, W. Bay St. (tel. 24233), for fire dancers, calypso bands, glass eaters, and limbo. Freeport/Lucaya—El Casino, Princess Hotel (tel. 352-7811), for a revue nightly in addition to the casino, and Uncle

Bill's Club Rolls-Royce, on Queen's Highway for American and Caribbean disco.

With the possible exception of its first settlers, the Arawak Indians, Bahamians have always banked on other people's money. Pirates like Henry Morgan, Blackbeard, Mary Read, and Anne Bonney, sought refuge in these numerous islands from man-o-wars. It took nearly a century to dislodge them, a feat finally accomplished by first Bahamian governor Woodes Rogers nearly 100 years after the British settled here in 1629.

Next in the line of privateers came American Civil War–era blockade runners, followed in the 1920s by bootleggers running demon rum into the States. Each time, the Bahamas made money as her hotels burgeoned with these neo-swashbucklers partying it up at the Royal Victoria and the British Colonial.

Finally, island citizens, seeing the profits in privateering, went into the shipwrecking business themselves, earning scads of dollars by luring ships onto the rocks and shoals that surround the islands. Even today modern smugglers find the thousands of reefs, cays, and coves a useful cover for nefarious activities.

A vast and far-flung country, the 700+ Bahamian islands and 2400 cays speckle 100,000 square miles of territorial waters of Atlantic Ocean. The islands and cays (pronounced "keys") are low and flat, actually the flattened tops of huge submarine mountains rising from the depths of the Atlantic Ocean.

Today the islands are a mecca whose muzzein is the sun calling faithful sunworshipers here from all over the world. Lying less than 100 miles from Florida's east coast, the Bahamas are among the most developed islands in the tropics.

Nassau is the nation's capital and offers sophisticated hotels with both native and chic nighttime entertainment in town and on Paradise Island, just a bridge away, while Freeport/Lucaya on Grand Bahama Island is more of the same. Resort complexes, duty-free shops, golf courses, tennis courts, international bazaars, casinos, nightclubs, and hundreds of restaurants cater to every whim of modern man.

British Crown Colony days ended in 1964 when the Bahamas were granted internal self-government. Five years later their constitution was in place, and on July 10, 1973, the islands became the world's 143rd sovereign nation. But two centuries of British rule have left such legacies of pomp and ceremony as the changing of the governor's palace guard, the uniforms of traffic police, and the powdered wigs in courts of law.

Nassau is the country's capital. It is a proud and historic city, both old and sparkling new. The waterfront architecture of Bay Street and Woodes Rogers Walk hasn't changed all that much in the last 200 years, but a successful tourist economy has changed many things. Resorts have brought new land- and cityscapes, and in the process given the people a new sense of worth and a new focus. Nassau today is a city alive and bustling, its citizens aware that they are forging a destiny as a country catering to the vacationing needs of the world.

Both the famous and the infamous have visited here. In the Senate Building on Parliament Square, Queen Elizabeth II delivered her Silver Jubilee throne speech in 1977, a big event in Bahamian history. Winston Churchill stayed at lovely old Graycliff Mansion, now a small but plush hotel and restaurant, more than 60 years ago. And in their time, Howard

Hughes and the shah of Iran have enjoyed the indolent life of these shores.

Visiting the island is easy. You dock right in the middle of things at **Prince George Wharf,** where your ship ties up just a step away from **Rawson Square,** Bay Street, and the center of town. From there you can roam the shops of busy Bay Street and visit the famed **straw market.**

"You can make anything out of straw if you just put your mind to it" is the conviction of the craftsmen in this sprawling expanse. Reputedly the largest in the world, the straw market has been relocated from its former Rawson Square location and is now just a few blocks west on Bay Street to the right of the pier. From miniature animals to placemats, dolls, handbags, baskets, replicas of the horse and surrey, and a thousand other items await your selection, including the work of some of the best woodcarvers in the country. Here you can bargain and dicker to your heart's content.

When the straw market moved, the historical value of the square was revealed. Now you can imagine the activities that must once have taken place in this old slave market, the large open building on the north end of the square. The building dates back to the early 1800s to just before abolition.

Just up from Rawson Square across Bay Street is **Parliament Square.** The House of Assembly, Supreme Court and the Library all front on this venerable old square under the watchful eyes of the statue of a young Queen Victoria, who sits placidly in the midst of these public buildings dating from 1812.

As you explore Nassau, seek out George Street, where you'll find **Government House,** an imposing structure with a pretty pink facade and green lawns rolling up to wide double doors. Once the governor's residence, this mansion atop a hill called Mount Fitzwilliam is where the Duke and Duchess of Windsor lived during the World War II years when he was governor. As imposing as its setting, the 12-foot statue of Christopher Columbus holds the commanding position in the center of the grand stairway. The **Changing of the Guard ceremony** takes place here on alternate Saturdays at 10 a.m.

Walking south on Elizabeth Avenue, you meet an unusual sight: the **Queen's Staircase,** 65 stone steps hand-hewn by slaves who carved them out of the solid limestone in the 18th century. They lead to crumbling Fort Fincastle and were carved as an escape route for troops stationed at the fort.

At the top of the Queen's Staircase is the 165-foot-tall **Water Tower,** offering the best panoramic view of Nassau, the harbor, and Paradise Island. Elevator up to enjoy a long view of the harbor.

Largest and most interesting of Nassau's fortifications is **Fort Charlotte,** built in 1789 and named after King George III's consort. Of particular interest are the many dungeons, underground passages, and the waxworks.

Next to Fort Charlotte is **Ardastra Gardens,** where flamingos steal the show as they parade from 11 a.m. to 4 p.m., walking and marching in unison.

Paradise Beach, a glorious strip of palm-fringed sand, is the best known of several island beaches. Get there on a ferry boat from the dock for $1 or by cab across the bridge ($2 plus cab fare). At Versailles Gardens nere, statuary adorns the long row of terraces leading to the **French Cloister,** originally built in Montrejeau, France, near Lourds, by Augustinian monks in the 14th century. It was disassembled and shipped here in pieces for reconstruction more than 600 years later.

The main sight in Freeport/Lucaya is the **International Bazaar.** More than 25 of the world's cultures display their architecture and wares in this world-famous bazaar. Built in 1967, this is the city's major sightseeing attraction.

Another favorite stopping spot is the **Garden of the Groves,** about seven miles from the International Bazaar. It's an 11-acre botanical garden, both tropical and subtropical, with waterfalls and ponds. The tranquil gardens are home to 10,000 plants and trees.

Out on East Settlers Way is the 100-acre **Rand Memorial Nature Center,** a place of unspoiled forest and trails. A 90-minute guided walk with a naturalist through this protected Bahamian forest is a top-flight chance to photograph Bahamian wildlife.

Cayman Islands

Capital and Port City: George Town, Grand Cayman.

Population: 15,000.

Size: 22 miles long by 8 miles wide.

Climate: 73° to 88°F year round.

Language: English.

Currency: Cayman Islands dollar C.D.$1 = $1.25 U.S.

Tourist Information: Government Administration Building, Elgin Ave. (tel. 949-4844).

Public Transportation: bus, taxi.

Car Rentals: Ace Rent-a-Car, N. Church St. (tel. 94158); Avis, Cayman Airport; and Coconut Car Rentals, Airport Rd. (tel. 949-4037). A driving permit costs $3. See Caribbean Motors, North Church Street (tel. 949-4051), for mopeds and motorcycles.

Shopping Specialties: Duty-free shops for bone china, British woolens, antique silver, cameras, French perfumes, Irish linens, Waterford crystal, Swedish cutlery, sculptured and black coral jewelry.

Restaurants: The Cayman Arms, Harbour Drive on the waterfront (tel. 949-2661); the Almond Tree, North Carolina Street (tel. 949-2893).

Some 500 miles due south of Miami lies a tri-island country that is one of the more unusual in the Caribbean, but for a strange reason—money!

The low-lying coral limestone Cayman Islands contain luxuriant foliage of mangroves, sea grapes, palms, breadfruit, mangoes, oranges, limes, grapefruit, and almonds, but what has put them on the map is an offshore banking-secrecy law that has lured thousands of corporations and monied types here.

Grand Cayman, largest of the three islands in the group, is only 22 miles long by 8 miles wide. Little Cayman and Cayman Brac lie 80 miles northwest of Grand Cayman.

Columbus recorded in his ship's log on May 10, 1503, on his fourth and last voyage, that he passed between two of the Cayman Islands, which he called Las Tortugas (the turtles) for the large numbers of turtles in the water and on the beaches.

The Caymans have a long history as a freebooter's haven. Henry Morgan and Blackbeard are believed to have cached some loot on Cayman Brac, and to have hidden out here while waiting to snag a gold-laden Spanish ship on its run up the gold route.

Most of this British Crown Colony's 15,000 people live in and around

George Town, the port and capital on Grand Cayman. Most of them are descendants of soldiers AWOL from Cromwell's army in Jamaica or shipwrecked sailors. Although the early settlers brought a few slaves from Jamaica and elsewhere, they did not develop a plantation economy here so only a few islanders are of West Indian or African descent. Today's Caymanian speaks with a lilting Welsh accent overlaid with a trace of Scottish brogue intermixed with plenty of American slang.

This speck of an island is famous throughout the Western Hemisphere as a banking center. After tax law changes in 1966, Grand Cayman became known as an offshore tax haven, and at last count had registered 16,500 companies and 400 banks! All that on a vestpocket island.

Those who come with money (or without it) will delight in wide, often-deserted beaches with plenty of nearby wrecks to explore—and on slow evenings you can always visit your money, or somebody else's. Just looking at the hundreds of brass "company" plaques can be quite an amusement.

With a claimed 200-foot water visibility and 300 known shipwrecks, the Caymans are world renowned as a **diving** capital. Seven Mile Beach, with its sugar-white sand, is one of the most beautiful **beaches** in the Americas.

Outside of that silica, there's not a great deal to see or do in George Town: the village is easily explored in an afternoon. After you've checked out the **Clock Monument** to King George V, you might wander over to the **post office** on Edward Street to see one of the oldest government buildings in the Americas still in use today.

Out on the island, the **Cayman Turtle Farm** is interesting and has some handsome tortoise products on sale. For more of the same, catch a bus near the Buy-Rite Market on Panton Avenue and go out to Northwest Point. Here are over 60,000 of the green beauties growing from a few ounces (at hatching time) to 600 pounds or more. Their life cycle is spent in tanks from 30 to 70 feet in diameter. Islanders now make a profitable venture of raising turtles, primarily for food.

Pedro's Castle, a few miles outside of Bodden Town, is the oldest standing building in the Caymans. Originally called St. James Castle, the building was erected by slave labor and today houses a restaurant.

And while you're on the island, **go to Hell!** Everyone does. It's a tiny village with an even tinier post office where you can have your postcards postmarked . . . well, Hell.

Curaçao

Capital and Port City: Willemstad (pop. 40,000).

Size: 38 miles long by 7½ miles wide; 180 square miles.

Island Population: 160,000.

Climate: 82°F on the average day.

Language: Dutch, English, Spanish.

Currency: Netherlands Antillean guilder; NA 1 = $1.75 U.S. Both U.S. and Canadian money circulate freely.

Tourist Information: Curaçao Tourist Board, Schouwburgweg, z/n (tel. 34046) with several offices in Willemstad.

Public Transportation: bus, taxi (fares set).

Car Rentals: Hertz, Kiosk Wilhelminaplein (tel. 613686); Avis, Plesman Airport National, Plesman Airport (tel. 613924); Budget, at the airport (tel. 83420); also several local firms.

Dress: shorts at pool and beach only.

Shopping Specialties: The main shopping area is in the Punda section along Heerenstraat and Breedestraat. Best bets: Swiss watches, French perfumes, English china, Irish crystal, jewelry, Italian and French designer clothes, Norwegian ceramics, silver, English cashmere; for luxury items, Spritzer & Fuhrmann is on Breedestraat. Try the floating Obra di Man handicrafts center for gift items of local handicrafts.

Food Specialties: conch stew, red snapper in créole sauce, fried plantains, keshi yena (a Dutch edam cheese stuffed with meat or fish and spices), rijsttafel (Indonesian-style banquet, with up to 24 dishes), erwensoep (a thick, savory pea soup).

Restaurants: French, Italian, Swiss, Indonesian, and South American cuisines available. Try Fort Nassau, near Point Juliana overlooking the harbor (tel. 613086), or Indonesia Restaurant, 3 Mercuriusstraat (tel. 70917), to sample the Indonesian rijsttafel.

Old World and New blend in the Dutch-colonized islands creating a sophisticated and cosmopolitan collage. Nowhere is this more in evidence than on lovely pastel Curaçao. Expatriates from no fewer than 79 nations make their home on this antique, sun-bleached island that lies just 35 miles off the Venezuelan coast. Reason for the polyglot? In 1915 Royal Dutch/Shell arrived to build a refinery near Willemstad to process crude oil from Venezuela.

Willemstad, the island's capital and for centuries the Dutch seat of government for the Netherland Antilles, was named after King William II in 1647, only 13 years after the first Dutch settlement here. Red-tiled, stepped roofs of Dutch colonial houses face bright pastel facades of 17th- and 18th-century homes on clean, orderly streets.

Out on the island, windmills and plantation houses stud the landscape. Some of these *landhuizen* date back to Curaçao's settlement in 1634. They perch on the hilltops much as they did 300 years ago, and many are still in use as private homes today.

Arawak Indians were the first Curaçao settlers, and gave the tribal name to the island. The design and decoration of their pottery, the craftsmanship of their tools, and the artistry of the hieroglyphs decorating the walls and ceilings of their caves can still be seen in 14 locations on the island.

A long spine of an island, Curaçao stretches 38 miles to the north and is 2 to 7½ miles wide. Three-armed cacti and spiney aloe plants sprout from a sere landscape that is a study in browns, russets, and cactus greens.

Cooling trade winds blow steadily, bending the divi-divi trees at the waist. Flat arid countryside sweeps up toward the western end of the island where Mount Christoffel rises 1300 feet. Over it all, the sun welcomes and warms visitors who roost contentedly along miles of beaches.

A long trading history, the arrival of Royal Dutch/Shell, and a generous infusion of Dutch hospitality have created a population attuned to sharing the delights of their homeland.

From the ship's deck as you enter the harbor you'll catch a good view of Willemstad's 200-year-old storybook waterfront buildings and narrow immaculate streets. These red-tiled, stepped roofs impart the old-world atmosphere for which Curaçao is famous.

Ships dock just a few minutes' walk from downtown and the curious **Queen Emma Pontoon Bridge,** a pedestrian bridge that joins the two halves of Curaçao. First built in 1888, the bridge still swings open 20 to 30 times a day for ships. Pause for a few moments in the center to get your bearings and view again the lilac, ultramarine, and pinks of the lovely old buildings that front the harbor.

Next stop should be the 300-year-old **Temple Mikve-Israel Emmanual,** on Columbusstraat at Kerkstraat, one of the oldest synagogues in the Western Hemisphere. Consecrated on the eve of Passover in 1732, it is today one of the better examples of Dutch colonial architecture. The complex now covers a square block in Willemstad's business district. In the 18th century it was sanctuary to Spanish and Portuguese Jews seeking refuge.

Allot 45 minutes to see a good historical show at **De Tempel Theatre,** a restored landmark on Wilhelminaplein. Built in 1867, the theater projects Curaçao's past and present on a 38-foot screen. This modern theater is located at the waterfront.

A "must see" are the **Floating Schooner Markets,** at the north end of Handelskade, Here, scores of schooners from all over the Caribbean and South America tie up to offer their colorful wares. Tropical fruits and vegetables can be yours at normal cost, and make wonderfully colorful photographs.

Fort Amsterdam, at Breedestraat and Handelskade, is center for both church and state: the fort encloses the Governor's Palace, the 1769 Dutch Reformed church, *and* the seat of the Netherlands Antilles government.

In the Otrabanda section, the **Curaçao Museum** is a former military hospital, built in 1853, that now houses historic artifacts of island's history.

On the road north to Westpunt is one of the oldest buildings on the island, the **Jan Kock House,** constructed in 1650 and now a private home, restaurant, and museum. Many of the furnishings date to the 18th century. To add even more interest, the house is said to be haunted.

Chobolobo Mansion, a 17th-century landhuiz, offers Curaçao orange-flavored liqueur for sip and sale, as well as a tour of the house. The liqueur is a distillate of dried peel of a strain of orange found only in Curaçao!

St. Christoffel Natural Park is a 3500-acre preserve with rare orchids growing near the upper reaches of the mountain. There are also four caves containing Arawak petroglyphs in the area.

Golfers will find tees here in Aruba, and there are courts for tennis, horses for riding. Water sports? Of course!

Dominica

Capital and Port City: Roseau.

Size: 29 miles long by 15 miles wide.

Population: 81,000.

Climate: 75° to 90°F year round (cooler in the mountains); dry January to June on the west coast, rainy in the mountainous areas.

Language: English, French patois.

Currency: Eastern Caribbean ("beewee") dollar (E.C.$). $1.00 U.S. = E.C.$2.60.

Tourist Information: Tourist Information Bureau, 37 Cork St., Roseau (tel. 445-2351).

Public Transportation: unmetered taxis, minibuses, trucks.

Car Rentals: none.

Shopping Specialties: vertivert grass mats, soaps made from fresh coconut oil.

Restaurants: Anchorage, two miles south of Roseau (tel. 445-2638); La Robe, 23 Cork St. (tel. 445-2896).

Until the story of Grenada hit the international press there wasn't one person in 100 who could tell you where or what Dominica was, let alone pronounce it right (it's Do-men-*eek*-ah). Then the island's feisty prime minister, Eugenia Charles, somehow managed to convince U.S. President Reagan that conditions in Grenada were threatening all the Caribbean, and *violà*! instant notoriety for her and for this tiny island.

As the story goes, Dominica was named by Columbus who discovered it on a Sunday in 1493, naming it Sunday Island. Like so many islands in this region, Dominica was the scene of many battles for possession between the British and French, finally paying a ransom to get the French to go home.

In 1978 the country acquired its independence, but it's far from financially stable. A severe hurricane that devastated tourist facilities in 1979 even dashed the island's tourism dreams, at least for a time.

Despite its difficulties, Dominica is one of the loveliest and most unspoiled islands in the Caribbean. The only remaining Carib Indians, a tribe that once populated all these islands and after which the Caribbean Sea was named, still live here. Nearly 3000 of them dwell on a reservation in the northeast sector of the island, where they live much as they always did, weaving baskets and vertivert grass mats, even making dugout canoes.

Morne Trois Pitons National Park is an ancient rain forest, a deep green jungle lying at the foot of peaks that have caused Dominica to be called the Switzerland of the Caribbean. You'll get a look at wild orchids and a rare species of parrot here, hear a waterfall roaring, and see some of the island's 365 rivers, one for every day of the year, as they rush to the sea. Hiking can be quite an experience in Dominica, but it's only for the hardy and only with a guide.

At the island's **Sulfur Springs** you can see the offshoot of underground volcanic activity, and at **Trafalgar Falls** you can visit the world's second-largest boiling lake, splattering gray mud in fat bubbles. Again the region is difficult to visit, but it can be done with some determination and a guide.

Shopping will probably be the best bet for most people visiting the island. Native handicrafts are available at several stores, including Dominica Handcrafts, on Hanover Street; Caribana Handcraft, on Cork Street; Island Craft Co-operative and Bernard's, both on King George V Street; Tropicrafts, on Turkey Lane; and Bon Marché, on Old Street.

You'll see the island's few dining spots as you roam about: Mouse Hole, La Robe Créole, Guiyave, Ti Kai, Vena's Garden Bar and Restaurant.

You'll find natural swimming pools in some of the rivers, and underwater in the ocean is a wide variety of sponges, some of them fluorescent. Divers will find particularly good **skin-diving** areas at coral reefs off the west coast from Castle Comfort to Scottshead, and at Cabrits, where remains of sunken ships can be seen.

Dominican Republic

Capital and Port Cities: Santo Domingo (pop. 1.3 million); Puerto Plata (pop. 45,000).

Size: 20,000 square miles.

Climate: 75° to 80°F in winter, 80° to 90°F in summer.

Language: Spanish; English widely spoken in the resort areas.

Currency: Dominican peso; $1.00 U.S. = DP 1.75.

Tourist Information: Dominican Informatiin Center, near the cathedral in Santo Domingo; The Ministry of Tourism, Separacion 12 (tel. 586-2177).

Public Transportation: buses, taxis (not metered, so determine the cost to your destination in advance).

Car Rentals: Hertz, Ave. Independencia 454, Santo Domingo (tel. 816883).

Shopping Specialties: Best buys: native handcrafted jewelry, especially amber and larimar (a variety of turquoise), rum, coffee, handknits, ceramics, mahogany crafts, and wicker. In Santo Domingo, El Conde Street is the main shopping street. In Puerto Plata, at the Factory Gift Shop, 23 Duarte, the master jeweler Ramón Ortiz fashions larimar, amber, and rare black coral into works of art in gold and silver settings.

Food Specialties: chicharonne (pieces of chicken, fried green bananas, and spices), platanos, sanchocho (a meat and vegetable dish).

Restaurants: Puerto Plata—Hotel Castilla, just off the main square at 34 John F. Kennedy St. (tel. 586-2559); Portofino, Ave. Hermanas Mirabel; Montemar, Ave. Circunvalacion del Norte (tel. 586-2800).

For nearly a century Spain dominated the Caribbean and the New World through Hispaniola, the island shared by the Dominican Republic and Haiti. Columbus first landed on the coral-edged northwest coast of the island on December 5, 1492. Less than a year later he established the first European settlement in the New World on the south coast. In time this settlement would become Santo Domingo, Spain's gateway to colonization of the Caribbean, South America, and Mexico.

But Spain's fortunes ebbed, and with them went those of the oldest country in the Western Hemisphere. Its palaces and forts became the siege ground for buccaneers, privateers, and the fractious monarchs of Europe. In 1697 Spain agreed to France's demand for the western third of the island, today's Haiti. But the squabbling persisted well into this century until the United States felt called upon to institute a military occupation to secure peace for the country and, no less important, to provide security for American shores.

In 1966 a president and legislature were democratically elected and the economy began stablizing. Today the Dominican Republic, which boasts some of the most spectacular but least developed terrain in the Caribbean, is setting up to capitalize on it through tourism. All the elements are here: lush tropical forests grow right down to soft golden beaches; the highest mountain range in the Caribbean moderates the tropical temperatures. The upward sweep of **Pico Duarte** stops at 10,417 feet, the tallest mountain in the West Indies, and the **Valley of the Cibao**—the rich sugarcane country—winds its way through the island.

At the center of this new republic is the jewel of the Caribbean that started it all, **Santo Domingo,** port city and capital of the Dominican Republic. Founded by Columbus's brother Bartholomew in 1496, the restored colonial Old Town is the bustling heart of this city of contrasts. Art galleries, museums, parks, restaurants, shops, hospitals, fortresses, university—all these were "firsts" in the New World. And the first cathedral, Cathedral de Santa Maria la Menor, is said to hold the remains of Christopher Columbus.

On the north coast at Puerto Plata, Columbus's first landing site, a gigantic statue of Christ rises atop **Isabel de Torres,** the 2575-foot mountain he named for Spain's queen. Arms wide, it welcomes the world to the Dominican Republic's shores. Frequently hidden by dawn's mists, the statue shares the spectacular view of the Amber Coast and the surrounding botanical gardens with the many visitors who get up here on a stately cable-car ride each day.

Green forested mountains swoop down to an indigo sea and the crescent harbor. Nestled between the mountain's foot and the bay is Puerto Plata, a historic city whose streets are cobbled with ballast stones from treasure galleons that swapped their stones for gold and silver to take back to Ferdinand and Isabella. This was Columbus's intended site for the first settlement of the New World, but fate intervened when gold was found on the south coast and Santo Domingo went on to become the leading city of the New World.

Puerto Plata, founded in 1502 by Nicolas de Ovando, means Port of Silver. Located 130 miles northwest of Santo Domingo, the city was named by Columbus, who saw silver reflections of the mists on the mountaintop. The cruise-ship pier is just a few steps from the center of town.

Have a look here at **Fort San Felipe,** at the harbor end of the Malecon, the road that rims the sea and leads to a beautiful beach, Playa Dorado. Built in 1540 as defense against fierce and sometimes cannibalistic Carib Indians and marauding bands of English privateers, the fort guarded a city that was the last stop of the Spanish treasure galleons before they breasted the Atlantic for Spain and so was of keen interest to privateers.

A **cable car** takes you to the top of Isabel de Torres, where you'll have a magnificent view of the Amber Coast.

In Santo Domingo, see the **Alcazar de Colón,** a restored castle originally built by Columbus's son Diego in 1514. Located at the end of Las Damas Street, it's built of solid coral rock and furnished as it might have been when Columbus and his bride Dona Maria de Toledo lived here.

La Atarazana was once a military depot and is now a hive of shops and small restaurants. Although the construction is mostly new, the effect is true 16th century in appearance.

Casa de Bastidas, on Calle Las Damas, a former mayor's home, is now a museum for sunken ships' treasures.

Cathedral of Santa Maria la Menor is early 16th-century Romanesque in style and is said to contain the bones of Columbus, although no one knows for sure just where the adventurer is really buried. You can visit what Dominicans claim are Columbus's caskets—there are three, lead inside crystal inside bronze—on your tour of the church.

Best buy on the island is **amber,** the semiprecious stone that is actually petrified resin. It is found only on this island in all the Caribbean, and in few places in the world. The most valuable specimens of amber contain the remains of tiny insects or animals trapped for eternity in the clear golden resin.

Larimar, often called Dominican turquoise, is a semiprecious stone, pale blue in color. It was first uncovered by a Santo Domingo jeweler who named it after his daughter Larissa and the sea (*mar* in Spanish). Both stones are set into jewelery by island craftsmen. Amber that has a red or blue hue is considered the most valuable, but other lighter colors are equally lovely.

Mahoghany rocking chairs also are a favorite local buy, and President John F. Kennedy is said to have ordered some of these comfortable chairs.

Grenada

Capital and Port City: St. George's (pop. 9500).

Size: 21 miles long by 12 miles wide; 133 square miles.

Country Population (three islands): 85,000.

Climate: 83°F annual average, with low humidity.

Language: English.

Currency: Eastern Caribbean ("beewee") dollar; $1.00 U.S. = E.C.$2.60.

Tourist Information: Grenada Tourist Office, Church St., past the Careenage behind the public library, St.George's.

Public Transportation: taxis (not metered, so agree on a price first); buses not recommended.

Car Rentals: Juliana Aird Agency (tel. 2504).

Shopping Specialties: spices (fresh bay leaves, nutmeg, ginger, ground coriander, pepper, cinnamon sticks, among others), all in neat baskets; duty-free shops; the Straw Market, on Granby Street at Market Square; Yellow Poui (Sendall Tunnel exit) for a good selection of local art; Charles of Grenada (Cross and Melville Sts.) for a wide selection of English woolen imports, and Granby Stores (Granby St.) for crystal, Wedgwood, china, and watches.

Food Specialties: lambi (conch) dishes, callaloo soup, West Indian dishes, seafood.

Restaurants: Rudolf's, at the Careenage (tel. 2241); Nutmeg, at the Careenage (tel. 2539).

Call it Gre-*nay*-da (*not* Gre-nah-da), and recall that this was the mouse that roared for the U.S. in 1983 when President Ronald Reagan ordered troops onto the island to wrest it from what that administration called a threat to the peace of the Caribbean.

After a brief flurry of fighting and some internal struggling, the leftists who had controlled the island were ousted. Within weeks little Grenada, long an outpost of civilization, was the place everyone wanted to go. Cruise ships that had been coming here for years returned to the island soon after the battling halted.

Grenada is a spectacularly beautiful island, where fertile valleys nestle amid green-clad mountains. The island's rugged volcanic interior is a jungle of palms, oleander, bougainvillea, purple and red hibiscus, crimson anthurium, bananas, breadfruit, birdsong, and ferns. Green mountains swoop to the sea, carving a dramatic coastline of coves, cliffs, and beaches.

Its stunning beauty is enhanced by attractive hotels and a local cuisine that is hard to beat. Known as the Spice Island, Grenada is fragrant with clove, cocoa, cinnamon, ginger, and vanilla—12 different spices in all—including nutmeg, of which it is the world's largest producer.

Located 100 miles north of Venezuela, Grenada was settled in 1650 by the French, who established a peace of sorts with the Carib Indians. But peace didn't last long and the struggle soon resumed. Finally the Caribs, pushed to the cliffs at Sauteurs in the north, rather than submit to enslavement, cast their women and children into the sea, and in a mass suicide leap threw themselves from the cliff onto the jagged rocks.

Columbus's log says he first sighted Grenada in 1498, on his third voyage, but passed it by. Its strategic location as a gateway to the Caribbean and South America later made it a focus for Europe's monarchs, and it changed hands many times over the next two centuries.

A sugar-producing colony, first under France and finally, after 1783, under Britain, the island gained independence in March 1979 when a People's Revolutionary Government, that often flirted with Cuban influences, was established and the island became a part of the British Commonwealth. Today Grenada is the chief island of the three-island independent country of Grenada, Carriacou, the Petit Martinique.

St. George's, the capital, is a hilly port city which flows around a horseshoe bay. Houses of yellow, blue, and pink, their red-tiled roofs a stark contrast to a backdrop of dark-green mountains, gaze across the bay. In the city's center, clusters of quaint, bright-roofed buildings of Georgian architecture line steep narrow streets reminiscent of the Italian town of Portofino.

In St. George's, stop by old **Fort George.** This French-built fort has subterranean passageways and old guard rooms and cells open to visitors, but the fort is now police headquarters.

At the island's **Botanical Gardens and Zoo,** tropical flora, although needing attention, is well labeled. There's a lovely vista from **Fort Frederick,** built by the French in 1779.

Out on the island, **Annandale Falls** offers a cascade that tumbles 50 feet into a basin in a tropical wonderland.

At **Dougaldston Estate** you can see most of the island's spices in their natural form, and at Grand Étang Lake you can visit a **rain forest** at 1800 feet. Cobalt-blue waters here flow over 13 acres.

Carib's Leap, in the north at Sauteurs, is the great cliff from which the Caribs leaped to their death rather than face enslavement.

At Gouyave, a **spice factory** welcomes visitors, and at Grand Anse you'll see what many consider one of the **most beautiful beaches** in the West Indies. Beach lovers will freak over **Point Saline** too: here, two beaches, one gleaming white and one volcanic jet black, meet.

Guadeloupe

Capital and Port City: Pointe-à-Pitre.

Size: 687 square miles on two main islands.

Population: 300,000.

Climate: 70° to 80°F year round; most rain during September to November.

Language: French Créole.

Currency: French franc; $1.00 U.S. = 8.5 F.

Tourist Information: Office du Tourisme, 5 Place de la Banque, Pointe-à-Pitre (tel. 82-09-30).

Dress: beach wear and scanty clothes not considered proper for urban areas.

Documentation: proof of U.S. or Canadian citizenship required.

Public Transportation: buses, taxis (unmetered, so agree on a price in advance).

Car Rentals: Avis, Hotel Frantel (tel. 82-64-44); National-Europcar, Aeroport du Raizet (tel. 82-60-74); Jumbo Car, Aeroport du Raizet (tel. 82-60-74); Hertz, route de la Gabarre (tel. 82-88-44).

Shopping Specialties: exotic spices, voodoo dolls.

Food Specialties: Créole and French cuisines; curries, stuffed crab.

Restaurants: Auberge de la Vieille Tour, in Gosier (tel. 84-12-04); La Plantation, in the Bas du Fort Marina (tel. 82-32-21); Chez Rosette Rte. de Gosier (tel. 84-11-32) and L'Enfer Vert (tel. 91-53-82), on the second floor of the Gallerie Nozières, rue Nozières, in Pointe-à-Pitre. Le Gommier, 3 rue Jacques Cazotte (tel. 71-88-55).

If your thoughts sometimes turn to a tiny cove with warm waters lapping at your toes and a sailboat skittering by on the horizon, your thoughts may be turning to Guadeloupe. If your thoughts turn to a monokini or less, you're definitely thinking of Guadeloupe.

Little known to most U.S. travelers, this cluster of five islands is a fantasyland for those who seek beautiful, unchallenging scenery, back-to-nature magic, and some wonderfully spicy Créole cooking.

Not as sophisticated as its fast-lane neighbor Martinique, Guadeloupe seems to snooze in the sun, its beauty running rampant but unassisted around it.

Still, there's more than a touch of the insouciant in Guadeloupe, as there always has been: when Martinique was adjusting happily to French rule, Guadeloupe was aligning itself with the enemy English. Paris did not take kindly to that and shipped out an enforcement squad that erected guillotines and promptly dispatched 4000 Guadeloupeans.

In topography Guadeloupe is much like its sister island right down to a matching volcano, Soufrière. It's actually two islands, Grand-Terre and Basse-Terre, separated by a channel.

Here you can explore lovely waterfalls and deep tropical forests, banana plantations and, of course, beautiful beaches. Known to the Arawaks as Karukera, "island of the beautiful waters," Guadeloupe was named by Columbus in 1493 when he dubbed it Santa Maria de Guadelupe de Estramaduros, after a saint in his homeland.

French settlers led by two Martinique men established a colony here in 1635. On and off, Guadeloupe belonged to the British, finally returning once and for all to the French in 1815.

Until 1946 the island was a dependency of Martinique, when it became a département (something like a French state) of France.

Pointe-à-Pitre, the port city, is not the most picturesque of places but it does have an interesting **covered marketplace** filled with exotic fruits, spices, and vegetables, and often some pretty exotic people too. Both market and nearby port can be good stops for photographers. You can pick up some of the best in Caribbean spices here: vanilla, nutmeg, bois d'Inde peppercorns, cinnamon bark, cloves.

Martinique has better buys and a far wider selection of china, crystal, and the like, but on Guadeloupe you'll find good bargains on imports from France—perfumes, Dior, Lalique, Baccarat, Hermès, and the like. Shops usually give big discounts on prices if you're buying with traveler's checks in dollars or in U.S. cash. Shops are generally closed from noon to 2 p.m. and on Saturday afternoon and Sunday. Your ship's presence in port may change that, however.

Among the **shops,** of interest are: Les 7 Barils des 7 Pêches, 6 rue Frébault, for liquor; Vendôme, 7 rue Frébault, for fashions; Elstel, near the Ecotel at Gosier, for appliquéed wall hangings. Island-made favorites include pointed straw hats of split bamboo which can make interesting planters, and native voodoo (*voudou,* in French) dolls.

Dining is elevated to sport here. There are dozens of restaurants large and small, all serving fiery-hot Créole food or gentler French concoctions. Even tiny snack shops on the beaches can be trusted to produce some memorable goodies.

As for **beaches:** one of the best island beaches is La Plage du Souffleur at Port Louis; another is Plage du Grande Anse, a mile of curving sand with a grove of palms and sea grapes and a small restaurant, Karakoli.

Two very dramatic spots on a drive around the island are **Anse Bertrad,** about five miles from Port Louis, and **Pointe de la Grande Vigie,** about 280 feet above the sea and reached by four miles of gravel road. You can see Antigua from this vantage point.

About four miles south you'll find **Porte d'Enfer,** where waves crash against narrow cliffs at a spot called the "gateway to hell."

On Basse-Terre you'll pass **Deshaies,** home of a Club Med. About three miles away is a beautiful beach called **Grand Anse,** shaded by trees swaying in the breezes. This is a popular diving beach too. At Mahaut, four miles from Pointe Noire, you travel through a **rain forest** and past two hills called Les Deux Mamelles (the two breasts). Jacques Cousteau spends some time at nearby Îlet du Pigeon.

Farther along the road you reach **Basse-Terre,** the main government enclave for the islands, but best known as the home of **Soufrière,** the smoking **volcano,** dormant now. Banana trees and tropical jungle cover the sides of the 4800-foot-high volcano which you reach by a road from St. Claude, an upper-crust suburb. You can travel to the 3300-foot mark where you can feel the heat of the volcano beneath your feet and watch steam puffing out of fumaroles.

Continue your drive along the coastline to Trois-Rivières where you can still see **Arawak rock carvings** and on to Chutes du Carbet, three pretty **waterfalls,** but you'll have to do some long and determined climbing to find them.

If you are by now hot and tired, you can take it off—all off—on one of the island's beaches where **nude swimming** is, if not encouraged, quietly (although probably not literally) overlooked. Among the spots for al fresco bathing on Basse Terre are beaches near hotels like the Club Med, or the Plage de Clugny between Ste-Rose and Deshaies; on Grande-Terre, Caravelle Beach and hotel beaches.

Snorkeling and scuba diving are wonderful here, and you can arrange trips through the tourist office, Club Med, or Pigeon Island.

Fishing, boating, and waterskiing are also readily arranged, as are tennis and horseback riding. If you're ready to try out your land legs after a few days at sea, plan a hike through the trails of the Parc Naturel in Basse-Terre.

Haiti

Capital and Port City: Port-au-Prince.

Size: 10,714 square miles.

Population: 5 million.

Climate: 70° to 80°F year round; about 20° cooler in the mountains.

Language: Créole, French.

Currency: Haitian gourd, but the U.S. dollar is accepted everywhere.

Tourist Information: Office National du Tourisme, Av. Marie-Jeanne, Port-au-Prince (tel. 2-17-29).

Dress: avoid revealing shorts and abbreviated outfits.

Documents: proof of U.S. or Canadian citizenship required.

Public Transportation: taxis (unmetered, but the government sets the rates; ask cost in advance, and bargain if you wish), colorful tap-tap buses.

Car Rentals: Avis, Duvalier Airport (tel. 7-1325); Hertz, Delmas 27 (tel. 61132); Chatelain Tours, rue Geffrard, in Pétionville (tel. 2-4469).

Shopping Specialties: oil paintings, woodcarvings, Haitian cotton fabrics, straw baskets.

Food Specialties: Créole and French cuisine, tropical fruits.

Restaurants: Belvedere, Kenscott Rd. (tel. 7-1115); La Lanterne, 14 rue Borno (tel. 7-0479); and La Recife, rue de Delmas (tel. 6-2605)—all in Pétionville.

Mountains rise to the sky in a blue haze, golden sands stretch for miles along glittering blue waters, and colorful blossoms run riot across the land. Haiti is a place of haunting beauty, but a place shocking and often depressing for travelers unprepared to stare poverty in the eye. It is indeed sad to see a land of such natural beauty and such cheerful, artistically talented people so unable to overcome the economic malaise that has long plagued this tiny nation.

Once a French colony, Haiti occupies the western third of the island of Hispaniola, sharing it with the Dominican Republic. It became the first independent black republic in the world when in 1801 its black slaves, led by Toussaint L'Overture, adopted a constitution and named a governor. Napoleon sent 25,000 men and 70 warships to bring the Haitians back in line, but they were unsuccessful and a year later the French signed an armistice and removed their troops. Independence was proclaimed on January 1, 1804.

Haiti's two victorious generals, Jean-Jacques Dessalines and Alexandre Pétion, ruled, followed by the rise to power of Henri Cristophe, who crowned himself emperor and ordered the creation of a mountaintop citadel at Cap-Haïtien. You can still visit that sky-high fortress that was said to have taken the lives of 20,000 men during the decade of its construction. You get there atop a small but footsure donkey led by energetic and equally footsure youngsters.

On this mountainous third of the island of Hispaniola, **Port-au-Prince** is the principal city, a teeming metropolis that is not large in land area but is gigantic in population, all of which seems to be crammed into the narrow downtown streets of Port-au-Prince.

For beautiful views you'll want to ride up into the mountains where you'll find the resort village of **Pétionville,** home of a number of small, pretty hotels, restaurants, and boutiques, and the wealthiest residents of the country.

Still higher on the mountain is **Kenscoff,** a small village in which you can visit the Mountain Maid shop, a Baptist-supported crafts center featuring some of the finest examples of Haitian woodcarvings, pottery, paintings, embroidery, and cottons. Kenscoff is the end of the road, by the way, and you'll see some beautiful views on your way there.

Haiti is a bargain hunter's paradise. Here you can buy massive woodcarvings for a few dollars and brightly colored Haitian oil paintings by local artists, some of whom have become famous for their primitive styles. To get a look at the best of what's available, stop by the **Musée d'Art Haïtien du College St-Pierre** (the Museum of Haitian Art) in downtown Port-au-Prince at Place des Héroes, Champs de Mars. Dewitt Peters, an early collector of Haitian Art and the operator of Centre d'Art, has helped oversee the compilation of this collection. A boutique here at the museum offers some of the finest handcrafted items in Haiti at very reasonable prices.

The **Centre d'Art** should also be a stop on any art enthusiast's list too. Peters, an artist himself, discovered and encouraged many Haitian artists who are today famous, and his Centre d'Art features the best in Haitian artwork. It's at 56 rue Roy.

With the rise to prominence of Haitian artist Philome Obin and others, every Haitian who can hold a paintbrush seems to have taken to the easel. You'll see hundreds, perhaps thousands, of these colorful paintings being sold everywhere you go. While most are not likely to become collector's items (unless you have an excellent eye for art), all of them are very colorful reminders of a visit here.

Well-known **shops** at which you may buy some of the better examples of Haitian artwork of all kinds include Nader's, Issa's, and Claire's Galleries downtown; Red Carpet, Panaméricaine, Rainbow Art Display, and National Art Galleries in Pétionville.

A shop called El Cano is quite near the docks (taxi drivers will know it) and features gorgeous rugs, pillow covers, and fabrics, all made from the nubby Haitian cotton and woven by a cooperative of workers. Carvings and straw work here are of high quality too, but the very best offerings are heavy cotton products in striking contemporary colors and patterns. The Salvation Army handicraft shop, off Delmas Road near the airport, has some quality items too.

You can bargain, bargain, and bargain in Haiti, securing yourself some bargains in the process. Offer the seller about half of the original price and work up very slowly. When you hear the word "finish," you know you've gotten about the best price you're going to get.

I recommend a visit to the **Iron Market** in Port-au-Prince only to my enemies. If you're very brave and don't mind being importuned from all sides and crushed in a mass of buyers and sellers, go . . . and good luck. It's an interesting place to walk through briefly, but I think you'll be very glad to get out of it and into a less frenetic shop. It's called the Iron Market, by the way, because it's built of ornate ironwork.

If you have read Graham Green's intriguing novel about Haiti, *The Comedians,* and would like to meet the character who provided the inspiration for Green's Petit Pierre gossipmonger, look for him at the not-to-be-missed Olaffson Hotel. Here you can have a lovely elegant lunch inside or out, and see the best of Haiti's impressive **gingerbread wood-trimmed architecture** all in one fell swoop. The Olaffson also was a central "character" in the novel, and has been the vacation home of an impressive array of celebrities. The hotel is surrounded by jungley growth and is one of the most interesting sights in the city. (Petit Pierre's real name is Aubelin Joliecoeur, and if you see him—he always wears a spotless three-piece white suit and carries a walking stick—just go over and introduce yourself and he'll happily take you to visit his home and art gallery where he has an impressive, if high-priced, collection of Haitian art. He's the epitome of an old-world gentleman, right down to kissing the hand of any ladies present, and is as much a "sight" in Haiti as any tourist attraction. He also knows everything that's going on practically before it occurs.)

Cathedral St-Trinité is an interesting stop and features a painting of Christ the way Haitians see him: as a black man.

If you take a city tour of Port-au-Prince or drive around on your own, you'll see the gleaming white **National Palace,** home of President Duvalier, better known as Baby Doc (his father, a man greatly feared for both his political and his voodoo power, was called Papa Doc). In front of the palace is a bronze statue called **The Marron,** which represents a slave holding a conch shell used to sound the call to arms for the revolution of 1791.

Swimmers and divers can dabble at **Sand Cay Reef** or at **Le Grand** Banc, whose shallow waters are visited by a catamaran sailboat called the *Yellowbird* docked at Beau Rivage Marina. It's a 90-minute ride to Sand Cay Reef on boats that depart from docks at the International Casino.

Rum lovers can sample to oblivion at the **Jane Barbancourt Distillery,** where some of the world's most unusual, indeed collector, rum is made. Haitian rum is a high-quality product much admired by rum drinkers. In addition to the basic aged rum, you can also buy hibiscus, mango, mint, coconut, cashew, and a dozen other flavors of rum. Samples are served to you in a lovely setting reminiscent of an 18th-century distillery.

Cap-Haïtien, a town of about 30,000 on the northwest tip of Haiti, is a much smaller and quieter town out in the Haitian countryside. French pirates once lived on the nearby island of Tortuga, and raided so often that the French finally ended up controlling the mainland. In the 1700s Cap-Haïtien was a fancy place for wealthy planters who drove around the streets in gilded carriages and built furbelowed mansions. You can still see some of them here today, although they don't exhibit much of their former grandeur.

Don't miss a trip to **La Citadelle,** whose 12-foot-thick walls took ten years to build and could house 10,000 people, with 40 rooms allocated to the "royal" family alone. (Cristophe-created "royalty" was unusual: Henri created some unique royal names, Prince Lemonade for instance.) As seen from above the fortress, from which no shot was ever fired, forms the outline of a pistol, with the longest side measuring more than 450 yards. In the center is Christophe's tomb (he killed himself with a silver bullet).

Below the Citadelle, which bristles with cannons and has a room containing 45,000 cannon balls, are the ruins of the **Palais de Sans Souci,** a place designed to rival Versailles. From what is left you can tell that once it was really something, but it was badly damaged by an earthquake. Historians say that it was three stories high with silk curtains on every one of the 23 windows on each floor, panels of inlaid mosaic or polished mahogany on the walls, and gilded mirrors reflecting fabulous tapestries. Cristophe even had streams diverted to help keep the palace cool in summer, an early air conditioner.

La Badie and Cormier Plage are two lovely swimming and snorkeling spots in Cap-Haïtien, which has some fascinating hoteliers who run lovely and often historic operations. One hotel here, the Roi Cristophe, was once the property of Pauline Bonaparte, Napoleon's reportedly nymphomaniacal sister, and was built in 1724.

As you may have gathered, Haiti is a most unusual place, changing like a chameleon to fit the circumstances. One of its most unusual aspects is the practice of **voodoo,** a religion that seems to have adapted itself easily to Catholicism and other religions represented here while not relinquishing its importance in Haitian life. Derived from the word "voudoun," meaning spirits, voodoo is designed to keep the individual in harmony with a raft of spirits, or loas. Head of the temple is the hougan priest or the mambo priestess, who oversees complicated ceremonies that can be as brief as an hour or as long as a week or more. Offerings are made to a loa, and symbols are drawn on the ground to lure the spirits. Drums beat as initiates prepare their bodies for possession by the loa. Voodoo ceremonies are held for tourists, but at night you can often hear the beat of real voodoo drums high in the hills.

St. Kitts, Nevis, and Anguilla

Capital and Port Cities: Basseterre, St. Kitts; Charlestown, Nevis.

Size: St. Kitts—65 square miles; Nevis—36 square miles.

Country Population: 48,000.

Climate: 68° to 80°F year round, with low humidity.

Language: English.

Currency: Eastern Caribbean ("beewee") dollar; $1.00 U.S. = E.C.$2.60.

Tourist Information: St. Kitts/Nevis/Anguilla Tourist Board, Pall Mall, Basseterre (tel. 2620).

Public Transportation: taxi (point-to-point rates are fixed by the government), ferry (between Charlestown and Basseterre, daily).

Car Rentals: Sunshine Car Rentals, Lesmike Auto, Cayon Rd. (tel. 2193). A local driver's license must be obtained from the Traffic Office, Pall Mall. (tel. 2642); fee: E.C.$4.

Shopping Specialties: in Basseterre's duty-free shops—batik prints, coppercraft, rum, colorful cottons with embroidered designs.

Food Specialties: roast suckling pig, turtle steaks, crab backs, curried lobster, pawpaw, christophine, breadfruit, plantain, guavas, mammy apples, soursop, pixilated pork.

Restaurants: Ocean Terrace Inn, Harbor St., Basseterre (tel. 2754); Avondale House, George Square, Basseterre (tel. 7406); Rawlins Plantation; Mount Pleasant, (tel. 6221); Ocean Terrace Inn, at the Post, Basseterre (tel. 2380).

Life is slow and quiet on these two beach-trimmed islands, moving slowly along much as they always have since Columbus stopped by here for a visit 500 years ago.

It was 389 years after Columbus spotted and named St. Kitts after his patron saint, St. Christopher, St. Kitts/Nevis achieved its freedom. In 1623 the first successful English Colony in the West Indies was established on St. Kitts and in 1983 the island acquired independence from the United Kingdom.

St. Kitts, with a 65-square-mile area, has a central mountain mass rising 3792 feet at Mount Misery, and a narrow peninsula to the southeast, where you'll find salt ponds and the island's best beaches. Although the British were there first, in 1623, the French Navy also landed a force. After a four-year tug-o-war the two forces decided to divide the island and to unite against the intruding Spaniards and the uncontainable Carib Indians. The British finally won the island from all, including the French, in 1783.

Nevis, with only 36 square miles, rises from the sea as a single dominant volcanic peak, reaching a height of 3542 feet, its summit usually encircled with clouds. Just two miles off St. Kitt's south coast, Nevis was settled in 1628. This small island had two big events: British Admiral Nelson married Fannie Nisbet in an island church, and Alexander Hamilton was born here.

In 1967 **Anguilla** broke away from the Associated State of St. Kitts–Nevis–Anguilla, and since that time has enjoyed separate administration and a continuing relationship with Britain. Its 5000 people live on a tiny island measuring 16 miles long and barely 4 miles wide.

At **Basseterre** on St. Kitts, in **Pall Mall Square** you'll still see the sectioning lines that in the 18th century delineated special areas for slaves and freemen. Other interesting sights include: antique **St. George's Anglican Church,** on Church and Cayon Streets, first built in 1670 and rebuilt in 1867; and **Brimstone Hill Fortress,** a mighty fort once known as "The Gibraltar of the West Indies," and surrendered to the French in 1782 but returned a year later to the English.

You can descend into a dormant **volcano** on St. Kitts and visit a museum outlining that steamer's history. The way down descends from the top of the crater at 2600 feet into the crater itself, but you have to hold onto roots and vines to get there. (Perhaps you might skip this adventure.)

At **Charleston,** on Nevis, you can visit the birthplace of the American patriot, **Alexander Hamilton,** on the waterfront, and the Hamilton Estate, once owned by Hamilton's father, above the town. Lovers should stop at **St. John's Church,** in Fig Tree Village, for a look at the marriage record of Lord Horatio Nelson and Fanny Nisbet of Nevis, who were married here all those many years ago. Their marriage certificate still reposes in the church register.

Jamaica

Capital and Port Cities: Kingston, Montego Bay, Ocho Rios.

Size: 4,411 square miles.

Population: 3.3 million.

Language: English.

Currency: $1.00 U.S. = $3.50 Jamaican dollars.

Tourist Information: Jamaica Tourist Board, Cornwall Beach, Montego Bay (tel. 952-4425).

Public Transportation: bus, taxi, mini-van.

Car Rentals: Hertz, Montego Bay, Casa Montego Arcade, Kent Ave. (tel. 952-4471).

Shopping Specialties: straw goods, woodcarvings, coffee, batiks.

Restaurants: Half Moon Hotel, Ocho Rios Rd. in Montego Bay (tel. 953-2211); the Plantation Inn, in Ocho Rios (tel. 974-2501); Trident Villas Frenchmen's Cove (tel. 993-2602) and De Montevin Lodge Private Hotel, 21 Fort George St. (tel. 993-2604), in Port Antonio. Richmond Hill Inn, Montego Bay, Richmond (tel. 952-3859).

Deep green forests, silvery beaches, sparkling waters, jungle-sided mountains, cascading waterfalls, meandering rivers, antique plantations. This is Jamaica, one of the jewels of the Caribbean, breathtakingly beautiful and endlessly surprising.

Most cruise ships stop at only one of the three major Jamaican ports. More's the pity, for each of the three has its own brand of magic, the kind of siren's call that has been luring travelers here for generations.

It started eons ago with the Arawak Indians, who named the place Xaymaca, a word for wood and water. There are of course plenty of both here, which is why the next visitor of note was Columbus, who stopped by in 1494 and presumably raved on about it so convincingly that a bevy of Spaniards came here and remained here for 161 years.

Towering over the island are the **Blue Mountains,** some of which rise as high as 7400 feet. On the slopes, banana groves spread over vast acres and sugarcane waves in the wind. Mango and lime trees add splashes of green, and nutmeg drops casually to plop unceremoniously but amazingly at your feet. In the mountains are born 126 rivers, some of them cascading down to the sea over gentle waterfalls and in meandering streams. Amid all the green are violent splashes of color from magenta bougainvillea, bright-yellow alameda, and rose hibiscus.

Sugar turned Jamaica from a little outpost to a massive plantation. When the British invaded the island in 1655, Jamaica's economy depended on the continued success of sugar, whose production was controlled from plantation homes called Great Houses. In 1673 there were just 57 of these massive estates, but 65 years later there were more than 400 of them! Sugar planters accumulated the wealth of kings but the abolition of slavery in 1838 was also to spell an end to plantation life.

An independent state since 1962, Jamaica is a laughing, loving place of gentle, proud people whose charming British lilt is a delight to the ear and whose humor is quick and bubbly. From their melting-pot ancestry that included Spanish, English, African, and Indian—traders, slaves, settlers, pirates, and merchant kings—the island has developed some distinctive music and dance that has recently become the rage in international circles. Jamaica's national dance company, which performs in Kingston and occasionally elsewhere on the island and in the U.S., is marvelous. Reggae has taken both European and U.S. music circles by storm.

From this polyglot background has come some very interesting English too. You'll hear some strange words and sounds, and if you're lucky you'll be able to listen to some hilarious folk stories, each with its carefully constructed moral expressed in riotous Jamaican slang. Ask someone to tell you a "duppy" story and you'll see what I mean.

While you're here, you'll want to try some Jamaican food and sample some of the island's exotic tropical fruit. Lobsters are wonderful; akee looks like scrambled eggs and is served with codfish; escaveche is marinated fish; curried mutton and goat are favorites; callaloo is something like spinach; and jerk pork is barbecued pork grilled over wood fires; breadfruit, jack fruit, and cho-cho defy description and jelly coconuts are to die for, especially when filled with rum punch. In Montego Bay, try patties at a bakery. Tía Maria is made here in Jamaica from coffee beans, and the local beer is Red Stripe.

Kingston, the island's capital city and home of an outstanding art gallery, was once the haunt of English buccaneers who harassed the Spanish from Port Royal with such success that the town came to be considered the richest and most wicked city in the world in its day. Capt. Sir Henry Morgan was even made governor of the island.

But while Kingston is the island's governmental capital, **Montego Bay** is its tourist capital. Here life flows at a lively pace on pretty Cornwall or Doctor's Beach, and in the city itself which offers plenty of shops and sidewalk vendors to keep you occupied.

In town, a brick **Georgian town house** at 16 Church St. has been restored to its original splendor, and in Charles Square you can see a small building once used to incarcerate runaway slaves.

To get a look at life as lived in the sugar plantation days, take a shore excursion or taxi to **Sign Great House,** seven miles outside town, where smiling helpers will take you on a well-informed guided tour of the plantation house.

Rose Hall Great House has quite a reputation in Jamaica (or rather, its owner does). Built in the 1750s at a cost of 30,000 sterling (and that was a ton of money in those days!), the house became the home of the island's most notorious female, Annie Palmer, made famous in a novel by H.G. deLisser called *White Witch of Rose Hall*. She was said to have taken slaves as lovers and killed them off when a new one appeared on the scene. Annie treated her several husbands similarly, and was supposed to have played with the fire of voodoo as well. Nasty Annie met an end like that of her several paramours. Now restored, Rose Hall can be visited daily from 9 a.m. to 5 p.m.

Greenwood Great House occupies a pretty hillside location 14 miles east of Montego Bay and is open from 10 a.m. to 6 p.m. daily. Once the home of a relative of Elizabeth Barrett Browning, the house was recently restored and opened to public view. You'll see some lovely music boxes and elegant furnishings, and in the back room, some good-looking ironwood carvings are sold.

While you're here, treat yourself to a long, lazy float down the Martha Brae River—on a raft! **Rafting** begins about three miles from Falmouth, and they'll even give you a certificate to prove you really did it.

Cornwall and Doctor's Beaches have been a favorite haunt of the famous and infamous for years. Lovely strips of sand with dressing cabanas, they're in or close to the city, and at Cornwall there's an interesting underwater marine park.

City Centre is the center for shopping, but you'll find plenty of interesting shops along the streets and in the straw market.

If you're docking in **Ocho Rios,** you'll pull up to some of the loveliest sand in the Caribbean. Off on both sides of the ship you'll see beautiful beaches just begging you to kick off your shoes and your inhibitions.

As you walk off the ship on the pier, you're just steps away from the city's **straw market,** an open-air group of stalls where sellers with their babies, dogs, and assorted hangers-on patiently weave straw creations and just as patiently ask you to buy. You'll find some interesting baskets in unusual shapes and plenty of small gifts for the folks back at the office.

Farther afield in Ocho Rios, a "must-do" trip is to **Dunn's River Falls.** Here a river tumbles to the sea, falling in gentle splashes over boulders that tumbled down eons ago. Wear your swimsuit, for you first descend to the sea; then, accompanied by a guide, clamber back up the "steps" of the falls, holding hands with other climbers. It's not a strenuous climb, although it's a merry, slippery trip. There's no need to know how to swim. All you need is a ready laugh and a desire to be a splashing child again.

On the way here you'll pass through **Fern Gully,** once a riverbed, now a fascinating rain forest filled with huge wild ferns and trees.

Some shore tours visit **Prospect Plantation,** for botany fans the best way to see and learn about the flora and fauna of the island. Tours by open jitney take you through this still-working plantation where you can watch a skilled climber shinny up a banana tree, and see coconuts, cocoa, coffee, sugarcane plants, and some beautiful views stretching as far as Cuba more than 90 miles away. Horseback tours also are available along the White Ri ver.

Shaw Park Gardens is another favorite shore excursion stop. It's a beautiful garden set into a cliff, with representatives of hundreds of different plants, each carefully explained and described by a young guide.

Not far from Ocho Rios, above Oracabessa, stands the **home of Sir Noël Coward,** in which everything has been kept just as he left it in the days when he entertained Britain's Queen Mother among others. You can visit it Wednesday through to Sunday.

Brimmer Hall Estate, near Port Maria, is a working plantation too, and offers a similar experience to that of Prospect Plantation. Here you can also sit around the pool and sample some interesting beverage concoctions or shop in a souvenir gallery.

Port Antonio is a dramatic harbor where great cliffs rise from the sea. A small town, Port Antonio is better for sightseeing than for shopping, although there's an interesting native market where straw goods and famed Jamaican Blue Mountain coffee can be purchased quite inexpensively—especially if you take time to bargain.

Far and away the number one favorite activity in Port Antonio is **rafting on the Rio Grande River.** Once the method used to transport bananas from the plantation down to the ships, the rafts were "discovered" by swashbuckling actor Errol Flynn, who lived here and hired rafts to amuse his friends. The rafts are about 30 feet long and 3 feet wide, and are poled down the river by rafting experts, some of whom have been working here for 20 years or more. There's usually a stop about midway in the three-hour trip to keep you supplied with the potables necessary to continue the journey. If you go on your own, you'll drive or take a taxi to Rafter's Rest at Burlington on St. Margaret's Bay and someone will take your car to the other termination point of your cruise.

On a drive around this lovely little village, you'll get a chance to visit **Somerset Falls,** about ten miles west of Port Antonio. It's a seductive spot that makes you want to curl up with a cool drink and just watch as the falls cascade down a gorge through a rain forest and into a deep rock pool.

Another popular stop is the **Caves of Nonsuch** and the **Gardens of Athenry,** a working banana plantation where a cave full of stalagmites and stalactites once shielded Arawak Indians who lived in the area. From the gardens there are beautiful views from an open-air lounge out across this lovely island.

One final stop is the **Blue Lagoon,** near Frenchman's Cove Hotel. A lovely, tranquil spot meant for lazy contemplation of life's mysteries (with some serious thought to how you can quit everything and spend the rest of your life here!), the Blue Lagoon also offers scuba diving and waterskiing. A mineral spring here is said to be good for rheumatism, but whatever the truth of that, the Blue Lagoon is good for the soul.

Martinique

Capital and Port City: Fort-de-France.

Size: 50 miles long by 19 miles wide.

Population: 100,000.

Government: Martinique is not a colony but a département of France, so all residents are citizens of France.

Climate: 70° to 80°F year round, with some rain June through September.

Language: French, Créole.

Currency: French franc; $1.00 U.S. = 8.5 F.

Tourist Information: Office du Tourisme, Bord de Mer, B.P. 520, Fort de France (tel. 71-79-60).

Public Transportation: taxis (unmetered, so agree on a price first), native buses, launch to Trois-Îlets.

Car Rentals: Hertz, 1 rue de la Liberté (tel. 71-42-44); Avis, 26 rue Lazare Carnot (tel. 71-12-34); Budget, 7 rue de la Liberté (tel. 71-91-19).

Shopping Specialties: pottery, straw items, Martinican dolls, woodcarvings.

Food Specialties: French and spicy Créole cuisines; crab, turtle, conch, octopus, curries, blaff (fish stew).

Restaurants: Pointe Simon—La Grand'Voile (tel. 71-29-29); Fort-de-France—D'Esnambuc, 1 rue de la Liberté (tel. 71-45-51); La Madrigue, 11 boulevard Chevalier-Sainte-Marthe (tel. 71-48-79); Pointe du Bout—Chez Sidonie (tel. 76-30-54) and La Marina (tel. 76-30-33).

Martinique is the Paris of the Caribbean, a sunny volcanic island that celebrates joie de vivre in lifestyle and culture.

Looming over the island is fierce Mont Pélée volcano, which erupted in 1902 to kill 40,000 inhabitants in a fiery display of nature's violence. On the slopes of this 4656-feet-high peak, deep-green rain forests thrive.

Martinique's most famous export was the Empress Josephine, consort to Napoleon, who hailed from the island of Trois-Îlets. Another famous French royalty groupie, Madame de Maintenon, mistress of Louis XIV, also came from Martinique. Some say those two are testimony to the outstanding beauty of Martinique women, and go so far as to claim that the island shelters the most beautiful femmes of the Caribbean. Here beauty is indeed in the eye of the beholder, for topless beaches are common.

Discovered by Columbus, the island was taken over by French settlers early on, in 1635 to be exact. Sugarcane plantations and rum distilleries have kept the island thriving over the years, and now tourism is doing its part.

This is an island of mountains, from its highest, **Mont Pélée,** to the 3960-foot **Carbet Peak.** The southern part of the island is hilly, where the land rises to about 1500 feet. Along the edges of the sea tiny coves provide intimate swimming spots, and beautiful bays are a photographer's dream.

You'll see fabulous flowers everywhere, adding their splashes of color to the pastel loveliness of sleepy villages. Tropical birds of all kinds, including hummingbirds, live here, flitting happily among shrubs that may shield a mongoose, imported here decades ago to rid the island of snakes. Mongoose-snake competitions are still a favorite sport on the island (although baseball is the national passion).

In Fort-de-France you'll find yourself strolling the island equivalent of New Orleans or Key West: ornate iron grillwork, tropical flowers, café au lait, great French and Créole cooking. If by now you're thinking it might be nice to skip a ship meal in favor of shoreside flavors, this is the place to do that.

Be prepared for some healthy hiking here—most of the streets climb steep hills—and some beautiful views as a reward.

In town you'll see a white marble statue of Josephine in a park called **La Savane,** and nearby at the Palais de Justice a statuary tribute to Victor Schoelcher, who worked to free the slaves a century ago.

If you'd like to see more Josephine mementos, take a 20-minute drive or a ferry to **Trois-Îlets,** where an estate about a mile out of town features a collection that includes the empress's bed, a letter from Napoleon, and some other remnants of her time. It's called La Pagerie, and is open daily (except Monday) from 9 a.m. to 5:30 p.m.

St. Louis Roman Catholic Cathedral was built in 1875 of iron and is certainly an unusual church. Stop by and you'll see what I mean. Overlooking the town is **Sacré-Coeur de Balata Cathedral,** a copy of Montmartre's Sacré-Coeur in Paris.

Fort St-Louis is the guardian of the port and stands on a cliff overlooking it. Once called Fort Royal, the fortress was the scene of fierce battles among the Dutch, French, and English as the island changed ownership in the 17th and 18th centuries. A sound and light show takes place there each night, and there's a new restaurant inside the fort, Le Lotus. Two other bastions, **Fort Tartenson** and **Fort Desaix,** offer plenty of exploration possibilities for fortress fans.

One very colorful spot you're sure to notice as you stroll the narrow byways here is **Library Schoelcher,** which features a red and blue portal in fancy furbelows, lotus-petal columns, and turquoise tiles. All of it was imported from Paris where it was part of the Paris Exposition of 1889.

History buffs should head for the **Musée Departementale de la Martinique,** where you'll see remnants of the early Arawak and Carib Indian tribes who once inhabited this island and many others in the Caribbean.

If you'd like to be more active, there is horseback riding, waterskiing, scuba diving, golf, tennis, and sailing. You can even try some airborne sightseeing, offered by Heli Antilles International and arranged at the Hotel Bakoua.

An "Aquascope" **glass-bottom boat** with gull-wing sides has taken up residence here recently and will take you on tours of the fish and coral which you view through the craft's windows.

You can hardly go wrong on restaurants here—they all offer good French cooking or Frenchmen cooking Spanish or Caribbean style. Don't panic if the restaurant looks like a roadside shack; the food's good and life is casual here.

A local **market** at Quai Desnambuc features local handicrafts and souvenirs, and in the **shops** you'll find some of the best of French imports: Vuitton, Limoges, Lalique, at prices often well below what you'd pay at home. Among the more interesting shops are Les Puces, 26 and 28 rue Victor-Hugo, two old mansions filled with antiques; Chantilly, on rue Victor-Hugo, for fashions; Gigi, 53 rue Lazare-Carnot; Au Printemps, rues Schoelcher and Antoine-Siger, a branch of the Paris department store although more modest; and Prisunic, on rue Lamartine, a cheaper version of Au Printemps.

For **island crafts,** try Calypso at Pointe du Bout, which is a bit out of town but has beautiful handicrafts and batik-ed silks; or the Caribbean Art Center, facing La Savane in town, where some of the best in island craftsmanship is displayed and sold. Rum's a good buy too, and comes in some unusual colors and types. Try a bottle of Bally from Boutique du Rhum, 41 rue Victor-Hugo (upstairs from the tea house below).

If you're going out on the island to explore, you'll see some plush hotels at Pointe du Bout, beautiful Diamond Beach with its grove of palms and towering **Diamond Rock, Savane de Petrifications,** a "forest" of petrified rock; Mont Pélée, and in **St-Pierre,** the town destroyed by the lava flow, the **Musée Volcanologique,** featuring relics dug from this Caribbean Pompeii.

Puerto Rico

Capital and Port City: San Juan (pop. 1 million).

Size: 100 miles long by 35 miles wide (about half the size of New Jersey).

Population: 3 million.

Climate: 70° to 80°F year round; rain forest in interior.

Language: Spanish, but many also speak English in the urban areas.

Currency: U.S. dollar.

Tourist Information: Puerto Rico Tourism Co., 301 Calle San Justo, about a block from the pier in San Juan (tel. 809/721-2400).

Documents: proof of citizenship required for non-U.S. citizens.

Public Transportation: taxis (metered), buses, jitneys, (called publicos).

Car Rentals: Hertz, 1365 Ashford Ave. (tel. 725-2027 or 5537); other major companies as well.

Shopping Specialties: chic clothing and shoes, jewelry, antiques, carved wooden santos (saints), china, silver, crystal, rum (you can take back to the States as much Puerto Rican rum as you want, duty free).

Food Specialties: rice and beans, ropa viejo, picadillo, arroz con pollo, paella, tostones, fried bananas, pork; plus a variety of international cuisines.

Restaurants: Los Galanes, 65 San Francisco St. (tel. 722-4008); Mallorquina, 207 San Justo (tel. 722-3261) for casual dining; Butterfly People, 152 Forteleza (tel. 723-2432).

Puerto Rico is at once ancient and modern, its lovely old historic district surrounded by the most modern of cities.

You'll dock right at the entrance to Old San Juan, the city's oldest quarter and its most interesting shopping area. The best way to see the old city is on foot, but wear your most comfortable shoes as you'll be doing some serious, but wonderfully rewarding, hiking.

And, yes, Christopher Columbus was here too. (As you travel the Caribbean you begin to think Columbus must have commuted! He seems to have been everywhere, but then getting everywhere in the Caribbean isn't all that difficult as you're discovering aboard your very own *Niña, Pinta,* or *Santa Maria.*) On his second voyage to the New World in 1493 that man happened upon an island he called San Juan in honor of St. John the Baptist. Ponce de Leon (of Florida's "fountain of youth" fame) was the first governor of the island, which later was called Puerto Rico or "rich port."

Trade winds cool cosmopolitan Puerto Rico year round so it's never blazing hot. In fact in the mountains out on the island temperatures are as perfect as they could be all year long.

Out on the island are deep, damp tropical rain forests, arid deserts, beautiful deserted beaches lined with swaying palms, even a phosphorescent bay filled with tiny organisms that glow in the dark when you swim there!

To get a look at lovely **Old San Juan,** let's begin with a stop at the tourist office, just up the street from the docks at 301 Calle San Justo. Called the Puerto Rico Tourism Co., the tourist office can supply you with a copy of "Que Pasa," which tells you everything that is going on in Puerto Rico and highlights a walking tour of the city. Here are some of the most interesting sights:

Nearest to the pier is **La Fortaleza,** on Calle (*calle* is "street" in Spanish) Fortaleza, the first castle built here by the Spanish in 1533. Now the home of the island's governor, it is one of the oldest executive mansions in this hemisphere. Tours in English are every half hour from 9 to 11:30 a.m. and 1:30 to 4 p.m.

San Juan Gate, Calle San Francisco and Calle Recinto Oeste, is more than 300 years old and was the main entry to San Juan in the 18th century.

City Hall, on Calle San Francisco, was completed in 1789 and has guided tours Monday through Friday from 8 a.m. to 4:15 p.m.

San Juan Cathedral, Calle Cristo and Caleta San Juan, was begun 400 years ago but suffered damage from 16th-century looters and storms. Ponce de Leon was buried here after he died from an arrow wound received in Florida.

Casa Blanca, on Calle Sol, was home to the descendants of Ponce de Leon for generations, although never to the governor and explorer himself. It now offers a fascinating look at life and homes of the 16th and 17th centuries. Tours are given daily from 9 a.m. to noon and 1:30 to 4:30 p.m.

Case de los Contrafuertes, on Calle San Sebastian, is a museum of pharmaceuticals and has a sensational collection of "santos," saints carved in native woods and now one of the great Puerto Rican collectibles, It's open from 9 a.m. to noon and 1 to 4:30 p.m. daily (except Monday and Thursday).

Pablo Casals, the renowned cellist, was a Puerto Rican, and his work and memorabilia are displayed in the **Pablo Casals Museum,** a tiny 16th-century house, lovely in its own right. Open 9 a.m. to noon and 1 to 4 p.m. Tuesday through Saturday, from noon to 5 p.m. on Sunday.

Dominican Convent, Calle Norzagaray, was begun in 1523 by Dominican friars and was often a refuge for San Juan residents attacked by Carib Indians. It is now the Institute of Puerto Rican Culture.

City walls 20 feet thick at the bottom, about half as thick at the top, protected the town against invaders and pirates. You can see the remains of these impressive walls between San Cristobal and El Morro Fortresses.

If you like forts, you're going to adore San Juan. No fewer than three well-preserved fortresses guard this island harbor. By name they are San Cristobal Fort on Calle Norzagaray, Fort San Jeronimo at the entrance to Condado Bay near the Caribe Hilton Hotel, and the granddaddy of them all, **El Morro,** on Calle Norzagaray. The most spectacular is El Morro, which looms above the harbor atop a vertical cliff. Ordered built in 1539, it was originally a single round tower which you can still see inside the main part of the fort. In those days it was called the Castle of San Felipe, and from its walls were fired the cannons that drove away Sir Francis Drake in 1595. Guided tours are conducted at 9:30 and 11 a.m. and at 2 and 3:30 p.m., but you can wander around on your own and figure most of it out yourself. In the small museum inside the fort, all the major battles that took place are described in English and Spanish.

From the ramparts here you get a spectacular view of the glittering waters that surround the island and of Old San Juan. There's even a dungeon for your peering pleasure. If you're tired from your explorations, outside the wall massive lawns shaded by an impressive row of casuarina trees stretch to the sea—a lovely place to rest, picnic, even nap a bit.

As you walk through the old town, you will see ornate wrought-iron balconies above you, pretty painted doors with fancy brass hardware, and houses in all colors of the rainbow. Scarlet bougainvillea and deep-green vines climb the old walls, and tiny flower-filled window boxes add splashes of unexpected color.

You'll find intriguing **shops** by the dozens, so many it would be impossible to outline them all here, but I've picked out a few of my favorites. For hammocks, hanging woven chairs, all kinds of string, cord, or yarn things to sit and lie in, the Gentle Swing, 156 Calle Cristo, is wonderful. A hammock chair you hang from the ceiling is possibly the most comfortable seat you'll ever sit in, and costs about $50. It was invented by the Taino Indians in pre-Columbian times!

Butterfly People, 152 Fortaleza, offers the most interesting creations in the Caribbean. Two Americans with the unusual names of Drakir and Attendaire Purington buy the most gorgeous butterflies you've ever seen from special farms in New Guinea and South America, treat them with chemicals to preserve the color, and frame them in Lucite boxes. These are not just pinned-up butterflies but signed and numbered artworks in which the shimmering iridescent creatures seem to be suspended in flight, their wings glowing like jewels, never looking quite the same twice. This handiwork is expensive, but it's worth every dime if you're in search of mementoes more meaningful than an ashtray labeled San Juan. Butterfly People is also housed in a lovely old building with a pretty courtyard and an enchanting small restaurant.

Collecion d'Aqui, 204 Forteleza, has fine, quality Puerto Rican handicrafts including pottery, metalwork, and woodcarvings.

Crazy Alice, 196 Fortaleza, has a shop packed with everything from Panama hats to papier-mâché fruit. Reinhold, at 201 Cristo St., is an old-line jewelry store.

You don't pay duty on purchases you take back to the mainland because Puerto Rico is part of the U.S. You also may find bargains as impressive here as in the Virgin Islands, and the shops are every bit as chic.

Sports enthusiasts will find golf, tennis, riding, and watersports of all kinds in and around San Juan. Details are available at the Puerto Rico Tourism Co. and in the "Que Pasa" publication.

Ships often remain overnight in San Juan so passengers can take in the lively **San Juan nightlife.** Shore excursions generally are a choice between a flashy flamenco show at the Condado Holiday Inn and a Vegas cabaret revue on ice(!) at the Palace Hotel. Both are top-notch entertainment. A nice club in Old San Juan for an intimate evening with piano music and quiet talk not far from the ship is called La Violeta, Calle Forteleza near Calle Cristo, and some top discos include La Vista Disco, Juliana's in the Caribe Hilton Hotel, and a disco in the Condado Plaza Holiday Inn.

Casinos are active in San Juan at several major hotels.

Authentic folklore entertainment is provided by a group of folk dancers who perform in the **LeLoLai Festival** at large hotels on the island. To discover where and when the show is playing call 809/722-1513 or 809/723-3135.

St. Lucia

Capital and Port City: Castries.

Size: 27 miles long by 14 miles wide.

Population: 120,000.

Language: English, Créole.

Currency: Eastern Caribbean ("beewee") dollar (E.C.$); $1.00 U.S. = E.C. $2.60.

Tourist Information: Tourist Office, Castries (tel. 2479).

Documents: passport required.

Public Transportation: unmetered taxis (verify whether price is quoted in U.S. or "beewee" dollars), jitney buses.

Car Rentals: St. Lucia Car Rental, Caribleu Hotel, Cap Estate (tel. 8551). Note that driving is on the left, and that a local license must be obtained from the Traffic Department, on Bridge Street in Castries (tel. 2455).

Shopping Specialties: sea island cottons, silkscreened fabrics, chic cottons, flour-bag clothing, shell jewelry, island perfumes.

Food Specialties: West Indian cuisine, curries.

Restaurants: Green Parrot, Le Morne (tel. 2869); Rain, Columbus Square (tel. 3022); The Still, Soufrière (tel. 7224).

You've heard of active volcanoes and quiescent volcanoes and now you're going to hear about a drive-in volcano! Yes sir, step right and drive into the volcano, but sorry, you can't drive out the other side with a grilled burger. Another of the Caribbean's Mt. Soufrières, St. Lucia's volcano is one of those bleak moon-landing landscapes steaming and fuming its way into the future.

You can drive a car right into it, parking and walking between sulfur springs and whooshing jets of steam. It makes a big stink, literally and figuratively, but this **Mount Soufrière** has never yet followed up its steaming threats.

Millions of years old, the volcano has two sisters, or brothers if you will, called **Petit Piton** and **Gros Piton,** both volcanic cones rising more than 2400 feet, shooting right up out of the sea and visible for miles around. You'll probably see them first while you're still at sea.

All this area is a huge rain forest in which the annual rainfall is something like 150 inches.

Here I've been talking about it all this time and you don't even know how to say it: it's pronounced St. *Loo*-sha. The island's capital, Castries, was named for an early French secretary of state to the colonies.

Nobody is quite sure who happened upon St. Lucia, which is about 20 miles from Martinique, but it was settled by some St. Kitts colonists in 1605. Over the years it was a favorite battleground for the French and English, and actually changed hands 14 times!

In 1967 the island became part of the British Commonwealth. Although it has a long history, the capital city has been destroyed by fire several times so there's not much left of the early colonial architecture.

Among the things you'll want to look at here are the Saturday morning **market,** and **Morne Fortune** ("Good Luck Hill"), an 18th-century barracks with its "Four Apostles" cannons and a lovely view of the harbor.

From the fort you can spot **Pigeon Island,** where pirates and British sailors gathered in days past. It's no wonder they picked this meeting spot: there are lovely beaches here.

Marigot Bay may just look a little familiar too, but it's not an attack of déjà vue. Rex Harrison's *Dr. Doolittle* was filmed here, and Sophia Loren came here to star in a movie called *Fire Power.* Admiral Rodney hid his ships under palm leaves here and lay in wait for the French frigates. You'll see some of those same palms along the shoreline.

As you can see it won't take you long to get a look at most of the sights. Then you can get down to what is serious business on St. Lucia: swimming, snorkeling, scuba diving, tennis, golf, horseback riding, sailing, windsurfing, and deep-sea fishing.

St. Maarten / St. Martin (and St. Barthélemy)

Capitals and Port Cities: Philipsburg, St. Maarten; Marigot, St. Martin.

Size: about 7 miles long by 6 miles wide.

Population: 21,000.

Climate: 70° to 80°F year round.

Languages: Dutch, French, French patois (called Papiamento).

Currency: St. Maarten—Netherlands Antillean guilder (NA 1 = $1.75 U.S.); St. Martin—French franc ($1.00 U.S. = 8.5 F).

Tourist Information: St. Maarten—St. Maarten Tourist Bureau, De Ruyterplein, Front Street, Philipsburg (tel. 2337).

Documents: proof of U.S. or Canadian citizenship required.

Public Transportation: taxis (unmetered, but the governments set the rates; agree on a price in advance for special tours), buses.

Car Rentals: Avis, Le Pirate Hotel, Marigot (tel. 87-52-38); Hertz, Cape Bay Rd. (tel. 5995); plus local companies. For mopeds, try Carter's Rental, Bush Rd., Cul-de-Sac (tel. 2621).

Shopping Specialties: St. Maarten—Indonesian batiks, Delftware, Dutch dolls; St. Martin—chic French designer clothes, jewelry, perfumes.

Food Specialties: conch stew, lobster, Javanese peppersteak.

Restaurants: in Philipsburg—West Indian Tavern, Front St. (tel. 2965); Le Pavillon, Simson Bay Village Beach (tel. 4254); Oyster Pond Hotel, Oyster Pond (tel. 2206); in Marigot—Le Vieillard, rue de la Liberte (tel. 875033); Chez René, Marigot Bridge (tel. 875280); La Maison sur le Port, Marigot (tel. 879150).

This is the split-personality island, half Dutch, half French. Legend has it that it got that way when the Dutch and French settlers here each picked a "citizen of sound wind" and had him walk around the island. Where the two met became the border.

That French walker must have been of very sound wind for he carved out the bigger slice of the island, about 21 of the 37 square miles, while the Dutch stroller was certainly of sound mind: he (or she) saw to it that the lovely harbor of **Philipsburg** was included in the Dutch sector.

That's why today you are likely to land on the Dutch side, called Sint Maarten, but it's no trick at all to hop a local bus and hie yourself off to the French side, St. Martin (pronounced on this French side San Mar-*tan*). Sint or St., the island is believed to have been named by Columbus in honor of the saint whose saint's day it was when he landed here.

Admittedly, that legend is more tale than truth. After Columbus sailed in and officially discovered the islands, Dutch and French settlers moved in and might have clashed if they had not gotten together to write a "mont des accords" agreement that established the two territories as separate but equal—and friendly—sectors.

Often a hideaway for pirates who found its horseshoe-shaped bays as accessible as modern sailing craft do, this craggy, hilly island for years sported tobacco and sugar plantations run by Dutch and French settlers who had become so close some residents weren't sure which nationality they were!

You can move from side to side here with no concern for Customs or red tape, and I certainly suggest that you do so. Both sides of the island have beautiful beaches, 32 of them in all, and both sides have scads of interesting shops.

You may be relieved to know that you'll have few sightseeing obligations here. Very little remains of the plantation era and there are no archeological sights of note on the island.

Shoppers, however, will be busy. This island is a veritable treasure trove of duty-free goodies ranging from beautiful batik-ed cloth from Indonesia (try Java Wraps) to jewels of all kinds and the best of Dutch imports, things like Delft Blue ware and Dutch dolls. In the village of Grand Case live many painters whose work makes a handsome souvenir of your visit here. You'll find the buys on Front and Back Streets in Philipsburg.

When you cross over to **Marigot** on the French side of this mountainous island dotted with salt ponds, you'll find some beautifully stuffed string bikinis romping on the sands, often topless. You'll also find some beautiful beaches obviously designed by nature especially for you beach-sitters.

Snorkelers and scuba divers can visit some of the clearest waters in the Caribbean and poke around the 1801 British man-o-war wreck, the *Prostellyte,* complete with cannons and anchor.

Tennis and golf are available, as are waterskiing, boating, and fishing. Ask at the Tourist Office in Philipsburg for details on how to organize these activities.

And casinos here for gambling fans.

Lobster lovers should head for the West Indian Tavern, Front Street, an intriguing spot that occupies the site of a 150-year-old synagogue and has as much local color as it does rainbow-hued decor. Le Pavillon and Oyster Pond Hotel are other pleasant spots. In Marigot, try Le Vieillard, Chez René, or La Maison sur le Port.

Few cruise ships visit **St. Barthélemy** (pronounced Bar-tell-*emmy*), more's the pity. This island, most often called St. Bart's, has been a retreat for millionaires for generations and nobody ever said they don't know how to live!

Populated since the early 1600s, St. Bart's was owned by the French until they turned the island over to Sweden, which ruled for 100 years or so after exchanging trading rights in Gothenburg for possession of this sunny spot. Britain was in charge for a time, but in 1878 the island was returned to France and is today a satellite of Guadeloupe.

David Rockefeller and Edmond de Rothschild occupied some plush real estate here, lured by the beauty of the tiny island's beaches and its intriguing Breton and Norman fishermen who still speak with those accents and dress in costumes of France's northeastern countryside. You can still see some of that Swedish ancestry too, in blonde, blue-eyed residents.

You can get here from St. Maarten on a 145-foot motor yacht that makes the hour-long journey to the tiny harbor at St. Bart's Tuesday through Saturday at 9 a.m., returning at 3:30 p.m.

You'll land in **Gustavia,** testimony to the island's Swedish connections, where there are shops and taxis that can take you on an island tour or to one of the pretty beaches here. If you're hungry, try La Cremaillère.

You can get some good buys here on imported French perfumes and the like. Everything's sold without duty, so often the prices are lower than they are in France (not a wide range of choices, however). A St. Bart's straw hat is a must.

All the usual water sports, plus tennis and horseback riding, are offered.

St. Vincent (and the Grenadines)

Capital and Port City: Kingston.
Size: 18 miles long by 12 miles wide.
Population: 120,000.
Climate: 70° to 80°F year round.
Language: English.
Currency: Eastern Caribbean ("beewee") dollar (E.C.$); $1.00 U.S = E.C.$2.60
Tourist Information: Department of Tourism, Kingstown (tel. 61844 or 457-1502).
Documents: proof of U.S. or Canadian citizenship required.
Public Transportation: taxi, ferry.
Car Rentals: Choice Garage, Grenville St., Kingstown (tel. 61883).
Shopping Specialties: sea island cotton fabrics, native pottery, weavings, jewelry, wall hangings, baskets.
Food Specialties: seafood, tropical fruits.
Restaurants: Cobblestone Inn, Kingstown (tel. 61532); Pink Dolphin, Villa Area (tel. 458-4238); Ikahaya, Halifax St.

Throngs of tourists have not yet hit the serene beaches of St. Vincent, but throngs of other less-welcome visitors have stopped by here over the years to wreak a little havoc. The Carib Indians were living here peacefully until they made the mistake of taking sides in the constant feuding between France and England. In 1795 French revolutionaries allied with the Caribs burned some British plantations, but lost the war and the Caribs ended up being deported to British Honduras, where their descendants remain.

Since then the island has been allied to the British and is now a British Commonwealth country. You can still hear some French in these islands, however, although the primary language is English. Spanish is not heard at all, although the first visitor here was Columbus, stopping by to plant the flag as he explored this part of the Caribbean on his third voyage to these waters.

As part of the Windward Islands, St. Vincent and the Grenadines—which include Mustique, Bequia, Cannouan, Mayreau, Union Island, Palm Island, and Petit St. Vincent—are cooled by trade winds that keep the temperature a steady gorgeous here all year long.

Tiny as St. Vincent is, it's a study in varied terrain ranging from valleys to peaks, waterfalls to silvery beaches, lush jungles to coral reefs—even a volcano and something called a crater lake 4000 feet high. It's even sometimes called the "Tahiti of the Caribbean" for the groves of breadfruit trees that grow here. Legend has it that Captain Bligh of *Mutiny on the Bounty* fame (or infamy) brought them here on his return from Tahiti.

A volcanic island, St. Vincent is a sailor's heaven. You will see many a mariner here, some of them natives sailing produce off to other islands, some of them yachting fans here for the day or the week or the month.

Among the sights everyone will be looking at are **Fort Charlotte,** which isn't much of a fort anymore but does have a beautiful view of the sea from an aerie more than 600 feet above it, and **St. Mary's Catholic Church,** an improbable melange of architectural styles that's both weird and wonderful.

The **Botanic Gardens,** about a mile from downtown, is the oldest such garden in the West Indies and will give you a look at some of the spices you use in your cooking while they're still on the trees.

Budding archeologists will want to take a close look at **Carib Rock,** one of the Caribbean's most outstanding petroglyphs, dating to A.D. 600. A human face stares back at you from the rock. There's an **Archeological Museum** in the Botanic Gardens too.

Barrouallie is a **whaling village** and for the Caribbean that's *unusual!* Whales are hunted here with harpoons, but don't worry too much about saving the whales. So few are seen here that it's a very big moment when one is actually spotted, let alone harpooned. Barrouallie also has a Carib stone altar.

A waterfall called the **Falls of Baleine** is accessible by boat, so check at the tourist office for arrangements if you want to see it.

A drive down the **Windward Highway** along the Atlantic coast is a study in crashing waves and rocky shoreline, plus arrowroot, coconut, and banana plantations.

You'll see massive **La Soufrière** volcano in the distance. It's accessible to hikers, but makes a full day's journey and you will need a guide (who can be secured from the Department of Tourism). The volcano erupted in 1979 sending a shot of steam 20,000 feet in the air. An earlier eruption in 1902 killed 2000 people and created Rabacca Dry River, a lava flow, and an eruption in 1972 created Crater Lake, actually an island of lava rock.

Queen's Drive around Kingstown is another breathtaking series of beautiful views, and **Mesopotamia Valley** offers a panoramic view unexcelled anywhere in the Caribbean. Dominated by Grand Bonhomme at 3181 feet, the valley is rich with plantations, and rivers and streams tumbling to the sea over the rocks of Yambou Gorge.

Sports fans can take to the tennis courts, the golf course, go snorkeling and scuba diving or fishing. Sailing buffs can rent a boat from Caribbean Sailing yachts at the Blue Lagoon. Horseback riding and windsurfing are also available.

Shopping choices are sparse in St. Vincent, although you can buy some pretty sea island cotton fabrics and even have something made to order. The St. Vincent Handicraft Centre has interesting native crafts.

South of St. Vincent, the **Grenadines** stretch along in the ocean like a ribbon trailing from a package. Called the Grenadines because they are on the route to Grenada, these tiny islands are really sleepy places you can visit by boat or air if you're in the area long enough.

A few cruise ships stop at **Mustique,** a seductive enough spot to have lured Princess Margaret (who managed to find herself in a scandal even way out here). Another visitor, at the other end of the royalty spectrum, was Mick Jagger.

Here you'll find golden beaches, sand roads lined with a sentinel array of palms marching alongside, waters striated in what surely must be all the shades of blue invented, and one single resort, Cotton House.

You're on your own here, gloriously . . . and that's what it's all about, after all.

Trinidad and Tobago

Capital and Port City: Port-of-Spain.

Size: 50 miles long by 38 miles wide.

Population: 1.1 million.

Climate: 70° to 80°F year round, with some rain June through September.

Language: English, plus Hindi, French patois, Spanish, Chinese, Urdu.

Currency: Trinidad/Tobago dollar; $1.00 U.S. = TT$2.40.

Tourist Information: Trinidad and Tobago Tourist Board, 56 Frederick St., Port-of-Spain (tel. 62-31932).

Documents: passport required.

Public Transportation: unmetered taxis (ask if the fare is quoted in TT$ or U.S.$), pirate taxis (route taxis, which pick up and drop off passengers as they go, and are cheaper), buses.

Car Rentals: Hub Travel, 44 New St. (tel. 62 53011); Mike's Taxi, 37 Industry Lane (tel. 62 41590). Note that driving is on the left.

Shopping Specialties: Steel drums, banana leaf weavings, Oriental imports, cascadura jewelry, straw and fiber goods.

Food Specialties: Indian roti and curries, callaloo soup, stuffed crab backs.

Restaurants: in Port-of-Spain—Mangal's, 3 Queen's Park East (tel. 62-23904); Copper Kettle Grill, 66-68 Edward St. (tel. 62-44432); Le Cocrico, 117A Henry St. (tel. 62-23444).

These islands are the home of the steel drum, so expect to hear plenty of that intriguing calypso music while you're here. Steel drums, which Trinidadians claim are the only new instrument invented in this century, were originally made from the tops of steel oil drums. So good are these Trinidadian drummers and calypso balladeers that they almost always win the annual Caribbean Islands' calypso competition.

Trinidad and Tobago are harmonious in other ways as well. As the melting pot of the Caribbean, these two islands are inhabited by the wildest variety of nationalities of any nation in the region. Among those who call these oil-producing islands home are Americans, Europeans, East Indians, Venezuelans, Syrians, Lebanese, Chinese, Hindustanis, Javanese, Créoles, descendants of slaves and of early Indian settlers. Christian, Hindu, and Muslim live side by side, and the language is . . . well, even pronouncing the name of the language is difficult so you can imagine what the tongue itself is like. It's called Trinibagianese, but English is widely spoken as well.

Located just ten miles off the coast of South America, Trinidad has a government perpetually feuding (verbally) with others in the Caribbean, but that shouldn't affect your enjoyment of a stop here.

You can explore **Port-of-Spain**, the capital, on foot beginning at **Queen's Park Savannah,** once a plantation until it was destroyed by fire in 1808. You'll hear the chimes from pink and blue **Queen's Royal College** on Maraval Road, which is also home to a gingerbready house that's quite a sight indeed.

Whitehall Mansion, home of the prime minister, is a Moorish-style building, while the home of the German Stollmeyers, built in 1905, is a Caribbean German castle. These three and some others you'll see in a row here are called the **"magnificent seven."** (It won't take you long to figure out why.)

If you'd like to see what Carnival is like here—and it's *really* something —you can ogle some of the costumes at the **National Museum and Art Gallery.**

The main shopping street is Woodford Square, where you will see the **Red House,** built in 1906. It houses the governmental activities of the islands.

On one side of the Cathedral of the Immaculate Conception is a street leading to the **Central Market,** on Beecham Highway, where the spices for which Trinidad is famous are sold—very colorful and picturesque.

Is there a Caribbean island without a botanic garden? There may be, but it isn't Trinidad which has a 70-acre **Botanic Garden,** including an orchid house and cocaine bushes! In the garden is the official residence of the president of the islands.

Fort fans get yet another chance here, at **Fort George,** which occupies a peak 1100 feet above the city and was built in 1804. It's about ten miles out of town, a long trip in these parts.

Birdlovers will enjoy the **Caroni Bird Sanctuary,** where flocks of scarlet ibis settle each evening, or the **Asa Wright Nature Center,** where all kinds of exotic tropical flyers nest, including the only accessible colony of cave-dwelling guacharo birds.

Most cruise passengers are driven along the **Skyline Highway,** a seven-mile trek across a pass called "The Saddle" that runs between two valleys. You'll pass through Santa Cruz Valley where huge stands of bamboo tower over you and go back along Beecham Highway. This route is the way to **Maracas Beach,** the best beach near the city.

Sports enthusiasts can play tennis, go fishing, try hunting alligators or wild hogs, shoot a round of golf, or attend the horseraces. Water sports are, of course, readily available, as are horseback riding and cricket matches.

Shoppers are in for a treat: this is one of the biggest and most elaborate **shopping** areas in the Caribbean. You'll find exotic treasures from all points of the globe here—saris, crystal, silver, china, Swiss clocks, gold jewelry, sisal items, woodwork, ivory and brass, Irish linens.

Local items made from dried banana leaves are available from the Trinidad and Tobago Blind Welfare Association, 118 Duke St., and a Trinidad and Tobago Handicraft Cooperative, on King's Wharf, sells small steel drums, hammocks, carved wooden items, and straw creations.

Tobago, Trinidad's sister island, is 27 miles long and 7½ miles wide. You can get to this former sugar empire 20 miles from Trinidad by air. So rich and powerful were those who once lived here that an expression "rich as a Tobago planter" was a favorite saying.

Unlike Trinidad, this is a quiet island, a frequent retreat for Trinidadians. Water sports, including pretty beaches and very good scuba and snorkeling waters, are the primary reasons for a stop here.

Trinidad, trivia lovers, is also the home of **Angostura Bitters,** dreamed up by a Venezuelan doctor who brought his still closely guarded secret here.

U.S. Virgin Islands

Capital and Port City: Charlotte Amalie (pronounced Ah-*moll*-ya).

Islands: St. Thomas, St. Croix, St. John, plus about 50 smaller islands.

Size: St. Thomas—32 square miles; St. Croix—82 square miles; St. John—19 square miles.

Population: 70,000.

Language: English.

Currency: U.S. dollar.

Tourist Information: U.S. Virgin Islands Office of Tourism, Department of Commerce Bldg., Back St., Charlotte Amalie (tel. 774-8784).

Public Transportation: taxi ($3 per person from dock to town).

Car Rentals: Hertz, Truman Airport (tel 774-1879). Mopeds and scooters are also available for rent.

Shopping Specialties: duty-free imports of all kinds—jewelry, gold, silver, wools, china, watches, perfumes, etc.

Restaurants: St. Thomas—L'Escargot, on Creque's Alley; Sebastian's, on the waterfront (tel. 774-0533); St. Croix—Sprat Hall, two miles north of town, a former Great House famous for island cooking (tel. 772-0305); Barb McConnell's, 45 Queen St. (reservations are a must; tel. 772-3309); St. John—The Out, an alfresco café, Islandia at Mongoose Junction (tel. 776-6644); Rick's Hilltop, behind the public school (tel. 776-6341); Meada's, ferry docks, Cruz Bay.

Got your wallet and credit card ready? Welcome to St. Thomas, St. Croix, and St. John, the duty-free shopping mall of the Caribbean. Cruise passengers can hardly wait to get down the gangplank to begin spending that cash on birthday presents for Peter, Christmas gifts for Aunt Maude, and a little something for everyone they know. Indeed St. Thomas and St. Croix make the pursuit of purchases very easy. There are, I think, more shops here than people.

If you're not a shopper, rest easy. There are plenty of beautiful—no, gorgeous—beaches here, and some interesting sailing trips too. I can't imagine the hardy soul who could pass up at least a look at the bargains, but if you're dedicated to sun and surf, you'll be just as ecstatic as the shoppers in the crowd.

Let's take a look at the islands separately, because each has a quite distinct personality.

First, a little historical background. Here's Columbus again! That man certainly did get around, and is said to have gotten around here in 1493 when he was so moved by the beauty of these emerald isles he named them after the virgins of St. Ursula, a group of beautiful women who were martyred in the early days of Christianity.

Part of the Antilles island chain that extends from south of Florida 1500 miles east and south in a huge arc that divides the Caribbean from the Atlantic Ocean, the Virgin Islands are the tops of a submerged mountain range. All these islands and many more besides are called the Antilles, a name derived from a mythical continent believed to have existed in the Atlantic. Could this be mysterious Atlantis?

Along the north side of this arc of islands are the large islands of Cuba, Jamaica, Hispaniola, and Puerto Rico, called the Greater Antilles. East of Puerto Rico, stretching in a shallow croissant shape through 1000 miles, are smaller islands called the Lesser Antilles, among them the Virgin Islands.

Just sailing among these islands is a treat. You may occasionally see a dolphin splashing and you'll often be within shouting distance of tree-covered, sand-rimmed islands—although there probably won't be anyone on them to shout back!

It won't take you long to decide you'd just like to abandon ship here and take up residence on one of the skittery little sailboats darting about the harbor in St. Thomas or sling your hammock on a deserted island and play Robinson Crusoe.

On St. Thomas, cliffs drop into the sea creating tiny coves with crescents of sand, one of which has been named one of the world's most beautiful beaches by people with the enviable job of judging such things.

Although you can fairly drown in gold chains here these days, Columbus is said to have given these islands short shrift because the Indians who lived here told him there was no gold. For decades after their discovery the Virgin Islands lay languishing in the sun, just as they had before Columbus happened along.

Danes, perhaps in search of some of the Virgin Islands' never-ending sunshine, sailed over in 1665 to colonize the islands, but the settlers did not fare well. Their ship was destroyed by two storms, a fire almost blew up their powder stores, their settlement was sacked twice by English pirates, diseases decimated their tiny colony, and finally a hurricane whipped through, after which they gave up.

After the Danes and the English made a deal permitting the Danes to settle in St. Thomas, colonial life improved. In 1672 a little cluster of colonists built Fort Christian and began what was to be a long association with these islands.

Danes are a shrewd lot, no less so these settlers, who soon made a deal with marauding pirates offering them refuge and a stronghold. Pirate booty was sold and traded openly in the streets, which rather discouraged legitimate shipping from pulling into port here. Slave traders took up the slack at the docks, however, and were an important economic force on the island for more than a century. Slaves brought here were used to work extensive sugar plantations that created many a millionaire.

While a few of the planters were Danes, they were by now joined by a polyglot of people from Holland, England, France, Ireland, Germany, and Sweden. Language was always a problem, so many residents scrapped multilingualism for Créole, a combination of many languages including African slave dialects.

Créole was even taught in schools, but eventually English won out over the other languages and is now the only language spoken here, although most streets retain Danish names and the "Gade" appellation, Danish for "street." English as spoken here is distinctly West Indian, so expect to hear some very odd colloquialisms.

In the intervening years **St. Thomas** had its economic peaks and valleys, perhaps a little heavier on valleys than on peaks. By the time World War I broke out, Denmark had come to look upon these islands as a liability, while the United States eyed them as back-door protection against any moves Germany might make. Intent on securing this security real estate, the U.S. bought the islands from the Danes, who had ruled for more than 200 years, for $25 million in gold. A condition of sale saw to it that the islands retained their free-port status. When air transportation increased after World War II and Cuban doors were closed, St. Thomas and St. Croix boomed once again.

To get a look at some of this history, go on a walking tour of downtown **Charlotte Amalie,** which is located about a mile from the docks. All the shops you will see there are housed in what were once pirate warehouses, later used to offload legitimate goods. These storage spots were crumbling into ruin until a few years ago when an enterprising island developer revamped them and leased them to shopkeepers. If you wander down the tiny alleyway to the right of A. H. Riise Alley as you face the town, you can still see one of the rails and flat cars used to roll goods from the waterfront to the warehouses.

Sir Francis Drake, Edward "Blackbeard" Teech, Henry Morgan, and their bands of pirates strode through the narrow streets and alleyways of St. Thomas, and galleons unloaded gold booty right where your ship is docked. They saw the same colorful native marketplaces and rough sailing craft along the waterfront that you see today, although they didn't have a handy little pocket camera to record it all!

[illegible] ont just opposite King's Wharf, you'll see [illegible] gs of the island's **Legislative Building,** with [illegible] the elegant architecture of a century ago. [illegible] center of the island's political life.

[illegible] square surrounded by tooting cars and the [illegible] s July 3, 1848, when a courageous, or [illegible] prompted by a slave revolt on St. Croix, [illegible] er. He was recalled in shame, suspected by [illegible] volt to make emancipation possible! In the [illegible] berty Bell and a stand of old lignum vitae, a [illegible] iron wood."

[illegible] **ian**—it's red. It has served as governor's [illegible] arters, jail, and now Virgin Islands Muse-[illegible]

[illegible] **n,** just across Norre Gade from the Grand [illegible] as hardly changed in the nearly 200 years [illegible] hind it, **Hotel 1829,** once the home of a sea [illegible] e of island architecture with its open-air s[illegible] l courtyard.

[illegible] **Steps,** one of the world's more perfect ex[illegible] cracy can create: Danish engineers who had ne[illegible] omas decreed that the city should be laid out in [illegible] y to accomplish that was to build steps into nea[illegible] steps. Bricks used to build them came from Den[illegible]

[illegible] top of the steps is **Crown House,** built in 1750 and one of the few Danish mansions left on St. Thomas. It was home to island governors and still contains a Versailles crystal chandelier, a hand-carved four-poster, and beautiful domed ceilings.

The present governor lives at the bottom of the steps in **Government House,** the center of Virgin Islands life since the time of the American Civil War. Paintings by Camille Pissarro, one of the founders of French impressionist art and a former St. Thomas resident, are on display here. Pissarro lived at 14 Dronningens Gade, which now houses shops just as it did when Pissarro's father ran a shop there. Pissarro himself began his art career here on St. Thomas sketching native scenes. He left when he was 22.

On Raadet's Gade near Dronningen's Gade is a **synagogue** first built in 1796 and reconstructed in 1833. Pissaro, a sephardic Jew whose real name was Jacob Pizarro, probably attended this temple.

Some other sightseeing stops:

Coral World, an underwater observatory, is an interesting place in which you actually go beneath the water, descending an enclosed staircase 15 feet into the center of a coral reef where you look through windows at the flora and fauna of the deep.

Bluebeard's Castle is now a hotel, but was inhabited in the 17th century by Bluebeard and his wife who, legend has it, invited Bluebeard's six girlfriends to tea and poisoned them! Beats talking.

Blackbeard's Tower is the second stone tower you see looming over the city.

Drake's Seat is a stone bench from which you will have a dramatic view across **Magens Bay,** rated by *National Geographic* as one of the world's six most beautiful beaches. Drake is supposed to have reviewed his fleet from this aerie as it hid there prior to an attack on San Juan in 1595.

Most shore tours or taxi tours visit **Mountain Top,** a dramatic observation point that also thoughtfully offers you legendary banana daiquiris to keep you going as you stroll through boutiques and shops selling perfumes, jewelry, liquor. Jim Tillett, a dedicated art supporter, runs a batik fabric operation here to help native artisans perfect a craft. Their attractive fabrics and the clothing made from them are for sale here.

As for the downtown **shops:** well, I'm not about to try and tell you where to shop! There are hundreds of boutiques and tiny shops in St. Thomas, each lovelier and more intriguing than the last and each seeming to offer a better bargain. I will go this far, however: among the more unusual shops in town are Java Wraps, at Palm Passage, specializing in Indonesian batik-ed fabrics in beautiful jewel tones; Colombian Emeralds; St. Thomas Fragrance & Cosmetic Factory, for unusual island flower scents like frangipani and ginger; Animal Crackers, for kid stuff; Guitar Lady, for island instruments like steel drums, bongos, and mandolins.

Among the good buys in these islands are table linens, emeralds and some other precious gems, liquor, crocheted and embroidered clothing from China, as well as the usual duty-free items. Amber and larimar, the rare and unusual semiprecious stones of the Dominican Republic, are not as good a buy here as they are in their native island, but if you're not stopping at that island you might take a look at the stones here. They are among the few things from the Caribbean that are native to the islands.

If you're planning a big shopping trip to the Virgin Islands—and remember, you can bring back $800 worth of duty-free goods for each person, even children, in your party—you would do well to check the prices at home before you sail so you know when a bargain is a bargain.

Sadly, few ships stop at the other two Virgin Islands, St. John and St. Croix, although the brand-new upper-crust *Sea Goddess I* has decided to use lovely St. Croix as it winter base in the Caribbean.

On **St. Croix,** life and the land move at a much more stately pace. You will see gently undulating hills here, many of them crowned with the remnants of windmills once used to irrigate the sugar plantations. There are two primary settlements on the island, **Frederiksted** on the west and **Christiansted,** once the capital of the Danish West Indies, on the east. Each offers a full array of duty-free shops and each has its charms.

So well preserved are some of the 18th-century buildings here that they have been designated National Historic Sites. Among these buildings are **Government House;** the **Steeple Building,** now a museum of St. Croix history; **Fort Christiansvaern,** complete with bastions, dungeons, and war relics; the **West India and Guinea Co.** warehouse; the **Customs House,** now the library; the **Old Scale House,** used to weigh rum barrels; elegant **Government House,** whose ballroom chandeliers were the gift of the king of Denmark; and the building where American patriot Alexander Hamilton worked as a boy.

Outside of town, beautifully restored **Whim Great House** is not to be missed, and St. George Village offers an interesting look at botanical gardens and relics of cane-growing and Arawak days, as well as an intriguing gift shop.

Frederiksted has another of those red Danish forts and lots of frilly, gingerbread-trimmed houses. Barb McConnell's restaurant here is a "must-do" experience, but call ahead for reservations.

Take the road called **Scenic Route** up 900 feet to the observation point above Davis Bay and drive through the rain forest.

For golfers there are two golf courses, one of them a Robert Trent

Jones design called Fountain Valley. Tennis and horseback riding are available, and of course water sports are everywhere.

Once in a great while a cruise ship stops at **St. John,** home of beautiful scenery and **Virgin Islands National Park,** the only national park in the Caribbean. But even if yours doesn't, you can go there on day-long shore excursions to the island or on your own by catching the ferry boat from Red Hook docks (a taxi will take you there).

St. John's fabulous park, which includes an **underwater park** with visits to sunken wrecks, spreads over 9500 acres, covering most of the center of St. John. It was given to the government by Laurance Rockefeller, who is also responsible for the construction nearby of famous jet-set haven, Caneel Bay.

In the park you can explore the crumbling remains of old Danish sugar **plantations,** hike or go horseback riding, visit a delightful **waterfall,** and see carvings left by prehistoric Indians, not even to mention superb beaches. Orchids are as common as toadstools here, and ferns come in the giant economy size. Virgin forests mix with wooded areas more than 150 years old, enclosing more than 260 kinds of plants.

British Virgin Islands

Capital: Road Town, Tortola.

Population: 11,000.

Language: English.

Currency: U.S. dollar.

Tourist Information: British Virgin Islands Tourist Board, Road Town, Tortola (tel. 494-3134).

Public Transportation: ferries, a few taxis (agree on a fare in advance).

Car Rentals: on Tortola—Dennis Alphonso (tel. 4-3137); De Castro Honda (tel. 4-2182). Note that driving is on the left, and a temporary local driver's license must be obtained at the police station in Road Town; fee: $2.50.

Shopping Specialties: straw products, shells.

Food Specialties: roti, fungi, seafood.

Restaurants: on Tortola—Prospect Reef, Road Town (tel. 494-3311); Sugar Mill Estate, Apple Bay (tel. 495-4440); on Peter Island—Peter Island Yacht Club, (tel. 494-2561).

From the hills of St. Thomas and St. John you can see all 36 of the eastern Virgin Islands, a crown colony of Great Britain and known as the British Virgin Islands, or BVI to devotees.

The main island is **Tortola,** about the same size as St. John, 12 miles long and 3 miles wide. Wooded peaks rise to more than 1700 feet at Mount Sage and the terrain is rugged. Picturesque **Road Town** is just a small village, but it's the biggest spot on the island.

Other inhabited islands in the group include Virgin Gorda, Jost Van Dyke, and Peter Island. One more, Anegada, has big, beautiful reefs and off them lie more than 500 wrecks, some of which reputedly hide treasure. Seek and perhaps ye shall find. Everyone at Peter Island knows where the treasure is: it's home in the bank or in Switzerland. A posh resort here is a well-loved retreat for well-heeled jet-setters.

As cruise ships go farther afield to find interesting spots to take their passengers, these small islands are becoming what some people in the industry irreverently call "barbecue ports." What they mean is that when the ship anchors off one of these tiny islands, passengers go ashore to swim, sun, wander about a bit, and later to partake of a barbecue or shore picnic, with lots of rum punch and beer. Then it's back on the boat and off again to the next stop.

One could hardly think of lovelier, more lusciously remote places for these picnic treats than the British Virgin Islands, each of which looks exactly like the place you'd dream up as an I-want-to-get-away-from-all-this-and-go-live-on-some-deserted-island spot.

If you'd like a few names to add to that fantasy, try these uninhabited, or hardly inhabited, British Virgin islands: Beef, Salt, Dead Man's Chest, Ginger, and Fallen Jerusalem. (Tortola, by the way, means "dove of peace," and Virgin Gorda is a "fat virgin"!)

These islands have been in the possession of the British for many, many years, although poor soil and limited rainfall kept them from supporting major plantations. When sugar declined as a profitable crop and slavery was abolished, plantation agriculture was abandoned and most of the British residents left, leaving ex-slaves behind to eke a living from the land.

What to do here has much to do with sun, sand, and surf, and little to do with historical markers.

The Baths, on Virgin Gorda, formed by mammoth granite boulders and carved by wind and waves, make lovely labyrinthine swimming holes. The scenery is superb, sand beaches sparkle, and tropical rain forests cover some of the islands. Charter boats will take you sailing or fishing. You can get there by plane from Beef Island off Tortola, or by a boat called Speedy's Adventures.

Mount Sage is a national park 1780 feet high overlooking tiny islands. Head west from Road Town. Out this way you'll also see "the Dungeon," the island's oldest fort, built in 1640. A rare wild West Indian cherry tree grows here.

A few boutiques on Tortola offer treasures, but this is not a duty-free port, although British items are not taxed. Shell jewelry made here is one of the more interesting buys, and hand-printed fabric at Caribbean Hand Prints is pretty.

Small shops can fit you out with **diving** equipment or you can participate in a diving shore excursion with shipmates. Most ships have them. A sunken wreck, the R.M.S. *Rhone,* off the west end of Salt Island, was called "the world's most fantastic ship wreck dive" by *Skin Diver* magazine. Aquatic Centers in Road Town (tel. 4-2858) can take you there.

Sailboats are available for rent too. Try the Moorings (tel. 4-2332).

On Jost Van Dyke, stop for a drink at Foxy's—everybody does. On Tortola, Sir Francis Drake Pub is a hangout, and Cell 5 is a good, very casual spot. The Ample Hamper can provision a picnic.

On Virgin Gorda, Little Dix Bay is a very posh and lovely place with an excellent dining room, Biris Creek is dramatically located atop a cliff, and the Bitter End Yacht club appeals to the yachting crowd.

3. Mexican Riviera / Yucatán Peninsula

Acapulco. Puerto Vallarta. Names that conjure up images of tanned bodies, daring high divers, a balcony perch for a mariachi serenade, legendary silvery beaches gleaming in the sunlight, and the moonlit, nonstop evenings of dancing and laughter with days to match.

Mexico is as modern as a jet ski and as ancient as 10,000 years of history can make it. It's as changeable as the chameleons that sun themselves on remote rocks and as everlasting as the surf that breaks ceaselessly on its sandy shores.

Come here with preconceived ideas of its people and its way of life and you will find those conceptions fulfilled. But come here with an open heart and this land will steal into it, weaving a golden web of memories that will remain with you forever, returning at unexpected moments to shed a glow of delight on the gloomiest day.

It has been ever so in this changeable land that stretches across the Texas, Arizona, New Mexico, and California borders, through desert into mountains and finally to the Pacific Ocean on one side, the Gulf of Mexico on the other.

Countless ages ago early sunseekers crossed the Bering Straits and wandered far down to these southern reaches, hunting what moved and gathering what didn't. Later the ancestors of these early settlers began planting some of the crops they gathered and creating pots in which to store them. Pots dating as far back as 2400 B.C, nearly 4400 years ago, have been discovered here.

More than 3000 years ago in the Preclassic Period from about 2000 B.C. to A.D. 300 a tribe called the Olmecs, who were the first known people to use a 365-day calendar, lived near today's Veracruz. Here they created mammoth 40-ton basalt sculptures that remain a mystery: How were they cut and carved with only primitive implements, and why? What are they?

In a few thousand years the pastoral life of these early people had been supplanted by ancient cities. From A.D. 300 to 900 in the Classic Period, Maya tribes moved into prominence, creating outstanding scientific and artistic achievements ranging from complex calendars that could predict astronomical activity to arithmetic calculations that made the first known use of the mathematical concept of "zero."

Other cultures joined the Olmecs and the Mayans: the Toltecs, Zapotecs, the Totonacs, each adding to the artistic and cultural history of this land.

Historians call the period from A.D. 900 to 1520 the Postclassic Period. During it the joy-filled, fun-loving life disappeared, replaced by war, migration, and social dissolution.

In the 1300s the warlike Aztecs ascended to supremacy near Mexico City, building a city huge for its time and creating a society rich in gold and material goods.

By the time the Spaniards arrived in the early 1500s the Aztec state was ruled by the Montezuma we've all heard so much about (although his name is said to be correctly spelled Moctezuma). When he tried to bribe them to leave, he only succeeded in tantalizing them, and finally was tortured by Cortés for information about his fabulous store of gold.

These Spaniards conquered Mexico and were soon followed by priests and brought Christianity here in the form of Franciscan and Augustinian friars. Silver and gold from this land turned Spain into the most formidable power in Europe.

Led by a priest, Father Miguel Hidalgo, the man now honored as the father of modern Mexico, the nation gained its independence in 1821. Turmoil reigned for several years during which, among other odd incidents, the Habsburg Archduke Maximilian ruled Mexico during three years of civil war.

Benito Juarez, another important figure in Mexican history, led the nation through some troubled times, followed from 1877 to 1911 by the legendary Porfírio Díaz whose dictatorship spawned the rise of another legendary figure, Pancho Villa, whose real name was Doroteo Arango. In the final ten years before the fall of Porfírio Díaz the nation fought a battle called the Mexican Revolution, a historic period that laid the foundation for the progress that was to come.

Today the 30 United Mexican States are guided by an elected president and a bicameral legislature quite similar to that of the U.S.

If there is one thing most travelers have heard about Mexico, it is tales of a malady known variously as *turistas,* "Aztec Two-Step," and/or "Montezuma's Revenge." To avoid this unpleasant memory of Mexico, which takes the form of diarrhea, nausea, vomiting, and fever, doctors say it is wise to skip uncooked vegetables, unbottled water, and ice. If you do succumb anyway, take it easy for a day and avoid food, drink lots of liquids for 24 hours. Ship doctors often suggest Kaopectate and Pepto-Bismol.

The weather is tropical on the west coast, which is protected from fierce *nortes* (northern) winds by high mountains, except in Mazatlán, which is often chillier than other regions. On the east coast along the gulf, the unprotected shoreline can have temperature drops as great as 40°F in an hour, although the Yucatán Peninsula is usually spared by the warming effect of gulf waters. The rainy season in Mexico is May through September, with June and September the worst for water.

Living here are nearly 60 million people, spread out across a land that encompasses 760,373 square miles nearly three times as large as Texas. Most people here speak Spanish, but there are also more than 50 different Indian dialects spoken in the country. In all but the most remote spots, however, everyone will know enough English and hand signals to exchange messages with you.

Mexican currency is the peso, and at last count you got 172 pesos for $1.00 U.S. Note that the dollar sign ($) is also used in Mexico to indicate peso amounts, so a sign that says "$75" most likely means 75 pesos . . . usually.

The capital city of this vast and varied land is Mexico City, but everywhere you go the shopping is wonderful. Specialties you can buy at very, very reasonable prices include pottery, cotton clothing, colorful glass, baskets, serapes, huaraches, rebozos, straw hats, embroidered dresses, silver, brass and copper, hammocks, tequila and mescal, and Guayabera shirts. Bargaining is expected and enjoyed.

To get around in Mexico you can rent cars, bicycles, motorbikes, and mopeds in most large cities, but you'll probably have to depend on taxicabs and local buses in the smaller towns. It's wise to work out the price of a trip to everyone's understanding before you get into the cab in all but the largest cities, and sometimes even there. Bargaining is quite permissible, particularly if you're in search of a regional tour.

Car-rental companies in Mexico include Avis, Hertz, Dollar, and Budget, plus local companies which may be cheaper.

You can get scads of information about Mexico by contacting the **Mexican National Tourist Council,** which has offices in 17 cities in the U.S. and Canada from Atlanta to Chicago, Miami, New Orleans, and San Francisco.

Although it is wealthy in natural resources ranging from silver and gold to the black gold of oil, Mexico still suffers from an inequitable distribution of wealth that creates a wide social gap between the have-a-lots and the have-nothing-at-alls. Poverty is commonplace, but so is pride. You'll find a few, but not many, beggars, plenty of insistent urchin entrepreneurs, and determined salesmen of all ages. Treat them all gently, without rancor, and you'll both be the better for it.

Enseñada

Population: 10,000.

Tourist Information: Tourist Office, via Oriente 1, Canalizacion rio Tiajuana, Baja Calif Norte (tel. 3-10-13).

Public Transportation: taxis, buses.

Car Rentals: Scorpio Rent-a-Car, Alvarado 95-2 (tel. 83275); Hertz, Calle Alvarado Local 4 (tel. 8-37-76).

Shopping Specialties: straw baskets, brass, silver, shells, piñatas.

Restaurants: Casa Mar, Blvd. Costero y Blancarte 499 (tel. 70-66-7); Restaurant Casa Argentina, 213 Balboa.

Enseñada is part of Baja California, a long, witch's-finger peninsula of land that points the way to Acapulco and the Mexican Riviera. A favorite weekend "quickie" trip for Southern Califorians, this village just 67 miles south of the border is quintessentially Mexican, with tourist touches.

As the start of the sand strip Mexicans like to call their Riviera, Enseñada has been luring visitors since 1542 when adventurer Juan Rodriguez Cabrillo first stopped by here. No one stayed long in those days for a good reason: they couldn't find water.

Today there's plenty of water, both fresh from underground and salty from the Pacific Ocean that borders the long peninsula. A quiet spot, Enseñada is proud of its crescent-shaped strip of gleaming white sand. Its harbor, dotted with colorful sailing craft, is a pretty place too.

You can visit the old **Santo Tomas Winery,** and if you have time, go on an excursion to the picturesque Baja countryside.

There's not a great deal to do here, nor rafts of things to buy, but it's a lovely place to wander around, savor the flavor of Mexico, and get in some serious beach sitting.

Cabo San Lucas

Most cruise ships include this on their list of ports of call, adding "cruising by" when you look closely at the itinerary. Tide and water conditions sometimes preclude a stop here, and really the area is quite as lovely a sight from offshore as it is if you anchored there.

Located on the very tip of the Baja Peninsula where the waters of the Pacific and the gulf mingle, Cabo San Lucas is a study in green sea and white sand. Springing up from the desert-like sands hereabouts are some intriguing homes and hotels, glittering white in the sunshine. Mexico's tourist interests are trying hard to make this a popular tourist attraction, and are succeeding to the extent that certainly thousands more people know where the place is, thanks to the cruise industry.

Keep an eye out for **Los Arcos,** arches created by the rush of water against stone.

Mazatlán

Population: 200,000.

Tourist Information: Mazatlán Tourism Office, Paseo Claussen of Zaragoza (tel. 14966).

Public Transportation: buses, taxis.

Car and Moped Rentals: Hotel Playa Mazatlán, Avenida del Mar (tel. 34754), for bicycle, moped, and sailboat rentals. Hertz, Hotel de Cima (tel. 16303).

Shopping Specialties: local handicrafts at the Arts and Crafts Center, on Avenida del Mar about two miles north of town near the Hotel Playa Mazatlán.

Restaurants: El Shrimp Bucket, in the Hotel La Siesta, Blvd. Olas Atlas II (tel. 16350).

Mazatlán is a typical seaside village, quintessentially Mexican Riviera. People here live for the sea, on the sea, and sometimes, it would seem, in the sea!

Sabalo Beach, at the northern end of town, is considered the best beach by locals. You can get there from the main square downtown, the Basilica, on the Basilica-Sabalo bus for about just a few pesos.

You can also get around in rather grand rickshaw style on a contraption called a *pulmonia,* which is an open-air, motorized vehicle that carries three people (bargain to get a good price on a ride around town or out to Sabalo). What a way to go!

If you'd like to get a closer look at this lovely bay, you can sail about on a double-decker boat. The **Fiesta Yacht Cruise** leaves at 10:30 a.m. daily from the south beach near the lighthouse, and tickets are available at hotels. On a three-hour cruise, bilingual guides tell you about the bay while musicians serenade you. There's a short swim stop at a small island too.

Top-flight **fishing** has long been one of the lures of Mazatlán, and remains a popular sport hereabouts. You can catch some whoppers here, including marlin, for which you can fish year round. If you'd like to rent a fishing boat, look for the lighthouse on the south side of town and you'll find the boats moored at the bottom of the hill. A trip, including equipment, will cost a few hundred dollars a day, but if you can round up a group you can share expenses. A fishing license is necessary, and can be obtained by writing Unifleet, Box 1035, Mazatlán, Sinaloa, México, or calling 1-51-21 in Mazatlán for information.

Shoppers should make a beeline for the **Arts and Crafts Center,** where you'll find a sprawling complex of shops inside and out, up and down: pottery, straw, leather, papier-mâché, dolls, brass, glass, embroidery. This is the Riviera shopping spot, and bearable even for shopper companions: they serve free beer and marguerita at the beverage bar. If the shops there are jammed with cruise passengers, wander a few blocks to Las Gaviotas, Designer's Bazaar, with Vercellino designs for stylish cottons.

You can rent diving and snorkeling equipment at a number of small shops in the area too. Or watch someone else do the diving at El Mirador, where daredevil divers plunge 40 feet into the surf.

On a shore tour here you'll want to see the lovely **Malecon,** or seaside walk along the Olas Altas beach area, watch the **cliff divers** at Glorieta's Rocky Promontory, or visit beaches at the north end of town. Las Gaviotas Beach is a pleasant spot too.

In winter there are **bullfights** on Sunday, and the rest of the year there are some rousing rodeos.

Puerto Vallarta

Population: 60,000.

Tourist Information: Tourist Office, Libertad 152 y Morelos (tel. 20242).

Public Transportation: taxis.

Car Rentals: Avis, Carrerter al aeropuerto (tel. 21412); Hertz, Hotel Oceana, 538 Ave. Presidente Diaz Ordaz (tel. 2-00-24).

Shopping Specialties: embroidered clothing.

Restaurants: El Patio, 78 Díaz Ordaz, La Iguana, 167 Lázaro Cárdenas (tel. 20105).

You can have it all in this city, which may very well be why practically every west coast cruise ship stops here: old-world elegance and charm, fast-paced city excitement, terrific lobster and shrimp, even the setting for the film *Night of the Iguana.*

Snuggled in beneath the tropical Sierra Madras mountains with the glittering Bay of Banderas stretching out before it, Puerto Vallarta is a photographer's paradise: scarlet bougainvillea glowing against whitewashed walls . . . a Malecon oceanside walkway rimming the bay . . . in the air the scent of jasmine.

Most everything in Puerto Vallarta is within walking distance since the town is hardly more than five or six blocks wide.

Beaches along the Malecon are lovely, but most bathers head across the Cuale River about a half mile south to the **Playa del Sol.** If you get hungry on a day's beach outing, you can buy a piece of fish grilled on a stick for next to nothing from one of the small boys who grill and sell them on the sand.

Boats depart from the Hotel Delfin just off Olas Altas at 10 a.m. (except Saturday) to take you to **Yelapa Beach,** and return about 4:30 p.m. There's a band on board and a free bar.

Most visitors take to the streets here, however, roaming about the cobbled streets, photographing donkey carts, admiring from a hill the panorama of Banderas Bay and the red-tiled roofs of town.

Hiking, tennis, golf, and horseback riding are popular pastimes, the details of which can be secured from the cruise director. Amuse yourself with a parasailing adventure or try burro polo on the sands.

Sights to see include the **Church of Guadalupe** with its crown-shaped spire, the **Municipal Marketplace,** the Handicrafts Center, the **Malecon,** Vallarta Water Sports Center and the Marina, and **Children's Island,** a cluster of shops and amusements on an island in the Cuale River. History buffs will enjoy the nearby village of **Yelapa,** where artifacts of this land's native Indians are preserved; nice beaches and great lobster feasts there too. Posh villas here are located in an area called "Gringo Gulch."

Manzanillo

Population: 36,000.

Tourist Information: Tourism Department, 111 Avenida Juarez at the corner of 21 de Marzo (tel. 22090), open from 9 a.m. to 3 p.m. daily (except Sunday).

Public Transportation: taxis (unmetered, bargain in advance), buses (called camionetas).

Car Rentals: Auto Rentas de Mexico cruceiro las Brisas S-N (tel. 21495); Hertz, Hotel de Cima, Ave. del Mar (tel. 1-63-03).

Restaurants: Hotel Colonial, 100 Calle México 100 (tel. 21080); La Chiripa, Costa Azul between Manzanillo and the Santiago Peninsula (tel. 20722).

Once a harbor for the Spanish fleet, Manzanillo has come a long way from those 17th-century beginnings—it was recently a movie star! To be a bit more accurate about that, it was Bo Derek who was the star (*10* was the name of the movie), but part of the film was made here at the posh Las Hadas resort.

Until cruise ships began calling at this port, like many other Mexican stops it was a quiet fishing village and a resort visited mostly by Mexican tourists. Now you'll be welcomed here with the bong of a great bronze bell.

Manzanillo's lure is a seven-mile curve of beach with the lovely name **Playa Azul** (it means "Blue Beach" in Spanish) that ends right at the Santiago Peninsula. You'll find two lovely lagoons near Manzanillo, one right behind the city and the other behind the beach.

Downtown, the plaza (zócalo) is the center of life as it always is in Mexican and Spanish cities, but it's separated from the waterfront by railroad and ship yards.

Fishing and swimming are the major attractions of this port. You'll find **charter boats** for the former along the waterfront and a beach for the latter at San Pedrito, close to the downtown area. At **San Pedrito** the ocean is shallow for a long, long way out, which makes it a great splashing place for the kids and nonswimmers. Serious ocean enthusiasts may prefer **La Audiencia Beach,** on the way to Santiago.

A note on taxicabs: They don't have meters so make your deal before you close the door. You'll find a cab stand in the plaza and plenty of cabs waiting to take cruise-ship passengers anywhere they might like to go. A ride out to Las Hadas makes a nice trip and its Moorish domes and minarets are quite a sight, not even to mention its yellow sand streaked with black.

If you're here on a Sunday night, you'll find a small dance band playing at the downtown breakwater called the Rompeolas.

Most evenings you'll also find carriages waiting to take you on a sunset ride along the sea boulevard.

Zihuatanejo/Ixtapa

Population: 18,000.

Tourist Information: Tourism Office, Paseo del Pesador (tel. 422-07), open from 9 a.m. to 1 p.m. and 4 to 6 p.m. weekdays, half day on Saturday (closed Sunday).

Public Transportation: taxis, buses.

Car Rentals: Avis, Juan Alvarez 10 (tel. 42275); Hertz, (tel.).

Shopping Specialties: carvings, woven rugs.

Restaurants: Restaurant Don Juan Vicente Guerrero y Ejido (tel.

43210); La Mesa del Capitán Nicolas, 18 Bravo (tel. 42027); El Pescadór, right along the waterside (tel. 42133).

If you can pronounce these two spots you're already well ahead of most of your fellow passengers. So let's have a stab at it: Zihuatanejo is pronounced See-wah-tan-nay-ho, and Ixtapa is *Iks*-tah-pa.

These two small villages are, like many others along this coast, in the throes of development by a government anxious to lure tourists beyond the usual Acapulco–Taxco–Mexico City stops.

Nestled at the base of Mexico's Sierra Madre del Sur, **Zihuatanejo** is quiet, simple, peaceful, unchallenging. Until a few years ago there wasn't even a paved road here and they turned the lights out at 11 p.m.! People touting the spot like to say that this little village is what Acapulco was like before the onslaught, and when you see a sloe-eyed burro clomping down the avenue, you'll believe it.

Certainly I wouldn't quarrel with that description. This is indeed a tranquil village with all the ambience of "Fantasy Island." Slip into something simple, stretch out on a beach, buy a coconut from a local vendor, and stare out over the coral reefs.

If you're more energetic, roam into the central market square (zócalo) or catch a boat over to the beach at La Ropa or Las Gatas, where you can repose in the shelter of a thatched hut.

Coconut plantations stretch out around the town and craftsmen offer carvings and woven rugs.

Zihuatanejo's **beach** is an entrancing spot, curving around a small bay where sailboats with colorful sails zip in and out among the fishing boats.

Ixtapa was discovered by computer! Government computers put to the task of finding the perfect resort location chose this beach-trimmed spot, and shortly thereafter the government created this resort about eight miles north of Zihuatanejo. The famous and the infamous visit here, so who knows what "name" you'll get to see.

You can get there on a bus from the market in Zihuatanejo or by taxi. As you enter the village you go over a small rise in the ground from which you see this lovely bay stretched out before you like a silver-blue carpet. Waves roll over the sands, palms sway gracefully along the edges of the beach—paradise found!

Acapulco

Population: 600,000.

Tourist Information: Department of Tourism, Costera Miguel Aleman 187 (tel. 2-21-70) and at Río do Cameron (tel. 2-22-46).

Public Transportation: buses.

Car Rentals: Hertz, 1945 Costera Miguel Aleman (tel. 56942); other major companies.

Shopping Specialties: pottery, silver, embroidery, haute couture.

Restaurants: Sanborn's, Costa Aleman (tel. 26167); Carlos 'n Charlie's, Costera Aleman (tel. 41944); Beto's, five miles east on Costera Aleman (tel. 40473).

Acapulco is as chic and trendy as the other Mexican Riviera ports are simple and old-fashioned. Here you'll see slick grande dames and dons turned out in clothes that may be casual but didn't have casual price tags.

Life is casual here too, starting late and often ending about the time most people are just starting! Daytime to Acapulco dwellers is what you have to get through before the fun begins.

Beach lovers will find plenty in this handsome, busy city to keep them occupied. So many beaches are there, in fact, that Acapulco dwellers have **favorite beaches** they visit only in the morning, others for afternoon, and others for sunset, 23 of them in all!

Here are some of them, moving from west to east around the bay: Playa Langosta, Caleta, Caletilla, Terraplen, Clavelito, Carabali and Hornos, Paradiso, Condesa and Icacos and Guitarron, not far from the showplace hotel Las Brisas where some *rooms* have their own swimming pools!

Of all those, **Playa Langosta** is my choice. It's a small sheltered cove near La Quebrada, and if you're lucky you won't find many other people there. (Just don't stay on it too long or you'll look like the boiled langosta for which the beach is named.) Caleta and Caletilla are similarly tranquil spots popular with families.

You can also try **parasailing** here, go to the **bullfights,** ride a balloon-strewn buggy down Main Street at night, try **jet skis.** You'll find golf courses and tennis courts, sailing, fishing, and all the usual resort activities. Ask at the purser's desk for specific recommendations, or call the Tourist Office at 2-21-70 (located on Miguel Aleman) or 2-22-46 (located at Río do Cameron).

An open beach called **Revolcadero** has an intriguing woodsy lagoon, and **La Pie de la Cuesta,** although it's about eight miles from town, is simply not to be missed at sunset. You rock in a hammock, preferably with a companion and a coconut full of rum, and watch the sun flame into the sea.

Jillions of **cruises** operate from the pier called Bono Batani just west of the zócalo offering everything from glass-bottom boat rides to moonlight cruises with dancing.

This is a great place for the ship's city tour shore excursion, and the easiest way to see it all, unless you want to rent a car which is fun but means contending with traffic and parking.

Early in the evening you might consider a stroll up to the Mirador Hotel at the top of the hill at the end of La Quebrada, where you can plunk down at the bar to watch the sunset and then stay on for a good view of the famed **high divers** of Acapulco.

In case you have somehow missed hearing about this event: each night every hour from 8:15 or so to 11:30 p.m. an intrepid diver who suffers not at all from acrophobia steps out onto a spotlit ledge just below the Mirador's terraces, raises his arms dramatically, and plunges with much fanfare and applause into the sea—130 feet below! With a prayer before and some pesos from onlookers after, he accepts congratulations and returns again the following evening. Occasionally some up-and-coming adventurers try their luck too.

Mirador's La Perla Supper Club has music and reasonably good food with a minimum in the restaurant, but if you've seen enough here and are ready to see what all the **Acapulco nightlife** fuss is about, head for the Costera Aleman area. Here you'll find UBQ (at 115 Costera Aleman), an up-market spot frequented by the highest of society (or trying to be); Baby Q, not far down the street (it comes complete with Jacuzzi); or Carlos's Chili 'n' Dance Hall 'n' Bar 'n' Grill, or D Joint, two whoop-de-do spots.

Nightlife changes about as rapidly as the faces in this tourist haven, so some or all of those may have different names or not be around anymore by the time you get there. Ask around, though, as everyone will have an opinion on the best or at least some very good sipping and soirée spots.

Mexico's Ballet Folklorico entertainment appears at one of the large hotels nearly every night of the week.

Cancún

Population: 70,000.

Tourist Information: Tourist Office, 13b Avenida Tulum (tel. 30123).

Public Transportation: buses, taxis (agree on the fare in advance).

Car Rentals: Hertz, Calle Guava, 25 Manzana (tel. 988-30938); local companies. Bicycles and motorbikes also available for rent.

Restaurants: Chocko's and Tere, Claveles 7 (tel. 41394), for mariachis, cowboys, and guitarists; La Longosta Feliz del Carib, Tulum 33-c (tel. 43316).

Cancún has sprung up out of the sands like a glittering mushroom. Chosen by computer as a lively spot for a government-backed resort development, this island in the sun has proven the computers right. It's skyrocketed to fame in recent years and is now the favored destination for ships cruising in gulf waters as well as for jet-set travelers.

Soft, fine, even delicate, sand is a feature of the beaches here, and the Caribbean waters on this side of the world are just as devastatingly blue as they are in the eastern sector of the Caribbean Sea.

Cancún is in the heart of a historian's paradise. Ruins, comparatively recently discovered and still not fully explored or excavated, are everywhere. The most accessible, and some say the most spectacular, of these is **Chichén-Itzá.** Getting there is not everyone's cup of tea—until they get there and discover what a wonder they are beholding. Every ship that sails to the region features a shore excursion to the ruins, about a three-hour bus trip away (and three hours back too). Grueling as that may be, it's well worth it, for this site is one of the wonders of this ancient world. More on that in a moment.

Some cruise ships sailing in the area are considerate enough to stop at Playa del Carmen, a small beach village about 44 miles from Cancún—and 44 miles closer to the ruins.

Once you reach Chichén-Itzá you'll see why I think it worth the journey. Here is the Aztec pyramid you've seen in many a history book and even reproduced on the deck of Norwegian Caribbean Line's *Skyward.*

Originally a Mayan city, Chichén-Itzá became part of the Toltec Empire in A.D. 987. Their leader, Kukulcán, built a sprawling city, part of which is Toltec in style while the other sector features Mayan Puuc (a word taken from the hills in southwestern Yucatán) architecture.

The most outstanding feature of the ruins is the 75-foot stepped **El Castillo temple,** which features a stair for each of the 365 days of the year. This temple is evidence that the Toltecs had a firm grasp on the concept of the passage of time and calendars. It also has 52 panels on each side representing the 52 years of the Mayan calendar, and 18 terraces (nine on each side of the stairways) to represent the 18 months of their calendar.

To prove they really knew what they were doing, if you watch the sun set here on March 21, the spring equinox, you'll see the serpent head carving at the base of the stairs descend into the earth as the sun moves slowly down each stair, signaling to the Mayas the start of the corn-planting season.

At the top of the **Temple of the Warriors** is a Chacmool, the reclining figure so often reproduced as a symbol of Mayan culture (you've probably seen the figure with a pot of flowers sunk into its middle).

On the north side of the plaza you'll see a pathway leading to the sacred well, called a cenote. Sacrifices of young women often took place here, and excavations of the walls have dredged up scores of bones and gold objects. Don't miss the ballcourt, the largest in Central America, with two stone rings through which the ball was thrown. Cheering your favorite player on must have been quite an experience here: if you stand at one end of the court and speak in a normal tone, you can be heard at the other end.

Tulúm, another fascinating archeological sight, is about an hour's drive from Cancún. Spread over several acres and walled on three sides, this "walled city" (which is what Tulum translates to in English) is the only remains of a Mayan coastal town. Here you'll find the crumbling remnants of 56 structures, the best known of which is El Castillo or Temple of Kukulkán, a small temple-crowned pyramid on a bluff overlooking the Caribbean 40 feet below.

Constructed in the tenth century, Tulúm was built to serve as a fortress city overlooking the Caribbean. At one time 600 people lived here, according to an early Spanish bishop, in houses set up on platforms along the street. Tulúm was inhabited until about 70 years after the Spanish conquest, when it was abandoned.

Although these ruins can't compare with the drama and magnificence of Chichén-Itzá, if you use a little imagination and look carefully at what you see, you'll be rewarded. Note the red stucco that still remains in places, and imagine what this spot must have looked like when all the buildings here were painted in the same bright red!

Take a look at the Mayan city walls constructed of limestone, and don't miss the interesting frescoes dating from the 13th century inside the Temple of the Frescoes. Sadly, these are difficult to see in the dark temple, so if you're especially interested in getting a good look at them, bring a flashlight along. Look carefully on the cornice of the building and you'll spot a Mayan god staring down at you.

Cozumél

Population: 5,000.

Tourist Information: Tourist Office, Calle 1 Sur, near the plaza.

Public Transportation: taxis, buses.

Car Rentals: Hertz, Hotel Cozumel Caribe (tel. 2-01-00), and smaller companies. Bicycles and motorbikes are also available for rent.

Shopping Specialties: coral, local handicrafts.

Restaurants: Restaurant El Portal, Avenidas Juarez and Rafael Melgar (tel. 20227). Sheraton Sol Caribe, Playa Paradaiso at the port (tel. 987-20700); Pepes Grill, Avenida Melgar 220 (tel. 20213).

Cozumél is to Cancún as private plane is to Concorde: not as flashy or as publicized, but it gets you there just the same and with less huzzah.

Life in Cozumél is quiet, elegant, serene. While the jet-setters are out-statusing each other over in Cancún, people at Cozumél are using their energy to explore the sea, this island, and their own place in the world.

Sailing, snorkeling, scuba diving, and swimming, and elegant restaurants are the ingredients of your day here. You can plunk yourself down in a little bistro and watch the world go by or grab your snorkel and fins and watch the underwater world swim by on three-mile-long **Palancar Reef.**

You can get to Tulúm on a ferry boat or with a shore excursion, or take off on a Robinson Crusoe adventure complete with beach picnic.

There's something tranquil and determinedly unrushed about this seaside resort that may tempt you to get off and just let the world sail on without you.

4. Mississippi and Ohio Rivers

Hum a couple of bars of "Up the Lazy River" and you have an immediate idea what life is like as you meander slowly through the waters of the mighty Mississippi. Life on the banks is as serene and intriguing as life on this busy river which has provided the nation with folklore and fancy for generations. Tom Sawyer and Huck Finn are the river's two most famous sailors; New Orleans, Natchez, Memphis, and St. Louis some of its most famous ports.

On a cruise upriver or down, you will step back into the world of Panama-hatted, derringer-carrying riverboat gamblers whose dashing good looks turned hearts to jelly and aces to their advantage. Sonorous tones of a rumbling calliope welcome you aboard gleaming white paddlewheelers that chug merrily up and down the river like floating white wedding cakes. In an instant you are no longer part of this world but are time-warped back to the days of cotton plantations and hoop skirts, flirty fans and flighty ladies whose soft drawls hid iron wills.

Things haven't changed all that much along this 2047-mile-long river. Life still moves slowly in many cities along its banks and people still talk softly. You'll settle into the tranquility the minute you step aboard a Mississippi River cruiser, and soon you too will be drawling an occasional "y'all."

In **New Orleans** you'll hear the wail of a clarinet and the hoofbeats of a carriage horse echoing through the narrow streets.

Upriver you'll visit **Houmas House,** star of that spooky film *Hush, Hush, Sweet Charlotte.* A Greek Revival mansion, Houmas House can trace its history to 1840 when it was the center of life for workers on 20,000 acres of sugar plantation, the most productive plantation in the nation. Owned by a quick-thinking Irishman, Houmas House was saved from destruction in the Civil War when its owner claimed that as a British citizen he—and the house—were immune from the Americans' troubles. Postwar changes took their toll on this plantation as on many others, and little by little it declined until in 1940 a New Orleans doctor restored it to its former glory.

At **Baton Rouge,** 230 miles upriver, you'll see more of those hauntingly lovely plantation houses, and at the Louisiana Rural Life Museum you'll get a look at the working side of plantation life. Here you can visit a reconstructed plantation settlement complete with workers' cabins, blacksmith shop, and sugar house, the world plantation workers knew so well.

Named after a red post (a *baton rouge*) that was constructed to divide two Indian settlements here, Baton Rouge was founded in 1719 and was the center of fighting in Revolutionary and Civil War days. These days you'll

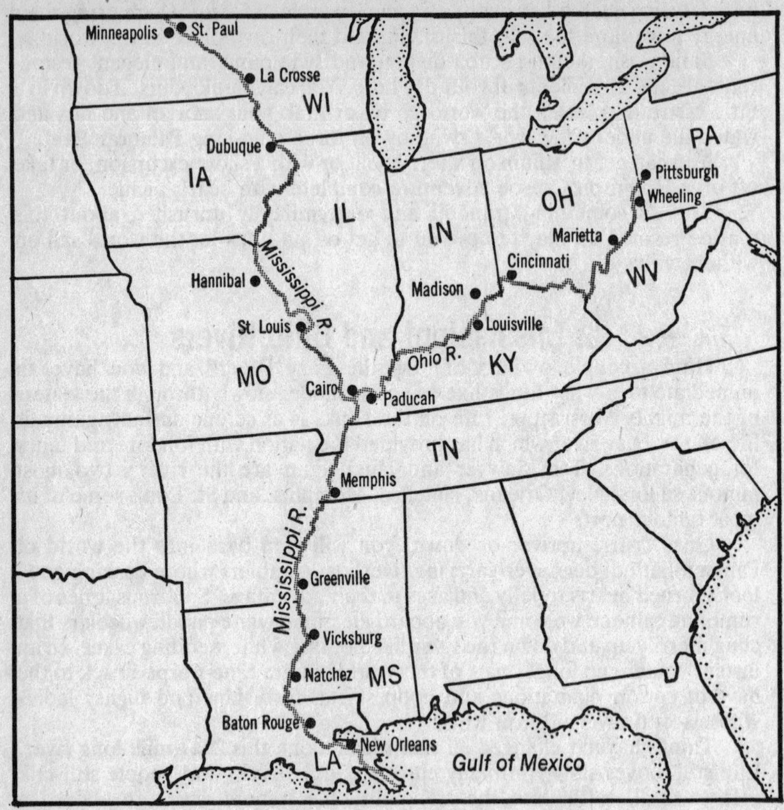

stroll down wide boulevards lined with former plantation homes so carefully restored that you can practically imagine yourself dancing in a candlelit ballroom there or placing your afternoon calling card carefully on the butler's silver tray.

Don't miss the Old State Capitol, reconstructed in 1882 after it was destroyed by Union troops during the war. It's one of the most unusual architectural creations in the South.

If you like rubbing elbows with money, even if it's historic money, you'll love **St. Francisville.** Here lived nearly half the nation's 19th-century cotton millionaires, ensconced in the splendor of glamorous plantations like the exquisite Rosedown Plantation and Gardens. In its parlors you'll see priceless furnishings brought here from France in 1835, gilded chandeliers, looping drapes, glittering crystal. At a similar plantation house, The Myrtles, you may even meet the ghost said to roam the massive halls and veranda.

In those elegant old days when King Cotton was growing up, **Natchez** was too, which accounts for the presence here of still more classic antebellum mansions. Spared by Gen. Ulysses S. Grant when he marched through the city during the Civil War, Natchez today sports some of the finest examples of antebellum architecture remaining in America.

You can ooh and ahh—and believe us you will!—over more than 200 massive plantation houses and gorgeous gardens that have made this city's semi-annual Natchez Pilgrimage festivals one of the most popular of all U.S. tours. On one of these you may visit Stanton Hall where hoop-skirted damsels will escort you graciously through the high-ceilinged, antique-laden rooms of this block-long plantation house. On the floors of a Georgian manor called Rosalie you can still see the scars left by the spurs of Union officers who strode through these hallways. At D'Evereux you will attend in your imagination one of the elaborate balls whose elegance earned the hostess here the title of grandest partygiver in the city.

Don't forget to sniff the air if you're here in spring: the heady scent of thousands of the city's famed magnolias fills the air.

More than 400 miles upriver is **Vicksburg,** where the sound of booming cannons seems still to haunt this tragic ground on which so many Americans fought each other. Surrounded for more than three months during the siege of 1863, Vicksburg natives refuse still to celebrate the Fourth of July, the day their ancestors surrendered to the Union Army.

In the Old Court House Museum are grim reminders of the past in small memorabilia that somehow seem to carry a more poignant message than battlefields and history books can provide: Confederate money, old war uniforms, receipts from slave sales, faded photographs—the tiny human touches so often lost in stories of the national tragedy that was the Civil War.

Its strategic location on the river and in the heart of cotton country made **Memphis** by 1873 the world's largest cotton market. Located 736 miles upriver but still part of the area known as the lower Mississippi River, Memphis is still a cotton center and its Cotton Exchange handles more than 4 million bales annually. You can visit the Exchange here, then go out and have a look at how the product that has made it famous grows and is worked in the fields.

A musical haven for generations, Memphis's Beale Street was home to blues musician W. C. Handy, while farther out of town another musician lived in considerable splendor: this is Elvis Presley's home, Graceland mansion.

Moving on upriver, you'll visit the now-quiet town of **Cairo,** Illinois, a city that once rivaled Chicago as a commercial center. As center of the steamboat trade, Cairo declined rapidly after the Illinois Central Railroad was built in the mid-1800s. You can still see wisps of the city's intriguing past, however, in the lovely restoration of Magnolia Manor and in Holiday Park.

When you reach the often-photographed Gateway Arch of **St. Louis** you're on the upper Mississippi River and at the old gateway to the west. There is much to see and do in this city, ranging from a visit to the largest brewery in the world. Anheuser-Busch, to a look at some of the trophies given aviator Charles Lindbergh who, you may recall, named his history-making aircraft *The Spirit of St. Louis* in honor of his St. Louis backers.

When the West was about to be won, pioneers gathered here to prepare for the trek onward through the wilderness. Traders, trappers, gamblers, dance hall girls, and all sorts in between made this a thriving city that remains to this day unexpectedly tolerant of the wide variety of adventurers who find their way here.

Another 300 miles up the upper Mississippi will bring you to **Hannibal,** Missouri, Mark Twain's boyhood home and the land that inspired his amusing tales of life on and about the river he loved. When you spot the first picket fence, you'll giggle at the memories of those young pranksters you once knew so well they seemed almost family: Tom Sawyer, Huck Finn, and Becky Sharpe. (Mark Twain was born Samuel Clemens but acquired his unusual name when he worked as a riverboat pilot on a sternwheeler bound for New Orleans.)

Water seems to affect the fate of many a Hannibal resident: this is also the birthplace of a lady known as *The Unsinkable Molly Brown* (her real name was Margaret Tobin).

Upriver you'll dock at **Burlington,** Iowa, but be sure to cross the river for a look at **Nauvoo,** Illinois, temporary home for Joseph Smith and his group of Mormon settlers. A dispute with the rest of the community here sent them on their way west, but before they left they constructed some interesting homes and buildings that have been restored by their descendants. Sip a glass of local wine while you're here in this vineyard capital of Illinois.

Next stop upriver is **Dubuque,** Iowa, nearly 600 miles into the upper Mississippi River. A vaudeville opera house built in 1910 is still in use here and is now listed on the National Register of Historic Places. You'll see more delightful 19th-century architecture in **Galena,** Illinois, a short bus ride away.

Victorian architecture begins to turn up regularly in this upper half of the Mississippi. You can see some interesting examples of it at Villa Louis in **Prairie du Chien,** Wisconsin, a quiet town near the confluence of the Mississippi and Wisconsin Rivers. Villa Louis was built by a representative of John Jacob Astor, the fur millionaire, who moved here to act as Astor's agent in the 1800s. Indian tribes lived in this area 10,000 years ago and the Hopewell culture settlement here features huge burial mounds 2000 years old.

Logging and furs were important industries in this area in the early 19th century when the river was used to float logs downstream. Steamboats like the one you're traveling on were an important part of that history. You can learn something about their role in life on the Mississippi at the Wabasha Museum at **Wabasha,** Minnesota, where you can also visit Suilman Antique Museum and an antique hotel, the Anderson House, which opened in 1856. Wabasha is also a cheese-manufacturing center, so you can visit a cheesery and nibble some samples.

Finally you come to **Minneapolis/St. Paul,** the twin cities 839 miles up the river and as far north as you can go on it. To head north or west from here people once had to travel by ox cart, and the traffic even in those days was terrific! Points of interest in this city include the renowned Guthrie Theater, Minnehaha Falls, and Fort Snelling, which dates back to 1825. Both these cities played a vital part in the opening of the Northwest Territory.

On some cruises you can branch off the Mississippi and head up the Ohio River all the way to **Pittsburgh,** where three rivers, the Allegheny,

Monongehela, and Ohio, merge. On the way you will travel up 1000 miles of the Ohio River, home of the first steamboat (built in Pittsburgh in 1811 and named the *City of New Orleans*).

On this river the mileage counting begins at Pittsburgh and rises as you move toward the river's confluence with the Mississippi at Cairo, Illinois. Stops on the Ohio include **Evansville** and **New Harmony,** Indiana, established in the early 1800s and once a major shipping center for coal. This is Abraham Lincoln Country, where the former president spent much of his early life. New Harmony gets its name from the Lutheran colony that settled here hoping to create a perfect community. Certainly they built a lovely one, and many of the early homes have been restored by proud homeowners.

Its annual "Run for the Roses," the famed Kentucky Derby that pits the best of the nation's thoroughbreds against each other in the most famous horserace in the nation, brought fame to **Louisville.** You can even cruise here for the race on a special four-night Cincinnati-to-Cincinnati Kentucky Derby Cruise that includes seats at the Derby plus a call at Madison.

In Louisville, 603 miles up the Ohio from Pittsburgh, you can see memorabilia of past races at Churchill Downs Museum and get a look at one of the few remaining examples of Thomas Jefferson designs at the Manor House.

Eclectic architecture is a much-loved feature of **Madison,** Indiana, a town established in 1810 and once the largest city in the state. You'll see all styles of architecture here, from Federalist to an Italianate villa with all the best known American styles in between. Many of the homes are open for tours.

Cincinnati is an industrial center. But while steel is the backbone of the Cincinnati economy, the city has also produced a lustily supported baseball team, the Cincinnati Reds, some outstanding art galleries, a symphony orchestra, and opera and ballet companies.

Once upon a time a gentleman who knew how to combine a closed mouth and some open doors lived in **Ripley,** Ohio. He was the Rev. John Rankin, one of the leaders of a liberation movement that became known as the Underground Railroad. Rankin is said to have provided a railroad "station" in his home or the homes of his friends for more than 2000 escaped slaves headed north to freedom. You can still visit his house, which once welcomed Harriett Beecher Stowe, who heard the story of one slave's escape and wrote about it in a novel that was to exacerbate an already explosive situation—*Uncle Tom's Cabin.*

Ripley is now also home to Arabian stallions, many of which are bred and raised here, carrying on the town's long history as a breeding ground of fine horses.

As you near the end of your Ohio River cruise, you will dock in downtown **Gallipolis** (pronounced Gala-*police*), Ohio, a French settlement that can still show you the first log cabin built here. If you look in the phone book, you'll still see plenty of French names, belonging to descendants of those early settlers, some of whom once played host to the Marquis de Lafayette. While you're here, stop in at "Our House," a brick riverside mansion and a tavern filled with intriguing antique furniture and unusual china, and don't miss the bevy of beautiful 19th-century homes surrounding Gallipolis City Park.

5. Bermuda / Northeast Passage / Inland Waterways

In summer there are a few ships sailing in these northern waters, calling at Bermuda, one of the most popular ports, and at small islands off the U.S. East Coast, places like Newport, Nantucket, Block Island, and Martha's Vineyard.

A fleet of small cruise ships carrying 100 passengers or less also visits ports along the Hudson River, up through Canada's Thousand Islands and into Québec.

Bermuda

Capital and Port City: Hamilton.
Size: 20 miles long by 1 mile wide.
Nickname: "The Onion Patch."
Population: 70,000.
Language: English.
Currency: U.S. dollar.
Tourist Information: Bermuda Department of Tourism, Old Town Hall, Front Street (tel. 809/292-0033); also offices in New York, Atlanta, Boston, Chicago, and Toronto.
Public Transportation: buses, taxis, horse-drawn carriages, ferries.
Car Rentals: none.
Shopping Specialties: British imports, including china, crystal, wools.
Restaurants: in Hamilton—Plantation Club, Bailiff Bay (tel. 293-1188); Penthouse Club, Punch St. (tel. 295-3410); in St. George—Fort William, Government Hill (tel. 297-0904).
Pubs: Loyalty Inn, Somerset (tel. 294-1398); Country Squire, Somerset (tel. 294-0105); Village Inn, Somerset (tel. 298-9401).

Bermuda is an artist's palette of rainbow colors mixed with abandon and applied with glee. Vivid scarlet and magenta blossoms cascade down the walls of frilly but stately homes painted buttercup yellow, mint green, and sky blue. Even the sand is pink!

Human plumage matches nature's. You'll see men in some of the most outrageously colored trousers and shorts ever invented, and women that match, sometimes literally. To make matters even stranger, many of those men are garbed in knee socks and knee-length shorts so popular they bear the name of this island: Bermuda shorts. Atop these knee-ticklers they're wearing button-down shirts, ties, and suit jackets. This predilection for unusual outfits sometimes seems to us to be a perverse reaction to the formality that continues to pervade this island settled 300 years ago by the British and still possessed of much British formality.

Britain's oldest colony, Bermuda approaches the U.S. geographically about where Bermuda shorts touch the body: a little south of halfway. Located about 600 miles east of Savannah, Georgia, this 21-square-mile island is about 775 miles southeast of New York.

That means that in winter Bermuda is quite a bit cooler than its neighbors in the Caribbean, hence the summer cruise season. Ships call at Bermuda between May and October when the average temperatures range from 74° to 85° and lows average 66° to 75°.

Quaint British customs live on in Bermuda, which still has a bell-ringing town crier, afternoon tea, snappy British accents, and rent of one peppercorn paid each April for use of the State House.

Lovely beaches are of course the lure here, so be sure to take a look at a couple of these strips of sand, scenically tucked in among cliffs and craggy rocks or stretched out with nothing to see but the glittering ocean beyond.

A glass-bottom boat ride out to the **Sea Gardens** is an intriguing trip, and the **Maritime Museum** at the Naval Keep Yard on Ireland Island features whaling mementos and antique boats, plus doubloons and jewels from a sunken treasure ship.

Life is not cheap on Bermuda, and few of the "bargains" are as much of a bargain as they may once have been. You'd be wise to check the prices at home before investing here. Some things are a bargain and some aren't. (If you're buying liquor, you need to order it from the store "in bond" at least 24 hours before departure to take advantage of the greatest bargains.)

Bermuda is actually the largest of 300 islands hereabouts, only 20 of which are inhabited.

Go exploring on this island Mark Twain once called "the biggest small place in the world." You'll want to see the **Crystal** or **Leamington caves,** where you can wander through glittering stalagmites and stalactites, and the **Blue Grotto Dolphins,** where trained dolphins perform five times a day in a natural limestone grotto. Good walkers might try a climb up the 185 steps leading to the top of **Gibbs Hill Lighthouse,** now more than 100 years old.

In **Hamilton,** the capital city, you'll dock on Front Street right in the heart of the downtown shops, where you'll find Shetland and cashmere sweaters, Harris tweeds from Ireland, leather goods, bone china, crystal, Irish linens and glass, antique silver, French perfume. And, naturally, Bermuda shorts.

To experience the Britishness of the island, visit **Sessions House,** where the Bermudian Parliament and wigged Supreme Court justices convene. A block away, City Hall features a landmark *Sea Venture* weather vane.

Golf and tennis are available on the island, and horseback riding is a favorite sport, as are sailing and water sports too, of course. You can even don one of those Jules Verne-ish diving suits and walk on the floor of the ocean with diver Bronson Hartley (and you don't even have to know how to swim).

You won't find any rental cars in Bermuda, but if you want to explore you can rent a motorbike to scoot about the island. A hilly but not mountainous speck in the Atlantic, Bermuda is said to be the flat top of a submerged mountain.

The former capital of the island and a charmer of a spot, **St. George's** seems to us far more intriguing than Hamilton. Here along **Somers' Wharf** old warehouses have been converted into a cluster of small boutiques intertwined with narrow alleyways. These branches of Hamilton stores are much less crowded than their counterparts in the capital city.

Here the island's history lives on in churches, graveyards, museums. In **King's Square** you can be photographed in pillory and stocks, and in the **Print Shop** you can see a working model of a 17th-century press.

To get a look at an old English church, visit cedar-lined **St. Peter's,** the oldest Anglican church in the Western Hemisphere.

At the **Carriage Museum** you can see the style to which earlier settlers were accustomed—and the elegant transport they used (until cars came to the island in 1945).

Nearby, at the **President Henry Tucker House,** you can hear some interesting Revolutionary War stories from a different point of view and see some exquisite furniture and portraits. In St. George's you can also see the **Deliverance,** a replica of the ship built in 1609 by 150 passengers of the shipwrecked *Sea Venture.* Until these early British settlers arrived, the island had been visited by the Spanish but never inhabited.

Wander narrow old lanes with names like One Gun Alley or Shinbone Alley and visit elegantly restored homes and small pubs like the Country Squire.

Many ships stay overnight in this harbor, so if you're looking for a place to party at night, try any of the larger hotels or the Clay House Inn for steel band entertainment, Robin Hood for folk music, Le Club, the Hotel Sonesta's Electric Rainbow, and Papillon's French Connection for dancing.

Northeast Passage

Although this is a bit of a manufactured name, it aptly describes the route some cruise ships take along the northeast coastline up the St. Lawrence and Saguenay Rivers.

History buffs will adore this section of the nation, which retains all the best of its years as the home of sea captains and whalers.

On a cruise in this area you'll want to find yourself a good seat on deck and just watch the scenery float by your chair. Emerald islands, deep-blue waters, fancy furbelowed old houses capture your senses and your imagination. It's not at all difficult to imagine yourself hurling a harpoon or spinning the polished wheel of a sailing ship, a nor'wester beating spray into your eyes as you trim the sails and head home.

On a stately steam through this region you'll pass by **Martha's Vineyard,** Massachusetts, a major whaling center in the 18th and 19th centuries, and home to many sea captains and ship owners who built elaborate and beautiful mansions here.

Other whalers lived on nearby **Nantucket,** another frequent port of call on Northeast Passage voyages. At the Whaling Museum you can get a close look at the life led by those fearless souls who went in search of ambergris and whale oil. You can read about the island in Herman Melville's novel *Moby-Dick,* the story of a whale of a whale.

Newport dates from colonial times, but really "made it" when the super-rich (and even some of the merely wealthy) of the late 19th and early 20th centuries built summer cottages here (some of these "cottages" had 30 or more rooms!). A number of these old homes are open to view. But Newport was perhaps best known as the site of an annual jazz festival, and for almost a century and a half (until 1983 when the Australians triumphantly carried off the trophy) as the home of the America's Cup yachting races that were held offshore every four years.

Boston was, of course, a pretty important place to the first settlers in America when they arrived in 1623. The city has recently done wonders with its waterfront, which is now one of the loveliest harbors in the nation. True sailors will want to get a look at the restored U.S.S. *Constitution,* "Old Ironsides," at the waterfront, and historians will want to walk the 1½-mile Freedom Trail that outlines some of America's earliest and most lump-in-the-throat history.

Waves crash off the rocky coast of Maine today just as they have for generations, and much else here is just as it was a hundred or more years ago. You can visit some of that changeless Maine seaside at **Bar Harbor** on Mount Desert Island off the east coast of Maine. Once the retreat of the very, very rich, Bar Harbor remains the summer getaway spot for some of the nation's fortune-eers.

Sailing in this area has the added benefit of an abundance of huge fresh

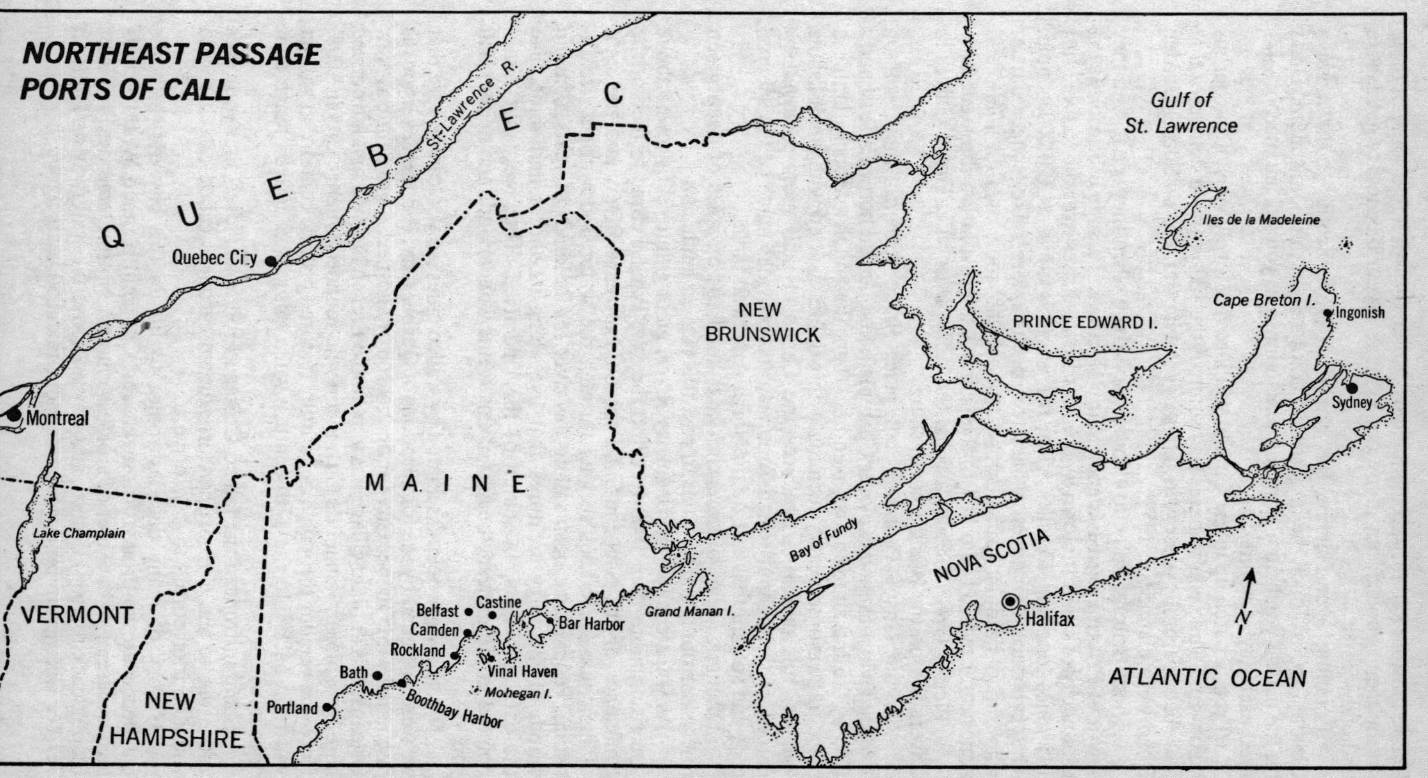
NORTHEAST PASSAGE
PORTS OF CALL
Q U E B E C
St. Lawrence R.
Quebec City
Montreal
Gulf of
St. Lawrence
Iles de la Madeleine
Cape Breton I.
Ingonish
Sydney
PRINCE EDWARD I.
NEW BRUNSWICK
M A I N E
Lake Champlain
VERMONT
NEW HAMPSHIRE
Portland
Bath
Boothbay Harbor
Rockland
Camden
Belfast
Castine
Vinal Haven
Mohegan I.
Bar Harbor
Grand Manan I.
Bay of Fundy
NOVA SCOTIA
Halifax
N
ATLANTIC OCEAN

Maine lobsters and fat succulent clams. No doubt you'll find some of these on the menu aboard, but if you don't, make it your business to get ashore and chow down.

Looming over **Halifax,** the capital of Nova Scotia, is the massive Citadel fortress, once the largest British fortress in this hemisphere. Don't hit the deck if you hear a giant cannon booming as you sail into harbor—it's fired each day at noon!

From a perch up in the Citadel you'll have a lovely view of the harbor below, and while you're here, visit some of the 100-year-old structures that have been carefully preserved. Halifax's Public Gardens on Spring Garden Road were planned in 1753.

Those Britons really do know a good thing when they see it, and they saw it at **Prince Edward Island.** Many Northeast Passage cruises visit the capital city of Charlottetown where Fort Edward rises over the harbor. Just 145 miles long and 40 miles wide, the island is home to 120,000 people. They can trace their ancestry back to French explorers like Jacques Cartier who sailed here in 1523, British troops who took over in 1758, and American Loyalists who fled to the island when revolution threatened.

Anne of Green Gables, a delightful story, lives on at Green Gables in Cavendish, on the island's north shore.

On the **Gaspé Peninsula** tall pines shade streams where salmon spawned when French explorer Champlain first landed here. Called Land's End by the Indian tribe that lived here then, this rough and rocky land is a place of awesome beauty teeming with wildlife. Dotted with small fishing villages, this peninsula produces the Canadian peat moss so loved by gardeners throughout North America, and provides much of the salmon, cod, and shrimp that end up on North American tables.

Dramatic views of bare cliffs and hundreds of miles of deep green forests surround you as you sail past this rugged land.

As you steam up the **Saguenay River,** giant granite cliffs tower above you rising more than 1000 feet into the sky. Whales come to feed at the confluence of the Saguenay and the **St. Lawrence River,** and the sight of their massive bodies surging through the water is downright breathtaking. People have been sailing this river for hundreds of years, some in search of the furry creatures that live along its shores and some, like the early explorers, in search of the land itself. They were not disappointed in the majestic beauty of this scenic wonderland, and neither will you.

We've always been fascinated by walled cities, so you can be sure that we were intrigued by the fortifications of **Québec City.** But then everyone is fascinated with Québec City for one reason or another! As romantic as New Orleans, this antique village has kept to the French lifestyle first introduced here by explorer Samuel de Champlain who founded Québec City in 1608. Here you wander through a beautifully restored historic center that will set you right back into the 17th century when this village looked much as it does now.

Stand in front of the famed Château Frontenac Hotel, shut your eyes and listen to the clop of the horse-drawn carriages called calèches, and you'll be transported to days of yore.

History of many decades comes to life in this city of which the Québecois are so proud: Roosevelt and Churchill planned World War II tactics here; North America's oldest church, Notre-Dame des Victoires (dating back to 1688) is here, and way up above the waterway on Dufferin Terrace Champlain built a fortress more than 350 years ago.

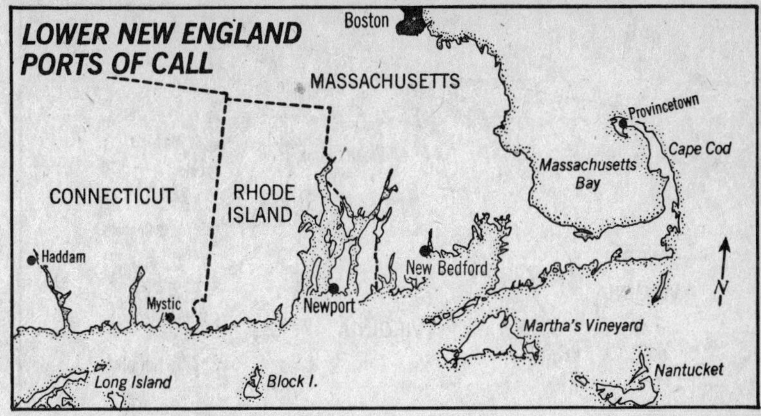

You'll run out of energy long before you run out of restored homes, beautiful architecture, and intriguing sights to explore.

Finally you reach **Montréal,** home of some of the finest cooks in Canada, perhaps even in North America. It gets cold up here in winter so you'll find much of this city's life underground, where shops, restaurants, boutiques, and amusements of all kinds abound.

The most historically interesting spot in this huge city, now the second-largest French-speaking city in the world, is the Place d'Armes, a central square where you can sit in a small sidewalk café and drink history with your café au lait. Roam the streets nearby to get a look at some beautifully restored old homes and typically Québecois architecture.

Not many cruise ships visit this appealing northeastern region of the hemisphere, but those that do offer their passengers a look at some of the loveliest landscapes and most intriguing lifestyles, past or present, of any region of the world.

Inland Waterways

As cruise lines begin to look farther and farther afield for new ports to visit, many areas of the country that have rarely or never been visited by a cruise ship are putting their best pier forward to attract sailing tourists.

A few small cruise ships, usually carrying fewer than 100 passengers, are U.S.-registered ships and are thus permitted to sail between these American ports. Among the lines making calls at places like Savannah, Yorktown, Williamsburg and Charleston are American Lines, American Canadian Lines and Clipper Cruise Lines.

Those inland waterway sailings most often occur on cruises called "positioning" cruises, which are created as a means of setting the ship from its winter schedule in the Caribbean, for instance, north to its summer schedule in the northeast.

To set there the ship usually heads north in the spring through Florida's Intracoastal waterway. (In the fall the itinerary is reversed.) Stops along the way often include posh **Palm Beach,** home of the Kennedy clan and scads of other millionaires, and historic **St. Augustine,** the nation's oldest city. Occasionally ships also stop at **Titusville,** gateway to the space shots at Cape Canaveral (and, of course, to inland Orlando, home of the world's most

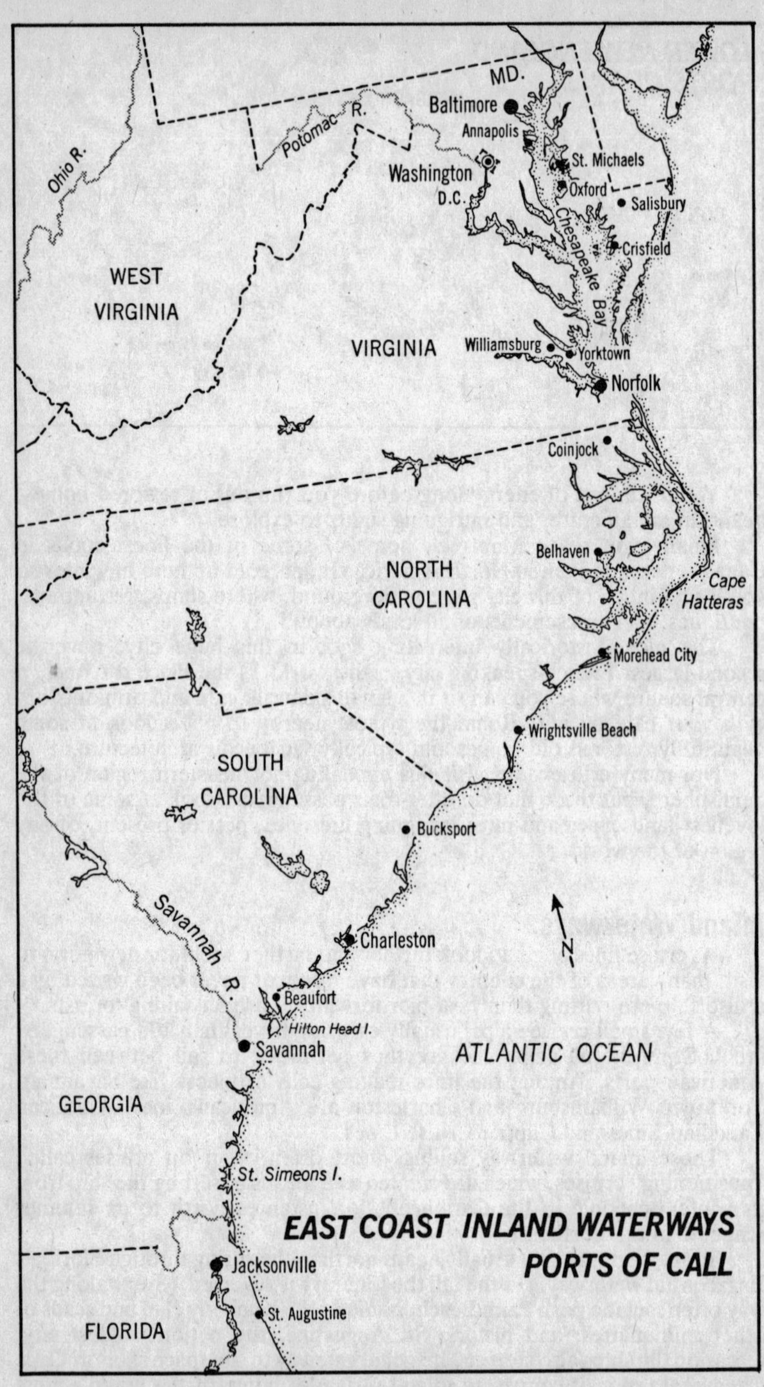

EAST COAST INLAND WATERWAYS PORTS OF CALL

famous mouse) and at tiny **Vero Beach,** a pretty seaside city much-loved by Floridians for its casual informality and beautiful beaches.

Then it's on to **Savannah** where on a day-long stop you can visit that city's cobblestone streets and stately plantations. From there the next stop may be **St. Simons Island,** a jet set playground, then on to **Beaufort** where restored Greek Revival antebellum homes provide a fascinating look into the glamor of the Old South.

At **Charleston** you'll dock near the city's famous Battery and visit Fort Sumter where the first shot of the Civil War was fired. At nearby **Hilton Head,** the largest sea island south of New Jersey, miles of beaches beckon.

Ships head inland again at the Chesapeake Bay visiting **Baltimore's** much-touted new Inner Harbor waterfront revitalization project. Then it's on to **Yorktown** and **Williamsburg** where Revolutionary War history comes to life.

At **Crisfield** you can gorge on those famous Chesapeake Bay oysters and crabs. In **Oxford** the days of pirates Stede Connet and Blackbeard Teach come alive as you visit the places these buccaneers swaggered through while their ships were being built and outfitted.

Nearby **St. Michaels** earned itself a place in history when its citizens hung lanterns in the treetops to deceive the raiding British fleet which shot its cannonballs at the lights and missed the town! In a stop at **Annapolis,** Maryland's capital, you can visit the U. S. Naval Academy where those swabbies toss their caps in the air each graduation day and roam this lovely old city which was the site for the final declaration of the end of the American Revolution.

6. Panama Canal

There may be no single cruise experience more memorable—or more frequently related—than a passage through the Panama Canal. In eight amazing hours you will move from the Atlantic to the Pacific (or vice versa), traversing a man-made body of water often fondly called the "big ditch."

Opened in 1914, the Panama Canal took 10 years to build and 400 years to get started. Way back in the early 1500s Spain's King Carlos V ordered his minions to begin looking into a way to cut through the narrow neck of land that prohibited Spanish sailors from extending their explorations to the Pacific Ocean by sea.

Sailing from the Atlantic to the Pacific (but not from east to west; check a map—it's northwest to southeast), your ship will enter the channel in Limón Bay at **Colón.** During the passage across the isthmus heading for the Bay of Panamá at Balboa on the Pacific, you will cover 40.27 miles of water with a minimum depth of 41 feet.

At Gatun you enter the first of a series of six locks, huge chambers each 1000 by 110 feet, where millions of gallons of water surge in to lift your ship a total of 85 feet above sea level, so that it can move into **Lake Gatun,** a 21-mile-long man-made lake. This basin is one of the largest artificial bodies of water on earth, covering 166 square miles. (Ships that sail on what are called "double transits" of the canal—that is, into the canal, through a portion of it, and returning the same way—use this massive basin to turn around in.)

Beyond the lake your ship navigates the narrow **Gaillard Cut,** an awesome eight-mile channel blasted through the solid rock of the Continental Divide, named for the engineer who presided over the creation of the canal.

On all sides throughout this journey you can see birds of flaming plumage flying through deep-green jungles sparked with the splashy colors of tropical flowers.

Finally, after your passage through **Miraflores Lake** and the **Miraflores and Pedro Miguel Locks,** you reach the Pacific Ocean at **Balboa.**

As beautiful and awe-inspring as it all is, there is a sobering side to this magnificence. Hundreds of men lost their lives to malaria, yellow fever, and other diseases during the canal's construction. In the long run, one of the most beneficial offshoots of the canal may well have been the study of these diseases and their eventual eradication or control.

7. South America

Huge as it is, South America is still a mystery to most North Americans who haven't yet discovered the many and varied enchantments of this vast southern neighbor.

Most cruise passengers don't get to see much of this huge continent either. Those lucky souls on world cruises will get a look at South America, but only a few harbors are regular ports of call on shorter voyages from the U.S. Among those are Caracas in Venezuela and Cartagena in Colombia, both of which are easy stops for ships making voyages through the Panama Canal.

One line, Sun Line, is now also featuring several voyages to the east coast of South America, exploring the remote Orinoco River and sailing down to Rio for the annual Carnival. Just reading the company's brochure for these cruises is a trip you make without leaving your chair!

Let's take a look at the two most popular South American ports visited on voyages leaving from the U.S.

Caracas/La Guaira, Venezuela

Population: 900,000.

Climate: 70° to 80°F year round.

Language: Spanish.

Currency: Venezuelan bolívar; $1.00 U.S. = 12.5 bolívars.

Tourist Information: Corporación de Turismo Venezuela, Centro Capriles, Piso 7, Plaza Venezuela (tel. 572-4196).

Documents: valid passport required.

Public Transportation: taxis, buses.

Car Rentals: Hertz, Edificio Hertz, Avenida Principal del Bosque (tel. 71-79-01).

Shopping Specialties: straw bags, hammocks, semiprecious stones, ponchos, sculpture.

Food Specialties: pabellon (a beef-bean casserole); multinational cuisine.

Restaurants: Coq d'Or Calle Real y Sabana Grande 90, Bolivar Shopping Gallery (tel. 579-9444); Sorrento, Avenida Manscal, Francisco Solano 42 (tel. 579-7983).

The capital city of Venezuela, this thriving oil metropolis is visited by a number of cruise ships sailing deep into the Caribbean or on their way to the Panama Canal.

You'll dock at La Guaira, a shabby spot that's really nothing but the port (and *that's* not a particularly lovely place). You can catch a local bus to ride into town or hire a taxi driver to drive you around the city and show you the sights. Most speak fair English and are pleasant, smiling souls anxious to tote you around and keep you happy. Fix your price before you begin your tour, however.

Drivers and shore excursions alike will take you to a glass factory that does some ordinary bibelots and some very attractive ones. You can also see the glass objects being created by glassblowers.

Looming over the city is **Mt. Ávila,** a 7000-foot peak that in the past has featured a cable ride to the summit. It hasn't been working for years, however, so don't count on riding it during your visit.

Founded in 1567, Caracas was named after a patron saint Santiago de Leon de Caracas, but no longer exhibits much of its original colonial architecture. About as close as you can come is the home of South American hero and liberator Simón Bolívar. Called **Casa Natal,** it's next door to the **Bolivarian Museum** which outlines South America history from its conquest by the Spanish to its colonial period, and finally its independence.

Bolívar, born here in Caracas, is the city's favorite son, so you will see statues of him and hear his name in many places in the city, one of the more interesting of which is **Plaza Bolívar,** the traditional center of Caracas.

At the **Colonial Art Museum** you'll find a restored mansion filled with art and objects from the Spanish era. Top that with a visit to **Quinta Caracas,** where artists are at work in the gracious antique patio.

You'll see just the opposite kind of architecture at **University City,** where 50,000 students attend classes. (Very contemporary styling here). Nearby you can roam through 175 acres of **Botanical Gardens** replete with orchids and a flurry of exotic tropical plants.

While there are not masses of things to see in Caracas, a drive through this city, with a stop at the central plaza, is pleasant. Ask the driver to show you the posh suburb that is home to some of the oil entrepreneurs, and to drive through the bustling and modern downtown past miles of parkland on the outskirts of the city.

Beaches in the area include Marina Grande, Playa Sheraton, Macuto Beach, and Los Angeles Beach.

Shoppers will want to check out the jammed **shopping area** on the Sabana Grande stretching from the Plaza Venezuela along Avenida Lincoln to the **Centrol Comercial Chacaito.** Gold and natural pearls from Margarita Island are good buys, as are hand-woven rugs made by Guajiro Indians. Piñatas are popular, as are high-fashion couture items.

Cartagena, Colombia

Population: 500,000.

Climate: 70° to 90°F year round.

Language: Spanish.

Currency: $1 U.S. = 15 bolivares

Tourist Information: Corporación Nacionál del Turismo, Palace of the Inquisition, Plaza Bolívar (tel. 44921).

Documents: valid passport required.

Public Transportation: buses, taxis.

Car Rentals: Hertz, Hotel Capilla del Mar, 8-59 la Cartagena (tel. 42921).

Shopping Specialties: wall hangings, ceramics, ruanas, pre-Columbian artifacts and reproductions, coffee, emeralds, aguardiente liquor.

Restaurants: Capilla del Mar, Avenida Chile (tel. 42921); Pavillon de France, San Martín at Calle 8 (tel. 41504).

Walled cities seem romantic and mysterious, and none in the Caribbean is more intriguing than Cartagena, whose walls rose 300 years ago as protection from pirate raids.

Cartegena's a walking city best seen on foot, so we'll outline a couple of walking tours for you.

Begin at the **Tower of the Clock,** called La Boca de Reloj in Spanish, one of the city's landmarks and a favorite meeting place. This clock tower is at the city's main gate called La Boca del Puente (which actually has three gates). Inside is the Plaza de Los Coches, where if you turn left at the gate, in a block or so you'll come across the old Customs House. There's a statue of Columbus there.

A little farther along you reach the **Church of San Pedro Claver,** which honors a priest who cared for African slaves imported to Cartagena by the Spanish.

Let's hope you haven't attended too many midnight buffets—some of the streets here are so narrow they're barely wide enough for one. See if you can squeeze through Calle de Boloco, for instance.

In the **Parque Bolívar** you'll see two-story houses with fancy balconies. At one end of the plaza is the **Palace of the Inquisition** (site of the Tourist Office), and at the other end is a basilica, a mosque-like structure. There's a 300-year-old sundial here too.

On Calle Santo Domingo is the **Santo Domingo Church and Convent, a** 16th-century creation housing a statue of the Virgin Mary with a crown of gold and emeralds. Nearby is the **Plaza de La Merced,** on Calle Factoria. From the wall here you'll see a beautiful view of the bay. Follow the wall and you're back on Avenida Venezuela near Boca del Puente.

Once there were two walls in this city, an outer and an inner wall. The inner, gone now, was designed to separate the wealthy from the hoi-polloi.

The outer city was called the **Getsemani Barrio,** and if you begin at the Tower of the Clock near the docks your first stop will be the **Parque Centenario,** where the independence fighters are commemorated. On Calle Larga, the main street in this part of the city, is a yellow bridge (the Roman Bridge) which crosses to the island of Manga, once a fort.

There you can see **San Felipe Fortress,** a mammoth fort rising 135 feet above sea level and completed in 1657 after 18 years of construction. Don't cross the Roman Bridge. Instead follow the outer wall to the left along Calle Lomba to another bridge, Paseo Heredia, where you will see a monument to a Colombian poet Luís Lopez de Mesa, who described the city as a pair of comfortable old shoes. Across the Paseo Heredia bridge is San Felipe Fortress, with some interesting underground tunnels and a good handicraft shop.

Among the other sights of interest in the city are **San Fernando Castle,** built 200 years ago and complete with dungeons; **Fort San José,** with 21 cannons and valves to control waves and tides; **Fort San Sebastian,** completed in 1743; **Bovedas,** the dungeons, which feature 22 shell-proof cells from the 18th century that now house boutiques; **La Popa Monastery,** on a promontory overlooking the city and still used for more than 375 years as a chapel and monastery.

Beaches in Cartagena feature dark sand, but the sun's just the same as elsewhere in the Caribbean. For snorkeling and diving, the Islas del Rosario are just off the coast.

If you're dining ashore try the local seafood, particularly pargo (red snapper).

Colombia produces more **emeralds** than any other country in the world, so if you're in the market for an emerald, this is the place to look. Emerald quality depends on the depth of color—the darker the better, without blue or yellow hues. Crystallization marks are not a flaw but an expected part of a good emerald and part of what makes it glow with what connoisseurs call green fire.

Pre-Columbian pottery, some of it 2000 years old, is also a popular purchase in Colombia, although it would be wise to deal with only the most reputable dealers.

Chapter II

RITES OF PASSAGE: HOW MUCH WILL IT COST?

1. Help from Travel Agents
2. Comparing Costs
3. Seasonal Sailing
4. More Budgetwise Tips
5. Fly-Free and Air/Sea Programs
6. When Is a Bargain Worth the Price?
7. Tipping
8. Shore Excursions
9. Fun and Games and Other Expenses

SOONER OR LATER the moment of truth comes! What is it going to cost?

Well, there's good news tonight: You can afford it!

Ship trips that once were the private preserve of royalty and the rich are now the playground of Mr. and Ms. Middle America. These days that "cruise revolution" so optimistically hyped by cruise lines draws its recruits from young singles, middle-aged marrieds, retirees, children, and every age and income bracket in-between.

Part of that, it must be admitted, is a spin-off of the baby boom which has left us with a population curve that bulges, literally and figuratively, in its early 30s. With masses of the population now falling in that 30 to 40 age bracket, the cruise industry is using all its considerable wiles to appeal to the pleasures and the pocketbooks of a wide range of travelers.

So somewhere, on some ship, there is a cabin that will fit your budget. Everything that comes afterward—all the mid-morning bouillon, afternoon tea, gorging midnight buffet, and showgirl entertainment—will cost you not one penny!

Yes, it's indeed wonderful to be living in this age of fierce competition and oversupply. No matter how your eyes glaze over when someone mentions the law of supply and demand, in this instance that law is working for you. Those supply and demand principles are what have made cruises affordable even down into the lowest reaches of nonrich pockets.

To explain it in a few words, there are now so many ships, and so many more under construction, that cutthroat competition for your dollars is pushing prices hard—down.

Even better for you, ship lines are not only fighting each other, but are also battling hotels, resorts, destinations, and all kinds of other leisure lures determined to convince you to spend your money on them.

Because all of those other forms of vacation entertainment are better known to most people than cruises, cruise lines must try just that much harder to tempt you into trying their fascinating kind of vacation. One way they do that is with very affordable prices and plenty of special promotions.

That desire to lure travelers away from the traditional two weeks in a heart-shaped Poconos bathtub has led to a proliferation of special money-saving deals that will warm the cockles of your bankbook. In recent memory there have been special offers for the third or fourth passenger sharing a cabin, deals for those over 40, specials for kids, specials for singles, specials for book-at-the-last-minute travelers, even let-us-choose-your-ship-and-save-you-money offers.

Every one of those deals offers you a chance to live like royalty for a day or a few weeks at a price even your gnomish banker would approve.

One of the keys to this money-saving business is your fertile brain, which ought to be reading the travel pages of the local newspaper in search of cruise bargains.

1. Help from Travel Agents

Another, and equally important, key is a travel agent. If you don't have one, get one. Never in history have these people been more wonderful—and necessary—to have around than they are now as prices and special promotions proliferate.

Agents spend many hours, most of them in their so-called free time, attending endless industry seminars at which cruise companies promote their products and their prices. Travel agents are dedicated to absorption of these quantities of information—after all, that's their business. Best of all (and here comes a lovely word), they'll offer you the benefit of all that knowledge for *free.* They're paid, of course, but not by you. Cruise lines pay them a percentage of your fare as a commission, just the way you pay a real estate agent for selling your house.

In their offices are brochures from all the cruise lines. In their heads are reams of detailed information about ships and prices, seasons and ports.

You may also save yourself money by reading newspaper ads run by travel agencies. If an agent says a special rate is available on a ship but doesn't quote the price, call. You may find that the agent has secured a price so low it couldn't be advertised without undercutting published rates.

Your first step in figuring out what a cruise will cost, however, is to decide how much you have to spend. Now that sounds pretty basic, but it's surprising how many people reject the whole idea of a cruise because they equate a cruise vacation with megabucks. It just ain't so anymore.

2. Comparing Costs

No one can help you find a cruise in your price bracket until you know what the bracket is. Once you know the top figure you can afford to spend, then you can begin the fun part—perusing the options.

That's when you'll discover fantasyland.

If you have $16,000 you can go around the world. If you have $1000 you can visit the Caribbean or Alaska or Canada or Mexico. If you have only a few hundred dollars you can spend three or four days on a cruise at least.

In the cruise business prices can range from the sublime to the ridiculous (well, they'd be ridiculous for *us,* but perhaps not for you). As you begin to see what you get for your dollar, however, you'll discover that what you spend on a cruise is about what you'd spend on any similar vacation. In fact you'll often discover that you spend less for a cruise and get a great deal more for your money.

One of the best loved selling points of the cruise industry is that a cruise vacation—with all its ports, nonstop food, and entertainment—is the world's only prepaid vacation. As Madison Avenue as that sounds, it's quite true that you can compute your cruise vacation almost down to the last penny and you won't find a host of small hidden extras cropping up to haunt you.

To get a handle on cruise costs, and to convince yourself what a bargain you can get on a cruise, you should learn how to compute the average cost per day, or *per diem* as they say in Latin.

To do that, take a look at the brochure of the ship you're interested in and find the cost of the cabin you think will be a suitable nest for you. If port charges are levied, you'll find a notation of the amount in the brochure. Look for it so you're not surprised to discover another $25 or more tacked onto your ticket price.

Now add port charges to cabin fees. Next look in that same brochure for information on air fare add-ons from the city in which you live. Add those air fares, if any, to the total and tack on about $5 a day for tips. Here's how these computations look:

7-day Caribbean cruise	$1600	per person
Port charges	$25	
Air fare add-on, if any	$75	
Tips	$35	per person for the cruise
	$1735	

Divide that $1735 per person total by seven (the number of days of the cruise) and you'll find that you're paying about $248 per person daily, double occupancy. That figure includes transportation, all meals, all ports of call, entertainment, and tips for the duration of the voyage.

You'll need to add on those things you must add on to any vacation: gifts for Aunt Millie and Mom, drinks and tips for the bartender, taxis or buses you take in port, photographs you buy from the ship's photographer, postcards.

There is one more cost and it's an important one: shore excursions. For those, you need to figure about $20 a person in each port, although you need not take the planned shore excursions. If you do decide to take one of the ship's tours ashore, you can find out from your travel agent or the cruise line what those excursions cost and pay for them when you book your cruise. Thus again there will be no surprises.

To satisfy your penurious soul, make the same kind of computation for any other kind of vacation you might have in mind, adding the costs of transportation, seven nights at a hotel, seven nights of entertainment, meals for seven days, and tips (and don't forget all those doormen, bellmen, and maids). Divide your total cost by seven and compare.

If you're bringing children along on your cruise or traveling with friends, you'll find that the rate per person decreases, thanks to the discounts offered for third and fourth passengers sharing a cabin.

You can see that if you're on a strict budget you can figure the price of a cruise vacation right down to the last Indian head penny. Cruise lines are quite up-front about prices, and don't toss in a raft of extra hidden fees. Just read the brochure carefully and you'll be able to tally the total cost of your vacation right there at the kitchen table.

3. Seasonal Sailing

If you've ever traveled to places where sunshine lives all year round, you've discovered there's a definite on-season and a just-as-definite off-season. When you begin to look at the prices of cruises, you find that the best cruise bargains occur in the off-seasons.

When are those? Well, in the Caribbean and Mexico peak season is the dead of winter when everyone wants to escape the cold, and off-season is from about April through October.

Alaska cruises are cheapest before the weather begins to heat up or when it starts to cool down, roughly early in June and late September.

Best prices on cruises in the northeastern part of the United States and Canada are also at the beginning and the end of the sailing season, say, in June, September, and October.

If you want to cruise the Mississippi River, you'll pay the highest prices in the summer months when everyone else has the same idea. The cool fall and winter months are ideal for budget-watchers.

If you want to travel in the highest priced season, don't despair. Even then, many fares can be as little as $100 higher per person.

4. More Budgetwise Tips

You can also often save money if you can be flexible. Norwegian Caribbean Lines, for instance, offers a deal on which they pick the ship, you pick the sailing date. If ports aren't of primary interest to you and you're willing to let the cruise line decide which ship they'll send you on, you can save money with this deal.

No one in the cruise business is going to like this advice, but it's true: if you want to take the risk of waiting until the last minute to book your cruise, you can often walk right up to the booking desk with cash in hand and tell them how much you're willing to pay. Because the cheapest cabins are among the first to sell, those less costly accommodations are likely to be sold out well in advance of sailing. That means you may be able to get a very nice cabin in a higher price category for the minimum price. Cruise lines want to fill those ships, and not all lines are scrupulous about how they do it. On the other hand, not all lines will go for this bluff, so be prepared for a rebuff.

5. Fly-Free and Air/Sea Programs

Far and away the best thing that has happened to pennywise cruisers, and to the cruise industry in general, is something called "fly free."

Born in this era of lively competition, **fly-free programs** were devised by cruise lines to lure Californians, for example, to Miami for a cruise on a Miami-based ship, and vice versa (that is, to lure Miamians and New Yorkers to the West Coast to a cruise line based there). In what seemed like minutes these kinds of programs expanded to include Omaha, Des Moines, Toledo, Dallas, Raleigh, Louisville, Savannah, Pittsburgh, Podunk, and your hometown.

Air/sea programs sometimes refer to getting on at one port and flying home from another, with air travel in only one direction. Usually they are programs that include air fare in both directions. These fly-free or air/sea programs fly under all sorts of names too, but you won't have any trouble recognizing them in the brochure, which will spell out the deal in detail.

Now we all know there has been no free lunch for many a blue moon. Cruise companies are not going to break their banks to provide you with free or almost-free air fares. So somewhere along the line those costs are covered. Very large cruise lines, however, move such volumes of people that they are able to make some excellent deals with airlines. You get the benefit of their clout and of their subsidies. So let's not question how those air fares are subsidized. Let's just take advantage of the all-in prices now available to you wherever you live.

Not all lines are offering fly-free programs, but every line we know provides some kind of package that helps you reduce your air fare. These programs are called **air/sea packages.** They offer you air fare and often airport-to-ship transfers for a rate you add on to the price of your cruise. Sometimes they're also called "air add-on rates."

Whatever you call them, they're an excellent bargain, enabling you to go on cruises originating at ports thousands of miles from your home. Once again there are no hidden extras, so you can figure your costs ahead of time.

We've mentioned that point about "hidden extras" so many times that perhaps we just ought to remind you of the time you went off to that sun spot for a vacation. Remember how you thought you had figured the cost of everything right down to the crystal swan for Grandma, when all of a sudden someone totaled up your bill with a 10% government tax and a 15% fuel surcharge and $5 a day for a chaise lounge, and a $20 cover charge in the nightclub, not to mention the three-drink minimum? Whoops, there went $50 a day you hadn't figured on, and/or there went the old credit-card limit.

Absence of just such dismays is the very best part of a cruise vacation, as cruise sellers will be quick to tell you.

So popular have air/sea programs become, in fact, that even Amtrak has gotten into the act with a program it calls—are you ready?—"rail-sail"! Call Amtrack, toll free, at 800-872-7245 for information.

6. When Is a Bargain Worth the Price?

While you're mulling over all those glossy brochures full of romantic pictures of tempting ports and moonlit moments, keep in mind that the old saw about getting what you pay for is most often spoken in moments of serious displeasure.

Ships are as different as people. Each one is designed especially to appeal to a certain market, and it behooves you to know what kind of market that is. In our outline of the ships and the lines (coming up in Chapter V) we have tried to indicate what you can expect of the line and your fellow passengers.

In general, cruise lines charging very low prices will attract passengers in concomitant social, economic, and educational levels. Often those ships are among the older ships afloat as well. Entertainment is nonstop and geared toward beer-drinking competitions, pillow fights, bawdy contests.

Lines with prices in the middle bracket generally feature less raucous entertainment, although every bit as much of it. Overused as is the term "laid-back," this is one place it cannot be topped. Activities are simply more laid-back, quieter, more sedate. On these ships your fellow passengers will be a bit older and more sophisticated, probably in a middle to upper income bracket.

Ships that charge the highest prices are, of course, luxury cruisers aiming their appeal at sophisticated, high-income travelers with time and money to spend. Life is more formal aboard and the masquerade party, if there is one, is more likely to star historical characters than male hula dancers. Afternoon tea is actually attended and enjoyed. Activities are generally quite genteel, with an emphasis on elaborate candlelit dinners, lectures, showy evening entertainment, casinos.

Each of the three has its own kind of appeal, but only you can know which will be of most interest to you.

7. Tipping

Here comes that dreaded subject. One day near the end of your cruise, your cruise director will drop his voice a level or two and intone: "Now, ladies and gentlemen, on this matter of tipping. . . ." You begin to squirm. But fear not. It's really much easier than you think.

Every cruise ship distributes cruise information brochures on board, and one of them is sure to contain what the line considers the basic tip for your cabin steward, and your dining room waiter and busboy. On some lines the business of tipping seems to have become just that: a business. Some cruise directors are downright tacky in their outline of what to tip their fellow workers and so pushy as to make you want to keelhaul them all the way back to port. This is a rarity, however, and we feel sure the line would like to know if its cruise director is offensive in his handling of the delicate matter of tipping.

Most lines recommend a minimum of $2 per person a day for the cabin steward, $2 a day per person for the dining room steward (i.e., your waiter) and $1 a day for the busboy. A few lines recommend tips of $2.50 and $1.50.

Greek lines traditionally ask you to collect all your tips together at the end of the voyage and turn them in to a central source, from which they are evenly distributed to the crew.

On the *QE2*, recommended daily tips are $10 per person divided between the cabin steward and the waiter for passengers in upper-price levels. If you're traveling in a middle-bracket cabin, the recommended daily tip is $8 (same split), and for those in the lowest priced cabins, $6 per person daily. Add to that $3.50, $2, and $1.50, respectively, for the busboy.

If the maître d'hôtel in the dining room has been particularly pleasant and/or attentive to some special request, you could slip him something appropriate to the situation.

Wine stewards, or sommeliers as they are often called, and bartenders on the ship are generally tipped 15% of the bill each time you order wine in the dining room or a drink at the bar, just as you would on land. You can tip them at the conclusion of the voyage too if you like.

Those are the basic recommended tips. If a cabin or dining room steward has been particularly wonderful—and they are often awesomely courteous, friendly, and out-of-their-way helpful—you can, of course, tip more lavishly.

Now, wasn't that painless?

Small as it may seem, a brief letter in praise of a particularly outstanding employee is a wonderful gesture that will earn you a lifelong friend and may earn that friend a promotion. Cruise lines put much stock in letters and comments from passengers, so if you want to give a newfound friend a lasting remembrance in addition to your financial one, send that letter or mention the name of that outstanding worker on your end-of-cruise comment sheet.

One more thing: Ignore all this tipping advice on Holland American Cruises. This chic and forward-thinking cruise line has a no-tipping policy, for which we offer them a 21-gun salute and a series of enthusiastic hip-hip-hoorays.

Still one more thing: Never, never, but absolutely *never* ever offer the captain or any of the ship's officers a tip. It is gauche beyond words.

8. Shore Excursions

Happy as you are sailing along in your little 30,000-ton cocoon, sooner or later you will hear the chains rattling and clanking as the ship's anchor drops into the sea. Land ho, maties.

You will not arrive unprepared. First, you will have this guide to every port we could think of; and second, you will have heard a little when-we-dock-tomorrow lecture from the cruise director.

Some of those presentations are so detailed that they become a mini-marketplace. On one ship we sailed, the presentation lasted well over an hour and included 5 minutes of local history and 55 minutes of shopping advice. You could, however, hardly call it *good* shopping advice since nearly every store in that port was recommended, and some were pushed with such fervor we began to wonder if this was a paid advertisement.

We regret to say that many cruise lines do a poor job of preparing you for the ports you are to visit. Most cruise directors certainly seem to know where every shop is located, but they know—or at least they tell passengers—very little about the history and cultural background of ports.

That generalization is particularly true of Caribbean cruises, less true on Alaskan voyages where some quite interesting wildlife talks are presented by a naturalist. His presence there is required by the park through which the ship cruises, however, so perhaps cruise lines should get less credit for these outstanding presentations.

You will also find, particularly on Caribbean cruises, some very enthusiastic sales of shore excursions. These are sometimes worthwhile, but more often, sadly, are not.

As a rule of thumb, if the shore excursion goes to a particular place of interest—Dunn's River Falls in Jamaica, for instance—go along. Hiring a taxi to get you there will probably cost nearly as much or more, and will be less convenient.

Otherwise, your enjoyment of a shore excursion will depend on how much you hope to get from it. Most do a very superficial job, ferrying you around the highlights with a few minutes here and a few minutes there.

If you're a shopping fanatic, you'll probably want to skip most shore excursions since they often leave you only a short time for shopping and/or take you to one store and herd you in there to vie with a busload of other travelers for the attention of harried clerks.

If you want to go shopping, walk, hail a cab, or take bus from the ship to town (if necessary) and go shopping. Your time will be your own and you can muse over the relative merits of those two gorgeous straw baskets for hours if you like.

If you're a history buff, you might do well to bone up on the sights you'll be visiting and go on your own walking or driving tour to those sights. Most shore excursions are not history oriented. A shore excursion is a must in Cancún, but be prepared for a two- to three-hour trip in each direction (well worth it, however, for a look at one of the architectural wonders of the Western world).

Garden and flower enthusiasts often really enjoy Caribbean island tours, for instance, as they generally include a look at and a description of odd tropical vegetation.

Look over the ship's description of shore excursions carefully, however, and ask for some very specific information on just what you will see and do.

A shore excursion we took on one Caribbean island drove endlessly around in a barely air-conditioned bus, visited a tiny, smelly, and downright depressing zoo, and stopped at a hotel for drinks. A final stop at an island church would have been the ultimate boring blow had not a lady at the back of the church been performing a pagan healing rite on a parishioner, offering us a look at the cultural elements that have been successfully assimilated on the island. That hot and dusty bus ride cost about $20 each, and was a most miserable way to blow $40.

Don't be afraid to talk with other passengers who might have visited the port before to find out whether a shore excursion is worth the money. In most small Caribbean islands you'll do just as well or better by rounding up a couple of other adventuresome types and dividing the cost of a taxi or a car. Seek out a driver with air conditioning and make sure he promises to turn it on (fuel charges are high in the Caribbean and drivers will leave the cool off if you don't make a point of it).

Don't be afraid to bargain on the price of a taxi for the day or half day, but make sure that the final amount you negotiate is as clear in the driver's mind as it is in yours. If there's a bit of a language barrier, write the numbers down on a piece of paper. Money numbers are an international language! And pay at the end of the agreed-upon time, not at the beginning.

Shore excursions are usually $20 to $35 a person, but can be $10 less or umpteen dollars more if the tour takes you a very long distance from the ship.

Don't think you are leaving civilization behind because you are visiting Mexico or the Caribbean. Rental cars are ever with us and available in practically any port. In most your Stateside driving license will get you on the road in the flash of a credit card or cash.

It may also be wise to make rental-car reservations through a travel agent or an international company before you leave on your trip. That way you can be sure a car, and the kind of car you want, will be there when you arrive. You can also pay for the car in advance. That little bit of planning cuts down wasted time too.

Rental-car rates are generally more expensive in the islands than Stateside, and cars are often not the clean and serviceable autos you've come to expect here. You aren't likely to have any problems, but allow yourself plenty of time to get back to the ship just in case something breaks or goes flat. And write down the telephone number of the rental-car office.

Some travelers have been known to take bicycles with them on their journeys, wheel them off to the dock, and just ride off on their own excursions. We've never tried it, but it sounds interesting.

Among the better bargains in shore excursions, especially for first-time cruisers, are the dive-in expeditions now offered by nearly every Caribbean cruise line. These provide you with snorkel and flippers and sometimes even a commemorative T-shirt that will be instant status back in the old neighborhood. On board the day before you reach port, diving instructors who are certified scuba divers will brief you in the best way to avoid snorkeling up half the ocean and how to keep your diving mask unsteamed while breathing heavily at the sight of a bikini atoll.

Once the ship has docked in port, you meet your diving cohorts and instructors at a specified time for the minibus ride to the best diving areas. After hours of diving and pointing and playing with starfish, you return exhausted to the ship where you try unsuccessfully to describe the wonders you've seen in that glittering and indescribable underwater world.

Excursions like that cost about $20 to $25 on most ships, and are worth the money. If you're an experienced diver and/or know your way around an island, you can often find your own good reef since there are a lot of fine places to dive not far from the ship on many islands. Just don't go diving alone under any circumstances. *Ever.*

9. Fun and Games and Other Expenses

While none of your food or entertainment on board will cost you a cent, you should budget some money for other small expenses.

You'll probably want to play Bingo, for which you pay about $1 a card. Bets on the ship's horse races are usually at least $1 each. There's betting on the distance the ship will travel that day aboard some ships too, and of course, betting in the casino.

Photographs you buy from on-board photographers will cost about $4 each. You'll probably be tempted to buy at least a few of the many that will be taken of you just to be sure you have some record of this vacation event.

Shopping on board and in port will require some dollars, as will taxis or buses you take to and from the docks at some ports.

Drinks, wine, and champagne are generally cheaper aboard cruise ships than they are ashore, but will still cost something. Mixed drinks are usually less than $2, although some fancy concoctions may be $3 or so, but sometimes that includes the fancy glass in which they are served. Bottles of wine can range from a reasonable $8 or $10 to the heights of fancy, as can champagne.

You pay for, and tip for, drinks when they are served, unless you're traveling on one of the ships that permits you to settle your account at the end of the voyage.

Credit cards? Yes, in most ships' gift shops, maybe in the bar, maybe not. Yes, on shore in almost all shops. Check with the line for its regulations on the use of credit cards aboard and in payment for tickets.

If you're planning to call home while you're on board or in port, budget some money for the calls. They are quite expensive, so if you can avoid them, do. If it's absolutely necessary, figure at least $10 for a three-minute conversation.

Chapter III

IS THAT YOUR SHIP COMING IN?: SELECTING YOUR CRUISE

1. Price
2. Entertainment
3. Crew Nationality
4. Ports
5. Fellow Passengers
6. Long vs. Short Cruises

THAT "CRUISE REVOLUTION" the cruise industry touts is occurring for the same reason there are horse races: a difference of opinion. It won't take you long to discover that a discussion of the perfect cruise ship is a little like talking politics or religion. People may not agree, but they will certainly have something to say on the subject.

Naturally such a wide range of opinions on what makes a cruise perfect has led to a proliferation of cruise ship marketing approaches. Those variations in approach determine a ship's personality, and that personality determines what your fellow passengers will be like and what ambience you will find on board.

No matter what kind of personality *you* have, there is a ship that will offer you food, activities, ports, accommodations, and service that will bring you joy and memories. Some will do that better than others, but all will accomplish the goal to some degree. So now's the time for a little personal assessment of your own personality and the personalities of those traveling with you.

Ships aren't anthropomorphized with that "her" label for no reason: they really do have personalities. To be perhaps a bit more accurate about that, it's really the crew, the officers, and the philosophy of the ship's owners that impart "personality" to the vessel. Food, entertainment, crew nationality, crew-to-passenger ratio, cruise length, and even historical factors all play a part in the creation of a ship's personality too.

Basically those personalities break down to informal or formal atmosphere on board. That formality, or lack of it, is reflected in luxuriousness of accommodations, cruise price, on-board entertainment, and often in crew-to-passenger ratio.

Let's take a look at some of the things that determine a cruise ship's personality.

1. Price

It probably will come as no surprise to you that price is an important determinant of a cruise ship's personality. On ships too, price is a very good guideline as to the kind of atmosphere you'll find on board. Luxury ships that charge high prices are quite like their counterparts in the hotel business. Those who can afford them are often older, more sophisticated travelers in search of a quiet, refined atmosphere with plenty of good food and good service. You can see that price helps determine the kinds of passengers who will be sharing your cruise.

That brings us to crew-to-passenger ratio, another indicator of personality. All ships these days tend to offer quite a lot of service and have the staff to maintain it. Those with a crewman for every two passengers or fewer are likely to offer you more, and more thorough, service than those with a lower crew-to-passenger ratio. That ratio is closely related to the price you pay for the cruise as well.

Price also determines the luxuriousness of your accommodations aboard. Luxury cruise ships with the highest per diem rates offer you very spiffy quarters that are not only attractively decorated but are also clean, neat, well cared for, and large.

2. Entertainment

Surprisingly enough, the kind of entertainment offered on board is often a good indicator of a ship's "personality."

Some ships offer lots of crazy, ringy-dingy, ice-breaker party games on board, so naturally the atmosphere on those vessels is relaxed, casual, informal, chummy. Low- and mid-priced vessels are generally characterized by this emphasis on on-board activities.

On the other end of the spectrum are higher priced vessels that stick to educational lectures, fine musical entertainment, and quieter pursuits that tend to lure more sophisticated, upscale travelers who expect a certain degree of decorum from crew and other passengers. That generally sets the stage for a more formal atmosphere aboard.

In the middle are those lines, usually the mid-priced ships, that juggle a combination of the two, offering both quiet pursuits and lively ones in an atmosphere that's formal on special evenings, unstructured and informal all the rest of the time.

3. Crew Nationality

Relax, we're not going to get into any ethnic slurs here. But it is true that certain nationalities create certain atmospheres. And nowhere will you be more aware of that than on a ship.

Italians, for instance, are exuberant, volatile folks who would jump ship if there weren't good food aboard. When the dining room staff or a majority of the crew is Italian, you can be sure the food will be wonderful.

You can also be sure that your waiter will be as solicitous as Mom, admonishing you to eat your pasta or you won't grow up to be big and strong. (These fellows seem to get as much pleasure out of your meals as you do!) Italians control the dining room or the ship on Sitmar Cruises, Costa Lines, Carnival, and Home Lines.

Greeks are much like Italians, although one suspects they will not be thrilled with that assessment. They are most hospitable, full of flashing good humor and quite attentive to your every wish. You'll find Greeks aboard Paquet's *Dolphin,* Royal Cruise Lines, Sun Lines, and Chandris, among others.

French crews are often quite provincial in their conviction that anything that isn't French is questionable. On Paquet's *Mermoz,* even line officials admit that it would be well for you to at least *appreciate* things French. The French joie de table attitude, however, means that you'll find the highest quality cuisine aboard, and plenty of yummy French pastries and sauces. What's more, if you manage a few words of broken French, they'll adore you forever.

We are convinced that Scandinavians run the cleanest, most organized ships afloat. Dust is the enemy aboard Scandinavian-operated ships, so you'll never see any. Norwegians, who run many of the ships operating in North American waters, have a droll sense of humor too. It creeps up on you when you're not expecting it. They love a good joke as well, so have a few ready. Scandinavian officers run the show aboard Norwegian Caribbean Lines, Cunard/North American Cruises, Royal Caribbean Lines, and Royal Viking Lines.

Indonesians are much loved by many cruise enthusiasts for their polite and courteous service. Many of them work as cabin stewards on board quite a number of ships.

Dutch officers aboard the Holland America Line ships run very handsome, clean, and efficient ships.

British personnel are typically British, either quite formal or just the opposite. Of the Cunard vessels, the *QE2* is often said to have a formal stiff-upper-lip crew while the smaller ships, the *Princess* and *Countess,* are considered more casual operations, much more informal. Of Princess Lines' three seven-day cruisers the *Pacific* and *Island Princess* are somewhat more staid than the *Sun Princess.*

On many Caribbean ships much of the staff hails from one of the many islands you'll be visiting. You can learn much from them about the history of their islands, so don't be afraid to ask what life is like in Trinidad or Jamaica.

Americans are often part of the ship's crew, particularly in hosting duties assigned to employees known as the cruise staff. That often includes the fitness director, the children's program staffers, cruise director, and on-board entertainment staff. The theory is that they understand Americans well, if that's possible, and are better prepared to deal closely with them as this part of the staff must. You'll find American crews on board the small coastal cruisers that operate in the south and northeast—American and Clipper Cruise Lines, for instance—and on the *Delta Queen* and *Mississippi Queen* which ply the Mississippi River. Americans, many of them from Hawaii, staff American Hawaii Cruises' *Independence* and *Constitution* too.

4. Ports

Some cruise lines want to emphasize your on-board experience. These offer you little time in port in comparison to the amount of time you spend on board. Carnival Cruise Lines, for instance, is dedicated to this precept of maximizing the on-board experience and minimizing time in port.

Other lines figure you want to see ports, so they take you to three or more on a week's voyage, offering you a day or so in each. One cruise line president makes frequent speeches in which he maintains that ports are what sell cruises. Consistent with that philosophy, his Royal Cruise Line offers you a choice of many, many exotic stops. Others, Sun Lines, for example, on its South American cruises offers you a new port each day of your cruise with only a few days spent solely at sea.

In general, ships that offer quite a number of ports tend also to offer longer and higher-priced cruises that appeal to older, well-heeled travelers.

If you love beaches, Norwegian Caribbean Lines started quite a trend recently when it bought a Bahamian Out-Island for its very own and began spending one cruise day anchored off that island. Now Eastern/Western Cruise lines, operators of the *Emerald Seas,* have bought an adjacent island and Paquet Cruises has announced it is about to do something similar.

If shopping is your first and foremost interest, you'll want to sail on a ship bound for Mexico, the Bahamas, or the Virgin Islands, each of which offers you duty-free treasures, lovely straw goods, very good liquor bargains, or in the case of Mexico, some indigenous craftwork and silver at very good prices.

5. Fellow Passengers

It's a maxim in the cruise industry that the longer the cruise, the older the passengers. That figures. Younger passengers, however much they may dream of long journeys, have neither the time nor the money to do so. Retired couples, on the other hand, often have both, so they can sail off on a two- or three-week journey (or longer) with nary a second thought. And why not? They've certainly earned it.

That means that if you're looking for a youthful crowd you'll want to search for your perfect ship among the three- or four-day voyagers or the week-long cruises.

On Inland Waterway, coastline, and Alaska cruises, you also will find an older clientele and/or people interested in natural beauty, history, and fascinating ports like Annapolis, Boston, Québec City, and Newport.

It's an old and overused joke in the cruise industry that the average age aboard used to be "deceased." We say "used to be" because the times they are a-changing. These days 60% of the world's cruise passengers are younger than 55 and 30% are younger than 35. So there! Whatever ship you take will probably have a wide variety of ages on board among both passengers and crew.

If you're looking for a gambling, drinking, and fun-loving crowd, you'll be happiest on one of the partying three- or four-day cruise ships or a seven-day sailer. On those you'll be caught up in the fun of Bingo and horse races, sports competitions and trivia contests, dance lessons and hula instructions, steel bands and rum punch.

Water babies should look for ships that visit several beach destinations, places like Jamaica, Grand Cayman, Cozumél. Most of the seven-day ships offer supervised diving programs that even the rankest underwater amateur can participate in and enjoy.

Ah, yes, what have we for lovers? A recent issue of *Cruise* magazine, a bimonthly publication for cruise enthusiasts, carried some amusing letters from lovers protesting the absence of love on all these "love" boats. How, readers asked, can you carry on a romance in twin beds, or worse, upper and lower berths? Inconveniently, that's how.

There is, however, some good news. Cruise lines in search of younger faces have realized the appeal of king-size, queen-size, and double beds, and are acting accordingly. New ships, ships being renovated, and even some of the older craft are outfitting at least some cabins with double beds or twin beds that can be pushed together to create king-size sleepers.

Regrettably for the future of love afloat, there are still not many of those cuddle quarters available. If you are thinking of a honeymoon or anniversary cruise, or think the joy of a cruise is related to the sleeping facilities, you should read the cruise line brochures carefully, speak to a travel agent, and book early.

Sad to say, you can no longer be married on board a ship, but some lines will arrange for you and the bridal party to exchange *dockside* vows, then all sail away into the sunset together, if you like! At least one line, Norwegian Caribbean Lines, even has a special honeymooners program, and most lines will offer you some special recognition if you're on your honeymoon. Tell the line or your agent about your wedding trip plans.

If just the opposite is what you have in mind—single blessedness—fear not, you're in the right place. In fact there may not be a better place to meet likely eligibles than on a cruise ship. Small ships carrying lots of passengers throw you into close proximity with hundreds of potential friends, and every ship we've ever sailed has had at least one get-together for single passengers early on in the cruise.

Norwegian Caribbean Lines and Carnival ships are good hunting grounds, as are Cunard's *Countess* and *Princess,* Princess's *Sun Princess,* and three- and four-night party cruises aboard Eastern/Western Lines' *Emerald Seas* on the East Coast and *Azure Seas* on the West Coast, and Paquet's *Dolphin* from Miami. For huntresses, there are some marvelous goodlooking crewmen aboard all the ships—just pick your nationality and go for it!

If you have a handicap that makes it difficult for you to move about, you will need to check ship brochures carefully. You'd be well advised to seek the help of a travel agent and to check with the line before you buy your tickets. Newer ships tend to have the wide hallways necessary to accommodate wheelchairs, and none of the high steps and barriers that make life so difficult for people with mobility problems. Older ships tend to be less accessible. If you travel by wheelchair, most lines require you to be accompanied because there is simply not enough staff to help you get from place to place. (Some lines also are quite definite about the measurements of the wheelchair too.)

Ask a travel agent or the line if the ship docks in port or anchors out and takes passengers to shore by tender. Travel by tender is difficult if not impossible for handicapped travelers. Check too on the presence or absence of elevators, and find out which (if any) of the ship's facilities may be denied you if you cannot walk to them.

Even geography will affect the kinds of passengers you find on board.

Westerners are different than easterners, there's no doubt about it. On ships based in California most of your fellow cruisers will be from the western states, and will appreciate western humor, music, and Las Vegas-y entertainment. On the East Coast passengers seem to share an interest in beautiful beaches, sports, and fitness activities, along with the usual drinking, gambling, and general partying.

Kids? Kids on a cruise? Did we say bring the *kids?* Certainly we said bring the kids. Get them across the gangplank, enter them in the youth program, and don't plan to run across them for the rest of the voyage.

Once again, the changing age patterns of the traveling public have led to the emergence of cruise ships that have extensive programs for youngsters. Sitmar, Home Lines, Cunard's *QE2,* and Holland America all welcome the young ones, and have full schedules of activities for them, often in port as well as on the ship. Youngsters of all ages become quite popular people on board a cruise ship, both with the crew and with other passengers. They get into everything, know every inch of the ship better, it seems, than some of the crew, and they know every shred of gossip practically as soon as it's born. And they have a wonderful time too, making new friends of all ages.

6. Long vs. Short Cruises

Naturally, the first two things you'll have to consider when you begin planning a cruise are time and money.

If you don't have much of either, you might want to get your feet wet, so to speak, with a three- or four-night cruise. Most of those will take you to the Bahamas or Mexico. There are even a few one- and two-night cruises—Scandinavian World Cruises, for instance—sailing from Miami or Cape Canaveral on one-day journeys to Freeport and back, or to nowhere at all. Some cruise lines, stuck with a day before a major cruise begins or after one ends, also will feature a day or two voyage to nowhere, cruising aimlessly around out of sight of land but still offering you all the sun and fun amenities of life on a cruise ship.

If three or four days sounds altogether too short to you, try a seven-night cruise. You'll have a wide range of choices from the huge *Norway* to the small *New Shoreham* or *Newport Clipper,* among others. In five nights at sea you can become a transatlantic traveler, sailing on the *QE2* from New York to England or France. On a seven-day cruise you can visit sunny Caribbean islands, Mexico, Canada, the Yucatán Peninsula, Alaska, or explore the Hawaiian Islands.

On most seven-day cruises you'll have the fun and relaxation of two or three days at sea and two or three days in port, sometimes at night, sometimes by day, sometimes both. That way you get all the experiences rolled up in one week's journey.

If you have ten days or two weeks available, you might consider cruises from San Francisco or Los Angeles to Alaska or Mexico, from New York to the Northeast and Canada, from Miami to South America and the Caribbean.

In two weeks you can also sail from Florida or California on a thrilling journey through the Panama Canal or to South American up the remote Orinoco River. You can paddlewheel your way up the Mississippi River all the way from New Orleans to Minnesota, or sail down the Intracoastal Waterway from the Northeast to Florida. In ten days you can also sail on a transatlantic trip from Florida to Europe.

Beyond two weeks the world is yours. In three weeks you can go deep into South America, sail to Europe from California or from Florida through the Mediterranean. Longer than that and you can go on an around-the-world voyage, visit the Arctic Circle and the fjords of Scandinavia, cruise to fabled ports in India, the Far East, even Russia, or sail lazily about the South Pacific visiting dream-finder ports like Tahiti and Bora Bora.

Chapter IV

YOUR HOME IS YOUR CABIN: CHOOSING QUARTERS

1. How It Will Look
2. Cabin Location
3. Sharing a Cabin

THE SELECTION OF YOUR CABIN is important, as you can see by a quick check of the title of this chapter. This is why we're discussing the ins and outs of cabin selection before presenting detailed descriptions of those dream cruise ships that you're waiting for. Just hang in through this material, for we think it will make the next chapter more useful and meaningful to you.

There are two schools of thought about cabins. One maintains that the size of the cabin is of little or no importance because you'll be spending almost all your time in the ship's bars and lounges, dining room and nightclubs, decks and swimming pool, saunas and gymnasium. Ships that feature dawn-to-dawn activity encourage you to get out of your cabin shell and come join the fun. Some not only encourage you verbally, but their encouragement takes the form of cabins that are small enough and/or so lacking in lounging spaces you wouldn't want to spend much time in there anyway!

The other school of thought maintains that your cabin will be your home away from home and ought to offer you the option of spending as much or as little time in it as you like.

Your personality and the personality of those with whom you are traveling ought to be taken into consideration when you are selecting a cabin. If you are a reader or a crossward-puzzle fanatic, for instance, your idea of a paradisical cruise may be a thick novel or the London *Times* puzzler—and the time to pursue those amusements. If that's the case you'll probably be happier with a cabin that has a chair or two or a bed that can be converted by day into a sitting area.

A small cabin is less important on a week-long voyage where you will be too busy to spend much time in it.

To a great extent the kind of cabin you book will depend on how

Song of America

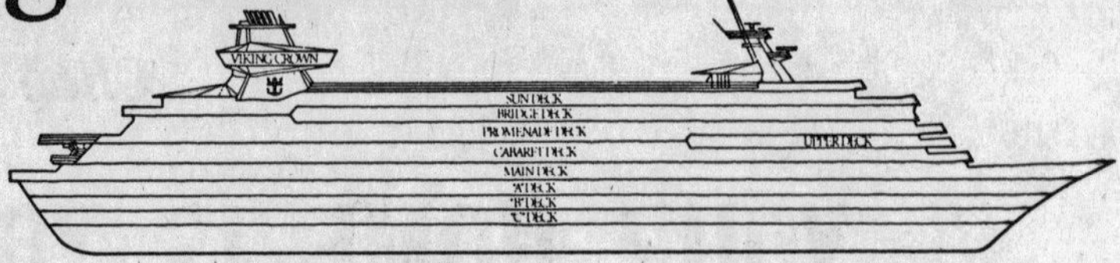

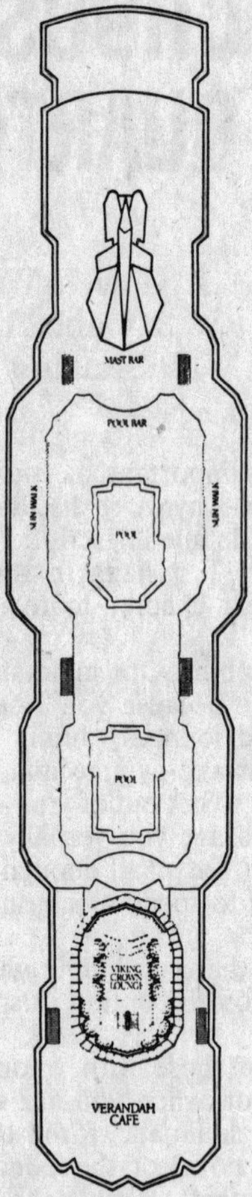

Sun and Compass Decks

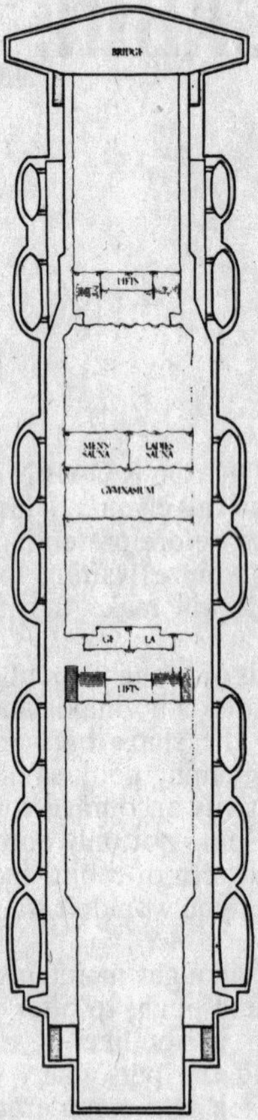

Bridge Deck

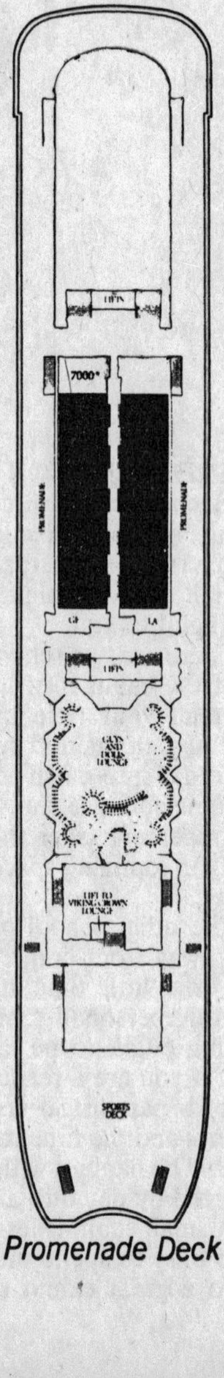

Promenade Deck

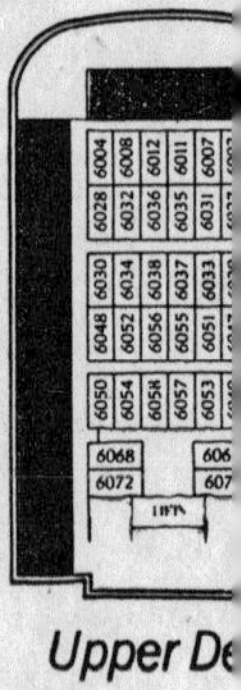

Upper De

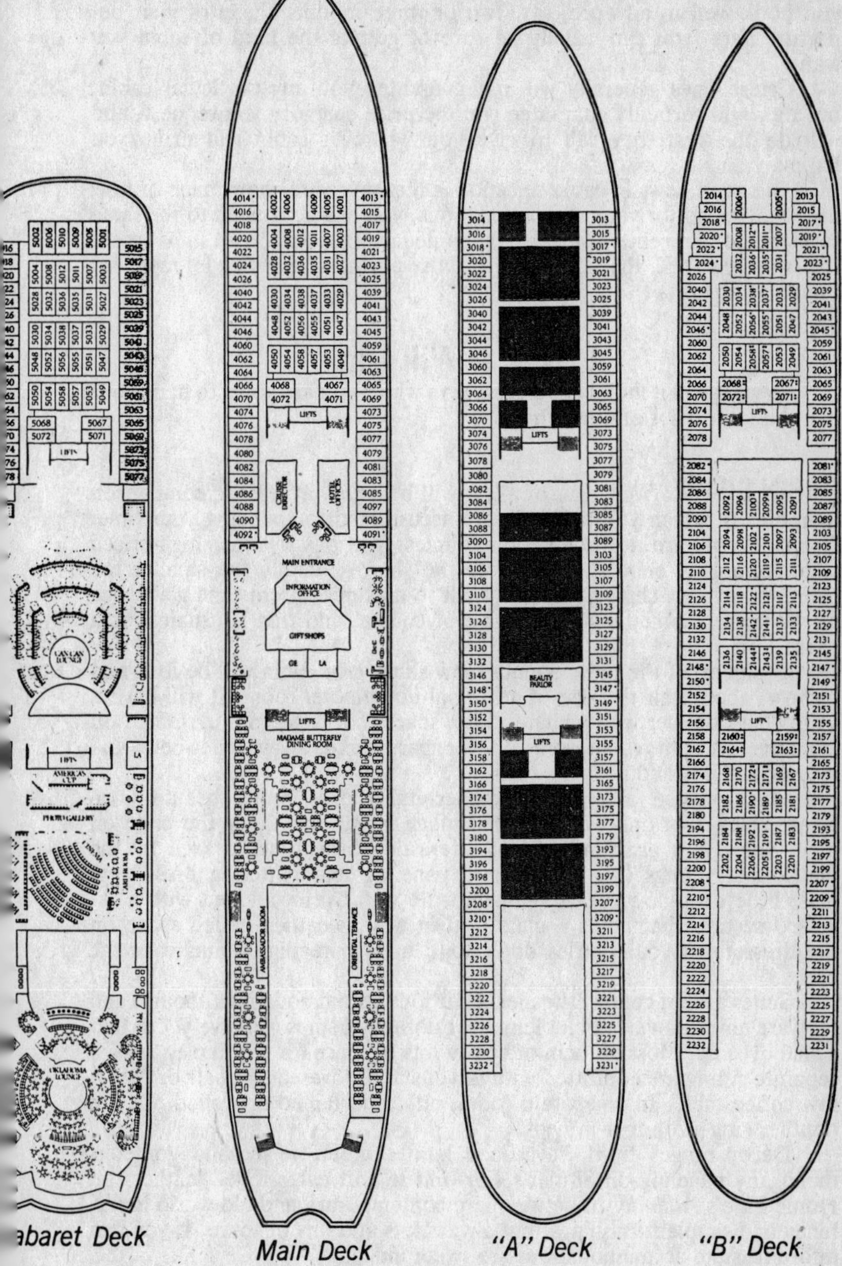
LIFTS
AMERICA'S CUP
PHOTO GALLERY
CINEMA
OKLAHOMA LOUNGE
CRUISE DIRECTOR
HOTEL OFFICES
MAIN ENTRANCE
INFORMATION OFFICE
GIFT SHOPS
GE
LA
MADAME BUTTERFLY DINING ROOM
AMBASSADOR ROOM
ORIENTAL TERRACE
BEAUTY PARLOR
abaret Deck
Main Deck
"A" Deck
"B" Deck

much money you have to spend and how soon you decide to spend it. If you book well in advance, say, two or three months ahead of your departure date, you can usually be sure of getting the kind of cabin you want.

Cruise lines generally will not guarantee you any particular cabin, but they will certainly guarantee you the price category you request, and will do the best they can to give you whatever cabin will make you happy.

The good news in cabin selection is that no matter how much or how little you spend for your accommodations, you will be treated to the same service, the same entertainment, the same facilities, and on all ships except the two-class *QE2*, the same food as those paying a little or a lot more for their stateroom.

1. How It Will Look

So what will it look like, this place in which you are going to hang your hat and quite a lot of other things?

CABIN SPACE: Well, first of all, it will be *small*, at least in comparison to rooms in which you probably are accustomed to spending your time. Cabins simply are not hotel rooms, unless you buy a large, high-priced suite. Strangely enough, the newer the ship, generally the smaller the cabin. Many new ships have been built to maximize profits and glamorize public space. Something has to give of course, and that is usually cabin space.

On many of the most popular new ships your cabin will be long and narrow, about half the size of a normal hotel/motel room. It will have a vanity/desk/dresser with a chair, closet space that is perhaps curtained off from the rest of the room, some drawer space tucked away somewhere, and usually a nightstand near the beds.

Much as we all worship modernity, old is really beautiful on cruise ships. Not only will you find much larger cabins for the price on older ships, but also find lots of interesting little touches axed by the plastic age: things like shiny wood paneling and glittering brass edgings; little drop-down trays built into the wall over your bed with a recessed section that holds a glass firm in wavy weather; railed space on the dressers so your bottles don't spill; built-in reading lamps over the bed.

Suites are, of course, the most luxurious accommodations aboard, and they are always lovely. In looking over dozens of ships we have yet to find a shabby suite. Most of them offer you lots of space for the money, with a separate sitting area outfitted with full couch or loveseat, a chair or two, a low coffee table. In a separate room, either curtained or walled off, are double, king-size, or twin beds.

Decor ranges from, say, deep hunter green velvet and gorgeous mahogany paneling on Sitmar's *Fairwind* to soft earth-toned leathers on Home Line's *Atlantic*. In between are contemporary and old-world looks, fancy and simple furnishings, but always lots and lots of space. If you can afford it, suite accommodations are sweet indeed.

New ships feature cabins so alike in size it seems to us ridiculous to pay for a higher priced cabin. All you're buying is a cabin on a deck closer to the public rooms. If you'd like to save some money on one of these ships, book the least expensive inside or outside cabins—but book them early because they go fast.

To figure out how much space you are likely to have in your cabin, look at the deck plan, find the cabin category you're interested in, and examine those cabins closely. If you assume that the beds are about two feet wide by six feet long, then you'll be able to figure out how much empty space, closet space, etc., there is in the room.

On some ships you really won't notice much of a difference between your cabin and a higher priced one. You can tell which ships these are when you see the deck plans. Deck plans are to scale, so if you can't see much or any difference in size among the cabins, it's safe to assume that there is none or so little as not to make any difference.

In general we'd say that if you're going on a long cruise of ten days or more, you probably should try to eke out a few dollars more for larger accommodations. On long voyages you'll probably want to spend more time in your room. On a short cruise you'll be home before you've tried out all the activities the ship has to offer.

BATHROOMS: These days nearly every ship afloat has a private bathroom for every cabin. If there are a few cabins available without private baths, they are noted in the ship's brochure (there will be shared facilities nearby). If that arrangement is acceptable to you, you can save quite a lot of money on accommodations without baths. Once again, very, very few ships have cabins without baths.

Bathrooms on most ships are just big enough for one, but don't drop anything—most of the time they're not large enough to bend over in without bumping into something.

Generally, more expensive cabins will have a bathtub as well as a shower. If you think you cannot get along without your bubble bath, be sure to look over the ship's brochure carefully to see exactly what you're buying. Showers are tiny, and on some ships feature hand-held shower heads that can be snapped into the wall so you don't have to hold them. These may sound strange to you, but they're a godsend if you want to shower without getting your hair wet. On a few of the very smallest coastal sailing ships the shower is not enclosed and sprays all over everything (not ideal, but you do eventually learn to cope).

You will see some very unusual plumbing aboard some ships, particularly those built a decade or three ago. We've seen ice-water spigots in the bathroom, skinny foot-long spigots, spindly legged sinks, and some real antiquarian hardware. It all worked, however, and that's what really matters. On some ships you may find a bidet in the bathroom. No, it isn't a footbath.

BEDS: That brings us to beds. On cruise ships these come in all shapes and forms. In the wake of "Love Boat" many more ships are now beginning to include some double beds in their cabin rosters. These are still comparatively rare, however, so if you want cuddle quarters you should book them well in advance of your sailing date.

Twin beds are in most middle-priced cabins. On some newer ships, like the *Tropicale,* for instance, they can be pushed together to form a king-size bed, but on most ships that's not possible.

Cheaper accommodations have upper and lower berths. A berth is a mattress tucked into a wooden frame. Pullman berths usually refer to beds of this kind that flip up during the day, more or less the way a Murphy bed does, and tuck away against the wall out of sight. Your cabin steward will see to it that the bed is flipped up in the morning and flipped down at night. You climb up to the bed on a ladder. Youngsters adore these aeries, though adults are a bit less keen on them.

On some ships you'll find a high-backed couch or two in your cabin. At night the cabin steward pulls down the back and the whole business becomes a bed. These are strictly a ship invention, quite different from convertible couches.

On some ships the bed flips up from the floor to tuck away against the wall with one edge designed to hold your champagne bucket in daylight hours!

Beds are most often parallel to each other, but sometimes are placed at right angles, in an L shape. That latter configuration gives you more floor space and makes your quarters look larger. It's preferable if you can get it.

ELECTRICAL OUTLETS: On the most modern ships you won't blow fuses all the way down the hall if you plug in your hair dryer, but on older ships that can happen. In deference to the widespread use of hair dryers, however, all ships have made some kind of arrangements for their use. Exactly what that arrangement is will usually be detailed in the ship's brochure. If it isn't, call or write the line and ask, or ask your travel agent. (Some ships have vanity rooms in fairly convenient locations and require you to go to one of these to use your hair dryer. It's not convenient, but once again you do eventually adjust.)

Outlets for electric razors seem to be available on every ship, but if the line's brochures don't answer your questions, call or write and ask.

Most ships frown on the use of travel irons in your room, but some provide small rooms set up with irons and ironing board. You can have the pressing, as well as laundry and sometimes dry cleaning, done for you on most ships too.

You may also find some ships with European outlets that require converter plugs. These are available in some drugstores and many travel shops. Little gizmos that step down the voltage also are available.

ATYPICAL STATISTICS: To give you an idea what a massive place a cruise ship can be, we thought you might be interested in taking a look at some of the things in the linen and china closets aboard the *Norway,* the largest ship afloat:

Pillows	3,600
Curtain fabric	4.38 miles
Furniture fabric	3.75 miles
Bath towels	12,000
Sheets	21,000
Napkins	18,000
Tablecloths	3,160
Glassware	32,880 pieces
Silverware	52,000 pieces
China	92,500 pieces
Art objects	1,800 pieces

2. Cabin Location

As long as you're looking at those deck plans, take a look at the deck above and below you.

If you're a nightowl you may not care that your room is located near the disco which howls to the wee hours. If you rise with the robins, however, you'll go nuts in that room.

Rooms low in the ship are best for those who fear they may suffer from motion sickness. Cabins near the middle of the ship also offer a smoother ride. On most cruises you'll hardly notice the roll of the ship, but transatlantic crossings, particularly in spring or fall, can be rough. (See Chapter XII on mal de mer.)

If you have any kind of handicap that makes walking difficult, book a cabin near the elevators. However, cabins beside or behind elevators can be good price and size bargains but may also be noisy.

On some ships cabins near the ship's engines or anchors can be noisy, and cabins near the galley likewise.

Generally, the higher the deck on which your chosen cabin is located, the higher the price. That's thought to be a leftover of old transoceanic days when higher cabins were sunnier, farther away from engine noise, and the coolest or warmest aboard, depending on where you were. Today all these conditions are controlled in other ways (air conditioning, soundproofing, etc.) but the high prices remain. If you like the status of a good address, book a cabin high up on the ship. Otherwise don't bother.

Families or friends traveling together can often book connecting cabins, but you should know that the door between connecting rooms lets you *both* hear what's being said next door. Give up catty remarks and/or avoid connecting cabins.

You'll often find cabins in the bow or stern of the ship are less expensive than those in the center. That's because the ship narrows at those points, curving inward. Cabins in those areas curve right along with it so they're often, but not always, a few feet smaller and crescent-shaped.

On some ships this kind of "smaller" means very small indeed (Sunward II, for example) while on others (the Vistafjord, for instance) the loss of space is barely noticeable, thanks to clever interior design that turns lemon into lemonade. You can often save quite a bit of money on one of these cabins but you'll need the help of a travel agent or someone else who has seen the ship and knows if a miracle has or has not been wrought.

Obviously, if you get the least feeling of motion amidships, you get more in the bow or stern, but, once again, let us stress that the kind of rough seas that cause most people's motion sickness are really quite rare in today's cruise world.

INSIDE VS. OUTSIDE: Old hands at cruising may skip this sentence, but if you're new to cruising you'll want to know that outside cabins are those located on the outer edges of the ship, inside quarters are those that run down the middle of the ship, tucked in between the outside rooms.

Which is better is a source of continuing debate that boils down to your need for a view of the outside world versus your desire to save money.

Inside cabins are darker and usually, although not always, smaller than outside quarters. If you don't care about light or space, and/or don't plan to spend much time in your cabin, go ahead and book the inside room. You may save yourself quite a lot of money. Inside cabins are great for late sleepers too—absolutely no fear of the sun's waking you.

If, on the other hand, you worry about claustrophobia, stick to outside cabins where a full-fledged window or a small porthole will let in the light and let you see what the weather is like today. Generally, the more expensive the cabin the bigger the window and/or the more of them you have in your room.

Ships are air-conditioned these days and portholes are almost always sealed shut, so don't expect to enjoy the sea air through them. Out on deck is all the sea air you can breathe.

Many ships now use contemporary lighting so cleverly that inside cabins are so bright and cheery you never miss the window. Cunard/North America Lines' *Vistafjord,* admittedly a luxury ship, has many inside cabins every bit as attractive as outside quarters.

There is one drawback to outside cabins. If the outside cabin you are considering is located on a deck (as opposed to directly on the side of the ship), other passengers strolling by can see into it. If that bothers you, either look for a cabin that's not located next to a promenade or try inside quarters.

If you're dedicated to outside cabins, you're in for a treat on the Princess Lines' new ship the *Royal Princess*—every cabin on board is an outside cabin.

3. Sharing a Cabin

If you don't mind sharing a cabin with one or several other travelers, you can save money. Most cruise lines will assign you a roommate of the same sex (they haven't gone coed yet), which means that you pay the normal per-person rate in that cabin price category instead of the 150% to 200% of the price levied on single travelers occupying a two-person cabin alone.

Some lines will even assign you, or you and a friend, to a cabin for four. That way each person pays a much lower rate than if you shared a cabin. If you're lucky the line won't find two others and you'll end up paying the lower rate but not sharing after all.

Ships are very competitive these days, so if they at first refuse to book you into a shared cabin until they can guarantee a roommate, persevere. Try calling closer to the sailing date. By that time your half price may look better than none.

Just as in any roommate situation, however, the shared-cabin experience can be wonderful or wearying. There are no guarantees that you and your cabinmate(s) will be compatible. At least in the beginning of your newfound friendship, however, you will have someone to talk to until you meet other new friends.

If you do share a cabin with one or more strangers, it would be wise to put your valuables in the ship's safekeeping. See the purser for information on the availability of safe-deposit boxes or other storage facilities on board.

Some ships—but not many—have cabins designed especially for single travelers. They have one bed and are, naturally, smaller than double cabins but are quite adequate for a single traveler. You'll find single cabins on Home Lines, among others.

Chapter V

THREE SHEETS TO THE WIND: CHOOSING A SHIP

1. American Canadian Lines
2. American Cruise Lines
3. American Hawaii Cruises
4. Bahama Cruise Line
5. Carnival Cruise Lines
6. Chandris Cruise Lines
7. Clipper Cruise Line
8. Commodore Cruise Line
9. Costa Cruises
10. Cunard Lines
11. Cunard/Norwegian American Cruises
12. Delta Queen Steamboat Co.
13. Eastern/Western Cruise Lines
14. Exploration Cruise Lines
15. Holland America Lines / Westours
16. Home Lines
17. Norwegian Caribbean Lines
18. Paquet Cruise Lines
19. Premier Cruise Lines
20. P & O / Princess Cruise Lines
21. Royal Caribbean Cruise Lines
22. Royal Cruise Lines
23. Royal Viking Lines
24. Scandinavian World Cruises
25. Sitmar Cruises
26. Sun Lines
27. Sundance Cruises
28. Sun Goddess Cruises
29. World Explorer Cruises

HUGE SHIPS AND TINY SHIPS, tall ships and small ships, aging ladies of the sea or young whippersnappers, elite fleets and fun ships, happy ships and world-class cruisers, river trippers, island hoppers, and floating fantasylands—just as there is said to be a match for every lonely heart, there is a ship for every dreamer.

You can sail with potentates or plumbers, retirees or those who don't retire until dawn. You can travel on a budget or break the bank. You can play at sea for days on end or set foot ashore every day of your cruise.

Somewhere, right this very minute, a cruise ship's foghorn is bellowing across the water, playing your tune.

Come with us now to see what's at sea.

1. American Canadian Lines

Contact: American Canadian Lines, P.O. Box 368, Warren, RI 02885 (tel. toll free 800/556-7450, or 401/245-1350).

Cruising Grounds: The Bahamas, Jamaica, U.S. East Coast, the Great Lakes.

Itineraries: *New Shoreham II*—

IN SUMMER: Warren, R.I.–Newport–Martha's Vineyard–Block Island–Warren *Or:* Warren–New York–Waterford–Oswego–Saguenay River–Prescott–Montreal–Quebec City–Tadoussac

IN WINTER: Nassau–Spanish Wells–South Palmetto Point–Eleuthera Bluffs–Governor's Harbour–Cape Eleuthera–Exuma Sound–Sampson's Cay–Staniel Cay-Hall's Pond Cay–Highbourne Cay–Nassau *Or:* Nassau–Spanish Wells–Lanyard Cay–Little Harbour–Hopetown–Green Turtle Cay–Treasure Cay–Man 'O War Cay–Marsh Harbour–Walker's Cay–Freeport–Nassau

Caribbean Prince—

IN WINTER: Montego Bay–Orange Bay–Savannah La Mar–Black River–Carlysle Bay–Port Royal–Kingston Market–Port Morant–Port Antonio–Port Maria–Ocho Rios–Discovery Bay–Montego Bay

IN SUMMER: Warren, R.I.–Hudson River–Toronto–Niagara Falls–Buffalo–Detroit–Alpena–Mackinac Island–North Channel–Algoma–Manitoulin Island–Georgian Bay–Owen Sound–Detroit and return same route

---

Mini cruise ships are a specialty of Luther Blount, president of American Canadian Lines and one of the pioneers of the mini-cruiser concept. Just 70 cruise fans sail aboard either of this line's two small ships, the *New Shoreham II* and the brand-new *Caribbean Prince.*

If you're looking for unusual destinations not too far from home, this cruise line may be the place to begin your search. For instance, the line's 72-passenger *New Shoreham II* spends the winter in the Bahamas, where its shallow six-foot draft allows it to stop in Exuma and Eleuthera, two lovely beach-lined destinations visited by no other cruise line. *New Shoreham II* docks in Nassau and takes her passengers on trips 12 sun-filled days long.

Meanwhile that new ship, the *Caribbean Prince,* plies those seductive Jamaican waters on stop-every-night voyages, exploring this island's enchanting villages far more extensively than any other cruise line.

Both ships return to Florida in April and May to sail on what cruise lines call a "positioning cruise" from West Palm Beach to Warren, R.I., the ship's home base.

New Shoreham II has been around for many years, sailing the crystalline waters of the Bahamas in winter. There the ship sails on two different itineraries. The first of those visits Spanish Wells, the Bluffs on Eleuthera, Governor's Harbour, Cape Eleuthera, Exuma Sound, Staniel Cay, Highbourne Cay, and Nassau. The second itinerary also departs from Nassau, calling on a number of intriguing island villages including Spanish Wells, Little Harbour, Hopetown, Green Turtle Cay, Treasure Cay, Marsh Harbour, Walker's Cay, and Freeport.

Those cruises run from the end of November through April, when the ship moves north to Rhode Island. From there it sails up the Saguenay River and back on 12-day cruises via Narragansett Bay and Long Island Sound to Waterford, N.Y., through the Erie Canal to the tip of Lake Ontario, past the Thousand Islands and on to Prescott, Ontario, Montréal, and Québec City. You return by bus from Montréal, or take the bus to Montréal and join the cruise there, reversing the route back to Warren. It's a six-hour trip on the air-conditioned bus from Warren to Montréal.

Fall-foliage cruises begin when trees along the waterways are shining like jewels. These are particularly spectacular sailings on this line. On many summer weekends the ship features cruises from Warren to Newport, Martha's Vineyard, and Block Island.

The new addition to the line, the *Caribbean Prince,* spends the winter circling Jamaica, the only cruise ship to explore these waters so thoroughly. Among the stops on a 12-day circumnavigation of the island are Montego Bay, Orange Bay, Savannah La Mar, Black River, Port Royal, Kingston Market, Port Antonio, Negril, Port Maria, Ocho Rios, and Discovery Bay.

Cruises around that lovely isle begin in December and continue through April, when the ship travels to West Palm Beach before heading north to Warren, R.I., up the Intracoastal Waterway on a 15-day cruise. From its base there it sails up the Hudson River, through the Erie Canal to Lake Ontario, visiting Toronto and Buffalo, and transiting Lake Erie to Detroit. From there the vessel sails through Lake Huron to Alpena, Michigan, and Mackinac Island, then into Georgian Bay. It returns along the same route.

You can join it in several 12-day segments, including Warren to Buffalo, Detroit to Owen Sound, or the reverse. In the fall the ship sails up the Saguenay River on a 12-day cruise and back on a similar journey.

CARIBBEAN PRINCE / NEW SHOREHAM II: Because these ships are so similar in size, shape, and price, we'll describe them together.

Activities/Public Rooms

Summer or winter, life aboard is casual with the scenery and ports providing entertainment. You don't need an extensive wardrobe. You won't have all that much room to store it anyway, so stick to basic sportswear.

Each ship is about 150 feet long (*Caribbean Prince* is 10 feet longer) and 35 feet wide. Because they draw only about five feet of water, the ships can sail in shallow waters inaccessible to larger craft.

A special feature of both is a bow ramp that lets you walk right off the ship down a ramp and onto the beach. How's that for service? And you can clamber around off the back of the ship and drop right into the sea from a platform at the stern. Imagine *that* some sleety Sunday when you're cooped up and freezing!

Dinners are served family style in the ship's small dining room. Big bowls and platters of, say, fresh lobster or papaya or mangoes right off the trees, are passed down around the tables until everyone's stuffed.

Cabins

Caribbean Prince offers you quarters in 32 staterooms with big picture windows or in six other cabins below the deck. Staterooms look a little like the compact quarters you see on a yacht, and are decorated in handsome colors echoed in fiberglass paneling trimmed in teak.

Above-deck cabins come with twin beds that can be made into a double, although that doubling up means someone has to sleep on the inside and crawl over the other. Or a double can have a small table and two chairs, with a bed for a third person included. All rooms have private bathrooms and are carpeted.

Cabin size ranges from 7 by 11 feet to 9 by 11 feet.

After dinner everyone moves into the lounge where talk, games, and cards are the order of the day. This is a BYOB ("bring your own bottle") ship; it doesn't serve liquor but does provide the setups. You can go ashore and explore too, of course.

On the *Caribbean Prince*'s Jamaica run the top-priced cabins are $1349 per person for a 12-day voyage. Smaller outside cabins on the main deck are $1279 per person for 12 days, and windowless inside cabins (no smoking in these) are $849.

On those summer voyages in the Great Lakes the same prices apply.

In Jamaica the line also provides taxi chits to get you from Montego Bay airport to the ship. Because the ship is in port on Wednesday and Thursday between its Friday departures in Jamaica, you can arrive early and move right into your cabin. The fee for those boat-as-motel days is $45 for a couple, $30 single (no such deals on the northern cruises).

New Shoreham II has five cabin classifications. Most of the accommodations on this ship are outside rooms, some with full windows, some with a porthole too high up to serve as a window. Most also can accommodate three travelers. And most, but not all, cabins have private baths. One, cabin "A," which is not available on northern cruises, does not have a private bathroom but has a bath across the hall.

Starting at the top, the two best staterooms on the ship, Cabins 91 and 92, feature twin beds, an easy chair, picture windows on two walls, and private bathroom. Located aft on the Sun Deck, these are roomy accommodations and cost $1379 per person for an 11-night, 12-day voyage in the Bahamas.

Just a little smaller are two cabins with single berths and a picture window: Cabins 81 and 82 are $1279 per person for the trip.

The next price category down has two lower berths, a picture window, and a private bath; it can accommodate a third passenger. The rate is $1209 per person.

Cabins 14 to 19 and 22 to 28 have two lower single beds and a porthole. Although smaller in size, these can also accommodate a third passenger (but it will be *very* cozy). The price for these is $879 per person.

The lowest priced cabins on board, Cabins 31 to 34, have upper and lower berths, a porthole, and private bath. One of these cabins will cost $799 per person for the 11-night, 12-day Bahamas trip.

When the ship travels to northern waters, most of its cruises are 12-night, 13-day sojourns. The top price for these is $1459 per person, ranging down to $1359 for the slightly smaller deluxe cabins, $1309 in the double cabins with picture windows, $919 for smaller cabins, and $869 for the smallest quarters on board.

Fall cruises to the Erie Canal and on foliage expeditions are $40 to $100 per person cheaper. The 14-night trips between Florida and Rhode Island are $50 to $270 more, depending on the size of the cabin.

Summer weekend cruises, 3 nights and 2½ days, are $300 per person for the top-price quarters, $220 to $285 for less expensive cabins.

On those long summer cruises, rates include the bus trip to or from Montréal.

If a third person shares your cabin, each person gets a 10% reduction on the price of the cabin.

Singles pay 175% of the per-person fare in the lowest priced accommodations, 200% for other quarters.

On the *New Shoreham II* a round trip minibus ride from the airport to the ship is included in the price.

On the Saguenay River trips there's a $30 Canadian surcharge per person.

One further note: You make your own beds.

2. American Cruise Lines, Inc.

Contact: American Cruise Lines, Inc., One Marine Park, Haddam, CT 06438 (tel. toll free 800/243-6755, or 203/345-8551).

Cruising Grounds: U.S. East Coast, Mississippi/Ohio Rivers.

Itineraries: *America/Independence/Savannah/American Eagle*—

IN WINTER: Savannah–St. Simons Island–Fernandina Beach–Jacksonville Beach–St. Augustine–Port Canaveral–Vero Beach–Lake Okeechobee–Fort Myers and return same route

IN SPRING: Baltimore–St. Michaels–Oxford–Cambridge–Yorktown–Crisfield–Annapolis–Baltimore

IN SUMMER AND FALL: Haddam, Conn.–Block Island–Martha's Vineyard–Nantucket–New Bedford–Newport–Haddam *Or:* Haddam–Boothbay–Rockland–Camden–Belfast–Castine–Bar Harbor–Haddam

---

Not all ships are huge floating hotels filled with a thousand or so fun-seekers. Some are small, cozy craft dedicated to simple, casual trips to interesting ports.

American Cruise Lines offers just such cruises. Now operator of four small ships, all of which were built and are operated by the company, America Cruise Lines is headquartered in a spot called Steamboat Landing in Haddam, Conn. Owned by a gentleman named Charles Robertson, the line specializes in sailing trips in and around New England, although it now branches out to the Chesapeake Bay and recently began sailing the Mississippi River. In winter one of the ships sails south to cruise the inland waterways of Florida too.

All the ships are small, and we do mean *small.* The first ship in the fleet was the *American Eagle,* which carries 49 passengers. By 1980 the line had added the 85-passenger *Independence* and introduced its twin ship, the *America.* In 1984 the brand-new 132-passenger *Savannah* joined the family.

You won't find any spangled dancing girls or poolside pillow fights aboard these ships. These cruisers are specifically designed for inland, coastal cruising to visit intriguing waterways inaccessible to larger ships.

Passengers aboard are in search of "a different type of experience than those who want to go gambling or to a disco," says a company official. Your fellow passengers will tend to be well-traveled people who have sailed on larger ships and are now in search of a small-ship experience.

Itineraries of the ships are carefully planned to provide you with just the right amount of time needed to see the most interesting features in the area. In some spots the line may stay a day or two; in others, just long enough for a brief shore excursion.

On these intriguing itineraries, the ships are always in sight of land, so you can expect to dock each night and spend your days gazing at the lovely scenery along the shores. In fact these cruises are about as close as you can come to the European waterway cruising experience—kind of an American Rhine River cruise.

On the *American Eagle,* the *America,* the *Independence,* and the *Savannah,* you sail the Maine coastline, visit Chesapeake Bay, chug along the rarely visited waters of Florida's giant Lake Okeechobee, or drop in on southern plantations. Because the ships are small, they can call at harbors the big-bruiser cruisers cannot negotiate.

This winter the *America* will be exploring southern waterways on ten-day trips between Savannah, Georgia, and Fort Myers, Florida, sailing down the Intracoastal Waterway and through Lake Okeechobee. In April the ship leaves Savannah for a "Colonial South" cruise that takes her to Hilton Head Island, Beaufort, and Charleston. After a few sailings from Baltimore to Savannah, and some seven-day trips around Chesapeake Bay, she heads north to New England where she'll spend the summer cruising the islands and exploring the Hudson River. In November the ship returns to its winter schedule.

Meanwhile the *Independence* follows a rather similar course, sailing those "Colonial South" cruises in April and May, Chesapeake Bay in June, and the New England islands throughout the summer. In October the ship returns to Chesapeake bay, sailing there until mid-November. Ports of call include Bar Harbor, Bath, and Rockland, Maine—quaint coastal villages, home to lobster fishermen and shipbuilders.

In 1984 the *Savannah,* largest of the four, joined the fleet. She will be sailing year round from New Orleans in 1984–1985, visiting ports as far north as Minneapolis.

Don't hold us to these itineraries, however. Because the ships are quite similar they sometimes exchange the line's 13 basic itineraries.

Activities

On board these ships you'll make your own fun—quiet talks with new friends, card games, a good book, a movie, perhaps nothing more rousing than a long, long look at glittering lights twinkling along the coastline.

Most of your days will be spent ashore, visiting the historic plantations of the Old South or the intriguing bays and coastline of New England. On the fall-foliage cruises, nature provides a flaming show more spectacular than any Broadway revue.

You'll have to bring your own alcoholic beverages aboard these ships, but setups are complimentary.

Friendly and efficient pursers and hostesses are on hand to serve you, but don't look for a disco or casino aboard.

At night the ships pull up to a dock so you can go ashore and explore, then return to your floating hotel.

AMERICA/INDEPENDENCE/AMERICAN EAGLE: Although these three vessels are not quite identical, they're very similar in appearance, facilities, cruises, and prices. Let's take a look at what they have to offer.

Public Rooms

On ships as small as these, spending an evening in the public rooms is like going over to a friend's house for coffee. Indeed you may be traveling with only 48 other passengers!

All three ships have a cozy Nantucket Lounge lined with windows and furnished with comfortable couches and easy chairs. You can settle in here for a pre-dinner libation or play cards or games later on a couple of low wood tables with little built-in checkerboards. You'll find an electric player piano aboard and a self-service bar, plus a tiny library.

In the ship's dining room, everyone dines at the same time on the family-style meals ranging from lots of ham and eggs for breakfast, soup and sandwiches or salads for lunch, American favorites at dinner. If you're touring Maine you'll find fresh Maine lobster on the menu, and in the Chesapeake some of those famous Baltimore crabs will turn up on your plate. And, of course, there are always the American beef and poultry favorites.

Two sundecks aboard offer plenty of space for sun lovers to seek the perfect shade of tan.

Cabins

On each of these ships you are guaranteed an outside cabin for a very simple reason: all the cabins are outside quarters! While they're not elaborately furnished—just twin beds, a small vanity with a built-in sink, a nightstand with several drawers, and a bathroom with shower—they're pleasant and clean.

Cabin prices are divided into three categories AA, A, and B, and in descending order. Let's look at the price of a week-long cruise aboard any of the three ships.

On the *America* most of the AA cabins are on the same deck as the lounge, although a few are down on the main deck. The price for a week-long cruise in one of these is $1050 per person. Figure $400 to $500 more per person for a 10-day cruise, and double the cost for a 14-day journey.

Category A cabins vary little except in price. For these cabins you pay $994 for a seven-day cruise.

Category B cabins are on the boat deck, a few on the main deck, and the price for these smaller quarters is $945 per person for a week's cruise.

Prices are the same on the *Independence* and the *American Eagle,* although cabins in the various categories are on different decks than on the *America.*

On the *Independence,* which has space for 78 passengers, you'll also find some cabins that can accommodate three. For one of these the fare is $798 per person for a seven-day cruise, $1140 for a ten-day journey.

Single fares on all three ships pay $1225 for a seven-day cruise, $1750 for ten days.

Two-week cruises are double the price of one-week voyages.

Per diem rates then work out to a low of $135 to $150 per person for a seven-day cruise.

SAVANNAH: Newest ship in the fleet, the *Savannah* carries 132 passengers. She's 213 feet long and, like all the ships in the line, has all outside staterooms. On this ship, however, they're quite large accommodations, averaging 11 by 17 feet—and that's bigger than some ocean cruiser staterooms.

You'll find your entertainment in four lounges on board with big picture windows, and there are also three sun decks for tanning or watching the shoreline slip by. (No gambling, however).

Because the ship is so frequently in port, you can go ashore for entertainment. If you stay on board, however, there are movies and a player piano for amusement. Guest lecturers and musical entertainers come on board occasionally too. And you won't have to BYOB on this ship—two bars will do that.

Cabins

All cabins aboard are outside quarters, some of them entered from the outside decks, some from central corridors on the ship. All are located above the main deck so you have a nice view from the windows in your room as well as from the public rooms. And all have picture windows that open if you want the breezes to cool you, although there's air conditioning aboard. Some cabins have queen-size beds, and all have private showers and toilet facilities.

The *Savannah* has some handsome American artwork aboard too, much of it in cabins.

Prices begin at $1015 per person for a week's cruise in a cabin with twin beds. Slightly larger rooms are $1085 per person for a seven-day cruise and the top-priced cabins aboard are $1155 per person. Ten-day cruises are $335 to $495 more, depending on your choice of cabin, and 14-day cruises are double the one-week rate.

Suites on board this vessel are $1470 per person for a seven-day cruise while triple cabins are $875 per person for the week-long trip. Single cabins are $1344 for seven days.

3. American Hawaii Cruises

Contact: American Hawaii Cruises, Three Embarcadero Center, Suite 2500, San Francisco, CA 94111 (tel. toll free 800/227-3666, or 415/392-9400).

Cruising Grounds: Hawaiian Islands, with occasional Pacific Ocean cruises.

Itineraries: *Constitution*—Honolulu–Hilo–Kona–Maui–Kauai–Honolulu Occasionally trans-Pacific cruises from San Francisco and Los Angeles

Independence—Honolulu–Kauai–Hilo–Kona–Maui–Honolulu Occasionally trans-Pacific cruises from San Francisco and Los Angeles

---

Aloha, mai e 'ai, e alu, and especially *le 'ale 'a!* That's what American

Hawaii Lines, owners of two historic U.S. vessels, wishes you. And come to think of it, they provide it for you too.

From sunup to sunset Hawaii is in evidence aboard this line's *Constitution* and *Independence,* so when your island cruise ends you'll be able to say all those words and know that they mean "Greetings, come and dine, relax, and have fun!" The *Constitution* and *Independence* provide all that and more for you, and toss in visits to those palm-fringed Hawaiian Islands, home of hula hands and silver sands.

Created in 1978, American Hawaii is a comparatively new line operating two elegant craft built in an American shipyard. They have the distinction of being the only craft operating as American-flag vessels. One of them, the *Constitution,* was thought lovely enough, in fact, to carry Grace Kelly and her wedding party across the sea to Monaco for her marriage to a prince.

American Hawaii bought the *Independence* from a Hong Kong shipping company and began operating her in Hawaii on seven-day inter-island cruises. Success on that front led the company to purchase the *Constitution,* sister ship to the *Independence,* and in 1982 this ship also became an American flag carrier.

Now both ships are sailing the Hawaiian Islands, with occasional Pacific Ocean cruises from California. Built in 1951 to carry 1000 passengers on long Mediterranean cruises, the ships' passenger load has been lowered to 800, so cabins and public areas are spacious. The *Constitution* was refurbished in 1982 and the *Independence* was redecorated in 1980.

Glenn Ford, Anthony Quinn, Alan Ladd, Peter Ustinov, and Ronald Reagan have sailed aboard the *Constitution.* And if she looks strangely familiar to you, it may be because she's also a film star: Cary Grant and Deborah Kerr filmed *An Affair to Remember* aboard this ship. She was also the star of a recent "Real People" television segment.

If you like numbers, you'll find the statistics the same on both ships: both are 30,090 tons, 682 feet long, and 89 feet wide.

Thanks to the ships' U.S. flag and an act of Congress, American companies can now deduct the cost of conventions aboard ship from their taxes. American Hawaii thought that was very good news and has aimed some of its marketing programs at conventioneers, so you may find yourself at a meeting aboard one of the ships.

Both sail on Saturday from Honolulu, calling at Nawiliwili in Kauai, at Hilo and Kona on the big island of Hawaii, and at Kahului in Maui. The *Constitution* reverses that order.

Activities

In 1983 the ships began operating occasional Pacific Ocean cruises called "Sentimental Journeys." Big bands play and passengers are invited to swing through the '40s on their way to Hawaii. These special events, which include old radio shows, movie posters, dance contests, and '40s costume parties and swimsuit parades, recently took place in July and December. A travel agent can pinpoint dates for you.

On island cruises, Hawaii and things Hawaiian are the theme. An award-winning Polynesian revue sizzles with grass skirts and swaying hips. Big pineapples and luscious island flavors turn up at meals. Those Hawaiian shirts and muu-muus are everywhere you look, adorned with leis and boutonnieres.

Name entertainers like Rosemary Clooney, Ginger Rogers, Gisele

MacKenzie, and the Dukes of Dixieland may turn up on some cruises. There's always dancing in the lounges and disco music far into the night.

Days, you can learn how to hula or create a flower lei or play the ukulele. You can try making a hat out of palm fronds, play golf and tennis in port, watch the whales, play cards, Bingo, or shuffleboard.

Or shed a few poi pounds at exercise and dancercize classes.

Movies? Of course. Food? Endless.

INDEPENDENCE/CONSTITUTION: These sea ladies are not only sister ships, they're twins. So alike are they in spirit and in statistics that we can explore both at once.

Public Rooms

You'll never lack for a place to play aboard the *Independence* or the *Constitution.* Every deck has a handsome lounge, each different, each offering entertainment, be it quiet pursuits or lively ones.

Up on the Sun Deck is one very popular place, the swimming pool, and nearby the inevitable snackbar and libations arena. On the *Independence* it's the Barefoot Bar; on the *Constitution,* the Beachcomber Bar.

One deck down is the ship's main showroom, the big Pacific Showplace on the *Independence,* Tropicana Showplace on the *Constitution.* Both have a lovely curving glassed-in section called the Commodore's/Tradewinds Terrace.

Amidships on this Promenade Deck is the *Independence/Constitution* Lounge, where great curving banquettes divide the room into cozy sipping spots.

On the *Constitution* a small room has been set aside to honor Princess Grace. Understandably, it's called the Princess Grace Room. There are lounges called Latitude 20 Degrees on the *Independence* and Lahaina Landing on the *Constitution.*

Children are much loved by this cruise line, which provides children's playrooms on both ships and a youth recreation center on the *Independence.* In school holiday seasons youngsters have a full range of activities every bit as ambitious as those offered adults. Recreation directors oversee the activities both aboard and ashore, planning disco nights and beach parties, pizza events and even appearances by youthful stars like Todd Bridges of "Different Strokes" and Kim Fields and Mindy Cohn of "Facts of Life." Video games too, of course.

You'll be dining in the pretty Palms Dining Room on board the *Independence* and in the Hibiscus Dining Room on the *Constitution.* Favorite American steak and seafood selections are supplemented with exotic island creations: things like lomi-lomi salmon, cream of coconut aloha, crabflake cocktails, mahimahi, ono, ulua, or opakapaka. What's that? Try it and find out!

Both ships have theaters too.

Cabins

On board both ships you'll find some very attractive quarters ranging from suites to simpler quarters. Some have king-size beds and some have nifty beds that flip back to become a couch. As is usual with older ships, spacious quarters prevail but rooms come in all sizes and quite a variety of shapes.

Prices are same on both vessels, divided into cabin Categories A (the highest price) through L (the lowest). There are no seasons to be dealt with in these balmy all-year-round tropics.

To get an idea of what a Hawaiian Island cruise on the *Constitution* or the *Independence* will cost, here's a look at prices for a week-long island cruise. If you want the very best, book a suite, a very roomy stateroom indeed, with a separate sitting room you can close off from the bedroom. Two lower beds can be pushed together to create a king-size sleeper. For one of these you pay $2295 per person for a week's cruise.

Three categories of outside rooms, Categories E, F, and G, all feature two lower beds or a double bed, and begin at a high of $1895 per person, dropping $100 in each category to a low of $1695 per person for the seven-day cruises.

Three categories of inside rooms have twin beds or a double bed, and the prices for these (Categories H, I, and J) cabins are $1495, $1425, and $1345 per person, for the island voyage.

On the *Constitution* some cabins in Categories E, H, I, and J have king-size beds. Prices are the same, however.

One additional category of inside room has upper and lower berths and is $1095 for the week-long trip.

The lowest price on the ship is a Category L cabin on Coral Deck with one lower bed and one upper berth—$995.

Third and fourth adults sharing a cabin pay $595; children under 16 pay $395.

Single travelers have accommodations designed for them in Categories C and D. These cabins have one lower bed and bathroom and are $2195 in Category C, $1895 in Category D.

Per diem rates range from a low of $156 to a middle range of $242 to $270 per person, and a high, excluding suites, of $313 per person for a seven-day cruise. All prices are a bit higher in December. Port and service charges are $19 per person.

Air/sea packages offering round-trip air fare from a number of mainland cities let you fly to join the cruise for less than $400 per person.

Rates for Pacific Ocean cruises range from a low of $1000 to a high of $2345 per person (excluding suites) for a seven-day cruise.

4. Bahama Cruise Line

Contact: Bahama Cruise Line, 61 Broadway, Suite 2518, New York, NY 10006 (tel. toll free 800/223-3223, or 212/785-1090); or Bahama Cruise Line, 4600 West Kennedy St., Tampa, FL 33609 (tel. toll free 800/237-5361, toll free in Florida 800/282-4766; or 813/879-3470).

Cruising Grounds: Mexico, U.S. East Coast, Bermuda, New Orleans.

Itineraries: *Bahama Star—*

IN SUMMER: New York–Bermuda–New York

IN WINTER: New Orleans–Cozumel–Cancun–New Orleans

Veracruz—

IN SUMMER: New York–New Bedford–Cape Cod Canal–Sydney–Saguenay Fjord–Quebec City–Montreal and return same route; occasionally other stops

IN WINTER: Tampa–Playa del Carmen–Cozumel–Key West–Tampa

Until 1984 Bahama Cruise Line operated one ship, the *Veracruz,* moving her in winter to Florida's west coast and in summer to New York. In 1984 the fleet doubled with the addition of Holland America's *Veendam,* henceforth to be known as the *Bermuda Star.*

A branch of a New York transportation company, Bahama Line, despite its name, does not sail to the Bahamas. Instead, *Veracruz* has been sailing for years from Tampa to the Yucatán Peninsula with stops at the silvery jet-set beaches of Cozumél, archeologically oriented Cancún, and historic Key West.

In summer months the ship sails on week-long voyages from New York up the St. Lawrence to Montréal. You can embark in New York or in Montréal and get to one of those cities on Amtrak's *Adirondack* day train or *Montrealer* night train. Several fall cruises visit Bermuda, Cape Cod, Martha's Vineyard, and Nantucket.

The latest addition to this line is the *Bermuda Star.* In the summer of 1984 the ship was scheduled to sail between New York and Bermuda, a familiar itinerary for this craft. Now owned by the Tung Group of Hong Kong, which bought the *Veendam* and its sister ship the *Volendam* from Holland America, the *Veendam* is on a long-term lease to Bahama Cruise Line which renamed it the *Bermuda Star.* In the 1984–1985 winter season it is also scheduled to sail to Playa del Carmen, Cozumél, and Key West, but from New Orleans, one of the few ships to call that lacy old city home.

The *Bermuda Star* has an unusual summer itinerary, featuring trips from New York to two ports in Bermuda—St. George and Hamilton—so you can get a look at the colonial charm of St. George and still not miss the cosmopolitan glitz of Hamilton. These cruises sound interesting: arriving in St. George's in the afternoon and spending the night and next day there, leaving at 3 p.m. for the two-hour sail to Hamilton, where the ship remains for two nights, spending a day at sea on either end of the cruise.

Both these ships are venerable old ladies offering all the basic amenities, more of them on the *Bermuda Star* than on the smaller *Veracruz.* Cabins and public rooms sometimes show their age on both ships.

One cannot fault the crews, however. On both ships they work hard to keep you happy and provide you with plenty of pampering.

Activities

As with many Caribbean sailers, activities on board begin early and end late, if at all, on the *Veracruz.* Each evening there's entertainment in the ship's lounge and dancing in several sections of the ship, not the least of which is the Disco just off the Lido Bar.

Life is very casual aboard this ship. You can dress to the nines on one or two evenings if you like, but you won't feel uncomfortable in jacket and tie even on formal evenings.

You won't find a full-fledged midnight buffet on board the *Veracruz,* but you can get pizza at the witching hour and stave off night starvation with some hot snacks. A coffeeshop (in which you pay for what you want, a rarity on a cruise ship) is open to 2 a.m. too.

Casino fans will find a small game room with slots and four blackjack tables.

If you think you have talent, you can find out whether others agree at a talent show. There's also a costume party.

A popular family ship, the *Veracruz* has a nanny on board in summer.

One interesting party aboard this ship is a scavenger hunt—quite an interesting environment in which to search.

The *Bermuda Star,* at 23,000 tons, is a much larger ship but one that carries about the same number of passengers. She has had quite a respectable career, much of it sailing the Caribbean. It seems likely that the ship will retain the play-as-you-go atmosphere that's so popular in Caribbean sailing, but as we went to press there was no word yet on what plans the line had, if any, for changes aboard ship.

VERACRUZ: Built in 1957 by a German shipbuilder, the *Veracruz* was constructed for transatlantic service and was once known as the *Freeport.* She was refurbished in 1975 and measures in at 10,595 tons and 487 feet long, and carries about 700 passengers.

Public Rooms

The first thing you'll see aboard is Bimini Deck. It's also the place you'll visit most often during your voyage—most of the ship's playing places are on this deck. For openers there's the big Dolphin Lounge, with bars at both ends and a dance floor in the middle. This is the place to head to see the evening's entertainment, which ranges from singers to dancers to comedians. Two bands perform here each night as well.

On the other end of this deck is the bright Casino Lounge, where piano-bar fans will find some of their kind of music going on. Big curtained windows here make this a cheerful room in which to while away the day. There's a small dance floor tucked away in this room too. On really romantic evenings you can move out to the nearby observation area and dance there in the moonlight.

The main staircase on board is attractive, with bright mirrors and glowing chandeliers.

Between the two major rooms on this deck is a shopping arcade where you can pick up the gift you forgot in port. The beauty salon and barbershop, and the information offices, are here too.

One deck up and aft is the disco tucked in beside the circular Lido Bar.

Still one more deck up is the sunning space including a glassed-in solarium and another observation area.

Swimmers will find the ship's small round pool down on Calypso Deck. The main part of the pool is rectangular, but two eyebrow arches on either side offer shallow splashing water perfect for children and nonswimmers. Nearby is the New Orleans Terrace, home of a snackbar and purveyor of hamburgers and hot dogs.

Amidships on Delta Deck is the Bahamas Dining Room, a U-shaped room with two wings down the sides of the ship. And down in the depths of the vessel you'll find the Cinema Theater.

A simple ship, the *Veracruz* is not a luxury liner and doesn't pretend to be, so don't expect glitter.

Cabins

On board you'll find 367 cabins designed to serve as sitting rooms by day and bedrooms by night. They're equipped with a sofa bed and a recessed bed, or sometimes with a double sofa bed or two lower beds. All have private bathrooms with a shower and sink. You can use your electrical appliances here too. Some, of course, have upper berths accommodating a third or fourth person.

Once again, don't expect luxury. Cabins are small, with basic accoutrements like carpeting and private bathrooms but nothing fancy.

Cabin prices run from Category 1 (the highest prices) through Category 10 (the lowest). There are three seasons aboard the ship, low (November to mid-December), middle (mid-December to February and late April to June), and high (February and March).

On its New England summer cruises the ship also has three seasons: early summer (June to mid-July), high summer (late July through mid-August), and late summer (late August through September).

Let's look at some of the prices for a week-long Caribbean cruise in peak winter season. (In low season you will pay a flat $545 per person for all inside cabins, and $625 for all outside quarters except suites, which are $725.) Some two-room suites are available. These are quite spacious, with separate sitting areas. One of these costs $905 per person in Caribbean high season.

Moving down a bit, the outside cabins are in Categories 1 through 5. The best and most expensive of these are on Aztec Deck, where the price is $805 per person. Others are located along the sides of the ship on Calypso Deck, the main passenger deck aboard. Those are $775 per person for the week-long Caribbean trip in high season.

More outside cabins are on Everglades and Fiesta Decks. As you go down in the ship the cabins get smaller and less expensive, ranging from $775 per person on Delta to $675 per person on Fiesta for the one-week trip in peak season.

Inside cabins fall into Categories 6 through 10 and are scattered about the ship. They range in price from a high of $645 per person on Aztec Deck (where the largest inside accommodations are found) to $615 on Fiesta Deck for a week's voyage in high season.

Third and fourth persons sharing a cabin are $395 for each adult, $190 for each child under 12. Four berths are found in inside cabins only.

Some outside staterooms have double beds.

Budget an additional $20 per person for port charges ($5 each in New England).

Single travelers pay an additional 50% in any category of cabin.

As you can see, per diem costs range from a very low $88 per person to a middle price of about $96 to $110 and a high of $143, excluding suites, making this ship one of the best budget buys afloat.

Some discounts are often available for senior citizens on certain sailings, and for payment 90 days or so in advance. On New England cruises you also get a discount if you take the two-week cruise.

Air/sea add-on rates are available too.

BERMUDA STAR: Built in 1958, the former *Veendam* was once known as the *Argentina* and briefly as the *Monarch Star*. She weighs in at 23,500 tons and carries 728 passengers and a crew of 340. Her officers are Dutch and the crew is Indonesian (or at least was when the ship was purchased).

Public Rooms

Most of your playtime will find you on Promenade Deck, where the public rooms are located. There are several shops and a newstand on board so you can buy and read whenever you like.

Sports fans will head straight up to the Sports Deck, where the ship has set up a small putt-putt golf course, one of the few (if not the only) such courses afloat.

Tan fans will find quite a number of open spots in which to seek the sun, but the biggest and best is on the Promenade Deck where you'll find the ship's swimming pool. A canopied area accommodates those who want the air but not the sun, and of course there's the usual snackbar and Lido Lounge right nearby.

At night the Lido Lounge turns on to the music of a dance band, and this attractive bright room is usually packed with dancers.

Up on the Promenade Deck you'll also find another big lounge and polygonal dance floor surrounded by long banquettes that snake about the room creating several intimate corners. Just off the open promenade at the bow is the ship's casino (which features the usual slots and blackjack tables) located not far from yet another lounge and dancing spot. The card room and library are nearby.

Look up on the Sun Deck for a quiet spot with lots of windows and a semicircular seating area that's a pleasant place for a chat with friends.

Bermuda Star's long rectangular dining room is on the main deck, and down a deck is the ship's theater. Up a deck is a health center.

Cabins

Cabins aboard this aging lady are quite comfortable, many of them large as befits a transatlantic cruiser. They were decked out in attractive batiks, but may be changed by the time you read this.

The top cabins are deluxe outside double rooms with two beds, full vanity, large wardrobes, comfortable sitting area with a couple of chairs and a table, and a full bathroom with both bathtub and shower.

Dropping a category, you'll find outside double rooms with twin lower beds and similar accoutrements, but in these the sitting area is smaller. Some have double beds.

Inside double rooms are smaller but still have adequate space, with twin beds, a vanity, plenty of wardrobe space.

The lowest priced accommodations have one lower bed, or lower and upper berths, but still have a vanity, closets, and bathroom.

The following prices are for a cruise on board this ship in peak summer season, from June through mid-August. (You will pay $50 less in late summer from mid-August to mid-October.) Cabin price categories are numbered from 1 through 10 (Category 10 is the lowest priced cabins, Category 1, the highest priced).

The most expensive quarters feature two lower beds and a sitting area, and cost $1350 per person in peak season.

Larger cabins, in Categories 2, 3, and 4, most of them outside cabins, are $1350, $1275, and $1225 per person for a week's summer trip.

Three cheaper categories of outside cabins also feature two lower beds and are $1125 for Category 5, $1075 for Category 6, and $1025 per person for a week's voyage in an outside Category 7 cabin.

Cabins in Categories 8 and 9 are inside quarters with two lower beds, and are $975 or $925 per person for the week's voyage in high summer season.

The least expensive cabins on board feature upper and lower berths and may be inside or outside cabins. These quarters are $895 per person in peak summer season.

Singles pay $1395 for inside or outside single rooms on the upper and main decks.

5. Carnival Cruise Lines

Contact: Carnival Cruise Lines, 3915 Biscayne Blvd., Miami, FL 33137 (tel. toll free 800/327-9051, toll free in Florida 800/432-5424; or 305/576-9260; for bookings within 30 days of sailing, 305/327-2058).

Cruising Grounds: Mexico (from both Florida and California), Bahamas, Puerto Rico, U.S. Vigin Islands, Cayman Islands, Jamaica.

Itineraries: *Carnivale*—Miami–Nassau–Miami or Miami–Freeport–Nassau–Miami year-round

Festivale—Miami–Nassau–San Juan–St. Thomas–Miami year-round

Mardi Gras—Miami–Cozumel–Grand Cayman–Ocho Rios–Miami year-round

Tropicale—Los Angeles–Puerto Vallarata–Mazatlan–cruising by Cabo San Lucas–Los Angeles year-round

---

Carnival Cruise Lines vessels are the fun ships, folks. Nonstop activity is the watchword here, so if you're looking for action days—and nights—you'll want to see what's going on at Carnival.

Carnival's execs know exactly what market they're aiming at and they know just how to satisfy it: fun, fun, fun, and sun, sun, sun. Carnival cruisers want to get away for a week or so, see a few ports, and play to the max.

Much of the success of Carnival's fleet must go to its sometimes controversial marketing executive Bob Dickinson. The Carnival marketing staff pursues potential passengers with enthusiasm, and with some very affordable prices that get even better when business is slow.

So intent is Carnival on marketing "fun" that it has made that somewhat nebulous concept part of its theme: the line's vessels call themselves "the Fun Ships," which says much to many. It should say something to you about the whoop-de-do atmosphere you'll find aboard the line's four craft, the *Carnivale, Festivale, Mardi Gras,* and *Tropicale.*

So successfully have they pursued this sun and fun market, in fact, that the company now boasts nine straight years with occupancy rates above 100%! (If you're wondering how they manage that, it has to do with the presence of third and fourth passengers in a cabin.) Not bad for a company that once thought its ship would never come in. When Carnival first appeared back in 1972 with one ship, the aging *Empress of Canada,* things did not go well at all. As a matter of fact, they did not *go* at all: the ship ran aground. Nothing improved much for Carnival's first ship, by now called the *Mardi Gras,* until 1975 when the line's ship came in to the tune of 100%-plus occupancy.

So shoestring was the company when it first began operating that it didn't want to spend the money to do a whole new paint job on the ship's stack, so just altered the Canadian Pacific line logo enough to make it look different. You can still see the resemblance in the line's red, white, and blue funnels.

From there the wave of success rose higher as the company bought the *Empress of Britain* to turn it into the *Carnivale,* then used profits to buy the *S. A. Vaal,* renamed it the *Festivale,* and treated it to a $20-million facelift. In 1982 the line floated the brand new *Tropicale,* now sailing from California.

In recent years Carnival has been a strong and vocal supporter of the free air fare concept. That means that if you decide on a Carnival ship, even one on an opposite coast, you pay nothing (or almost nothing) to fly to that other coast to board the ship. Nothing's for nothing, they say, but these offers (also made by other middle-market cruise lines) come close.

Carnival's ships seem to us best suited to young and/or first-time cruisers willing to forgo elegance for a relaxed fun-jammed, action-packed week filled with plenty of piña coladas and late nights. Still, Carnival cruises attract plenty of the not-so-youthful as well. In fact one of the scheduled parties aboard is a grandparent's bragging event, so you'll find all ages aboard.

You'll also find honeymooners and singles, swingers and quiet types, midwesterners and Yankees—everyone in search of a week of fun and frolic on the high seas. Unlike many cruise ships which sell the fascination of their ports of call, the emphasis on board these ships is on the shipboard experience.

It seems fair to say, in fact, that they do all they can to keep you at play aboard the ship, with about 80% of the cruise spent on board and 20% in port. So nonstop is activity aboard, in fact, that your shipboard experience sometimes seems to mimic what the ships' names suggest: a lively, party-up Mardi Gras, carnival, and festival.

Italian officers and many Italians in the crew ensure that there will be good food and plenty of pasta aboard.

All the line's ships feature Carnival's distinctive red, white, and blue smokestack, and all are painted a snappy white to go with it.

Carnival's schedules have been quite predictable: from Miami all three ships sail to islands in the sun. *Festivale* goes on seven-day voyages from Miami to Nassau, San Juan, and St. Thomas. *Mardi Gras* makes seven-day trips to Cozumél/Playa del Carmen, Grand Caymen, and Ocho Rios. *Carnivale* sails on three- and four-day cruises to Nassau and Freeport.

On the West Coast of the U.S. the *Tropicale* is now on regular runs from Los Angeles to Mexico and back, in seven days.

Now the line is planning still another ship, the 45,000-ton *Holiday,* expected to go into service in July 1985, and has two more ships, the *Jubilee* and the *Celebration,* on the drawing boards for 1987 and 1989. Those last two will be 48,000-ton ships, the largest ever built specifically for cruising. All will be seven-day ships, line executives say, but ports are undecided.

If Carnival completes its plans, by 1987 the line will have seven ships and something like 8000 beds in its fleet, and will be carrying half a million passengers a year.

Activities

So what is all this activity we're talking about? Well, for openers there are movies going in the ships' theaters all day and most of the night, nonstop.

There's always a party somewhere on board, be it grandparents bragging, beer drinking, pillow fighting, plank toppling, or champagne celebrations for honeymooning couples.

Following through on their "Fun Ship" theme, the line figures fun has no age limit so plans something for absolutely everyone from the youngsters to the oldsters and back again. As line executives like to say, at any given moment "the ship really cooks." There are bands playing outside, the casino is going, continuous movies, activities in and outdoors, a disco rolling.

Even on its new three- and four-day schedules Carnival keeps the Nassau visit to one day and then spends all day Sunday at sea to, as Carnival executives put it, "showcase" their product.

At dinner every night there's a theme evening, something like Texas night, for instance. And here's an interesting touch: if you have a certain age preference in dinner companions you can request that when you book your cabin.

Cruise staffers must be entertainers as well, so some nights you'll see them performing magic tricks, singing, and dancing.

Entertainment is slightly different on the *Tropicale,* where the western audiences are accustomed to glitzy Las Vegas shows and mariachi bands. You'll find both on board that ship, and sometimes even a steel band, which proved so popular in test runs that it just stayed. Definitely there will be a calypso band on Caribbean voyages.

CARNIVALE: Launched in 1957 as the *Empress of Britain,* this 27,250-ton "Fun Ship" carries 950 fun-seekers to such fun spots as Nassau and Freeport. Renovated in 1976 and refurbished a bit in 1984, the ship retains many '50s touches, and in cabins some dated, if unabashedly tropical, color schemes.

Wood, wood, and more wood is a watchword of this ship. Fabulous light-wood paneling lines the hallways, and corners are often trimmed in contrasting dark woods. You'll see polished wood handrails and handsome wood head and foot boards everywhere you look.

Electrical connections aboard are such that it's necessary to leave your room and go to a nearby vanity room if you want to use your hairdryer. It may not be convenient, but you get used to it after a while—or give up drying your hair. Those vanity rooms also have ironing boards and a gizmo that remains a mystery touch: a chrome cabinet with spigots on the doors (we still haven't found anyone who knows what on earth that is).

In some of the hallways aboard you'll find taps for ice water, and in a couple of corners you can spot little lighted alcoves labeled "cigarette ends." Antique buffs will love exploring this ship.

Public Rooms

Carnivale's International Dining Room is down on the main deck, a dark spot lined with beautiful woods and wood columns. A burgundy color scheme here is sparked up by white linens.

Dance buffs should head straight for the circular Fly Aweigh Disco, where the floor lights up, old windows feature etched glass, old fittings hark back to days gone by, and there's even a jukebox. Woodworking fans ought to love the burl door too.

Mardi Gras Nightclub is also a circular spot, but this lounge is done up in blues with chairs that give a giant pouf when you settle into them. The stage is trimmed in shiny stars and there's live entertainment in this room, which also features a circular parquet floor.

On the same Promenade Deck you'll find the cinema not far from the children's playroom, and the ship's gift shop and boutique.

Between the Mardi Gras Nightclub and the disco (of all places!) is a small library.

As you might have guessed by now we're very partial to those long enclosed promenades, one of which you'll find here. You shouldn't have any trouble finding your way around the walkways either—big marquee signs identify public rooms like the casino, which by the way features a bank of impressive brass doors.

Art deco turns up on the doors to the cinema, which looks its age, but then how beautiful does a movie theater have to be anyway?

The largest lounge aboard is the Showplace, which seats 550 and is done up in plastic chairs in shades of burgundy and tan and features lots of windows.

Swimming pools? Good grief, yes. Up top on the Lido Deck the Lido Beach Club features no fewer than three pools and a wader, and way down on Riviera Deck there's yet another pool, the Coral Pool, near the ship's gym and sauna.

Cabins

If you like an early-morning dip in private, some of the ship's lowest priced rooms—$290 to $310 per person for a three-day cruise—are not too far from the indoor pool.

There are 12 rate categories aboard, with most expensive price in Category 12, the least expensive in Category 1. Cruises also are divided into "season" prices and "base" prices. Base prices are in effect in the slow tourist season in these waters and season prices are in effect in the most popular winter months and June through August. Exact season dates had not been set when this book went to press, but figure January to April as top-price months along with those summer months already mentioned, and everything else at base prices.

The following are the *Carnivale*'s prices for a three-day cruise in peak summer season, from late May through August.

Top dollar for a three-day cruise at that time will buy a veranda suite, a very spacious suite with a big separate sitting room and a twin-bedded room with lots of closet and drawer space. Despite the veranda tag, these do not have an open balcony. They do, however, have big French doors that close one room off from the other, thus giving two couples or a family more privacy than is available on any other ship we know. That could make this a bargain for you if you're traveling with others. The price for this suite on a three-day cruise is $575 per person.

Because rooms differ so widely aboard the ship it's really quite impossible to begin describing them. Suffice it to say that the more you pay the more space you buy, and on this ship more is plenty! Cabins are quite spacious, even in the lowest categories, and not uncomfortably crowded even at the minimum rate. That's one of the reasons some people are so partial to older ships like this one.

Outside cabins from Category 11 down through Category 6 will cost from $535 per person for a three-day trip to $495 per person, not a large gap. Cabin E73 seems a good example of Category 10, and a particularly good example of a room with lovely wood headboards. You'll also find a matching dresser, and triple mirror, plus a full-length mirror, amid an orange and gold decor. There's a separate sitting room and twin beds in this outside deluxe double which can be yours for $535 per person for the three-day trip.

Nearby E69 is a veranda suite with aging furnishings, a sitting room, and more of that same beautiful wood. Tub and toilet are each in separate rooms here, as they are in many cabins throughout the ship.

Category 6 cabins (inside) and Category 8 (outside) feature twin beds. One of those folds up to become a couch and one upper pulls down. A shower shoots right into the floor, testimony to the aging plumbing aboard. Of these cabins, 41 is nice. The cost of a Category 6 inside cabin is $495, and for a Category 8, $515 per person for the three-day voyage.

Category 5 inside cabins with twin or double bed are $465, and again are pretty spacious quarters.

Categories 4, 3, 2, and 1 include both outside cabins with upper and lower berths, and inside cabins with upper and lower berths, a double bed, or twins. Those with double or twin beds cost the most: $465 per person for three days. Those with upper and lower berths, or inside rooms with double beds, range from $290 to $365 per person for three days.

Third and fourth persons sharing a cabin pay $190 for adults, $95 for children, on a three-day trip.

Single occupancy of a cabin costs 50% of the price of that cabin in Categories 1 to 3, and 200% in other categories.

If you're willing to share a cabin with three other people, you pay $250 for a three-day cruise, and you must pay $18.75 for gratuities in advance for the three-day cruise.

Port charges are $17 for adults, $11 for children under 16 for the three-day cruise, $18 and $12 for the four-day trip.

Per diem rates on the ship work out at a low of about $96 per person, rising in the middle price ranges to $148 to $168 per person and a high of $185, excluding suites.

FESTIVALE: Carnival has adapted some aging craft to its purposes, which means that you can expect some unusually large cabins aboard. Not that they're all huge, by any means, just that you'll find more large cabins than you might find on some other newer ships never built to pamper the demanding, transoceanic traveler.

On the other hand you'll have to accept a few of the less desirable elements imposed by this antiquity. For instance, you'll have to get used to visible sinks right in your room rather than tucked away in separate bathrooms, aging electrical and plumbing systems, and dining rooms well below decks with no windows.

Public Rooms

Festivale's very best feature, to my mind, is a long, long deck, glassed floor to ceiling, where you can sit in windless, rainless comfort and watch the world go by—shades of "Bring me my tea, Jeeves."

The Tradewinds Club is a very Sidney Greenstreet spot in which to perfect your Bogart imitation, and the Copacabana Lounge features contemporary wicker decor in tan.

The Carnivale Lounge, with its deep-burgundy accents and low contemporary chairs, art deco wood design, and tinted mirror, is the best place on the ship (nobody said we have to be objective here). The Gaslight Saloon is a good match for its name, with two big lanterns that give you the feeling of that era.

An entrance/reception area aboard is quite contemporary with red furnishings and attractive murals.

Backlit figures etched on glass in various colors are a don't-miss in the round Le Cabaret Room, where evening entertainment is presented. Lighted floors in the Fanta Z disco produce a light show timed to the music, and you can watch yourself at play in the mirrored ceiling. Finally, the shiny steel art deco stairways aboard ought to be designated a national treasure.

Those who visualize heaven as a place in which you drape yourself over a lounge chair beside the pool can practice up here. There are three pools aboard, two outside, one in, and one with a slide that slips you into the wet stuff, screeching with the joy of it all.

Seek out the Lido Lounge, near the indoor pool, for a look at some interesting brass ship steering equipment, not to mention snacks.

Plastic is a very common substance aboard. You'll find it covering chairs, on walls—just about everywhere. We point that out only to indicate that while appealing to the budget traveler, the Festivale is offering budget-y looking accommodations. There's often a bit of a thrown-together look about the color schemes that may be a reflection of the line's ongoing renovation projects.

While her antiquity is fascinating to those of us who did not live in that era, some older, more affluent travelers may not be as enchanted by this lovely old lady. Oddly enough, the *Festivale*'s antiquity appeals mightily to young travelers. One barely bearded fellow raved on and on to us about his adoration for this ship, whose best point, he said, was "its ambience, its amazing old-world travel feeling." Indeed.

Cabins

Some cabins on the *Festivale* feature double beds and even king-size sleepers, which on cruise ships is a very rare feature indeed. Upper and lower bunks are quite common aboard this craft, which makes up for its small and often dated bathroom facilities with plenty of closet space.

Let's look at some of the accommodations and the prices you'll pay for a week's cruise aboard this venerable aging lady in peak winter season (figure $50 and $100 less in the off-season).

The price categories are once again divided into 12 options, with

Category 12 the highest priced accommodations. There are two seasons aboard, base and the season. Base includes May and September to December; the season is mid-January through most of April and June through August.

Those Category 12 cabins are veranda suites, very large accommodations, which sport a divider between beds and the sitting area. They're quite spacious and some even have private outdoor verandas! For one of these cabins you pay $1795 per person for a week's cruise in peak season.

Accommodations known as demi-suites are every bit as nice as the suites. V34, for instance, has wood bedsteads and is very spacious. For that you pay $1595 per person for the week-long trip.

Outside cabins in Categories 10 and 9 are very large outside cabins, some with queen-size beds, some with twins. One of these rooms, in either configuration, will cost $1475 or $1395 per person for a week's voyage in peak season.

Cabin U3 is a Category 8 cabin with a queen-size bed and an unusual arcing wall. It's small but nice for honeymooners and others who value togetherness. It's also a bit cheaper because it's smaller: $1335 per person for that week's journey in peak season.

Cabin E147 is a basic Category 7 cabin, large with twin beds, and costs $1295 per person for a week.

Cabin U137, a Category 6 cabin, is one of the mid-priced accommodations aboard, and has a sink in the bedroom, a queen-size bed, and a somewhat barren look to it with minimal decor elements. That one goes for $1245 per person on the week's trip. Others in this category also have queen-size beds, but generally someone will be sleeping next to the wall.

Inside cabins with twin or queen-size beds in Categories 5 and 4 are $1195 and $1135 per person. An inside Category 3 cabin with upper and lower berths is $1075 per person for the trip.

A Category 2 cabin, Cabin U143, just a few steps away, has upper and lower berths in an inside cabin and is one of just a few low-priced cabins on that deck. By low we mean $1025 per person for a week's cruise in high season.

Lowest price accommodation on board is an inside cabin with upper and lower berths, small but not tiny. One of those cabins is $950 per person for the peak-season voyage.

As you can see, per diem rates range from a low of $135 to a high of $210 per person for a week's cruise in high season, excluding suites.

Third and fourth persons sharing a room pay $395; children under 16, $195.

Port charges are $22 for adults, $20 for children.

Single-occupancy rates are 150% of the fare in the three lowest priced categories, 200% for higher priced categories.

If you go for the sharing plan, four to a cabin, assigned by the line, you pay $495 per person for a week's cruise in high season—not bad at all.

MARDI GRAS: First of Carnival's ships, the *Mardi Gras* is thought by many to be an oldy but goody. She's an incredible study in Le Style Grande, probably the most evocative-of-days-of-yore ship of any craft afloat. It takes no imagination at all to picture the fabulously wealthy trailing merrily down these wide, wide hallways or drifting about in cabins practically large enough to get lost in!

This ship is a woodworker's dream—and in fact pretty dreamy for anyone with an interest in antiques and the woods of which they were made. You'll see endless miles of wood aboard this ship, streaking down long wide hallways in massive stretches of paneling, and in almost all the cabins.

If you look very closely in the higher priced cabins you'll find a tiny plaque telling you what kind of wood you're looking at—each room is different. We spotted one done in something called "grey harewood dyed," another in figured silver birch, another in "one-quarter figured mottled white ash"! None of those slick but plastic new ships can match that.

A twin to the *Carnivale* in most aspects, the *Mardi Gras* features the same beautiful woodsiness with lots of brass accents. Once known as the *Empress of Canada,* she was built in 1961 and refurbished in 1973 and again in 1982. Today her public rooms look surprisingly contemporary, although cabins hark right back to the '50s in both colors and furnishings.

At 27,250 tons, she carries 1100 passengers and shows her age in many places, almost always charmingly. She's kept neat and clean too, which makes those few antiquities bearable.

Public Rooms

Gamesters can while away the wee hours at the glassed-in Bourbon Street Arcade while dance fans can trip the light fantastic until the wee hours at nightclubs and discos. Three bands—steel, orchestra, and "loverly"—attend to your musical needs.

In summer and for holidays there are special programs for children, and at any time of year there's plenty to keep both adults and children occupied. There are, for instance, three swimming pools aboard, two outside and one inside. One pool aboard is especially earmarked for the youngsters, who also have a playroom near the sports deck and near that youngster's-only pool.

There's a fully equipped gymnasium on the Sun Deck, a sauna near the indoor pool, and a cinema (with a balcony) on the main deck, where movies are shown continuously.

Another of Carnival's enclosed promenades turns up on the Empress Deck where the Point After Club is a lively meeting spot. On that same deck you'll find the grand ballroom and some shops.

Mardi Gras's dining room is small and inside, but comparatively bright and cheerful. Mirrors help make it look larger than it really is, and contemporary furnishings and a red decor brighten it still more.

In the Grand Ballroom you'll find brass-trimmed glass doors with a double-winged staircase leading to a balcony that rims the room. Quite an impressive spot, it features circular banquettes in deep burgundy and a deco-ish pattern in the carpet. Way up in the ceiling tiny lights glitter.

More of that glowing burgundy shade turns up in the nearby Carousel Lounge, which features windows down both sides overlooking a closed promenade. A black-lacquered piano bar captures center stage in this attractive room.

Disco fans can dance up a storm in the Point After Club where a mirrored ceiling and matching columns glitter. There's a wall of windows here, so as you're dancing you can look out over a swimming pool. A massive woodcarving is a focal point on one wall of this red and black room.

A small nook called The Den is brick lined on three sides, but opens to the deck through a glass wall. Pretty carved-wood furniture gives the room a European bistro look. Look for it up on the Promenade Deck.

Up there too you'll find a long enclosed promenade known as El Patio Grande. Nobody seems to have known quite what to do with this section of the ship, so it now sports a gaggle of ice-cream-parlor chairs and tables in bright yellow, plus a couple of one-armed bandits. El Patio Grande encircles the ship's Showboat Club Casino, a huge casino with one of those big roulette wheels, craps tables, table roulette, blackjack, and slots.

Cabins

As with many old ships, the *Mardi Gras* has quite a number of cabins that are larger than some you'll find on newer ships. All of them have private facilities and the 24-hour room service offered on all Carnival ships. Many, many cabins have sink and shower in one small room and toilet in the other. Many, many bathrooms are tiny creatures, barely big enough to turn around in and certainly not ideal for the hefty.

If you're partial to king-size beds, you'll find some of those on Riviera Deck. They're inside cabins in Category 6 which is about mid-price for this ship. Be prepared to find that there's not a great deal of room left over, however. Some cabins also have double beds, the less expensive being inside cabins on upper, main, and Empress decks.

Again there are 12 price categories (the highest priced is 12; the lowest is Category 1). And again there are two seasons: high season (mid-January through April and June through August) and low or base season (May through June and September through mid-December). You'll pay $50 to $100 less if you're not sailing in peak winter or summer seasons.

Suites much like those on the *Carnivale* are $1795 per person, and a demi-suite is $1595 per person, for a week's trip in high season. The best thing about these suites is this: if you're traveling with a family or another couple, you can have absolute privacy by closing the paned-glass doors between the two separate rooms. You'll save lots of money on those third and fourth fares too.

Categories 10, 9, 8, and 7 are all outside cabins with double or twin beds, and they are big, big, and bigger. Look at the line's brochure and you'll be able to spot the largest ones. All look much the same, outfitted in orange or blue bedspreads with a wavy pattern. Prices in these cabins range from a high of $1475 to a low of $1295 per person, less than $200 difference per person for the week-long trip. Cabin E28, a Category 9 cabin, is very large, large enough to accommodate two cots at night (the steward will remove them in the morning). This room is paneled in figured mottled white ash and it will cost $1395 per person for a week's journey in high season.

In Category 6, Cabin E30 is a good example of an inside cabin in this price bracket. It's small, but not uncomfortably so, and features a double bed, with a sink in the room rather than in the bathroom. There's a bathroom too, of course.

Categories 4 and 5 are inside cabins with double or twin beds. One of these costs $1195 or $1135 per person.

Categories 3, 2, and 1 include both inside and outside cabins, but all have lower and upper beds. Category 1 cabins have a sink in the room, but there's still plenty of space. Bathrooms are small, however.

Some of these lower priced cabins are in a section of the ship that has wall coverings or plastic panels on the wall, so you won't see the woodwork here that you see in higher priced cabins. Upper berths flip back against the wall during the day so there's a bit more space then. Even these quarters usually are reasonably spacious for the price. The price in these three lower categories ranges from a high of $1075 to a low of $950 per person.

Third- and fourth-person fares and single-occupancy rates are the same as on the *Carnivale* and *Festivale.* Per diem rates are the same as well.

TROPICALE: In 1984 the *Tropicale* spent its first full year as a California-Mexico cruiser, abandoning the Alaska sailings it had done under charter to another company.

Line officials are dedicated to a philosophy they call "keep it simple," with few or no itinerary changes for each ship and a steady pattern of cruising all year long to and from the same destinations. Nevertheless, Carnival was premiering summer cruises to Mexico, something rarely done in the past and never done previously by Carnival.

The entertainment on this ship is slightly different, flashier, more Las Vegas in style, tailored to the western audience which has come to expect that kind of evening showbiz. Here too you'll see a salute to Mexico with a mariachi band on board, often in addition to the steel band which met with success on some trial runs.

Public Rooms

Public rooms on the *Tropicale* are very contemporary. In the Palm Restaurant you'll find sweeping circular lines, rattan furnishings decked out in rust and gray, recessed ceiling lights. In the Islands in the Sun Lounge, trendy Lucite discs trim the ceiling line and orange couches encircle a grand piano that forms one of the focal points of the room.

In the Tropicana Lounge, deep blues and a jewel-toned aquamarine are so blue you sometimes feel as if you're snorkeling your way through your margarita. Slick brown plastics are a highlight of the Boiler Room Bar and Grill, where hi-tech touches carry out that mechanical theme. Exta-Z Disco is a favorite spot for the late-night set.

Tropicale seems a well-thought-out ship, with a game room, library, card room, casino, two lounges, and a swimming pool all located on Promenade Deck. Part of that deck features an enclosed promenade and part of it is open.

One deck higher on the ship, the Lido Deck features another pool and that casual Boiler Room snackbar. Atop that the veranda and sports decks feature a gymnasium with all the required shiny equipment plus ladies' and mens' health clubs, two saunas, and lots of deck room for sunning. On the sports deck you can practice your golf drive across the biggest water hazard of them all, or try trap shooting, table tennis, and shuffleboard.

For the youngsters there's a children's playroom tucked away on the Empress Deck right near a wading pool for the pint-size water baby.

Shops? Of course, including a beauty salon and barbershop.

Cabins

Because this ship was built for the line and not reconstructed from an older ship, every cabin on board—except suites, of course—is similar in size and shape, planned rather than carved from available space.

In the outside cabins the portholes are often long windows rather than the brass-trimmed circles of days past. And almost all rooms on board have twin beds that convert to king-size beds by the simple expedient of pushing them together.

Outside cabins on the *Tropicale* are very large, and suites are really something. Cabins have closed-circuit televisions too, mounted high up in the corners of the room, so you can watch a film right in your room. There's a full television production studio aboard too.

The price ranges are very similar to those aboard the other ships—in fact they're identical, except that the two upper level categories, 10 and 11, are missing on this craft. Veranda suites are $1795 per person, but there are no demi-suites or extra, extra-large outside cabins.

Outside cabins begin in Category 9 and range down through Categories 8, 7, and 6. Prices go from $1395 per person in Category 9 to $1245 per person in Category 6, and there's little difference except overall size of the cabins.

Inside cabins begin in Category 6, but these also have twins that can be pushed together to become king-size beds.

The five lowest categories aboard begin at Category 5 and go down through Category 1, just as they do on the other ships. Prices for those categories range from a high of $1195 to a low of $950 per person. In Categories 3, 2, and 1 the beds are upper and lower berths, and the top price in those categories is $1075 per person for the week's cruise in peak season.

Single rates and charges for a third or fourth person sharing a cabin are the same as on the other ships. Children's fares are also the same.

HOLIDAY: Not yet completed when this book went to press, the *Holiday* is scheduled to be a $170-million ship Carnival is calling their "superliner." It's slated for delivery in mid-1985, so you'll be hearing plenty about this 45,000-ton craft built in Aalborg, Denmark. Recent reports indicate that the new ship will be 742 feet long and 94 feet wide, meaning she will be large indeed. Her 725 cabins will accommodate 1450 passengers, about 350 more with all the upper berths filled.

In 95% of the cabins, the line says, twin beds will convert to king-size beds as do the sleepers aboard the *Tropicale*. In fact nearly all the cabins aboard will have that configuration, with only about 25 of the total also equipped with upper and lower berths. All cabins will have closed-circuit television, stereo, telephones, and 110-volt AC current too.

I've never quite understood who cares how many outside and inside cabins there are aboard a ship, but if you're curious: about 62% of the cabins will be outside accommodations and 10 of those will be veranda suites with balconies overlooking the sea.

Two decks aboard the new ship will be devoted to public rooms, including two restaurants, each with seats for 450, six bars, a full casino, three outdoor pools, and a children's playroom. Such names as Casablanca Bar, Library Bar, and Bus Stop Café may give you a bit of an idea how they'll be trimming out these rooms. In fact it's likely that the decor aboard will be similar to what you'll find on the *Tropicale* since the same design team has been hired for the new ship.

Fitness enthusiasts will find a gymnasium aboard. All the usual shipboard games from shuffleboard to skeet shooting will be available, and there will be some sort of golf facilities, a putting green perhaps, on board. When you've worn yourself to a frazzle, you can relax it off in the sauna.

Unless the line makes a radical alteration in course, prices on this ship will be the same as the line's other seven-day cruisers.

6. Chandris Cruise Lines

Contact: Chandris Cruise Lines, 666 Fifth Ave., New York, NY 10019 (tel. toll free 800/223-0848; or in New York 212/586-8370, in California 213/272-2141, in Florida 305/371-7620).

Cruising Grounds: Bahamas, Mexico, Puerto Rico, several Caribbean islands (itineraries vary, so check with Chandris).

Itineraries: *Britanis*—

IN WINTER: Miami–Nassau–Miami *or* Miami–Cozumel–Cancun–Key West–Miami

IN SUMMER: New York–Bermuda

Victoria—San Juan–St. Thomas–Martinique–Grenada–La Guaira (Caracas)–Curaçao–San Juan year-round

---

Chandris is a Greek line better known in Europe than it is on this side of the Atlantic. It's particularly difficult to keep up with what Chandris is doing: first, because they seem to have a small labor force Stateside that doesn't spend much time publicizing the line; and second, because they move their vessels around often and lease or sell them frequently. That makes it hard to say just what Chandris will own, operate, or otherwise have an interest in when you read this.

Don't get the idea that what you are about to peruse is written in stone. Chandris is changeable. It's a good idea to check with Chandris to see where they're going, if you have some specific ports in mind. Let's take a look at the line just so you'll have some idea what to expect generally, if not specifically.

Chandris was first organized, so the story goes, way back in 1915 by a gentleman named John D. Chandris, who sailed into the passenger cruise business in 1922. Born in the eastern Mediterranean area that has been home to such shipping magnates as Onassis and Niarchos, Chandris also made a foray into the hotel business in the Greek islands and on the mainland.

Meanwhile Chandris Cruise Lines bought, sold, and operated a raft of ships, including the *Ariadne, Monterey, Lurline, America, President Hoover, Aurelia,* and the *Dunottar Castle,* which were later to be renamed the *Amerikanis, Ariane, Britanis, Ellinis, Italis, Regina Prima, Romanza,* and *Victoria,* with a few names in between.

At this moment the only two Chandris vessels sailing in North American waters are the *Britanis,* which was booking two- and five-night cruises to the Bahamas and to the Yucatán Peninsula respectively; and the *Victoria,* which was sailing from San Juan to a variety of ports in the Caribbean on three slightly different itineraries.

To give you an idea how things change while staying the same, the *Britanis* once plied the routes the *Victoria* sails.

In Europe, the Chandris' *Romanza* sails the Mediterranean, concentrating on the Greek islands.

Two other ships, one of them the *Amerikanis,* returned to Chandris by Costa, and another ship, the *Galileo Galilei,* are scheduled to join the line in 1984.

BRITANIS: Like other Chandris vessels, this venerable old lady is showing her age. Built in 1932, this 25,245-ton ship has 552 cabins and carries twice that many passengers, and can carry even more in cabins outfitted with additional berths.

Public Rooms

This is no luxury ship, but then it doesn't pretend to be. It is, however, about as perfect as you can get for a first-time sailing trip, particularly if you work all week and can't get much more than a weekend off. When we sailed on a weekend cruise aboard this ship, a dozen people told me they were on their first cruise and having the time of their lives!

The food aboard the *Britanis* gets special kudos from many who sail on her. Greeks love their food almost as much as Italians, so it's easy to understand why they cook well, if not showily, aboard.

You dine in one of the two dining rooms, the Waikiki or the Coral Dining Room, the latter the smaller, more intimate of the two. Both are down on a lower deck (Barbados Deck to be exact), so they're not as glassy and as showy as those you'll find on other ships.

Activities

Just behind the casino is a nice card room, and on the opposite side of the ship the Gallery Bar is an attractive hideaway for a quiet post-dinner drink. If you smoke and are tired of hearing snide remarks from those who don't, you can join other protesters at the Smoke Bar which features a special smoking room at one end.

Of course there's a swimming pool, complete with Marine Bar, adjacent to the disco, and on the main deck the youngsters will find a playroom for their sailing pleasure.

You can work off the calories at dancersize classes, visit the sauna, try skeet shooting or table tennis, go to the movies, or do nothing at all—in the sunshine.

Each night there's a different show in the nightclub ranging from high-kicking showgirls in sparkles to dance bands and singers. A casino provides gamesters with craps, slots, blackjack, and roulette to while away the evening.

Cabins

Most of the cabins on this ship are inside sleepers and not all of them have private facilities. Many have one or two extra berths, and some can even accommodate six!

One large cabin we saw had an upper and lower berth, a chair that converted into a bed, and a couch that flipped over to become a sleeping spot. It also featured two very large closets and a third all fitted out with a bevy of drawers, obviously designed to accommodate the trunkloads of clothes travelers once packed on long transoceanic voyages.

The cabin price categories range from A to M, with A the lowest and M the highest prices aboard. Peak season aboard is the last week in

December and February through April. In the off-season you pay about $20 to $30 less per person for a two-night cruise. Five-night sojourns in peak season are $130 and $210 more per person than a two-night cruise in the same season.

Let's look at some of the prices for a cabin on a two-night cruise in peak winter season. Decks on board are named after popular Caribbean ports—Aruba, Barbados, Caracas—and the highest prices are to be found on the main and upper decks where large suites and junior suites with two lower beds and a sitting room are $385 or $455 a person for the two-night cruise to Nassau. Categories J and K are outside cabins with two lower beds, somewhat larger and more elaborate than other outside quarters on board. For one of these cabins you'll pay $315 to $345 per person for a two-night trip.

Two categories of large inside suites, Categories H and I, also feature two lower beds and are $275 to $295 per person for a two-night cruise.

Outside cabins with a double bed are $295 per person for the trip and similar inside quarters with double beds are $255 to $275 per person for a two-night cruise. If you don't mind sleeping in upper and lower berths, outside cabins with those accommodations are $240 per person for a two-night cruise in peak season. Similar inside cabins in Category C are $225.

Category B cabins are smaller, inside, and have lower and upper berths. One of those is $189 per person for a two-night cruise.

To partake of the rockiest of rock-bottom rates aboard you will have to give up a private bath, although there'll be a bathroom and shower nearby and a sink in your room. For one of those outside or inside cabins with two lower beds and lower and upper berths, the cost is just $169 per person for a two-night cruise.

Single rates are double the price for the cabin if there are two lower berths in it, 150% of the fare if the cabin has upper and lower berths.

Budget $17 for each adult for port taxes, $11 for each child under 16. On a five-night cruise those charges are $24 for each adult and child.

Third and fourth adults sharing a cabin pay $140 for a two-night cruise, and children under 16 are $80 each (under 3 they cruise free).

VICTORIA: Chandris's *Victoria,* once known as the *Dunottar Castle,* weighs in at 14,917 tons and is fitted out to carry 500 passengers. Her size helps her work her way into small ports, so the ship follows some interesting itineraries.

In fact she has three different itineraries. All begin in San Juan, where you board anytime after 3 p.m., have dinner on board, and sail at about midnight. The next morning you're in St. Thomas for the day, followed by a day in Martinique, a day in St. Vincent, a stop at La Guaira (the port for Caracas), then on to Caraçao. After one day at sea you arrive back in San Juan early Monday morning.

On another *Victoria* itinerary you visit Aruba instead of Curaçao, and on a third you substitute Barbados for St. Vincent, Antigua for Aruba or Curaçao, and add a stop at St. Maarten in place of a day at sea.

Public Rooms

Built in 1939 and refurbished in 1975, this ship offers a gym and sauna, plus a playroom for children. Her cinema is a two-story spot with a balcony.

Swimmers will find two swimming pools aboard. Oddly enough, they're back to back on the Lido Deck, with a cute little arching bridge crossing between the two. To reach this pool deck from the upper deck you can make quite a grand entrance on a swirling staircase. There's not a great deal of sun space aboard.

If you like to read or join some new friends for bridge games, there's a large library and card room just off an enclosed promenade area known as the winter garden.

Nights begin with dinner in the Roman Dining Room. Later the ship comes alive with some rousing Vegas-y entertainment. The click of the little white ball spins into the wee hours in the casino, and a nice hideaway spot is the small bar just off the Bamboo Club on the Sapphire Deck.

Cabins

One of the line's more contemporary ships following a renovation in the '70s, the *Victoria* has a very large number of outside cabins, so you have a good chance of seeing the Caribbean from your cabin window. That's especially nice when you're sailing, as the *Victoria* does, among many small islands.

The rate range aboard the *Victoria* begins at $599 per person for inside cabins with private bathroom and shower, and rises to $999 per person for a large two-bed outside suite with bath. There are six of those suites aboard, each named after a Bahamian island—Bimini, Eleuthera, Antigua, Inagua —and two mini-suites, Andros and Abaco, that are about $79 cheaper.

Cruise rates begin with Grade VC16, the highest priced cabins, and move down to VC1. Cabins aboard are quite simply laid out and there are quite a large number of outside accommodations.

The next price down from suites are two-bed outside cabins, which range in price from $870 per person in Grade VC14 down to $760 per person in VC7, with each price category dropping about $20 to $25.

Those in the mid-priced VC11 category ($799 per person) are outside cabins on the Emerald Deck, have two beds, and measure about 22 by 9 feet. Those with the letter C (for Coral Deck) ahead of their number are similar and a bit cheaper; a sample size would be 15 by 9 feet. If you like a double bed, there are some available aboard on C and E decks. Several of those double-bedded accommodations are quite reasonably priced too, at $715 per person for the week-long cruise.

Inside cabins range from Grade VC7 to VC4 and are $715 to $695 per person. The lowest priced accommodations on board are upper- and lower-berth accommodations inside, with bathrooms, for $649 to $549 per person.

Some cabins aboard have upper berths to accommodate a third sailor, and if there's a fourth, that person occupies a portable bed. Third and fourth passengers travel at the minimum rate of $599. If they are children between ages 1 and 12, they pay only 50% of the minimum fare.

Some cabins have been set aside for singles. Those are on the Coral, Emerald, and Sapphire Decks, and are priced at $870 to $999 for the week-long cruise.

In the late spring the ship sails to Europe where she spends the summer cruising the Mediterranean with some trips to Scandinavian ports.

As you can see, prices aboard are quite reasonable. Per diem rates begin at a low $85 per person, rising in the middle ranks to $114 per person for an outside cabin and in the very highest realms to $142 a day per person for a suite. Budget an additional $25 per person for port taxes.

7. Clipper Cruise Line

Contact: Clipper Cruise Line, 120 South Central, St. Louis, MO 63105 (tel. tol free 800/325-0010, or 314/727-2929).

Cruising Grounds: summer—U.S. East Coast and Northeast; winter—Caribbean islands (itineraries vary, so check with Clipper).

Itineraries: *Newport Clipper—*

IN SUMMER: Boston–Plymouth–Nantucket–Martha's Vineyard–Newport–New Bedford–Boston

IN SPRING AND FALL: Baltimore–Yorktown–Crisfield–Oxford–St. Michaels–Annapolis–Baltimore

IN WINTER: St. Thomas–Tortola–Virgin Gorda–Jost Van Dyke–St. John–St. Thomas

---

In 1983 with considerable fanfare a new cruise line was born in, of all places, St. Louis! The first of the Clipper Line ships is the *Newport Clipper,* a sparkling vessel outfitted in contemporary fabrics and lovely bleached maple trim.

Aboard you'll find a clubby atmosphere enjoyed by those in search of visits to interesting ports—particularly historic American ones.

Built in St. Louis, the ship has an all-American look too, from the fresh-faced young midwesterners who man her with a smile to the delicate pastel decor, wide open spaces of public rooms, and sleek contemporary furnishings.

This spiffy new line is a departure from the norm in cruise lines in many ways, not the least of which is the size of its one ship. Only 207 feet long and carrying just 100 passengers, the *Newport Clipper* is something between a private yacht and a full-fledged cruise ship. In fact they call this ship, which is small enough to negotiate inland waterways between New England and Florida, an "ultra-yacht."

"One of the worst mistakes we ever made was to call this Clipper *Cruise* Lines," a line executive told us. "While it was still being built (in 1983), we found ourselves saying 'No' to 'Does it have a casino?' and 'Does it have elevators?' We should have called ourselves Clipper Yacht Line."

Two more facts: you'll find stewardesses, rather than stewards, taking care of your cabin and serving meals and drinks; and there are no facilities for children.

NEWPORT CLIPPER: The *Newport Clipper* travels a sedate ten miles an hour, and because it has a flat hull and a mere eight-foot draft, can sail into shallow waters denied larger craft. That's why you'll find the ship visiting such exotic ports as Tortola and Peter Island during its winter in the Caribbean. Intriguing ports are indeed what lure most passengers aboard.

Itineraries of this very handsome new craft vary widely. In the spring and fall she's likely to be sailing on cruises the line calls its "Colonial South" journeys, from historic Savannah, Georgia, to St. Simon's Island, Charleston, antique St. Augustine, Palm Beach, and Fort Lauderdale on the way from and to its winter itinerary, which in 1984 included stops in such offbeat Virgin Islands waters as Bitter End on Virgin Gorda, Road Town on Tortola, and Caneel Bay, that posh Rockefeller enclave on St. John Island.

In summer the ship can be found touring some of the nation's historic spots: Williamsburg, Yorktown, Baltimore, Annapolis, Boston, Nantucket, Newport, New Bedford, Nantucket, Martha's Vineyard.

Because the ship has such a variety of itineraries, one of its selling points is that repeat passengers can sail different itineraries four times a year if they've a mind to do so—and at about $180 a day per person.

In December 1984 a sister ship, the *Nantucket Clipper,* joins the line, and a third vessel, the *Charleston Clipper,* is slated for delivery in 1985.

Activities

Not even the line denies that this small ship is designed in every way—including cost and ambience—for a certain kind of person. If you want lots of nightlife, plenty of rip-roaring on-board activities, bars, games, and organized events, the *Newport Clipper* is not for you.

If, on the other hand, you like to keep reasonably early hours and to fill your days and nights with some fascinating sightseeing, quiet walks and talks, you ought to adore this sparkling new seafarer.

Most of your fellow passengers will be retired, affluent folks who are also sophisticated travelers to whom the intimacy and interesting itinerary of this small craft are particularly appealing. Those we've talked to who have sailed this ship seemed quite enthusiastic about the young crew, despite some inconveniences attributable to inexperience.

This is no ship for the handicapped as there are no elevators and the stairs are steep. There's also no doctor aboard, although daily port stops mitigate this lack.

Entertainers are brought aboard at some ports, and video movies are shown on two televisions aboard. You can also tune in the morning and evening news on these televisions.

Public Rooms

Throughout the vessel you'll see beautiful blonde bleached-maple trim and light contemporary earth tones. Big, big windows everywhere make this ship as open in feeling as any craft we've ever seen.

The main gathering spot is a forward lounge that's decked out in pale pastel shades of aqua and peach. It has a small bar, some comfortable low chairs and couches, and a bookcase in the corner that serves as library.

Sports fans can swim in the pool or jog around the deck (18 times around is a mile—that's how small we're talking about here!) or work out on the Sun Deck.

Life aboard is casual, with one seating at dinner and no formal nights. They do draw the line at jeans for dinner, although your Calvins will do just fine for the occasional barbecues on deck or ashore on some of the more remote Caribbean islands visited in winter.

Decked out in green and white, the dining room is small and intimate, with tall windows, tables for four and six, chic hunter-green china. With the small number of passengers there's just one seating for dinner and assigned seating only for that meal. Breakfast is at 8 a.m., lunch at 12:30 p.m., and dinner at 7:30 p.m.

Beige carpets run throughout this ultra-yacht, which has some cabins that can be converted to accommodate three. Radios in each cabin bring prerecorded music, including a jazz channel, to your room.

Lots of handsome little touches make this small cruise ship a very special place. Baskets of African violets adorn the pretty pastel lounge, and contemporary artwork is subtle and serene.

Cabins

Every cabin on board is an outside cabin, many opening onto an outside deck (not ideal on rainy days). Each has its own small bath and is decorated in those same light beiges and delicate earthy tones. Big windows let in lots of light and three closets offer ample space for even the most extensive wardrobes. Cabins on the forward end of the ship are quietest, and a real blessing during early-morning departures.

In the cabins you'll find a very light and airy look created by tailored cream-colored bedspreads in a heavy cottony fabric sparked with soothing earth tones. More of that handsome bleached maple appears in the dressers, wardrobes, and trim around the beds. Beds are only about six feet long, so really tall folks will have to scrunch up a bit. You can tuck your luggage in beneath the wood-trimmed beds. Pleated fabric blinds on the windows are an interesting touch.

Cabins are divided into five price categories, one of those for single staterooms. The highest price category is Category 5 (for singles) and Category 4, with prices descending from there. To give you an idea what you'll pay, let's look at the rates for a seven-day cruise.

The prettiest cabin aboard—and the most expensive—is L24, which features huge windows, a desk (that's a feature in all rooms), dresser, and triple mirror, plus a full-length mirror. It can accommodate three, with the third occupying a pull-down bunk. For one of these outside double staterooms measuring 138 square feet the cost is $1325 per person for a seven-day trip.

Slightly smaller outside double rooms with two lower beds are located on the bow end of the main deck and the aft end of the lounge deck. For one of these you'll pay $1275 for a week's cruise.

Category 2 quarters are a bit smaller yet, about 121 square feet, and cost $1235 per person for a week-long trip.

The lowest priced category on board, Category 1, features cabins the same size as Category 2 cabins, but located toward the bow where the ship begins to curve inward so they seem a bit smaller. One of those is $1195 per person for a week's cruise.

Single travelers will be happy to hear that there are single rooms aboard, but you pay a premium for them: $1695 for a seven-day cruise, as compared to double stateroom rates which range from $1195 to $1325 per person for week-long voyages. A third person sharing a stateroom pays $500.

8. Commodore Cruise Line

Contact: Commodore Cruise Line, 1007 North American Way, Miami, FL 33132 (tel. toll free 800/327-5617, toll free in Florida 800/432-6793, or 305/358-2622).

Cruising Grounds: Haiti, Jamaica, Grand Cayman, Mexico (Cozumél), St. Thomas, Puerto Rico, Dominican Republic.

Itineraries: *Boheme*—Miami–Port au Prince–Port Antonio–Grand Cayman–Cozumel–Miami year-round

Caribe I—Miami–St. Thomas–San Juan–Puerto Plata–Miami year-round

---

Commodore likes to call its two vessels the "Happy Ships" and why not? Aboard the *Caribe I* or the *Bohème* you'll be visiting some of the Caribbean's best loved ports and traveling on a line that's been around long enough to know how to create "happy."

The line aims to please a lively young crowd looking for a few days of fun and sun at reasonable prices, and it does that very successfully.

Based in Miami, Commodore's rainbow-striped funnels have been seen here since 1966 when a Miami Beach hotel developer named Sanford Chobol saw the wave of the future and surfed it. He bought a ship, named it the *Bohème,* and began sailing it on cruises from Miami to the Caribbean. Now owned by a Swedish company, the line operates two ships, the *Caribe I* (once known as the *Olympia)* and the *Bohème,* both of them registered in Panama.

Of the two, the *Caribe I* is the larger, weighing in at 23,000 tons and carrying 900 passengers, with space for 300 more in extra bunks. Her smaller sister, the *Bohème,* is an 11,000-ton ship and carries 438 passengers.

We'd say the line's best selling point is its reasonable price, which at last check, for a week-long cruise ranged from $649 per person for inside staterooms with upper and lower berths to $999 for deluxe suites with two lower or one double bed and honeymoon staterooms with double bed and sitting area.

Special prices for third and fourth passengers sharing a room make these ships particularly attractive to families. You'll see many aboard. Commodore also has some very attractive money-saving fly/cruise programs from 84 gateway cities across the U.S.

Commodore has a reputation for good food, and is proud to say that it produces all its own goodies rather than offering the cooking duties to a concession operator as many ships do.

The *Bohème* sails on week-long Saturday-to-Saturday cruises from Miami to Port-au-Prince in Haiti, Port Antonio in Jamaica, Grand Cayman, and Cozumél. Her sister ship, the *Caribe I,* also departs on Saturday from Miami for week-long cruises to St. Thomas, San Juan, and Puerto Plata, Dominican Republic.

Activities

Commodore wants to create happiness aboard its ships. One of the ways it does that is with some interesting theme cruises. For example, in the fall there's an Oktoberfest complete with om-pah-pah band, German beer, and fat pretzels. In the traditionally slow months the line also revs up business with a popular country and western cruise with all the requisite nyah-nyah-nyah wailing songs and lots of clogging and cowboy boots.

In spring the line, which was once registered in West Germany, takes its cue from what goes on in Europe each spring: wine. Commodore sponsors a Mayfest featuring European wine and cheese tasting and plenty of Alpine music. On national holidays like the Fourth of July, New Years' Eve, and Easter, there are appropriately themed festivities.

Even if you don't make a theme cruise, you'll find plenty of fun aboard—casinos, giftshops, snappy productions in a double-deck theater, intimate entertainment in a piano bar, steel band entertainment from the very first second aboard.

BOHÈME: Commodore's small 11,000-ton *Bohème* came to Miami as a new ship and went into service here in 1968. That means that for more than 15 years she's been sailing the seas between Florida and the Caribbean, so you can certainly rely on the line's familiarity with this kind of cruising.

On board you'll find that *La Bohème* opera theme reflected in the names of many of the ship's public rooms. Not only are they named after characters in the opera, but also for Paris landmarks frequented by artists of the romantic period of the early 1800s.

Public Rooms

On the Promenade Deck, for instance, you'll find the Café des Artistes, a small snackbar perky with flower-sprigged red and yellow print on white-metal furniture. An interesting Mondrian-like graphic is painted on a bright-blue wall. There's an antiquey jukebox in the corner. Nearby is the ship's tiny swimming pool and small open deck area.

On the main deck you'll find the Puccini and Paris Dining Rooms, both pretty rooms, although we prefer Paris. Puccini features lacquered metal furniture upholstered in gray velvety fabric offset by a gray and russet carpet. A small semicircular room, this dining room is all glassed in with tinted windows, and is very bright and lively.

Meanwhile the Paris Dining Room offers one wall of big windows, but is a darker, more intimate dining room with natural wood featured in stylized captain's chairs decked out in shades of rose. Round wall lamps add a golden glow to the room, and the blue napery picks up colors in the carpeting. The windows have pretty drapes drawn to the center and tied.

The food served in both dining rooms is basic American cuisine, which might include such choices as yellowtail, loin of pork roast, baked chicken, and roast prime rib with all the usual starters, salads, soups, and desserts.

A small shop near the dining room is little more than a well-equipped drugstore.

The best spot on the ship is Le Club Mimi, where you can settle into small couches facing each other strung out along a bank of windows draped in pretty blue and white curtains and trimmed with plants. This long room with its equally long bar is so quiet and attractive you won't want to leave. Certainly it's far superior to the adjoining, and much larger, Rodolfo Lounge, which has similarly showy draping on the windows and is decked out in red and white. An attractive ceramic wall hanging at the back complements the room's blue tweed and metal furniture.

On an upper deck the ship's Marcello Lounge is a pretty glassed-in room with a serene green-and-rose decor that's bright and attractively decorated. At night the room becomes the ship's disco.

Carrying just 500 passengers, the ship is often called "cozy" and "intimate" but we're afraid that some people might find it a trifle claustrophobic.

Cabins

Most of the really tight quarters occur in the cabin areas of the ship where the corridors are narrow and dark. Cabins are small and drably decorated in olive chenille bedspreads and dull, dated colors. Orange plastic chairs are often teamed with these spreads.

You won't find modern quarters aboard, although the ship was refurbished in 1977 and goes in for some minor spiffing each year. Many of the bathrooms on board feature hand showers. Bathrooms also contain something we've never seen: foot-long spigots in the bathroom sink.

As in most elderly craft, there is plenty of closet space and some goodlooking wood paneling here and there. If you like a double bed, you'll find some cabins aboard with those accommodations.

If you can secure a cabin with furnishings in an L shape, Cabin 247, for example, you'll have more floor space and the feeling of more space in general.

Even the top suite on board, the Royal Poinciana, is a small spot, although it's quite attractively decorated with creamy bedspreads and pale seafoam green and rose upholstery on the armchairs and couch, plus lots of storage space and a big window. (Would that the line would replace some of that olive drab and puce green with some of these attractive colors.)

Cabin prices aboard are divided into a simplified structure of four categories: inside cabins with upper and lower beds, inside cabins with two lower beds, outside cabins with two lower beds, and suites.

Commodore changes its rates frequently, often lowering them, but for recent winter season sailings they were $999 per person for suites, $899 per person for outside cabins with two lower beds, $799 per person for inside staterooms with two lower beds, and $649 per person for inside rooms with upper and lower berths. Singles pay $799 or $899.

CARIBE I: One of two ships operated by Commodore Cruise lines, the *Caribe I* can trace her ancestry back to 1953 when she was known as the *Olympia.* Much bigger than her sister ship in the line, the *Caribe I* weighs 23,000 tons and carries 900 passengers. You'll see fabulously beautiful signs of her age aboard in acres of handsome polished woods and curving art deco lines that can rival anything Radio City Music Hall has to offer!

Wood is everywhere, absolutely everywhere. There are wooden columns here, wood trim there, marquetry on the walls of the dining room, even an inlaid wood wall clock. As you enter the ship, a brass information desk glitters and huge brass-and-glass doors feature a deco design. Passageways are lined in wood and there are gleaming brass touches everywhere you look.

Scheduled for a refurbishment in 1984, this handsome aging lady can use the facelift in some areas, but they'd better not touch all those woods and deco furbelows. Antiquarians, arise.

Public Rooms

Our favorite spot on the *Caribe I* is the library, which surely ranks as one of the most plushly-comfy reading rooms afloat. You sink right into the overstuffed flower-print chairs scattered about this rose and gray, wood-paneled room. If you can stay awake, you'll think you've dropped back an eon or two into the days of quill pens and old English manse libraries where Heathcliff brooded—a dreamy spot indeed.

If you're not of a reading-meditating-napping turn of mind, head for the Grand Lounge, where chrome glitters amid beige and pink furnishings. Tall windows give this faintly circular room an airy look similar to what you'll find in the Caribbean Dining Room, where gray, peach, and rust create a look that's contemporary, if a bit shopworn. No doubt the refurbishing project will improve this high-ceilinged room, which already features beautiful marble tiles and pretty tinted mirrors etched with mermaids.

There's a full casino aboard with all the requisite blackjack, roulette, and other gambling games, plus a striking black and red carpet adorned with hearts, clubs, spades, and diamonds.

A small showroom up high on the ship has tiny unusual hexagonal marble tables on tall spindly brass legs and chrome chairs upholstered in a pink that matches the drapes on a bank of windows down both sides. Burgundy and gray complete a very slick color scheme here.

In the Out Island Disco you can dance until you drop, and in the Out Island Club, also up there on the Sun Deck, you can have a quiet drink.

Two small shops can help inveterate shoppers pass some time, and there's plenty of deck space for strolling and sunning.

Cabins

Cabins on board this ship are roomy. Many of them feature pretty wood paneling, and all have some wood trim. Outside staterooms have about 200 square feet of space, inside cabins about 142 square feet. All have wall-to-wall carpeting, radios with music channels, telephones, old but serviceable private bathrooms, and plenty of storage space.

Commodore recently introduced a simplified pricing structure which divides prices into four categories: inside cabins with upper and lower beds, inside cabins with two lower beds, outside cabins with two lower beds, and suites. Rates for winter-season sailings were $999 per person for suites, $899 per person for outside cabins with two lower beds, $799 per person for inside staterooms with two lower beds, and $649 per person for inside rooms with upper and lower berths. Singles pay $799 or $899.

Deluxe suites feature two lower beds or a double bed, a separate sitting area, big closets, and a comfortable couch.

Moving down a category, outside staterooms are large enough for a family, with two lower beds and an adjoining stateroom with one lower bed that becomes a sofa. Some rooms in this category have three or four lower beds.

Single travelers can choose from two categories of cabins: Category 11, all outside staterooms with one lower bed, or Category 12, all inside accommodations with one lower bed.

Third and fourth adults sharing a stateroom with upper berths pay $395 each. Children under 12 sharing a stateroom with folding upper berths pay $295 each. Add $20 per person for port taxes.

Per diem rates begin at a very low $93, rise to $114 to $128 in the middle ranks, and finally to about $143 for the highest-priced accommodations aboard.

9. Costa Cruises

Contact: Costa Cruises, One Biscayne Tower, Miami, FL 33131 (tel. toll free 800/462-6782, or 305/358-7325).

Cruising Grounds: Cartagena (Colombia), Mexican West Coast, Panama Canal, Alaska, Puerto Rico, Curaçao, St. Vincent, St. Maarten, Barbados, St. Lucia, Antigua, Grenada, Martinique, Guadeloupe, St. Thomas.

Itineraries: *Carla Costa*—San Juan–Curaçao–La Guaira (Caracas)–St. Vincent–Guadeloupe–St. Thomas–San Juan year-round

Daphne—

IN WINTER: San Juan–St. Maarten–Martinique–Barbados–St. Lucia–St. Thomas–San Juan

IN SUMMER: Vancouver–Wransell–Endicott Arm Fjord–Juneau–Skasway–Davidson and Rainbow Glacier–Ketchikan–Vancouver

---

Costa's yellow smokestack with its big blue "c" in the center is a familiar sight in the Caribbean, and has recently become a familiar sight in Alaskan waters as well. It has long been a common sight in the Mediterranean, birthplace of this large fleet.

Among the world's largest passenger lines, with six ships in its fleet, Costa has just signed up a seventh craft. This winter the line is expecting delivery of a new addition to the line, the former *Marconi,* which will be renamed the *Costa Riviera.* Extensively renovated in 1983, the *Costa Riviera* is scheduled to begin sailing from Florida to the Caribbean in late 1984.

Rumor has it that the line's new ship—and perhaps some of its others—will be sailing from Port Everglades. In this case there's a very good chance rumor might be right—the new president of the line, Howard Fine, a former Cunard executive, has himself moved to Fort Lauderdale recently and says there's a "strong" possibility the ship will do likewise.

Wherever it docks, Fine says, the new *Costa Riviera* will feature a very special itinerary on a liner offering "European luxury unlike anything now sailing the Caribbean."

A family-owned company, the Costa can trace its history as far back as 1860 when two Costa brothers began an import business in the Mediterranean. That business eventually extended to passenger ships and soon there was a fleet of Costa ships. That large fleet, some of which bear the names of Costa grandchildren, is now spread around the globe.

There are always lots of changes at Costa Lines too. Ships sail under the aegis of the line for a time and then are sold or chartered by another line, or another line's ships are bought or chartered by Costa. For instance the *Amerikanis,* which was operated by Costa in 1983 on three- and four-day sailings from Miami to the Bahamas, is no longer part of the line. A sister ship, the *World Renaissance,* also has disappeared from the line's roster. Or at least those two statements were true when this was written.

There are still plenty of ships remaining, so many that the line's officials remember them as two Cs, two Ds, two Es, and an R. Here's what that means:

Those two Cs are the *Columbus,* which sails in South America in the winter and in Europe in the summer, but rarely if ever stops at any North American port; and the *Carla C,* which sails on from San Juan to Curaçao, Caracas, St. Vincent, Guadeloupe, and St. Thomas.

The two Ds are the *Danae,* which sails in Mediterranean waters in the summer and often to South America in the winter and the *Daphne,* a winter Caribbean sailor that returns to the Mediterranean in summer. Both are luxury cruisers carrying only 400 passengers on longer-than-average cruises. (In 1985 the *Danae* is scheduled for a world cruise, perhaps beginning in Florida.)

Daphne, twin to the *Danae* and at 16,330 tons one of the line's smaller ships, is scheduled for two-week Caribbean cruises from Florida in the winter of 1985. Both the Ds are luxury vessels but the *Daphne* is the one you'll see in North American waters. In summer the ship heads for Alaska where it sails on weekly voyages from Vancouver to Skagway, Ketchikan, Endicott Arm, and Davidson and Rainbow Glaciers. Prelude and prologue voyages take her through the Panama Canal and on Mexican Riviera cruises.

Two Es are the *Enrico C* and the *Eugenio.* The *Enrico C* sails from Venice through the Mediterranean, and the *Eugenio C,* flagship of the line, sails in South American waters in winter, in the Mediterranean in the summer.

R is for *Riviera,* a ship scheduled to go into service from Florida to the Caribbean, probably on week-long voyages beginning in late 1984.

Activities

On many of its ships the crews *parla l'italiano, grazzie,* and cook *italiano* too. That *cucina italiano* is one of the line's strongest selling points, backed by some good international cabaret entertainment and a wide variety of destinations encircling the globe.

Here's a shopping tip for Costa sailors: look for goodies emblazoned with this line's logo. It's one of the spiffiest logos afloat, and Costa is so proud of it that they devote an entire shop on some ships to the sale of their logo-ed T-shirts and ashtrays, duffle bags and pencils.

Like other Caribbean vessels the Costa ships offer a full round of entertainment. On the *Daphne,* a more luxurious ship, that entertainment is apt to be just as steady but a bit more refined.

Among the activities that will fill your days are skeet shooting, shuffleboard, movies, and of course those daily port stops.

At night, consumption of some sensational dinners occupies a couple of hours, made even more entertaining by special theme evenings. Every night at midnight there's a bountiful buffet, and one night you'll be treated to an on-deck barbecue. Another evening a sumptuous spread is presented right on the polished galley so you can see what goes on behind the scenes.

In the evenings glittery showgirls dazzle you with song and dance. International performers sing, dance, and laugh it up for your entertainment, aided and abetted by masquerade evenings, a captain's dinner, and a farewell dinner. Every night there's a show on deck too.

CARLA C: Be at the docks in San Juan on a Saturday, summer or winter, and you'll see the *Carla C* readying for her midnight departure to such alluring ports as Curaçao, La Guaira in Venezuela, Grenada, Martinique, and St. Thomas. What this ship lacks in glamor she makes up with a bubbly Italian crew, good food and wine. Like the cheerful crew, life aboard is informal, with two formal nights scheduled to let you play at dress-up.

Public Rooms

You'll find plenty of public places to while away the hours. Certainly there's plenty to do aboard, and plenty of public rooms in which to do it. Most of those are on the ship's Lido Deck, where a huge circular Observation Lounge features an orchestra for entertainment and a sensational view of emerald isles on the horizon.

At the bow of the ship is the swimming pool, and in between, a balconied theater, a gift shop, several bars, and the Grand Salon, where there's always something happening.

Below on Continental Deck is the ship's dining room, where you'll always have a selection of wonderful pastas plus the usual fancy continental cooking, ranging from succulent beef and veal choices to luscious frilly sinful desserts.

There's a casino aboard too, for those who like to while away the hours with Lady Luck as a companion.

Cabins

All the ship's cabins have private bathrooms and are divided about equally between inside and outside cabins. Those quarters are large, as they are in most older ships, but to our mind they're spartan, a bit dated. If you don't plan to spend much time in your cabin, then this may be just the ship for you.

Cabin prices run from Category 1 (the least expensive quarters) through Category 15 (the costliest spaces). The *Carla C* also has a "value season" and peak-season price. Figure value season as January, late April to mid-June, and August through mid-December. Peak season includes the last week in December, February through mid-April, and late June through mid-August.

Let's look at the price of cabins for a one-week cruise from San Juan in peak season (about $100 less in value season). Free or low-cost air add-on rates are available.

The most luxurious cabins are on the Promenade Deck, where quite large suite accommodations bear such names as Portofino, Acapulco, Puerto Vallarta, Balboa, Tahitian, Cabo San Lucas, Monterrey. These feature two lower beds, a sitting room, and a sofa bed, and are of course quite spacious. For these you will pay $2215 per person for a week's cruise.

If you want to go in style but just a little less in cost, you might consider a Category 12, 13, or 14 cabin on the Promenade Deck. In the price Category 12, outside cabins with two lower beds or a large double bed plus bath/shower combination are $1695, and some of those are extra-large accommodations. In Categories 13 and 14 you are buying a deluxe outside cabin with two lower beds and a sofa bed, or a suite with sitting room and sofa bed, for $1735 or $1865 per person for these more elaborate accommodations. Measurements on one Category 12 outside room are 12½ by 24 feet, and that's very large by anyone's standards.

Three categories of smaller outside cabins (Categories 8, 9, and 10) with two beds, and additional berths if you want to include a third or fourth person, are $1485 to $1595 per person for a week's cruise.

Four categories of inside cabins (Categories 4, 5, 6, and 7) include two lower beds and are $1325 to $1485 per person. Mid-priced inside cabins, those in Category 7, for instance, are $1485 per person and can measure as large as 14 by 23 feet, quite substantial. Two of those are even located up on the Boat Deck where there are only a dozen or so other cabins, all of them outside sleepers with a $1665 per-person price tag in peak season. Down on the main deck a cabin in that price category that seems especially spacious is 401, which has two additional berths as well.

Category 3 is a value-wise selection. In this category are outside cabins, but they have a lower bed and an upper berth. For one of these you'll pay $1270 for a week's cruise.

The lowest prices on the ship are on Pacific Deck, way down in the ship where the cabins are inside cabins and some are very small indeed. However, the price is just $995 to $1095 per person for a week's cruise. Some of these lowest priced accommodations have lower bed and upper berth; others have two lower beds, and sometimes upper berths as well.

A bargain aboard this ship is a special offer for third and fourth occupants of cabins on sailings from late April to early June: they pay just $100 each, making the sharing of a cabin quite economical for four friends or a family. At other times the third- and fourth-person rate is $495 for adults, $250 for children under 12 sharing a cabin with adults.

Per diem prices on this craft range from a low of $156 to a mid-price in the $212 to $272, and deluxe suites at $266 to $316 per person daily. Budget $35 per person for port charges.

Singles pay 150% of the rate for a cabin.

The *Carla C* sails from San Juan to Curaçao, Caracas, St. Vincent, Guadeloupe, and St. Thomas on one-week cruises beginning each Saturday. And don't forget that you can combine the voyage with a week on the *Daphne* if you have two weeks to spare.

DAPHNE: Big staterooms are the pride of this cruise ship, which boasts that even the smallest quarters measure in at 260 square feet. And some of the spiffiest—and most expensive—even have private balconies!

In winter, from about December to April, this sparkling-white craft is in San Juan each Saturday preparing for her midnight sailing to St. Maarten, Martinique, Barbados, St. Lucia, Antigua, and St. Thomas. And these appealing stops can be combined with a week's cruise on the *Carla C* to make a fascinating two-week sojourn.

In summer the ship heads for Alaskan waters, where she sails merrily through the glaciers on glittering seven-day Alaskan sailings. To get into position for those sojourns, in spring and fall the ship features a 17-day Panama Canal odyssey visiting six ports of call between Miami and Los Angeles. Some of the stops on that voyage: Cozumél, Montego Bay, Cartagena, Acapulco, and Mazatlán.

Once in Alaska the *Daphne* sails from Vancouver every Friday from mid-May through mid-September on cruises through the Inside Passage to Wrangell, Endicott Arm, Juneau, Skagway, Davidson and Rainbow Glaciers, and Ketchikan.

Built in 1956 and rebuilt and relaunched in 1976, the *Daphne* is 432 feet long with five passenger decks. Life aboard is casual, but on two nights you can break out the wing collars and long gowns.

Public Rooms

The *Daphne,* at 16,330 tons, is one of the line's smaller ships and Costa likes to call her a "seagoing yacht." While that phrase has a touch of Madison Avenue to it, it is true that all cabins have two lower beds and bathtubs as well as showers, and that the ship is small enough to accommodate all 425 passengers at one sitting in the bright glass-walled Symposium Dining Room.

It's also true that some vessels of comparable size carry nearly twice as many passengers. On this ship you will find one of the highest ratios of space to passengers of any cruise ship. You are practically guaranteed an outside cabin too, since about 90% of the ship's quarters—190 cabins—are outside doubles.

Decks aboard this ship have some tongue-twisting names—Polymnia, Euterpe, Melpomene—evocative of the Greek origins and crew of this ship. Once you've mastered Euterpe (it's pronounced you-*tur*-pea) you'll discover that it's the place to look for almost all the ship's public rooms.

Here you will find the Symposium Dining Room, a pleasant little dining veranda, a shopping arcade, card room, library, and the big main lounge where the nightly action takes place.

Fitness buffs will find a gymnasium aboard, and up top on the Thalia Deck there's space set aside as a sports deck. Something for everybody: gamblers will find a casino aboard.

Fittingly enough the discothèque is up on Terpischore Deck, where you'll also find the swimming pool. On Polymnia Deck the ship's theater is backed by a playroom for the youngsters.

Cabins

Cabins aboard are quite spacious, and with only 400 other passengers you'll find plenty of open public spaces aboard too. A low passenger count means you'll get some very good service as well, a pride of this ship.

Let's look at some of the prices you'll pay for a week-long voyage in Alaska's peak season from the end of June to September. (Value season runs roughly from the end of May through mid-June and the first few weeks of September. At that time you pay $100 less than peak rate.)

To show you what we mean by luxury ships, for openers there are four categories of deluxe suites on board this vessel. All of them have separate living room, refrigerator-bar, television, attractive contemporary decor, plenty of space, and a lofty view. Deluxe suites even have a private balcony for some very private stargazing! Quarters like these range in price from $1850 per person down to $1450 per person for a week-long peak-season Alaska cruise.

Outside doubles in the next six categories (Categories 8, 7, 6, 5, 4, and 3) all have two lower beds. For one of these you pay rates ranging from $2680 per person for a week's cruise to a low of $2090 per person on the Alaska voyage.

Finally, the least expensive quarters on board are inside cabins with two lower beds. The price for one of these Category 1 or 2 cabins is $860 or $945 per person.

Third and fourth adults sharing a cabin are $860; children under 12 are charged $430. Port charges are $30 per person on the Alaska cruise, and single occupants of a double cabin pay 150% of the applicable rate.

Per diem rates for this ship on its peak-season seven-day Alaska cruises run from a low of $123 to $150 to $193 in the mid-price range, and a high of $207 to $264 per person.

COSTA RIVIERA: Once known as the *Marconi,* the 28,000-ton *Costa Riviera* carries 1000 passengers on nine decks. This ship will henceforth be operated by Costa on week-long cruises to the Caribbean. She was scheduled to go into service in the winter of 1984 from a port in South Florida, either Miami or Port Everglades.

10. Cunard Lines

Contact: Cunard Lines, 555 Fifth Ave., New York, NY 10017 (tel. 212/880-7500) for general inquiries; for the *QE2*—tel. toll free 800/221-4700, 800/221-4400 in the Northeast, 800/522-7530 in New York state, or 212/661-7500 in New York City; for other Cunard ships—tel. toll free 800/221-4800, 800/221-4444 in the Northeast, 800/552-7520 in New York state, or 212/661-7505 in New York City).

Cruising Grounds: *QE2*—transatlantic New York—Southampton run, various Caribbean ports, and an around-the-world cruise; other ships—Alaska, Mexican Riviera, La Guaira/Caracas (Venezuela), Grenada, Barbados, St. Lucia, St. Thomas, St. Maarten, Îles des Saintes, Guadeloupe, St. Kitts, Tortola.

Itineraries: *Cunard Countess*—San Juan—La Guaira (Caracas)–St. Vincent–Barbados–Fort de France–St. Thomas–San Juan *or* San Juan–Tortola, Nevis–St. Kitts–Guadeloupe–St. Lucia–St. Maarten–St. Thomas–San Juan year-round

Cunard Princess—

IN SUMMER: Vancouver–Alert Bay–Ketchikan–Tracy Arm–Juneau–Skagway–Haines–Glacier Bay–Petersburg–Ketchikan

IN WINTER: Los Angeles–cruising by Cabo San Lucas–Mazatlan–Puerto Vallarta–Manzanillo–Acapulco–Zihuatanejo–Puerto Vallarta–Mazatlan–cruising by Cabo San Lucas–Los Angeles

Queen Elizabeth II—

IN SUMMER: New York–England

IN WINTER: World cruise from New York, Fort Lauderdale and Los Angeles and some Fort Lauderdale–Caribbean cruises

---

To say Cunard is to say *Queen Elizabeth II,* flagship of this venerable old British line. No other ship is as famous as this queen of the seas whose namesake predecessor set the standards for transatlantic sailings and for cruises of all kinds.

You can see the massive 67,140-ton *QE2* in Florida's Port Everglades several times each winter season, and in summer you can spot her tooting in and out of New York Harbor.

If you're very, very lucky—and quite well-heeled to boot—you can sail with 1700 or so other infatuees on the *Queen*'s annual dream-machine, around-the-world-in-89-days sojourn. For a lot less money you can join one of the shorter Caribbean cruises in early winter or her regular series of five-day New York—Southampton voyages each summer.

If you're treating yourself to the best of everything, you can even combine the elegance of the *Queen* with the very New World pizazz of that needle-nosed, sound barrier–blasting Concorde airplane on a special fly-cruise program.

So huge is the reputation of the *Queen* that even seasoned sailors sometimes forget that there are two other ships in this fancy fleet: the *Cunard Countess* and the *Cunard Princess.*

If this year is like other years, the *Countess* will be sailing on 7- and 14-day journeys through the Caribbean from San Juan all year long, while the *Princess* will alternate between summer Alaska sailings and a winter program of Mexico visits.

Cunard, which is part of Britain's Trafalgar House conglomerate, recently acquired two more top-of-the-line vessesl, the *Vistafjord* and the *Sagafjord,* a beautiful duo formerly operated by Norwegian American Cruises.

Whichever Cunard ship you sail on, you'll become part of a fascinating history that stretches back nearly a century and a half to a far-sighted Nova Scotia merchant named Samuel Cunard. Back in 1839 Cunard dreamed up a plan to operate a mail service on the North Atlantic between England and North America. First he talked the British bureauracy into a mail contract, then he launched a 1150-ton paddlesteamer called the *Britannia* which sailed to Boston from England in the summer of 1840. Fourteen days later the *Britannia* reached American shores, where Cunard was presented with a huge silver cup to commemorate the historic moment. You can still see that cup at the Columbia Dining Room of the *QE2.*

Eight years later Cunard began carrying mail to New York and in 1856 he launched a ship called the *Persia.* That craft was quite a vessel for its day: with paddles 40 feet in diameter, it was twice as long as the *Britannia* and had a speed of 14 knots.

Soon the race was on. Speed became the issue and was to remain a competitive necessity through many a decade. So important was transatlantic speed, in fact, that an award called the Blue Riband was given to the fastest ship on the Atlantic. Cunard disdained participation in that race, but one of the Cunard ships always won it anyway!

It wasn't long before Cunard built two new ships that were to become the yardstick by which ships were to be judged for many a decade to come: the *Queen Elizabeth* and the *Queen Mary.* Built for speed, the two ships could travel at 28.5 knots. The *Queen Mary* was launched first in 1937, followed a year later by her sister ship the *Queen Elizabeth.* By the time the *Queen Elizabeth* rolled off the launching pad, however, the world was at war, so she spent her early history racing across the North Atlantic ferrying troops between England and the U.S.

Tales of the ships' near-misses are legion, but both made it safely through that bitter conflict to receive the praise of a grateful Prime Minister Winston Churchill, who pointed out, quite accurately, that "the world owes them a debt it will not be able to measure."

After the war the two royal sailers began boarding royalty and servants, famous and infamous, and anyone with masses of money, for the transoceanic passage. What an elegant scene it must have been: Afternoon tea on delicate china, violinists playing softly in the background, long lazy days in the sea air, long elegant nights amid fluttering fans and exotic perfumes.

Sadly, it ended in the late 1960s when the *Queen Mary* sailed on her final voyage across the sea to a new life in California, where she remains today, a tourist attraction and hotel.

Her sister ship came to an even more bitter end. She was sailed to Hong Kong to become a floating university, but sank in the harbor there, consumed by fire.

Cunard met the challenge, however. In 1967 the line launched the brand new *QE2,* sent down the rails after a champagne christening by Queen Elizabeth II, granddaughter of the lady who christened the first *Queen.*

You'll now find the *QE2* still making those transatlantic voyages in summer. Just as Cunard was the first, it is now the last remaining line to run a regularly scheduled service from New York to England. In winter the

Queen heads south to Port Everglades for several Caribbean voyages, and to begin her around-the-world trip, usually in early January.

Meanwhile the *Cunard Countess* is a familiar sight in Puerto Rico where she sails year round from San Juan to a variety of interesting Caribbean islands. The *Cunard Princess* spends the summer in Alaska, the winter on Mexican Riviera cruises.

QUEEN ELIZABETH II: There is no more famous ship afloat than this great beauty, which since her construction in 1967 has gone around the world and gone to war. Flagship of Cunard Lines and indeed the flagship of jolly old England herself, the *Queen* is the reigning queen of the seas, no doubt about it.

It makes no matter that the *Norway* is larger, that others are newer, fancier, or more dramatically appointed. This handsome navy-blue vessel with the distinctive red-and-black Cunard funnel carries with her a history and mystique that cannot be touched by any other craft afloat.

She is magnificent, no question about it, and the sight of her sailing majestically off into the sunset is heart-stopping. There's never been one like her, and it's likely there will never be another.

Aboard the *QE2* the British caste system is firmly in place. You travel first class or tourist class, just as passengers did a generation or two ago. Those who pay the most dine in the choicest of the four dining rooms on board, and are treated to cocktails and afternoon tea in a private sitting room, invited to a private party with the captain.

Frankly, we don't think you'll notice these small discriminations. If you're very observant you're even likely to see some of those first-class travelers joining the tourist class fun!

All the restaurants on board are pretty places, and there are plenty of lounges just as beautiful, if not even lovelier, than that first-class haven which was looking a bit worse for the wear before the ship's last round-the-world cruise. So, fear not, you'll never even notice that some people are getting something you're not. And if you do, just contemplate what they're paying for it!

One cannot help but be amazed at the sheer size of everything about this ship. On a recent visit we were overwhelmed to discover the size, of all things, of the ship's hospital! When you stop to think about it, extensive medical facilities are, of course, to be expected on a ship whose long cruises naturally attract older travelers who have had the time to acquire the money and now have the time to stay floating for two or three months. Still, who'd expect to see 15 hospital rooms, plus examining rooms for the crew, a dentist's office, a pharmacy, and finally, a complete operating room!

There are many more examples of the *Queen*'s huge size: she measures 67,107 tons, is 963 feet long and 105 feet wide, and carries a crew of 1000 to serve 1815 passengers! She can trot right along at 28.5 knots, and has 13 decks, 22 elevators, and a 530-seat theater! There are four swimming pools aboard, one of them indoors, plus four dining rooms and seven bars.

Activities

Not even the most blasé soul could fail to be impressed by the sheer numbers of things to see and do on this ship, not to mention the sheer beauty of her deep-blue hull steaming through the seas like a great whale.

Down by the inside pool is a branch of the posh Golden Door Spa, which will coddle you and whip you into shape, not necessarily in that order. Use of the recently expanded Golden Door Spa at Sea is included in the cost of your voyage, so you can justify your cruise by figuring you saved the $2500-a-week that a trip to the land-lubbing Golden Door would cost! That spa includes an exercise area, sauna, massage center, 16 daily exercise classes, a hydrocalisthenics pool, whirlpool baths, yoga, aerobics, and ballet.

A new addition to the ship is a personal computer learning program at sea, equipped with six personal computers, videotape machines, and a library of educational films. Every day there's a seminar showing you how to use the computers, and the center is open 12 hours a day so you can play between sessions.

Another new addition to the ship is a glass "Magrodome," a sliding roof that can be rolled out to cover one of the swimming pools if rain dares fall on the sunseekers below. At night the area becomes an indoor-outdoor disco.

Film fans will find a big balconied theater aboard where top films are shown. Of course there are church services, and there's even a small paneled synagogue tucked away on the ship.

Cunard is proud of its Life Enrichment Program, which in 1984 invited more than 300 stars and experts on board to discuss everything from financial success to psychological well-being. Among those who were featured in the program were Helen Gurley Brown, Vida Sassoon, and Dr. Christiaan Barnard.

The entertainment on board is fabulous.

Top-name entertainers appear: Rita Moreno, Ben Vereen, George Burns, and the orchestra that plays at Buckingham Palce soirées. On her world cruise this year, the *QE2* featured Patti Lupone, star of *Evita,* plus a magician, a French singing star, Latin American dance champions, two comedians, a guitarist, the *QE2* dancers, a variety act, and a classical artist. That's not even to mention lecturers, who have included Maxene Andrews of the Andrews Sisters, a photographer, a television actor, a financial lecturer, a computer expert, and a psychotherapist.

Recent renovations have expanded the Club Lido into an entertainment complex with a sound-and-light show. Decorated in red and black with some gray touches, the room is brand new.

Bridge players will disappear for the whole cruise, participating under the tutelage of expert Ernest Revere. Crafts enthusiasts can learn everything from macramé to woodwork, and photographers can shoot 'em up at photography classes. Joggers have a track to trot on, and get this—a mere 3½ times around is a mile!

Dining Rooms

Dining is more than an event aboard the *QE2*; it's a status game as well. Where you dine on this ship determines who you are.

The Queens Grill seats the 188 top-paying passengers aboard. The Princess Grill serves 102 of the next fiscal group down the line, followed by the Columbia Restaurant which provides for 610 diners. Tables of the World serves the 828 Transatlantic Class passengers.

If you book one of the ship's five lowest priced cabins you'll join those 827 other diners in the Tables of the World Dining Room, a bright and cheerful room with themed decor. Here you'll find five theme areas—British, French, Spanish, Oriental, and Italian—each decked out in representative colors. Cheery square umbrellas reign over these colorful regions.

Tall windows run down both sides of the rooms, and tables for two, four, and six are available, along with some banquette seating. Lamps created from straw fans are an unusual touch. You can select the theme area you prefer. (France's sector is quite pretty.)

On the menu is an impressive list of juices, first courses, soups, fish, entrees, grills, cold meats, vegetables, salads, desserts, fruit and cheese. Dining is more informal here than in the other dining rooms on board, but that certainly doesn't mean you wear your cutoffs and sandals. American entrees predominate too.

The Queen's Grille is a study of royal blue and mahogany, where drapes cover the windows and chandeliers glitter from the raised ceiling. Chrome-framed Erte posters add a contemporary touch to this English library–like room, and a centerpiece made of huge seashells is a showstopper.

In this formal spot you can order anything you can dream up and it will magically appear. We're not guaranteeing ostrich eggs, you understand, but there are all manner of strange delicacies that can be produced with the wave of a whisk.

Outside the Queen's Grille is a sitting room with marble tables on which afternoon tea and pre-dinner cocktails are served.

Next down in the pecking order is the Princess Grill, which has seats for 102 diners. A subdued room, the Princess Grill is an intimate spot offering fine food in beautiful surroundings enhanced by a view of the ocean through broad windows.

The Columbia Restaurant has two graceful statues looming over one end of the dining room and a huge silver urn with dolphin handles at the other. On the tables are stacked-glass lamps that look like little skyscrapers.

Sunlight streams through tall windows down both sides of the room. Tables for two, four, six, and eight are available, and there's a pretty wing off to one side for some very private dining. If you select a cabin in Category E, F, G, or H (toward the lower end of the price list) you'll dine in this serene, and somewhat more casual, setting.

On this ship, as on all cruise ships, all your five or six meals a day are included in the price of your passage. However, on the *QE2* you can sometimes dine in the Queen's Grill if you like by paying a hefty cover charge.

You may think we're going on and on about restaurants here, but remember that where you dine determines your status aboard the *Queen*. So far does the dining connection go, in fact, that some Cunard brochures refer to cabins not by category or type but as "Columbia cabins" or "Tables of the World cabins."

Worry not, however. Any of these restaurants is as lovely as anything the average hometown can boast, and the food varies some but not greatly. Service is good anywhere.

Other Public Rooms

Without a doubt the best shopping area afloat is here on the *QE2*. Located on a mezzanine overlooking an equally dramatic public room, the glittering shops fill an entire floor. Even the most antishopping soul will be lured by the sheer beauty of the displays in windows here—Cartier, Gucci, Adidas, leather wallets with an embossed *QE2* label, lambswool sweaters,

Royal Doulton china, formal wear, golf shirts, you name it. You could come on board without luggage and have no trouble outfitting yourself here.

At one end of the shopping arcade you can make a grand entrance down an arching steel staircase to the dance floor in the very contemporary room below. Decorated in a dramatic burgundy theme, this multilevel Double Down Room is furnished in slick contemporary style with several three-quarter-circle banquettes, a raised stage, and raised wings on either side of a big, big dance floor. Way at the back is our favorite seat, a big semicircular banquette where you can watch everything at once.

Want to send someone flowers? Drop by the complete flower shop on board.

Want to retreat to a small drawing room with a large something-cool? Try the Double Down Bar, where long sheer curtains maintain a sunny atmosphere while keeping out the glare. Beige, wood, and plenty of seductive upholstery make this spot one of the best rooms aboard. If you must, you can watch the sportsters batting tennis balls and working out on the putting green just outside the windows of this getaway spot.

Another top lounge on board is the Midships Bar, a satisfyingly dark spot decked out in velvet so deep green that drinking there is like sipping in a tree house. Tinted-glass doors keep it cooly verdant at any hour, and brass accents glow with constant polishing.

Another huge public area on the quarterdeck is called the Queens Room, and features a soothing tan-and-white decor that's very contemporary. Chairs swivel so you can keep an eye on what's going on anywhere in the room. A beautiful lighted ceiling reigns over a big dance floor with a raised bandstand.

If your idea of paradise is hours and hours of uninterrupted reading, you'll love the library here. While its big windows offer some minor distractions, its incredible array of book titles balances those negatives nicely. This is a full-fledged library, with comfortable couches to sit in, a writing area, and walls and walls and walls of books. What's more, there's even a librarian who really looks the way you'd think a librarian should look, and she keeps things in apple-pie order, all carefully placed by subject. Books with large print are available, as are books in German, Japanese, French, probably Swahili. Beautiful paneled walls make the room a pleasure to look at whether or not you're checking out a book, and the beamed ceiling just adds to the joy of it all.

For gaming amusement there's a handsome room designed in pale olive green velvet with chess, backgammon, and of course, card tables available. If you like games with financial rewards, there's a full casino on board as well.

For youngsters there's a big playroom with a staff dedicated to childhood amusements. Kids even have their own cartoon cinema.

There's a gym, saunas, indoor pool, casino, cardroom with rosewood tables, bank, on-board newspaper, paddle tennis court. There's a kennel in which to park your toy poodle, even an 80-car garage to park your Toyota!

Cabins

As for cabins, well, they come in all sizes, shapes, and prices. All have private facilities and direct-dial telephones that will connect you to anyone in the world. Some even have their own private veranda.

If your ship has really come in, you can book one of the *Queen*'s balconied suites on an around-the-world cruise for a mere $216,000. Prices *start* at $16,085 per person.

Don't panic. Cunard sells the Big Trip, but is smart enough also to sell it in small segments, 10 days to here, 30 to there, 5 to there, all the way around.

Cunard is also smart enough to sell quite a number of other cruises ranging from five-day transatlantic voyages back and forth between New York and England, and delightful Caribbean junkets in the winter sunshine.

You need not be 103 and a zillionaire to sail on the most famous ship afloat. But you can live like one: in 1984 if you sailed one way on the *QE2* New York–England voyages, you could buy a ticket back on the supersonic Concorde for just $499! You can in fact go from New York to London on the *QE2* for as little as $760. Or from Fort Lauderdale to Los Angeles on a 12-day cruise through the Caribbean and the Panama Canal for a low of $2620 per person for an outside cabin.

So for purposes of dreaming and scheming, let's look at the price of a five-day transatlantic trip from New York to England on the *Queen*. Besides the 19 categories of cabins available, the *QE2* also has four fare seasons, known as super-thrift, thrift, intermediate, and high. Super-thrift is in effect on only one sailing in late November, thrift on one in late October, and intermediate from late April through June and mid-August through the first week of October. High season applies to two New York–England sailings in July.

Let's look at the prices of cabins in the intermediate season, which covers most of the ship's voyages.

Top cabin in both location and price is the Queen Mary or Queen Elizabeth suite. These are split-level apartments no less, in which you will luxuriate in newly refurbished quarters decorated in soothing earthy colors. For one of these suites (and most definitely an invitation to cocktails with the captain) you will pay—are you sitting down?—$22,000 for the suite, which you can share with three others. Dropping down a tiny peg, the Queen Anne and Trafalgar Suites are $19,590.

Moving right along now, we get into figures we can at least absorb, if not afford. Luxury outside cabins with private verandas onto which you can sweep majestically range in price from $4510 to $6215 per person for the trip. The next three categories of deluxe outside cabins with two beds are $3550 to $4215 per person for the voyage. In all these aforementioned accommodations you dine in the plush Queen's Grill, and are of course recipient of the best of everything.

The next category down, Category D, is deluxe outside cabins with two beds and dinner in the very pretty Princess Grill. For one of these you pay $3275 per person for the five-day crossing.

In the next four categories in descending price order you dine in the Columbia Restaurant and sleep in outside quarters with two beds. For those accommodations you pay a high of $2930 in Category E, dropping about $100 in each category to a low in Category H of $2590 per person for a five-day transatlantic cruise.

Now we come to the passengers traveling in a class known as Transatlantic Class, as opposed to all you've read about so far who are considered First Class.

Transatlantic travelers have a choice of three categories of outside cabins, Categories I and J, either of which has two twin beds, and Category K, also an outside cabin but this time with lower and upper berths. In Category I and J cabins the cost is $2060 or $1745 per person; in Category

K, $1710 per person for the five-day transatlantic crossing in intermediate season.

The lowest price categories on board are Category L at $1625 per person for an inside cabin with two beds and Category M at $1440 per person for an inside room with lower and upper berth.

Cabins for single travelers are available on board in both First and Transatlantic class. For one of those in the intermediate season you will pay a high of $4670 for a deluxe outside cabin and dinner in the Queen's Grill, dropping to $4280 for an outside cabin and dinner in the Princess Grill. An inside cabin with assignment to the Columbia Restaurant is $2825 and an outside Transatlantic Class cabin is $2485. The lowest single price on board is an inside cabin for $1800 for the five-day intermediate-season crossing.

Third and fourth persons sharing a room pay half minimum fare in Columbia and Tables of the World cabins. In Grill cabins third and fourth passengers pay 50% of Category D cabins, or $1637 in the intermediate season.

As long as you've gone this far, budget another $60 per person for port taxes.

You can save some money on air fares with the ship's air/sea programs.

If you can sail in that super-thrift season, rates are substantially cheaper, beginning at $760 per person for an inside cabin and rising to $3275 per person for luxury outside veranda suites. The middle bracket in that season is $1085 to $1870 per person.

Per diem rates on those five-day voyages across the Atlantic in intermediate season work out to a low of $360 per person, rising in the middle ranges to about $415, and in the highest priced cabins, excluding suites, to $843 per person.

CUNARD COUNTESS: Some dreary day in February when the snow has piled into great gray piles of mush and your feet are freezing, into your ungovernable imagination will come a picture of palm trees and balmy breezes. That's as good a time as any to consider the *Countess*. Heading right into the trade winds is where you'll find this Cunard ship, which sails from San Juan all year round on cruises to fabled Caribbean isles.

Built in Italy and launched in 1976, this 17,500-ton ship carries 800 passengers to La Guaira (the port for Caracas), Grenada, Barbados, St. Lucia, and St. Thomas. An alternate itinerary takes her on what the line calls its "Seven Plus" cruise to St. Maarten, Îles des Saintes, Guadeloupe, St. Lucia, St. Kitts, St. Thomas, and Tortola.

If you're looking for a two-week vacation, you can do those cruises back to back or get off in Barbados or St. Lucia and spend a week ashore at Cunard's Paradise Beach Hotel in Barbados or La Toc Hotel in St. Lucia.

Public Rooms

Last year Cunard embarked on a $7.5-million refurbishing project which has added a new indoor-outdoor center the ship likes to call its "theater-in-the round." Translate that to mean you can sit inside or out to view the ship's cabaret entertainment. There's dancing under the stars too, and a late-night disco featuring the latest in electronic sounds, lights, and special effects.

Although we haven't seen the results of this multi-million-dollar refurbishment, you can trust Cunard to do whatever it does right. For openers, all the ship's decks have been replaced with teak. See what we mean?

Fitness fanatics can play in a new area called the fitness deck, where you'll find an outdoor pool, sauna, air-conditioned gym and exercise room, even a whirlpool bath. Built in several tiers, the pool is lined in mosaic tiles.

On those teak decks you can play volleyball, table tennis, and drive golf balls.

The theme aboard this ship has a celestial focus: you'll find a Splashdown Bar, a Gemini Dining Room, a Nova Suite, the Galaxy Lounge, and Club Aquarius, even a Starlight Lounge.

As part of the renovation the ship's Splashdown Lido Bar and Satellite Outdoor Café have been redesigned. Cedar blocks line the ceiling and whirring paddle fans cool the air. Decked out in yellow, blue, and white, this section of the ship is a gathering spot for sun worshipers.

In the forward lounge you can watch through tall windows as the ship plows through glittering Caribbean waters. You can play casino games or have a quiet talk in the piano bar. Some interesting glass cocktail tables convert to chess and backgammon game boards.

If you have youngsters hooked on electronic games (and enough quarters to support their habit), send them off to the new Milky Way Arcade video arcade where Pac Man and Ms PC chase those ghosties.

Meanwhile, you can escape to the newly remodeled theater where tiered seating offers a more comfortable seat for the ship's shows and movies.

In the Meridian restaurant you'll now dine amid a pretty brown, pink, and salmon decor with soft romantic lighting.

Activities

You can get in shape in the ship's gym, swim in the pool, try life in a hot tub. All day long there's a round of activity aboard, ranging from dancing classes to lectures, movies, paddle tennis, volleyball, skeet shooting, and a golf driving range.

Nights, there's a cabaret show in the ship's nightclub and festivities in the new theater-in-the-round. Or dance under the stars in the ship's new instant disco, alive with flickering lights, special effects, and plenty of rhythm.

Cabins

The cabins aboard this ship are newly redecorated too. Now they're fitted out in soft pastel colors. All cabins have private bathrooms.

The *Countess* offers both one- and two-week fares, and divides its year up into three seasons. The cheapest of these runs from July through mid-December. Slightly higher rates—about $30 more per person—apply April through mid-June and in September. High season is from Christmas through March, late June through August, and October through mid-December. At that time you'll pay $100 more per person above the low-season rates.

There are eight cabin categories aboard. Category A and B cabins, which are deluxe outside double cabins with bathtub and shower, cost $1715 to $1915 per person for a week's cruise in the peak winter and summer seasons.

Category C and D cabins are outside doubles with shower, and cost $1590 and $1540 per person in peak winter season for a seven-night cruise.

Inside double cabins with a shower fall in Categories E, F, and G, and cost $1564, $1489, and $1364 per person, depending on size and location of the cabin.

Finally, double cabins with upper and lower berths and shower are $1239 per person for the week-long cruise.

A third person sharing an outside cabin pays $499 to $599 depending on season, $548 to $648 in an inside room.

On this ship two-week fares are substantially less than twice the one-week rate. For instance, if you decided to book a cruise in February, the peak season, in a Category C or D outside double, you'd pay $1540 to $1590 per person for a week's cruise. For a two-week cruise in the same month you'd pay just $2310 to $2385, a 50% reduction! And those prices include round-trip air fare and transfers to the ship in San Juan too.

Back in Chapter II you'll see more about fly/cruise programs. Suffice to mention here that if you can leave from some of the most popular gateways (New York, Newark, Philadelphia, Boston), you can buy a cabin for $50 or $100 or more less on the line's bargain-conscious "Selected Gateway" fly/cruise programs.

Better still, the price per person goes down rapidly if you're booking four or five people into two rooms.

Cunard is focusing on younger travelers aboard this ship, and at one point was offering anyone under 40 the chance to take a friend along for free.

If you're making your first foray into the lower Caribbean, this ship provides a comparatively economical way to do it. Per diem rates range from a low of $177 for a week's cruise to a high of $273, with the middle falling somewhere in the $220 range.

CUNARD PRINCESS: The *Princess* is now the line's Mexico and Alaska sailer. Launched in 1977, she weighs in at 17,500 tons and carries 800 passengers off on 7- or 14-day voyages to such exotic Mexican stops as Mazatlán, Puerto Vallarta, Manzanillo, and Acapulco.

A special feature of the ship's week-long Mexican trips is an overnight stopover in Acapulco, where you have plenty of time to sample the restaurants and nightlife. The ship docks on Friday morning at 10:30 but your cruise doesn't officially end until 8 a.m. on Saturday so you can stay aboard and use the ship as your hotel that final night.

On the northbound trip from Acapulco you can board the *Princess* at 4 p.m. on Saturday so you have a pillow for your weary head after a night—and a day—on the town before the ship departs at 7 p.m. on Sunday. On the northbound leg of the journey the ports change to Zihuatanejo/Ixtapa, Puerto Vallarta, and Mazatlán, cruising by Cabo San Lucas before arriving on Saturday in Los Angeles.

In June the ship points her bow north and heads for the icebergs of Alaska. In those waters she sails on one-week cruises through mid-September. On those voyages you embark in Vancouver, British Columbia, get off the ship in Alaska, and then fly home from there. The *Princess* sails back from Anchorage, of course, so you can turn the sojourn into a two-week trip if you like. (There's quite a price break if you do.)

You can even decide to tour Alaska, visit Mt. McKinley, Nome, Fairbanks, Denali National Park, and then rejoin the ship two weeks later for its return voyage. Cunard makes that easy for you by providing a variety of land tour programs outlined in the company's Alaska brochure, and of course, by giving you a break on the price.

Cunard likes to say that you see more of these waters on the *Princess* than on any other Alaska cruise ship because you spend a full seven days getting to Anchorage. Other ships, they point out, sail for three days or so and then turn around. They do have a point there.

Another high point of the ship's Alaskan journey is its passage up Tracy Arm Fjord, a waterway few cruise ships visit.

As for the ship itself, it can be called a princess with impunity—it was launched by the late Princess Grace of Monaco in New York Harbor in 1977.

Public Rooms

The *Cunard Princess* is a twin sister to the *Cunard Countess,* so you'll find similar public rooms, some of them even bearing the same name.

Exploring your way down from the funnel, amidships is the *Princess*'s oval swimming pool, surrounded by open deck and protected from the breeze by long windows down both sides. A pool bar nearby dispenses food and drink to tan seekers.

On those Alaska voyages the Observation Deck gets crowded, for this is a prime vantage point from which to view passing glaciers.

Nights, you'll play in the Topsail Lounge, which is enclosed with windows and features a piano bar for quiet entertainment. The ship's casino, with blackjack tables and slot machines, is up here too.

At the stern you can thump away on the paddle tennis courts, visit the Outrigger Café for an alfresco lunch or breakfast, or curl up in a cozy corner of the library/writing room.

You'll dine in the Meridian Dining Room, a handsome glassed-in area with banquettes as well as chairs.

The largest lounge aboard is the Showboat Lounge, where the evening's cabaret entertainment takes place along with musical entertainment and speciality acts. A focal point here is a shining black marble dance floor. Oval windows are an unusual feature.

If you're sailing in Alaska, you can amble into the Eight Bells Club for hot spiced wine at 10 a.m. and stop by again in the afternoon to hear the naturalist's talk on whales. Later, there's easy listening music in this lounge.

Cabins

Like the *Countess,* cabins aboard the *Princess* are not as elaborate as you'll find on some of the other ships in the Cunard family. They're convenient though, in that beds become couches when you're not sleeping in them so you can have a sitting room without paying for a suite. All are carpeted, and have a radio, telephone, and bathroom.

For a week-long cruise to the mariachis of the Mexican Riviera, peak season runs from the end of September through mid-March. From March through May you pay about $70 less for a similar cruise, and from October through mid-December the rates drop an additional $30 per person.

The two top cabins aboard are Category A deluxe outside rooms with a sitting area, twin beds, and a refrigerator/bar unit. For a week's cruise in peak season prices are $2065 per person, dropping in some smaller Category B rooms to $1915 per person.

Outside double rooms in Category B have twin beds and perhaps also an upper berth accommodating a third person. Those are $1715 to $1590 per person, depending on location of the cabin.

Categories E, F, and G are inside double rooms with twin beds, some with that additional upper berth for a third person. These accommodations range down from $1564 to $1489 to $1364 per person, according to the size and location of the cabin.

The least expensive rooms on board are double inside quarters with shower and upper and lower berths, and are located where the ship's structure begins to curve, thus reducing space a bit. One of these rooms is $1239 per person for the week's cruise to Mexico in peak season.

A third person sharing a room is $599, and singles pay $2132 to $3614. Some holiday cruises tack about $100 onto cabin prices. Cunard also includes round-trip transfers from the airport in the price, and has air/sea programs that can save you money on air fares to Los Angeles. Add $30 per person for port taxes for a one-week cruise.

Two-week fares are also tempting, ranging from $1785 to $2873 per person, with a third person paying $849 in high season. Occasionally the line has special promotions on two-week fares, one of which offered the two-week journey at the one-week rate plus $99!

Alaska sailings are close to the same price, running from a low of $1225 per person to a high, excluding those two suites, of $1805 per person (suites are $2445 per person).

11. Cunard/Norwegian American Cruises

Contact: Cunard Lines, 555 Fifth Ave., New York, NY 10017 (tel. toll free 800/221-4800, 800/221-4444 in the Northeast, 800/522-7520 in New York state, or 212/661-7505 in New York City).

Cruising Grounds: varied itineraries, usually including Alaskan and Caribbean ports.

Itineraries: *Sagafjord—*

IN WINTER: Transcanal cruise from Los Angeles to Fort Lauderdale and return followed by world cruise

IN SPRING: Los Angeles–Fort Lauderdale and return and Los Angeles–New Orleans and return

IN SUMMER: San Francisco–Victoria–Alert Bay–Ketchikan–Endicott Arm–Juneau–Columbia Glacier–Whittier–Yakutat Bay/Hubbard Glacier–Sitka–Vancouver–San Francisco

IN FALL: San Francisco-Far East

Vistafjord—

IN WINTER: Fort Lauderdale–Santo Domingo–St. Vincent–Bridgetown–Antigua–Tortola–St. Thomas–San Juan–Fort Lauderdale

IN SPRING: Fort Lauderdale–Mediterranean

IN FALL: Fort Lauderdale–St. Croix–St. Maarten–Martinique–Devil's Island–Fortaleza–Salvador de Bahia-Rio de Janeiro and return

IN SUMMER: Mediterranean cruises

Now there are two slick new additions to Cunard, the *Sagafjord* and the *Vistafjord*. These two floating palaces joined Cunard's fleet when the company took over the operations of Norwegian American Lines in 1983. Highly rated for their elegance and élan, these luxury cruisers have an interesting history too, if perhaps not quite as romantic as that of the *QE2.*

Both these sleek cruisers have been highly rated, and no wonder: where else can you find ships that offer such impeccable elegance and service: terrycloth bathrobes and Lancome soap, even personalized stock quotes and a Chinese laundry man?

And talk about dream cruises—in 1984 the *Sagafjord* sailed from Port Everglades on January 10 on an 84-day trip around South America to India, Singapore, Yokohama, and Honolulu.

If you don't have 84 days to spare, try the 25,000-ton *Vistafjord,* which sails from Port Everglades this winter on a series of 8- and 13-day voyages to a variety of Caribbean islands.

SAGAFJORD: Numbered by her fans—and probably even her competitors—as among the top ships in the world, the *Sagafjord* is a classy operation, no doubt about it. Step aboard and you'll soon see why she's so beloved by her often-repeat customers. Copper and enamel sculptures grace the Veranda Deck, where elaborate woodcarvings are a feature of the Garden Bar, decked out in deep blue with tiled tables and big beautiful windows. A trio keeps 'em dancing on the circular dance floor by night, and presents concerts for afternoon tea.

Sweep up the swirling staircase from Veranda Deck and don't miss the absolutely sensational dark-wood paneling you'll see throughout the ship.

Public Rooms

Speaking of that dining room, aboard the *Sagafjord* there's only one sitting. You dine anytime you please (at tables for two, four, six, or eight) between 8 and 10 p.m. Whatever time you arrive, you will be enchanted by an open airy room done in a contemporary beige shade with just a hint of pink to it. Long windows, lighted pillars, and a raised ceiling almost two stories high add drama to dinner.

Shops aboard the *Sagfjord* are especially nice, with a very wide open and airy feeling to them, quite a contrast to some ship's shops which are so tiny and crammed you sometimes feel a little like a mole.

There's a spa program aboard if you'd like to limber up and slim down, offering an indoor pool and a complete spa operation with fancy weight-lifting and workout equipment, bicycles, massage rooms, even a hot tub.

The tiny Lido café is a comfortable place to settle into the air conditioning while not sacrificing the feeling of being outside. Besides, the pool is just beyond the glass doors that sets off this café. Out on deck plastic pipe furniture cushioned in orange and browns is pulled up under patio umbrellas.

A brand-new nightclub was being carved out of some extra space recently, so if you're aboard this year you'll be among the first to see it. Meanwhile you can dance the night away in the ballroom, decked out in a lovely sprigged orange-and-red pattern on a beige background. Big curving banquettes are a special feature of this room, which has long narrow windows and a raised bandstand, plus a big, big dance floor.

You'll also find a launderette aboard with washing machines for do-it-yourselfers, as well as the usual ship's laundry services.

Cabins

The cabins are very spacious aboard the *Sagafjord,* as they really ought to be at these prices. The top of the line, number 129, an outside double, features a suede couch and chair in a delicate pink-beige color with chocolate and rust accents. A divider sets off a sitting room from the sleeping area, which features twin beds with velvety velour spreads in a similarly delicate pink-beige.

There's a full-length mirror over a long dresser and a refrigerator built into a bar. A large table with drawers provides a nightstand between the two beds, and three very large floor-to-ceiling wood closets equipped with shoe racks offer plenty of place for everything you'd need on a cruise. Baths have tiled floors and many have tubs as well as showers.

On the Sun Deck, Cabin 105 is one of several new suites just carved out aboard the *Sagafjord.* It's decorated in rust and blues, and has a couch, two chairs, one flanked by an end table, and—get this—a private terrace with patio chairs and a table. Closets on this ship are rigged out with sliding wire baskets that help compartmentalize your belongings, and rooms have full-length mirrors.

Cabin 102 is a terrific corner suite with completely separate sitting room and two big picture windows. Decorated in rust and beige, it features walk-in closets and a very large bath, plus three more closets. This is a very, very special cabin.

Cabin 343 is an example of an outside double with twin beds and an emerald-green decor. Very trim heavy woven bedspreads are the focal point of this room, which offers plenty of space between the beds and two portholes for light. There's a dresser with a mirror, a full-length mirror, and four closets, plus a bath with tub too.

Even smaller quarters are far from small. Cabin 305, for instance, is much smaller than some but is by no means tiny. You enter this one down a hallway, one wall of which has a small closet draped off with a floral curtain in place of a door. There's a tub and shower in the bath, and three full-length closets with doors. One bed turns into a couch during daylight hours, and there's a chair, table, two small dresser-like storage pieces (one with a mirror), and a full-length mirror.

Newly redecorated cabins are done in contemporary pastel shades—dusty roses, light blues, grays. Cabin 233 is a good example of the gray theme, and features gray and blue stripes in the carpeting, a similar color combination on the heavy checked spreads. This small corner room also sports lots of closet space and a bath with shower only.

Cabin 227 is a monster accommodation "as big as my first apartment" laughed one awestruck peeker. This suite features beige carpets, twin beds, armchairs, dressers, and closets in one room, separated by sliding doors from an adjoining sitting room with more chairs, lots more closets . . . well you get the picture. If you can afford this one, don't let it get away.

If you're looking for a double bed, you'll find one in Cabin 438, among others.

Because itineraries and prices vary so widely it's difficult to select a representative price, but let's look at the price for a 14-day Alaska cruise from San Francisco.

The top rate for a suite on that long voyage is $10,590 per person, followed by outside doubles for $6870 or $5490 per person.

In Category D, four categories down from the top-priced A suites, you pay $4510 per person for the 14-day trip. In Category E, also outside doubles, the price is $4120.

Category F outside doubles are $3930 per person for that 14-day Alaskan trip, while Category G inside or outside doubles are $3730 per person.

Category H outside doubles, which are naturally smaller than the more expensive cabins, are $3530 per person, while inside doubles in Category K are $2950 per person for the 14-day journey.

Singles have a number of options on board, with prices ranging from a high of $6870 to a low of $3730 for an inside single cabin for 14 days.

A third person sharing the cabin pays $1475 for the 14-day trip.

Per diem rates then range from a low of $210 to a high, excluding suites, of $490 per person for a 14-day Alaskan cruise. Rates include air fare from a number of cities, and transfers to the ship and back to the airport. A trip to Anchorage, including transportation from the coast, is also included in the price.

VISTAFJORD: Like the *Sagafjord,* this is one of the most beautiful vessels afloat. From your first glimpse of her trim gray-and-white hull topped by the bright-red Cunard funnel, you'll know you're seeing a very special cruise ship.

Launched in 1973, the *Vistafjord* is as close as most of us can come to a floating palace: for openers, a bottle of champagne, set in a bucket of ice, awaits you in your cabin on departure day.

Beyond that, a magnificent arching staircase twists majestically through the middle of the ship, each of its steps lighted from beneath and on the sides by small white lights.

The cabins are a study in gray, peach, salmon, and meltingly lovely pastels. Brass sparkles, glass shines, everything is as perfect as a spiffy Norwegian crew can keep it—and that is spiffy indeed!

Public Rooms

Club Viking is a handsome enclosed garden room where you can watch the swimmers outside in air-conditioned comfort. Contemporary chrome and reed chairs are cushioned in eye-stopping lime greens in this café overlooking the pool.

More of those arching staircases turn up on this deck, winding their way to the galleried nightspot that surely must be the most dramatic nightclub afloat. Behind a wall of tinted glass here you'll see a two-story room flashing with chrome and mirrors. Decked out with high-backed gray swivel chairs, the room centers around a lacquered gray piano and white marble dance floor.

Wide glass doors at the head of the dance floor open onto a small balcony to let ocean breezes cool fevered brows. To take advantage of those tropical evenings, seek a seat on one of the two glassed-in but unroofed outside wings to this room, where you can cuddle into beige-cushioned chairs and sip something cool as the ship steams through a starry night.

Sun buffs will find plenty of deck space and pools aboard, and movie fans can see current favorites in comfortably cushioned theater.

For more contemplative moments, head for the Norse Lounge where a deep-green decor plays counterpoint to brass-trimmed tables and watercolors adorn the walls. Nearby is a game room, and just beyond that you'll find another lounge and dance center, the Garden Room. Green predominates, from the masses of plants that encircle the white marble dance floor to the upholstery, to the accent colors on the tiled tabletops. Lamps trimmed in brass add a metallic glint to this sweeping circular room enclosed in windows.

Those streamlined lines you find everywhere on the ship extend even to the craft's boutique, where shining treasures are displayed in a glittering glass counter that swoops across the entrance.

Deep down in the ship you'll find a goodlooking indoor swimming pool backed in vivid navy tiles sparked with fiery touches of orange and lined with orange circles. In the nearby spa you can get a facial, have your eyebrows shaped, get a massage, or have some infrared heat treatments.

Everywhere you look on this ship is beautiful woodwork and lighting, cleverly designed to give the ship an airy, wide-open look. Which, come to think of it, this ship would have even *without* that subtle lighting.

Beige and orange play counterpoint in the dining room, where you'll dine on a wide range of continental delicacies and get an opportunity to try some Scandinavian specialities too.

Much of the action aboard occurs in the big orange-and-gold ballroom in which a massive vase of silk flowers provides a focal point.

Cabins

Kept spic and span by a bevy of cheerful stewardesses, this ship has some of the loveliest accommodations we've ever seen in a hotel, let alone on the high seas. Naturally, cabins get bigger, better, and infinitely more elaborate as you rise in price category, but we've never seen an unattractive one aboard.

On this ship you'll find real wood beds with wood headboards and footboards, and wood circling all around. In the tall closets are lights that switch on automatically when you open the wood paneled doors. In there too you'll find a metal bar over which to hook your shoes, hooks for hangings things, and shelves that swing up and lock out of the way or swing down for extra storage. In some of the more elaborate cabins you'll even find walk-in closets, and in many you'll find closets big enough to stroll in, plus beautiful dark-wood nightstands and dressers, all with a key-locked drawer too.

All cabins have full-length mirrors, and many have both tub and shower. In the bathroom a three-sided mirror stretches across the wall above a thoroughly modern sink outfitted with lots of storage space for shaving and makeup needs. Cabin 242 is a good example of this kind of cabin. It's decorated in soothing grays and dusty-rose shades, and features a big window, piped-in music, and an interesting chalk drawing on one wall.

The most beautiful rooms aboard are those that have obviously been recently redecorated. In those, pink and gray are the dominant colors, with drapes that blend those shades with a pale mauve hue. Older quarters are outfitted in those colors commonly thought of as tropical: orange, royal blue, gold, green. Cabin 240 is one of those gray and salmon creations with a couch that converts to a bed, set at a 90-degree angle to a twin bed.

The smallest cabin we saw aboard was Cabin 333, done in gold and blues. Nearby, Cabin 343 is another small nest with one lower bed done up as a couch in royal blue and an upper berth that pulls down. Here you'll find the same dresser and closets as are found elsewhere on the ship, plus a tub and shower in a spacious bathroom. Similar cabins: 345 and 353.

Even inside cabins are lovely on this ship; in fact some of them could challenge the outside quarters any day. Cabin 653 is an attractive inside accommodation decorated in gold. Drapes run clear across a wall behind the bed and are backlit so cleverly you're not sure there isn't a porthole behind them.

Many cabins aboard make the best possible use of whatever space could be found. Cabin 679, for instance, is an unusual shape with a couch angled to a twin bed, the whole a study in royal blue and white. Life jackets are stowed away in a nightstand. Behind the couch in this cabin, as in many similar accommodations, the curve of the ship has been traced with a shelf so you have lots of room to store the treasures you pick up along the way—then just close the drape and all the jumble disappears! Two similar examples: Cabin 690, which is a very private place off by itself, and Cabin 684, an unusual room decorated in contemporary off-white checks.

Many rooms aboard, like Cabins 676 and 678, are tucked away at the end of a small private foyer. These two are long rooms with berths that convert to a couch set at right angles to a twin bed. These two, and others like them, seem perfect for two couples or a family traveling together.

One cabin we thought especially nice for a single traveler was 576, which featured that contemporary gray and pale-pink color scheme again, with one bed tucked away so invisibly it served as a counter for the champagne and ice bucket. If you frequent the beauty salon you should like thls one: it's just steps away.

If you have plenty of mad money to spend on your cruise, consider one of the suites. The Mediterranean Suite is dove gray from stem to stern, with two chairs in chrome and gray velour, a couch that becomes a bed, a dresser, lighted mirror, big closet, nightstand by one bed, two huge windows, and a lot of space. A nearby suite, the Baltic, is similarly gorgeous. If you like pink, the Atlantic Suite is outfitted in pale hues of that color with darker pink accents.

A little lower in price, but not much, Cabin 108 features a built-in refrigerator, and like other suites, can be connected to create two massive living, sleeping areas. Numbers 103 and 104 nearby are other top-of-the-line accommodations.

Our special favorite aboard is Cabin 174, a super-long suite trimmed in gray with three windows, a full couch, two beds, a chair, coffee table, full-length mirror on a deep-green wall, and a refrigerator built into a cabinet. The best feature of this one is its sitting area which, because the room is long, is quite separate from the sleeping area. If we can't have this one, however, we'll settle quite happily for its only neighbor, 176, which comes complete with huge walk-in closet and pink decor. It's quite similar in design to 174.

One final mention for really comfortable sailing: Cabin 175 features a built-in wall unit in lovely blond wood and glass, salmon and gray color scheme, two beds that can be joined to create a king-size sleeper, two chairs, and a curving love seat.

Once again cabin prices vary widely because the ship sails on so many different itineraries. It is only to be expected that you'll pay top dollar for the elegance you get aboard this ship. On eight-night cruises in the Caribbean, for instance, per-person rates begin at $1390 and rise to $4970 for very elaborate suites. Mid-price accommodations for the eight-day voyage are in the $1750 to $2210 range per person.

12. Delta Queen Steamboat Co.

Contact: Delta Queen Steamboat Co., 511 Main St., Cincinnati, OH 45202 (tel. toll free 800/543-1949, 800/582-1888 in Ohio, or 513/621-1445).

Cruising Grounds: Mississippi and Ohio Rivers.

Itineraries: *Delta Queen—*

IN SUMMER: New Orleans–various cities along the Mississippi and Ohio Rivers

IN WINTER: New Orleans–Houmas House–Baton Rouge–Natchez–St. Francisville–New Orleans

Mississippi Queen—

IN SUMMER: New Orleans–various cities along the Mississippi and Ohio Rivers

IN WINTER: New Orleans–Houmas House–Baton Rouge–Natchez–St. Francisville–New Orleans

---

There survives in the South a sweet, slow way of life that is both scorned and coveted by those who pursue—or is it endure?–the rapid and demanding pace of the megalopolis.

When you board one of the furbelowed steamboats operated by Delta Queen Steamboat Co., you drop instantly out of frenzy and into the world of yesteryear where Scarlett dallied and Rhett romped.

In long, lazy days chugging up the Mississippi past sprawling columned plantations and rainbow gardens, slowly, slowly, you sink back into the glamorous world of the riverboat, a world of glittering chandeliers, shining brass, oak beams, and satin drapes.

A day or so into a trip aboard one of these craft and the sudden appearance of a white-suited riverboat gambler wouldn't even garner a second glance.

Romantic as the days of flirting fans and hooped gowns, Delta's two steamers are wonderful anachronisms authentic enough to please "Maverick" fans yet modern enough to satisfy "Love Boat" enthusiasts. These two steamboats can trace their history back to 1890 when a riverboat captain named Gordon Greene began operating packet steamers on the Ohio and Mississippi Rivers.

Riverboats remained in the Greene family until 1973, when the *Delta Queen* became part of Overseas National Airways. That company began construction of a second vessel, the *Mississippi Queen.* For a few years in the late 1970s the two ships were owned by the Coca-Cola Bottling Co. of New York. In 1980 the Delta Queen Steamboat Co. became a publicly owned company operating the only two remaining overnight passenger steamboats in this nation.

There's something magical about sailing on one of the very few remaining American flag vessels, something that can be equalled nowhere in the world. It can be an especially inspiring voyage if you take the time to read a little of the history and folklore of this river that has over the centuries played such a vital part in the history of this nation.

Arise early some morning when golden rays of sunlight peek through pines along the shore as you steam along deep dark waters. Suddenly you will know why a fellow named Mark Twain never lost his fascination with this mighty waterway and the craft that ply it.

Plunk yourself down in a deck chair and lose yourself in the churning white wake foaming out behind the spinning paddlewheel. Sink into the emerald shade of giant live oak trees spreading their ivy-covered branches over sweeping columned verandas of massive antebellum mansions. All around you is the haunting melody of the nation's most elegant and most tragic historical moments: the grim, silent battlefields of Vicksburg, the sugary sweetness of Natchez, whose stately homes were spared the ravages of the nation's most bitter conflict.

Unfetter your imagination aboard either of these two elegant ladies of the river and you'll become part of the best of the Old South for a few leisurely days up the lazy river from New Orleans, or down it from St. Louis, Cincinnati, or Pittsburgh on cruises that vary in length from two to ten nights.

There are some exciting special cruises aboard both the ships. In June the duo race each other up the river from New Orleans to Cincinnati—although at speeds that don't exceed a stately 12 mph . . . you certainly won't get any stockcar sensations!

In February the vessels, which spend much of their time in the New Orleans section of the river to catch the best weather, celebrate Fat Tuesday with a couple of Mardi Gras celebrations, followed by trips that will appeal to the gardeners among us: Spring Pilgrimage Cruises, when riverside cities open their homes, their hearts, and their gardens in a celebration of their dramatic history.

Something similar happens in fall when nature turns the Ohio into a flaming carnival of autumn leaves. Finally, from Thanksgiving through New Year's the line brings out the turkey and trimmings for trips they call Old Fashioned Holiday Cruises, when you can see the plantations dressed in holiday best.

Activities

On board either of these two ships you not only see history along the shoreline, you become part of it in a way that is at once antique and modern. Fly a kite over the paddlewheel, whizz a mean shuffleboard disc, dip in the Jacuzzi, work out in the gym, relax in a sauna, head for the golf courses and tennis courts of Vicksburg or Natchez.

On your way to dinner, sweep down the glamorous Grand Staircase for your own grand entrance. The *Delta Queen* gets our vote for the most beautiful staircases afloat.

Aboard either of these two vessels you'll savor American flavors, things like Louisiana oysters, Arkansas catfish, Créole flavors, crunchy pecan pie.

After dinner, get in on the fun as riverboat becomes showboat, celebrating American–Old South style with Mardi Gras parties, Dixieland bands, bluegrass banjos, a steamboat cabaret, ragtime, singalongs, dance music. You can even learn to play a real oldtime "Steam Pianna," otherwise known as a calliope, one of the rarest instruments around. Steam pressure produces the tunes on calliopes, which were invented by a fellow who figured they could replace church bells. His idea never quite caught on, and when you hear one of these wheezing, tooting whistlers, once called a cross between an organ and a fire engine, you'll get an idea why not!

It isn't all history aboard this line. In 1983 the line's *Mississippi Queen* was featured on NBC's "Today Show," which came aboard to film the vessel's computer-learning seminars. Talk about leaping time zones!

Life is casual and for the most part informal on these riverboats, although gentlemen will feel better in jackets and ties, ladies in the feminine equivalent, at dinner.

DELTA QUEEN: In the glow of stained-glass windows and under the glitter of crystal chandeliers, you'll find it hard to believe this steamer hasn't been cruising these waters for generations. Truth is, she's been around only since the 1920s when she was built on the River Clyde in Scotland—Glasgow to be exact. Well, not built exactly but composed of a bunch of prefabricated pieces that were shipped to California where all the puzzle parts were put back together for cruises between Sacramento, Stockton, and San Francisco.

Used to ferry troops during World War II, the ship was purchased by the Greenes in 1946 and moved to the Mississippi River. That may sound simple, but it was quite a project: the boat was towed for 5000 miles down the Pacific coast, through the Panama Canal to New Orleans. After refitting in Pittsburgh, she began in 1948 to sail on cruises between Cincinnati and Cairo, Illinois. So authentic is the *Delta Queen* that she's entered in the National Register of Historic Places.

For those who like to see a lady's figures, the *Delta Queen* is 285 feet long and has a 7½-foot draft. She weighs 1650 tons and her paddlewheel is 18 feet wide and 20 feet in diameter. When she's pouring it on, she can go as fast as 12 m.p.h. but most of the time she sails along at a sedate 7 m.p.h. She carries 190 passengers in 95 cabins, and has a crew of 77 to serve them.

Public Rooms

Public rooms aboard are a study in teardrop chandeliers, intricate wrought-iron staircases, stained glass, polished woods, and heavy ornate moldings everywhere.

From the top down, you'll find the Sun Deck, which, interestingly, houses all together the two top-priced cabins, some mid-priced quarters, as well as several G category, much more moderately priced rooms. Next comes the Texas Deck, where you'll find most of the riverboat's staterooms and the Texas Lounge, where the ship's entertainment takes place.

One deck lower, Cabin Deck, are two more lounges aptly named the Forward Cabin Lounge and the After Cabin Lounge so you can't get lost no matter how many Planter's Punches you've had! On this deck are the purser's office and gift shop too. Follow the heady perfumes of good cooking and you'll find the Orleans Dining room on the Lower Deck. Tables for four predominate here, although two can sometimes find a private spot.

All in all, we think that the *Delta Queen* is not as elaborate, nor as slickly turned out, as her *Mississippi Queen* sister, but that absence of modernity is the very thing that makes her every bit as charming as the *Mississippi Queen.*

These days you can find the *Delta Queen* sailing up and down the Mississippi and Ohio Rivers all year round on cruises on the lower Mississippi, the upper Mississippi, and the Ohio, with stops at places like Houmas House, a classic southern mansion; St. Francisville, site of Rosedown Plantation; magnolia-trimmed Natchez; and the ramparts of Vicksburg. Other cruises stop in at Baton Rouge or journey to Memphis, Cairo, or St. Louis.

Cabins

The quarters you'll find aboard range from two big snappy staterooms overlooking the paddlewheel to an economical—and small—upper/lower bunk-bedded inside room in which you share a bathroom a few steps down the hall. All of them have beautiful moldings, oval mirrors, brass fittings, and wooden shutters, which reinforce the historic feeling aboard.

If you elect the top-of-the-line Sun Deck cabins, A339 and A340, you'll certainly be in good company—former President Jimmy Carter and his family once occupied those two. To sleep where a president slept, in a double brass-bedded room with a sofa bed, shutters on the windows, wall-to-wall carpeting, polished wood dresser, and bath, will cost you from $650 per person for a two-night cruise to $2275 for a seven-night journey.

Price categories aboard begin at the top with A and work down to the low category I rates, so you have nine price options. You also can sample the ship on a two-night cruise (although there aren't many of those) or try a four-night Kentucky Derby journey, or longer voyages lasting 5, 7, 10, 11, or 12 nights (although there are only a few of the latter lengths).

Way down the price range in those super-budget quarters you'll pay $230 per person for a two-night cruise, rising to $1265 per person for 12 nights on the river. For a seven-night cruise, the most common offered by the company, one of the six cabins in this bottom range will cost $805 per person.

A cabin in the middle price range (Categories C, D, E, and F), which includes the majority of cabins on the *Delta Queen* (62 of the 95), costs $1365 to $1960 per person for a seven-night trip in peak season (which is just about every month except February and the beginning of December). Five nights aboard in that category of stateroom will cost $975 to $1400.

All cabins have washbasins in the room (they're not in the bathroom, which in some of the lower priced cabins is just as well since some of those bathrooms are quite tiny indeed). From Category F on down cabins have upper and lower berths, although a few queen-sized sleepers are available. Some rooms also have extra-wide lower beds enabling the cabin to accommodate three if one is a child. Third persons sharing quarters pay $75 a night if they're more than 16 years old; under the age they sail free!

If you want cabin sizes, figure a very compact 44 square feet or so for the smallest quarters, 68 square feet for mid-priced quarters, and 135 to 156 square feet for the very top bracket. But whatever accommodations you select will contain room-to-room telephones, and at night there will be a chocolate on your pillow.

Single travelers pay 175% of the regular per-person fare if they want exclusive occupancy of a room. The line will try to match you up with another passenger traveling alone if you'd like to share a room.

You can save 10% to 15% on either the *Delta Queen* or the *Mississippi Queen* by booking and paying half the fare six months or more ahead of your sailing date.

MISSISSIPPI QUEEN: What a beauty we have here! Launched in 1976 at the height of the Bicentennial celebration, the *Mississippi Queen* is about twice the tonnage of her fellow sailer, the *Delta Queen.* She weighs in at 3364 tons, and carries 424 passengers in her 216 cabins.

New deluxe suites were recently added to the top of the vessel by cranes that lifted the new quarters into place on the Promenade Deck. Furnished to a contemporary faretheewell, the new suites offer the lucky the same view as the ship's pilot, six flights up, through huge windows that let you look upriver and off to the sides. In that same year all the public rooms, which were lovely to start with, were redone over again.

Unlike the *Delta Queen,* this $27-million craft sports an all-steel hull and superstructure, and about all the modern conveniences the modern mind can conjure up: a movie theater, a swimming pool, a sauna and gym, a beauty salon, elevators. And all that's tied together with brass, mirrors, chrome, steel and brass, parquet dance floors, beautiful contemporary colors.

Exterior design was by James Gardner, a London designer who helped create Cunard's *Queen Elizabeth,* and the ship was built in Jeffersonville, Indiana, at the Jeffboat Shipyard that has created more than 4800 steamboats over the years.

Public Rooms

Most of the action aboard takes place on the Observation Deck, five decks above the waterline, a lovely aerie from which to get a gull's eye view of the river below. Here, perched over that churning paddlewheel is the Paddlewheel Lounge, a dramatic two-story room with a shining tile floor. Tall windows soar two stories up to give you a magnificent view of the shoreline sliding by outside. Contemporaray chrome chairs are upholstered in cherry red, and from a seat on the second-level balcony you can look down on all the world, for a while at least.

Farther forward is the ship's dining "saloon," as they call it. Decked out in linens and flowers, this handsome room has windows all down the sides so there's a good view from all tables as you dine on crayfish bisque, chicken breast Lafayette with sauteed almonds, or a brace of roast quail with wild rice. Traditional southern riverboat culinary treats—things like shrimp remoulade—are specially marked on the menu where they're called La Bouche Créole, with a tip of the hat to that Louisiana cuisine which grew from classical French cooking.

If you're looking for an intimate hideaway bar, try the Center Bar, located fittingly enough right in the center of Observation Deck, just short of the Grand Saloon where you can get comfortable in a plush couch or circular armchair. Nearby, the Starboard Gallery has tall windows—and more of those fancy ceilings—through which you can watch the lights glittering in plantation windows.

One deck higher, the Calliope Bar is a pleasant aerie. Not far away you'll find a full-fledged gym, with massage facilities too. A Jacuzzi on board makes a nice afternoon dip in summer when temperatures rise.

Way down on the Lower Deck you can take in a movie in the ship's theater, and back up on the Cabin Deck, the Forward Lounge is a good place for the faster of the two cohabiting travelers to await the slower. If you'd like to curl up with a good book, you'll find a cheerful library on board too.

Cabins

All the cabins on the vessel are located on three decks separate from all those public rooms. That means you'll spend your sleeping hours on the Texas Deck, Cabin Deck, or main deck (the one closest to the water).

If you can afford the tariff, the top-priced rooms here are worth the money, if for no other reason than that they have lovely private verandas. There are actually quite a number of these available, 80 in fact, ranging in price from $1820 to $2450 per person for seven nights (about $550 less per person in the December and February off-seasons). These upper bracket quarters also have a sofa bed, dressing area with vanity, lots of closet space, and tubs as well as showers in the bathroom.

From there down in price we'd suggest that you spend your looking-time up on deck. Although cabins in Categories F, G, H, and I are outside accommodations and do have large windows, they're not always in convenient places for comfortable observation. Inside cabins, of course, don't have windows.

You'll find twin beds pushed together to create a king-size sleeper in the upper price categories, twin beds or double with an upper pullman berth in less expensive veranda quarters, and outside cabins without verandas. In some Category H rooms you'll find the river view partly blocked by outside stairs.

Families will do well with adjacent Category A, B, D, and K rooms, and some in the lower priced Category I rooms that share a common entry hall.

If you want to sail on this ship on a budget Category J, K, and L cabins are the most economical. Some have twin beds, some upper pullman berth and lower twin bed. For one of those you will pay $665 to $980 per person for a seven-night cruise.

The *Mississippi Queen* sails the variety of 2- to 11-night cruises to the same destinations as her smaller sister. If this year's cruises match last year's, as is likely, the ships will be sailing round trip from New Orleans most of the year. There are some special cruises to St. Louis, St. Paul, Memphis, Cincinnati, and Pittsburgh, but most of these sojourns take place in the fall when the foliage is putting on its flaming free show.

13. Eastern / Western Cruise Lines

Contact: Eastern Cruise Lines, 1220 Biscayne Blvd., Miami, FL 33101 (tel. toll free 800/327-0271, 800/432-9552 in Florida, or 305/373-1611); Western Steamship Lines, 140 West 6th St., San Pedro, CA 90731 (tel. toll free 800/421-5866, 800/262-1128 in California, or 213/548-8411).

Cruising Grounds: Bahamas, Mexican Riviera.

Itineraries: *Azure Seas*—Los Angeles–Ensenada–San Diego–Los Angeles or Los Angeles–Ensenada–Los Angeles year-round

Emerald Seas—Miami–Nassau–Bahamian Private Island–Freeport or Miami–Nassau–Bahamian Private Island–Miami year-round

---

Eastern has been sailing its *Emerald Seas* between Miami and the Bahamas for so long the Atlantic would look empty without her. On this run since 1971 when Eastern/Western Cruise Lines bought the ship from Chandris, the *Emerald Seas* offers three- and four-night cruises to Nassau and Freeport, and the line's new pride its deserted Bahamaian Out Island.

As one of the oldest lines in the country, Eastern can trace its history back to 1868 when the company was incorporated in Massachusetts and had ships plying the islands off the New England Coast. During World War II most of the company's ships had negative encounters with German subs. Two, however, the *Evangeline* and the *Yarmouth,* managed to escape the

German navy and returned to Boston where they sailed for some years between New York, Bridgeport, and Canada.

In 1954 F. Leslie Fraser, a Jamaican living in Miami, purchased the two cruisers and brought them to Miami where they were docked right downtown in the middle of what is now Bayfront Park. (In those days three-night cruises cost a lordly $39 to $54!)

By the 1960s Fraser had bought another ship, the *Arosa Star,* renamed it the *Bahama Star,* and was doing a booming business on three- and four-night cruises to Nassau. Meanwhile the line's two original ships cruised to the Caribbean and Central and South America on longer voyages. This line also owned the *Ariadne* at one time, but eventually sold those ships, ending up with their present vessel, the *Emerald Seas.* In December of 1982 she began sailing to the Bahamas.

Once known as the *President Roosevelt,* the *Emerald Seas* was built in 1944 with an eye to sailing her around the world, and she served the country in World War II as a troopship. Broad abeam and deep of draft, she can provide a smooth ride in the worst weather.

This year the line added a new twist—its own Out Island in the Bahamas. Called Little Stirrup Cay, this island in the Berry Island chain is for many passengers the highlight of the trip. Why? Because there's absolutely nothing to do, thus relieving you from any duty to get out there and sightsee. In fact, a tiny, long-abandoned stone cottage, thought to have been built by early settlers is the only point of interest. Except, of course, crystalline waters, sands warm as Hades, coral reefs populated by the flashiest floor show afloat, and sun, sun, and more sun.

Little Stirrup Cay's absence of sights means you can, without guilt, obtain a frothy rum punch from the thatched gazebo, stretch out on silver sands, and tan, while you catch up on the naps you missed after two busy days aboard the ship and in Nassau.

Explorers should take a look at the ruins then head off for the far end of the island where some thoughtful soul has strung up a couple of hammocks where you can meditate while swaying gently in the breeze.

Meanwhile on the west coast, the line's *Azure Seas* has for several years been operating similar three- and four-day sailings from Los Angeles to Enseñada. Like the *Emerald Seas'* cruises, these voyages are nonstop parties that just happen to be floating. Nightclub entertainment, a big and busy casino, lounges, a disco, a theater, library, card room—see what I mean?

On three-night cruises the ship leaves Friday evening and spends the next day in Enseñada, where most passengers drink tequila and go on buying sprees, then heads for home in the wee hours of Sunday morning (late Saturday night), spending Sunday at sea and arriving back in port early enough on Monday morning so you can get right off and almost make it to your office on time.

That same day it leaves about sunset, spends Tuesday at sea, Wednesday in Enseñada, and Thursday at sea, returning on Friday morning.

Activities

Entertainment is nearly nonstop aboard these ships, which feature a lively show each evening, two seatings at dinner, a very busy casino, and the usual array of shipboard activities from gong show to trivia contest. Activities at sea and in port run from Bingo to skeet shooting and dance lessons.

In the shops on board the *Emerald Seas* you'll find some bargains on duty-free liquor and perfumes in case you forgot something on shore in Nassau.

Life aboard ship is very casual, and because the cruises are short, you don't have to pack for formal evenings. As a matter of fact, sportswear covers just about everything except the captain's cocktail party, when a suit for the gentlemen and dress for the ladies is the furthest you need to go in the direction of formality. If you like dressing up, of course, you can do that to your heart's content in port or at dinner on the ship.

EMERALD SEAS: This is a newly redecorated craft featuring spacious and well-maintained cabins. If you can afford the fare for a suite on this short voyage, you'll be rewarded with a huge room with beautiful floor-to-ceiling glass windows, a seating area, twin beds, even closed circuit television for watching on-board entertainment in the comfort of your own quarters. All 245 outside and 145 inside cabins have private baths.

Recently painted stem to stern in a pale-green hue and renovated to the tune of $2 million, the ship now has a contemporary look.

The food aboard is just fair, but a new chef recently joined the line so it's likely some changes will be made. One couldn't fault the quantity, however: breakfast buffet style on deck or in the dining room, mid-morning bouillon, lunch, afternoon tea, dinner, midnight buffet every day, and snacks in machines in the hallways.

If you're sailing on a budget and/or new to the whole business of cruises, the *Emerald Seas* may be just the introduction to the high seas you've been seeking. At 24,458 tons, she's quite a big ship, carrying 800 passengers and 400 crew, any one of which may be just the person you've been wanting to meet.

Public Rooms

The public rooms aboard got most of the attention in the recent renovations so you'll find a nice contemporary look throughout the ship. The Aquarius Club is particuarly attractive, with a dance floor flanked by comfortable conversation areas where passengers often gather for pre-dinner cocktails.

Four dance bands should be enough to provide the kind of music you'd like to hear, or you can buzz down to the theater and watch a movie. There's an amateur talent night and professional entertainment on nights the ship is at sea.

There's a similar contemporary look about the disco that spreads across the aft end of the ship on the Sun Deck. Just outside here you'll find a cute little French café that's a favorite gathering spot for swimmers in the pool just beyond.

The *Emerald Sea* sails on Friday afternoon, drops anchor in Nassau early on Saturday morning, and stays there until the wee hours of Sunday morning when she sails on to the Out Island, returning to Miami on Monday morning. Her four-night sojourns begin on Monday, end on Friday, and include Freeport. They naturally attract an older crowd more able to schedule free time on working days.

As one first-time sailor told us: "I didn't know whether I'd like a cruise or not but I had the best time of my life! I'm going to start saving this week to go on another one." Enough said.

Cabins

You won't find this a fancy ship, but it is quite spacious. That's particularly true of the cabins, which are among the largest of any cruise ship afloat—and one of the prides of the line. To give you an idea what that means, lanai suites are about 11 by 20 feet, mid-priced double cabins are 16 by 13 feet or 20 by 9 feet, and less expensive quarters measure about 12 by 16 feet, some smaller.

Suites are good buys for the money, but then you have to have the money. A three-night cruise in one of these will cost $630, and four nights is $755 per person in winter season (February through March). They're very comfortable, however, with as much space as some hotel rooms.

Prices aboard are highest in the winter months (February through March) and in summer (from June through mid-August). Off-season aboard is January, April to June, and mid-August to the end of December.

You'll find rooms with queen-size beds aboard too, although those tend to be in the highest price categories.

Budgetwise cruisers will do well on the Emerald, Ruby, and Topaz Decks, where an outside cabin with upper and lower berths costs $415 per person for a three-night cruise in peak season. Cabins E77 and E76, which are smaller rooms wedged in among the suites, might be good choices in this bracket. Rock-bottom budgets can find quarters here for $310 a person for a three-night cruise in peak season, $270 per person in summer.

Children under 16 pay $150 each; those under 3 are free. If an adult and child under 16 are sharing a room with upper and lower berths, you pay half fare for the youngster. Third and fourth occupants of a cabin pay the minimum rate. Singles are charged 1½ fare for a cabin with upper and lower berths, two full fares for a cabin with two lower beds.

AZURE SEAS: Western Steamship Lines, a subsidiary of Eastern operating on the West Coast, operates this cruise ship with similar three- and four-night cruises. On these you visit Enseñada in Baja California on the three-day cruise. On four-night sailings the ship stops in at San Diego too.

Like the *Emerald Seas,* the *Azure Seas* is a party ship, designed to provide you with three days of fun, frolic, and food. Built in 1955 as the *Southern Cross,* this 21,486-ton vessel (later known also as the *Calypso*) carries 728 passengers so there's plenty of opportunity to meet fun and frolic. An interesting historical note: she was the first ship afloat to be christened by a reigning monarch, Queen Elizabeth II. Refurbished in 1976 and again in 1983, the ship is clean and contemporary looking, with lots and lots of deck space for sunning.

While it's no luxury ship, it's popular with first-time cruisers, who have a rip-roaring weekend while they're discovering what cruises are all about.

Public Rooms

If you like to play the slot machines, you can pull until your biceps fail at the bank of one-armed bandits in the ship's casino. All the other casino games are available too.

Three nightclubs ought to provide plenty of places to play, and there's always the disco for late-night howling. It's way down on its own deck so the partying goes on well into the a.m. here.

You can tone up in an exercise room, then recuperate in the whirlpool and a small spa. You can round up a fourth for bridge or go see a movie in the ship's balconied Rialto Theater.

Most of the action occurs on the Promenade Deck, where you'll find the ship's show lounge, the Rendezvous Lounge, where a Broadway revue provides evening entertainment. Not far away, the Mayfair Lounge offers a piano bar and soft lighting. Nearby are gift shops and the theater, and back aft is the smaller Café Miramar, a self-service dining room. St. Tropez Bar is a popular gathering spot too. It's decked out in contemporary furnishings with a bright awning overhead.

Weekend cruisers can come aboard the ship at 5 p.m., although it doesn't sail until 7:45 p.m., and enjoy a buffet dinner at an open sitting. Bars are open too, although you'll have to wait until the ship's at sea to have a go at the casino.

In the ship's 1983 renovation the Caravelle Dining Room and the Miramar Lounge, the ship's nightclub, were revamped with colored lights that bounce off the ceiling of the room. Mexican tiles at the entrance and new carpets give the room a distinctly western look, abetted by wall graphics of California scenes, Mexican villages, tropical flowers and birds.

Cabins

In 1983 the line refurbished the cabins on board the *Azure Seas* so these days they're looking prettier than ever, all outfitted in contemporary earth tones. On large old ships like this one you can expect ample quarters too.

Cabins begin one deck down, on the Atlantis Deck, and continue on the Barbizon Deck, Caravelle Deck, Dolphin Deck, and Emerald Deck. All the cabins on board have two lower beds or a double bed, plus plenty of closet and dresser space. Some have a pullman upper berth or two so you can take the kids along if you like. All cabins are carpeted, and they all have private bathrooms with shower, telephone, and piped-in music on two channels. Bright tropical colors and lots of blue are featured in the decorating schemes.

If you elect an outside cabin, you'll find big rectangular portholes offering a nice view of the passing scene.

Prices are divided into nine categories, with Category 1 cabins the costliest, Category 9 cabins the least expensive. There are also two seasons aboard. Off-season is April through June and September through late December, plus mid-January through March. Peak season begins in mid-June and lasts through September, including some Christmas holiday sailings.

The following prices are for a three-night cruise to Enseñada from Los Angeles in peak season. You'll pay $20 to $25 less in off-season, and four-day cruises cost about $55 to $70 more than three-night cruises.

The top cabin aboard is the owner's suite on Atlantis Deck. It has a convertible sofa in the separate sitting area and costs $825 per person for a three-night cruise in peak season.

Outside cabins in Categories 1 through 4 have two lower beds or a double bed, and range in price from a high of $590 per person to a low of $545 per person. Inside cabins begin in Category 5 and go through Category 9. These quarters feature two lower beds or a double bed, and cost a high of $520 per person, dropping to a low of $440 per person for a three-night cruise in peak season.

Third and fourth persons sharing a stateroom pay the minimum rate for the cruise, and singles get quite a break on this ship: they pay only a

10% surcharge in Categories 1, 2, 4, and 5, except during holiday sailings. Those cabins are limited though, so it would be wise to book early.

Children under 16 are charged $150 when traveling with two adults. Those under 3 are free, but a port tax is levied on everyone. (Port taxes are an additional $21 per person.)

14. Exploration Cruise Lines

Contact: Exploration Cruise Lines, 1500 Metropolitan Park Building, Seattle, WA 98101 (tel. toll free 800/426-0600, or 206/625-9600 or 206/624-8551).

Cruising Grounds: U.S. West Coast, Alaska, Pacific Northwest inland rivers, Panama Canal, Tahiti.

Itineraries: *Pacific Northwest Explorer—*

IN SPRING AND FALL: San Francisco–Sausalito–San Joaquin River–Stockton–Sacramento River–Sacramento–Locke–San Francisco

IN SUMMER: Portland–Columbia River–Astoria–Bonneville Dam–The Dalles–Snake River–through several dams–Lewiston–Kennewick–Multnomah Falls–Portland

IN WINTER: not in service

Great Rivers Explorer—

IN SPRING AND FALL: Portland–Columbia River–Astoria–Bonneville Dam–the Dalles–Snake River–through several dams–Lewiston–Kennewick–Multnomah Falls–Portland

IN WINTER: Balboa–Panama Canal–Colon

Majestic Alaska Explorer—

IN SUMMER: Ketchikan–Misty Fjord–Wransell–Sitka–Tracy Arm–Juneau–Skasway–Haines–Glacier Bay–Petersburg–Ketchikan

IN WINTER: Cruises from Tahiti

Glacier Bay Explorer—

IN SUMMER: Ketchikan–Misty Fjord–Wransell–Sitka–Tracy Arm–Juneau–Skasway–Haines–Glacier Bay–Petersburg–Ketchikan

IN WINTER: not in service

Exploration Cruise Lines got its start a decade ago as Alaska Tour and Marketing Co., operating land tours to the dramatic Alaska, Arctic, and northwestern U.S. scenery. In 1981 the company bought its first ship, the *Pacific Northwest Explorer,* and began sailing from Seattle on cruises to the San Juan Islands and Puget Sound.

Combining a familiarity with the region and a belief in its saleability, a year later the company bought two more ships, the *Great Rivers Explorer* and *Majestic Explorer.* Family owned, Exploration Cruise Lines is operated by Robert Giersdorf, president of the line, and his son Dave and their families.

Cruises on these ships are for people who want to combine a look at the stupifyingly impressive scenery of this region with the ease and comfort of ship travel. These are not large ships, so your entertainment will be almost solely scenic, although the line does have a cruise director.

In the summer months a cruise aboard the *Majestic Explorer* will take you to Alaskan waters, including some of the more remote spots larger ships cannot negotiate. In winter the ship heads for artist Paul Gauguin's paradise, Tahiti.

Pacific Northwest Explorer and *Great Rivers Explorer* spend their summers in Portland, cruising up the Willamette River visiting logging towns and beautiful valleys, traveling downstream on the Columbia River, just the way explorers Lewis and Clark did it generations ago. These cruises continue down the Oregon coast, then transit eight locks and dams which lift the ship 730 feet above sea level on its way to Lewiston, Idaho, the Northwest's most inland seaport, 465 miles from the Pacific!

In winter *Pacific Northwest Explorer* visits the California Delta from San Francisco on three-night trips to Sausalito, Stockton, and Old Sacramento. *Great Rivers Explorer* shares summer duties in the Columbia and Snake Rivers, then moves south in winter to the Panama Canal where the ship visits an Indian village in the Darien Jungle on four- and five-night cruises that include a Panama Canal transit.

A special feature of these ships is a plated bow piece that can be slid aside to allow stairs to be lowered so you can walk right off the ship and onto an iceberg!

Activities

As on most small ships you won't find a raft of lounges, discos, or gymnasiums, so don't expect a round of rousing entertainment or a daily schedule of events. Cruises on these vessels feature the destination more than cruising itself, concentrating on offering passengers a close-up look at awesome scenery and some interesting shore excursions. Many of those shore excursions, by the way, are included in the price of the cruise.

On small ships like these, cruises are also more casual. Passengers spend more time together and get to know each other better than they would on a large cruise ship. To encourage friendships, the ships plan entertainment that gets passengers mingling and mixing. Activities on board are coordinated by a cruise director, and include things like talent contests, Bingo, and slide shows or movies. In some ports—Tahiti, in particular—the line brings entertainers on board several different evenings. A player piano often gets the fun going, and there's a full-service bar open whenever anyone wants it to be.

There are some attractive sun decks where you can pull up a chair and gaze at snow-clad mountains rising in regal splendor along sapphire waterways.

Life aboard is very casual, so don't bother to pack a black tie. You can dress up for the Captain's Gala dinner if you like, but you won't feel the least bit out of place if you don't.

At happy hour you'll find trays of appetizers circulating, and you can get tea, coffee, or hot chocolate at any time of day or night.

PACIFIC NORTHWEST EXPLORER / GREAT RIVERS EXPLORER / MAJESTIC EXPLORER: So much alike are these three small sailers that we'll explore them all at one time. All are about 150 feet long and carry about 90 passengers.

Public Rooms

Dinner in the Explorer Dining Room is the main event of the evening, followed by some congenial gatherings in the Vista View Lounge. Both are on the main deck, and feature big windows on both sides so you need never miss any of the view passing by outside. In the lounge you'll find a small bar dispensing libations and some comfortable chairs and banquettes. A piano sets off occasional singalong evenings, and cards games are popular.

Dining is family style at long tables down which are passed the dishes de jour. Those will include fresh fish and fruit or the speciality of the region. Cooking is basic American, with the emphasis on foods favored by American diners.

There is no beauty salon or barbershop aboard, and no laundry facilities. Most electrical equipment can be used, but no irons or small appliances exceeding 500 watts.

Cabins

All cabins aboard are outside accommodations, brightly decorated in cheerful colors. While not elaborately appointed, they're clean and cheerful, and seem quite comfortable for the amount of time you'll be spending in them (who would want to miss this scenery?). All are carpeted and have private bathrooms, mirror, and individual reading lights.

It seems quite amazing that with just 40 cabins aboard there could be four price categories, but that's the way it is. The top-of-the-line cabins are deluxe staterooms on the Bridge Deck. They measure 10 by 11½ feet, and include a small table and chairs by the window, a double bed, sink in an alcove, and shower in the bathroom. A closet in one corner provides for your storage needs. Biggest draw here is the view through big windows on both sides of the room. A pullman can accommodate a third person. For one of these cabins the fare on a six-day, five-night trip from Seattle through the San Juan Islands to Vancouver, Princess Louisa Inlet, Alert Bay, and Knight Inlet, is $1079 per person. For a four-day, three-night trip the rate is $659 per person.

On the main deck are rooms with double beds, but here one person will be next to a wall, creating the crawl-over problem. These quarters also have a small table and chairs that can be converted to a pullman berth (which might solve the aforementioned problem). One of these Category AA staterooms is $979 per person for the longer cruise, $599 for the shorter.

In Category A staterooms twin beds set at right angles to each other, leaving the maximum floor space visible. A small bathroom with a shower is off one side of the room. The fare for one of these cabins is $889 per person for a five-night trip, $549 for three nights afloat.

The lowest price on board is a Category B cabin, with two lower berths, one of them extra wide. Although there's a window, it's high on the wall so it's more for light than for view. These are small rooms, measuring 7 by 10 feet, and there are no closets—just some hangar-bars for your clothes.

A third occupant of a stateroom, adult or child, is charged the minimum cruise fare (the cost of a Category B cabin). Single travelers occupying a stateroom alone pay 130% of the price per person for a Category B cabin, 150% for all other categories.

15. Holland America Lines / Westours

Contact: Holland America Lines / Westours, 300 Elliott Ave. West, Seattle, WA 98119 (tel. toll free 800/426-0327, or 206/281-3535 or 206/281-1970).

Cruising Grounds: itineraries vary, but will likely include Mexico's Yucatán Peninsula, Jamaica, Grand Cayman, and other Caribbean islands; a 95-day around-the-world cruise; the Mexican Riviera; and Alaska.

Itineraries: *Nieuw Amsterdam—*

IN SUMMER: Vancouver–Ketchikan–Juneau–Glacier Bay–Sitka–Vancouver

IN WINTER: Tampa–Playa del Carmen–Cozumel–Montego Bay–Grand Cayman–Tampa

Noordam—

IN SUMMER: Vancouver – Ketchikan – Juneau – Glacier Bay – Sitka – Vancouver

IN WINTER: San Francisco–cruising by Cabo San Lucas–Puerto Vallarta–Zihuatanejo/Ixtapa–Acapulco–Puerto Vallarta–Mazatlan–Cabo San Lucas–San Francisco

Rotterdam—

IN SUMMER: Vancouver–Ketchikan–Juneau–Glacier Bay–Sitka–Vancouver

IN SPRING AND FALL: Fort Lauderdale–St. Maarten–St. Thomas–Nassau–Fort Lauderdale

IN WINTER: World cruise from New York, Fort Lauderdale and Los Angeles

---

The newest star in the firmament of this elegant old line is the *Nieuw Amsterdam.* Christened in 1983, this brand-new, 32,000-ton French-built vessel is a smashing beauty Holland America describes as "an extraordinary marriage of art and technology." But the *Nieuw Amsterdam*'s sparkling newness will shortly be upstaged by yet another new Holland America ship, the *Noordam,* a twin to the *Nieuw Amsterdam* and her replacement on cruises from the U.S. West Coast.

Holland America is inordinately proud of its big luxurious ocean liners, so proud, in fact, that the line has trademarked the term Ocean Liner Service. Oldtime elegance is the watchword of Holland America, and that isn't just Madison Avenue hype either. You can sample the finest example of that service in glamorous style aboard the company's oldest and most stately vessel, the world-cruising *Rotterdam.*

In 1985 the *Rotterdam* has once again scheduled a real dream-machine cruise: a 96-day around-the-world sojourn that will travel 32,700 miles and visit dozens of countries. You can take any of several segments of the cruise, or catch this elegant lady on one of her Caribbean sailings from Port Everglades before she leaves on that fantasy journey.

Aboard the line's two brand-shining-new other ships you'll find that same touch—or touches—of class. Holland America spent thousands of dollars to equip the *Nieuw Amsterdam* with a fortune's worth of historic art treasures: museum-piece glassware and silver from the 17th and 18th centuries is displayed in glass showcases outside the dining room. You'll see navigation instruments from those long-gone days proudly on display in the ship's Crow's Nest Bar. A massive wooden mermaid looks soulfully down from her perch in the Lido and a 16-foot mosaic mural graces a balcony perch.

And to make matters even classier: there's a welcome no-tipping policy aboard all Holland America ships, so the crew work for your smiles instead of your little white end-of-cruise envelopes. You can, of course, cross some palms with green, but you won't have to endure any of the tacky talks on tipping that are so prevalent on many cruise lines these days.

Dutch officers keep things humming, and a smiling Indonesian crew can't seem to do enough for you. They are there to escort you to your room when you step aboard that first day, and they're there every minute thereafter to see to your every whim.

Once you're aboard you can sign for purchases, then pay your bill on your last day—no cluttering your pockets with wrinkled bills.

Holland America has quite a fascinating history, one that stretches back to 1872 when two Dutchmen from Rotterdam began sailing the first *Rotterdam* from the Dutch city after which it was named to the U.S. In those days eight lucky passengers could travel first-class, about 400 others went in steerage, and the cargo was what kept it all afloat financially.

A year later the two formed the Netherlands-American Steam Navigation Co., which became known in 1896 as Holland America Line. It has kept that name all these years and bears it still, although the company is now owned by Seattle-based Westours, which first found its niche in the travel marketplace selling Alaska tours. Westours backed into the shipping business, acquiring this famous line after having chartered her ships several times for Alaska voyages.

Over the years Holland America has owned ships called the *Noordam, Maasdam, Statendam, Ryndam, Potsdam,* and more recently the *Veendam* and *Volendam.* If you've loved cruising for a long time, you probably recognize some of those famous names.

HA's original *Statendam*—all 32,000 massive tons of her—had the misfortune to be launched about the time the Germans were discovering U-boats. She was sunk by one of those lethal craft before she could board her first paying passenger. A namesake ship was launched in the late 1920s, sadly at the opening of a miserable economic decade and just prior to another World War that was to force the Dutch company's operations out of the land of dikes to the Dutch-owned isle of Curaçao.

The latest of the *Statendams,* a 24,294-ton vessel carrying 850 passengers, is now sailing under Paquet Cruise Lines colors as the *Rhapsody.* Meanwhile the *Maasdam* and *Rundam* went off to become the *Stefan Batory* of Polish Ocean Line and Epirotiki Line's *Atlas.*

In 1983 Holland America became part of Westours and sold its *Veendam* and *Volendam* to shipping magnate C. Y. Tung, who in turn leased the *Veendam* back to Bahamas Lines. The future of the *Volendam* after the 1983–1984 winter cruises was undetermined.

The current *Rotterdam* is the fifth ship to carry that venerable old name. Launched in 1957, this 38,000-ton cruiser, christened by Queen Juliana, has been the flagship of the fleet for nearly three decades.

This season the *Rotterdam* will be based in Fort Lauderdale's Port Everglades, where she'll be sailing on Caribbean cruises from late September to December, when she sets off on that 95-day journey around the world, returning through the Panama Canal to Port Everglades. In April and May she returns to the Caribbean for several voyages, then sets off in late May to go through the canal again and up to Alaska, where she will spend the summer. In the fall the process reverses, giving you lots of chances to sail to many ports on segments of this ship's busy schedule.

The *Nieuw Amsterdam* will spend her first-ever winter in Tampa, sailing from that west coast Florida city to the silvery beaches and swaying palms of Jamaica, Grand Cayman, and the Yucatán Peninsula. She's scheduled to return to Alaskan waters for the summer of 1985.

Nieuw Amsterdam's twin sister, the brand-new *Noordam,* will head to San Francisco where she'll sail on seven-days-there, seven-days-back cruises along the Mexican Riviera to Acapulco, shifting operations to Alaska in summer where she'll join the *Rotterdam* and the *Nieuw Amsterdam.*

NIEUW AMSTERDAM: As the new twins of the line, the *Nieuw Amsterdam* and *Noordam* replaced former ships of the same names. These two ships, built in French Chantiers de l'Atlantique shipyards, are look-alikes right down to the last inch of their 33,930 tons.

The *Nieuw Amsterdam* spent her first days in North American waters in the fall of 1983 after some construction delays nixed her scheduled summer appearance in Alaskan waters. In the summer of 1984, however, she sailed those matching glacial waters before she set sail for a winter of Mexican Riviera cruising.

This winter you can see her in Tampa where she'll be sailing into the sunshine of Grand Cayman, Jamaica, and the Yucatán Peninsula with a special 14-day Christmas journey to—and through—the Panama Canal with stops at several Caribbean islands.

And she's worth seeing! With a deep-blue hull topped by a white superstructure, she slips through the seas carrying 1200 passengers in considerable splendor.

Activities

You'll find all the usual exercise classes, gymnasium, crafts classes, and deck games, but life aboard these ships is not typically seven-day raucous. There's plenty to do and plenty of lovely places to do whatever you like to do, but you probably won't find any male nightgown competitions.

In the evenings, dinner is a production and features some wonderful Dutch and Indonesian treats as well as the more familiar continental flavors. Later, bands play, the casino clicks and whirrs, and flashy shows take place in a beautiful showroom.

Public Rooms

There is no more beautiful lounge afloat than the *Nieuw Amsterdam*'s Stuyvesant Lounge with its shining dark woods and high ceilings. A massive lion-bedecked gold crest backs the raised stage where gleaming chrome trims the band's royal-blue music stands and flashy entertainers perform. Subtly tasteful woven fabric covers wood-trimmed armchairs. A shining wooden dance floor, glittering in the glow of round lights set into chrome squares, is a sight to behold. On a glass-trimmed balcony, named Minnewit Terrace in honor of that shrewd trader who spent $24 to buy Manhattan, you can peer down at the dancers swirling below.

A look at some of the room names on board will quickly clue you in to the theme aboard: Old New York a/k/a Nieuw Amsterdam. That, thank goodness, is as far as the resemblance to the *old* of Old New York goes.

Everything else aboard this ship is spanking new, with the best of the Old World represented in polished wood, shining brass, acres of teak deck, and some very courtly service.

We could go on rapturously here with description after description of handsome public rooms, but our vote for the best home-away-from-home drawing room on any ship afloat goes to the Explorers Lounge. Settle into an earth-toned, wood-trimmed couch or chair here, turn on one of the shaded brass table lamps, open a Robert Ludlum thriller, and lose yourself in scrunchy comfort. Or if you're not the reading type but do occasionally interrupt your pursuit of activity for a breather, take that breather here, where you can gaze through tall curtained windows at sapphire seas below. Afternoon tea, complete with violins, is served here too.

Fittingly, the serene Explorers Lounge merges right into the ship's Book Chest Library and an adjoining card room. A few steps away you'll find the Princess Theatre, where films are shown daily. This general area also makes a good waiting spot for those whose contribution to the shopping expeditions in nearby boutiques is to sit and wait patiently. Nothing on this deck is far from the popular Henry's Bar, where a long bar streaks in marine-blue splendor down one wall and comfortable chairs in the same riveting hue pull up to small square tables.

Nine decks high and 704 feet long (that's only 4.3 times around for a mile, joggers!) this glamorous ship could be overpowering, but clever designers have turned her busy Promenade Deck into a series of unusually shaped nooks and crannies.

No matter how many fun seekers there are aboard you can always find a quiet spot somewhere for an intimate tete-à-tete. If you're looking for such a spot, try one of the remoter corners of the Hudson Lounge. Or go way up to the Sun Deck where you can become part of the big circular bar in the Crow's Nest, or find a spot near the windows for a magnificent ocean view.

Exercise buffs can tone up in the ship's outdoor pool, then snack and drink at the Lido Restaurant and Bar, just steps away. Right here's where you find the 60-foot buffet presented for breakfast, lunch, or late-night supper. Three decks up on Navigation Deck there's another swimming pool and a flashy gym. In salute to the nation's fascination with physical fitness, the *Nieuw Amsterdam* now features an ocean-going gym. In it you'll find Universal weight machines, a treadmill, bicycles, dumbbells, and an inclined plane. If it's any consolation, you can enjoy a lovely view out over the navigation deck and swimming pool as you huff and puff.

One deck up, on the appropriately named Upper Promenade Deck, you'll find the balcony half of that gorgeous Stuyvesant Lounge and a gambling spot called the Wampum Casino. That name carries this theme thing to ludicrous depths but this spot nevertheless offers attractive quarters in which to take your best shot at a lady named Luck.

During blackjack breathers you can hoist one at the glowing wood Partridge Bar which is (get this) just off the Peartree Club. Both are named after a pear tree old Peter S. planted a couple of centuries ago. Plump with comfortable barrel chairs and ocean shades of blue and green, the Peartree grows on you.

Disco fans can boogie to their heart's content in the Big Apple Lounge, a rip-roaring spot that, thankfully, is tucked away on one remote end of the Boat Deck so the vibes need not be shared by earlier-to-bed birds.

When the sun drops over the yardarm you will dine under the sparkle of dozens of contemporary chandeliers glowing over the massive Manhattan Dining Room that seats more than 700 diners. Tall windows fill the room with light at lunch and give you a glimpse of the stars at dinner.

Most of the tables in this restaurant room are for six, but down the center you'll find some tables for two and four. Two wings on one end of the room are called the King's and Queen's Rooms. Wherever you sit, you'll dine on top-quality cuisine, sometimes featuring some of those delectable Indonesian dishes so popular in Amsterdam, and even occasionally get to try some Dutch treats. You'll also dine on Rosenthal china with silver created in the same mold that formed the silver on the original *Nieuw Amsterdam.*

Cabins

When you're finally beginning to flag after a long luxurious day of dance lessons, bridge tournaments, deck sports—you can even practice your service on tennis practice courts—trap shooting, golf lessons, nightclub entertainment, and sightseeing, it's off to sleep in the most contemporary of cabins. For openers (literally and figuratively), you get into your cabin by inserting a little plastic card in a slot until you hear the door click open.

So many cabins are there aboard this huge ship that you'll find some on nearly every deck (except Promenade). No matter what kind of sleeping arrangements you prefer, you're sure to find them here: king-size beds, queen-size beds, a room with a king-size bed and a sofa bed, a room for four with two lower beds and two pullman uppers, connecting rooms, nonconnecting rooms, rooms with bathtubs, rooms with showers, rooms with both.

Of the 600 or so rooms on board, more than 400 are outside cabins. All of them have a multichannel music system piped in, closed-circuit television, telephone, and individually controlled air conditioning. All have pretty plush carpeting on the floor, and bright contemporary colors abound. You'll find lots of green, striking red with white accents, earthy contemporary tones, delicate floral prints. Drawer space is tucked away in nightstands and beneath vanity/writing tables.

In some rooms couches flip over to become beds; in others, beds with flouncy skirts serve as pillow-backed sitting areas during the day. Outside cabins feature long rectangular windows rather than portholes, the walls are covered with light paneling, and there are lots of closets too. Many rooms have a couple of deep easy chairs or contemporary tub chairs for extra seating.

The least expensive rooms aboard are, as usual, inside cabins. There are some on every level from the main deck down to and including C Deck. Even in these cabins you'll find two double closets, a contemporary bathroom, a lighted makeup table, and a big dresser. Of the two lower beds, one serves as a sitting area during the day.

These are the smallest rooms aboard, and the beds are often placed in an L-shape to give you the most walking-around space. They're small, yes, but we've seen tinier. Cabins 705, 702, and 661 offer a little more space than others. The price for accommodations in these cabins is $1255 to $1355 (the extra $100 buys you a bit more space) per person for a seven-day Caribbean cruise in peak season.

Which brings us to peak versus off-season aboard, and thank goodness, it's simple. For a one-week cruise you pay $60 more for any room in peak season, which begins in late January and lasts through most of March.

Moving up the cabin ladder there is one more category of inside double rooms. These are a bit larger, large enough in fact for some to accommodate a queen-size bed. For these accommodations you pay $1435 per person. For just $20 more you can have an outside cabin of the same size, although with twin beds (seems worth it to us, especially for cabins 620, 621, 618 and 619).

From there on up prices range from $1535 to $1795 per person for a seven-night voyage in cabins called outside double, large outside double, and deluxe outside double, in ascending price order.

The outside doubles in the lowest of the upper price categories offer two beds and four double closets. Two particularly good buys in this category are Cabins 064 and 067, which are way up on Navigation Deck, just down the hall from the ship's highest priced quarters.

Large and deluxe double rooms, which range in price from $1635 to $1795 per person, are very pretty, quite large, and furnished with twin or queen-size beds, and the higher of those two prices includes sweeping picture window, a separate sitting area, dual dressers, and bathtub as well as shower.

Suites? Of course, 20 of them in their own private wings on the Boat and Navigation Decks, with a king-size bed, twin dressers, a separate sitting area with couch and chairs, lots of space, and costing $2050 per person for a week's Caribbean cruise in high season.

For that 14-day Christmas cruise, per-person prices range from $2510 to $3590 for cabins, $4100 for those 20 suites.

Third and fourth room-sharers pay $350 to $400 for seven-day cruises, $700 for that holiday voyage.

And here's a bargain break: if you don't need transportation to or from Tampa (which usually applies to those who drive in from other parts of Florida or places nearby), you get a $50 credit toward the price of your stateroom. (What they're really offering here is a $50 credit to anyone not participating in the line's air/cruise programs.)

Single sailors pay an additional 50% to inhabit a cabin alone.

If you're figuring per diem charges, in peak season you'll pay a low of about $179 per person for a week's cruise, to a middle range of $208 to $244, and a high of $248, excluding suites which are $292 per person daily.

Add about $19 a person for port charges on a 7-day cruise, $30 per for a 14-day sojourn.

ROTTERDAM: As grande dame of the fleet, the *Rotterdam* has been riding the waves for a quarter of a century. In an age that venerates youth, the *Rotterdam* retains an aloof disdain for discussion of age and even goes so far as to celebrate her years. In 1983 the ship's glamorous 96-day world cruise saluted what it called the "Vanity Fair Years . . . a time of charm and splendor, of laughter and elegance, when the world was younger and a shade more innocent."

Whether or not the world was more innocent in those days (or just choosier about the people with whom it shared secrets), the *Rotterdam* seems the perfect place to glorify those Roaring '20s and '30s "when evening meant black tie and long gowns, champagne and caviar . . . a time of tea dances, the Charleston, Fred Astaire, the Ziegfeld Follies, a Gershwin tune," as the cruise ads said.

Cruise ships somehow seem to epitomize that bygone era when the rich were richer, or at least far more innovative in their use of wealth. And what better place to celebrate the creative use of wealth than aboard this massive ship where it requires very little effort to imagine Fred and Ginger floating down the great curving staircase that sweeps up to the balcony of the Ritz Carlton Room.

At 38,000 tons, the *Rotterdam* is 6000 tons heavier than her sisters in the line, and carries fewer passengers—1114—which of course means more space for everyone.

Public Rooms

Ten decks high and three-fourths as long as the Empire State Building is tall, the ship combines the extravagance that could still be afforded in the '50s with the contemporary look that was born in those days. You'll still see unmistakeable signs of the '50s on board in things like tapered chair legs, but the ship was designed with such clean simple lines that she looks almost as modern as her newer sisters.

In the Ocean Bar, for instance, you'll find big windows sweeping to the ceiling, circular tub chairs decked out in red plaid, and a long arching bar under a shining ceiling scattered with small spotlights.

Acres of wood spread throughout the ship on swirling polished dance floors and what seems to be miles of paneling. So civilized is life on board that there's even a handsome smoking room filled with plushy velvet armchairs gathered into cozy circles. Beautiful wood paneling provides a backdrop for an intricate metal sculpture, one of many you'll spot on the ship.

On the glass-enclosed Upper Promenade Deck you'll find the ship's big 610-seat CinemaScope Theatre with its second-level balcony. Here too you'll find the ship's flash-and-dazzle center, the slick Ambassador Room. A rocking spot, this room's a study in circles, from divider walls of glass circles to a circular dance floor filled with a myriad of starburst-inside-starburst, and overhead a spiffy white circular ceiling.

Gift shops, a boutique, even a drugstore are tucked away on this deck, and it's here you'll go to find something to read in the ship's library or to gamble on your luck in the casino.

One deck lower, on the Promenade Deck, you'll dance away the evenings in the big Queen's Lounge with its kidney-shaped polished-wood dance floor and elegant grand piano. Or sneak into the Ocean Bar for a quiet moment. If you play cards you'll have plenty of space to play them at the big card room set off the glass-enclosed promenade. There's a shopping center on this deck too.

Finally the Lido with its semicircular bar and big Lido Terrace café winds about the swimming pool so you need not fear starvation or thirst after a day in the sun. (There's an indoor pool too.)

While you're out in that sun, by the way, you might as well make the most of your time and get in a little tennis on the practice courts, take a couple of golf lessons, or try trap shooting or weightlifting. Send the kids off to the video games.

Perhaps the single best-known spots on the ship are down on B Deck—the bright and elegant La Fontaine and Odyssey Dining Rooms. Decorated in red and royal blue, this domed dining arena is lined with golden columns lit by dozens of upturned glittering lamps that bounce light off the ceiling. The dining rooms offer mirrors and murals, red-jacketed sommeliers, shining gold buttons, white gloves, and course after course of delectable treasures ranging from lobster to steaks to kiwi fruit and chocolate mousse pie. Chefs on this ship and all others in the line are members of the select Confrerie de la Chaine des Rôtisseurs; the international group of gifted chefs and food lovers.

Dinner is even announced with elegance: not the usual loudspeaker to disturb your meditation but the soft ring of brass chimes.

Activities

Evenings find a pianist/singer in every lounge, a dancing-singing revue in the main lounge, the usual sounds in the disco, a string quartet, big-band sound, even a midnight show. Not to mention the casino.

If you like quiet spots, stop up to the small Sky Room on the Navigation Bridge Deck where you can sit out on the observation deck or terrace and, well, muse.

If you're wondering how your wardrobe is going to stand up to all th is, let it be known that the *Rotterdam* gets rave reviews for its laundry and dry cleaning service. So good and so inexpensive is it that some people say they have contemplated saving up their laundry and bringing it on board to have it done here.

Cabins

At last the full days become full evenings and turn finally into exhaustion. You wend you way back to your cabin, a spot that can come in many sizes and shapes.

If you've secured one of the top cabins aboard, an outside double room in Category B, you'll be returning to a room with twin beds outfitted in a contemporary print. Off to one side of the room, built-in wood cabinets rise to the ceiling matching the tiny strip of molding that edges the ceiling. You're likely to have two portholes, covered with tied-back curtains that match your bedspread and the drape that sets the sleeping area off from the couch and chairs in your sitting room.

If you have a slightly less expensive outside cabin, called a "large outside double room" on this ship, you're still likely to find one of those massive built-in wall units in your room, complete with drop-down bar/desk. Twin beds often sport a fluffy dust ruffle, while a couple of chairs provide a seating area for cocktail time. Signs of the '50s in these rooms range from Formica-clad furnishings to Danish modern chairs and the tapering wooden chair legs that were so popular in those days.

If you've chosen an inside double room, Category D, you'll be occupying a room with twin beds and often a couple of chairs in a small seating area.

The least expensive categories are economy outside or inside rooms that are compact with upper berth and lower bed. Some have bathtubs as well as showers.

On board this ship, as on few ships, there are single rooms designed especially for the unaccompanied traveler. Granted, they're small, but then the price is in line for single travelers who often have to pay much more elsewhere.

It's quite difficult to tell you just what a cruise will cost here since there are so many possible options on the ship's around-the-world cruise. For the sake of comparison let's look at the fares for a week-long trip aboard the

Rotterdam sailing from Fort Lauderdale to St. Maarten, St. Thomas, Nassau, and back to Fort Lauderdale.

On this cruise, one of those inside single rooms will cost $1395. An outside room for a person traveling alone is $1695.

Economy inside double rooms begin at $1095 per person, rising to $1250 per person for similar outside quarters. For $45 more ($1295 per person) you can have a slightly larger room but still inside, and for $100 more per person you can have a large inside double room.

Outside quarters range form $1475 to $1695 per person, depending on size of the cabin of course, and if you're really going first class, you'll pay $1990 per person for a deluxe stateroom with separate sitting area and the best of everything.

As you can see, that works out to a minimum of about $156 per person a day, rising to $185 to $210 in larger or outside quarters, up to $284 per person daily for a week's cruise in a suite.

Extra passengers sharing a stateroom with two full-fare guests pay $350 for a week's voyage, proportionately higher on longer trips. On those week-long trips, by the way, there's a $50 credit for those who do not require transportation to or from the embarkation point (no similar deal on longer trips, however).

NOORDAM: The sister ship, make that identical-twin, to the *Nieuw Amsterdam,* this flashy lady will be sailing to Mexico this winter on 14-day voyages

On this new 33,000-ton ship, cabin sizes and layouts are the same, deck plans are the same, public rooms are the same, and some may even have the same name as on the *Nieuw Amsterdam.*

Public Rooms

None of that makes her any less glamorous, however. Just as on the *Nieuw Amsterdam* you'll find museum pieces from the 17th and 18th centuries carefully scattered about the ship to keep you aware of the line's Dutch East India Company theme. After all, that historic old firm spurred the creation of early trading routes and encouraged seafaring adventures that were to change the world.

The *Noordam,* which carries 1214 passengers, features 11 passenger decks and two swimming pools.

On board you'll find more than 20 public rooms, places like the Amsterdam Dining Room where 106 floor-to-ceiling windows overlook the shining sea below. In the Admiral's Lounge an atrium soars two stories high. Tasman's Terrace (named for Albert Tasman who discovered Tasmania) is one of many cozy lounges aboard. Dancing? Of course, in the Hornpipe Club.

Cabins

You don't have to stay on board as long as 14 days—or spend that much money—because the *Noordam* will be sailing those 14 days in 7-day segments: seven days from San Francisco to Acapulco, with stops at Puerto Vallarta and Zihuatanejo/Ixtapa on the southward journey; seven days back with stops in Puerto Vallarta and Mazatlán on the northward leg. On both journeys you cruise by the glittering white architecture of Cabo San Lucas.

The tab for the seven-day cruises in either direction begins at $1300 to $1480 for inside double rooms, rises to $1580 to $1680 for outside doubles, and plateaus at $1780 to $1930 for large or deluxe outside doubles—all per person of course. Top-of-the-line staterooms are $2130 per person.

All those prices you just read are for seven-day cruises in off-season, but don't panic: there are only two peak-season seven-day sailings, one on December 22 from San Francisco and the other on December 29 from Mexico.

A third or fourth person sharing a stateroom pays $675, $725 more on those two peak sailing dates.

Naturally, you save quite a lot of money on the two-week cruises if, of course, you can afford the cost of the saving. Rates for the round trip range from $2010 to $2910 per person, with suites at $3240. Those two peak sailing dates will cost you $175 more in each category. Third and fourth persons sharing a cabin with two full-fare passengers pay $425 each, $525 for the peak sailing dates.

Per diem rates range from a low of about $185, rising in more expensive quarters to $225 to $275, with a high of about $304 per person per day for the largest cabins on board. And on both these ships that price includes a Dutch (what else?) chocolate on your pillow each night!

Singles pay 150% to inhabit a cabin alone.

Budget $14 per person for port charges on a 7-day cruise, $31 per person for a 14-day voyage.

16. Home Lines

Contact: Home Lines, One World Trade Center, Suite 3969, New York, NY 10048 (tel. toll free 800/221-4041, 800/522-5780 in New York state, or 212/432-1414 or 212/775-9041).

Cruising Grounds: Bahamas, Bermuda, St. Croix, St. Thomas, St. Maarten, Aruba, Puerto Rico, Jamaica, Curaçao, Grand Cayman, St. Kitts, Nevis, Antigua, Cartagena in Colombia, Panama Canal, Mexican Riviera.

Itineraries: *Oceanic—*

IN SUMMER: New York–Bermuda–Nassau–New York

IN WINTER: Fort Lauderdale–San Juan–St. Thomas–St. Maarten; occasionally Antigua, St. Kitts

Atlantic—

IN SUMMER: New York–Bermuda–New York

IN WINTER: Fort Lauderdale–Caribbean on varying itineraries, including San Juan, St. Thomas, Cozumel, Grand Cayman, Ocho Rios, San Andres Islands, Cristobal, St. Kitts, Nevis, St. Maarten, Curacao

---

Although the Home Lines fleet is small, its reputation is quite large. Both the *Oceanic* and the *Atlantic* receive top marks for good food, good service, and good-looking ships.

This small but significant line got its start in the 1940s providing passenger service between Italy and South America. Soon that service spread to providing oceanic connections between Europe and New York on two ships, the *Italia* and the *Atlantic*.

Home Lines' 39, 241-ton *Oceanic* was launched in 1965 and was among the first ships built especially for cruising, as opposed to providing transatlantic passenger service. These days the ship spends winters in the Caribbean and in summer she and the 1034 passengers she carries steam from New York on summer cruises to Bermuda and Nassau.

In days gone by Home Lines also operated another ship called the *Doric,* which now sails as the *Royal Odyssey* under the flag of Royal Cruise Line. After the line sold the *Doric,* it paid more than $100 million to a French shipyard commissioned to build the *Atlantic,* a 33,800-ton vessel that can carry up to 1150 passengers. Launched in 1982, the *Atlantic* can trot right along if she's of a mind to: the ship has a cruising speed of 23.6 knots.

An interesting feature on both Home Lines ships is a swimming pool with retractable "magrodome" which rolls right over the pool on rainy days, enabling you to "make a splash in any weather," the line proudly claims.

An enthusiastic crew of Italians provides top-flight service in dining rooms, lounges, and cabins aboard Homes Lines ships. People rave over the culinary offerings, beginning with the breakfast buffet and going right through a midnight buffet to 2 a.m. pizza!

You'll often find some interesting lecturers aboard too. Not long ago Dr. Isaac Asimov, science-fiction writer and astronomy lecturer, made an appearance at the line's annual "Astronomy Island" cruise in July. That trip even included solar- and star-viewing sessions on a private estate in Bermuda!

If you like numbers—and even if you don't—you'll be happy to discover that there's a crew member for every two passengers on board and lots of space on both. Interestingly enough, cabin size tends to be just a bit smaller aboard the newer *Atlantic.* A mid-priced cabin on that ship measures about 190 square feet as compared to 200 square feet on the *Oceanic,* while inside cabins in the budget price measure in at about 140 square feet on the *Atlantic,* 188 on the *Oceanic.*

Home Lines has one of the most detailed deck plans of any cruise line. Each cabin and its bed-bath-closet-etc. contents is sketched in with a legend provided to help you figure out just how your cabin will look. Price listings are detailed too, with each cabin both listed by number and keyed to the deck plan by color.

Prices are right in line as well, with perhaps just a bit wider range than on other ships in these waters. A six-day Caribbean cruise aboard the *Atlantic* in what the line calls its intermediate season (January and April) ranges in price from $930 per person double to $1885 per person for a fancy suite. On the *Oceanic* a seven-day sojourn in similar season is priced from a $955 per person minimum to $2325 per person for a suite.

December through April the *Atlantic* sails in the Caribbean on cruises of varying lengths. The most spectacular of those are two-weeks-plus cruises they call Pan-Atlantic, Pan-Pacific, and (teamed up for 32 days of sailing) Panorama Cruises. Those voyages depart from Port Everglades in February, traveling to St. Croix, St. Maarten, Cartagena, the Panama Canal, Acapulco, Zihuatanejo, and ending in Los Angeles. On the return voyage to Port Everglades the ship substitutes stops in Puerto Vallarta and Manzanillo for Zihuatanejo, and calls at Aruba skipping St. Croix and St. Maarten on the return journey.

During the rest of the winter season, cruises vary from 6 to 11 days, visiting well-known ports like San Juan, St. Thomas, Ocho Rios, Curaçao, and Aruba, and some less well-known stops like St. Kitts, Nevis, St. Maarten, and Grand Cayman.

The *Oceanic,* meanwhile, sails in winter from Port Everglades on seven- and eight-day cruises to Nassau, San Juan, St. Thomas, and St. Maarten, skipping Nassau on the shorter trips. One special cruise in April adds St. Kitts and Antigua to the eight-day itinerary.

In spring both ships return to New York where they sail from about the end of March through November on seven-day cruises from New York Harbor to Bermuda and Nassau. The *Atlantic* provides passengers with about four days in Bermuda. Rates on those cruises begin at $855 to $925 per person, depending on the date of the cruise.

OCEANIC: To me that phrase "Old World" comes closest to describing the feeling you get aboard this vessel. Velvets and sheer curtains, columns and shaded lamps, Austrian pleats and fancy furbelows combine in lounges and dining rooms aboard to evoke an atmosphere redolent of elegant old European hotels.

Somehow the ship seems to me a bit more formal in demeanor, exuding a refined elegance that's more conducive to quiet talks in the salon than goombay bands on the fan tail. In fact they require a jacket and tie in dining room and public rooms after 6 p.m., and nix T-shirts, tank tops, and the like at any time in the dining room.

Activities

This line has long since learned how to cater to its audience, however, so amid the velvet chairs and looping Austrian drapes you'll find all the usual fun and games from bridge and exercise classes to Bingo (one jackpot was $2400!), rum and singles parties, chess tourneys, and even Italian lessons. Entertainment is provided by a dedicated staff and features spangled dancers, singers, and a witty and popular cruise director.

Public Rooms

The best known feature of this alluring craft is the dramatic Lido Deck, where twin free-form swimming pools nuzzle back to back across 10,000 square feet of the ship's midsection. A massive sliding glass roof called a "magrodome" spreads across half the deck and can be closed so you can keep on swimming even if it's raining.

Enclosed in glass on both sides, this intriguing sunning-swimming section of the ship is rimmed by a promenade one deck up, a perfect aerie for girl-watchers to look over the options. At night circular silver plates reflect colored lights, turning the deck into a fairyland of color.

At one end of this twin-pooled area you'll find the line's Italian Candy and Ice Cream Bar, where a smiling candy man purveys what the name suggests. Those Italian ices are homemade too.

Not far away, the youngsters will soon discover, the Fun-O-Rama Room offers electronic games and pinball machines set up around a tiny lighted glass dance floor where a jukebox provides pint-size entertainment. Clever designers have carpeted a raised platform and cut out a hole in it so you can sit on the floor and dangle your feet into the empty space below the table. An adjoining table is set close to the floor so once again you pull up a piece of floor for sitting. What teenager could resist it!

Away at the other end of the pool is the ship's plush Escoffier Grill. In this circular, formal dining room trimmed in brown and beige velvets, Austrian drapes swirl across tall windows. The *Oceanic*'s other dining room, called fittingly enough the Oceanic Restaurant, is much larger and seems to us straight out of a Victorian novel. Sun streams through rows of portholes down each side of the room, glinting off wine glasses and silver, crisp white linens, velvet chairs and long sweeping benches upholstered in rose and mauve shades. Shaded floor lamps, just like the ones you see in elegant old European restaurants, add a golden glow to it all. Glass doors at the dining room entrance are curtained in silk, and if you like model ships, you'll find a huge glass-encased vessel stealing center stage.

One especially nice touch for late sleepers: open sitting for breakfast. Another nice touch: lots of tables for two down both sides of the room, and the usual assortment of tables for four or more, some of them grouped together to accommodate a cluster of up to 12 diners in a cozy setting.

Pasta lovers will be happy to find a "farinaceous" course—fusilli amatriciana, for instance—always available at dinner, and the presence of all those Italians guarantees some good food with an Italian flavor.

Far and away the most beautiful of the public spaces aboard is the Aegean Room, a serene spot filled with plush velvet chairs in glowing shades of fuschia and lavender. Tall windows make this main entertainment room a bright, airy place to gather. Rows of gold anodized columns are topped with lighting that glitters through Lucite icicles dripping down the sides—unusual indeed.

As you roam the ship, be sure to look for the striking artwork and ceramic creations that are a trademark of this line. The full-sized folkloric lasses gracing a landing near the dining room are particularly impressive examples of Italian ceramic talent.

Just outside the Aegean Room, you'll find a comfortable seating area with a dramatic metal sculpture that sweeps across a red velvet wall. (Take a good look at what the Neptunian goddess is cuddling under the arm that isn't holding a baby!)

Some artistic soul has made good use of a long, dark corridor aboard the ship by lining it with glass cases filled with tempting treasures available in the ship's shop. Intricately enameled music boxes, amusing ceramic sculptures, hefty Italian pottery, mosaic-lined picture frames.

The sound of clinking coffee cups will lead you to the Mayfair Bar, a cozy spot decorated in gray and burgundy velvet with a long bar set up to dispense that strong Italian coffee and other potables.

Just beyond you'll find Italian Hall, a circular room rimmed with windows and decked out in white tweed and aquamarine carpets and drapes. A handsome circular wood floor made of small squares of polished dark woods marks this as the dancing spot on the ship. Overhead a circular ceiling features a chandelier created from hundreds of small tubes that catch and reflect the light. A very large painting of a bacchanalian event covers one wall of this bright meeting spot.

Nearby there's a game room with felt-topped tables, camel-colored chairs, and something you may never see again: a built-in wall unit covered in leather. There's also a small library on board with some comfortable seating and lots of writing desks.

Casino fans will find their toys in the Skal Bar, and inveterate shoppers can browse the ship's perfume shop nearby. Fitness buffs should wend their way to Belvedere Deck for jogging. Film lovers can see some fairly current films in the big balconied theater way below decks.

Whether or not you're a churchgoer, take a look at the chapel on board. It's one of the most elaborate afloat, and comes complete with stained glass and brocaded altar.

You pay $6 for a week's use of a deck chair, but in one respect at least it's worth it: the chairs are those antique-y slatted wooden chairs, just like the ones you see in the movies, complete with little brass nameplate.

All through the ship you'll find similar touches of the past, from varnished wood doors to brass doorknobs and portholes.

Cabins

As for the cabins, well, ample seems the best overall description. The Sun Deck suites, for which you'll pay top price of $2325 to $2450 per person for a week-long Caribbean cruise, have huge private balconies carefully screened from adjoining rooms—great for all-over-tan fans. They're very large indeed, and come complete with living room furnished with a sofa bed, plus a bedroom with twin beds.

That price is hardly indicative of the line's cruise prices, however, since it's about $600 higher than the next lower price. So let's look at what most people will pay on this ship which divides its prices into 16 categories. Here as on most ships prices are highest on the highest decks, get lower as your go deeper into the ship. On the *Oceanic,* however, cabin prices can range widely on the same deck, so expect to spend some time looking over the deck plans.

The lowest rates ring in at $955 to $1015 per person for a double inside room and bath on Oceanic Deck, $1290 to $1365 for single accommodations. The highest price, short of a suite, is a Belvedere Deck outside cabin with bedroom, sitting room, and bath, for $1805 to $1895 per person, about $600 less for an inside stateroom.

From there down each price category drops about $100 a person, with average mid-price rates about $1500 per person for an outside cabin on a week's journey, about $300 less for a comparable inside cabin.

If your budget is aimed at something less elaborate, you'll find both inside and outside cabins quite spacious. Simply decorated in golds, browns, and burgundy, many cabins have beds that flip up by day to become high-backed couches. In some cabins the upper berths swing back against the wall. There's plenty of closet space, dressers, and nightstands, and often a writing desk/vanity and a couple of chairs.

A couple of standout cabins: A9 (a price Category 11, near the bottom of the 15 price categories available) is a spacious inside room that will cost $1070 to $1110 per person for a week's cruise; A2, a slightly more costly Category 10 inside cabin with an attractive burgundy color scheme, is $1195 to $1130 per person for a seven-day cruise.

A couple we talked to in C50 seemed happy with this ample inside cabin with sofa bed and twin beds upholstered in gold (also a Category 9 cabin, at $1195 to $1265 per person). Elsewhere on the Continental Deck a giggling group of youngsters was happily ensconsced in two rooms across the hall from each other, C109 and C115. We'd call those two cabins typical examples of inside cabins in a mid-price Category 8 bracket—sofa beds and pullman, a bank of three closets, plus a desk/vanity and chair, for $1255 to $1320 per person for a seven-day voyage.

Third and fourth occupants of a cabin, regardless of age, pay half the minimum rate.

Divide any of those numbers by seven and you'll discover a daily rate in Caribbean high season from $125 to $176 per person, less of course at less popular times of year.

ATLANTIC: Launched in 1982, this snappy new craft was designed inside and out by a bevy of architects and interior decorators. Said to have the largest outdoor deck of any cruise ship afloat, the *Atlantic* sports that same sliding glass "magrodome" roof you see on the *Oceanic*.

This is one beautiful craft, so stunning in decor that each room you visit seems more beautiful than the last. With no fewer than 23 public rooms, the ship offers plenty of places to see and be seen, to meet and to greet, to play and to do nothing at all.

Public Rooms

For openers, it seems safe to say that there's more leather aboard this ship than on any other craft afloat. Everywhere you look are acres and acres of glove-soft leather chairs, and in at least two of the lounges even the bar is made of silky leather.

Among the cozier places on board is the Rendezvous Bar, where you can plunk down in a tan leather chair—or a matching leather bar stool—while a small combo entertains for dancing on the postage-stamp dance floor. This lounge runs right down the side of the ship, so you can watch through tall windows as the *Atlantic* pulls out of port.

On the opposite side of the ship you'll find another lounge with an odd name: the Quiet Room. What exactly makes it quiet is anyone's guess, but it certainly is attractive. Those same tan leather chairs appear here, but now in a setting replete with cream-colored drapes and matching wallpaper of tranquil waterside scenes.

Between the two is the spectacular glassed-in Observation Lounge, furnished wall to wall with black and beige leather tub chairs.

In the evenings you'll be entertained in the Atlantic Lounge, a handsome multilevel room with white translucent lights overhead, comfortable couches and chairs in beige tweedy fabric, a raised stage, and a dance floor. Tinted-mirror cocktail tables are rimmed in chrome, and a steel bar shines at the rear of the room. Banks of windows stretch down both sides of this very contemporary setting that's an all-day meeting spot as well as an evening haven.

Throughout the ship you'll see beautiful contemporary glass and metal sculptures, the most impressive of which is a giant bronze Atlas holding up the world. Look for it in the main foyer, where you can settle into a dark-brown leather chair and meditate upon the difficulties of Greek gods.

It's difficult to meditate much on board this ship, however. There's always some temptation to lure you away. Tops among those are the ship's shops, which are certainly among the most spacious and beautifully designed shops afloat. One purveys perfumes, another those delightfully humorous Italian ceramics. Both are glass enclosed. Unlike some vessels where shops are tucked away in dark corners, the *Atlantic* puts them right down the side of the ship alongside big portholes that let light stream in to bounce off shining crystal and porcelain treasures.

Even the youngsters have been considered here: there's a small electronic game room.

For adult gamesters there's a spacious two-room casino featuring slot machines in one room, blackjack tables in another.

Card and Scrabble players have a room all to themselves, too, a beautiful spot decked out in green and gold with dark-wood furniture and brass-trimmed tables. This bright, airy corner with its shaded wall lamps is as quietly lovely as a library in an English manor house.

When quiet is not what you have in mind, head for the Disco Nite Club, yet another gorgeous room. This one is outfitted in deep-burgundy velvet banquettes and chairs, and lit by U-shaped graphic designs on the walls. Overhead a black ceiling is dotted with round white lights. Take all this glamor in, then step up to the S-shaped bar and run a hand over its silky surface—yes, the entire bar is glove-soft burgundy leather!

If you're looking for sports, there are plenty: in the ship's big gym you can bike on the exercycles and lift on the weight machines, then ease the pain at a massage room or in the sauna. Walk a few steps farther back on the Lido Deck and dive into the Veranda Pool, surrounded by that movable "magrodome" roof. Or walk a few steps in the other direction and splash in the Lido Pool, then sun on the open end of the Lido Deck.

If you're feeling particularly martyred after your efforts, drop by the soda fountain or try a long cool one in the cheery La Baracca snackbar or at the soda fountain in the Lido Bar.

Even the theater is something to see: its 250 seats have cocoa-brown velvet upholstery andd leather arms. Small white lights on the dark-brown walls create a graphics effect. Look for it on the Pacific Deck.

Some of the deck names aboard the *Atlantic* are twins to those on the *Oceanic*—Belvedere, Continental, Oceanic, and the easy-to-remember Restaurant Deck.

On that latter deck is the *Atlantic*'s 600-seat restaurant. It's quite similar in layout to the one aboard the *Oceanic,* but on this ship you'll find a deep-purple decor sparked with lavender and rose touches. A high domed ceiling in the center features indirect lighting to highlight the silver sculptures that adorn the room's silver pillars.

One final spot to explore: the Bermuda Lounge, a vast, glass-enclosed room in tropical orange, lime, and gold velvet decor that is continued in the adjoining Hamilton Bar. In that bar be sure to look up at the very unusual windmill-like copper lighting fixtures hanging over the (you guessed it) all-leather bar!

Activities

La dolce vita aboard this ship begins whenever you want it to, but always with a couple of cheerful *buon giornos* from this Italian crew.

You can start the day with breakfast in the Observation Lounge and move on later to a swim in one of the two pools. That sliding glass roof over one splashing spot guarantees swimming in any weather.

Golfers can drive a few off the deck into the sea while games fans plot strategy in a backgammon tournament.

Afternoons you can nibble on some delicious Italian ice cream at the Lido soda fountain or browse in the ship's shops.

An energetic crew provides plenty of other distractions as well, ranging from afternoon tea to fashion shows, trap shooting, a white elephant sale.

Every evening there's entertainment in all the ship's major show rooms, so much of it in fact that you'll be humming a variety of Italian favorites—maybe even in Italian—by the time you get back home.

While there's plenty to do aboard, the number of ports visited on this ship's cruises means you'll find fewer on-board competitions and scheduled events, at least during daylight hours. This is a somewhat more formal ship too, one on which you can expect to put on your finery every night the ship is at sea for the whole day, about three nights in ten. As is customary aboard cruise ships, dinners are informal when the ship has been in port that day, but gentlemen are requested to wear jacket and tie every evening.

Each evening dinner is a theme event too. One night there's a Mexican dinner, another a Bahamas celebration, still another a French feast. Halloween fans can think up a costume for the masquerade evening, and one evening you'll be treated to bottles of bubbly champagne.

Each evening the disco goes on to the wee hours, accompanied for many of those by the action in the casino. Night snackers will be relieved to know they can always sneak out for a 2 a.m. pizza!

Cabins

All this glamor extends to cabins too. For openers, more than 75% of the ship's 543 cabins are outside, and they're big: deluxe cabins feature 200 square feet of space with bedroom, sitting room, and full bath with tub and shower.

All cabins feature piped-in music (three channels of it), and many even have closed-circuit television.

Try as we would, we couldn't find one really undesirable cabin aboard this gleaming vessel. Every one we explored was large, comfortable, bright, and contemporary, and the suites—well, some apartments are not as gorgeous as these suites!

To travel in one of these suites is to know you've arrived: two full couches upholstered in soft butterscotch leather and a big matching easy chair, beautiful walnut paneling, a television on a stand that opens to reveal a small refrigerator, twin beds in subtle earth colors occupying a big walled-in alcove that closes off from the rest of the room with both a door and a drape, bright mirrors, a bank of tall windows, contemporary shaded lamps, a low coffee table, and a walk-in closet practically big enough to jog in! In the bathroom are sleek bright-blue contemporary fixtures, a floral bouquet painted on the mirror . . . well, you get the picture. These suites are simply the best of everything. You can occupy one of these beautiful suites on a ten-day high-season cruise for $3240 per person.

If that's strictly Dream City for your budget, don't despair. There are lovely quarters on every deck of this ship and in a comparatively wide variety of price brackets.

You'll discover shortly that reading the rate sheet for this ship is a day-long job. There are 14 categories of cabins, and prices for cruises of varying lengths from 6 to 16 days in high winter season and a season the ship calls "intermediate." No matter what category of cabin you select on this contemporary ship, you'll find lovely quarters. Even the single cabins, which are often either nonexistent or stuck in some dark corner, are lovely on the *Atlantic*

Each cabin deck features different colors, so you'll find some cabins outfitted in apple green with cream-colored drapes that feature a palm pattern in coordinating shades of green. Outside rooms on the Oceanic Deck, 036 for example, look just like that, but also have a seating area with two comfortable armchairs, a couch, television, small cocktail table, and a big mirror that makes all this look even larger. In the big bathrooms, coordinating wallpaper carries out the color scheme amid very modern plumbing. For a room in that price category, Category 6, about midway in the list, you'll pay $1155 per person for a six-day January cruise.

An outside room for a single traveler, Cabin 012 for instance, is much smaller but plenty of room for one. It has all the same amenities too: a small dresser with a slide-out board that converts it to handy desk space, another dresser in the foyer, big closets, even a green telephone. That and similar cabins are $1125 for a six-day Caribbean trip.

The lowest priced cabins on board are inside quarters that are a bit more spartan but nothing you'll find oppressive. These cabins feature the same lovely color schemes, but in these you'll find one twin bed at a right angle to the other with the second fitted out with big blocky cushions so it doubles as a couch in daylight hours. You'll still have plenty of dresser and closet space, and a reasonably sized bathroom. For one of these you pay $930 per person for a six-day cruise.

In the middle ranks are inside cabins similar to the one we just described, barely varying in size. Outside quarters are quite similar in size throughout the ship too, and even those in Category 7, a mid-priced category, include sitting areas. The cost of one of those is $1115 per person for a six-day cruise.

Prices go down as you go lower in the ship. Deluxe outside cabins in a top price category with two beds and sitting room on the Belvedere Deck ring in at $1365 per person for a six-day cruise. Prices drop $100 for similar accommodations on Pacific Deck, and finally go as low as $1155 for an outside room with two beds and bath on Oceanic or Pacific Decks.

Singles get what seems to us to be a bit of a price break on this ship. Single outside cabins can be found at the bow of the ship on Pacific, Oceanic, Restaurant, and Europe Decks with those on Pacific priced at $1125. That's within $100 of what a couple pays per person for an inside room of quite similar size nearby.

The rate range then goes from $930 to $1885 per person double for a six-day cruise in intermediate winter season, and from $1125 to $3150 single (the latter price provides you with an outside room with two beds).

The daily rate per person for a winter Caribbean cruise runs $155 to $227, excluding suites.

With such a variety of cruise lengths available (6, 9, 10, 11, 13, and 16 days), you ought to be able to find a cruise and a cabin that fit right into your bankbook.

17. Norwegian Caribbean Lines

Contact: Norwegian Caribbean Lines, One Biscayne Tower, Miami, FL 33131 (tel. toll free 800/327-7030, 800/432-9696 in Florida, or 305/-358-6680).

Cruising Grounds: Bahamas, St. Thomas, Puerto Rico, Dominican Republic, Grand Cayman, Jamaica, Key West, Mexico's Yucatán Peninsula.

Itineraries:

Norway—Miami–St. Thomas–Nassau–Private Bahamian Island–Miami year-round

Skyward—Miami–Cancun–Cozumel–Key West–Private Bahamian Island–Miami year-round

Southward—Miami–Puerto Plata–St. Thomas—San Juan–Miami year-round

Starward—Miami–Private Bahamian Island–Ocho Rios–Grand Cayman–Cozumel–Miami year-round

Sunward II—Miami–Nassau–Private Bahamian Island–Miami Or Miami–Nassau–Private Bahamian Island–Freeport–Miami year-round

---

As one of the largest and most successful cruise lines in the world, Norwegian Caribbean Lines makes it their business to know where and how people want to play. That's why you'll find this line offering cruises to the Caribbean's best loved destinations aboard ships that feature nonstop and showy, often top-name, entertainment.

The flagship of the line is none other than the massive 69,500-ton *Norway,* the world's largest cruise ship, home to as many as 1800 passengers. Six city blocks long, the former S.S. *France* has more than a million dollars worth of art on board, and features some of the biggest names in show biz in her huge Saga theater. If you like your entertainment intimate, you can play tête-à-tête in a dozen different lounges or "21" in a full-fledged casino.

The *Norway*'s smaller sisters are just as popular. NCL's *Southward, Starward, Skyward,* and *Norway* all sail on seven-night sojourns from Miami, while the line's fifth and smallest ship, the 14,100-ton *Sunward II,* features three- and four-night getaways to Nassau and the line's Out Island, Great Stirrup Cay.

This conglomerate of cruisers got its start nearly 80 years ago when a seafaring Norwegian named Lauritz Kloster bought an 830-ton steamer to haul ice and coal between Norway and Great Britain. Ten years later that one vessel had been joined by a merchant fleet, seemingly invincible even during the tribulations of World War II.

In the mid-1960s the company, now known as Klosters Rederi A/S, began examining the opportunities for specialization and shortly established a U.S. cruise division, Norwegian Caribbean Lines. Over the years the leadership of this influential shipping company has passed from its founder to his son, Mogens Wiig Kloster, and in turn to his grandson Knut Utstein Kloster, current board chairman of Klosters Rederi A/S.

In 1966 NCL brought the 11,000-ton M.S. *Sunward* to Miami, where she was the first ship to call this then-small port home. In those days the ship pulled into a berth at what is now Bayfront Park in the middle of downtown Miami!

People laughed. How could a shipping company be successful in a little port like Miami, which in those days was about as important a cruise center as Des Moines. But NCL was to prove them very, very wrong, as it turned its single one-class little ship into a fleet that today includes the largest ship in the world.

With all those experiences under its waterline, the company has learned many things about its marketplace. It has used those lessons to keep its fleet filled with laughing passengers in search of fun and frolic on the high seas, some intriguing port visits, and enough rum punch to fill the Atlantic.

When it feels things are slowing up a bit, NCL may switch a few itineraries around a bit to give its significant nunbers of repeat customers some place new to explore. Generally, however, you can depend on the ships to maintain regular schedules from Miami year in and year out, all year around. "White" ships in the fleet (the *Norway*'s blue hull has earned her a "blue" ship nickname) are switched about on different itineraries occasionally, but the vessels are so similar in ambience and size that you'll hardly notice the difference.

When NCL decided it might be time to try something really new, it just went out and bought its own island! Called Great Stirrup Cay, the island was one of hundreds of deserted Bahamian isles. It's deserted no more. These days you'll find it filled with sunning, swimming, snorkeling passengers having one whale of a time drinking in sun and rum punch on a one-day stop there.

The biggest surprise of all was last year's decision to take the massive *Norway* off her steady seven-day St. Thomas–San Juan itinerary and send her on a breathtaking Scandinavian sojourn for the summer.

Despite occasional surprises, the line sticks close to its successful formula which, in a nutshell, is seven-day Caribbean cruises to the best loved ports and to a deserted sand-trimmed island. Just to keep up with the competition and to give the first-time and/or low-budget cruiser a taste of the seafaring life, the line keeps its three- and four-day sailer, the *Sunward II,* plying the party-ship waters.

To give the cruising world something to ponder, the line in 1982 became the first cruise line to advertise on network television. And what spot do you suppose it chose? A couple of minutes right in the middle of "The Love Boat," what else!

What surprises does this line have in store next? That's anybody's guess but owner Knut Klosters has spent $1 million or more on construction of a model of a massive new cruise ship that will carry—are you ready—4000 passengers!

On this line you pick ports more than ship (except on the *Norway*) because the ships are so similar in all things from cabin size to on-board activities. When NCL hits on a good idea, it introduces it on every ship. Witness the ship's Olympic games, western evenings, Fit With Fun fitness programs, and Dive In snorkel-scuba shore excursions available on all ships.

NCL's ships are kept very clean, and they're decorated tastefully, if not always elaborately, a $62-million refurbishing campaign that will include decor updating in all the staterooms of every ship is well underway. We saw some of that renovation in its early stages and found it downright magical—from dated '50s to contemporary '80s decor in the flick of $62 million. When the job's complete these will certainly be among the best dressed ships in the Caribbean.

Cabins, with the exception of suites, are of just-average size, not what you'd call spacious but big enough to share comfortably with another sailor.

NCL's *Sunward II, Southward, Starward,* and *Skyward* are not elegant or formal ships, but they're solid, well-maintained contemporary craft sailing to appealing ports. On them you will find dedicated service, some good, simple cooking, and a delightfully international crew overseen by friendly Norwegian officers who speak perfect, delightfully accented English.

If you have only three or four days to spend, you can try life aboard the partying *Sunward II,* where spirits are free and the partying is nonstop. *Sunward II* travels to Nassau, Freeport, and the Out Island.

If you have a week, here are some tips to help you decide.

Norway, sailing to St. Thomas, Nassau, and that Bahamian Out Island, is spectacular in both size and variety of entertainment possibilities.

The *Southward* is relaxed and casual on visits to more ports than any of the other ships: sunny St. Thomas, old (and very new) San Juan, the mountains and silvery beaches of Puerto Plata, and romantic Nassau.

Skyward, the look-alike for the *Starward*, travels to less frequented ports, visiting the archeological treasures of Cozumél, the scuba-diving heaven of Grand Cayman, and the Old Florida antiquity of Key West.

Finally, the *Starward* is for beach lovers. It offers you a look at sand-trimmed Ocho Rios, a chance to dive in the crystal waters of Grand Cayman, and sun on the jet-set beaches of Cozumél.

NCL stays right with the competition in offering free or very low-cost air fare from dozens of cities across the U.S. Your travel agent can help, and the line's brochures will help you figure what your cruise will cost.

Activities

NCL has found a very secure niche by appealing to people who want to visit some interesting sun destinations without spending a great deal of money. It provides informal cruises jam-packed with day-into-night activities designed to appeal to those who love a casual party. There are, of course, a couple of dress-up evenings aboard, but you'll wear your flip-flop sandals and T-shirts much more often than black ties or glass slippers.

Passengers aboard these ships don't seem to fall as neatly into categories as they do on some other ships. Most, one would guess, are middle-income, middle-age-bracket travelers, many taking their first cruise, and all of them ready, willing, and able to have a good time.

NCL provides for that with masquerade parties and western night barbecue-hoedowns on deck; with a hilarious ship's Olympics that involves, among other games, carrying a balloon between your knees and passing it off to another Olympic star; and with professional entertainment every single night.

Now on the *Norway*, well, that's different! On that ship you'll often find top-name entertainment as well as the line's high-kicking, spangled Sea Legs Review, song and dance-sters that would do Broadway proud.

NORWAY: To speak of this ship is somehow always to say the *Norway* in awed if not hushed tones. There's no question about it: this stately grande dame can steal any show.

It's a trip just to tour this massive vessel and that's before she's even left the dock! How big is she? Well . . . once France's pride, *joie*, and national flag carrier, this 70,200-ton bruiser-cruiser is so large the *Sunward II* could fit inside just her forward engine room without touching any of the walls! To get this beauty on the road . . . er, sea. . . . takes 24½ gallons of gas just to move the ship her own 1035-foot length.

One crew member told us that when he met a friend in a corridor aboard one day, the other fellow welcomed him back from vacation. "But I wasn't on vacation at all," the crewman reported. "I just hadn't seen that guy aboard for three months!"

So huge is the *Norway* that the 800-person crew of this craft has an entire world of dining spots and lounges all to itself, while the 2000 passengers aboard can choose from a dozen bars, two perfectly gorgeous dining rooms, a maze—and we do mean maze—of public rooms and boutiques.

This ship is so big they have international symbol signs to help you find your way around. And that's not to mention 63 ship's directories, each with a locator map of key shipboard facilities and an overview of each passenger deck.

Public Rooms

So you'll know how to read those deck signs, starting from top deck down they show a sunburst for the Sun Deck, some pine trees and rippling water for the Fjord Deck, a snowflake for the Oslo Deck, a stylized globe for the International Deck, some waves and a railing for the Pool Deck, a Viking helmet for the Viking Deck, a Norwegian flag for the Norway Deck, lots of waves for the Atlantic Deck, a palm tree for the Biscayne Deck, and a jumping dolphin for the Dolphin Deck. Got it?

When you find your way to the shopping center on the International Deck, you'll discover not one small souvenir shop but an entire shopping center called International Promenade. Jade and Cartier gold, T-shirts and tennis shoes, aquamarines and aspirin, follies and furbelows, it's all there. You can browse in shops like Upstairs at the Downstairs, featuring everything from cameras to porcelain; Le Drugstore, for everything from basic toiletries to ashtrays; Dimensions, for swim wear and clothing; Scandavia, for those intricately knitted Norwegian sweaters, fashionable Swedish glass, or enameled jewelry from Denmark; East of Eden, for Oriental silks and jade; the Golden Touch for 18-karat gold jewelry.

If you don't care anything about shopping, fear not. There are 40 or 50 other things for you to do. For instance, participate in the line's Fit With Fun program, that works its way through weightlifting, to brisk walks and runs, and aerobics. Try arts-and-crafts classes in flower making, ice carving, collage, or magic. Or play Bingo—sometimes the jackpot is in the thousands!

Listen to the cruise director expound on the next port. Jog around the one-eighth-mile track on the Oslo Deck or on shore, using a handy Joggers Cruise News map provided by the line.

Take in a movie in the 500-seat theater or try trap shooting. Drop in on one of the multitudes of parties ranging from a Honeymooner's Champagne Party to a Grandparents' Party to an Unattached Party, or the ship's Olympic games.

You can play volleyball, nine-hole miniature golf, or golf ball driving. Or take aerobic or social dancing classes, inspect the bridge, or try on-board horse racing, with bets of course.

For you sedentary souls and anti-group-activity types, you can scrunch into an easy chair on one of the *Norway*'s huge enclosed decks and meditate on the history and glory of it all as you let the porpoises provide a floor show. Explore acres of polished wood rails and slate floors, marble-topped tables, and teak decks so long you think surely they must reach port hours before you do.

Stroll down one side of the ship and you're an entrepreneur exploring posh Fifth Avenue lined with ornate wrought-iron furniture. Walk the other side and you're a boulevardier on the Champs-Élysées. Or stop by the card room and its adjoining Henrik Ibsen Library, decked out in pale aquamarine velvet Austrian drapes set off by velvet-topped tables and find a like-mind player.

While you're having this marvelous time, rest assured that any youngsters you might have brought along will be doing even better. For the little ones there's Trolland, a playroom full of the child's equivalent of adult toys. It's open daily and when the ship's in port.

As you explore this massive vessel, whose funnel soars 17 stories high, you see a fortune's worth of artwork including beautiful tapestry weavings.

Three pools offer plenty of places to paddle, but if you're looking for the most swimming space, head for the pool near the Lido Bar—it's the largest sunning-swimming spot.

Will you starve? No way! Begin with breakfast in the dining room, or on deck in the ocean breezes, or in bed. Lunch on a cold salad bar, hot dogs, and hamburgers at the Great Outdoor Restaurant, or go for the full sit-down multicourse luncheon. As the sun slides gently over the horizon, you sip your final pre-dinner (or post-sun bathing) libation in the West Indies Bar, the Windjammer Bar, the poolside Sunspots Bar, the Café de Paris, the North Cape Lounge, or the Lido Bar.

Then it's on to dinner in the dramatic formal Windward Dining Room, where tiny lights sparkle in the huge domed ceiling and subtle scone lighting turns the room into a wonderland. Or in the Leeward Dining Room, where more than 500 diners can be accommodated in this two-story wonder that features a stunning brushed-steel circurlar staircase curving elegantly down from a second-level balcony to the main-floor dining area. Once upon a time this impressive dining room was for second-class travelers(!), while high rollers were assigned to the elegant Windward Dining Room with its wide and equally grand staircase.

Want something special that isn't on the menu? Seek and ye shall find it delivered.

Enough? Certainly not. After dinner it's on to the glittering sequined razzle-dazzle of the leggy Sea Legs Revue, equal to anything Vegas has to offer. Auditions for these shows' performers occur three times a year and are as competitive as anything *A Chorus Line* ever saw.

Or take in a show featuring Vic Damone, Shirley Jones, Diahann Carroll, Roger Miller, Buddy Greco, Jim Nabors, or the Smothers Brothers, among others. So top-notch is the entertainment aboard that seasoned cruise passengers book a cruise only after they've selected which performer they want to see.

There's a 15-piece band in the North Cape Lounge and piano players in the bars.

We don't think even the competition would argue with the *Norway*'s claim to the best entertainment afloat. The toppest in top-name stars make guest appearances aboard. If you love entertainment, you hardly need read further for you have found your dream boat.

The *Norway*'s Monte Carlo Room casino claims honors as the largest casino afloat, featuring 180 slot machines, eight blackjack tables, roulette, and craps.

Or make your way to any of a dozen lounges on board or to the A Club Called Dazzles disco where a rainbow-lit glass floor flashes, and the splashy neon trim is as contemporary as the silvery decor. While you're dancing, you can look through portholes into an illuminated swimming pool. Relax, the room's soundproofed so you can sleep even if you're in a nearby cabin.

At Checkers Nightclub you'll find deep-red decor trimmed with onyx black as night and a dance floor created with checks of black and white marble.

High ceilings, shining chandeliers, and great open spaces recall the vessel's venerable past in the ship's "living room."

From racquetball to clown-and-popcorn Carnival Night, from sequined showgirls to lazy afternoons on deck, you'll never want for something to see and do.

Cabins

Now primarily a seven-day sailer visiting St. Thomas, Nassau, and the line's Bahamian Out Island, the *Norway* has recently been redecorated so she's more luxurious than ever. The cabins are all decked out in contemporary plaids in deep blues or soft earthy shades. The walls are creamy white, making the rooms seem larger.

In peak Caribbean season, which on this line runs from about late December to April, cruise prices are grouped into 16 categories, with Category 1 the highest priced quarters and Category 16 the lowest.

So varied are cabins and prices, the mind boggles. There are fabulous suites with big separate sitting areas, billowing drapes, and touches of art deco in the decor. Those very grand suites cost $4875 per person for a seven-night Caribbean cruise. There are slightly smaller versions of that with a king-size bed, Moorish windows, big wardrobes, and contemporary sofas for $2710 per person—quite a drop.

As you move down to Category 3 cabins, you'll find junior suites with twin beds outfitted in the line's new-look tailored bedspreads with contemporary plaids in subtle colors. In these cabins there is often a loveseat and chair in a separate sitting area, and needless to say, big windows. These quarters are $1035 per person for a seven-night Caribbean cruise.

One category down, Category 4, in the ship's deluxe outside rooms, the cabins get a bit smaller and one bed serves as a couch during the day; some have a double bed. Outside cabins have a big window, however, and like all cabins on board, a closed-circuit television and telephone. A cabin in this price category costs $1885 per person for a week's Caribbean cruise.

In the next three categories, outside double rooms with twin or double bed, you'll pay $1635 to $1760 per person for a seven-night sojourn.

If you don't mind doing without a window, a superior inside room with twin beds is $1510, the ship's mid-priced cabin. These come in a variety of shapes and on several decks, but NO83, NO79, NO80 and NO84 are among the larger cabins in this category. Outside rooms with doubles beds are available for the same price—$1510 per person—but these are a bit smaller.

Three categories of inside rooms with twin or double beds—Categories 11, 12, and 13—range in price from $1360 to $1460 per person. Even cheaper is an outside room with upper and lower berth, available for $1235 per person for a week's trip.

The lowest-priced cabins on board are inside quarters on Biscayne Deck, Category 16, but there are only a few of these. For a seven-night Caribbean cruise in one of thse small cabins with upper and lower berth you pay the minimum rate available on board: $1095 per person. A few more inside rooms with upper and lower berth are available for $1210.

You can figure that prices on board for the usual seven-day cruise range from a low of $156 to a high of $269 per person daily, suites higher.

A third or fourth adult person sharing a room pays $570; children pay $375. The single rate is 150% of the fare in Category 11, 12, and 15 cabins, 200% in other categories.

SKYWARD: Perhaps the most unique element of the *Skyward* is an open-air, balconied lounge on the aft end of the ship. When this ship sails on its "Mexibbean" cruises to the Yucatán Peninsula/Cancún area, this tropical half-roofed three-story lounge is outfitted in palm branches and adorned with replicas of famous Mayan sculptures, one of which features a somewhat bemused fellow balancing a plant on his belly.

Public Rooms

Elsewhere on this 16,250-ton ship, look for a gorgeous Lucite etching of a ship under full sail and check out the brass sculpture in the Pot of Gold piano bar. In the Starlight Dining Room you'll find an impressive fiber wall hanging that plays perfect counterpoint to the soft pastel color scheme here.

For entertainment, head for the Lido Disco, which features tropical furnishings and a round steel floor. There's a flashy stage show, too, and it has something going on every single night. In addition to a masquerade ball and strolling Mexican singers at dinner, there's a Mexican folkloric show to get you into that "South of the Border" mood.

Here too, as aboard other NCL ships, one evening is devoted to a Country and Western Night. Jeans, boots, ten-gallon hats, sombreros, big belt buckles, and anything remotely western is dress of the day. Western dance lessons too. Barbecued ribs and chicken stave off midnight hunger pangs.

Dancing girls—and guys—put on a terrific show, similar to (but not as large as) the show aboard the *Norway*. It takes place in the Paradise Lounge, where you'll find an unusual color scheme that somehow successfully mixes burgundy and oranges around a parquet dance floor.

Just off that lounge is the Viking Bar, a smaller sipping spot that's a wonderfully intimate corner for private tête-à-têtes.

The Cumuku Bar up on Compass Deck is a pleasant hideaway, and in the Pot O'Gold Room down on Rainbow Deck you can pursue that glitter at the tables or machines. Or take in a movie at the ship's theater or go shopping in a row of gleaming shops and boutiques.

On every deck you'll find fiberglass walls depicting that Mayan theme too.

Naturally you'll find a swimming pool on board—this one's figure-eight-shaped to inspire you to match it.

Cabins

Cabins on the *Skyward* are done in the company's theme colors: blue and beige checks with cream walls—very contemporary, very attractive. Most cabins are medium-sized, long and narrow with two twin beds separated by a nightstand and often backed with a porthole. There's a desk/vanity in most rooms, and of course more space in the suites.

Rates aboard are divided into 15 categories, from Category 1 (the highest prices) through Category 15 (the lowest). There are two seasons aboard this Yucatán sailer: Season 1, the high season, roughly from late December through mid-April; and Season 2, a less expensive cruising season from late April to mid-December.

NCL has its rate categories divided up by decks which makes prices a bit difficult to ferret out, but if you want to be on a certain deck of the ship you can see what's available on that deck quickly.

All cabins are carpeted, and have private bath, radio, and phone.

Let's look at the price of cabins for a week's voyage in peak season.

The top accommodations aboard are big suites on the Boat Deck. The biggest of these has a sitting room with a convertible sofa, lounge chairs, bedroom area with double bed, and *two* private baths. For one of these suites you pay $1910 per person for the week-long peak-season trip to Cancún, Cozumél, Key West, and the line's pretty Out Island. Slightly smaller suites on this deck are $1655 per person for the trip.

Inside rooms on this deck occupy space between the suites. For this good address the cost is $1285 per person for a cabin with double bed and folding upper berth.

Outside rooms with two lower beds that can be pushed together to create a double bed are $1455 per person on Atlantic Deck, $1410 on Biscayne Deck, and $1335 on Caribbean Deck. Similar rooms with a double bed and folding upper berth range from $1355 per person on Atlantic Deck to $1320 on Biscayne and $1235 on Caribbean. Inside rooms with a double bed and folding upper berth are $1220, $1200, or $1135 per person on the three descending decks.

The least expensive cabins on board, and there are just four of these available—501 through 504 at the bow of the ship—have an oversize lower bed (not as big as a double) with a folding upper berth. These are $995 per person.

Finally, outside rooms with a lower bed and folding upper berth on Atlantic Deck or Biscayne Deck are $1160 or $1110 per person. These are located where the ship's structure begins to curve, so they have a bit less space than similar accommodations nearby.

A cabin for four on the *Skyward* has upper bunks that sport a slide-and-pull mechanism that lets you lower them and use them for storage of extra luggage if all four aren't being used for sleeping. That extra storage space may not seem important, but it's surprising how much you can acquire on even a brief voyage.

Third and fourth persons sharing a cabin pay $495 for adults, $295 for children under 17 in any season or category.

Single travelers pay 150% of the fare. If you share a cabin for four with others assigned by the line, you pay $595 per person.

Port charges on board are $24 per person, adult or child.

Per diem costs range from a low of $142 to a high, excluding suites, of $208, with middle bracket in the $165 to $183 range.

Very competitive air/sea programs are available from many cities in the U.S. to get you to Miami at little or no additional cost.

SUNWARD II: Once called the *Cunard Adventurer,* the *Sunward II* is the second ship of this name to sail under NCL colors. This *Sunward,* a 14,100-ton vessel carrying 718 passengers, was rebuilt and relaunched in 1977 when she was given her new name. Now she plies happily between Miami and the Bahamas, filled with sun-seeking passengers in search of a days-long "Bahamarama" beach party. They get just that at the line's Out Island Great Stirrup Cay in the Berry Islands.

A bit smaller than some of the line's other ships, the *Sunward II* offers dining in the Sunburst Dining Room, decorated in earthy colors with chrome accents. Etched-glass dividers add sparkle to the room, which has some unusual banquette seating as well as tables.

Aboard all NCL ships you'll see some handsome Scandinavian craft work. On this ship the rya wall hangings on each landing are particularly dramatic.

Public Rooms

The Bahamarama Lounge is a good-looking spot outfitted in burgundy upholstery and featuring a big ceramic sculpture as its focal point, lots of etched glass, and mirrored columns, plus a stainless-steel dance floor. In this room you'll watch the ship's nightly entertainment.

Another steel dance floor turns up in the Lido Café/Disco, and at horse racing time some ornate carved wooden equines provide an interesting departure from the usual plywood nags.

The *Sunward*'s movie theater has an unusual and bright decor, and frequent top-quality films. There's also a big swimming pool and plenty of sunning space, plus sauna and massage rooms too.

There are some homey touches aboard—things like sheer white curtains trimmed in burgundy and tied back around the portholes—that make this a particularly cozy weekend home.

A large casino offers five blackjack tables and two banks of slot machines, plus the ever-present roulette wheel.

An interesting feature aboard is an artist who occupies a kind of second-story den overlooking the casino. He'll whip up a portrait of you in practically no time at all.

In the Crow's Nest nightclub you can pretend you're captain at a big ship's wheel. Outdoor types can sip at the roofed-in outdoor Buccaneer Bar, snappily trimmed out in navy and white.

Shoppers will enjoy the impressive shopping arcade studded with treasures from around the globe.

Cabins

Most of the 359 cabins aboard the *Sunward II* are average or small in size, certainly not huge, and sometimes tiny, although some of the outside staterooms are quite spacious, as are the suites of course. Cabins that are small are *definitely* small, however. Don't plan on spending a lot of time in one of those.

High season aboard this ship is roughly the same as aboard the line's other cruisers. On the *Sunward II,* however, add sailings from mid-June to mid-August to the peak season. Favorite vacation periods turn those months into an extra peak season for these short party cruises.

Let's see how much you will pay for a cabin in that peak season for a three-night cruise to Nassau and the line's Out Island.

Top price aboard will buy you an outside stateroom with two lower beds and sometimes an upper folding berth. Again, all cabins have private bathrooms. One of these rooms will cost $595 to $615 per person for the peak-season three-night cruise.

Three more categories of outside cabins with two lower beds or upper and lower berths are $545 to $565 per person for the peak-season cruise.

Seven categories of inside cabins, ranging from Category 7 through Category 13, drop $10 in each category, beginning at $525 per person and ranging to $405. Some of these rooms have two lower beds and some have upper and lower berths (your travel agent can help you secure the kind of cabin you want). The lowest price aboard is $315 per person for an inside room with upper and lower berths for the three-night cruise in peak season.

Third and fourth adults sharing a cabin pay $240, while children under 17 pay $130 for a three-night cruise in any season or category.

Port charges on a three-night cruise are $18 per person; on a four-night trip, $20 each. Christmas and New Year's sailings are higher in price.

Per diem rates for a three-night peak-season cruise work out to a low of $105 per person, a middle range of $165 to $155, and a high, excluding suites, of $201 per person.

SOUTHWARD: This 16,607-ton craft is very like her three sisters, the *Starward, Skyward,* and *Sunward,* in size and ambience, and has an interesting intinerary that includes a visit to little-known Puerto Plata in the Dominican Republic. The *Southward* joined the line's fleet in 1972 and inaugurated a 14-day itinerary from the Port of Miami. In 1975 the line bet its future on seven-day cruises and the *Southward*'s since been sailing on week-long voyages.

This ship has an atmosphere very similar to that on the line's other vessels, and many of the same activities, ranging from a masquerade ball to a country and western evening and in-port Dive-In snorkeling excursions.

This is NCL's answer to those who love ports. The *Southward* stops at four—San Juan, St. Thomas, Nassau, and Puerto Plata—with three days at sea.

Public Rooms

The big and shining El Dorado Dining Room offers a lovely view of misty green islands sliding by outside. One evening during your cruise you'll be treated to a fiery display of baked Alaska, paraded around the room in glittering splendor by waiters who sometimes balance the trays on their heads.

A recent addition aboard is a set of shining exercise equipment tucked away in a corner of the ship. You'll find everything here from an exercycle to chin-up bar, with weights you add on with the flick of a key.

The main lounge aboard is the bilevel Clipper Lounge, the center of attention each evening for showy entertainment flown in from one of the other ships or some amusing slapstick comedy provided by a hardworking staff.

A bank of slot machines is set off in a small separate room that's a favorite spot for some of the more dedicated gamblers: we watched one lady work two machines at a time every night and many afternoons every single day of the cruise! (Yes, she won—quite a lot.) Others were content to climb up to a tiny couple-of-tables casino where blackjack players were busy computing combinations of 21.

You can find the young and young-at-heart set rocking in the Crow's Nest Nightclub, a lively spot so dark we couldn't tell you *what* color it is in there. Nearby there's a small but impressive observation post where tall, tall windows offer you a look at the same view the captain's seeing.

For an even better captain's-eye view, take one of the ship's tours of the bridge.

Up on one of the wings that rise at the rear of the main lounge aboard you'll find a small library and a card room. Lovers should head for the opposite side of the ship to search out a tiny lounge that's small as a cozy living room, with comfortable couches and chairs, a piano, and usually few other people.

If you don't want to leave the sunshine on Beach Deck (which is where you'll find the larger of the two swimming pools aboard), pick up a hamburger or hot dog or Danish at the casual Riviera Bar.

An energetic crew of all-American types keeps you going with all kinds of activities ranging from aerobics to arts and crafts. You can learn the merengue, that step-drag-step-drag dance so popular in the Dominican Republic, at dance lessons or try skeet shooting with one of the Norwegian officers. On shore, the cruise director can lead joggers in the best jogging directions and a couple of underwater enthusiasts will teach you how to snorkel.

Cabins

Cabins aboard are just about the same as on all the ships, although some are larger than average. An outside cabin will have twin beds, decorated (until the renovation is complete) in tropical colors, oranges, golds, and the like.

There's a desk/vanity, a couple of closets quite big enough for this short journey, and plenty of drawer space to stow your belongings. Portholes are the traditional circles rather than the large windows found on some newer ships, but they're large enough to keep things bright, especially in the fierce Caribbean sun.

All quarters on board have compact private bathrooms, some with both tubs and showers, others with showers only.

On the *Southward,* prices begin with Category 1 suites and work down through Category 15 cabins, which are the lowest priced accommodations aboard yet are outside cabins! That's quite a departure, but there's a catch: the beds in these cabins are what the line calls "oversize" lower beds. Translate that to mean a bed that's smaller than the normal double bed yet larger than a twin. Definitely not recommended for light sleepers or chunky folks.

On this ship too, Season 1, peak season, runs from the latter part of December through mid-April, and the low season begins in late April running through mid-December. Cabins do not differ much in size but do differ in price from deck to deck, decreasing as you go lower in the ship, farther away from the topside entertainment facilities. This means that cabins on Atlantic Deck will cost more than identical quarters on Biscayne Deck, one deck lower, which in turn cost more than the same quarters on Caribbean Deck.

To get an idea of what you'll pay for a cabin on board, let's look at the prices for a cabin on a seven-night cruise to Puerto Plata, St. Thomas, San Juan, and Nassau in peak season.

A suite aboard the *Southward* will cost $1910 or $1695 per person, depending on size of the accommodations. Both those suites include a sitting area with sofa, chairs, and tables either in the room or in a foyer. More expensive accommodations have a double bed; less costly suites have twins. Inside rooms up near these Boat Deck suites have a double bed and folding upper berth, and are $1320 per person for the peak-season cruise.

On Atlantic Deck, outside rooms with two lower beds that can be pushed together are $1485 per person, and similar accommodations with a full double bed and folding upper berth are $1385. Inside rooms here are $1285 per person and also have a double bed and folding upper berth. Outside rooms in Category 7 have those oversize lower beds we mentioned earlier, and are $1190 per person for a week's cruise.

One deck down, on Biscayne Deck, outside rooms are $1430 per person for a week's cruise and have twin beds. Outside quarters on this deck with double beds and folding upper berth are $1350 per person. Inside rooms have a double bed and folding upper berth and cost $1245 per person, while the budgetwise but very cozy outside rooms with oversize lower bed are $1135 per person in peak season.

You'll find the lowest prices aboard on Caribbean Deck, where outside rooms with two lower beds are $1380 per person and similar accommodations with full double bed and upper berth are $1280. Inside rooms here have a lower and folding upper berth, and are $1160 per person. The lowest price aboard for the week's cruise in peak season is for outside rooms with the small double bed, $995 per person.

Per diem rates run from a low of $142 to a middle price range of about $178, and a high, excluding suites, of $212 per person in peak season.

STARWARD: As the first ship to join the present fleet, the *Starward* bears a close resemblance to the *Skyward.* She weighs 16,000 tons, and carries 740 passengers and about half that many crew. The *Starward* joined the fleet in 1968, two years before the *Skyward.*

This is the beach lovers' ship. It visits the sands of Cozumél, Grand Cayman, and Jamaica, three very lovely beach spots indeed. If the line's Dive-In program sounded interesting to you, this would be the ideal ship to book. Its stops offer some of the best snorkeling and scuba diving in the Caribbean, in the world for that matter.

Starward sports a starstruck out-of-this-world theme. To give you an idea what that means, there's a Galaxy Deck on which you'll find the Neptune Dining Room, the Venus Lounge, and the Orion Club.

There are two swimming pools on board, one near a pool bar on the Boat Deck, the other one deck down near the Lido Bar.

If you're looking for an intimate get-together spot, the Garden Lounge gets our vote. It's a lovely spot, high up on the Compass Deck.

The major entertainment on board takes place in the Venus Lounge, a big room with tables and banquette seating in the center of the room and similar arrangements down both sides so everyone has a good view.

A few steps away is the Neptune Dining Room, where tables for four and six predominate. On this same deck, Galaxy Deck, you'll find the ship's small casino and the adjoining Orion Club, an unusually shaped room that winds around a dance floor and has lots of windows through which you can spot the real Orion.

There's even a two-level theater where you can catch that film you missed at home.

With a lovely name like *Starward,* it stands to reason that the ship would have more than a passing interest in those stellar glimmers. That's why you'll find on board an observation platform that's home to the *Starward*'s Star Planetarium! Now that's surely a first for a cruise ship.

Cabins

Cabins aboard are average in size, although larger outside cabins offer a bit of moving-around space. On this ship price is determined by the deck your cabin is on. As you go farther below in the ship, the price gets cheaper, although the sizes of the cabins do not vary. This means that a cabin on Atlantic Deck will cost you more than one directly beneath it on Biscayne Deck or Caribbean Deck.

Suites feature double beds and small sitting areas, but in some of the doubles the beds take up most of the room. Closet space is curtained off in some rooms, but there's enough wardrobe space to accommodate a week-long voyage.

All rooms have private bathrooms, some with tubs but most with shower only (no tub). In 1984 the line began its cabin renovation of this ship so you should now or soon see some of those pretty blue bedspreads, cream-colored walls, and coordinated draperies in *Starward* cabins.

Peak season (they call it Season 1) on this ship is late December through mid-April. Season 2, or low season, runs from late April through mid-December.

The fares below apply to a week's trip to Ocho Rios, Grand Cayman, Cozumel and the Out Island, in peak season.

Starting at the top on Atlantic Deck, you'll pay top price aboard for a week's cruise in the comfort of a suite with a double bed, sofa, chairs, sitting area, and bathroom with both tub and shower. Suites like this are $1760 per person, while somewhat smaller but similar accommodations (with a convertible sofa bed in the sitting area) are $1640 per person for the week-long trip.

Outside rooms with two lower beds that can be pushed together to become a double bed are $1560 per person on Boat Deck, $1510 on Atlantic Deck, $1455 on Biscayne Deck, and $1370 on Caribbean Deck. Slightly smaller outside rooms with a double bed and folding upper berth are $1405 per person on Atlantic Deck, $1370 on Biscayne Deck, and $1295 on Caribbean Deck.

Inside cabins with a double bed and folding upper berth are $1320 per person on Atlantic, $1300 on Biscayne, and $1230 on Caribbean.

The lowest priced cabins on board are outside rooms with upper and lower berths. These are $1205 per person on Atlantic Deck, $1150 one deck below, and $995 on Caribbean Deck.

Third and fourth adults sharing a cabin pay $495, while children under 17 pay $295.

Single occupants of a cabin for two pay 150% of the fare, although the line offers a share-a-room program in which you pay just $595 for a week-long cruise if you share a room with three other budget-conscious travelers assigned to that room by the line.

Port charges are $24 per person, adult or child, and Holiday sailings are $75 to $100 higher.

Per diem rates, as you can see, work out to a low of $142, rising to a middle range of about $172 to $200 per person, and a high, excluding suites, of $223 per person.

18. Paquet Cruise Lines

Contact: Paquet Cruise Lines, 1007 North American Way, Miami, FL 33132 (tel. toll free 800/327-5260, 800/432-3362 in Florida, or 305/374-8100).

Cruising Grounds: Mexico's Yucatán Peninsula, Grand Cayman, Puerto Rico, St. Croix, Curaçao, Martinique, Îles des Saintes, Bahamas, Panama Canal, Mexican Riviera, Alaska, Europe.

Itineraries: *Dolphin*—Miami–Nassau–Miami or Miami–Nassau–Freeport–Miami year-round

Mermoz—

IN WINTER: San Juan–St. Croix–Guadeloupe–Trinidad–St. Lucia–Iles des Saintes–Martinique–Iles des Saintes–St. Thomas–San Juan OR San Juan–St. Bart's–Guadeloupe–Curaçao–La Guaira (Caracas)–Barbados–Martinique–Antigua-St. John–San Juan

IN SUMMER: Mediterranean cruises

Rhapsody—

IN WINTER: Miami–Ocho Rios–Grand Cayman–Playa del Carmen–Cozumel–Miami

IN SUMMER: Vancouver–Juneau–Skagway–Glacier Bay–Ketchikan–Vancouver

---

Paquet Cruises likes to accent its French connections . . . with wine, what else? Every night at dinner the wine is French and free. Of course you'll have to cross palms with silver for Château Lafitte Rothschild, but at least you can rest easy knowing the wine cellar here does not lack.

If you like a little song with wine and thou, you won't want to miss Paquet's enchanting music cruises aboard the *Mermoz*. Some of the world's top musical artists appear aboard these voyages, and who could pass up a chance to jog Grand Salon Deck with flutist James Galway or a dancer from the New York City Ballet?

Paquet's *Mermoz* is a good choice if you like offbeat destinations. Because it's a comparatively small ship, just 13,800 tons, it visits some smaller harbors rarely reached by larger vessels, places like Martinique, St. Croix, Curaçao, Îles des Saintes.

If a quick getaway is about all you can see in your winter future, Paquet's *Rhapsody* features week-long cruises to the western Caribbean ports of Cozumél and Grand Cayman. In summer the ship sails into the icy waters of Alaska.

If all you can manage is a weekend, try a cruise aboard Paquet's *Dolphin,* which has three- and four-night sojourns to Port Canaveral and Nassau.

Modern cruise lines can often trace their roots back to the earliest days of steamshipping, and Paquet is certainly one of those. Back in 1860 a gentleman named Nicola Paquet got together with a few friends and chartered a 350-ton steam-sailer called the *Languedoc* for runs between Marseille and Morocco. Three years later Paquet and companions branched out to Senegal and the Canary Islands, forming a company called Compagnie de Navigation Paquet, or in less foreign terms, the Paquet Navigation Co.

That company remains in operation today under the same name, but it hasn't been smooth sailing all those years. During both World Wars the line's passenger/cargo liners were pressed into service by the Allies and they didn't fare well. But that didn't discourage Paquet, which just rebuilt its fleet and went back to business as usual. So vigorous has this company been over the years that it has operated 46 different ships! In the late '60s the company became a subsidiary of a conglomerate with interests in textile and cellulose products, and also operates container ships and UTA Airlines.

In 1966 Paquet introduced its first passenger ship designed solely for cruising, a vessel perhaps fittingly named the *Renaissance*. A short time later the company joined the activity in the Caribbean where it began its now-legendary Music Festivals at Sea, about which you will read more shortly.

By the beginning of the '70s Paquet had put the 13,800-ton *Mermoz* into service. Following a massive renovation in 1984, she returns to San Juan where she will spend the winter as usual, sailing to offbeat Caribbean ports. In the spring she heads once again to Europe where she spends the summer touring the fjords of the North Cape and sailing to Mediterranean ports.

Paquet also operates another ship, the 11,600-ton *Azur,* a super-casual craft that sails from Toulon carrying passengers and cars to Mediterranean ports.

In 1979 Paquet began marketing the *Dolphin* for Ulysses Cruises, calling the combination Paquet Ulysses, and offering weekend party seekers three- and four-night cruises from Miami to the Bahamas.

The newest member of Paquet's family is the *Rhapsody,* the former *Statendam,* which became part of the line in December 1982. This ship spends her winters in the Caribbean and her summers in the glacial waters of Alaska with, of course, Panama Canal voyages in between.

Paquet Cruises on the *Mermoz,* and to some extent on the *Rhapsody,* are what we would call adult voyages as compared to some of the fun-and-games sailings so common in the Caribbean. Entertainment on board longer cruises is shorter on beer-drinking contests and longer on more intellectual pursuits, things like lectures on art as an investment, lessons on creating the perfect omelet or learning more about French cheese—or even learning French itself. While there's no lack of things to do on board, a more refined demeanor prevails.

The *Rhapsody,* competing in a very tough seven-day cruise market, retains the usual sun-and-fun activities for competition's sake, but tries to add some esoteric elements, for instance, a spring cruise focusing on sea life in the planet's oceans.

The *Mermoz,* on which you'll pay higher rates, unabashedly aims its appeal at what marketers call the up-market, the more sophisticated and experienced travelers who want a more meaningful cruise experience than suds-swilling competitions can provide.

Paquet's *Mermoz* is praised to the skies for its outstanding French cuisine, and rightfully so. There are some superb cooks aboard this ship—and outstanding service to match. A nice additional touch: the ship serves you a bottle of very good French vin de table each night, no charge.

Most of the staff aboard the *Mermoz* and the *Rhapsody* are French with a sprinkling of Indonesians, but on the *Dolphin* you'll find handsome Greek officers.

MERMOZ: The *Mermoz* is a very French ship that's so appealing to Europeans you'll find everything aboard written in both English and French. So French in feeling is she that even the line's officials will tell you that on the ship's European cruises, you really ought to "have at least some appreciation for France and the French" to get the most from the cruise.

That's less true on Caribbean cruises, but even there you'll sniff the aroma of hundreds of croissants and brioches a-baking each morning, and be treated to a choice of no fewer than 36 cheeses every night! It won't be long before you're dunking your croissants in your morning chocolate and tucking into mouthwatering French pastries every night just like everyone else.

The *Mermoz* also makes no bones about the kind of passengers she attracted: those "who appreciate these unique refinements . . . the most sophisticated of travelers from both sides of the Atlantic." From the terry robe provided for you, to movies in both English and French, you know you're on a very special and sophisticated voyage.

Activities

There's just naturally something musical about the sea, something that inspires great music. It seems quite a logical step then to turn a cruise into one long round of glorious music under the stars, under the sun everywhere.

Sound enchanting? That's just what Paquet thought when it created the first of what were to become many musical cruises aboard the glittering *Mermoz*. Imagine a silvery beach stretching out before you, the inky-black night playing backdrop to twinkling stars, and the delicate notes of a flute floating faintly out into the night.

That is the *Mermoz*'s Musical Festival at Sea, an event now celebrating more than 25 of its twice-a-year festivals. Among the performers who have participated in the noteworthy event have been pianists Byron Janis, Joseph Villa, cellist Mstislav Rostropovitch, flutist James Galway, trumpeter Maurice André, singers Galina Vichnevskaya and Stafford Dean, the Eder Quartet of Budapest, the Norwegian Chamber Orchestra.

Granted, this is going to cost you, but there's practically no other way you could ever buy the chance to meet and talk with such performers during long sunny afternoons by the pool or quiet evenings at sea.

Exact dates for this year's cruise haven't been set, but the line usually schedules it in the first two weeks of February. In Europe this sonorous sailing last year took place in September. So well known among U.S. music lovers are these musical cruises that even on the European sailing the ship carries more American passengers than Europeans.

Evenings called Gala Nights provide special tributes to the regions of France—Bourgogne or Provence, for instance—and the wine and menus reflect that region. Other nights focus on the Caribbean's fascinating islands.

Whether or not you make that very special cruise, you'll find the *Mermoz* a welcoming craft with some of the finest food afloat.

Public Rooms

This floating feast begins at breakfast with those flaky croissants only the French can create perfectly and perhaps a cup of chocolate. If you want to stick with tradition, there's wine and Camembert and crusty French bread for lunch. If you don't, you can try one of the multicourse feasts in the dining room or the poolside buffet lunch. Everyone dines at the same hour aboard, either in the large Restaurant Deck dining room or in the Grill.

At dinner in the ship's Grill or Dining Room the menu includes such delicacies as foie gras, papillote of salmon poached in white wine, veal with apricot stuffing, and lobster in champagne sauce. Wine enthusiasts have not only the free bottle of wine at lunch and dinner, but thousands of bottles of vintage wines too, and 15 different champagnes to sip.

This feasting and sipping goes on all day—and night—long, performed with the grace and style the French bring to any event that includes food.

And on this ship everything, but absolutely everything from the sommelier to the maître d'table, is French.

As for the ship, she's a small craft, just 13,800 tons, and carries just 625 passengers in 321 cabins. With ten decks at the disposal of passengers, she provides all the amusements any cruise ship has to offer.

On the Sun Deck is a well-equipped gymnasium. One deck down, on the Lido, there's a swimming pool and the popular pool bar. One deck farther down, the Grill Deck, is yet another swimming pool, plus just what the name suggests, a little Grill for not-far-from-the-pool dining. Tucked away behind an elevator is the ship's small library.

In the evening you'll want to head for the Grand Salon Deck where the ship's bevy of entertainers appear in the 500-seat Grand Salon. Here too you'll find a dramatic arcade of glass-enclosed boutiques filled with treasures.

Le Club, a nighttime dancing and sipping spot, occupies a prime position on the Restaurant Deck, where the ship's big dining room features unusual domed lamps hanging down from the ceiling and shedding a golden glow on the spotless linens below.

For a sound and light event, head for the ship's Caverne Disco, way down on the Caverne Deck.

If your idea of an entertaining evening is a trip to the movies, rest easy. *Mermoz*'s Studio 240 Theater seats more than that number of people. And casino lovers will find games aboard, and plenty of opportunity to get your own card games started with like-minded souls.

Cabins

There's very little point in describing the decor of the cabins aboard this ship for the best of reasons: *Mermoz* was scheduled for a $10-million stem-to-stern renovation in preparation for the 1984–1985 winter cruising season.

All the ship's public rooms and cabins will be fitted out in contemporary colors and fabrics, polished and shined to a faretheewell, before her return to San Juan where she'll resume her winter schedule of 10- and 11-day cruises to romantic Caribbean islands.

With this line's talent for renovation, as witnessed on its *Dolphin* and *Rhapsody* cruisers, there's every reason to anticipate some very lovely quarters when the overhaul is complete.

We can still give you an idea what you'll be paying, however. Rate categories are numbered from 1A to 10, with Category 10 the lowest priced inside cabins (but still with two lower beds). Quite a number of rooms on board also have upper berths to sleep a third or fourth person. All rooms have private bath, telephone, two-channel radio, and wall-to-wall carpeting.

The top-of-the-line cabins on the Information Deck (1A) feature two lower beds and a bathroom wth both tub and shower. These cost $2570 per person for a ten-day winter-season cruise to Caribbean ports like St. Lucia and Antigua, plus six other stops. The next lower price category (Category 1) is a deluxe outside cabin with a double bed. One of these costs $2465 per person for a ten-day Caribbean cruise.

Categories 2 through 7 are all outside cabins. Accommodations in any of these will cost $1835 to $2360 per person for that same ten-day cruise, depending on the size of the cabin.

Finally, the three lowest prices aboard are all for inside cabins, ranging in price from $1510 to $1720 per person for a ten-day cruise.

Eleven-day cruises cost proportionately more, and third and fourth adults sharing a stateroom pay $1085 for ten days aboard. If that third or fourth occupant is a child from 2 to 12, the additional charge is $585 per child. For children under 2 you pay $10 a day.

Single travelers pay 140% to 150% of the per-person rate for double occupancy, depending on the price category of the cabin selected. You can also join the line's "Paquet Partners" program, which will team you up with a roommate of the same sex so you both can share a cabin and pay the per-person double-occupancy rate.

RHAPSODY: It's easy and also punningly tempting to wax, er, rhapsodic over this 24,500-ton vessel that spends its winters in the sunny Caribbean and its summers among the glaciers of Alaska. For one thing, she's had a long and fascinating history since her construction in 1957. Many of those years between then and now have been spent as one of the showpieces of Holland American Lines, which operated her as the *Statendam* on cruises to Bermuda and the Caribbean.

Those who book a Caribbean cruise this winter or next summer to Alaska will have the fun of being among the first to see the *Rhapsody*'s brand-new Promenade Deck, the third and final phase of a long renovation project on which the line has spent a great deal of money. In November the ship went into drydock where that deck was gutted and refinished stem to stern.

Public Rooms

When you step aboard this handsome vessel, you'll be greeted by white-gloved attendants who escort you to your cabin.

An intriguing feature on the *Rhapsody* is a glittering chrome lighting fixture that plunges down alongside the main stairway from top to bottom deck. Look up or down at it as you pass by and you'll gaze upon a maze of glittering metal and seemingly infinite white light.

Now all decorated in contemporary colors and fabrics, this Promenade Deck contains the ship's big Rhapsody Lounge, where you can see a wide range of lively entertainment from dancing girls and guys performing a Broadway Salute to a Carnival in Nice presentation. Windows down both sides of the room fill the lounge with light, and a big raised bar set with glass sculptures offers a nice vantage point for both interior and exterior sights.

If your knees are strong, you can sneak off for a nightcap in the Can Can Bar, where low, low, low seats settle you a foot or so off the floor beneath a miniature baby grand piano with a shining white lacquered finish.

You can usually find a quiet corner in the American in Paris Lounge, a cozy spot designed as a series of small living rooms separated by unusual hook-shaped room dividers. Mirrors that reflect the room's tweedy beige furnishing back at you are so artfully placed you'll think these small spaces are huge. There's even one completely enclosed seating area here if you're looking for a very quiet spot. This lounge gets our vote for the best sitting spot aboard.

For your spare moments there are plenty of shops, the library and card room, a Lido café for snacks.

Which brings us around to food, the very best part of a *Rhapsody* cruise. Throw away your scales and prepare to enjoy, for food aboard Paquet ships is outstanding, certainly the best of any seven-day cruise ships. You'll find all those marvelous French touches in things like duck à l'orange or flaming desserts, lobster or Kansas City beef. Every night you'll also find a bottle of red or white French wine on your table, and you'll never get a bill for it.

You'll be consuming all this in the ship's Cordon Bleu Restaurant, a pretty place filled with reed and chrome Breuer chairs upholstered in glowing navy blue offset by bright-pink napery. Windows down both sides of the room keep it bright all day long, and at night domed lights in the round ceiling create a golden glow.

Walk off some of those delicious calories on the Upper Promenade Deck where you can march on an open deck at the stern or take shelter from the breezes in a short glass-enclosed promenade. A casino filled with all the usual gaming devices is flanked by the card room and library where you can always find a good book—or a magazine from the nearby newsstand—with which to while away a slow day.

We saved the best for last: the Sun Room. Plunked down just aft of the observatory, this small semicircular room is a delight. It's glassed in, has comfortable contemporary brown leather chairs, and is one terrific spot to settle in for some dedicated sea-gazing.

Activities

From the moment you step on board there's always something going on. On Caribbean voyages a Calypso band gets things off to a rhythmic start with entertainment up by the Lido Café—and that's while the ship's still at the dock! You can get a preview of the ship's dining opportunities at a bon voyage snackbar, to which you can invite your friends, although they'll have to pay ($6) to partake of a big buffet of goodies prior to castoff.

Besides such special events the *Rhapsody* also provides plenty for you to do. It has a 330-seat theater, a gymnasium, and both an indoor and an outdoor swimming pool. There are even men's and women's saunas (although they still call them Turkish baths on the deck plans).

Scheduled activities aboard are unusual: lectures on investments or cooking classes that will help you perfect your omelet technique, French lessons or French cheese tastings. If you like films you can watch them two ways: in the ship's theater or on a big-screen television where video cassettes are played.

Speaking of theater, last summer the ship sponsored a Theatre at Sea production in which such stars as Orson Bean, Helen Hayes, Anne Jackson, Patrice Munsel, James MacArthur, and Eli Wallach participated. Presented by the Theater Guild, the cruise featured special presentations and lectures by the stars and discussions with *New Yorker* theater critic Brendan Gill. A repeat event is likely this year too.

Don't despair if you can't make that one, however. No matter when you sail you'll find plenty of activity going on around you: a Masquerade Night, a "Latin Fiesta," or "A Night in the Tropics," for instance. And bring something blue for the ship's "Rhapsody in Blue" evening.

With more than one crew member to every two passengers, you can expect—and get—very attentive service. "I got lost in one of the passageways one day," an enthusiastic passenger once told us, "and almost before I realized I was lost, I had a couple of crewmen come up and shake hands with me, laugh, and walk me to where I was going. They're wonderful!"

After you've worn off a few calories clapping for the showy entertainment in the Rhapsody Lounge or danced off a few, it's time to wend your way back to your cabin.

Cabins

Inside and outside cabins are about equally split here—264 outside and 193 inside cabins, for a total of 892 passengers (more if some share rooms with a third or fourth person).

Cabins on the *Rhapsody* come in a variety of sizes and shapes, but all are attractively decorated and most are quite spacious quarters. Refurbished in 1983, the cabins are now decked out in soft earth tones, beiges, browns, pale blues, occasionally a deep green or royal blue. You'll find new carpets underfoot, private shower and/or bathtub in every room, telephones, radios, and quite adequate space.

An intriguing new element in many rooms are double beds that flip back up into the wall like a Murphy bed. Once they're up, a small tweedy couch appears to provide additional seating, and with beds flipped up there's really quite a lot of space, even in smaller inside cabins.

Let's look at some of the quarters available and the prices you'll pay for a seven-day Caribbean voyage.

Deluxe suites on the Upper Promenade Deck are the top-of-the-line accommodations, with two lower beds, full bath, separate sitting area, and long built-in storage units with a drop-down desk/bar. Shutters keep out the morning sun and attractive paintings hang between wall lamps. Two really pretty ones are Cabin 48, decked out in a deep hunter green, and Cabin 55, a navy-blue beauty. Of course these are also the costliest quarters. For a week in one of these spacious cabins, you'll pay $1695 per person for a week-long Caribbean cruise in peak winter season.

Working down a bit in price, Categories 3 through 7 are all outside accommodations, all with two lower beds and some of those with a double bed. You may or may not have a bathtub and a shower, but you'll have one or the other, and of course, complete bathroom facilities. About the only difference in these classes is the price and the size of the cabin, although all these outside quarters seem quite spacious and there's not a great deal of difference in space. In this price bracket the Category 3 cabins on the main deck are very nice; Category 7 rooms like Cabins 110 and 104 are just a bit smaller. If you prefer the minimum of neighbors you might try Category 3 Cabin 134 or 135, both of which are just off the ship's reception area. In any of these categories you'll pay $1275 to $1545 per person for a week's cruise.

If you're keen on an outside cabin, Category 5 accommodations, located on several decks, seem to us very good buys, particularly those on the Upper Promenade Deck. Of those, Cabins 40, 41, 50, and 51 are spacious accommodations tucked in among the highest priced cabins on board, but you can get one of these for the medium price of $1395 per person for that week-long Caribbean sojourn.

Category 6 cabins are $85 less per person and offer some good-looking quarters. One we liked was Cabin 223, one of those flip-up double beds with full tub and shower and plush brown carpeting. An outside cabin, it features two portholes and quite a large bathroom, with the same big built-in dresser/wall units found throughout the ship. An intriguing feature in all rooms on board are small metal brackets that flip down to hold small bottles in place so they don't slide off the dresser.

Quite a number of inside cabins in Category 8 have double beds now.

That's good news for those in search of a real love boat and a bargain! Prices for these inside accommodations are $1195 per person for a week in peak winter season.

The least expensive outside cabins on board seem a good buy at $1095 per person, although there aren't very many at this price. Cabin 313, for instance, seemed a spacious twin room with upper and lower berths, that built-in dresser, a big wardrobe, chair, and small coffee table.

The rock-bottom rate on board, Category 10, will buy you an inside cabin with one lower and one upper berth and a shower (no tub) in the bath. You'll find these on Main and Allegro Decks, and the price is $995 per person for a sailing week in high season.

Third and fourth persons sharing a cabin with two full-fare passengers pay $485 each for a week's cruise, while children under 16 pay just $285 each. In Alaska you should budget an extra $26 for port charges, and in the Caribbean, $20 for adults and $18 for children under 16.

Good news for singles: There are cabins aboard for single occupancy. The bad news: There are very few of them. For one of those outside cabins you pay $1295 in peak season for a week's cruise. A group of inside cabins with upper and lower berths also are available for single occupancy and cost $1195 for a week's cruise. Otherwise, single rates in Categories 3 to 8 are 150% of the double occupancy fare, 200% in Categories 1 and 2.

Good news for everyone: You can often find some very good bargains on this cruise ship, which in the winter of 1983–1984, for instance, offered inside cabins with upper and lower berths or a double bed at $599 for a seven-day cruise! Better yet, for $699 you could have had an inside cabin with two lower beds, and for $799 an outside cabin with two lower beds. If one of those deals is in effect, your travel agent will know. Check.

DOLPHIN: The smallest of the line's ships, the *Dolphin* was built in 1956 and was once known as the *Ithaca*. She's a diminutive lady, just 12,500 tons, carrying 565 passengers. Rebuilt in 1973 and refurbished in 1984, the ship takes its 565 sunseekers on three- and four-day cruises from Miami to Nassau and Freeport all year round.

In the pre-plastic era shipbuilders created with wood, and you'll see what we mean aboard the *Dolphin,* which has acres of shining dark-wood decks, wood trim around the cabin doors, wooden wardrobes, lovely paneling, small round wood cocktail tables in one of its lounges, even some pine dressers and nightstands.

Greek officers add a pleasantly Mediterranean touch to the ship, while the best loved French flavor is added by complimentary French wines at dinner.

Under that distinctive red, white, and blue funnel with the flying white gull on it, you'll find a typical short-cruise party ship that concentrates on three days of fun and frolic. Many cruise lines like to keep at least one ship in the three- and four-day market to snag new cruisers who want to give this cruising business a try. Paquet is no exception to that, and the *Dolphin* is their response.

These days this small party ship is lovelier than ever, with a brand-new look from stem to stern. Redecorated in 1984, it now looks as shiny as a new penny, with delightfully plush fabric wall coverings in passageways and cabins, contemporary and colorful decor everywhere. Gray and rust tones predominate in the passageways, and rooms are now decorated in peach and russet or pale-blue and steely-gray combinations.

Lording it over the main entrance of the ship is a shining brass-and-steel sculpture of leaping dolphins at play in a sea of silver waves.

Activities

Although small, the *Dolphin* offers all the activities that characterize these short Caribbean voyages: plenty of sunshine, gambling in the casino, swimming in the pool, entertainment night and day.

Because so many single people like to take these cruises, the voyage begins with a party for the unattached.

In the mornings there are dance and exercise classes, and in the afternoon you can practice your putting on a golf green. Daily quizzes test your trivia knowledge and fashion shows give you a look at what the shops have to offer.

There are movies in one of the lounges and a tour of the bridge. Not to mention pillow fights, Goombay music, beer-drinking competitions.

One evening you'll be invited to meet the captain, and on the final evening of the cruise he'll preside over a farewell dinner. Most nights there are variety shows in the Rendezvous Lounge, movies, and dance contests. Before and after those evening shows, the Café Miramar is the gathering spot. Much later, the cine-disco is the spot aboard.

Public Rooms

There's a particularly handsome swimming pool on board surrounded by the most spectacular wood decking you'll ever see. It may be mahogany, but none of the crew was a woodworking expert so we never did determine that for sure. Whatever it is, it sweeps across all the decks, and provides a raised sitting area around the edge of the small pool.

If you're taking the youngsters along, you can deposit them in a small circular pool just three feet deep while you splash in the deeper water of an adjoining pool. A poolside bar? Of course.

One more toy for the youngsters (and perhaps the not-so-youngsters) is up on the Promenade Deck too: an electronic game room lined with 13 of those whirring machines.

Breakfast and luncheon buffets are available in Café Miramar so you don't have to miss a minute of sunshine. A big circular bar is the focal point of this room, which features an attractive contemporary decor of Breuer chairs and spacious banquettes, lots of mirrors, a handsome wood dance floor, and a huge wood wall hanging that combines the room's orange, beige, and brown color scheme. Lots of big windows let in the sunshine in daylight hours and a view of the stars at night, when this becomes a dancing spot.

You'll be dining in the Barbizon Restaurant, an attractive but small dining room serving excellent food up to and including some sinful French pastries. Low ceilings and dark gold decor make this room a rather dark spot, but the top-notch food aboard easily makes up for any missing decor pizazz.

From there, gamblers can head up to the Promenade Deck to the Monte Carlo Casino, where there's even a coin-operated roulette wheel. You pick the odds and the wheel automatically revolves, paying you off if you win. What next?

Those in search of the evening's entertainment will head for the pretty

Rendezvous Lounge. Velvet banquettes and chairs in handsome oranges and magenta encircle a central dance floor where the ship's nightly entertainment takes place. That show, by the way, might be a magician, a singer, or a comedian, or any combination of the above.

For a nightcap, try the Club Royal, a small cozy spot where the bartender will whip up a very satisfactory piña colada. Dancers will beat an immediate retreat way down to Dixie Deck, where the Disco is tucked away in a spot that doesn't keep anyone awake. You can party there until you drop—they'll go on just as long as you do.

A small shop aboard provides for basic needs.

Take the elevator on this ship only if you're an antiquarian or courageous or both. A real antique it is, with double doors and unpredictable behavior.

Cabins

When you do finally drop—after, we hope, the midnight buffet of French bread, fruit cheeses, pâtés, and a thousand or so other goodies—you'll do so in one of 284 cabins found on five of the ship's seven decks.

All the *Dolphin's* cabins were refurbished in 1984 so you'll find plush new carpets in contemporary gray or rust, and matching peach or misty-blue bedspreads with tiny cream leaves scattered across them. Coordinated drapes reverse the color scheme, and all the walls have been covered in earthy-colored fabrics.

The *Dolphin* recognizes two seasons it calls "value" season and "on" season. Value season includes January, late April through May, and mid-August through about mid-December. That leaves February through most of April and June through mid-August as "on" season, when prices in each rate category are about $30 higher for a four-night cruise, $20 more for a three-night voyage. As for the difference in price between a three-day and four-day cruise: you pay $115 more per person for a four-day cruise in value season, $125 per person more in peak season.

The top-of-the-line stateroom aboard is Cabin 511, a suite with a separate entrance to its next-door sitting area. And very pretty it is too, decorated in brown widewale corduroy and plush carpet. A handy built-in wall unit also houses dozens of glasses, each carefully set into a built-in holder to keep them steady.

Other top-price cabins are as usual located on the top decks of the ship. Aboard the *Dolphin* you pay the highest rate for a cabin on the Boat Deck, where outside rooms are extra-large with two lower beds and a full bath, including a hand-held shower, and more wardrobe space than you'll find elsewhere on the ship. Now all decked out in the line's new peach or pale-blue drapes and bedspreads, these are large and pretty quarters. For one of these cabins you pay $555 per person if you select a room with twin beds on a three-day high-season cruise ($20 less for a double bed).

The next four grades of outside cabins (Categories 2 through 5) will cost you $490 to $520 per person for a three night cruise in peak season, $610 to $640 per person for a four-night trip. The higher priced cabins are on Atlantis and Boat Decks, with lower prices in this category found on Barbizon and Caravelle Decks.

Quite a number of cabins, both inside and outside, have double beds. One particularly pretty one is Cabin 400, which follows the curve of the ship and thus has a most unusual shape. It also has its own porthole, but only a view of the deck beyond. A nice sketch of an old sailing ship hangs on one wall and there's a cozy feeling to the room that's appealing. It's $520 per person for a three-night cruise in peak season. Cabin 403 is also a pretty double-bedded room. Some inside rooms with double beds, however, are set up so someone has to sleep next to the wall and clamber out over the other sleeper.

The least expensive cabins on board are inside quarters with lower and upper berth. Some of those are almost as large as some of the more expensive accommodations, Cabin 411 for instance. That one is right near the center of activity aboard, Purser's Square, and quite close to many cabins costing almost twice as much. For one of these dollarwise choices you pay $300 per person for a three-night cruise in peak season.

Three or four adults sharing a room will do so only with good friends. While multiperson cabins are a good buy aboard and are larger than are found on some newer vessels, they're pretty close quarters for four. Nevertheless if you're willing to share your space, you'll save quite a bundle. Third and fourth adults pay just $200 ($250 for a four-night trip), and if those third and fourth passengers are children under age 12 the price is just $100 each for a three-night cruise, $125 for four nights.

Some of the more accommodating rooms we saw aboard include Cabin 421, with a fetching little shell-shaped lamp and lovely pale-blue decor and big porthole; Cabin 403, a nice double; Cabin 411, an inside cabin with more of that pale-blue decor, two lower beds, and a spacious feeling despite its small size; and Cabins 501 and 502.

Radios, complete carpeting, and telephones are in all rooms. Bonne nuit!

19. Premier Cruise Lines

Contact: Premier Cruise Lines, 101 George King Blvd., Port Canaveral, Cape Canaveral, FL 32920 (tel. toll free 800/327-7113, 800/432-2545 in Florida, or 305/783-5061).

Cruising Grounds: Bahamas.

Itinerary: *Royale*—Port Canaveral–Nassau–Andros (Bahamas)–Port Canaveral Or Port Canaveral–Nassau–Andros (Bahamas)–Port Canaveral year-round

---

Premier made its première in the spring of 1983 when it bought Costa Line's *Frederico C,* then painted, primped, and polished her up to present her to the cruise world as the *Royale.*

As the latest entrant in the three- and four-day cruise marketplace, the *Royale* was greeted with loud huzzahs by officials of Central Florida's Port Canaveral. They'd been trying for years to lure a cruise line to this small port hard by the Kennedy Space Center.

Rigged out in shiny red and topped by a red smokestack emblazoned with a red P for Premier, the *Royale* steamed into port to begin year-round cruises to the Bahamas. Owned by Greyhound Corporation (yes, the bus people), the ship is hoping to tap what it sees as a lucrative market of 24 million Central Florida visitors who come here to visit famed Walt Disney World.

That tie-in with Greyhound, by the way, goes even a step further. Greyhound has recently begun operating a fleet of express buses connecting Disney World with about 40 Florida cities. Needless to say, that system can also be used to transport visitors from other parts of the state to Central

Florida where they can experience both Disney World and the cruise world in which Greyhound now has an increased interest.

Premier has in fact worked out a package program in which you can spend four nights at sea with the dolphins and three nights on land with the Mouse.

ROYALE: Built in 1958, the *Royale* is a 20,410-ton ship designed to carry 689 passengers. She's carrying those passengers to Nassau and Andros Island, the largest of the Bahama Islands, on the three-day cruise, and increasing the journey by one day by spending an extra day in Nassau on the four-day trip.

Bruce Nierenberg, a top executive at Premier and one of the founders of the line, promises they're going all-out to provide the best of seven-day amenities—and then some—to passengers on these shorter cruises. Nierenberg, who for years was an executive at Norwegian Caribbean Lines, says Premier wants to bring some of the elegance to the three- and four-day cruises with things like real china and delicate little treats for tea time, "not a plastic cup and a Lorna Doone."

Themed dinners are another way they're adding that elegance, he says. Each evening will be French or Italian or some other ethnic night, and everything in the dining room, right down to interchangeable paneling on the walls, will reflect the theme. On French night just remember to call your waiter François, not Frank!

Public Rooms

On board this craft you'll find lots of deck space, probably the single most important item to cruisers looking for a couple of days of Bahamian sunshine.

This close to the Kennedy Space Center it's only natural to think celestial thoughts, which accounts for the interplanetary monikers that appear on every public room.

If you're sailing with children, send them on up to the Bridge Deck where the Big Dipper Ice Cream Parlor and Captain Video Arcade will keep them occupied tummy and soul.

One deck down, you can soothe away your tensions in a big oval whirlpool backed by a pool bar with the unlikely name of Mars Bar. At the bow on this deck, in the Apollo Observatory, you can get a look at the starry world that inspired the names aboard.

If you have something a bit more starstruck in mind, you might begin looking down on the Lounge Deck where the Starlight Cabaret offers an oval dance floor surrounded by a cluster of chairs and loveseats. On this deck you'll also find the ship's Casino, a big, wide-open spot with a bank of slots and the usual gambling games.

Search a bit off to the port side on this deck and you find a quiet piano bar that makes a lovely spot for post-prandial sipping. Off to the starboard side (that's the right side) you'll find another small watering hole, the Gemini Room.

Major entertainment on board occurs in the ship's big Club Universe, where a rectangular stage is the focal point for a room outfitted in snappy colors. Up here too you'll find a small Satellite Café for snacks.

Not worn out yet? Okay, on the Promenade Deck you'll find the Saturn Lounge tucked away near the ship's big swimming pool. Down a deck, on the Restaurant Deck you can watch a film in the Mercury Theater, and down one more deck, on the main deck you can party at the Outer Limits disco, a slickly contemporary circular room.

You'll dine aboard in the Galaxy Dining Room, a long U-shaped room featuring many tables for four and six, a few for two.

Activities

Nonstop entertainment is a feature of most three- and four-day ships, and the *Royale* is no exception.

You can rev up with an aerobic class out on deck at the Apollo Observatory, or nibble wine and cheese at a tasting. You can of course find suitable entertainment in those seven lounges on board, or listen to someone else entertaining at the piano bar.

There are first-run films in the Mercury Theater, big-band sounds in the lounge, movin' music in the disco. If you stay awake until midnight, you can nibble at the special outdoor midnight buffets.

When you get to Andros Island, home of little leprechauns called "chickharneys," you can walk a mile or so down an empty beach and see if one of the little creatures will come out to play.

Although Andros is the largest island in the Bahamas, it's one of the least known. Beaches are lovely here, and stretch for no less than 500 miles around the island! Andros is also tops for diving fans. Here you divers can discover a deep, deep ocean depression called the Tongue of the Ocean, a hole in the ocean floor so deep no one knows just how deep it really is. Although you won't see the bottom of that, you can get to the bottom of some coral reefs and explore deep troughs known as "blue holes," home to zillions of gaudily colored sea creatures.

Premier has come up with a Splash Down snorkel program that will teach you how to snorkel in shallow water just offshore and reward you with an official Splash Down certificate.

The *Royale* offers some amusing diversions for you on shore as well. You'll be greeted by a cannon salute as you step ashore, and later a gang of marauding "pirates" will visit. You can also go on a treasure hunt to pirate Henry Morgan's cave.

Cabins

Cabins are about equally divided between inside and outside quarters, with 192 outside accommodations and 155 inside cabins. That's as much uniformity as you'll find, however. To take a look at the ship's deck plans is to wonder if there are any two cabins alike on this craft.

So different are they, in fact, that there are 15 rate categories, and a 16th to cover family accommodations! (Here's where you'll really discover how wonderful your travel agent is.) To complicate matters further, the rate list is divided into on- and off-season departures. On-season runs roughly parallel to the prime season in Central Florida: June through mid-August, when the youngsters are out of school and visiting Disney World, and over Christmas. Off-season ranges from mid-April to June and from late August to about December 21.

The following prices are for a three-night peak-season cruise. Figure about $165 more per person for a four-night trip.

The top accommodations on this ship are outside suites on the Promenade Deck. These have two single beds and a sofa bed in a separate sitting area. They're decorated in tropical colors, and like all the cabins aboard, have a little wicker basket full of shampoo, fancy soaps, shower caps, and the like. The cost of one of these suites is $650 per person for a three-night cruise in peak season, $830 for a four-night trip.

Moving down a bit, Category 2 cabins are larger outside staterooms with two lower beds or a double bed. Four of these cabins (P17, P18, P19, and P20) have a queen-size bed. A Category 2 cabin costs $610 a person for a three-night cruise, $795 for a four-night trip in peak season.

Categories 3, 4, 5, and 6 are standard outside cabins with two lower beds or a double bed. These accommodations range in price from $530 to $560 per person for a three-night cruise in high season.

Three categories of larger inside cabins with two lower beds or a double bed—Categories 8, 9, and 10—are priced from $480 to $510 per person.

Among the better outside cabin buys on board, although they are narrow or oddly shaped, are Category 11 cabins, which have upper and lower beds. There are not many of these on board and they're scattered about on several decks. For one of these you will pay $440 per person for a three-night cruise in high season.

Finally, the lowest priced cabins on board are in Categories 12, 13, and 14. All are small inside cabins with upper and lower beds. These cabins are $400, $390, or $295 per person, depending on size.

It's possible to rent a cabin without a bathroom for $245. For $195 you can take the same cabin on a family plan and use it as a connecting room to a room with full bath.

Single rates are $660 for an outside cabin, $445 for an inside cabin, in peak season for a three-night cruise.

Port charges are an additional $20 per person.

Third and fourth persons sharing a cabin with two passengers paying full fare are $240 per adult for a three-night cruise, $130 for children under 17. For a four-night trip the fare is $325 for adults, $165 for children.

Premier has air/sea add-on fares from a number of cities, ranging from $175 from Atlanta to $300 in Chicago, Cleveland, and the like.

20. P&O / Princess Cruise Lines

Contact: P&O / Princess Cruise Lines, 2029 Century Park East, Los Angeles, CA 90067 (tel. toll free 800/421-0522, 800/252-0158 in California, or 213/553-1770 or 213/553-7000).

Cruising Grounds: Puerto Rico, St. Thomas, St. Maarten, Barbados, Martinique, Aruba, Curaçao, Cartagena (Colombia), La Guaira/Caracas (Venezuela), Panama Canal, Mexican Riviera, Alaska.

Itineraries: *Pacific Princess*—

IN SPRING/SUMMER: Mediterranean cruises

IN FALL AND WINTER: San Diego–Puerto Vallarta–Mazatlan–Cabo San Lucas–San Diego

Island Princess—

IN SUMMER: San Francisco–Vancouver–Prince Rupert–Juneau–Skagway–Glacier Bay–Sitka–Victoria–San Francisco

IN WINTER: Los Angeles–cruising by Cabo San Lucas–Mazatlan–Puerto Vallarta–Manzanillo–Acapulco–Zihuatanejo–Puerto Vallarta–Mazatlan–cruising by Cabo San Lucas–Los Angeles

Sun Princess—

IN SUMMER: Vancouver–Juneau–Skagway–Glacier Bay–Misty Fjord–Vancouver

IN WINTER: San Juan–Barbados–Grenadines–Martinique–St. Maarten–St. Thomas–San Juan *Or:* San Juan–Curaçao–La Guaira (Caracas)–Grenadines–Martinique–St. Thomas

Royal Princess—

IN SUMMER: Vancouver–Juneau–Skagway–Glacier Bay–Sitka–Vancouver

IN WINTER: Los Angeles–Acapulco–Panama Canal–Cartagena–Aruba–Martinique–St. Thomas–San Juan, returning same route to Los Angeles

---

Born in the early 1800s, the Peninsular and Oriental Steam Navigation Company grew and prospered over the years until today it owns and operates some of the finest ships afloat and is England's largest passenger line. In fact it was on P&O ships that a word you have heard many times was born: posh. Although posh now means something elegantly upper crust, the word has some very humble beginnings as nothing more than a four-letter designation stamped on certain steamship tickets. That POSH stamp on an Egypt to India ticket indicated the ticket was the possession of a passenger traveling Port Out, Starboard Home, the coolest, and thereby best, cabins on board.

Today P&O, as it is known, operates three big cruise ships, the *Canberra, Oriana,* and *Sea Princess,* but is better known in the U.S. for its ownership of what is now quite a famous cruise line. More on that in a moment.

The flagship of P&O is the huge *Canberra,* 45,000 tons of classic transoceanic traveler. On board you will find at least 1735 passengers, and more than 800 crew members. When you stop to think that many Caribbean cruise ships carry 800 or fewer passengers, you can see that this is one whale of a ship!

Officers on the vessel are Britons or Aussies, some of whom provided a couple of weeks of hilarious nonstop entertainment when we sailed this craft some time ago. Crewmen come from Goa, Pakistan, and China.

Sadly, the *Canberra* makes only a very occasional stop in North America, spending almost all her time on an annual—and fabulous—world cruise abetted by summer Mediterranean voyages. She does, however, stop in Fort Lauderdale's Port Everglades about twice a year, once in the fall prior to her world cruise and once in the spring on her return to England. You can, of course, join her then or anywhere in the world to participate in all or part of her transoceanic adventures.

Sister ships in the line include the *Oriana* and the *Sea Princess.* Of those two, the 26,700-ton *Sea Princess,* once known as the *Kungsholm,* sails in the South Pacific in winter and in the Mediterranean in summer. Meanwhile, the 42,000-ton *Oriana* takes 1750 passengers on cruises of Mediterranean and Australian waters.

Much better known in North America is P&O–owned Princess Line. Princess may in fact be the best known line in the world, thanks to television, for Princess is none other than . . . blare of trumpets, the "Love Boat" line!

Now, let's get what you really want to know right up front here. No, Gopher and Captain Stubing and Julie and Doc and Isaac are not real people and they do not spend their nonfilming hours working on the *Island Princess,* the *Pacific Princess,* or the *Sun Princess.* Travel agents tell us it's downright amazing how many people are crushed to discover that the stars of "Love Boat" do not actually work on one of the Princess ships! Which says a great deal, of course, for the talented performances staged by "Love Boat's" crew of actors in the series.

Now that we've crushed your fondest dreams, let us add that you can sometimes see the stars who play those parts on board one of the Princess ships. They go aboard regularly to film some of the location shots necessary for their popular "Love Boat" television series.

Even if you don't see your favorite stars on board, you'll hardly notice the difference—and hardly care. On these ships Gopher's equivalent actually does wear those knee socks and Bermuda shorts, although he's more likely to have a British accent than an American one.

What's more, these ships are downright gorgeous. They're contemporary to a fault, as bright and airy as a garden room and as elegantly appointed as a penthouse.

You'll feel like Midas aboard one of these showboats as you journey off to ports in Alaska, the Caribbean, and Mexico.

If you're looking for Caribbean sunshine your choice will be the *Island Princess* or the *Sun Princess.* From January through May the *Island Princess* sails on cosmopolitan 14-day journeys from Los Angeles to jet-set Acapulco, through the Panama Canal to Colombia's Cartagena, the Dutch island of Aruba, the French island of Martinique, the shopping paradise of St. Thomas, to historic San Juan. On return journeys the ship substitutes stops in Caracas, Curaçao, and Cabo San Lucas.

In June the ship moves to Alaskan waters where it sails on 12-night trips through mid-September, visiting Vancouver, Prince Rupert, Juneau, Skagway, Sitka, and Victoria on cruises that begin and end in San Francisco.

Meanwhile the *Sun Princess* does what her name suggests. She sails in sunny Caribbean waters from October through mid-May on two alternating schedules. Both itineraries begin and end in San Juan with one visiting such sunny ports as Curaçao, Caracas, Palm Island in the Grenadines, Martinique, and St. Thomas; the other substitutes stops in Barbados and St. Maarten for Curaçao and Caracas.

In mid-May the ship leaves the Caribbean to join both other Princess ships in Alaskan waters. There she sails on seven-night trips from Vancouver to Juneau, Skagway, Glacier Bay, Ketchikan, and Misty Fjord.

Finally, the *Pacific Princess* spends most of the year from mid-September to June sailing from Los Angeles to Acapulco and back. On the way south to Acapulco she cruises by Cabo San Lucas calling at Mazatlán, Puerto Vallarta, Manzanillo, and Acapulco; on the way back to Los Angeles she stops at Zihuatanejo/Ixtapa, Puerto Vallarta, and Mazatlán.

In 1985 she's going to try a change in home base, however. From January 12 she'll be based in San Diego, from whence she will make the same 14-day Mexican Riviera cruises. The change is an attempt to capitalize on the large population concentration in Orange and San Diego Counties, about a three-hour drive from Los Angeles.

In summer the *Pacific Princess* also heads north to Alaska, where she sails on 12-night round trips from San Francisco to Vancouver, Prince

Rupert, Juneau, Skagway, Glacier Bay, Sitka, and Victoria, and back to San Francisco.

Each of the ships breaks its steady pattern with one or more cruises of 9, 10, 11, or 14 days, and on some sailings you can combine voyages to create a two-week round-trip cruise.

So let's take a look at this famous Love Boat line and see if there is where your cruise future sails.

ISLAND PRINCESS / PACIFIC PRINCESS: As you might have noticed, we come to a bit of a departure here, describing two ships at once. That's because these two vessels are twins. What you find in one is found in the other, right down to the last lobster fork.

Both were built in West Germany, both are 550 feet long, weigh 20,000 tons, and carry 630 passengers plus 352 in the crew. Both have seven beautiful passenger decks. You may find a few color differences here and there, but the only real difference between the two is their itineraries—and in summer even those are almost the same.

Launched in 1972, the *Island Princess* carries 626 passengers off to what her name suggests—islands—all winter long, switching to Alaska in summer. Her sister ship, the *Pacific Princess,* was launched two years earlier in 1970.

If you watch "Love Boat" occasionally, by now you probably recognize the emerald-green and royal-blue Princess Line logo—a female face with streaming hair emblazoned on the ships' soaring funnel.

Once you've been aboard a craft sporting that logo on her smokestack, you'll be convinced that it really is royalty pictured up there!

Activities

Speaking of razzle-dazzle, wait until you see the entertainment here. Beautiful women and handsome men dancing and singing in full-production revues featuring some of the loveliest costumes afloat: not only glitter but beautiful feathery headdresses, period costumes, top hat and tails, professional singers, dancers, magicians, special lighting and musical scores, the lot.

If a cruise without a little casino action is unthinkable, rest easy. You can play the slot machines aboard until your biceps rebel. There are no other gambling games, however.

On board the *Princesses,* you'll never lack for things to do, from the early-morning deck walk to aerobics, dance classes, even a workout in the gym if you like. Bingo and backgammon, trap shooting or a ship tour, flambé cooking demonstrations or afternoon tea—it's all there to keep your every minute as jammed or as lazy as you like.

Public Rooms

Among the things that will convince you these are royal ladies indeed is the two-storied magnificence of the Pursers' Lobby with its glamorous staircase sweeping down from a mezzanine to a wide reception area.

Every bit as showy as any modern hotel lobby you've ever seen, this gleaming deck exhibits the loveliest architectural design afloat. Overhead, subtle lighting gleams down on bright-blue carpeting and accent lights focus on a shining contemporary sculpture. All around you glass soars to the ceiling and transparent surfaces gleam.

In the purser's office here you'll meet smiling faces prepared to produce all the information you need to know about anything on the ship. Shoppers will quickly find this spot too—a showy glass-fronted boutique here offers treasures from around the world.

After that glamorous introduction, sweep majestically (Loretta Young–Betty Davis style fits right in here) up that grand staircase. On the mezzanine above you'll find a long, library/writing room just begging for you to curl up with a good book or to get some of those postcards written. Nearby are beauty salons and barbershops, and the ship's photo studio.

Both these decks, Fiesta and Aloha, are lined with cabins that run down both sides of the deck, with some inside quarters tucked away in the center (more on that later).

One deck up, the Riviera Deck, is where all the fun begins. Here you'll find the handsome Carousel Lounge, where things go around in circles, literally and figuratively. Comfortable couches and chairs in bright jewel tones fan out in a wide arc from the circular dance floor fronted by a stage. Off in a corner you can huddle with new friends in the Carousel Bar.

Amidships you'll find the showy Princess Theatre, where both ships present what the line calls its Princess Discovery programs. Elsewhere these are known as port introductions, but on board this ship the cruise directors use slides and movies as well as words to tell you a little about the history and culture of each destination. The multilevel theater also doubles as a movie theater.

Flanking the theater are two wings in which you'll find on port side the International Lounge with an arching bar, on starboard side a matching reverse image of that lounge, this one called the Bridge Lounge. Both are wonderful places to watch passing scenery, both inside and out.

Amidships is the Skaal Bar, which by night becomes an action-packed disco.

While you're up on the Riviera Deck, walk toward the aft end of the ship and have a look at the Carib Lounge (called the Pacific Lounge on the *Pacific Princess*). Here's another sweeping staircase, this one joining this airy lounge to the smaller Terrace Room up on the Boat Deck. If you don't look beyond the soaring wall of glass here, you could swear you're in some posh penthouse lounge in Manhattan sipping a few while below the world scurries about on its mundane, trivial business.

Look around you and you'll see lovely aquamarine sectionals in channeled fabrics offset by creamy chairs, lots of shining chrome, a gleaming dance floor and stage. Slim glass panels soar two stories high to enclose both this lounge and the Terrace Room above, offering both a view out across a swimming pool and tanning deck to miles of glittering ocean beyond.

On the port side there's a lovely boutique where shoppers can lose themselves among the treasures after depositing nonshopper companions in cozy seclusion just outside the doors in the Veranda where they wait in royal splendor while gazing at nature's floor show slipping past outside the windows.

And there's a swimming pool here on the Riviera Deck, just outside the Carib/Pacific Lounge.

Up on the Sun Deck, amidships is the ship's cloverleaf (well, three-leafed clover) Crystal Pool swimming hole, a beautifully designed splasher that features a sliding cover called a Sun Dome. Naturally, sun is the name of the game on every cruise, so that dome remains open most of the time, closing only if you-know-what falls from the sky.

You'll also find another set of slot machines up here on the Sun Deck not far from a spot with the lovely name of Starlight Lounge. This is something to see: sunlight streaming through a curving wall of glass and glinting off the latest in contemporary chrome furniture in creamy earthy colors, glass tabletops, lots of growing things, a sweeping curve of bar, and a view that goes on forever. Also, don't miss the elaborate and perfectly gorgeous buffets on deck either.

That brings us ever so neatly to dining on board. Despite its British officers and crew, the ship has Italian personnel in the kitchen and dining room. Princess has a very good reputation for providing excellent cuisine, and pasta lovers certainly will never go hungry. Nor, of course, will anyone with five meals or snacking sessions plus midnight buffets available.

You'll dine in the Coral Dining Room, a handsome spot on either ship. You'll find quite a few tables for two aboard either ship, even more tables for four, fewer for six, all with small dome-shaded table lamps. International nights are celebrated each night aboard the ship. Some nights your waiters will turn up wearing French berets and serving soupe à l'oignon and peppered entrecôte. Another night they'll be serving beef Wellington, roast beef and Yorkshire pudding, or celebrating Italy with creamy fettucine Alfredo.

Cabins

On these ships the staterooms are comparatively uniform in size and shape, although naturally the more you pay the more space you get.

Basically there are three configurations of cabins aboard. First of these is an outside or inside twin-bedded room, with a sofa that converts to a bed by lifting off a cover and bolster, plus a recessing lower bed that folds neatly into the wall and out of sight during the day.

Next up in luxury is a "deluxe" outside twin-bedded room with two beds that convert to sofas for daytime sitting, plus a couple of chairs and a small table.

Finally, the top-of-the-line cabin is a deluxe suite with twin beds, a separate sitting area which includes a sofa that can be converted to a bed (and curtained off for privacy), plus a table and chairs for snacktime. These are fancy quarters like the ones you see on the television show.

All cabins have private bathrooms with a shower, and the more elaborate have tubs as well. A music system piped into your room provides music if you want it, and all cabins have wall-to-wall carpeting and telephones. They're decorated in handsome tropical colors, many of them deep greens or golds offset by subtle contemporary prints. The furniture has clean contemporary lines, often with brass trim, and every room has a dresser/vanity/desk combination with a big mirror. There's plenty of closet space too, and lots of light through big rectangular windows.

Naturally, with cruises of such different lengths the rate schedules are lengthy. Let's just look, however, at prices for a week-long cruise aboard the *Pacific Princess* to the Mexican Riviera. You will pay proportionately more for longer cruises, and also for a week-long voyage on the *Island Princess* Alaska cruises.

Rates on both ships are divided into ten price categories ranging from those deluxe suites at the top of the price range to inside twin rooms at the bottom of the range.

On the *Pacific Princess* Mexican Riviera cruises there are two fare seasons. You will pay less if you can plan to travel in January or April through mid-May, slightly more in February and March or October through mid-December.

Suites come in two configurations, one with a separate sitting room and one slightly more compact with just a sitting area. Both have refrigerators. For one of these two kinds of cabins you'll pay $2674 to $2856 per person in the lower priced season, $2821 to $3010 in the more expensive sailing season.

Singles are provided for on these ships as they are on few others. On both ships a number of cabins are designed for those traveling alone. For one of those outside rooms, which also feature in-room refrigerators, single travelers pay $3080 to $3241, depending on season.

The "deluxe" rooms, inside or outside, cost $2016 to $2478 per person. in off-season, $2121 to $2604 per person in high season for a week-long Mexican Riviera cruise. As you can see, you can save quite a bit of money if you're willing to settle for an inside cabin. There are very few of these in this price category, by the way, so you'd do well to book as far in advance as possible if you're hoping for one of these rooms.

Most of the cabins on the ship are located on Aloha and Fiesta Decks. On these decks you will also find the more moderately priced cabins, those in price Categories F to K (A is the highest priced category). Outside twin rooms will have two beds and a shower in the bathroom. They're not as large as those higher priced staterooms you've just been reading about, but as ship's cabins go they're spacious. For the higher priced among these cabins you will pay $1911 per person in off-season, $2009 in the more popular sailing months. Cheaper outside rooms can be had for $1750 to $1813 per person in off-season, $1848 to $1918 per person in peak times.

Dividing those numbers by seven, you get a per-day cost of about $198 to $208 per person in the minimum-price cabin, $273 to $287 in outside twin rooms in the middle-price bracket, and $354 to $372 per person for the highest priced outside double room, excluding suites.

Prices on the Alaska sailings of the *Island Princess* are slightly higher. For seven-day cruises in those waters prices begin at $1400 per person and rise to a high of $3213 per person for suites. In fact these seven-day Alaska cruise prices closely parallel the high-season rates for a Mexican cruise aboard the *Pacific Princess.*

The *Pacific Princess* sails on 12 night voyages from San Francisco during the summer months, and those cruises are priced at $2424 to $5448, which works out to a daily cost of $202 to $454 per person.

A third person sharing a room pays 50% of the minimum cruise fare and can take advantage of the line's fly-free programs which offer free or low-cost air fare from many cities in the U.S. and Canada. Children aged 2 to 12 pay half the adult fare (except in some of the higher priced accommodations where they pay the full adult fare). Children under 12 months old are not permitted on the ships.

Princess also has a quite liberal program for exclusive (that means single) occupancy of a double stateroom. The single supplement is just 10%, way below the 50% to 75% or more charged by many other lines.

SUN PRINCESS: Launched in 1972, the *Sun Princess* was once known as the *Spirit of London,* a monicker that rather typifies her current lifestyle if you visualize today's Londoner as contemporary, casual, and just a little jazzy, as they used to say.

Less luxuriously showy than her two sisters in the line, the *Sun Princess* is also smaller, just 17,370 tons. On board are 700 passengers in search of shorter, less expensive, fun-filled cruises typical of the middle-income bracket, seven-day market. Her interesting itinerary, which takes her to some of the less frequented Caribbean isles, makes this ship a good choice for port fanciers.

Perhaps the raciest looking of the three ships, the *Sun Princess* features streamlined long paned-glass panels that run the length of the ship, curving toward the aft end and making her look as sleek as a sportscar.

She's quite typical of many seven-day cruisers in that she carries a comparatively large number of passengers on short journeys at reasonable prices. What's more, she provides for those passengers just as sumptuously as the other ships in this line, offering them every bit as much service, food, and fun.

Public Rooms

Start your tour on the Riviera Deck, where most of the ship's public rooms are located. Here, for instance, is the Monte Carlo Room, housing the ship's slot machines. Those who like to keep their gambling to a marathon penny-a-point bridge game can do so in the card room nearby, while those who only want to read about the world's gamesters can do so in the reading room on the port side of the ship.

Before dinner, save a few minutes to stroll along the lovely open Promenade Deck, where cool evening breezes brush by as the sea, now as black as the night sky, rushes away beneath you in a cloud of white foam.

Then find your table in the ship's Continental Dining Room, plunked down right in the middle of this deck. This long room is now a study in contemporary elegance, with comfortable upholstered armchairs. Clever use of glass room dividers, each featuring a stained-glass landscape scene in glowing colors, helps keep the long room cozy and inviting.

As on the other two ships of this line, the *Sun Princess* presents outstanding cuisine, delicacies like beef Wellington, succulent lobsters, rosy Alaskan salmon, followed by desserts as elaborately picturesque as they are scrumptious—and calorically disastrous.

Evenings will most likely find you headed toward the International Lounge, home for some of this line's showy entertainment. A multilevel room, the International Lounge offers good views from every direction, a good thing since you won't want to miss the elaborate production numbers created for your entertainment.

Later, stroll up to the Observation Deck where you'll find the Starlight Lounge, a handsome spot that turns into a sound-and-light show for dancers each night. Or stop by the Union Jack Bar, a casual meeting spot whose decor is as red as the cross in the flag whose name it bears. Or—perhaps and—sip an after-dinner libation at the rectangular International Bar.

By day, it must be admitted, there are some people who don't partake of all the activities the ship has to offer. Instead these sluggards head straight for the pool as soon as the sun peeps over the horizon and there's no budging them from there until they can no longer feel the heat. If you know one of those, you'll likely locate the worshiper on the Lido Deck. It won't do any good to tell them lunch is served in the dining room because tan fans just stay right out there in the rays at lunchtime, partaking of the ship's on-deck buffet. The Union Jack Bar gets plenty of attention too.

If you've lost a shopper on board, begin your search on the Aurora

Deck where the ship's big Princess Boutique holds forth down one side of the ship; a Sundry Shop takes up some space across the way.

If it's a movie fan who's suddenly disappeared, you should begin searching on Baja Deck or Capri Deck, where the two-story Princess Theater can be found filling eyes and ears with top-flight movies.

Cabins

When you do finally give up and head back to your cabin, you'll find rooms a little less sumptuous than their counterparts on the line's other two ships. They're nicely if not elaborately decorated, however, and many have one or two upper pullman berths.

So here we are at prices again. In the Caribbean this ship features three price seasons: the cheapest in January and late April through the beginning of May; the next highest from February to mid-April; and the most expensive in the holiday period in the last two weeks of December. Sample prices we'll detail in the next couple of paragraphs will refer to the lowest prices available. If you want to sail in prime time, figure an additional charge ranging from about $70 to $150 per person for the lowest priced cabins and about $132 to $180 or so per person for the top-priced accommodations.

On this ship the most luxurious quarters aboard are several suites on the Promenade Deck. Two of the six suites available here (PR6 and PR7) have quite an unusual shape, with one wall sweeping around in a curve. Inside that curve snuggles a couch, coffee table, and chairs placed to form a separate sitting area. Called deluxe suites, these rooms also have double beds, bath with tub and shower, nightstands, lots of closet space, a refrigerator, and a curtain that pulls across to separate the sleeping quarters from the suite's living room. Room numbers of these accommodations are PR1, PR2, PR6, PR7, PR24, and PR21. The price for a week's Caribbean cruise in one of these top-notch nests is $2772 per person, a very nice buy if you can afford it.

Moving down a peg to a deluxe outside room with twin beds that can be converted to a double bed, a separate sitting area, and a refrigerator, you'll pay $2478 per person for a week's Caribbean cruise.

The *Sun Princess* also has some single outside rooms for those traveling alone. For one of those you'll pay $2555 to $2835, depending on season.

Outside cabins with twin beds, many of which can be converted to a double bed, are available in four descending price grades, Categories D, E, F, and G. Eight of the most expensive rooms in this middle price category are in a nice neighborhood up on the Promenade Deck snuggled in between the ship's big suites. For one of those the price in low season is $2219 per person, rising in other seasons to $2331 and $2471 per person for a week's Caribbean cruise.

Smaller rooms in this price bracket are located on Aurora Deck, Baja Deck, and Capri Deck, the three passenger decks deepest down in the ship. All of these rooms are outside cabins, however, which makes them quite a good buy for the money. Rates for these cabins range from $1820 to $1918 per person in low season, $2023 to $2471 per person for a week in holiday season, and $1911 to $2331 per person in the mid-priced season.

Finally, the four least expensive rates on the ship cover one category of inside double rooms and one (Category H) of outside rooms with double bed. That latter category, for which you pay $1764 to $1960 per person for a week's cruise (depending on season, again) is Category H, and there aren't a lot of those available. If you want a double bed, speak up early and take a deposit to your travel agent as far ahead of sailing as you can.

Inside cabins come in three price brackets. Categories I, J, and K, in descending price order. Once again, if you like a nice address, there are some Category I rooms up on the Promenade Deck near the ship's suites and deluxe rooms. The cost for one of those is $1617 to $1799 per person for a seven-night cruise.

Finally, for inside cabins in the two lowest priced categories you'll pay $1358 to $1512 in low season, $1426 to $1589 in middle-priced season, and $1512 to $1680 during those December holiday times. Cabin C13, despite the off-putting number, looks a good choice in this budget category.

As you will see when you look over the deck plans of these ships, the majority of cabins are in the middle price range. Dividing by seven to get per diem rates, you come up with a range of $194 to $365 per person, excluding the two upper brackets of rooms and suites.

Alaska cruises aboard this ship are also seven-night adventures, with one nine-night sailing. These are divided into two seasons, the least expensive running through most of June and September, the higher prices applicable throughout the summer months. Lower prices range from a low of $1267 to a high (for a suite) of $2919, with the middle ranges running about $1600 to $1800 per person for a week's voyage.

Most of the summer cruises, however, will cost a minimum of $1330 per person for a week's cruise, rising to $3073 per person for a suite. Middle-bracket prices are about $1700 to $1900 per person.

Third-person fares, children's fares, and single supplements for single travelers seeking exclusive occupancy of a double room are the same as aboard the *Island Princess* and the *Pacific Princess*. Fly/cruise programs also are the same.

ROYAL PRINCESS: This member of the royal family had not yet been christened when this book was being researched. Some christening it was scheduled to be too, with none other than Diana, Princess of Wales, heaving the bubbly at her bow.

From there the ship was headed to Miami where it was to spend three days before transiting the Panama Canal to take up residence in Los Angeles from which it will be sailing on a ten-day Christmas cruise to Mexico followed by two 14-day transcanal sailings.

Fares for the inaugural 17-night Miami to Los Angeles cruise range from $4029 to $10,319 per person, double occupancy. If you want to sail on the holiday Mexican voyage, the cost is $2180 to $5600 per person, and the New Year's 14-night transcanal cruise is priced from $3550 to $9114 per person, double occupancy.

What do you get for your money? Well, for openers this cruise ship is the first vessel afloat to have all outside cabins—every single one. By now you will have figured out that outside cabins cost more, so it's likely to cost you a bit more to travel on this ship than on some others. Those prices you just read bear that out, averaging out at $237 to $607 a day.

Public Rooms

A 45,000-ton ship, the *Royal Princess* is wide of beam, a feature that means you can expect lots of wide-open spaces aboard. Main public spaces will be located on the top decks, with accommodations for the ship's 1200 passengers in a narrow superstructure atop the wide hull. There will be a full casino on board.

Joggers will be thrilled to hear that a jogging track aboard completely encircles the ship, and is supplemented by a fully equipped gymnasium and health center, two Jacuzzis, two acres of open deck, and four swimming pools, including a lap pool for really serious swimmers!

Like the other ships in the fleet, the *Royal Princess* will have a British crew and staff, with Italian dining room personnel.

Besides cruising from Los Angeles to the Mexican Riviera, she will also visit the Caribbean, Alaska, and other destinations around the world.

Cabins

Every cabin in each of the ship's price categories is identical, however, so you don't have to wonder how your cabin will look.

And how will it look? Well, all cabins will have large picture windows, twin beds convertible to doubles, tub bath and shower, refrigerator, and television.

All suites, deluxe rooms, and some standard staterooms will have private outside balconies large enough to contain a lounge and two chairs. Furnishings in many cabins will be handsome dark-wood units with matching mirror frames.

21. Royal Caribbean Cruise Lines

Contact: Royal Caribbean Cruise Lines, 903 South American Way, Miami, FL 33132 (tel. toll free 800/327-6700 or 800/327-4368, or 305/379-2601).

Cruising Grounds: Mexico's Yucatán Peninsula, Bahamas, Bermuda, Grand Cayman, Jamaica, Puerto Rico, St. Thomas, St. Croix, St. Maarten, Martinique, Barbados, Antigua, Curaçao, Caracas (Venezuela), Key West, New Orleans.

Itineraries: *Nordic Prince*—Miami–St. Croix–Martinique–Barbados–Antigua–St. Thomas–Miami or reverse Or Miami–Nassau–San Juan–St. Thomas year-round

Song of America—Miami–Nassau–San Juan–St. Thomas–Miami year-round

Song of Norway—Miami–Grand Cayman–Montego Bay–Playa del Carmen–Cozumel–Miami year-round

Sun Viking—Miami–Ocho Rios–Curacao–La Guaira (Caracas)–Barbados–Martinique–St. Martin–San Juan–St. Thomas–Miami year-round

---

You can tell an RCCL ship anywhere: just look for the classy glassy "Crown" lounge that forms a shining coronet high up on the funnel stack of every RCCL liner. That ten-stories-up lounge is the line's trademark.

The pride of the fleet is the new 1400-passenger *Song of America,*

32,000 tons of Norwegian fun with twin swimming pools and a lounge/showroom that will knock your socks off—if you're wearing any, which on these casual sun sailers is unlikely.

On the other end of the size spectrum is the smallest ship in the fleet, the *Sun Viking,* an 18,559-ton ship specializing in longer cruises to fascinating Caribbean ports. This winter the *Sun Viking* will visit such different sun spots as St. Maarten, Martinique, Barbados, Caracas, and Curaçao on 14-day voyages.

Occupying mid-size space between the *Sun Viking* and the *Song of America* are the 23,000-ton *Nordic Prince* and the 23,005-ton *Song of Norway*. Both of these ships are fine examples of an innovative idea in ship construction called "stretching."

Here's what that means. Faced with a desire to carry more passengers but possessed of ships that simply couldn't accommodate greater numbers, the line charted an unusual course. It sent the ship back to the shipyard where it was cut in half. Then an 85-foot section was added to the middle of each of the two vessels and they were put back together again. *Voilà*! Two "new" ships and no stretch marks!

Thanks to those stretching changes, the *Nordic Prince* and *Song of Norway* are now 4500 tons larger, 85 feet longer, and can accommodate about 1000 passengers each, 300 more than pre-stretch. A similar stretching job was rumored to be imminent for the *Sun Viking* some years ago, but no talk of that lately.

Royal Caribbean Cruise Lines hoisted its sail in 1968 and is today owned by three Norwegian shipping companies. One of the first lines to take a shot at year-round seven-day cruises from Miami, RCCL maintains a very steady and predictable schedule, rarely changing itineraries or voyage lengths—but always keeping its spic-and-span craft up to date!

Ships and cruise lines have personalities, we keep saying, and the personality you'll find here is refined and classy. No, we don't mean stuffy. What we mean is, if this were humor we were discussing, Royal Caribbean's ships would be wit, while some other ships in similar cruise-length categories would be slapstick.

This cruise line must be doing something right. It's gotten special kudos for its food from La Chaine des Rôtisseurs, an esteemed gourmet group, and for its overall ambience from magazine readers and cruise enthusiasts around the world.

Service is very good on these ships, and you'll delight in the little extra touches: fresh fruit in a basket every night, a bucket of ice and a continental breakfast in your room until 11 a.m.

Even the youngsters are well looked after, with a carload of activities planned just for them in the usual summer holiday period. The line even provides incentive and performance rewards from T-shirts to watches and radios.

Ports are important to this line, which meets its competition by offering both the old-favorite ports and some less visited ones. On nearly any voyage on this line's ships you will visit at least three ports and often many more than that.

Air/sea programs, to which the line has been committed for years, enable passengers from anywhere in the nation to fly to Miami and cruise on these ships at no or very low additional fees.

As for itineraries, well, there's hardly anyplace in the Caribbean you can't go on one of these well-organized smooth-sailing ships. This year, for instance, you can expect to see the *Song of Norway* sailing her usual pattern of seven-day cruises from Miami to Grand Cayman, Jamaica's Montego Bay, Playa del Carmen, and Cozumél. She makes that stop in Playa del Carmen, by the way, so history lovers can go ashore and see the ancient Mayan ruins there.

Meanwhile the *Nordic Prince* will sail on eight-day cruises to the gleaming waters of the Virgin and Cayman Islands, Nassau, and Puerto Rico. On her ten-day sojourns the ship is a port-collector's dream. On those longer trips she visits Key West, New Orleans, Playa del Carmen, Grand Cayman, and Ocho Rios on one cruise; on another, St. Croix, Martinique, Barbados, Antigua, and St. Thomas. *Nordic Prince* also usually schedules a couple of interesting summer sailings from Miami to Bermuda, where she stays for two days before returning to Miami via Nassau.

The *Song of America* sails on a predictable seven-day itinerary that takes you to Nassau for the day then on to San Juan and St. Thomas, before returning to home port in Miami.

Finally, the line's longest cruise, a 14-day visit to eight ports on the *Sun Viking:* Ocho Rios in Jamaica, Curaçao, Caracas, Barbados, Martinique, St. Maarten, San Juan, and St. Thomas. Several of those 14-day trips can be booked as seven-day sailings. On those you disembark in Barbados and fly home, or fly to Barbados and get off back in Miami. Special air/sea free or low fares make that financially tempting.

Activities

In daylight hours the gamblers aboard will head for the pool deck where volunteers move wooden horses toward the finish line to the roll of dice. You can bet on the winner, and you're paid off at odds just as you are at a real racetrack. And whatever you may think of Bingo, you'll soon find yourself joining all the others and hoping you've got that magic winning card!

White elephant sales of all the things you bought—or brought on board—and now want to . . . um, well, unload, are popular events, as is the ice-carving demonstration out by the pool.

Every night at dinner all the restaurant staff dresses in costume to celebrate the theme of the evening. Just before dessert, waiters and assistants suddenly disappear to reappear again a few minutes later parading about the room to musical accompaniment. After you get into the swing of things aboard, this costumed nonsense is likely to become a high spot of your evening. Costumes and entertainment range from French berets on a Gallic evening to a fire-breathing dragon on a Chinese night. Passengers get so caught up in this entertainment, they cheer for "their" waiters, and are doing standing ovations by the end of the cruise. On Caribbean Night those talented islanders on the staff carry dozens of filled liqueur glasses on a tray—on their heads—while they dance!

Each of the ships features similar entertainment. RCCL jets its professional entertainers around so all passengers can see the talented singers, dancers, and variety acts. Performing cruise staffers sing and dance too, so you'll see them stomping up a storm during your cruise.

If you think you're as talented as anyone, you can prove it at passenger entertainment night. It's surprising just how talented some of your fellow passengers are too!

On all ships in the line there are the usual rounds of dance classes, aerobic exercises, arts and crafts, and special events like grandparent's bragging sessions, singles parties, skeet shooting. As with all ships, there's no charge for any of these activities (except trap shooting, for which you pay a small charge to cover the cost of the clay pigeons).

Every single night there's dancing in several places aboard, and you'll often have poolside entertainment as well.

If you can stay awake late one night during the voyage, you can listen to a comedian's adult entertainment (translate adult to some very risqué jokes and language, scheduled for late hours to be sure the youngsters are well tucked into slumberland). If you find this sort of entertainment offensive, you need not go, of course. You'll be told what's doing long in advance.

SONG OF NORWAY: With such a musical name it seems only natural that RCL's *Song of Norway* would have a special affection for music. Indeed it does, as you'll see aboard this ship where everything in sight seems to be named after something musical. There's the King and I Dining Room, the South Pacific Lounge, the My Fair Lady Lounge . . . well, you've got the picture (or should that be tune?).

This sleek craft offers much else that is harmonious, too: attractively decorated public rooms, a long hall of glittering shops, a delightful Norwegian crew.

Christened in December 1969, the ship made her maiden voyage almost a year later and sailed on week-long voyages for eight years before her return to the Wärtsilä Shipyard in Helsinki. There she was lengthened in 1978, returning to Miami in December to make what the line likes to call her "second" maiden voyage.

Public Rooms

As with all RCCL ships you'll find plenty to do aboard: slot machines, good-looking lounges, cafés, even a late-night spot called the Lounge of the Midnight Sun that rewards your staying power with a night-owl patch if you manage to stay upright, preferably dancing, until 1:30 a.m.

On this ship, as on others in the line, there is some lovely artwork. Handsome circular photographs hang on many walls aboard the *Song of Norway,* and some very colorful tapestries grace the stair landings. Our special favorite small touch on this ship is an etching of a fjord, the land of this line. You'll find lots of wood in the passageways of this vessel too.

If you like activity, you'll always find something going on in the My Fair Lady Lounge, a rather contemporary spot decked out in pink and orange with lots of shiny metal surfaces.

In the King and I Dining Room you'll dine each night to a different theme with seven appetizers and five entrees offered for your chowing pleasure, not to mention all the other courses. The decor is a smashing combination of black with navy-blue chairs and some green touches here and there.

You'll find a whole acre of deck space on this sun sailer, most of that right around the outdoor pool and its sidekick pool bar. Lounge chairs around the pool are outfitted in green and blue, and on the side decks is still more sunning space, decorated in gold and brown. The teak decks aboard are beautifully maintained.

The South Pacific Lounge is a pretty place, decked out in tropical oranges and golds and encircled by a bright-green rail. There's a different show here each night, some provided by talented staffers, some by professional entertainers—and some by you at the passenger entertainment night.

Disco fans will head straight for the Midnight Sun Lounge, where a slide show offers visual accompaniment to the music. Glass tables are cleverly lit from beneath, and there's a circular bar and dance floor rimmed by banquettes.

About 4:30 p.m., head for that circular Viking Crown Lounge way up on the funnel stack, where you'll have the loveliest of all possible views of the sun sinking slowly into the flaming sea.

There's quite a large outdoor swimming pool up on the sun deck, and it's accompanied by the inevitable pool bar and café where you can have breakfast, lunch, or dinner if you don't want to bother dressing for the dining room.

Activities

One special event much loved by passengers is a party the ship dreamed up to compete with all those Out Island "experiences" other lines are offering. "We call it our in-island experience," laughed one executive, adding, with an eye to the competitive aspects of all this, that passengers get both a visit to an interesting port and a beach party on this populated island.

Called a Buccaneer Beach Party, the soirée takes place on shore at two Grand Cayman hotels, the Holiday Inn and Colony Beach Club. You have to pay your own way there—all of $1.50 for the cab ride—but once there you're treated to "an all-day romp" complete with picnic buffet, music, games, even a beach towel.

Cabins

Pretty as are all the RCCL ships, their cabins are disappointingly small. Not uncomfortably, you understand, but far more compact than you'd expect on a ship with such elaborately decorated public rooms.

RCCL's response to this, of course, is that they want you to get out of your cabin and join the fun. And the ship does go out of its way to provide amusements that promote passenger togetherness and full use of the ship's facilities.

Cabins vary only a little in size and barely at all in shape. Most have twin beds that share a nightstand, a desk/vanity, a couple of closets, and a small bathroom. All have a three-channel radio by the bed, and reading lights that are ideally placed for some late-night reading. You'll also find full-length mirrors, wall-to-wall carpeting, and private baths. Electricity is modern too, so you can use your hairdryers and shavers in your room without blowing a fuse down the hall.

You'll be happy to discover that all the cabins—and every other room aboard the ship—display Scandinavian spic-and-span approach to living.

If you take a look at the deck plans of the ship, you'll see cabins so uniform in size it's difficult to tell the difference between the top accommodations and the lowest priced cabins aboard (good news for budget-watchers). You'll soon spot the largest accommodations and the smallest, and discover matching price tags.

There's only one suite aboard, so you probably won't have to worry about whether to choose that or not.

Beyond that, there are 352 outside staterooms and 183 inside rooms. If you want a double bed, you'll do well to book early as there are only about 60 of those cabins on board. If you're sailing with a family or a couple of friends, you might ask about the availability of connecting staterooms.

Price categories run from A to K (A is the most expensive) and the top three of those categories cover only a very few of the largest rooms. Off-peak rates are in effect most of the year, with peak rates beginning in mid-January and lasting through March. You'll pay $135 more per person in that prime-time period. You must also figure $85 to $210 per person more than the off-peak prices for sailings during the two-week Christmas holiday period.

In peak winter season, top dollar buys an outside deluxe stateroom on the Promenade Deck. The cost, depending on the size of the cabin, is $1825 to $1975 per person for a week's cruise. Cabins 840 and 838 seemed to us to be about par for this price category. The former features green and beige floral print, a very large louvered closet, and a small bathtub as well as shower; the latter is done in beige, light blue, and burgundy, with a large dressing area but limited sitting-around space. Either of those is $1770 per person in nonpeak season, $1905 in the winter months. Cabin 830 is nice too, and its about $80 cheaper.

You'd be hard pressed to see much difference between cabins in the next four price grades, Categories D through G. They're also outside quarters with two lower beds, and are rather uniform in size. About all that seems to differ is the price, which ranges from $1575 to $1685 per person in the winter months. In these price categories we found Cabin 536 and the similar Cabin 534 quite nice. The latter is decorated in green and blue, with twin beds set in an L shape so you have a little more moving-around space. Either of these is $1475 per person in low season, $1610 per person for winter sailings.

The configuration of the four lowest priced cabins aboard varies. In any one of four categories you'll find both inside and outside staterooms for the same price, and the bed setup may be one double bed plus a pullman berth or two lower beds. Naturally you can ask for what you want, and if you book early enough, you can get it. Cabins in these lower price categories range in those three winter months from $1275 to $1500 per person.

Third and fourth persons, including children, pay $525 for a week's cruise any time of year except the Christmas sailing when the fare for the extra person is $630.

Single travelers pay 150% of the fare for "accommodations available for single occupancy" (which means they're not giving up the possible sale of some cabins for two to one person, not even for an extra percentage).

Those rates work out to a per-person per-day average ranging from $163 for the least expensive cabins to about $205 to $237 for mid-priced accommodations, and a high of $241 to $263 for the top-of-the-line cabins.

SONG OF AMERICA: To us this is one of the most beautiful ships afloat. From the second you step on board this wide and glittering ship you'll know you're somewhere special.

First, the wide open spaces are really remarkable—none of those narrow, dark little corridors typical of some of the older craft; none of those dark dining rooms or cramped shops. Broad of beam and blocks long, this lovely beauty has made the most of her modernity.

Not only does the *Song of America* have one of those distinctive Viking Crown Lounges high above the sea, but on this ship it offers you a 360-degree look at that watery world you've come to see!

Christened in 1982 by opera star Beverly Sills—and who better to christen the *Song of America*?—this lovely lady of the sea was constructed in that same Helsinki shipyard. Registered in Norway, the ship has Norwegian officers and an international staff of 500 to care for 1400 passengers. She measures in at 32,000 tons, is 705 feet long, and is the largest passenger cruise ship ever built in Scandinavia—although she may be upstaged any minute by one of the new ships under construction.

She's very new, so of course she's very contemporary. You'll find lovely color schemes aboard, interior design that glitters and gleams, jewel tones that glow.

Public Rooms

As one of the widest ships afloat—line officials say it's the widest ever built—you get such a feeling of space that any claustrophic fears lurking in your subconscious will be instantly dissipated. There is a more spacious feeling here than you'll find in many hotels!

As on the line's other ships, public rooms aboard the *Song of America* are named for famous Broadway shows, so you'll find an Oklahoma Lounge, a Can-Can Room, a Guys and Dolls Lounge, the Madame Butterfly Dining Room.

In that Madam Butterfly Dining Room you can down banana pancakes for breakfast and coq au vin au chambertin or Kansas prime ribs for dinner. Whatever you choose, you'll consume in an elegant dining room decked out in dusty rose offset by deep red touches and brushed-brass accents. Tables for four and six predominate.

Off in two cozy wings of the main dining room are smaller tables, many of them along the big portholes here. Of the two wings, the Ambassador Room and the Oriental Terrace, the Ambassador seems the more darkly dramatic, decorated in royal blue with gold accents, while the Oriental Terrace is brighter with a lively gold decor accented with light blue.

As you wander along the passageways, you'll notice they're decorated in tranquil beiges with dramatic navy touches and plenty of brass accents. A special feature you'll see on this ship and no other is a Photo Gallery, hung with some eye-catching photographs of sea scenery.

If you love those machines with the single metallic arm and the three eyes that spin, head for the Oklahoma Lounge where there's a healthy bank of those bandits. There's also dancing on a big central dance floor here each evening.

Song of America is the only ship in the line with its own cinema (although the others show movies too). Pretty it is too, all done in blue and green.

Our special favorite place aboard is the Americas Cup Bar, a dark and dramatically decorated room outfitted in bittersweet chocolate-brown leather and a small piano bar. Sailing fans will love this intimate corner: the theme of the room centers on the New York Yacht Club.

The largest lounge aboard is the splashy Can-Can Room, where lively shades of lavender and hot pink adorn a multilevel room that encircles a round dance floor. Brocaded fabrics and velvets add a lush touch to swivel chairs, and atop it all is a huge chandelier made of shining glass bubbles.

The Guys and Dolls Lounge is perhaps the loveliest room on the ship. Outfitted in beige and hot pink with big circular banquettes, chrome-trimmed smoked-glass tables, and a steel dance floor topped by two flashing mirrored orbs, this spot is disco heaven for dance fans. A massive light-and-sound room keeps things lively. Nearby here you can catch an elevator up to that lofty Viking Crown Lounge.

On the main deck, which is, to put it mildly, simply sensational, don't miss the glass sculpture with royal blue accents. It's near Purser's Square, which is itself something to see: acres of glass and subtly muted colors that herald the kind of glitzy modernity you'll see throughout the ship.

Start at the top where you'll find not one but two big swimming pools perched up on the Sun Deck and surrounded on the next deck up by a delightful sun deck. That means, of course, that the pools are open to the sun above but carefully shielded on the sides by dozens of transparent panels.

One deck down, on the Bridge Deck you'll find the ship's snazzy gymnasium and saunas for both men and women.

Cabins

Cabins aboard the *Song of America* are almost evenly divided between inside and outside cabins, with 407 outside staterooms, 300 inside. Most cabins have two lower beds, some of which (especially in inside rooms) can be converted to double beds. Some staterooms have third and fourth berths, but those are in the minority so book early if you're planning on sharing your space with friends or family.

On this ship you'll find a three-channel radio in your room and individual controls for the air conditioning as well. Standard 110-volt electrical connections make it possible for you to use your hair dryer and other travel applicances without concern. All rooms have private bath, but only a few of the top-priced cabins have both bathtub and shower (others are showers only).

Once again, cabins (with the exceptions of suites) are not large. Many of them feature one twin bed with back cushions that turn it into a couch, plus a fold-down twin bed that flips up in daylight hours to give you extra floor space. The decor runs to bright blues and lively tropical colors.

There are four rate seasons on this craft too. Most of the year you pay off-peak rates, but in the winter months of January, February, and March, when everyone wants to sail away into the sunshine, rates rise. Prices are also higher during the three weeks around the Christmas holidays, roughly the last two weeks in December and the first in January. At that time of year figure to pay about $75 a person above peak-season rates, which are themselves about $135 more than off-season prices.

The following are the peak-season prices on the *Song of America.*

There's one giant suite on board, Cabin 7000 on the Promenade Deck, and it's as costly as it is lovely. You pay $2105 per person for a week-long voyage in peak season.

On the Promenade Deck you'll find the most luxurious quarters aboard. Each has twin beds topped by pretty cream and russet print bedspreads, a separate sitting room providing lots of space, plus a full bath and all the accoutrements for a week of plush living. A week in this lovely room will cost $1905 per person in winter.

Down the line a bit on a partial deck between Promenade Deck and Cabaret Deck you'll find a cluster of outside cabins that are a bit less costly. Called Categories B and C cabins, they're virtually the same size. For a cabin in either of these two categories in the height of the winter season costs $1625 or $1695 per person for a cruise.

A large number of mid-priced outside cabins fall in rate Categories D, E, and F. All have two lower beds and prices range from $1500 to $1600 per person.

Inside staterooms are of course less expensive. The *Song of America* has five prices for inside staterooms, all with two lower beds, some that convert to double beds and some that have one or two upper berths. For one of these you'll pay $1275, the minimum peak-season price on board, to $1455 per person.

An especially good buy on board is a Category 1 outside stateroom on B Deck. For an outside room with two lower beds you pay just $1350 per person in peak months (that's just $150 above the price of the lowest priced inside cabin on board). If you think an outside cabin is worth a little extra money but not a lot, this is the cabin category for you. There are quite a large number of these available too.

Third and fourth persons sharing a cabin—and that includes children—pay $525 all year long, except the peak holiday sailings in December.

Single supplements are 150% of the fare.

Per-person daily rates aboard range in peak season from $182 to $242. Suite prices get up into the range of $300 per person per diem.

NORDIC PRINCE: Christened in 1970 by actress Ingrid Bergman, this 23,000-ton ship made her maiden voyage in July 1971 from the Port of Miami. Stretched in 1980, she now carries 1038 passengers and 400 crew on her eight- and ten-day Caribbean voyages. That stretch project enabled the line to increase the size of the ship's public rooms, which are now quite spacious and lovely. While the number of cabins aboard increased by about a third, the size of the new cabins is about the same as those that were already there.

The real sailors among us might be interested to know that the *Nordic Prince,* like the *Song of Norway* and the *Song of America,* has two gizmos called "bow thrusters" that enable the ship to maneuver by itself without tugs. To see her and her sisters leave the Miami harbor is quite a miraculous sight. They just get those bow thrusters going, roil up the water a bit, and ease on out into the channel. What won't they think of!

Public Rooms

Way up top you'll spot that circular Viking Crown Lounge, lording it over the ship's seven passenger decks.

Among those decks, the top fun spot in daylight hours is the Sun Deck where everyone gathers about the big swimming pool. Like the *Song of Norway,* the *Nordic Prince* has a very large swimming pool, 598 square feet of watery fun. Only the center of the pool is deep, so even nonswimmers can enjoy just splashing about in the wide strip of shallow water around the sides. If you get hungry there's a Pool Café for snacks and a bar for a frosty daiquiri.

This deck is also home to the ship's well-equipped gymnasium. For the sore muscles you acquire in the gym, walk just a few steps away and steam in the sauna for a while. You'll also find a masseur and masseuse aboard; and they hold court up here on the Sun Deck.

Joggers will soon discover the wonders of the Promenade Deck. Those who only sit and wait for joggers to return can do so in the vicinity of a lovely lounge with an equally lovely name: Midsummer Night Lounge. This good-looking spot gets really lively at night when you can dance to the wee hours.

Most of the after-hours action occurs down on the Restaurant Deck, where you'll find the ship's Camelot Dining room. Here you gorge (and hate yourself for a few minutes, at least) on broiled lobsters and filet mignon, salmon and sauces, sinful chocolate creations. You'll do so in a room decked out in handsome contemporary furnishings. Most of the seating is in the main room, but some tables are tucked away in two side wings.

After dinner, stop in at the lively set in the Carousel Lounge, a circular room with a central dance floor flanked by banquette seating. And way on the other end of this deck is the Showboat Lounge, another showy room. There's dancing here every night too.

One deck down, on the main deck, the main entrance hall of the ship is right in the middle of a long hallway called Karl Johans Gate. Along this "Main Street" of the *Nordic Prince* are the information office and cruise director's headquarters, plus a beauty salon and a bank of gift shops.

Throughout the ship the main passageways bear names: there's Helmsman Lane, Sailmakers Lane, St. Olave's Gate, Kristian IV's Gate.

Cabins

Cabins aboard this craft are quite similar to those found on other RCCL ships. In fact, the cabins in various price categories seem so similar to each other that unless you can afford a full-fledged suite you might just as well go for budget quarters. There's not a lot of difference in size, and little or no difference in decor.

The *Nordic Prince* has 7-, 8-, 10-, and 14-day sailings, and peak or off-peak rates. Peak-season rates are in effect from about January through March, off-peak rates effective in other months. A special 14-day holiday cruise sails in December.

The following prices refer an eight-day cruise in peak winter season.

The suites (they're called outside deluxe rooms in the rate schedule) are gorgeous quarters, from the name on the door to the decor inside. Named after famous ships—*Golden Fleece, Cutty Sark, Great Republic, Flying Cloud*—each offers quantities of space and is decorated in striking colors: rose, burgundy, deep greens, light blues, mauve.

Suites contain beautiful wood paneling, plush carpets, big bathrooms with both tub and shower, four big closets, a television and stereo built into a wall unit, even your own refrigerator. Through portholes in the passageway here you can look right into the swimming pool. For an eight-day cruise in peak winter season one of these suites will cost $1825 per person.

Up on this same deck, a large inside cabin is a good buy at $1500 per person for that eight-day cruise. There are also somewhat smaller and less expensive outside quarters with two lower beds, which cost $1685 per person for an eight-day cruise in peak winter season.

Moving down a couple of decks you find outside cabins with two lower beds (Categories C and D) for $1575 and $1610 per person.

Category E quarters include both inside and outside staterooms, some with two lower beds, some with a double bed. They're pretty uniform in size and cost $1500 per person for that eight-day cruise.

The least expensive cabins on board are in Categories F, G, and H. Some of these are inside cabins, some outside; some have a double bed and pullman upper, some two lower beds. Prices in these categories are, in descending order, $1425, $1350, and $1275 per person for an eight-day cruise in peak season.

Ten-day cruises cost about $600 to $700 more per person in the least expensive accommodations aboard, about $1000 more per person in the highest priced cabins.

The per diem rates in peak season work out to a low of about $160 per person, a mid-price range of about $187, and a high of $228 per person. RCCL calls its low season "off-peak," which includes sailings from April through mid-December. In that time period you can subtract $50 from prices quoted above for an eight-day cruise. Ten-day sailings cost $110 less per person.

Third and four persons, including children, sharing a room pay $525 for an eight-day cruise in peak season, $750 for a ten-day voyage in any season.

Single travelers occupying a room alone pay 150% of the fare.

RCCL is promoting eight-day cruises on the *Nordic Prince* this year, and is offering an eight-day cruise for what it has been charging for seven-day voyages. That means, of course, that you're getting an extra day free.

SUN VIKING: This cozy ship is the line's smallest vessel and the one that makes the longest voyages. There's a solid marketing reason behind that: fewer people can afford the time or the money, so it makes sense to use the smallest vessel for the two-week trips offered by the *Sun Viking*.

You ought to know, however, that you can take just a week's cruise aboard this ship by flying to the ship or flying home from it. Tempting package programs called SunVenture tours make that possible.

If you can stay aboard, you'll visit some fascinating sights: the pastel loveliness of Willemstad in Curaçao, the busy streets of Caracas, the beautiful beaches of Barbados, Martinique, and St. Maarten, and the treasure-laden shops of St. Thomas and San Juan.

Life aboard this cruiser is a steady round of sun and fun. There's a polite but casual air aboard, and fine service tailored to passengers who are a bit more sophisticated. Thus there are fewer of the more rousing shenanigans that are such an integral part of some ships.

Ports play a very big role on *Sun Viking* cruises. It seems safe to say that most of the people aboard are here *just* because they want to visit these enchanting ports in the easiest, most satisfying way.

Public Rooms

The major passageways are named on this ship too: Court of the Antilles, Kon Tiki Passage, Prinsens Gate, Kristan Augusts Gate, and that RCCL "Main Street," Karl Johans Gate. Along "main street" are the ship's boutiques, where you can buy everything from a sailor's mug that's tilted so it won't slide off a table to fine perfumes and Ladro figurines. The shops' glass windows display all the treasures so you can window shop here even when the shops are closed.

Up on the Restaurant Deck is the ship's H.M.S. Pinafore Dining Room, a pleasant place decked out in tropical colors. A wing of the room extends down the port side of the ship and has quite a number of tables for four along the windows.

In the evening you'll probably head first for the Annie Get Your Gun Lounge, where the ship's nightly shows take place. A big multilevel room, the lounge is also the place to go for Bingo games and dance lessons.

If you're set on a dancing evening, head for the Merry Widow Lounge, where a combo holds forth to the wee hours in a big circular room. Disco fans will head for the Lounge of the Northern Lights, where pretty lighting almost makes you think you're seeing those northern lights!

For a quiet nightcap, the tiny Sitting Bull Bar is a cozy spot much loved by some of the crew too.

If someday you're looking for a quiet place to curl up with a book, the pastel shades of the tiny Sextant Room up on the Promenade Deck is one of the most tranquil hideways on board.

On those balmy Caribbean days a big swimming pool on the Sun Deck provides a cooling-off spot. If you select a perch on the surrounding sun walk on the Compass Deck you can snag some terrific photos of the ice-carving exhibition which, despite the sun's withering effects, takes place beside the pool. And naturally there's a pool bar, which is a good place to head after you've shed a few pounds of water in the saunas aboard.

Of course, there's one of the line trademarks: the Viking Crown Lounge. On this ship it's been newly redecorated in glittering chromes.

Cabins

As on other ships in the line, even the top-priced cabins here are not massive quarters. They really are *intent* on getting you out of your cabin and into the fun on board or in port.

You'd do well to seek a room with beds set in an L shape, for those offer more walking-around space. Otherwise, twin beds set parallel to each other have only a few feet of space between them.

Most of the *Sun Viking*'s 14-day cruises occur in off-peak season, so let's take a look at the price of a two-week cruise at that time, roughly mid-April through mid-December. (Peak charges are in effect from mid-January to mid-March. One of those latter cruises will cost $100 more per person.)

Keep in mind that you can take a seven-day SunVenture cruise aboard the *Sun Viking* if you fly to Barbados to join the ship or fly home from Barbados after a week aboard. Rates for those include air fare from many U.S. cities in the off-season. Prices range from $1215 to $1440 per person in off-season, $1350 to $1575 per person in peak winter months. And in peak winter season from October through March you must also add $75 to $175 for air fares, with the amount of the add-on depending on how far away from Miami you live.

A top-of-the-line cabin, a Category A outside deluxe stateroom with two lower beds and small sitting room—costs $3370 per person in off-season for the two-week trip. Outside staterooms in Categories B, C, and D are $3090, $2940, an $2870 per person for the 14-day trip.

In the mid-price bracket are both inside and outside cabins in Categories E, F, and G. Some have a double bed, some twins, and some of the rooms also include pullman upper berths. The highest price in these three categories is $2715 per person, moving down to $2565 and $2415 per person for a two-week cruise.

The lowest rate you can pay for the two-week cruise on the *Sun Viking* is $2265 per person, which will get you an outside stateroom with a double bed and pullman upper, or an inside stateroom with two lower beds or a lower bed and pullman upper.

The per diem rate begins at a quite reasonable $161 per person, rising in the mid-price bracket to $193 and in the highest rate level to $240.

Third and fourth travelers sharing a cabin pay $2265 in off-season, $100 more for a peak-season sailing.

If you don't need transportation to Miami, you pay $100 less per person for a 14-day cruise, $50 less each for a seven-day trip.

Single cruisers are charged 150% of the fare.

22. Royal Cruise Line

Contact: Royal Cruise Line, One Maritime Plaza, Suite 660, San Francisco, CA 94111 (tel. toll free 800/227-4534, 800/792-2992 in California, or 415/956-7200).

Cruising Grounds: Caribbean islands, Panama Canal, Mexican Riviera, Scandinavia, Mediterranean Sea.

Itinerary: *Royal Odyssey—*

IN WINTER: Miami–Ocho Rios–Cartagena–San Blas Islands–Panama Canal–Balboa–Costa Rica–Acapulco *Or* Acapulco–Costa Rica–Panama Canal–Cartagena–Aruba–Curaçao and return same route

IN SUMMER: Mediterranean and Scandinavian cruises

Royal Cruise Line's president Richard Revnes has become something of a phenomenon on the lecture circuit these days, and his popularity is well deserved: he's a top salesman and a very, very good speaker selling a top-notch product.

Revnes claims that ports sell cruises, which may be why this line's two ships visit the most fabled ports of history from the Mediterranean Sea to the Scandinavian fjords. With just two ships in its retinue Royal is not one of the world's largest cruise lines, but its marketing efforts and its fascinating itineraries have made it one of the most popular.

Royal Cruise Line is a comparative newcomer to the industry. It began operating in 1972 when a Greek company was formed by P. S. Panagopoulos, who dreamed of creating a fleet of deluxe cruise ships sailing to fabled ports. He carried that dream to its logical and luxurious conclusion with Royal's two ships, the *Royal Odyssey* and the *Golden Odyssey.* Two years later the U.S. branch of the company was incorporated, with main offices in San Francisco.

First to sail under the Royal flag was the *Golden Odyssey,* launched in 1974. Carrying just 460 passengers, this small, 10,500-ton ship concentrates on the Mediterranean, where you can see her in spring, summer, and fall. In winter she sails off to the Far East on cruises with evocative names like the Route of Marco Polo and Magnificent Odyssey.

Meanwhile, you can see the much larger 25,500-ton *Royal Odyssey,* formerly the *Doric,* here in the U.S., but you have to look fast. She too spends much of her sailing year in Mediterranean and Scandinavian waters, but in December she heads for the Caribbean sun. Once there, she cruises through the Panama Canal to Acapulco and back to Curaçao, stopping along the way at fascinating ports like Cartagena, Caldera in Costa Rica, lovely little Aruba. In March she sails away to the Mediteranean again.

You can of course join any of these cruises with the line's fly/cruise program, which offers reasonable air fares to passengers who join a cruise in Europe, the Far East, or anywhere. Royal Cruise Lines says it owes much of its success to its commitment to air/sea programs.

Activities

This cruise line presents what is certainly the most innovative and intriguing entertainment idea aboard any ship afloat: dance partners. Because so many women travel alone on cruises, Royal's creative and energetic staff one day dreamed up this idea: why not give some carefully screened gentlemen passage aboard the ship in exchange for their participation in what the line likes to call its "host" program?

The function of this gentleman—who must be over 50, single, a good dancer, and a gregarious type—is to dance with unaccompanied women, be a fourth for bridge, and provide some friendly conversation. Proper introductions occur early on in the cruise when all the single femmes aboard are invited to attend a special cocktail party at which the hosts are introduced.

Begun as a project designed to last only one season, the host program was so successful it was repeated and repeated and repeated. Hosts, often recommended by travel agents, are interviewed and screened by the line. Several hosts travel on each cruise and dance each evening with 25 or 35 women, (Now there's the perfect vacation!)

Late risers will be thrilled to hear that breakfast on board is open seating, meaning you can show up anytime during the two hours or so the restaurant is serving breakfast.

The *Royal Odyssey* maintains formality at dinner, so gentlemen will have to have a jacket, although there's nothing in the fine print about ties.

One night, the ship throws a Pastel Night party when everything's decked out in pale hues, so you might want to pack your pinks for that event. Costume-party fans, by the way, should begin dreaming up their outfit for that event (participation is strictly voluntary), although the ship's crew will be happy to help you with some props.

While we're on frivolous entertainment, you might like to know the line has special programs for children seasonally.

ROYAL ODYSSEY: Certainly the *Royal Odyssey,* built in 1964 and rebuilt in 1982 when Royal Cruise Lines bought the ship, is testimony to what this line and $20 million can do.

Showy entertainment, good food, spacious quarters, and dramatic contemporary decor are just the start of things. From there it goes on to soft leather furniture, polished woods, plush carpets, and lots of glitter chrome and steel. A Greek crew provides plenty of hospitality.

Particularly popular with West Coast cruise fans, the *Royal Odyssey* must be doing something right—some of its passengers are booked on their 14th cruise aboard!

Public Rooms

Let's start our tour on the Odyssey Deck, where most of the ship's public rooms are located. Under a high domed ceiling is the ship's big entertainment center, Odyssey Lounge, outfitted in dramatic plum, blue, and magenta decor. Thanks to the Greek origins of the line, you're likely to spend an evening here watching Greek dancers in native costume performing centuries-old dances. They'll even teach you how it's done! Other nights you'll see cabaret entertainers dancing and singing up a storm.

Not far away from the Odyssey Lounge is the Calypso Lounge, in bright pink and orange. Shining wood floors are reflected in glittering mirrors and big curving banquettes encircle the central dance floor. Afternoons there's a tempting luncheon buffet served here.

One deck up via a curving outside staircase, the Promenade Deck provides sunning space handsomely outfitted in brown and russet tones. Yet another deck up is more room for sunseekers, plus a snackbar and deck tennis courts, plunked loftily down atop the ship where it's protected from wayward breezes by glass walls.

Out on several other deck levels you'll find open sunbathing areas decked out in royal-blue cushions. Right up here, too, you'll find an unroofed but glassed-in sun deck where you can perfect your tan without ruffling your feathers. Unusual lounge chairs and the off-the-beaten-track feeling of this spot win it special honors.

Movie buffs will love the theater aboard. It features a raised wood platform that shines like a new penny and orange theater seats tucked in between long expanses of stained glass. First-run films are shown daily.

Those of you who can count to 21 faster than a speeding bullet can tote your winnings in the Monte Carlo Casino. You'll find it snuggled in between the lounge areas that rim Monte Carlo Court, a long central area of the ship focusing on a colorful purple and aquamarine bar and a flashy white piano that's the star of this entertainment area. A low silver ceiling is studded with round orbs that shed an intimate light over this dramatic lounging area.

Pink and lavender team up with a deep-purple shade in the Ambrosia Dining Room, which features a brushed-steel ceiling and tables for two, four, and eight. Low ceilings give this small but handsome room an intimate feeling, and at breakfast and lunch you have a nice view of the ocean from some tables.

Fresh flowers magically turn up on your table every day to compliment the pastel linens and shining crystal. While there are occasional Greek preparations on the menu, you'll find a rather continental selection, and plenty of American favorites like Kansas prime beef or filet mignon. So popular is the cooking aboard, in fact, that the ship has published its own cookbook, *The Odyssey Cookbook, A Culinary Cruise,* so you can go back home and whip up these goodies yourself!

Agora means marketplace in Greek, and it has a smiliar meaning aboard the *Royal Odyssey* where the Agora Shopping Arcade is a maze of reflective surfaces, glass, mirror, metal. Shops here offer a glittering array of treasures (we even spotted a bicycle for sale).

On Odyssey Deck you'll also find the handsome Panorama Lounge, where you can sink into a black leather chair and watch the dancers swirl amid chrome and glass accoutrements. It's a lovely place to while away the day watching the sea too.

Particularly good chrome deck maps show you just where you are on board, and help you figure out what's up and what's down from where you're standing. That may not sound like much, but on a ship of this size and complexity you'll be glad to see those maps.

If you like swimming but don't want any more sun, you can hike down a few decks to the ship's indoor pool. Here also are a gymnasium, and saunas for both men and women. Up on Odyssey Deck is the ship's outdoor swimming pool.

Cabins

Accommodations aboard are top-notch. For openers, there are 280 outside staterooms (plus 55 suites), and only 73 inside cabins. All feature wall-to-wall carpeting, two channels of music (if you like), a telephone for room service, attractive wood furnishings, and vanities. Most have a writing table and full-length mirrors. It you're a clothes hound, you'll find plenty of closet space, usually at least two full-length closets in each room, and modern baths with a dressing table extending across under the sink in the bathroom.

The decor differs from room to room, but all the most recently modernized rooms—which seems to be nearly every room aboard—feature quite contemporary decors in deep jewel tones or soft pastels.

Cabins are comparatively large, with the top cabins offering 268 square feet, the mid-priced quarters (Category L) offering 178 square feet, and the budget quarters (Category Q, for instance) measuring in at 122 square feet.

Room keys are color coordinated to deck colors, a nice touch that can help you find you way around as well.

Outlining the price is no easy task aboard this ship—there are 20 different rate categories and 13 different cruises! Here's where you'll learn to adore your travel agent.

To give you an idea what you'll pay aboard, let's take a look at the prices for a ten-day cruise from Acapulco to Curaçao through the Panama Canal, the shortest cruise available in North American waters. Price categories are lettered from A to Q, with A the highest price and Q the lowest.

If you're traveling really first class (and price), you could hardly do better than the Cannes Stateroom. It's a beauty, a study in beige with a semicircular look and L-shaped couches in a separate seating area. The Marbella Suite features a double bed and couch, and is also decorated in beige with a touch of blue. For accommodations in this upper price bracket a ten-day Acapulco to Curaçao cruise costs $3098 per person.

Cabin 5040, called a deluxe junior suite, is quite a comfortable spot, featuring a couch and two twin beds. The cost of that cozy quarter is $2838 per person for the trip.

Rooms in the 6000 and 7000 numbers (Categories B and E) are a bit lower in price and still quite lovely. Cabin 7019, for instance, features beige couches and a large double bed, while cabin 6005 is done in deep blues with one bed stretching along under the porthole, the other along a wall, with a bath tucked off to the side. Those rooms are all outside cabins on Promenade or Odyssey Decks, where prices range from $2578 to $2978 per person for that ten-day voyage.

Rooms in the 5000 numbers (on the Marina Deck) are stunners. Cabin 5056 (a Category F) is particularly lovely, decked out in a dark dusty-rose color teamed with brown in the carpet, bedspread, and accent pillows. It's very similar to other rooms in this price bracket, but in this one the bath is off on one end of the room so the cabin looks slightly larger. It features tub and shower too, if you're given to bubble baths. The price for rooms like this one, which is called a superior deluxe outside stateroom, is $2578 per person for that same trip.

A good mid-priced choice aboard is Cabin 4037 (or its counterparts in Category J), where burgundy and pink are teamed everywhere from the stripe in the carpet to the tiny pink dots in the bedspread. A ten-day trip in this attractive, long, narrow room is $2318 per person.

Down the line in Category M, Cabin 2061 features an orange decor and is equipped with a chair, desk/dressing table combination, and a drop-down third bed. Lots of mirrors, three closets, and plenty of throw pillows give this one a special ambience. The price for one of these outside cabins on one of the ship's lower decks (Coral, in this case) is $2148 per person for the ten-day trip. Cabins in this price category seem a good buy on this vessel.

Inside staterooms begin at $1898 per person for the ten-day transcanal journey. A somewhat higher priced inside cabin, called a deluxe inside stateroom—Cabin 5028 is an attractive example, with beds on either side of the room and a bathroom at the back—is priced at $2048 per person for the trip.

On a per diem basis this ship occupies a spot on the high end of the cruising market, with daily per-person rates beginning at about $189, mid-price in the $214 to $240 range, and top-of-the-line accommodations at about $300.

Third persons sharing a room pay $1650 for that ten-day cruise, and port charges are $42 per person. If you don't participate in the line's fly/cruise air fare rates, you can take $500 per person off the price.

If you're traveling alone and want to occupy a cabin by yourself, the single supplement to the fares is $900.

23. Royal Viking Lines

Contact: Royal Viking Lines, One Embarcadero Center, San Francisco, CA 94111 (tel. toll free 800/422-8000, or 415/398-8000).

Cruising Grounds: Panama Canal, Caribbean islands, South America, Mediterranean Sea, Scandinavia, Alaska, South Pacific (itineraries vary and are complicated, so check with Royal Viking or your travel agent).

Itineraries: *Royal Viking Sky*—

IN FALL: New York–Nantucket–Cape Cod Canal–Charlottetown–St. Lawrence River–Saguenay River–Montreal–Quebec City–Bar Harbor–Boston–Newport.

IN WINTER: Fort Lauderdale–St. Thomas–Curaçao–Cartagena–Cristobal–Panama Canal–Balboa–Acapulco–Zihuatanejo–Puerto Vallarta–Los Angeles–San Francisco and return

IN WINTER/SPRING: World cruise

IN SUMMER: Mediterranean and Scandinavian cruises

Royal Viking Star—

IN SUMMER: Vancouver–Juneau–Skagway–Glacier Bay–Sitka–Victoria

IN FALL: San Francisco–Far East
IN WINTER/SPRING: South Pacific and Orient cruises

Royal Viking likes to call its service "World Class," as opposed to mere first class, you understand. And when you step aboard one of these floating palaces, you'll soon find yourself agreeing.

Not even Royal Viking's competition denies that these are elegant, beautifully appointed ships on which there is only one class—first class.

As history goes, Royal Viking Lines is one of the newer kids on the block. Formed in 1970, Royal Viking was at first a composite of three companies—Bergen Line, Nordenfjeldske, and A. F. Klaveness—until Klaveness dropped out of the group. The line was recently purchased by J. H. Whitney & Co., a San Francisco–based investment company.

As you might have guessed from the names, this is a Norwegian operation, so you'll find delightful Scandinavians in charge aboard all the ships.

You'll see Royal Viking's white stack emblazoned with a soaring red sea eagle in such diverse climes as the Norwegian fjords, the Black Sea, the South Pacific, the Orient, and the Caribbean. So varied are the itineraries, in fact, that the line's brochure is thicker than most monthly magazines.

As for the ships beneath those smokestacks, well, prepare to be stunned. These are true luxury crusing ships. Contemporary and elegant, they're kept so spotless you'll be convinced an army of workers is on board picking up after each passenger. Everything from the brass trim to the glass portholes shimmers and shines, kept neat as a bandbox by smiling Norwegian stewardesses.

Royal Viking's three ships—the *Royal Viking Sky,* the *Royal Viking Star,* and the *Royal Viking Sea*—are identical, or as close to that as ships can get. Each was launched in the early 1970s, so they carry the latest in modern design, both in the public rooms where you can see it and below decks where you can't.

In recent years all the ships have been "stretched" with multi-million-dollar, 93-foot additions added to the midsection, enabling the vessels to carry more passengers and to expand the size of public rooms. That means you'll now find 725 passengers aboard each of the ships which measure in now at 29,000 tons and are 674 feet long.

The first launched of the three vessels was the *Royal Viking Star*, which set sail in 1972. Next to join the fleet was the *Royal Viking Sky*, launched in 1973, followed a few months later by the *Royal Viking Sea. Star* was expanded in 1981, *Sky* in 1982, and *Sea* in 1983.

It would take pages and pages to detail exactly where these ships go, but here's a general outline of the fascinating areas each of the vessels visits.

The *Royal Viking Sky* usually begins her year with a trip through the Panama Canal from San Francisco to Fort Lauderdale, with stops in the western Caribbean. Then she heads south on a 17- to 60-day cruise around South America, returning in April to Fort Lauderdale for Caribbean cruises. in spring she crosses the Atlantic to get into place for summer cruises in the Mediterranean and Adriatic Seas and up to the North Cape, returning to southern sunshine in late fall.

In 1985, however, this regal beauty will sail on a fantasy cruise—departing Fort Lauderdale on January 19 for a 99-day journey around the world! How much? Well for 99 days to remember for 99 years, begin thinking at $19,008 per person. If figures like that make your wallet curl, think about it in shorter segments. You can join the ship for any of the nine different segments ranging in length from 11 days (Athens to London) to 87 days (Fort Lauderdale to Athens).

The *Royal Viking Sea* begins her year with a series of Panama Canal cruises through mid-April, when she also heads across the Atlantic for a summer-long series of North Cape Cruises. In the fall she sails to New England and Canada, then through the Panama Canal again to the South Pacific where she spends the winter.

Finally, the *Royal Viking Star* begins her year in the South Pacific, staying there in the Orient through the frigid months. In summer she heads for Alaska where she sails on a series of 12-day cruises before returning to the Pacific and the Orient.

Because the *Royal Viking Sky* and the *Royal Viking Sea* are twins we'll look at both those ships at once, then meet the very similar *Royal Viking Star*.

Activities

Naturally, on a line that features many long cruises, a very elegant atmosphere, and some prices to match, most of the passengers aboard are likely to be more mature and sophisticated travelers who have spent years earning their right to this kind of luxury. That means that although there's no dearth of activities aboard, those you do find are quieter, more refined pursuits (definitely no suds-swilling competitions here).

Recently the line has been trying some interesting sports-oriented cruises focusing on tennis clinics presided over by top-ranked tennis players. Golfers have their day too.

You'll now also find new exercise and sports facilities aboard the ships, including Parcours equipment that leads you through a complete 30-minute workout.

A paddle tennis court offers you the opportunity for some exercise, and there's a ball machine for honing your tennis stroke. You can dunk a couple of basketballs on board or work out at jazzercize classes offered twice a day when the ship's at sea.

On board ships of this caliber dinner must be numbered among the day's activities, for it's a scheduled event, every bit as showy in its way as a nightclub performance. From Swedish pancakes with ligonberries or fruit-topped Belgian waffles in the morning to filet of beef tenderloin, poached ocean perch Florentine, or breast of chicken with wild rice and bing cherry sauce, you will wine and dine royally.

Royal Viking Line food has an outstanding reputation, and the surroundings in which it is served are equally outstanding. Ease into a comfortable chair by the window and gaze at the scenery passing by as you dine on Malasol caviar and beef Wellington prepared by top-ranked chefs. Royal Viking Lines even likes to say you can almost chart the ship's course by what you see at dinner—exotic fruits and herbs, unusual spices.

Lavish presentations of menu selections is a pride of the line too, so you'll see delicacies presented on silver trays and served on hand-painted china and delicate Scandinavian crystal. There's only one seating on board these ships, so you can enjoy a leisurely dinner and take all the time you like.

If you don't want to miss a minute of sunshine, you can visit the showy luncheon buffet on deck where immense bouquets provide a focal point for elaborately presented lobster salad or open-face sandwiches.

If you want something special, all you have to do is ask and it will be prepared for you.

A new feature of the line is the Supper Club, an intimate 60-seat room in which you can reserve a table, then dine and dance with new friends. There's a separate menu here, and entertainment too (no extra charges, however).

Guest speakers are often on board to discuss everything from home computers to financial planning, politics, or history. Vincent Price has been on board to talk about his life and times, as have astronaut Scott Carpenter and author Irving Stone. And with such exotic ports to visit, even the port talks are thrillers.

You'll get a chance to learn a little more about Norwegians when the crew dons traditional handmade costumes called *bunads* and invites you to join in for a festive evening of song and dance. Other nights dazzling stage shows will entertain you with feathers and sequins, glitter and glamor. Occasional theme cruises offer classical music or operatic presentations, and there are always movies, dancing, and nightcaps in cozy lounges.

Top entertainment aboard has included Tony Martin, Lainie Kazan, the New Christy Minstrels, and classical artists Anna Moffo, John Browning, and Victoria de los Angeles.

Sit back, sip an icy glass of Aquavit, and enjoy!

ROYAL VIKING SKY / ROYAL VIKING SEA: First, let's take a look at the ships' statistics. Both *Sea* and *Sky* are 676 feet long, the *Star* two feet shorter. All three ships are 83 feet wide, weigh 28,000 tons, and carry 725 passengers. As ships' ages goes, these are all among the newer ships afloat, originally constructed in the early 1970s.

Best of all, each of the ships is a luxury sailer and a study in small, thoughtful touches. Along the passageways are ceramic mosaics and delightful small decorative pieces. In the spacious cabins you'll find wooley afghans draped casually over the beds, one of which often also serves as a couch during the day. Everywhere you'll see shining brass accents, glowing carpets, fresh flowers, glittering crystal, acres of open space and extra touches that let you know in a wink that you're aboard a very special craft.

Public Rooms

Drama, tastefully executed, is in fact a byword of the decor aboard. On these ships you'll see leather and rosewood, teak and crystal, oil paintings and gold leaf. You'll find original artworks everywhere you look, and interior design so stunning you'll never quite get used to the luxury of it all.

In the airy dining room aboard the *Sky*, for instance, is a crystal fountain glittering amid the contemporary orange and brown decor. Glass dividers section off areas of the room, and a small dining area off to one side is a particularly intimate dining spot.

Perhaps the most dramatic room on the ship is the Discovery Room (called the Windjammer Room on the *Sea*), an oval room encircled by tall windows through which sunlight streams across a deep-green decor.

The furnishings throughout the ship are very contemporary. In the Prince Olav / North Cape Lounge dark red and marine blue play counterpoint and a ship's bowsprit in gleaming gold leaf provides a striking focal point. You'll get a look at this room if you attend one of two evening shows that take place here.

Curving leather loveseats are a feature here, and plush leather shows up again in the writing, card, and library rooms which are downright gorgeous, equipped with chess boards built into tables, a huge dictionary and atlas, comfy chairs.

If you're looking for a nice pre-dinner retreat, find your way to The Cove, a cozy, tiny room that has a couch, three chairs, contemporary paintings, a table for four, and plants in the windows overlooking an open promenade.

A similar getaway room is called The Snug, and is done up in olive and beige with cute etchings on the wall. One shows a musician haughtily intoning: "I really prefer to play here alone, then I can always play *first* violin." Talk about snug—there are just 11 seats here!

Among the larger public rooms is the Trondheim/Oslo Lounge done up on the *Sky* in a color scheme of orange, gold, and beige with lots of contemporary chrome accents and big windows. Filled with fresh flowers, this large two-level room is a study in shining brass. It's here you will head to watch the ship's main evening entertainment.

There's yet another show on board, this one in the Buccaneer Club / Emerald Club, not far from the striking blue-green and white Finlandia / Dolphin Bar where a pianist/singer performs before lunch and dinner. Complimentary cappuccino is a lure in that latter room.

Gamesters can spend their waking hours in the handsome Casino Royale playing blackjack, roulette, and slot machines (the croupiers wear white gloves). You'll find it tucked discreetly away on the Bridge Deck on the *Royal Viking Sea.* Meanwhile movie fans can head down to the Mediterranean Deck where they'll sit in the regal splendor of the domed Skylight/Saga Theatre and watch a top film.

Up on the Atlantic deck you can get all your questions answered in the wide-open reception area, and shop in the pretty glassed-in boutiques you'll find there.

One deck farther up, the Scandinavia Deck, you'll find a big heated swimming pool, one of two pools on board. Finally, up on the sports deck you can get some outdoor exercise and down on B Deck you can work out in the gym and recover in the sauna.

There are, of course, many things to do on these ships, but perhaps the most enchanting "do" of all is nothing more complicated than an exploration through the wide passageways and open promenade deck of the ship.

And don't miss sending a postcard, if for no other reason than the fun of dropping it into the cutest little red Scandinavian mailbox you've ever sen (it's outside the purser's office).

Cabins

As you would expect, your cabin will be as luxuriously handsome as everything else aboard this ship. You'll find a cozy afghan spread across a couch, a basket of fruit awaiting, a tiny mint on your pillow each night.

Every cabin has a private bathroom, and there are built-in bars, drawers you can lock, rosewood cabinets, a three-channel radio, telephone, and modern electrical outlets.

A nice touch aboard is a small laundrette where you can throw a few things in the washing machines for yourself, although those services are available from the crew too.

Because these are quite new ships, within each category accommodations are quite uniform in size and decor. What's more, prices on all the ships are the same for each cabin price category. For the sake of comparison with the majority of other ships, let's look at some of the cabins and the prices you'll pay for a week-long Caribbean cruise.

The top cabins are called Penthouse Suites, which are really quite something: twin or double bed in a separate room from the sitting area. A comfortable couch in glowing hues stands beside a built-in wall unit in which you'll find a television, refrigerator, telephone, lamp and plenty of storage space. Plunk down in a comfortable swivel chair and look out across your private veranda to the ocean beyond. Your ship has come in, no question about it. One of these elegant staterooms costs $4004 per person. (Don't panic, a suite is, after all, the very best you can buy.)

Moving down a bit, there are two additional categories of suites, which cost $2709 or $3080 per person for the week-long cruise, depending on the elaborateness of the cabin you occupy.

Deluxe outside bedrooms are the next two price categories, Categories A and B, on Promenade and Atlantic Decks. Each offers a small sitting room with a couch, a pretty wood desk, two chairs, and a small cocktail table by day, sleep in twin beds at night. For one of these handsomely decorated quarters you pay $2576 or $2254 per person for a seven-day voyage.

Single travelers get special notice, with cabins in four categories—CC, C, H, and N. The top-priced of these (CC) is an outside single with a bed that becomes a couch by day. Lots of closet space and a comfortable chair make these cabins very comfortable for the single traveler. In this price category singles pay $2513 for a seven-day voyage. Two more categories of single cabins are somewhat smaller but feature about the same furnishings, at a cost of $2212 or $2408.

Inside cabins for singles (Category N) are $1806 and can be found on Atlantic and Pacific Decks. All inside quarters and many outside single cabins feature shower only in the bathroom, no tub.

Moving on down the price and size brackets, there are a whole raft of outside double cabins, all with two lower beds and some with upper pullman berths to accommodate a third person. Some have both bathtub and shower, but most have shower only. These are really quite adequate in size, and carefully designed to offer you the maximum amount of moving-around space. Some, however, have quite small bathrooms, particularly in the new cabins aboard the *Star,* which may be a tight squeeze for heftier travelers. Prices in these eight categories of outside double cabins range from $1176 to $1757 per person for a week's voyage.

The lowest priced accommodations are inside double cabins on Pacific and Mediterranean Decks, two of the lower passenger decks aboard. These too feature two lower beds and have a shower, no tub in the bathroom. For one of these bedrooms you pay $1057 per person for a seven-day journey.

Dividing by seven to get a per diem cost on these voyages, the lowest rate per person is about $151, rising in the mid-priced cabins to $168 to $251 and in higher priced categories to $258 to $368 per person, excluding suites.

Single occupancy of suites and deluxe bedrooms is double the fare, and exclusive use of standard double cabins costs 160% of the per-person rate.

A third person sharing a stateroom pays the minimum fare for that cruise. If the third person is a child under 13, the fare will be half the minimum fare offered on that cruise. Children under 13 in a double room with an adult pay half fare while youngsters older than 13 pay full adult fare. In suites, deluxe cabins, and single rooms, children occupying regular accommodations are charged as adults. Infants under age 2 are charged $2 a day.

Royal Viking also has fly/cruise fares in which you add on varying amounts for air fare from your hometown to the embarkation point.

ROYAL VIKING STAR: If Alaska is your dream cruise, the *Royal Viking Star* may very well be your dream ship for that cruise. Certainly she is a lovely lady, very like her sister ships in size and exactly like them in elegance, price, and service.

There are a few differences in public rooms names, so let's take a look at the public areas aboard this cruiser.

Public Rooms

Once again fitness buffs will be working out in the ship's gym way down on B Deck and participating in their sunshine sports activities up on the sunny Sports Deck.

One deck lower, on the Sky Deck, is the slick Venus Lounge, a favorite evening meeting spot. Farther forward on the same deck, the Stella Polaris Room is a lovely spot to observe the world passing by inside and out.

Down on the Promenade Deck are two more lounges, the Galaxy Club with its circular banquette seating, and the Neptune Bar with its big arching sipping spot. The *Star*'s rendition of that tiny Cove sitting spot and a lovely promenade gallery are also on this deck.

The main entertainment deck is one deck farther down on the ship, the Scandinavia Deck. Here is the big Bergen Lounge, where the ship's major evening entertainment takes place. Here too is the handsome dining room, where you'll find more than the usual number of tables for two.

A library is tucked away near the dining room, and the tiny Ondine Room makes a cozy spot for a quiet conversation.

Cabins

Cabin accommodations aboard are just what you'll find aboard the line's twin ships. Prices are also identical, so please turn back a page or so to discover what you'll pay for accommodations aboard the *Royal Viking Star.*

24. Scandinavian World Cruises

Contact: Scandinavian World Cruises, 1080 Port Blvd., Port of Miami, Miami, FL 33132 (tel. toll free 800/327-7400, 800/432-0900 in Florida, or 305/377-9000).

Cruising Grounds: one-day cruises to the Bahamas or to "nowhere."

Itinerary: *Scandinavian Sun*—Miami–Freeport–Miami year round

---

Undisputed master of the one-day breakaway cruise, Scandinavian World Cruises offers the perfect solution to what to do with a beautiful day. Sail it away to the Bahamas.

While you're at it you can chow yourself into blimpdom, dance to the twangs of a steel band, rum punch yourself, sun the body beautiful, splash happily in the pool, find a quiet contemplation corner.

Scandinavian World Cruises operates the *Scandinavian Sun* in Miami and expects soon to add another ship which will operate from Port Canaveral in Central Florida, probably on one-day cruises to nowhere.

Novice cruisers may find this the perfect way to get an idea what this cruise business is all about while spending the least amount of time and money. On the other hand, a one-day voyage is a very minimal look at what cruise ships have to offer. Still, if you're not doing anything this Saturday (or any other day of the week), why not trip off to Miami and give this day of wine and sunshine a try?

The Miami-based *Scandinavian Sun* sails one-day sunseekers off to Freeport where they can stay for a couple of days, if they like, returning on one of the ship's other daily trips.

It has not been all beer and skittles for the folks at Scandinavian World Cruises. In fact when this cruise line got started just a few years ago, the industry broke out in one long guffaw. One-day cruises? It can't be done, the three-, four- and seven-night cruise executives snorted.

But it has been done and with comparative success; witness this ship still plying the waters between Freeport and Miami with plans to reenter the sailing world in central Florida soon.

This day-long cruise idea was born back in 1980 when an old and respected shipping company, United Steamship Company of Denmark, known as DFDS, backed the idea and launched Scandinavian World Cruises.

Scandinavian World Cruises purchased the *Caribe,* then being operated by Commodore Cruise Lines, and turned it into the *Scandinavian Sun.*

In 1982 the line began operating a new 20,000-ton vessel, the *Scandinavia,* on runs from New York to Florida. To avoid the constrictions of U. S. maritime laws, the company routed the voyage through Freeport, where passengers—and their cars, if they brought them along—got off and boarded the *Scandinavian Sun* for the run to Miami.

That nice try at the major New York-Florida market was a flop, so SWC abandoned the project in 1983, sending the *Scandinavia* off to Scandinavia where it now shuttles cars and people on a ferry run from Oslo.

On board the *Scandinavian Sun* you will find cabins-for-a-day, outfitted more as a resting and changing spot than as a place to spend much time. So it's not a cabin you're buying here but a round of activities that begins with breakfast in the sunshine and ends with dancing under the stars.

SCANDINAVIAN SUN: An 11,000-ton ship, the *Scandinavian Sun* leaves Miami each morning at 8:30 a.m., arriving at Freeport, Grand Bahama, about 2 p.m. She leaves Grand Bahama about 5 p.m., and gets back to Miami at 11 p.m.

The round-trip deck passage, including port charges, is $79 for adults. Meals are an additional $20 for each adult, and include full buffet breakfast, buffet lunch, and dinner. Children under 17 sailing with an adult receive free deck passage but pay $15 for meals and $12 for port charges, or a total of $27. Children under two pay only the $12 port charge.

Senior citizens get a 20% discount, so they pay only $63 passage, with the same fee for meals.

If you don't come back the same day, however, you pay twice the one-way deck passage fee of $59, plus a $20 meal-plan charge.

Cabins aboard cost $60 and suites are $100 for either one-way or round-trip voyages.

You'll find a full casino on board, a swimming pool, gift shop, cabaret, video game room, and disco. Use of all the facilities on board is free.

Periodically the ship sails from other ports around the state on cruises to nowhere, so you might be able to catch up with her in Jacksonville, Fort Lauderdale, or elsewhere. Any travel agent can tell you where she is this week.

Activities

Activities on board this ship go nonstop from departure to return.

You can party in any of four lounges on the *Scandinavia Sun,* watch a movie in the theater on board, play in the disco. There are games and activities out around the big swimming pool, snacks in the snack bar, elaborate buffets.

In 1984 the line, which calls its cruises SeaEscape had scheduled theme cruises for nearly every week of every month. Themes ranged from a soap opera week, with stars of those soupy soaps on board, to a Dolphin weekend featuring Dolphin football players, to Irish celebrations, and big band days.

Music from different eras and in different styles was featured one month with a Latin Week, Country Jamboree, Jazz Notes, even a Rock and Roll Revival.

25. Sitmar Cruises

Contact: Sitmar Cruises, 10100 Santa Monica Blvd., Los Angeles, CA 90067 (tel. toll free 800/421-0880, 800/252-0301 in California, or 213/553-1666).

Cruising Grounds: Caribbean islands, Panama Canal, Mexican Riviera, Alaska (itineraries vary, so check with Sitmar Cruises or your travel agent).

Itineraries: *Fairsea—*

IN SUMMER: Los Angeles-cruising by Guadalupe Island–Mazatlan–Acapulco–Zihuatanejo–Puerto Vallarta–Cabo San Lucas–Los Angeles

IN WINTER: Los Angeles–Cabo San Lucas–Acapulco–Balboa–Panama Canal–San Blas Islands–Cartagena–Curaçao–St. Thomas–San Juan, returning same route.

Fairsky—

IN SUMMER: San Francisco–Victoria–Johnstone Strait–Prince Rupert–Ketchikan–Juneau–Lynn Canal–Haines–Skagway–Glacier Bay–la Perouse glacier–Sitka–Victoria–Astoria–San Francisco

IN WINTER: Los Angeles–cruising by Guadalupe Islands–Mazatlan–Acapulco–Zihuatanejo–Puerto Vallarta–Cabo San Lucas–Los Angeles

*Fairwind—*Fort Lauderdale–Grand Cayman–Montego Bay–Panama Canal transit–San Blas Islands–Cartagena–Nassau *Or* Fort Lauderdale–Curaçao–La Guaira (Caracas)–Martinique–St. Thomas–St. John–Nassau (some cruises stop in Antigua, Barbados year round

---

Sitmar Cruises officials are as excited as a new daddy pacing outside the delivery room these days. What they're palpitating over is every bit as important to them as a new baby, and in fact is a new baby—a 38,000-ton,

$150-million cruise ship that will round this line's "family" of cruise ships out to three.

Sitmar already has twins: two historic turbine steam ships, the *Fairwind* and *Fairsea,* once part of the Cunard family of elegant vessels. And by the time you read this the *Fairsky* will have been delivered into the world of cruising where her glitter and gleam will lure passengers bound for Alaska in summer, Mexico in winter.

Meanwhile her twin sisters, both 25,000-ton vessels, will be sailing on warm-weather adventures, the *Fairsea* through the Panama Canal to San Juan and on summer Mexican voyages, the *Fairwind* to the Caribbean from Fort Lauderdale.

Sitmar Cruises is another of those cruise lines spawned in the 1970s during the renaissance of cruising in the Western Hemisphere. Begun by some former airline executives, Sitmar began operations with the purchase of two Cunard liners, the *Sylvania* and the *Carinthia,* which were built by the John Brown & Co. shipyard on the River Clyde in Scotland. Sitmar rebuilt and refurbished both vessels for cruising and renamed the *Sylvania* the *Fairwind* while the *Carinthia* became the *Fairsea.*

Now the new addition is due, and quite a big and handsome ship it is. Measuring in at 38,000 tons, the new ship will be 790 feet long and carry 1212 passengers on 11 public decks. Like its sisters the ship will have larger-than-average cabins and will have a laughing, dedicated Italian crew, including some outstanding Italian cooks to maintain the line's top reputation for outstanding cuisine.

Children get special attention from this line, which has set aside special play areas for youngsters from 2 to teens, and offers an impressive round of activities for sailing youngsters.

Finally, there's one special Sitmar trademark we especially love—each ship has a pizzeria!

Activities

Sitmar is one of the few lines around that has considered—and welcomed—the possibility of sailing with children, and then taken action to arrange as much fun for them as for their weary progenitors.

On these ships youngsters will find a Soda A Go-Go game room strictly for teens (adults need not apply), with all those whirring electronics the kids love, some game tables, soft drinks, and cookouts on deck. There's even a pool nearby earmarked for the youngsters. They're very strict about keeping out adults too, a rule the youngsters love, need we tell you?

So far do they go with this youth program (which is offered every day, not just on holidays, from 9 a.m. to midnight, in port and at sea) that the kids have their own specially printed activities schedule delivered to their cabin. On it they'll find a round of activity ranging from pizza parties to ice cream time, arts and crafts, board games, and story hours for the 2-to-12 set. There's even a nursery for the very small fry.

For those worldly teenagers there are dance contests, theatrical activities, beauty demonstrations, weight-training classes, games, and even Italian language lessons. In holiday season teens even have use of the ship's discotheque from 8 p.m. to midnight, and are treated to late-night movies on some evenings, as well as wide-screen video programs.

Fear not, Sitmar hasn't overlooked grownup entertainment. A speciality of the line is theme cruises like an Alaska "nostalgia" program and a trans–Panama Canal "Broadway at Sea" voyage.

There are five lounges and a raft of pubs, and entertainers have ranged from kootchy-kootchy Charo to Tony Bennett, Ben Vereen, Rita Moreno, and Florence Henderson.

You can win master points in bridge tournaments, take a shot at trap shooting off the stern of the ship, try shuffleboard or table tennis.

You can take a sedate stroll on four open decks, waltz to a dance band, or boogie up a storm in the ship's disco.

You can learn Italian, play Bingo, watch a first-run movie, work out in a gymnasium, steam in a sauna.

FAIRWIND/FAIRSEA: Once again we are going to introduce you to two ships at once because in everything except color schemes these vessels are twins.

Italians haven't come by their reputation as food fanciers for nothing, as you'll discover aboard these vessels. Meals are eagerly awaited events that feature everything from canneloni in lobster sauce to veal Oscar and cherries jubilee, even "Slim and Trim" selections for weight-watchers. Sitmar is proud that all the food aboard is prepared by employees of the shipline, not by the independent caterers that cook on some ships. Finally, of course, there's that delightful brick-lined pizzeria!

The *Fairwind,* which is based in Fort Lauderdale and sails on 7-, 10-, and 11-day Caribbean voyages all year round, recently celebrated the tenth anniversary of her sailings from that port.

It's no wonder she's such a familiar sight in this East Coast marketplace because she's quite an attractive craft, kept up to date with frequent renovations. When we saw her recently, the line had just completed a facelift on the dining room which is now all decked out in creamy beiges and contemporary chrome furniture. Yes, the food is very, very good indeed.

Public Rooms

From the moment you step aboard and are greeted by a bevy of white-gloved, smiling crew members you know some special things will be happening aboard. And as you explore the ship, you'll discover where some of those special things are happening—places like the splashy round Mistral Nightclub (it's called the Dolphin on the *Fairsea*), where you can watch the stars outside through tall windows as you dance the night away on a big round dance floor.

The ship's disco is decorated in burgundy with gray accents. Seating is on circular contemporary chairs plus cozy couches, and there's a stainless-steel circular dance floor.

The Windward/Seaward Lounge, a main show room aboard, features cocktail music before dinner and nightly entertainment à la dancing girls and guys in elaborate costumes. The room itself is entertaining, outfitted on the *Fairwind* in black and burgundy with comfortable U-shaped chairs and loveseats. And here's a neat trick: the stage show can also be seen on your cabin television!

For a more intimate setting, seek out the Caribbean / South Pacific Lounge, where a combo plays for quiet dancing on a steel floor and seating is on low modern chairs and loveseats in teal blue. The lounge is right on deck so you can dance out into the starlight glittering down on one of the ship's three swimming pools.

On both ships you'll find some gambling action in Le Petite Casino.

Shops on board are good-looking too, with floor-to-ceiling glass windows. That shopping area is called Fifth Avenue aboard the *Fairwind,* Bond Street on the *Fairsea,* which should give you an idea of the quality of the tempting merchandise. There's a shop for clothing, one for perfumes, one for china, all of them heaven for compulsive buyers. (On the line's new *Fairsky* the shops will be called Rodeo Drive!)

We're especially partial to the ship's Mediterranean/South Seas Lounge, where piano music tinkles as you relax in deep white or teal-blue chairs. Beneath your feet on the *Fairwind* is more of that lush burgundy carpeting you'll find in many places throughout the ship, and above your head a shiny black ceiling. It's a very understated and tranquil setting indeed, flanked by an equally sublime, petite cocktail lounge.

For quieter moments there's a very nice library aboard, complete with glass-enclosed bookcases, comfy armchairs, and paneled walls. There's also a card room for long-into-the-night bridge games.

One more small bar is a nice spot for post-show libations, the tiny Moby Dick Bar (called Harry's Bar on the *Fairsea*), where a few comfortable couches and chairs offer a quiet retreat.

And then there's the pizzeria. Open from 11 p.m. to 2 a.m. for adults only, this bilevel room focuses on its pizza ovens and smells wonderful all the time. Kids are welcome at certain times of day, but at night it's a strictly adult haven.

Down on D Deck you'll find the ship's balconied theater (the balcony's one deck up, of course, on the Continental Deck).

Finally, down on the Riviera Deck you'll find the ship's two dining rooms, the Ritz and the Lancaster on the *Fairwind,* the Grosvenor and the Dorchester on the *Fairsea.*

If you're one of those people who's always ready on time for dinner and your companion is just the opposite, seek out the tiny garden room for your toe-tapping wait. It's just a small spot, but the palms rustling in the background ease waiting pains.

Both ships are equipped for wheelchairs too.

Cabins

An especially nice touch occurs the minute you step aboard this ship: white-gloved attendants meet you and take you to your cabin so you're not left wandering aimlessly about. Cabin service is quite good and the accommodations are kept spic and span. A friendly steward will bring you fruit juice and small sandwiches.

The cabins are unusually large, due in part to the spaciousness you often find on older ships. Sitmar promises, however, that its brand-new *Fairsky* will have cabins every bit as roomy.

You'll find full-length wardrobes in your cabin, private bathrooms in all of them, and closed-circuit television in suites and mini-suites. All cabins are carpeted and feature four channels of music on the radio. Telephones let you call new friends aboard or at home, as well as on-board services.

Cabins with two lower beds also have two upper berths that swing back into the wall during the day so you don't even know they're there.

If there is a criticism of *Fairwind* cabins, it's the line's tendency to replace what needs replacing with little concern for the room's existing color scheme. One room ended up with a beautiful new burgundy carpet that looked very strange indeed under gold and orange furnishings.

Some outside cabins with portholes don't have much of a view but they do let in the sunlight. Sitmar is scrupulous in telling you, pre-purchase, about any obstructions to your view, so if you feel that's important, do inquire.

Electricity on the *Fairwind* is a little antiquated so you have to go to special hair-drying rooms if you want to use those powerful hair blowers. One very nice feature, to my way of thinking, is a self-service laundry with an ironing board and oldtime flat irons. You can also send your things to the on-board laundry which has rapid service.

The *Fairwind* is kept scrupulously clean and refreshingly shining, so her few signs of age are less apparent.

In the poshest cabins there are no fewer than three stewards to see to your every need, if you can come up with that many needs. In fact, so quintessentially Italian are they aboard this craft that stewards have been known to put the arm of Herbie's jammies around Molly's nightie when they turn down the bed!

Price categories are numerous aboard Sitmar ships, ranging from the top-priced Category A to the lowest priced Category P, a total of 15 price levels. To complicate matters further, there are peak and "value" seasons on all cruises. Peak prices are in effect in these time periods: mid-January through mid-March on trans–Panama Canal voyages; mid-December through February on Mexico cruises, and through March on Caribbean voyages; mid-June through mid-August on Alaska sailings. "Value" season is all the other months.

Let's take a look at some of the cabins and their costs for a seven-day Caribbean voyage in peak season. Figure about $70 less per person in "value" season.

If price is no object, the deluxe Ocean Capri Suite is a smashing sight—bath with bidet and tub, dressing area, refrigerator, built-in bar, large television, Haitian cotton bedspreads, a full couch, and two chairs, and all of it in brown, beige, and deep-green velvet. A special favorite is a suite called Ocean Antibes, a study in royal-blue carpet, burgundy velvet couches, and drapes screening off the sleeping area where a queen-sized bed reposes in regal splendor. Gorgeous dark wood, mahogany, rosewood perhaps, is everywhere. For one of these really magnificent and beautifully decorated suites you'll pay $2245 per person for a seven-day Caribbean cruise.

There are two mini-suites aboard, featuring twin beds with drapes that close off the sleeping area from the sitting area and its L-shaped couches and chair—very comfortable indeed. Televisions show closed-circuit movies. Mini-suites are a bit lower in price—$1855 per person for a seven-day cruise in peak season.

Cabin 0154 is a typical example of a Category C cabin, an outside double room with two lower and two recessed upper berths, a central dresser, a big window facing an outside stairway, and a nice long mirror for pre-dinner primping. The charge is $1730 per person for a seven-day peak season cruise.

Outside double cabins with two lower beds and two recessed upper berths range on down in price from Category D through Category G. One of those outside staterooms costs $1560 to $1690 per person.

Categories I and J are inside cabins with the same upper and lower bed setup, this time on Acapulco and Riviera Decks, comparatively high up on the ship. These inside accommodations are $1465 or $1495 per person for that week-long Caribbean trip.

Less expensive outside cabins in Categories K and L offer one lower bed and an upper berth. For one of these cabins the cost is $1360 or $1390 per person for double occupancy on a week-long cruise, $2040 or $2085 single.

On the Europa Deck Cabin 189 is long and narrow, a comfortable nest for a single person and quite spacious. This is also a low-priced cabin aboard, costing $1595 for a seven-day cruise in peak winter season.

If you like blues and golds, you'll like the accommodations on the Europa Deck, most of which feature those colors. The price for this Category N inside cabin with one lower bed and one upper berth is $1185 per person double for a week-long cruise, $1780 if you are occupying the cabin alone.

In a lower price bracket, Cabin 176 on the Ocean Deck is an inside single with an upper bunk. Although the room is quite small, it has a very good address if you'd like to buy a little status cheap. This Category P cabin is an example of the lowest priced quarters aboard, and can be yours for a seven-day cruise for $1065 in peak Caribbean cruising season.

Third and fourth adults sharing a cabin with two full-fare adult passengers pay $745 for the week-long cruise in peak season, while children between 2 and 18 pay $425. There is no charge for the under-2 crowd. In "value" season those extra person prices drop $50 for adults, $30 for children.

The per-person, per-day rate begins at about $152, rising in upper price brackets to $194 to $247 per person daily, higher in suites.

Sitmar has some money-saving fly-free programs designed to lure you to its cruises.

FAIRSKY: We can't tell you exactly what the *Fairsky* looks like yet because when this was written she had not yet begun her cruising career. However, the line previewed the ship with a flurry of films and photos. Judging from those, here's what you'll see aboard this brand-new sailing ship.

Constructed in a French CNIM (Construction Navales et Industrielles de la Mediterranée) Shipyard in La Seyne-sur-Mer near Toulon, the *Fairsky* will measure 38,000 tons and carry 1200 passengers. She cost $150 million at last count.

On board are 11 public decks with 606 passenger cabins, 350 of them outside cabins, 218 inside, plus 28 mini-suites and 10 larger suites. All cabins have color television and 110-volt current. Like her sister ships, she will have ceiling-recessed upper berths in many cabins, a particularly appealing feature for families.

For fitness fans the ship will have a jogging track, a sports deck for paddle tennis, and a health center with exercise equipment. Called "the Spa," this health center will include a whirlpool bath, two saunas, and a massage room, all on the Sun Deck.

You'll also find a complete casino with blackjack and roulette tables and 85 slot machines.

A main showroom on board is big: 11,000 square feet, one of the largest afloat and able to accommodate 800 passengers.

Special pains have been taken with a forward observation lounge where floor-to-ceiling windows offer a glamorous view the line calls a "captain's eye view" of the ocean outside. Two dining rooms aboard also will have tall windows.

Other public rooms include a piano lounge, meeting room, library, bridge and card rooms, and no fewer than six bars, a veranda lounge, and nightclub. And one more thing: a pizzeria!

The *Fairsky* was scheduled to depart from San Francisco on 14-day Alaska sojourns calling at Vancouver, Alert Bay, Prince Rupert, Ketchikan, Juneau, Sitka, Victoria, and Astoria. Cruises will include sailing in the Seymour Passage and Johnstone Strait, Grenville Channel, the Lynn Canal, Glacier Bay and La Perouse Glacier.

Rates for those two-week trips in "value" season range from $2395 per person to $5210, with peak season prices about $200 more per person.

26. Sun Lines

Contact: Sun Lines, One Rockefeller Plaza, Suite 315, New York, NY 10020 (tel. toll free 800/223-5670, or 212/397-6400).

Cruising Grounds: Caribbean islands, often including Puerto Rico, St. Thomas, Jamaica, Bequia, St. Vincent, Guadeloupe, and St. Kitts; Mexico's Yucatán Peninsula; South America, including the Amazon and Orinoco Rivers, Ciudad Guayana (Venezuela), Cartagena (Colombia), and various Brazilian ports; Panama Canal; Mexican Riviera; Mediterranean Sea (itineraries vary, so check with Sun Lines or your travel agent).

Itineraries: *Stella Oceanis*—

IN WINTER: San Juan–St. Maarten–Martinique–St. Lucia–Barbados–Tobago–Orinoco River–Ciudad Guayana–Bequia–St. Vincent–Guadeloupe–Antigua–St. Kitts–St. Thomas–San Juan

IN SUMMER: Mediterranean cruises

Stella Solaris—

IN WINTER: Fort Lauderdale–St. Thomas–St. Barthelemy–St. Maarten–St. Lucia–Barbados–Fortaleza–Salvador–Rio de Janeiro–Salvador–Fortaleza–Tobago–Martinique–St. Thomas–Fort Lauderdale

IN SUMMER: Mediterranean cruises

Sun Lines can trace its history back to the Aegean where warm waters and sunny islands have been luring adventuresome cruisers since the Phoenicians began touring here. But romantic and ethereally beautiful as those islands are, they are somewhat less interesting when visited on cargo boats, which are to cruises what cheap old hotels are to motoring trips: just a way to get there.

That's about how Greek entrepreneur Alex Keusseoglou sized it up in the early 1960s when he decided to do something about the quality of life on the Mediterranean Sea. Figuring it couldn't hurt to add a little elegance to Med voyages, Keusseoglou set out to create a cruise line of his own. He had plenty of background to give him a clue on how to go about this gargantuan task: he'd been an executive of Home Lines and helped develop that company into a major force in transatlantic cruising.

Beginning in 1960 with a vessel named *Stella Maris* which sailed on Aegean cruises, Keusseoglou soon had two ships, the second called *Stella Solaris I.* As time went on both those vessels were replaced with two new ships called the *Stella Maris II,* which became part of the line in 1965, and the *Stella Oceanis,* which joined the company two years later. And in 1973 the *Stella Solaris,* a new ship became the pride, joy, and largest vessel in the Sun Line fleet.

In 1971 the Marriott Corporation acquired an interest in Sun Line, but the company is still managed by the Keusseoglou family, which tends to all the details right down to the decor of the ship (coordinated by Isabella Keusseoglou, wife of the line's president).

Sun Line likes to call itself the "elite fleet" of the travel world, and it's certainly true that the line's three ships sail to glamorous places and are themselves good-looking ladies.

The largest of the three is the far-from-massive 18,000-ton *Stella Solaris,* which carries just 620 passengers and 330 staffers off to much-loved Caribbean ports like St. Thomas, Montego Bay, Cartagena, and Cozumél most of the winter, then takes time off for 23- to 48-day cruises that drop anchor at dozens of fascinating ports in the Caribbean and move on to cruise the Amazon River and visit Brazilian ports before turning northward for a transit of the Panama Canal. In spring she sets sail from San Francisco through the Caribbean and on to Europe for stops in the souks of Tangier, the beaches of Palma de Mallorca, and the ruins of Civitavecchia outside Rome.

North Americans don't see much of these ships, although we will shortly be seeing more: the *Stella Solaris* will make Fort Lauderdale's Port Everglades her home this winter, sailing from there to the Caribbean and on double transits (that's through and back again) of the Panama Canal. In summer she returns to European waters for Mediterranean cruises.

Meanwhile her much smaller sister ship, the 5500-ton *Stella Oceanis,* spends the winter cruising from San Juan through the Caribbean to some most unusual South American ports. She cruises up the remote Orinoco River never before visited by a cruise ship, visits Ciudad Guayana in Venezuela (where you can take a shore excursion to massive Angel Falls), then drops anchor in Bequia, St Vincent, Guadeloupe, and St. Kitts, among other Caribbean islands on 14-day round-trip journeys from San Juan.

Stella Maris II, yacht-like at a mere 3500 tons, sails in summer on Mediterranean itineraries that take its 186 passengers from Venice to Corfu, Malta, Costa Smeralda, Elba, and Portofino.

Activities

Ports are important to this cruise line which offers you many on every cruise. Those port visits fill almost every day on many cruises, so when you do have a day at sea it's probably not a round of activity you'll be seeking but a nice quiet place in the sun.

At night, however, the ship sizzles with zappy singers, dancers, and comedians, or dances to the music of an orchestra. Occasionally a concert pianist will turn up to turn passengers on to the music of Beethoven. More often a mariachi band or reggae dancers will come aboard to dazzle and amuse, since the *Stella Solaris* likes you to have a cultural taste of the countries you visit.

A special feature of this Greek line, of course, is a Greek night, when the staff offers you Greek wines at cocktail hour, then entertains you at dinner and later with Greek dancing, winding up finally in the disco where you can learn the syrtaki.

You can dress up if you like for the ship's masquerade evening. On other nights the ship celebrates French Night, Ladies' Night, Caribbean Night, and finally, throws a farewell banquet.

For quiet evenings there's music in the piano bar or dancing on deck.

Special pasta lovers alert! At midnight there's a spaghetti party.

On the *Stella Oceanis* too port visits are a very important part of this ship's cruises, so on-board activities are less frenetic and jam-packed than on some ships. In fact on Orinoco River cruises you are in port every single day of the journey so that leaves very little time for arts and crafts classes or nutty contests.

You can of course see a movie, visit any of several sipping spots on board, play cards or read in the library and card rooms, get some exercise in the ship's swimming pool or in the gym.

Nighttime activities begin with pre-dinner cocktails, work their way through a leisurely dinner, and then move into the ship's lounges where shows are similar to those aboard the *Stella Solaris.* Take a look at what's going on there and expect to see more of the same on this ship.

STELLA SOLARIS: Enter the massive reception area in the *Stella Solaris* and you'll know that there are some good reasons why this ship is so popular. Undoubtedly, this handsome craft has much to recommend it.

Public Rooms

First, it is elegant. From decks named after gems—ruby, emerald, sapphire—to a big cinema decorated in gray velvet to a below-stairs disco outfitted in white leather and featuring a steel dance floor, the 18,000-ton *Stella Solaris* is a ship at once cozy and contemporary.

Although not a particularly large ship—just 18,000 tons and carrying 650 passengers—the *Stella Solaris* has such an open airiness you often feel as if you're on a much larger craft.

The Main Lounge is a sweeping bilevel room with long expanses of glass and raised seating along the sides of the room. Front and center, a glowing parquet dance floor provides a focal point for a handsome tranquil room. An ornate open wall cordons off an adjoining lounge and bar where you can watch the sun setting over the stern through a bank of glistening windows. Leather banquettes add a contemporary touch to a room decorated in subtle orange and brown tones.

Up on the Lido Deck, the Lido Bar is a popular retreat for sunseekers who spend their days draped around the ship's eye-catching figure-eight, double-circle green mosaic swimming pool. It's built that way to help keep down the wave action in the pool as the ship plows through the water.

On the Solaris Deck is the ship's dining room, a tranquil spot decorated in a soothing blue and white theme.

When you see how well you eat on this ship, you may want to be introduced to the gymnasium, the saunas, and the massage room. The *Stella Solaris* provides quite a nice environment in which to huff and puff: carpets throughout, a big shiny set of chromed weights, rowing machines, mats, slant boards, bicycles, the lot.

Built for cooler climes, the *Stella Solaris* sports one of those covered promenade decks that can't help but remind you of old movies in which passengers sat sipping tea, their knees neatly covered with an afghan as they crossed the North Atlantic. (Just what you'd be doing with an afghan in the Caribbean is difficult to say, but the image is seductive anyway.)

Just around the corner from the purser's desk on the Solaris Deck is a handsome shopping area with wide windows displaying everything from showy caftans to pre-Columbian replica jewelry.

Beauty salons and barbershops seem to be the most neglected area on most ships, but not here—these are very classy operations, clean and shiny with marble floors.

Up top on the Boat Deck there's a comfortable reading and card room, and down on Golden Deck there's a special playroom for children.

Down on the main deck, which on this ship is beneath the ship's seven passenger decks, is that slinky gray and silver discothèque, and on the Sapphire Deck is the ship's big cinema. And a Monte Carlo Casino, of course.

Cabins

Cabins come in all sizes and shapes, but have one unusual feature: more expensive quarters have closed-circuit television sets in them, but there are hookups in every room so you can bring your own portable if you're a real television fan.

On this ship the cabins are down a short passageway that leads off the main thoroughfares of the vessel. All the ship's quarters are reasonably spacious, usually with twin beds, a couple of chairs, sometimes even a couch and coffee table. Large dressers and closets give you ample room to stow your belongings, and many of them have a special corner for storing your bed pillows during the day when you're using the beds as a seating area. All rooms have private baths.

Sun Lines keeps it reasonably simple with cabin price categories. There are just seven, Categories 1 through 7.

If you're really going first class, deluxe suites B6 and B8 are especially handsome quarters, the former smartly outfitted in a beige and brown diamond pattern and twin beds almost hidden from the sitting area. There's lots of storage space: a full dresser, three full closets. Suite B8 on the Boat Deck is decorated in soothing shades of deep burgundy, and similar quarters (suite B2) in deep blue and white. The main allure of B2 is its location all alone on a hallway, making it very private quarters indeed.

A ten-day Panama Canal cruise in one of those elegant Category 1 suites, which feature two twin beds or a double bed and both tub and shower in the bathroom, plus a spacious separate sitting area, will cost $4012 per person. Similar suites on the Golden Deck, two decks down, are $3662 per person for that same voyage. Still another group of suites is located on the Ruby Deck and is available at Category 3 prices: $3462 for a ten-day canal trip.

Moving down the price list, there are four categories of outside double cabins, all with two lower beds and private bath, of course. Categories 4, 5, and 6 range in price from $3012 down to $2912 or $2762 per person for the ten-day cruise. Category 7 cabins, which are called standard outside cabins (as opposed to the superior classification of the others), don't differ a great deal in size but two have two lower beds and two upper ones. One of those costs $2662 per person for a ten-day trip.

In Category 5 ($2912 per person for the ten-day cruise) cabin R67, decorated in burnt orange, is an attractive example of this mid-priced category (both tub and shower here too).

The remaining cabins—Categories 8, 9, 10, and 11—are all inside quarters. Inside cabins, of course, are smaller, but they are still roomy. Cabin R53 and its counterparts in Category 9 look comfortable. The top-priced accommodations among those inside selections have two lower and two upper beds and cost $2562 per person for a ten-day cruise.

Standard inside rooms have two lower beds and are either $2462 or $2262 per person, depending on size and location.

Category 8 cabins, which cost $2562 per person, are quite spacious, with shower only in the baths, two lower and one upper bunk, and two full-length closets. Cabin R69 is an attractive example of this category.

The lowest priced accommodations for this ten-day sojourn on the *Stella Solaris* are Category 11 standard inside cabins with one upper and one lower bed. They cost $2062 per person for a ten-day Panama Canal trip.

That works out to a daily rate beginning at $206 per person, rising in the more expensive cabins to $226 to $301 per person a day, higher for suites.

A third person sharing a cabin pays the minimum fare for that cruise, while children under 12 occupying a third or fourth berth in the same cabin pay 50% of the minimum rate.

Single occupants of a superior or standard double cabin pay 150% of the fare for that cabin, 200% in suites.

If you don't take advantage of the line's fly/cruise packages, you are given a $225 credit on the ten-day cruise, up to $550 on longer voyages.

You must also budget $55 additional for port charges on the ten-day cruise, more on longer voyages, to a high of $236 for a 48-day journey.

STELLA OCEANIS: A much smaller ship, the *Stella Oceanis* is just 5500 tons and carries 300 passengers, half that number of staff. On a ship this small you'll feel almost as if you're on a big yacht. Although we've never been on the *Stella Oceanis,* friends have praised the intimate feeling of this small ship.

Public Rooms

Greek history and culture play a big part in the theme aboard this ship, so learn your mythology.

You'll be dining, for instance, in the Aphroditi Dining Room, which seats 200 and is decorated in gold and blue. On the Oceanis Deck just outside the restaurant you can amuse yourself in a small casino or shop in a boutique with some interesting Greek creations for sale.

Entertainment takes place in the ship's Minos Salon, which is big enough for all 300 passengers. A tiny club at the back of the Minos Salon makes a good spot for quiet post-prandial sipping.

For more eventful evenings, head for the Plaka Taverna, which becomes the ship's disco at night.

Cabins

There are seven grades of cabins on board this small vessel, numbered Category 1 through 7 with the highest numbers the most expensive quarters on board.

The shortest cruise available on the *Stella Oceanis* when she's sailing on this side of the world is that enchanting 14-day Orinoco River trip, which stops in at least 12 ports and spends a couple of days cruising the river and waiting for passengers to return from thrilling trips to awesome Angel Falls.

The following prices are for one of these two-week sojourns.

If you opt for a deluxe outside suite with two beds and sitting room, you'll pay $4774 per person for the trip.

In three deluxe outside cabins you pay $3710 or $4088 per person, depending on the size and location of the quarters.

In mid-priced outside cabins in Categories 4 and 5 the two-week journey will cost $3402 or $3276 per person.

Categories 6 and 7 are inside cabins with two trim lower beds. The cost in one of those is $2842 or $2492 per person for the 14-day cruise.

Finally, a few inside cabins with one lower and one upper bed are available. The rate for these accommodations is $2492 per person for a two-week trip.

Third- and fourth-person prices are the same aboard the *Stella Oceanis* as aboard the *Stella Solaris,* minimum fare for the cruise. Children under 12 pay 50% of the minimum rate when occupying a cabin with two adults paying full fare.

Single travelers also pay the same aboard both ships, 150% to 200% of the fare for single occupany of a double cabin.

If you do not use the line's fly/cruise programs to get to San Juan to join this two-week trip, you can take $150 per person off the price.

Per diem rates run from a minimum of $178 per person to a high of $292, with the mid-price range about $234 per person.

27. Sundance Cruises

Contact: Sundance Cruises, 520 Pike St., Suite 1230, Seattle, WA 98101 (tel. toll free 800/222-5505, or 206/467-8200).

Cruising Grounds: Alaska, Mexican Riviera.

Itinerary: *Sun Dancer—*

IN SUMMER: Vancouver–Juneau–Haines and/or Skagway–Tracy Arm–Ketchikan—Misty Fjord–Alert Bay–Vancouver

IN WINTER: Los Angeles–Puerto Vallarta–Mazatlan–Cabo San Lucas–Los Angeles

---

Something new in Alaska cruises hit the marketplace in the summer of 1984 when Sundance Cruises began offering three-, four-, and seven-night voyages from Vancouver to Juneau, Skagway or Haines, Trace Arm, Ketchikan, and Misty Fjords.

Organized by Stanley McDonald, who was influential in the creation and marketing of Princess Cruise Lines, and by Scandinavia's Silja ferry line, Sundance offers you the opportunity to take your car with you, disembark in Skagway to tour the Yukon or Alaska, and then rejoin the cruise.

"This is a chance for the rank-and-file person, the ordinary, everyday person who doesn't have an awful lot of money but really wants to see this area," a line executive told us. "The idea is to put your automobile or camper on and then forget about it and have a posh cruise with saunas, barbershop, gym, full entertainment and gourmet dining. It's just like a regular cruise and you have the added attraction of taking a car north or southbound." He adds that the line hopes to lure passengers of varying ages and incomes (particularly incomes) with some very budgetwise fares.

Like what? Like a maximum of $1850 per person for a week-long Alaska cruise—and that's in the owner's suite! The minimum fare for a week-long Alaska cruise is $795.

SUN DANCER: As for the ship, the *Sun Dancer,* she measures 17,500 tons, is 500 feet long, and carries 700 passengers. Her officers are Scandinavian and the crew is international, with many Americans in that number, particularly in hosting positions.

Departing Vancouver on Friday afternoon, the *Sun Dancer* sails north, spending the following day at sea and reaching the Alaskan capital city of Juneau on Sunday afternoon. After a visit to the famous Red Dog Saloon and Mendenhall Glacier, you're back on board, arriving in Skagway, the gateway to the Klondike, or Haines, where a salmon bake is scheduled. Here you can leave the ship and tour the Yukon or the interior of Alaska for a few days or a few weeks. Just be sure to return to one of the two villages where you will reboard the ship and return to Vancouver via Tracy Arm, Ketchikan, and Misty Fjords. You'll also spend another day at sea.

In winter the ship is scheduled to sail in Mexico, probably from a berth in California.

Activities/Public Rooms

On board you'll dine on grilled salmon and the like in the ship's dining room or at a casual poolside grill and 24-hour deli.

There are three cinemas on board where you can catch all the latest movies. But the ship's pride is a nifty piano bar, the Sky Bar, overlooking the ship's bow.

Evenings, you can dance in the video disco, watch live entertainment in the nightclub, or have a go at it in the casino.

Out on Deck 5 there's an outdoor swimming pool complete with swirling waterslide, and up on Deck 1 is an indoor swimming pool, a flashy gym, a whirlpool, saunas, and masseurs.

On the Sun Deck you'll find a complete running track and a small spa operation, plus an oval bar.

Book fanciers will find a small library tucked away near the purser's office, and shoppers can ogle the scrimshaw in the shop not far away. For card and game players there's a card and game room, naturally.

Cabins

Although we haven't seen this ship, the cabins seem comparatively uniform in size and the ship's brochure carefully outlines what it considers typical outside and inside twins and deluxe staterooms.

All cabins have complete bath with shower, a dresser/vanity, closets, and usually an easy chair. Beds can be used as sitting areas during the day. Electrical connections will support most appliances, but ironing is out and high-wattage hair dryers are questionable (ask the room steward if you have any doubts).

Prices are grouped into ten categories and divided into two seasons, peak and "value." Peak season occurs in June, July, and August; "value" season applies to three sailings in September.

The prices below refer to a seven-night round-trip fare in peak season. Figure about $45 to $90 less in "value" season.

Two luxury suites are outside rooms, featuring two lower beds, a bathroom with shower, a sitting area with sofa, a refrigerator, and small mini-bar. All these are on a top deck of the ship, Deck 6, and cost $1850 per person for the trip.

Somewhat smaller and less elaborate but still nifty quarters are the deluxe staterooms, with two lower beds, bath with shower, sitting area, and refrigerator. These are $1625 per person for the trip in peak season.

Outside rooms with two lower beds come in four price levels—Categories C, D, E, and F—ranging in price from $1125 to $1525 per person, depending on size of the cabin. One more category of outside cabins, Category H, is called an "economy" cabin and has a lower bed and an upper berth. That room is $995 per person for the seven-night trip in peak season.

Less expensive inside quarters, with two lower beds or a lower and an upper berth, are $795 or $895 per person (the more expensive price is charged for two lower beds).

Single travelers pay 150% in Categories E through J and 175% in the upper categories.

Third and fourth persons sharing a room pay $55 each per night, same for children.

The per diem rate for these quarters for a seven-night voyage in peak season begins at $113 for the lowest priced quarters, rising to $178 in mid-priced quarters and $218 in higher price categories, excluding suites.

Transport of cars or recreational vehicles costs $954 round trip in either season.

Three-night northbound or four-night southbound fares are also available. Three-night rates range from $355 to $810 per person in peak season, $325 to $755 in "value" season. Four-night rates begin at $470 per person and rise to $1070 in peak season, $485 to $1005 per person in "value" season.

Air/sea rates range in price from $49 for round-trip air fare from Portland to $359 from Chicago.

28. Sun Goddess Cruises

Contact: Sun Goddess Cruises, 5801 Blue Lagoon Dr., Suite 360, Miami, Fl 33126 (tel. toll free 800/458-9000, 800/457-9000 in Florida, or 305/266-8705).

Cruising Grounds: itineraries vary; check with Sun Goddess Cruises or your travel agent.

Itinerary: *Sea Goddess*—

IN WINTER: St. Croix–The Baths–Gorda Sound–St. Maarten–St. Lucia–Mustique–Guadeloupe–Îles des Saintes–Guadeloupe–Antigua–St. Barthelemy

IN SUMMER: Mediterranean cruises

Okay, you've been introduced to some budget bargains, some mid-priced ships, and some luxury liners, so now you're ready to meet, in your dreams at least, a seaborne status symbol.

We're talking about the *Sea Goddess I,* first ship of a cruise line that unabashedly caters to zillionaires or to those willing to pawn the family jewels for a chance to live like one for a week.

Right up front, the daily rate here is $500—per person—and on their air/sea program you fly the Concorde!

Even to unflappable cruise-marketing executives Sun Goddess Cruises was a startling shot at one-upmanship. Founded about 1983, the company was created by a Norwegian shipping company A/S Norske. At the same time the line contracted for two small and exclusive ships, the first to go into service in the spring of 1984, the second in 1985.

Not content with just another cruise ship, the company created the crème de la crème of big, ocean-going yachts and began marketing it to those whose annual income is in the $100,000 bracket. (Higher than that is also acceptable, of course.)

SEA GODDESS I: So what do you buy for your buck in these lofty realms? Well, for openers, as you sit at the outdoor café, a waterfall splashes and tinkles behind you, pouring ceaselessly down a section of the ship's sleek smokestack.

When you anchor in some crystalline Caribbean waters or off a glittering Greek isle, a platform at the stern of the ship is lowered and you step right off into the sea for some snorkeling, or onto a windsurfing board or small sailboat.

Swimming in the ship's pool sounds a real yawner? Then try the whirlpool right there beside the pool. Or escape from the sun to the ship's secluded Greenhouse, where you relax on comfortable couches amid a profusion of exotic blooming plants.

You just want to relax in your stateroom? Of course. Would you like us to turn on the stereo or the video cassette player, fix you a drink from your stocked in-cabin bar, or turn on the television? Perhaps a little snack from your refrigerator carefully packed with assorted cheeses and garnis?

And what does your room look like? Well, there are no mere cabins aboard. Every one of the 60 staterooms is a suite, each has a separate living room and big wide windows overlooking the sea. You can't outclass anyone because each cabin aboard is the same size, about 50% larger than the usual cruise-ship cabins. You can take your choice, however, of twin or queen-size beds. Archways and built-in cabinetry are of white oak, the furniture outfitted in soft contemporary colors. Plus floor-to-ceiling mirrors, a coffee table large enough for dining, deep carpets, thick walls.

Small though she is, the *Sea Goddess I* is quite a bit larger than other luxury yacht-ships of this kind (about four times as large in fact): 4000 tons, 340 feet long, and designed for 120 passengers.

In the ship's bright dining room lined with moldings and mirrors, you dine when you please, not at some preordained hour.

After dinner perhaps you'll choose a game in the small casino, or some quiet music at the piano bar, some witty conversation with fellow passengers. Or nip into the circular Main Salon where the best of shoreside entertainers has been brought on board for your evening amusement.

You're looking forward to Bingo, grandmothers' bragging contests, arts and crafts? Then you are very likely not Sun Goddess material!

If you select this very posh way to sail the seas, you'll find yourself spending a summer week gliding to the very best and most exclusive ports of the Mediterranean from, say, Monaco to Ibiza, Mallorca, and St. Tropez, and wintering, as does anyone of any importance, in St. Croix and cruising from there to the best addresses of the Caribbean—Casa de Campo or Princess Margaret's Mustique hideaway.

And how much does this all cost? Well, if you have to ask. . . . But since you did, a week in the Mediterranean is $3600 per person, double occupancy; singles are $4400.

If you want to do this in real style, you can participate in a preplanned expedition that flies you to France on the Concorde, houses you at the

Hotel George V for a couple of days, flies you first class to Malaga to join the ship, and sends you home again on the Concorde. Price: $8000 per person.

29. World Explorer Cruises

Contact: World Explorer Cruises, 3 Embarcadero Center, San Francisco, CA 94111 (tel. toll free 800/854-3835, 800/222-2255 in California, or 415/391-9262).

Cruising Grounds: Alaska, South Pacific.

Itinerary: *Universe—*

IN SUMMER: Vancouver—Prince Rupert–Sitka–Skagway–Yakutat–Columbia Glacier–Whittier–Valdez–Juneau–Glacier Bay–Ketchikan–Vancouver

IN WINTER: San Francisco–South Pacific–San Francisco

In these pages you've read about floating hotels and love boats, mini-cruisers and maxi-yachts. Now it's time to meet a floating university campus!

Step right up and say hello to the 18,100-ton S.S. *Universe,* one and only craft of World Explorer Cruises.

We're going to go out on a limb here and *guarantee* you that no ship afloat has a larger library—and we mean that literally! How, after all, could you beat 11,000 volumes?

What's going on here? Well, half the year this ship is chartered to the University of Pittsburgh, which uses it as a floating campus for its Institute of Shipboard Education's Semester-at-Sea. (Where were semesters like that when we were in college?) If you missed that floating-semester era, you are about to get another chance.

In April, World Explorer Cruises gets its ship back from the university and takes 550 passengers on a glamorous 62-day trip from San Francisco to the South Pacific, calling at such fabled ports as Bora Bora, Tahiti, Tonga, Roratonga, Pago Pago, Fiji, Guam, Saipan, and the Hawaiian Islands. Now there's a semester at sea for you!

In late June the ship returns to Vancouver where it spends the summer cruising glacial Alaska waters on quite reasonably priced 14-day cruises. Of the ships sailing on 14-day Alaska cruises, this is the only one cruising 14 days from Vancouver which allows you to see more of Alaskan waters than do cruises from San Francisco or Los Angeles.

UNIVERSE: Formerly the S.S. *Atlantic,* this American-built ship went into service in 1959, and was bought by this cruise line in 1977 and refurbished throughout in 1983.

Activities

Aboard you will find 550 passengers intent on learning more, indeed as much as possible, about the lands they are visiting. To help them do that, the line brings lecturers on board for detailed discussions of the art, literature, and cultures of the people you'll be meeting at ports you visit.

You may hear an art expert lecturing on ceremonial art of the Mekoryuk or an oceanographer explaining how the Tongans trick an octopus into leaping at their lures. Anthropologists outline the possible meanings of petroglyphs and naturalists will explain the importance of the walrus to native Alaskans.

You'll find historians, political scientists, even musicians aboard to introduce you to the places you're visiting, offering you a firm foundation of knowledge on which to create your own cultural exchange with those you meet.

While these are not stuffy events, they're definitely meant for the person who wants more than the superficial cruise experience, the more sophisticated traveler with a strong interest in a cruise as an educational experience.

Line executives unabashedly admit that this is not an elegant luxury ship, adding that they consider the ship a "value cruise."

Cabins and public areas are spacious but not elegant, they point out, "and you won't find people wearing furs and diamonds." You will find many retired professional people, teachers, educators, people still active physically and mentally, and in search of an improvement in both.

All is not seminars, of course. Evenings there may be a classical guitarist or pianist performing in a quiet lounge, or a singalong going strong in the piano bar.

In keeping with the general atmosphere of the cruises, masquerade parties aboard are more likely to feature historic characters than pregnant nuns or big-bellied male hula dancers. Entertainment runs more toward quiet evenings of dance music and conversation than frenetic disco sessions.

As one line executive put it: "We offer a lot more steak and a lot less sizzle. We wine and dine and entertain, but don't serve flaming desserts or have Broadway revues."

Public Rooms

You'll find plenty of entertainment aboard, and plenty of places for it. For openers, there are seven decks, five lounges, a nightclub, bar, 200-seat theater, and glass-enclosed promenade deck.

Up in the Dolphin Lounge on the Boat Deck a piano is the focal point of a bright room flanked by the small Dolphin bar. Not far away is another small lounging area, outfitted with banquettes, comfortable chairs, and low tables.

Down a deck, on the Promenade Deck, there's always dancing in the Mandarin Lounge or quiet talks in the Jade Room or Anchorage Room.

Just off the open deck at the stern you'll find the ship's big Commodore Lounge, where an orchestra provides dance music for terpsichoreans who whirl on the big rectangular dance floor. The Commodore bar here is a favorite gathering spot, and has some cozy nooks and crannies for conversations with new friends.

Down on the main deck is the ship's dining room, a bilevel room lined with tables for four. Here you can dine on a wide range of American favorites, or try some new gustatory adventures created by the Chinese chefs aboard. Although the cruise staff is American, all the crew is Chinese, so you can be sure you'll get an opportunity to try some "different" Oriental specialties.

In the theater you can see some top films, and in the lounges variety shows, passenger talent shows, and entertainment by the cruise staff keep things hopping. There are some rousing bridge tournaments aboard too.

Naturally, you'll find gift and beauty shops on board, and way up top there's even a special room for the youngsters. For balmy days in the South Pacific there's a swimming pool in which to cool. Not to mention a hospital and that monstrous library, which, as a line executive pointed out to us, is bigger than the library of many a small town!

Cabins

All accommodations on board have private baths and are quite spacious as you would expect on a ship of this age and type. All are carpeted and feature simple furnishings, usually including a dresser/desk, a chair or two, and closet space. Following that recent renovation, all the cabins are decorated in soft and pretty earth colors.

Twelve price categories range from A through K, with an extra BB category tossed in to cover outside double cabins. All Alaskan cruises are 14-day trips, while the South Pacific voyages can be taken for the full 62 days, or in shorter segments of about a month.

Let's look at the prices for a 14-day Alaska cruise.

The top-of-the-line accommodations are deluxe cabins with two lower beds, a tub bath, shower, loads of space, and a long mirrored dresser. For that the cost is $3095 per person for a 14-day cruise.

Moving down in price a bit, outside staterooms with two lower beds are $2995 per person, and outside double cabins with similar accoutrements cost $2795 per person for the 14-day cruise.

Three mid-priced categories of outside cabins—Categories D, E, and F—differ a little in size but have about the same general look to them, many including a couple of easy chairs and two beds with really quite a lot of space in between. For one of those you will pay, in descending price order, $1545, $1345, or $2095 per person.

If you think you'll be happy with an inside cabin, you'll find them on the Upper, Main, and Promenade Decks, the latter sharing a deck with some quite high-priced quarters. Depending on what you ask for and what you pay, there will be either two lower beds or an upper and lower berth in these inside cabins. The price for one with two lower beds is $2095 per person for a two-week cruise, dropping to $1845 or $1745 per person for cabins with upper and lower berths.

The rock-bottom price aboard is a quite reasonable $1595 per person for the two-week cruise. (Elevators do not connect to this floor, but you can catch one on the next floor up.)

Single travelers have a choice of quite roomy outside single cabin in Category C for $2995 or an inside single cabin for $2395.

Third or fourth persons sharing a cabin are $395 per person for the Alaskan sojourn, and you'll also need to budget port charges of $29 per person in Alaska, $42 in the South Pacific.

On a per-person per diem basis, those figures work out to a low of $114, a middle price in the $149 to $182 range, and a top price, excluding suites, of $199. For Alaskan waters these are quite reasonable per diem rates. (Line execs claim they're the lowest for Alaska sailings.)

You're curious to know how much the South Pacific 62-day dream cruise is, right? Top-of-the-line cabins are $14,245 per person for 62 days of sunshine and orchids. The least expensive cabin on board for that long voyage is $7395.

Chapter VI

FARE WEATHERING: BOOKING YOUR TICKET

SO NOW YOU HAVE picked a ship, chosen a price category, pulled out your checkbook, and you're all set to commit yourself to a week as Captain Cook—or Captain Hook!

So now what?

If you haven't done it already, now is the time to see a travel agent. All along here we've been touting these travel agent people, and for very good reason: they can help you and they won't charge you a penny for doing so.

1. Working with a Travel Agent

As surprising as it sounds, travel agents tell us that there are still many people who don't really know what travel agents are or what they do, and who are afraid they'll have to pay them for help in booking tickets.

If you're not altogether sure just what an agent is, let it be known that travel agents' services are free. They will do all the work, share all their considerable knowledge, and probably even send you flowers or a bottle of wine when you book a cruise.

How do they earn money? Simple. Just like real estate agents, they are paid by the seller, in this case the cruise line, which pays them 10% to 15% of the cost of your ticket for having sent the line your business. Before you begin thinking that travel agents must be millionaires, figure that they must subtract all the costs of a business from their commissions, which doesn't leave many millionaires.

Many agents pay dues to belong to a group called the American Society of Travel Agents. Like any trade organization, ASTA offers its members educational seminars and lobbying services. An ASTA logo on the agency door or advertising at least means that that agency is serious about its business. Other trade organizations include the Association of Retail Travel Agents (ARTA) and the Institute of Certified Travel Agents (ICTA), which confers a degree, Certified Travel Counselor (CTC), on agents who have been in business for five years and have completed many hours of required courses.

While membership in any of those groups does not guarantee a good agent, it gives you a place to start looking. From there on, your personal assessment of an agent's talents and personality will help you decide if you want to do business with that agent or agency.

We really do advise you to seek an agent's help in booking a cruise. They have all the latest information on renovations, good and bad cabins, itineraries, and best of all, special price deals. What's more, they usually know the cruise lines' reservation agents and sales representatives well and will solicit their help on your behalf. That's especially nice if you have special problems or requests on a cruise.

Let's just say that travel agents are your business Mom (or Dad). They'll do their best to see that everything goes perfectly for you.

When you talk to your travel agent, don't be shy. Tell them how much money you have to spend. Holding back on that information is like refusing to tell your doctor where it hurts. As good business people and smart travelers, they may try to "sell up," that is, suggest that you pay a little more for a cruise than you'd planned If you absolutely can't afford any more, stick by your guns. If you can, listen to their reasoning. It's based on experience, both personal and through reports from other clients.

While you're unburdening your financial soul, tell them something about yourself and your companion, if you have one. Do you like to meet lots of new people and socialize with them or are you happier keeping to yourself? How fussy are you about your living quarters? Do you like things contemporary or antique? What kind of entertainment do you like?

Good agents will ask you many questions like that in an attempt to narrow down the numbers of ships they think you will enjoy. They know, after all, that if *you* aren't happy, you'll see to it that *they* aren't happy!

Which brings us to the final point in working with a travel agent: don't blame them if some shipboard employee was rude or the line couldn't find your ticket or some other major or minor calamity occurred. They are in the unenviable position of promising a product that will be delivered, but having no control over the successful delivery of that promised product. If you do have service or other problems with a ship, tell—but don't berate—your travel agent.

If you insist on booking your own tickets, you can do so by contacting the line and following their instructions. Booking specifics usually are detailed on the back of a line or ship brochure too.

2. Booking Your Ticket

When you've settled on a cruise and a cabin, you'll be asked to give the line a deposit, which varies from a set amount to a percentage of the total cost of each ticket. Your deposit will be confirmed by the cruise line and your cabin will be assigned, but no specific cabin number may be given to you until embarkation.

If you are determined to have a certain cabin, you can request it by number. Most lines will do all they can to give you the cabin you want—the more you pay for the ticket, the better chance there is that you'll get what you want. Money talks here as everywhere.

Travel agents can be really invaluable to those who want a specific cabin. In this industry, as in all industries, it's not what you know but *who* you know that counts. Travel agents know where to go with special requests, and their buying clout makes shipping lines eager to honor their requests.

You will be asked to pay the remaining amount at some time before a departure. Once again, when you must pay the full amount to reserve the cabin varies from line to line.

GROUP BOOKINGS: All lines sell at reduced rates to groups of 10, 15, or more, and many offer travel agents a free "tour conductor" cabin for every group they book. Agents often don't use the tour conductor cabin and pass the savings along to the group. Discounts for groups are usually 10% to 15% of the total, and each cruise line decides for itself how many people comprise a "group." If you are traveling with several other couples, read the ship's brochure information on group bookings and ask an agent how much you might be able to save.

Agents may also be able to team you up with a group the agency is booking on a certain ship. Ask about that possibility. Unlike group travel on the ground, ship groups are not herded about as a group and, of course, you have individual cabins.

MONEY-SAVING TIPS: Wherever money is changing hands, there are ways to secure a bargain.

Booking as far in advance as possible is one of the best ways to save money for two reasons: (1) cruise lines often offer a discount for early bookings (the definition of "early" varies); and (2) the least expensive cabins (and strangely enough, the most expensive quarters) are the first to be sold.

Another money-saving trick: Some lines will accept bookings known as "to be assigned," or TBA, at minimum or average rates. Such an arrangement stipulates that you will be given a cabin at least as good as the price category you paid. If you have paid a minimum rate and those cabins are all sold at the departure time, you will be "upgraded," as they say, and given a cabin in a higher price category. We've heard of some really lucky souls who have sailed in suites at the minimum rate! That's very rare, however, so don't be too optimistic. Do, however, ask about TBA arrangements on the line you're interested in sailing.

Single passengers have a similar opportunity. On ships that offer you the option of sharing a cabin—and that's almost all ships—you can ask your travel agent to specify that you will book only on a per-person double basis. If the line agrees and is unable to find someone to share your quarters, you pay only the per-person double rate instead of the 50% to 100% supplement required of single travelers occupying a double cabin by themselves.

One line, Norwegian Caribbean Lines, has a "Sea Saver" program in which you choose the cabin, they choose the ship. Designed to help them spread the passenger load over their sizable fleet, the program offers you bargain prices if you're willing to go on any cruise offered. Other lines may be working out a similar program even as you read. Look at travel ads in the newspaper and ask a travel agent about possible money-saving plans.

A real gambler (so some real gamblers tell us) can take cash in hand on the day he wants to sail (or perhaps just a few days before), walk up to the booking desk, and tell them that he wants to go on a cruise and has just this much money to spend.

Naturally, the amount you offer must be in the ballpark of at least the minimum price aboard (these people are not idiots). If a line is hungry and sailing emptier than it would like, however, there's a possibility you could get a nice cabin for the minimum price or less. We can't tell you if this rumor is true since no one will admit to it, but if you're very flexible—and prepared for rejection—it might be worth a try. Very risky though.

LOOK AT YOUR TICKET: Not only is it fun to hold that paper promise of tomorrow's pleasures in your hand and meditate on the fun ahead, it's vital to check it to make sure everything is right. In this heavily mechanized world mistakes seem to occur with more, instead of the promised less, frequency. So when you get your tickets, take a close look at them.

It's going to sound stupid for us to tell you to look at the name of the ship you're sailing on, but we've been told that many people who arrive at the bustling Port of Miami don't know what ship they've booked! Be sure you know the name of the ship, and that you've been booked on the one you requested.

A ticket is a valid contract between you and the cruise line. They must fulfill their obligations and you must fulfill yours. That means it would be wise for you to read the ticket (or passage contract accompanying it) to see what your cancellation responsibilities and expectations are and what will happen if you fail to sail or if you leave a cruise before it's over.

You'll also find in that contract the details of your fare, luggage restrictions (if there are any), line policy on cabin changes, information on what to do with money and valuables, details of what the line will do for you if it is forced to cancel or shorten a cruise, and warnings about illegal substances or dangerous items.

That brings up the matter of the line's cancellation of a cruise. Ships are, after all, mechanical creatures. Occasionally something major breaks down and the line is forced to cancel a cruise. In recent years ships have cancelled cruises when air conditioning broke down (and who would want to cruise the Caribbean without it?) and when a ship struck a submerged object and was damaged, among other incidents.

Cruise lines have bent over backward to be fair in those instances by offering disappointed passengers everything from a free hotel room for the night to future cruises at enormous discounts.

Let's hope nothing goes awry before or during your cruise, but if it does, rest easy. The line will try very hard to ameliorate your disappointment. After all, they want you to come back and sail with them again.

3. Cancellations

If you must cancel, do so as soon as you know you're not going to be able to go on the cruise. Cancellation charges vary widely, but most lines look kindly on refunds if you cancel more than 30 days before the scheduled date of departure. If there are medical reasons for your cancellation, ask your doctor for a brief note. That will also help you get your money refunded.

As your sailing date approaches it becomes more difficult to secure a full refund, but you can usually get a partial refund. Amounts vary from line to line.

If you miss the boat, you miss the boat. Don't expect to get your money back. Unlike planes, cruise lines can't count on overbooking and can't take standbys. Anyway, they promised *you* the space and kept it for you, so it's only fair that if you don't show up or cancel soon enough for them to sell the cabin to someone else, you are the one who should suffer.

Read the cancellation rules on the back of the ship's brochure and don't expect them to grant you any special favors, although if there are compelling reasons why you cannot go, your travel agent may be able to help you get all or some of your money back.

Travel agents and others also sell trip insurance. For a small fee, the insurance company will cover your losses if you should be forced to cancel. If you have any reason to believe you might have to cancel, this inexpensive insurance is well worth the cost.

Travel insurance covering any medical costs you might incur on a trip also is available. If you're going on a long cruise and/or have any medical problems, purchase of this kind of insurance is wise. Check your existing medical insurance policy, however. You may already be covered.

4. Dining, Mail, Special Plans

Once you've made a decision on line and price, it's time to think beyond the ticket to those wondrous moments known as meals. Just to reinforce what we've said elsewhere in this guide: all your meals and all your snacks—everything you consume on the ship—is included in the cost of your ticket. When you finish dinner or lunch or any other meal, you get up from the table and leave. No tipping, no cashiers, nothing.

Isn't that a pleasant thought?

Before you book your tickets, however, you might give some thought to your dining room seating arrangements. All large ships have tables for four or six, and many have tables for two or eight or ten as well.

If you like to meet people, you'll probably want to dine at a large table, while honeymooners may want only each other for company.

You can request a table for two, four, or whatever at the time you book. Dining room stewards and the maître d'hôtel will do their best to assign you to the kind of table you specify.

There is another consideration too: the hour at which you want to dine. On very small ships or very elegant ones, you will find only one seating so no decision is necessary. On large vessels, however, you will find two seatings at all or two of the three meals.

You can find a more detailed discussion of dining aboard in Chapter IX, so look that over, decide when and with how much company you would like to dine, and make your requests at the time you book the tickets. Late seatings are the most popular, by the way, so if you prefer to eat about 8 p.m. (as opposed to early seating at 6 p.m. or 6:30 p.m.), get in your bid for that seating now.

If you're going on a long cruise, you can have mail delivered to you at various ports. Now is the time to peruse the brochure and/or ask your agent or the line for the port addresses to which your friends and relatives can write.

If you want anything special aboard, now is also the time to indicate what those special needs might be. We are talking now about details on facilities for the handicapped; special diets (kosher, vegetarian, salt-free, oil-free, sugar-free, etc.), and any medical needs you might have or anticipate.

5. Documentation

If you're visiting countries that require a passport or a visa, you will need to have those papers. A travel agent or the cruise line can tell you what, if any, papers are necessary.

No passport is necessary for cruises to the Bahamas, Caribbean islands, Mexico, Canada, Hawaii, or Alaska (exotic as they are, those last two destinations are U.S. states, remember?), but it's always wise to have some proof of citizenship with you. Driver's licenses are not proof of citizenship, but a birth certificate, voter registration card, or citizenship papers are acceptable proof that you are indeed who and what you say you are.

If you're sailing to Mexico, you may need a Mexican Tourist Card, available through a travel agent or from the Mexican Consulate prior to departure.

We carry our passports in our wallets all the time. They are small enough not to take up too much space, and it never hurts to have it with you. Who knows when someone may offer to fly you to Tahiti for the afternoon (although, sadly, that hasn't happened yet).

Passports are, of course, the very best proof of citizenship of all. Take yours along. If you don't have a passport, write to the U.S. Immigration Service and they will send you the necessary forms to apply for one.

On some cruises to South America, a visa is required. When you book one of those cruises (Sun Lines makes several South American visits, for instance) the line will ask you to send them your passport and they will secure a visa for you. Travel agents also perform these services.

If you're sailing to some far-away port, you'd be well advised to ask a travel agent or the line what, if any, inoculations might be required. While smallpox vaccinations are no longer required in North or South American waters, malaria inoculations are sometime suggested in some areas, and other shots may be necessary or suggested if an outbreak of some illness has occurred there recently. If shots are necessary, take them *before* you go so you have time to recover from any swelling or other adverse reaction.

Chapter VII

SURELY YOU DIDN'T FORGET THE . . . : WHAT TO PACK

1. Shoes
2. Daytime Wear
3. Jewelry
4. Evening Wear
5. Rain and Glacier Wear
6. Laundry Facilities
7. Other Things to Pack

THE VERY WORD "CRUISE" conjures up visions of bejeweled ladies and handsome gentlemen fluttering off to dinner in floating organza dresses and white wing collars, dancing under the stars, gazing out to sea as balmy breezes ruffle their hair and moonlight glitters overhead.

Is it true? Yes . . . and no.

All that glamor can be there if you want it, or can be radically modified if the idea of a starched shirt and bowtie sends you into a paroxysm of panic.

In days of yore when people dressed formally for dinner at *home,* a cruise was an extension and expansion of that formality, a place to see and be seen in your finest. In those days of high tea and higher society, only the very wealthy could afford to take a sea trip. In these socially leveled days, cruises are available to a wide range of pocketbooks, the majority of which have no necessity to own paste copies of their jewels, for they don't own jewels.

Cruises have changed with the times and these days are much more informal events. Now one or two dashing evening outfits will be fine. On most ships, gentlemen, those outfits need not include a tuxedo or dinner jacket. A business suit, preferably a dark one, will do nicely.

It is interesting to note here that cruise line execs tell us the one thing that most quickly sells women on the idea of taking a cruise is anticipation of dressing up for formal evenings and for dinner. Conversely (or perversely), that is the single point they say is most likely to discourage the gentlemen of the species. C'mon, guys, shape up and ship out—you'll love it.

Okay, so let's get down to it. Just what should you pack and how much of it?

1. Shoes

Let's start at the bottom—your feet. Footwear can include rubber-soled shoes of any kind ranging from flip-flops to low-heeled sandals. If it rains or if there's water splashed on the decks, surfaces are often slippery, so don't plan on too many Miss America appearances in bathing suit and three-inch heels.

Lots of stairs—and we do mean lots—will make you happy to see those low heels too. Shoes, comfortable ones, are a very important ingredient in your cruise wardrobe. Many ports you visit won't have fancy sidewalks, and will be dusty in dry heat, muddy and sloppy in the rain. With that in mind, don't pack a raft of fancy new shoes for port visits either.

You'll also find that although you can take taxis, if you elect to walk from the ship to town or back again, the hike can be a long one. Add a couple of hours of shopping and sightseeing to that and whew! Comfortable shoes make it fun. Uncomfortable ones make it a Dante-an level of Hell.

Joggers should pack their running shoes and outfits. Nearly every ship has made some concession to this national fad and now either has a running track or an outline of how many times around Promenade Deck is a mile. Some lines, Norwegian Caribbean Lines, for example, has an on-shore running session when the ship is in port, and will even provide you with a map of the best running spots ashore. That same jogging outfit can be used in the gymnasium, one of which now appears on most vessels.

2. Daytime Wear

By day, T-shirts and shorts, bathing suits and cover-ups, low-heeled sandals and casual shoes will keep you chic. Do take something to cover your bathing suit when you're taking short cuts through the public rooms or having lunch on deck.

It's quite amazing how many times you can change outfits in a day if you're a real clothes horse. One outfit for breakfast, a swimsuit for sunning until lunch, another outfit for lunch and some afternoon games or port visits, still another outfit for dinner and dancing later.

Of course, you don't *have* to change for all those occasions, but you may very well find yourself doing so. Salt air is everywhere and does leave you feeling a bit sticky. In combination with hot sunshine . . . well.

If you've ever seen the March and April department store ads, you'll have an idea what they're selling as "cruise wear." Colorful is a prime ingredient: bright reds, plenty of white, marine blue, sunny yellow, apple green.

Very brief shorts or skirts are fine on shipboard—if you have the body to wear them—but are frowned on in some ports, notably Haiti, the Dominican Republic, and some parts of Mexico. Limit those scanty little nothings to the Sun Deck and don't wear them ashore.

Scarves are a necessity if you like to keep your hair in place. All but the tightest hats get blown off in the breeze. They're all right for port visits, however.

Don't forget your sunglasses. Or your prescription glasses. Two pairs. There's nothing as disconcerting as losing your glasses on a vacation and needing someone to read the menu for you.

3. Jewelry

You'd be well advised not to wear very showy and/or expensive jewelry in port. Many of the places you visit have high levels of poverty and it seems gauche somehow to flaunt scads of gold chains in front of people who are working hard to sell a string of shell beads for a quarter.

Some consideration should also be given to what a relative of ours calls the Eleventh Commandment: Thou shalt not tempt!

If you have beautiful jewelry and feel downright naked without it, of course bring it along, but keep it in the ship's safe when you're not wearing it, and wear it on board, not in port.

4. Evening Wear

At night, ships come alive. Big beautiful lounges that have been a little sleepy by day turn into glitter palaces. Your ship's dining room will gleam with silver and crystal, linens starched to wooden stiffness and napkins folded into pretty fans or angular geometric shapes.

About this time the company begins to glitter as well. The captain and officers roam in spotless white coats and gold braid, while passengers turn out in all colors of the rainbow.

Some ships are more formal than others, as we've pointed out in several parts of this guide. In general those include any ship that is sailing on cruises longer than seven days. Specifically, you'll find a more formal atmosphere on the *QE2,* the Royal Viking Line ships, Cunard/Norwegian American Cruises' *Vistafjord* and *Sagafjord,* Holland America Lines' *Rotterdam,* Sun Lines' *Stella Solaris* and *Stella Oceanis,* and Royal Caribbean Line ships that cruise for more than a week. Let's just sum that up with: the more expensive the cruise, the more formal the atmosphere.

On three- and four-day cruise ships, life is very, very informal so you need pack very dressy clothes only if you like the idea of getting dressed up for dinner. On most of these short cruises you won't see black tie at all, and sometimes you'll hardly see anything fancier than a sport jacket.

On your first night out and your last night aboard, you need not dress up for dinner. First night is always casual, a sensible tradition since most people have just flown or driven to the port and clothes are not yet unpacked and pressed. On your last night aboard, the theory is that your bags will be packed in preparation for the next morning's debarkation so you wear the clothes you'll be wearing for the journey home.

From there on each line differs, but on all ships dinner is the high point of the day. Men are requested to wear jacket and tie after 6 p.m. on most ships, although on some the absence of a tie is forgiven. For the ladies, this is the time to break out the silks and the satins, the chiffons and the high heels.

On a seven-day cruise you'll have two to four formal nights aboard, depending on how many days you spend in port. After a day spent in port, dinner is usually not a formal night.

Royal Caribbean Cruise Line, Inc.

DAILY CRUISE COMPASS

M.S. Song of Norway

Wednesday

CAPTAIN OSTEN ANDREASSEN - MASTER

WELCOME TO ST. THOMAS, U.S. VIRGIN ISLANDS !!

Approximately	7:00 a.m. -	M/S "SONG OF NORWAY" is due to arrive at Charlotte Amalie, St. Thomas.
8:00 a.m.	9:45 a.m. -	TOUR OFFICE IS OPEN - MAIN DECK, Purser's Square.
8:15 a.m.	9:45 a.m. -	THE MORNING CITY AND ISLAND TOUR - Leaves from "B" Deck, Forward.
8:30 a.m.	9:45 a.m. -	THE CORAL WORLD TOUR - Leaves from "B" Deck, Gangway
	9:00 a.m. -	The V. I. DIVING SCHOOL TOUR - Meet on "B" Deck
	9:00 a.m. -	THE SEA SAFARI TOUR - meets at Purser's Square
	9:30 a.m. -	THE V. I. DIVING SCHOOL SNORKEL TOUR - Meet on "B" Deck Forward.
	1:00 p.m. -	THE SEA SAFARI TOUR - is departing. Please gather at Purser's Square - Main Deck.
	1:00 p.m. -	AFTERNOON SCUBA TOUR DEPARTS - "B" Deck Forward
	1:15 p.m. -	THE KON TIKI BOAT TOUR DEPARTS - Please meet in the "South Pacific Lounge".
	1:15 p.m. -	ST. THOMAS - ST JOHN ISLAND TOUR - Please meet in the "My Fair Lady Lounge".
	1:30 p.m. -	AFTERNOON SNORKEL TOUR departs "B" Deck Forward.
	2:30 p.m. -	MOVIE - "THE CHAMP" - Starring Jon Voight and Faye Dunaway. Rated "PG". Ends 4:31 p.m. in the "South Pacific Lounge".
	5:30 p.m. -	ALL PASSENGERS ARE REQUESTED TO BE ABOARD NO LATER THAN ONE HALF HOUR PRIOR TO SAILING.
5:30 p.m.	6:30 p.m. -	Departure Music & Limbo Contest - Sun Deck, Poolside. (Weather Permitting).
5:30 p.m.	6:30 p.m. -	Supplies, ideas, and suggestions for all PIRATES in the "My Fair Lady Lounge", Port Side.
	6:00 p.m. -	THE M/S "SONG OF NORWAY" sails promptly for Miami Florida, (1,039 Nautical Miles).
7:00 p.m.	8:15 p.m. -	CASH BINGO for passengers on SECOND SITTING - In the "South Pacific Lounge".
7:30 p.m.	8:30 p.m. -	Supplies, ideas, and suggestions for all PIRATES in the "My Fair Lady Lounge". Port Side.
7:30 p.m.	10:30 p.m. -	Popular Dance Music - "My Fair Lady Lounge".
8:30 p.m.	9:45 p.m. -	CASH BINGO for passengers on MAIN SITTING - In the "South Pacific Lounge".
9:30 p.m.	12:30 p.m. -	Popular Dance Music and Disco - In the "Lounge of the Midnight Sun".
9:45 p.m.	10:30 p.m. -	Official Hanging of all Pirates in the "My Fair Lady Lounge".
	10:00 p.m. -	MOVIE - "IN-LAWS - Starring Peter Falk and Alan Arkin. Rated "PG". Ends 11:43 p.m. in the "South Pacific Lounge".
	10:30 p.m. -	"PIRATES PARADE" - All hands fall in for the Biggest Ball of all - "THE PIRATES PARTY". Dancing, Fun, Prizes, & Surprises for all hands! In the "My Fair Lady Lounge" and the "Lounge of the Midnight Sun".
	Midnight -	Floor Show - Night Club.
12:15 a.m.	1:00 a.m. -	Dance Music in the "My Fair Lady Lounge".
12:30 a.m.	1:15 a.m. -	The Pirates Parade to the "Lounge of the Midnight Sun" - and the PIRATES PARTY continues. Hidden treasure can be found.
1:15 a.m.	3:00 a.m. -	Popular Music and Disco. In the Night Club.

Among the events that are always formal are the captain's cocktail party and dinner and an event known as the Gala Farewell Banquet, scheduled near the end of the cruise.

Each day you'll receive a ship's newspaper alerting you to the activities of the day and outlining the formality of the evening. Formal, informal, and casual will be explained in that news sheet. "Formal" generally refers to tuxedo or fancy evening jacket for men, long or short dressy dresses for women; "informal" is dark suit for men, long or short dressy dresses for women; and "casual" is no jacket or tie for men, and slacks, good-looking jeans, or casual evening wear for women.

Many ships have theme evenings like country and western nights, and on those occasions your jeans and red kerchiefs, ten-gallon hats and sombreros are perfectly acceptable at dinner. Other speciality nights include masquerade evenings, pastel night, pink or blue night, at which the line would like you to dress in those colors.

Don't fail to read your cruise newspaper. Everything you want to know about what to wear is in there.

Except on the most formal ships, gentlemen need bring truly formal wear—the tuxedos and wing collars—only if they enjoy wearing them. Dark suits are now considered *de rigueur* on most ships. Many modern fellows are wearing, particularly in summer, formal pleated shirts with light or dark suits, a bow tie, even a cummerbund, in place of the traditional tuxedo or white dinner jacket. In winter, velvet smoking jackets have a contemporary look.

Long dresses have suffered a bit of a decline in recent years, but many people drag them out of the back of the wardrobe and bring them along on a cruise. If you have a lovely long dress you'd like to wear, bring it along. In warm climates and warm months of the year, some pretty candy-striped long cotton dresses and those long crinkled cotton dresses seem particularly appropriate. Short cocktail dresses and evening suits with silk or lacy blouses are always appropriate.

Silky or lightweight wool shawls are easy to pack and very convenient for cool evenings.

When you're planning your wardrobe, keep two things in mind; (1) travel irons are frowned on or downright forbidden on many ships, and shipboard do-it-yourself pressing facilities are limited and often antiquated, not ideal for fragile fabrics; and (2) storage space on modern cruise ships is, shall we say, compact. Older ships have much more closet space, but even there you've got to find some place to stick all those suitcases.

Suitcases, by the way, can often be stashed away under the bed, but if you've really overdone it and can't find another single inch in which to stuff the Samsonite, ask your cabin steward if he can find a place to store the beast. Stewards are ingenious.

Try to keep your wardrobe as coordinated as possible so you can make several different outfits from a minimal number of matching pieces.

5. Rain and Glacier Wear

Out on the briny blue evenings are a bit cooler than on shore. Although the temperature may be in the 70s (let's keep our fingers crossed), that constant breeze from the movement of the ship will make a shawl or sweater a welcome sight. Air conditioning on ships can be very, very good too, so plan on some kind of wrap for evening.

In Alaskan waters you'll definitely want a sweater and/or jacket for evening, and something similar for daytime visits to glaciers. If you have a fur jacket or stole, you could certainly wear it on many Alaskan and some transatlantic cruises. (Furs on Caribbean voyages? No.)

Raincoats and umbrellas always seem to be back at the ship when it rains on land so we just don't bother. One of those little pleated rainhats some company is always giving away to advertise itself is usually enough to keep you dry until you can run to the nearest shelter spot.

If you're very organized, plastic raincoats that fold up into little squares you can stick in a pocket or purse are clever and very convenient to carry along without fuss. Getting them back into that little square is quite another matter, however. (How *do* those things work anyway?)

Some very small ships, by the way, have a luggage limit, so if you're planning on traveling on one of the coastal sailing vessels, check the line's brochures for luggage restrictions.

Now that didn't hurt did it? Go ahead, pack it in and get out there and dazzle 'em.

6. Laundry Facilities

Dry-cleaning facilities are not available on most ships, although many offer laundry service for a small charge.

As cruises become more popular, some ships are beginning to add small laundromats on board, either coin operated or free. You might have to have your own soap, however, so if you've discovered a laundromat listed in the ship's brochure, pack a small box of soap.

Don't figure you're going to do what you did on your last European trip: hang all those clothes around the room on inflatable hangers with towels underneath to catch the water. There simply is no space in most cabins to hang up even your small washable items. Pack enough to last the voyage or plan to send your things to the ship's laundry. Your steward will give you a bag to pack them in, take them away, and bring them back.

So good are the laundries on some ships that they garner top praise from frequent cruise travelers. Some travelers claim the *Rotterdam*'s laundry is so skilled that they bring their dirty clothes on board with them just to be able to send them to the ship's laundry!

7. Other Things to Pack

Man (and woman) does not live by clothes alone. There are other things you should pack for your glorious adventure.

What? Well, for openers, a camera. If you like swimming, diving, and snorkeling, and plan to do lots of that on your trip, you might consider a waterproof camera. At least consider waterproof housings into which a camera fits. Tell your local camera store what you want to photograph and they can help you get outfitted with film and camera for some sensational shots that will be quite different from the pictures everyone else aboard is taking.

If you're strictly a snapshot-taker, Polaroids let you know immediately whether your magic moment has been successfully captured on film. Some of the new small cameras that fit in a pocket can be very convenient to carry around on port visits as well as on board the ship.

To dwell on that diving business for just a moment, if you're planning on learning or perfecting your snorkeling or scuba diving, don't forget to take whatever equipment you need. Some equipment is available on board, but it's nice to have your own, which will fit you better and have all the features *you* consider important. You can join in organized diving expeditions on most ships or head off with a companion—no diving alone, for safety's sake—to find your own no-traffic reef to explore. There are quite a lot of diving possibilities on most cruises, so even if you've never tried it before, sink a few bucks into snorkeling gear and get out there and look!

Binoculars may sound like a hassle, and they are on land trips, but at sea you can stow them in your room without difficulty. They're great for getting a good look at the shoreline as the ship enters or leaves port, for a closeup look at a whale or dolphin or sea bird, and for spotting promising bikinis.

A tote bag to carry beach gear, camera, and things you buy ashore is worth its weight.

If your idea of a marvelous time is hour after endless hour with a fascinating story, stock up on books. Books are available on many ships, but selections are often quite limited. There are, of course, bookstores in ports, but if you're visiting foreign ports most of what those bookstores sell will be written in that foreign language. Take your own or figure on heading for the ship's library the minute the ship leaves the dock.

With all the modern emphasis on fun and sun, many ship's libraries are woefully inadequate and open seemingly only for 20 minutes right in the middle of lunch. Scholars, arise and protest—but don't plan on finding much of a library aboard. Most ships' libraries, by the way, ask you to leave a $5 or $10 deposit to ensure that you'll return the book at the end of the voyage.

Which brings up another very important take-along: money. Although some ships will tally your bills as you sail and permit you to settle the whole thing at once at the end of the voyage, they are the exception rather than the rule. Most ships want to see cash or travelers checks in payment of bar charges and for items from the gift shops. Many ships accept credit cards, but not all. Once again the ship's brochures will indicate what form of payment is accepted on board and when.

Ships visiting countries in which foreign currency is required will have a bank on board to perform currency exchange for you. Once again they want to see cash or travelers checks, and are not prepared to advance you money on the strength of your credit card.

You may also need money for some special services like massages, beauty salon and barbershop services, special spa services like facials or manicures. On some ships, although very few, there is a small charge (about $5 a week) for use of a deck chair. All ships we know of also charge for skeet shooting, about $2 to pay for the clay pigeons on which you test your shooting skills.

If you take any kind of medication regularly, get your prescription filled before you go. Ships do not carry or dispense special prescriptions, and the difficulties of getting a prescription filled in a foreign country are virtually insurmountable. Pack more than enough medication to last the voyage in case you spill or lose it. There's nothing more frustrating than spending a day in port chasing around trying to get a prescription filled.

Basic medication like aspirin and sunburn relievers will be available on board or in port shops. You'll also find toothpaste, shaving cream, shampoos, and the like in shops on board.

Zip-lock plastic bags, big ones, always seem to come in handy, as do premoistened towelettes.

If you're a shopper, take an empty suitcase or totebag to pack your purchases.

And amateur archeologists should pack a tiny flashlight to illuminate caves and such.

Chapter VIII

GET ME TO THE PORT ON TIME: BON VOYAGE

THAT GLORIOUS DAY has arrived. You're going on a cruise and today's the day! Envious friends are all lined up to share the bubbly and watch you sail off into the sunset. Bags are all packed and checked and rechecked, tickets clutched, money counted, excitement mounting.

Now what?

Well, first you have to find the ship.

THE PORTS

In North America the main embarkation ports are first Miami, the nation's busiest cruise port, followed by Port Everglades, New York, San Juan, San Francisco, Los Angeles, Vancouver, Seattle, Cape Canaveral, and Tampa in Florida, perhaps Norfolk, not necessarily in that order. As you can imagine, we could go on and on here because you can get on ships in many places.

Far and away the largest number of passengers embark at the ports we've just mentioned though, and one has to call a halt to this somewhere.

So if you're anticipating boarding a ship somewhere in the Chesapeake Bay or at Warren, R.I., or in Nassau to join one of several small coastal sailers, the cruise line will provide you with maps of their dock sites.

Let's take them one by one then, beginning with the largest cruise port, for a look at some of the details of getting there, staying overnight, parking, getting to the port by public transportation, and getting back to the plane or home when the cruise is over.

1. Miami-Port of Miami

Getting to Miami by plane is quite easy. This city has an international airport served by more than 60 airlines including every major carrier in the U.S., Canada, South America, and Europe—even British Airways Concorde!

So many cruise ships depart from Miami that airport personnel here are quite used to dealing with the needs of passengers. Your luggage will be handled efficiently and usually quickly. Thanks to a new rapid Customs clearance program you should be into and out of the airport within an hour, even if you're coming here from a foreign country.

There is another advantage in sailing from Miami. Such a gaggle of cruise ships dock here that the competition is downright snarling-viscious at times, meaning you can be sure you will find bargain rates.

Recent years have seen the birth of a concept known as "free air" or "air/sea" or "fly-free" programs designed to offer you free or very low-cost air fare from perhaps as many as 100 cities across the country and in Canada.

Each cruise line has its own air fare deal, but every cruise line has some sort of program, and to Miami most of them have free air fare. Somewhere along the way it's built into the cost of course, but it's nice to know you don't have to pay a few hundred dollars more per person to fly to Miami to take a cruise. Your travel agent or the cruise line will be able to tell you all about the benefits of air/sea programs offered to Miami.

LINES SAILING FROM THE PORT OF MIAMI: More major cruise lines are based in Miami than in any other port on earth. These include the fleets of Royal Caribbean, Norwegian Caribbean, Carnival, Commodore, Paquet, Chandris, Costa, Scandinavian World Cruises, and Eastern Cruise Lines.

Miami is home to several fleets, so ships in those fleets have been assigned permanent docking spots, or as permanent as anything can be in this floating world. Here's a list of those pier assignments:

Piers 1 & 2:	*Scandinavian Sun*
Piers 1 & 2:	*Norway*
Pier 2:	*Skyward*
	Sunward II
Pier 3:	*Emerald Seas*
	Southward
	Starward
Pier 4:	*Nordic Prince*
	Rhapsody
Pier 5:	*Amerikanis*
	Song of Norway

	Song of America
	Sun Viking
Pier 6:	*Bohème*
	Dolphin
Pier 7:	*Scandinavian Sun*
Pier 8:	*Carnivale*
Pier 9:	*Festivale*
	Mardi Gras

PRE- AND POST-CRUISE STOPOVERS: If you must take a plane that arrives a day before the ship sails in order not to miss the boat, some lines offer special overnight packages that will save you money. In fact you can spend several days in the sunshine of Miami at quite reasonable rates with a pre-cruise package. Ask a travel agent what's available.

If you're not taking advantage of a package rate but do plan to stay overnight, hotels near the Port of Miami include the comparatively inexpensive and recently renovated Marina Park, where prices are in the $60 to $80 range, moving up to the Everglades, Dupont Plaza, Pavillon, Holiday Inn, Hyatt, Marriott Biscayne Bay, and Omni, where rates will range up to about $125 double in high season. Some hotels may offer special pre-cruise rates for cruise passengers.

Metro Dade Visitor and Convention Authority, 234 West Flagler St., Miami, FL 33100 (tel. 305/579-4694), can provide you with information on hotels and motels in the area. On Miami Beach the **Miami Beach Visitor and Convention Authority,** 555 17th St., Miami Beach, FL 33139 (tel. 305/673-7070), can do likewise.

SIGHTS: If you spend a few days in Miami before or after the cruise, you can visit lovely Key Biscayne, where beautiful beaches trim the highway and lush trees and vines will show you what tropical means.

Historic and posh Coconut Grove, the Greenwich Village of Miami, is now a top shopping spot too. Vizcaya, a huge Italianate mansion built by industrialist James Deering, is open to the public.

Miami Seaquarium features a performing killer whale, and at the new uncaged MetroZoo animals roam free, separated from you and from each other by moats. Parrot Jungle or Monkey Jungle or Orchid Jungle are fun, and in Miami Beach the delightful art deco district on the south end of Miami Beach is a don't-miss for art lovers.

You can also take a day trip to Orlando from Miami on special buses that go directly to Disney World early in the morning and bring you back about midnight.

If you have a full day or more in the city, you can visit that fascinating primeval swamp known as the Everglades and take a ride on a speeding airboat that "floats" over the swamp waters.

GETTING TO THE PORT: The Port of Miami is located on Dodge Island, an island in Biscayne Bay between downtown Miami and the island of Miami Beach.

From any of those downtown hotels (a five- to ten-minute drive) the taxi fare is not likely to be more than $5.

Red Top Limousine service (tel. 305/526-5764) is the cheapest way to get from the airport to downtown hotels for $6. Taxi service (Yellow Cab, tel. 305/633-3333) from the airport to the downtown area or the port is $15 to $20, from downtown hotels to the port about $5, from hotels on Miami Beach to the port about $15. If you want to stay in less expensive Fort Lauderdale (about a 45-minute drive), you can get a limousine from there to the Port of Miami for about $10 per person.

Miami will soon have monorails to take you from the airport to the downtown area.

Metrobus service (tel. 305/638-6700) from the airport to downtown and to the port (and vice versa) is Route 3, and costs 75¢ per person.

If you're driving to the port and leaving your car there while you're on a cruise, you'll pay in advance $3 a day. Parking is in an open lot (no covered parking), and there are security guards on duty at the port.

You get to the Port of Miami by car on I-95, exiting at the Port of Miami exit. At the exit, follow the signs to the Port, crossing over Biscayne Boulevard and, a block or so later, over Biscayne Bay.

At the port look for long narrow signs on which the names and pier numbers of the ships are listed and color coded. Follow the signs to the ship.

Some lines charge a small amount to arrange transfers from the airport to the ship. Once again, your travel agent can tell you if such a transfer program is offered by the line on which you're sailing. If it is, you'll probably be transported to the ship by van or bus.

Greyhound and Trailways buses both stop at major stations in downtown Miami, and from there you'll have to take a cab, although very good walkers with very little luggage could hoof the mile or so distance to the ships.

Amtrak trains stop west of the city at the new train station, and you can get a cab or bus from there.

AT THE PORT: At the Port of Miami the terminal facilities are among the most modern in the nation. Each ship has its own enclosed, carpeted waiting area on the second floor of new concrete buildings. There's plenty of sitting space on carpeted seating areas built along the sides of the rooms.

For that matter, there's even a jogging track, a picnic area, a football field, and a tennis area. (Officially they're for port employees, but no one will mind if you want to take a turn around the track while you're waiting for your ship.)

Porters will take your luggage right at the entrance to the terminal and see that it gets aboard the ship. There's next to no possibility that it could go astray and end up on some other ship because the next terminal down the line is a healthy block walk away!

Meanwhile you can take an escalator up to the second floor waiting area where your tickets will be checked and your boarding pass issued.

2. Fort Lauderdale / Port Everglades

About 40 miles north of downtown Miami is Fort Lauderdale's Port Everglades, where several new terminals were completed in 1984. One of those is a knockout *trompe l'oeil* (French for fool-the-eye) building on which columns, arches, and windows are painted so cleverly they make a solid concrete wall look like a Mediterranean villa!

Port Everglades, the second largest cruise-ship base in Florida and one of the top five in the world, is home to some very classy ships, in fact the classiest ships afloat, and brags about that at every chance.

Located in a quiet, posh community of higher than average per capita household income, the port has become increasingly alluring to cruise lines in recent years. That allure stems from its proximity to a small, comparatively hassle-free airport about a five-minute drive from the port, and to a seven-mile strip of palm-lined open beaches.

LINES SAILING FROM PORT EVERGLADES: When we say classy ships sail from here, we mean *classy* ships sail from here.

Start with Cunard's *Queen Elizabeth II* and move beautifully on to Royal Viking Lines, Cunard/NAC's *Sagafjord* and *Vistafjord,* Home Lines, Sun Lines, Sitmar, P&O, Holland America, Clipper Cruise Line, and Royal Cruise Lines.

Of these only Sitmar's *Fairwind* is based here year round, but the others make forays into the Caribbean or on trans-Panama cruises from this port all winter long.

Costa Lines is expected to join them in 1984 when it brings its new ship, the *Riviera,* to South Florida.

PRE- AND POST-CRUISE STOPOVERS: Port Everglades is within a 10- to 15-minute drive of the main Fort Lauderdale beach area, so your choice of hotels ranges from very large, top-notch hotels like Pier 66, Marriott, Sheraton Yankee Clipper, or Yankee Trader to small family-run properties a block or so west of the main beach highway, Route A1A.

Prices at those large hotels will run upward of $100 to $125 in high season, while prices at small properties a block or two off the beach like the Sea Château, Worthington, Palace Bleu, are about $40 to $50 a night double.

Taxi fares from that main beach area to the port are not likely to exceed $10 or so. Limousine service (tel. 305/764-2211) to Port of Miami is also available and costs $10 per person.

SIGHTS: Fort Lauderdale's pride and its selling point is its seven-mile beach, a glorious strip of sand trimmed with palm trees.

While you're here you can explore the city's hundreds of miles of canals—more than Venice!—aboard the *Jungle Queen,* a paddlewheel dinner/sightseeing boat, or a similar craft called the *Paddlewheel Queen.*

To get a look at the city's posh gas-lighted Las Olas Boulevard, take a ride on the Voyager Train. There's also a small but pretty historic district called Himmarashee Village, where the city's first hotel is still intact and operating as a small hands on museum called the Discovery Center.

From Fort Lauderdale you can visit Disney World on one-day or longer tours arranged by local tour companies, which also have tours to the Everglades, Miami, and the Keys.

GETTING TO THE PORT: Most major airlines offer service to Fort Lauderdale/Hollywood International Airport, including Air Florida, Delta, Eastern, Continental, Northwest, Ozark, Piedmont, and TWA, among others. Miami International Airport is about 25 miles away, $11 by airport limousine.

From Fort Lauderdale/Hollywood International Airport the taxi ride to Port Everglades will take about five minutes and costs about $6 to $8.

If you're driving to Port Everglades on the Florida State Turnpike, exit at the State Road 84 interchange. If you're traveling on I-95, you should also exit at State Road 84 and head east to the port, which begins at the eastern end of that highway.

You can park your car there for the duration of your cruise for $3 a day. Parking is outdoors in a locked and guarded area.

If you're coming to town by Greyhound or Trailways bus or on an Amtrak train, you'll need to get a cab from the station. The taxi ride will cost about $10, perhaps less.

AT THE PORT: Port Everglades has just spent a bundle of money building two new terminals, the newest of which was opened in 1983. Very contemporary buildings, these new bilevel terminals feature snackbars, lounges, and loads of comfortable chairs to sit in if you arrive before boarding begins on your ship. There are escalators so you don't have to climb stairs lugging your hand baggage. Plenty of porters see to it that your luggage gets safely onto the ship.

If you have to sit around and wait for boarding to begin, there could hardly be a more pleasant place to wait: good-looking contemporary seating areas, food and drink, even a pretty glassed-in wall-full of rare shells on display. We've seen airline terminals that aren't this pleasant. Also, there are covered walkways to the ships too so you don't get damp if it rains.

3. Cape Kennedy / Port Canaveral

This tiny port was strictly a "Port What?" until a few years ago when Scandinavian World Cruises began operating daily cruises to nowhere from here. Then other ships began making tentative forays into these Disney World waters, and in 1984 a new cruise line with high hopes and a bright-red ship began sailing from Port Canaveral.

Now the port has embarked on an ambitious building program that port officials hope will make it one of Florida's premier ports in just a few years.

There are certain drawbacks: Orlando's airport, the nearest one, is about an hour's drive away, although that drive is on a major expressway, no traffic lights. It's also more than an hour's drive from the tourist centers that have grown up around Walt Disney World, and about a five-hour drive from the major metropolitan areas of South Florida.

On the very positive side, it's comparatively easy to combine a cruise from this port with a trip to Walt Disney World's Magic Kingdom or EPCOT Center, but you will need to stay in the area at least a week to wedge in both activities.

LINES SAILING FROM PORT CANAVERAL: The biggest news in many a moon at Port Canaveral was the arrival of Premier Cruise Lines, a new cruise line operating an old but renovated ship, the *Frederico C.*, renamed the *Royale.* This flashy new cruiser sails on three- and four-night cruises from Port Canaveral to Nassau and a Bahamian Out Island.

Other lines occasionally call at Port Canaveral.

PRE- AND POST-CRUISE STOPOVERS: Beach lovers ought to settle in at nearby Cocoa, a beach and surfers paradise, for a few days. Hotels and motels in the area are listed in a publication produced by the **Cocoa Chamber of Commerce,** 431 Riveredge Blvd., Cocoa, FL 32922 (tel. 305/636-4262).

Those who want to meet the Mouse will head for any of hundreds of motels and hotels in the Orlando area. We really can't pinpoint the cost of hotels there. It ranges from a low of about $35 or so to a high well into the $125 range. The full story on all there is to see and do in Orlando is available in *Arthur Frommer's Guide to Orlando, Disney World, and EPCOT.*

It will take you an hour or more to get from the port to the Disney World area. Information on hotels and motels near the park is available from the **Kississimmee–St. Cloud Visitor and Convention Bureau,** US 192, Kissimmee, FL, 32741 (tel. toll free 800/327-9159, 800/432-9199 in Florida, or 305/847-5000).

SIGHTS: We hardly need tell you at this point that the chief sight anywhere hereabouts is Walt Disney World's Magic Kingdom and EPCOT Center. But that certainly is not all there is to see.

Cape Canaveral, home of the astronauts and site of the rocket launchings, is right here. If you time your cruise very carefully, you may even be able to go to sea to see a launch.

Over in Orlando, about an hour's drive away, is Sea World where sweet Shamu, the so-called killer whale, kisses pretty girls and toddlers; Circus World, where a blond lion tamer controls 13 of the big brutes at one time; Six Flags' Stars Hall of Fame, where you can see wax images of the stars and try out for a part in a national television show.

GETTING TO THE PORT: If you're coming to central Florida by plane, you'll fly to Orlando International Airport, a brand-new airport with whooshing monorail transportation and the latest technology everywhere. Most major air carriers fly there.

Transportation from the airport to the port is a bit shaky, although Premier will apparently be operating some buses on cruise departure and arrival days, and will book transfers for you when you buy your cruise tickets. A limousine service also operates from the airport to the ship, but you'd have to charter the car, an expensive proposition.

That leaves rental cars. Budget Rent a Car is scheduled to open a facility at the port which will enable you to drop the car off there so it isn't just sitting around costing you money while you're away on a three- or four-day cruise.

If you want to visit the wonders of Walt Disney World, you must make your way to a road called the Beeline Expressway (Route 528), which does indeed make a beeline across the state from Orlando to Port Canaveral. From other areas of the state you can take I-95 to the Cape Canaveral-A1A exits or I-75 from the northern parts of Florida to the Beeline and east on the Beeline.

AT THE PORT: Two dome-topped terminal buildings here were acquired by the port from Disney World and have a bit of a futuristic look. Inside these circular structures are just the bare essentials, not thrilling for long waits. Another similar structure is being built this year.

If you must wait a while, get in some beach time at nearby Jetty Park, where you'll find a campground, recreational facilities, concession stands, and showers. Now that's not bad!

Porters are available to take your luggage and see that it gets onto the ship.

Greyhound and Trailways buses stop in Cocoa Beach, but you'll have to take a cab from the station there.

Amtrak trains stop in Kissimmee and in Orlando, but you'll need to rent a car to go from either of those stations across the state to the terminal at Port Canaveral.

4. Tampa / Port of Tampa

Tampa is another newcomer port that pulled off its biggest coup in 1984 when it lured Holland America's brand-new liner, the *Nieuw Amsterdam,* to its piers.

Although the Tampa port area itself is huge, stretching for miles and miles, almost all of that is cargo area with only two passenger terminals, one of them constructed in 1982. Land has been purchased in downtown Tampa to provide another port in the area, but don't expect completion of that for years.

LINES SAILING FROM THE PORT OF TAMPA: Although Tampa would certainly welcome new cruise lines, at the moment it has only two: Holland America's *Nieuw Amsterdam,* which docks at the new terminal, and Bahama Lines' *Veracruz,* which ties up at a pier known as the Eller & Co. dock.

PRE- AND POST-CRUISE STOPOVERS: By Florida historic standards Tampa is a rather old city and has some interesting historical sights, as well as some very contemporary amusements.

If you're thinking of staying over for a few days before or after your cruise, nearby hotels include the Hilton Tampa, Hyatt Regency Tampa, Holiday Inn Downtown, and Sheraton Tampa, all of which are in the downtown area, about a $10 taxi from the airport. It will cost you about $5 or so to get from downtown hotels to the cruise terminals.

Hotel rates in peak winter season will be in the $60 to $100 range, although hotels in other price ranges are available in the city. If you'd like information on hotels in the Tampa Bay area, contact the **Tampa Chamber of Commerce,** 801 East Kennedy Blvd., Tampa, FL 33602 (tel. 813/228-7777), or the **Pinellas Suncoast Tourist Development Commission,**

St. Petersburg/Clearwater Airport, St. Petersburg, FL 33732 (tel. 813/ 448-2452).

SIGHTS: Busch Gardens' Dark Continent is Tampa's most famous sight and is an amusing way to spend a day. You'll find thrilling rides, several theme areas depicting parts of Africa in everything from shops to entertainment and food, wild animals roaming an open "veldt," and plenty of what made Busch famous.

History buffs should head for the University of Tampa, which occupies an historic hotel built by Henry Plante, a railroad kingpin on this coast. Built in the '20s, the structure's famous onion-shaped minarets can be seen from many parts of the downtown area.

Ybor City, once home to Cuban tobacco workers, is another intriguing historical site and home to several good restaurants and lots of interesting small shops.

GETTING TO THE PORT: Tampa's comparatively new international airport is still getting raves for its very contemporary facilities. So well organized is the airport that it's possible to get from plane to taxi in fewer than 700 steps and in just a few minutes. Most major U.S. airlines have flights to Tampa.

If you're driving here, you'll arrive on I-75 which stretches along the west coast of Florida, I-4 which connects Tampa with Daytona through Orlando, or on I-75 from points north. Exit any of them at 21st Street South and follow that road until it merges with 22nd Street. Turn right on Maritime Boulevard and make the first left on Verger Boulevard. Verger will take you right by the Holland America terminal and, further along, past the terminal for the Bahama Lines.

Parking fees in an uncovered lot are $20 a week at the new terminal, $21 at the Eller & Co. terminal, and there are roving security guards.

Greyhound and Trailways buses have terminals in downtown Tampa from which you will have to take a cab to the port.

Amtrak trains from the Northeast and from other parts of Florida stop in Tampa too.

AT THE PORT: Newest of the two terminals at the Port of Tampa sports a nautical theme. You'll alight at a canopy-covered entrance where porters will see to your luggage. If you're a bit early, you can wait in an attractive building with lots of windows through which you can watch the activity in historic Tampa Bay, visited by pirates and explorers for more than 400 years.

Baggage claims areas here feature colored stripes that correspond to colored arrows overhead, so it's quite easy to find your luggage when you return.

Smoky-gray carpets and blue and gray couches offer a pleasant place to wait, and there's a covered gangway to the ship so the weather's no problem.

That other terminal, located a mile south, is a great deal less impressive. It's just a converted cargo warehouse and has no facilities for waiting around or for anything else, so don't get there way ahead of time. There are no snackbars, lounges, or restaurants in the area, so bring your own snacks or diet.

A cruise shuttle between the port and Ybor City restaurants and shops was operating, but at last word wasn't in operation. It may be resumed. Ask.

5. San Juan/Port of San Juan

Lovely old San Juan has become almost as popular a starting point for cruises as it is an itinerary. There's a very good reason for that too: its location down in the middle of the Caribbean sea lets you explore, in a week or so, many island destinations that would take much longer to get to from Florida.

LINES SAILING FROM SAN JUAN: Ships that have settled here as home base include Cunard's *Princess,* Chandris's *Victoria,* Sun Lines' *Stella Oceanis,* Costa's *Carla C* and *Daphne,* Paquet's *Mermoz,* Princess Lines' *Sun Princess,* and Sitmar's *Fairsea.*

PRE- AND POST-CRUISE STOPOVERS: If you're taking a cruise from San Juan you'll surely want to spend some time exploring this old—and very new—city, and if you have time, the rest of this mountainous and very tropical island.

Several hotels, including El San Juan, Caribe Hilton, and Howard Johnson's, have special overnight packages and transfer arrangements for cruise passengers. Rates at those very large hotels will be in the $100-and-up range in peak season, but there are plenty of other accommodations in the city ranging from charming guest houses to mid-priced hotels and sprawling resorts. To find out about other hotels on the island, write to the **Puerto Rico Tourism Co.** at 1290 Avenue of the Americas, NY 10019 (tel. 212/541-6630). Ask for a copy of "Que Pasa?" a very informative brochure that will tell you what to see and do in San Juan and out on the island.

From San Juan International Airport, the ride to the port or to area hotels will take about 35 minutes and costs about $3 per person by airport limousine, the cheapest way to get there.

Taxi fare from the airport to downtown San Juan is about $10, less if you're staying closer to the airport.

Some cruise lines offer transfers by charter bus, and on cruise departure days the line will have a representative in the baggage claim area. At the docks, you can get airline help from airline representatives stationed there.

SIGHTS: San Juan's port is located right in old San Juan, the most picturesque part of the city and one of the best shopping areas as well.

You can spend days exploring among the tiny lanes and pastel town houses with beautiful ornate wrought-iron balconies. A must-see is placid El Morro fortress. Other interesting sights: Pablo Casals Museum, the 400-year-old Dominican Convent, La Fortaleza (the oldest executive mansion in the Western Hemisphere), and El Convento, an old convent turned hotel.

GETTING THERE: American, Capitol, Delta, and Eastern fly into Puerto Rico from many major cities in the U.S. San Juan's airport is a reasonably hassle-free spot, although parking there is chaotic, to put it mildly.

You can rent a car from a variety of all the usual major U.S. car-rental companies if you want to strike out across the island for a few days before or after a cruise.

AT THE PORT: San Juan's port is a really lovely place, open, clean, and well attended by taxi drivers who will want to take you on sightseeing tours. If you don't want to strike a deal with one of them, a simple "No, thanks, we're walking" will discourage them.

Piers in San Juan are equipped with bright and clean terminal buildings where you will find food, drinks, and small shops to keep you busy if you're waiting to board a ship. Escalators are available to get you up to the second-story gangways, but not all of the area is covered so you might have to dash a bit between the ship and the door to the terminal building.

You're right at the edge of Old San Juan, so if you're very early, walk around a bit or find a spot in one of dozens of nearby cafés and watch the passing parade. In San Juan that can be very colorful.

6. New York / New York City Passenger Ship Terminal

The Big Apple's passenger ship terminal is a popular and often crowded place in summer when a number of cruise ships sail from here on trips to Bermuda or on transatlantic journeys.

One of the greatest cruising thrills you'll ever have is the one you'll see as you enter this harbor area: the majestic Statue of Liberty greeting you as she did many of our forefathers.

LINES SAILING FROM NYC TERMINAL: In spring and summer you'll see the *QE2* steaming grandly in and out of this port, joined by smaller counterparts, Home Lines' *Oceanic* and *Atlantic,* and occasionally by Paquet's *Rhapsody,* Cunard/NAC's *Sagafjord,* Royal Viking Lines' ships, and the Bahama Lines' *Bermuda Star.*

PRE- AND POST-CRUISE STOPOVERS: To be in New York and not take advantage of all the dining, entertainment, theater, museums, etcs., of the nation's busiest city would be a shame indeed. If you can, spend a few days in the city before or after your cruise, and perhaps move on to New England if you have time.

Hotels in New York are easily in the $100 to $150 a night range, although there are some budget spots in slightly lower brackets. Midtown hotels and those in the Central Park area are reasonably close to the port, about a $5 taxi ride away.

Transportation from La Guardia or JFK International Airports to downtown hotels will run from about $15 to $20 for a taxi from La Guardia to $10 for bus service from JFK.

From there to the port will cost you another $5 or so in cab fares.

SIGHTS: New York City's multitudes of sightseeing options are so numerous people have written books about them! Certainly we can't tell you here all the things to see and do in New York, but top sights include the Empire State Building and the World Trade Center, the Statue of Liberty, Central Park, the United Nations, the Metropolitan Museum of Art, the Museum of Modern Art, Wall Street, Rockefeller Center, Greenwich Village, Lincoln Center.

GETTING TO THE PORT: Every major airline in the world flies into New York City, either to La Guardia, the airport closest to Manhattan, John F. Kennedy International, farther away, or Newark International, the most distant of the three.

From La Guardia Airport, Metropolitan Limousine Service (tel. 212/476-5515) provides service to the terminal for $7 per person.

From Newark International Airport, limo service provided by the same company (tel. 201/961-4250) is $10 per person, and from JFK (tel. 212/656-5980) the fare is also $10 per person.

If you're driving there are many ways to make your way to the port, which stretches from 48th to 55th Streets on Twelfth Avenue. A brochure available from the New York City Passenger Ship Terminal, Port Authority of New York and New Jersey, Marine Terminals Dept., 1 World Trade Center, New York, NY 10048 (tel. 765-7437) will detail how to reach the port area from the Henry Hudson Parkway (West Side Highway); the Holland, Lincoln, Queens Midtown, and Brooklyn Battery Tunnel; the Major Deegan Expressway (New York State Thruway); from northern New Jersey and Rockland County; and from the Triborough Bridge.

Open parking on the roof of the building is available for those who are seeing you off, using the automobile ramp at 55th Street and Twelfth Avenue. Long-term covered parking is available next to the terminal at Pier 94, and there's a free courtesy car to and from the terminal.

Enter the parking area adjacent to the automobile ramp at 55th Street and Twelfth Avenue. Write Kinney System, Inc., New York City Passenger Ship Terminal, 711 Twelfth Ave., New York, NY 10019 (tel. 212/757-4936), for reservations. The charge is $8 a day. In prime months like June and July when there are likely to be quite a number of ships in port, you would be well advised to reserve a parking space well ahead of time.

Long- and short-term insured parking is also available at the Oil Market Garage. Write or call the garage at 575 Eleventh Ave., New York, NY 10019 (tel. toll free 800/223-6384, or 212/245-0170), and a red-jacketed attendant will meet you at the ship and drive your car off to the garage. When you return, an attendant will meet your ship and take you back to the garage to retrieve your car. The rate varies but is $42.50 for five days, $68 for seven days, including tax.

AT THE PORT: New Yorkers always see to their creature comforts, albeit varying degrees of that comfort. That means that at the ship terminal you'll find places to sit, places to eat and drink, and you'll have some very nice views of the ships while you're waiting to board.

Negotiating your way to the port can be a mind-boggling traffic experience, but once you're there you won't starve or die of thirst or be forced to stand up.

Porters are available to help you with your luggage.

To help you plan, the Port Authority has a number you can call to discover arrival and departure times of vessels: 212/765-7437.

7. New Orleans / Wharves

New Orleans doesn't have a huge fleet of ships or flashy passenger-ship terminals, but it makes up in charm what it lacks in size.

There are just two passenger wharves here, one called the Poydras Street Wharf, the other called the Robin Street Wharf. At either one you are just blocks from the city's intriguing French Quarter.

LINES SAILING FROM NEW ORLEANS: Delta Cruise Lines' two old-timey sailing craft fit right into this antique and charming atmosphere. The *Delta Queen* and *Mississippi Queen* both sail from the new Robin Street Wharf on trips up the Mississippi River as far as Pennsylvania and even into Minnesota.

In 1984 Bahama Lines announced plans to sail its *Bermuda Star* from New Orleans on week-long winter cruises to the western Caribbean and Yucatán Peninsula. And American Cruise Lines also is now operating a ship on the river in summer months. Both Bahama Lines and American Cruise Lines will be sailing from the Poydras Street Wharf.

PRE- AND POST-CRUISE STOPOVERS: One could hardly think of a lovelier place to get into the mood for a cruise up the lazy river. New Orleans's French Quarter, with its wrought-iron balconies and slow-talking, slow-walking ways, looks as if a Mississippi riverboat gambler might step out of one of the taverns any moment.

Hotels quite near the wharves include Bienville House Motor Hotel, Marriott Hotel, Monteleone Hotel, International Hotel, and New Orleans Hilton, which is the closest to Poydras Street Wharf. At these you will pay about $100 to $150 in the busiest seasons. Many other smaller hotels and guest houses are available in New Orleans. You can get a list of those by writing the **New Orleans Tourist and Convention Commission,** 334 Royal St., New Orleans, LA 70130 (tel. 504/566-5011). Another excellent source is, of course, *Arthur Frommer's Guide to New Orleans.*

Taxis from the airport to the old section of the city will cost about $15 and take about 30 minutes.

SIGHTS: By day New Orleans offers narrow streets, lovely old restored homes, lacy wrought iron, and flower-filled courtyards. History lives here, and its address is Vieux Carré. You can discover it tucked away among the boutiques, streetside artists, and conventioneers in such pretty and historic places as Jackson Square, St. Louis Cathedral, Ursuline Convent, the Old Absinthe House. Walking tour maps and other historical background materials are available from the Tourist Commission.

By night the city turns on its steamy and seamy side to provide you with some of the world's greatest jazz clubs, renowned Preservation Hall, and a raft of dives and nudity shows that are more fun hearing about from the hawking doormen than they are to attend.

GETTING TO THE PORT: Major air carriers across the nation will take you to the city's Moisant International Airport, about 15 miles from downtown New Orleans and the wharves.

Airport limousine transportation costs about $7 to the Hilton Hotel. From there you'll have to walk the final block or so to the wharf, so if you have quite a lot of luggage and want to be delivered right to the Poydral Street Wharf, you'll have to take a taxi from the airport or from the Hilton. Taxi fare from area hotels will be about $5 to the wharves, but from the airport will be about $20.

The Robin Street Wharf is about a mile upriver from the Poydras Street Wharf. Taxi prices will be similar, and Orleans Transportation will take you to the wharf from the airport for $7 per person.

Greyhound and Trailways buses have terminals in the city, but you'll have to take a cab from the bus terminal to the wharves. Amtrak has service from a number of points in the Midwest to New Orleans.

If you're driving into the city, you can reach the wharves by taking the Poydras Street exit from I-10 for the Poydras Street Wharf. You can park your car in the area at Rivergate Building or International Trade Mart, 2 Canal St. (tel. 504/529-1601), for $5.50 a day. The Hilton Hotel, which is right at the wharf, also has parking.

Delta Lines is now docking at Robin Street Wharf, a new facility at the foot of Thalia Street. To reach it, drive down Magazine Street, turn left on Race Street to Tchoupitoulas Street, and left again on Celeste, which will take you to the river. Follow the signs from there to the Robin Street Wharf.

AT THE WHARVES: Some facilities are planned for the wharf, but until they're completed there are no waiting facilities. Check with the line to see if the wharf facilities have been completed if you're arriving early.

8. Los Angeles/Port of Los Angeles

Los Angeles has quite a busy port, and a growing one, now looking forward to the appearance of several new cruise ships. Popular for its weather and its proximity to the Mexican coastline, Los Angeles is another port city in which there is much to see and do.

LINES SAILING FROM THE PORT OF LOS ANGELES: Los Angeles has its fair share of cruise competition these days as three lines move new ships into this port: Princess Lines' *Royal Princess,* Holland America's *Noordam,* and Sitmar's *Fairsky*. Those join Carnival Cruise Lines' *Tropicale,* Western Cruise Lines' *Azure Seas,* Sitmar Cruises' *Fairsea,* Cunard's *Princess,* and Royal Viking Lines ships.

PRE- AND POST-CRUISE STOPOVERS: According to all the jokes, it's worth going to Los Angeles once in your life just to play in the traffic on the freeways! Traffic games notwithstanding, there are enough interesting things to do in this city and in the general area to make a pleasant stop before or after a cruise. In this far-flung city, elevations range from sea level up to 5000 feet, and the inhabitants are every bit as diverse as the landscape.

If you're flying into the city or coming in from out of town, taxi fare to downtown hotels will cost about $20 to $25.

Included among downtown hotels are Westin Buenaventura, Sheraton, Hilton, Hyatt Regency, and Biltmore.

Information on the city and its hotels is available from the **Los Angeles Chamber of Commerce,** 404 South Bixel St., Los Angeles, CA 90017 (tel. 213/629-0711).

Downtown hotels are about 25 miles from the port, so you'll have to figure about $25 to get to the port from downtown. The airport is about a hour's drive from the port. Airport vans take you to hotels, but you'll have to take a taxi or bus to the port. Long Beach has some hotels about a 15-minute drive from the port if you can arrange to fly into Long Beach Airport.

If you are really saving pennies, the Southern California Rapid Transit District can give you information on what buses to take from the airport to downtown and then (on another bus) to the port.

Amtrak goes into downtown Los Angeles, and Greyhound buses will bring you to the city too.

SIGHTS: More is new than is old in Los Angeles, but you can still see a little of the antiquity of this city on Olvera Street, at Old Mission church and Avila Adobe.

La Brea Tarpits will be of interest to archeology buffs, and Chinatown is fascinating to everyone for one reason or another.

In nearby Anaheim is Disneyland, and every bit as fantasyland as Disneyland is Hollywood.

What else? Marineland, restaurants, nightclubs, theater, the Rose Bowl, a zoo.

GETTING TO THE PORT: Like everything else in Los Angeles, getting to the port involves miles of travel—after you've found your way to Los Angeles.

Dozens of national and international air carriers land at Los Angeles International Airport, one of the nation's major gateways.

Taxi fares from the airport to the harbor area are about $20 to $25. You can also catch buses that will take you to the pier area for about $5. Kiosks outside each terminal area at the airport can give you information on what buses to take and the price.

Mini-van services operate an airport-harbor shuttle service too, and can be reached on a courtesy telephone located in the baggage pickup area of the airport. Call one of those, Super Shuttle, at 213/777-8000. The rate is $20 for one person, $5 for each additional person, from airport to pier.

For information on transportation and other services provided by the Los Angeles Airport, call the airport referral system (tel. 213/646-5260).

If you're traveling to the port by car, drive south on the San Diego Freeway from the airport, or south on the Harbor Freeway from downtown, toward San Pedro or Wilmington. Berth 93 is used by Carnival,

Cunard, Princess, and Western Cruise Lines, and is located off Harbor Boulevard at Swinford Street. Berth 195 is used by Sitmar Cruises and Royal Viking Line, and is reached off John S. Gibson Boulevard at Matsonia Way.

Parking is available at Catalina Terminal, Harbor Boulevard at Swinford, in San Pedro, next to Berth 93 (tel. 213/832-1718), and costs $3 a day. Although this parking area is about a 15-minute drive from Berth 195, most passengers park their car at this lot and take a cab (about $10) over to Berth 195.

Another parking lot, called the Seventh Street Garage, is located about a mile from the port area at 777 South Centre St. in San Pedro (tel. 213/833-1338). The charge is $4 a day plus $5 to $9 for a taxi ride to the harbor.

AT THE PORT: Los Angeles doesn't run a showplace port area, but it could be worse. Near Pier 93 is a cluster of shops and restaurants called Villages at Ports of Call, which features architectural elements of New England, Polynesia, and Cannery Row. It's about a mile from Berth 93, about four miles from Berth 195. A cab will get you there for about $5.

Los Angeles also is developing a region known as West Channel / Cabrillo Beach, which by 1986 will sport a complex featuring beaches, marinas, restaurants, and eventually a small hotel. Development of what the city calls its World Cruise Center at what is now Berth 93 is also under way, and by 1986 will be home to all the cruise ships permanently based here. (Berth 195 will be closed and converted to an automobile import handling center.)

All those things are in the future. For now you'll find no food or beverage centers at the terminal, just basic seating areas, if you have to while away a few hours until your ship departs.

Berth 195 is the older of the two with a nice view out over the channel, but at Berth 93 you can begin your cruise experience without ever leaving shore—have lunch on the *Princess Louise,* a cruise ship-turned-restaurant! It's within easy walking distance of the pier.

9. San Francisco / Port of San Francisco

The best thing about San Francisco's harbor is that it's right in the middle of things. When you're standing at the harbor you're right on the city's Embarcadero, not far from Telegraph Hill, and not all that far from Chinatown and Nob Hill, a quick trip away from Fisherman's Wharf. And if you want to get right down to it, not far from Alcatraz either!

LINES SAILING FROM SAN FRANCISCO: Many ships make a stop in San Francisco, but most of them are just passing through on their way to somewhere else. American Hawaii Cruises, although its ships sail almost solely in the Hawaiian Islands, is officially based in San Francisco. Others calling at this port include Cunard/NAC, Exploration Cruise Lines, Holland America, Paquet, Princess Cruises, Royal Viking Line, and Sitmar Cruises.

PRE- AND POST-CRUISE STOPOVERS: It's not so much one or two single sights that make San Francisco so intriguing, but the collage of all the sights in this hilly bayside city where the slopes seem to go straight up—and straight back down the other side.

Plenty of hotels in the downtown area offer you a wide variety of places to stay, ranging from small inns to huge hotels. Among the hotels nearest the port area is the Hyatt Regency, and in the Fisherman's Wharf area are the Sheraton, TraveLodge, Holiday Inn, Howard Johnson's, Ramada Inn, and San Francisco Marriott.

For more suggestions, contact the **San Francisco Chamber of Commerce,** 465 California St., San Francisco, CA 94103 (tel. 415/974-6900), or the **San Francisco Convention and Visitors Bureau,** 201 3rd St., San Francisco, CA 94103 (tel. 415/974-6900).

SIGHTS: Put on your mountain-goat shoes and take to the hills in this up-and-down city. Better yet, see it by cable car. San Francisco without a cable car ride is . . . well, you know, unthinkable.

Chinatown is a fascinating melange of sound, color, and scent, and is said to be the largest Chinese community in the world outside Asia.

The Golden Gate Bridge is a smashing sight, and so is Sausalito on the other side. Golden Gate Park will please open-space enthusiasts, and the Fisherman's Wharf waterfront area, where you catch the ship, is a must-do on every tourist's list.

Don't bother with the boat trips, though; you'll shortly be doing one of your own. Do bother with a little paper cone full of fresh seafood.

Other favored stopping spots: Seal Rocks, the Opera House, Wells Fargo Historical Collection, Cliff House.

GETTING TO THE PORT: All major airlines fly into San Francisco International Airport, and from there airport buses will take you to the downtown terminal at $6 for adults, $4 for children. A cab from there to the docks is $10 to $15. Lorrie's Tour has direct airport service to hotels at $6.50 for adults, $4 for children, and also to nonhotel destinations like the pier for $11 to $15 (tel. 415/826-5950).

Amtrak trains run to Oakland and then buses automatically bring you to San Francisco.

Greyhound buses also have terminals in the city, but you'll have to take a cab from there to the pier.

If you're driving into town, you'll find Pier 35 at the foot of Bay Street where it meets Embarcadero. Off I-80 (the James Lick Freeway) or the Bay Bridge, take the Main Street exit to Mission Street and go north on the Embarcadero.

There is no parking on Pier 35, but you can park between Piers 31 and 33 after dropping off your luggage on Pier 35. Parking fees at San Francisco Parking Garages, 923 Folsom St. (tel. 415/495-3909), are $7 a night for indoor security-guard-protected parking, $4 if you want to leave your car in a fenced outdoor lot. If you contact the company, they'll send you a form letter to fill out specifying when you'll be departing and arriving back from your cruise. A valet parker will then meet you and take your car to the garage, and meet you when you return too.

To get to downtown hotels from San Francisco International Airport by cab will cost $20 to $25.

AT THE PORT: Once you've found your way here, you'll discover a new $1.5-million terminal building, modern, with lots of windows and open space inside an old-fashioned transit shed. A two-story building, it features a downstairs Customs area and room upstairs for passengers. There are bars and restaurants in the neighborhood, but not in the terminal. That doesn't matter much, however—you're just minutes away from famous Fisherman's Wharf.

10. Vancouver / Port of Vancouver

It's certainly not surprising that Vancouver has emerged as one of the most popular ports in North America, and the number one departure point for cruises to the glacial waters of Alaska.

There's water, water everywhere in these parts, and what isn't water is lovely pastoral countryside given to picket fences and privet hedges, shades of old England.

A new passenger terminal is under construction in Vancouver, but in the meantime Centennial Pier and Ballantyne Pier will serve as temporary anchoring spots until 1986.

LINES SAILING FROM VANCOUVER: Ships from a number of lines call in here in the summer months. In fact you can catch an Alaska cruise from this port on almost any day of the week! Among the lines sailing from this port in the summer months are Cunard, Costa, Princess, Paquet, Holland America, Sundance, World Explorer Cruises, and Royal Viking Lines.

PRE- AND POST-CRUISE STOPOVERS: This is a city with spectacular scenery, and it knows just how to take advantage of it. As long as you're way up here on the edge of the world anyway, you really ought to spend a few days exploring this watery wonderland.

Hotels in the area are very near the harbor. You'll find such luxury hotels as the Four Seasons, Hotel Vancouver, Westin Bayshore, Holiday Inn Harbourside, Hotel Georgia, Sheraton Landmark, Granville Island Hotel, and Hyatt Regency just a short distance away and featuring prices in the $80 to $100 range (in U.S. dollars). Some of the hotels have some terrific bargains on weekends, so be sure to ask.

You can find out more about hotels in this city by writing or calling the **Greater Vancouver Convention and Visitors Bureau,** 1055 West Georgia St., Vancouver, BC V6E 4C8 (tel. 604/682-2222).

Transportation from the airport to the downtown area on Airporter Bus costs $5.25.

SIGHTS: Vancouver's top sights seem to be places you go to look at the sights! For instance, Harbour Centre is a soaring tower where a glass skylift takes you up 40 floors to look at awesomely lovely scenery in every direction, or Stanley Park, the park lover's paradise, has everything from a giant checkerboard to a miniature railroad.

A pride of the city is the renovated brick-lined Gastown district, where a steam clock plays Westminster chimes on steam whistles. Nearby is North America's second-largest Chinatown (San Francisco's is the largest).

The Capilano Suspension Bridge is a wonder indeed, dangling across a canyon like a steel spider web, and the city's Aquarium is *some* goldfish bowl—9000 species of fish and a couple of white whales!

GETTING TO THE PORT: Air Canada offers service to this city and is backed by a host of other airlines connecting Vancouver with U.S. West Coast cities and with the world.

From the airport you can take the Airporter Bus for $5.25 to downtown hotels, and from there go by taxi to the pier (about $6 to $8). A taxi straight from the airport will cost $12 to $15.

Train service is available from points across Canada but not from Seattle. A cross-Canada Via Rail train from Québec City to Vancouver takes five nights and four days to cross the nation.

If you're coming up from Seattle, which has Amtrak service, you must take a Greyhound bus from Seattle to Vancouver. It's a 3½-hour trip by express bus, an hour longer by regular motorcoach. Greyhound provides bus service to the city.

If you're coming here by car, take Kingsway, Burrard, or Seymour Streets to Hastings Street, then proceed east to Heatley Street. Both piers are at the foot of Heatley Street.

Parking is available at Downtown Parking, 107 East Cordova St. (tel. 604/682-6744) or at Imperial Parking, 400 West Cordova St. (tel. 604/681-7311). The cost at either is $3 a day. You'll have to transfer from there to the passenger terminal, about six blocks away from Downtown Parking, and about $3 to $5 by taxi. Some very obliging people at Downtown Parking say that if an attendant is available, they'll drive you over to the port.

AT THE PORT: A new pier is under construction in Vancouver and is expected to be completed in time for the 1986 Exposition. It will be in the city's downtown Convention Center. In the meantime, facilities are train station–basic with some simple seating areas and a small standup snackbar. It's not a place you'd want to hang around for long, so plan your arrival accordingly.

GETTING ABOARD AND SETTLING IN

So you've gotten to the port city your ship will be sailing from, and you've managed to find the right pier. Perhaps you've even had a chance to see some of the local sights or get a bite to eat. But departure time is drawing near and you're eager to get aboard.

11. Getting Your Luggage Aboard

The next step is to find a porter for your luggage. That won't be difficult. There are porters at the entrance to every port and they'll jump to attention to take your baggage.

There seems to be rather a lot of debate about how much you should tip this streetside porter who really only takes your luggage to a conveyor belt or to a crewman who then takes it on board. Some people seem to think you should tip these porters not at all, others say the usual $1 a bag or so is the correct thing to do.

As far as we're concerned, we have yet to meet the sturdy soul with nerve enough to ignore a porter. In fact a friend of ours, whose job is to plan and pay for convention arrangements, steadfastly refuses to let a hotel bill him in advance for porter services. No one, he says, can look a porter in the eye and fail to tip him—even if the tip has already been paid!

That leaves us at square one. Make your own decision to tip or not to tip, but do feel justified in tipping lightly.

12. Bon Voyage Parties

No matter how unselfish you are, one of the high points of a cruise is sailing off into the sunset leaving envious friends behind! This right of passage is known as a bon voyage party, an event that can be great fun for all concerned until the moment the "all ashore" sounds and nonsailors have to stand on the dock watching you sail away.

If you'd like to share your excitement with some friends, go ahead and arrange an on-board bon voyage party and watch the ship's crew go into action even before you sail. Most cruise lines will happily arrange all the details of your party for you—everything from a tray of bon voyage goodies to that golden bubbly—if you let them in on your plans far enough in advance.

Lines differ on their requirements, so the advance notice can range from 24 hours to 14 days. How elaborately they prepare for your party is an arrangement that must be worked out between you and the line too.

To get your friends on board for the party it will also be necessary to arrange for boarding passes for them. Once again, each cruise line has its own attitude toward boarding passes, some issuing them in advance, some on the day of sailing, some both ways. Some have a limit to the number of guests you may have board too. Ask the line or a travel agent what the policy is on the ship you're sailing, then make your arrangements with friends.

Once you're well into your bon voyage party, keep an eye on the clock.

In answer to the question you're now mulling: No. If your friends don't get off the ship, they cannot sail with you. They will be taken off on the pilot boat or dumped unceremoniously ashore at the first stop, from whence they will have to foot the bill to get themselves home.

13. Exploring the Ship

Despite the "Love Boat" image, it's most unlikely that there will be a Julie Cruise Director standing at the gangplank to welcome you aboard. Generally, however, there will be someone there to tell you where your cabin is located and at least point out the direction in which you should begin looking.

On some lines your welcome may be a wondrous event. European lines, in particular, station a horde of room stewards at the entrance to the ship, outfit them in snappy uniforms and white gloves, and instruct them to meet you with a smile and brain in gear.

That white-glove service is a lovely welcoming touch that ought to be followed by all lines but isn't. Some just leave you milling about looking for someone who knows what, if anything, is happening. So we can make no blanket pronouncements on what kind of greeting you'll receive or how much help you'll get in locating your stateroom. If you don't find a welcoming committee, ask the nearest person for the purser's office and there you'll find some help.

After all you went through selecting the ship on which you're sailing, you will be familiar with the line's brochure. Somewhere in that brochure, or readily available from the line or travel agent, is a deck plan of the ship. It would be well to bring that on board with you. Locating your cabin will be much easier if you have one of these ship "maps."

After you've located your cabin and explored all its nooks and crannies, why not spend some pre-departure time exploring the rest of the ship? The deck plan shows all the ship's public rooms and outlines all the facilities, so go have a look at them.

If you're hungry or thirsty after a long plane ride, you'll usually find a bar open on board. Some ships even serve a pre-departure buffet, free to you, a small charge for your guests. A band will probably be playing somewhere on the ship. Up on deck, crewmen will be distributing the streamers and confetti and paper horns you'll use to signal your departure.

As you board the ship or as you prepare to sail, you'll also find photographers taking your picture. These will be posted later in the cruise and you can buy one of them to record the magic of these moments in your scrapbook. Photo charges are usually about $4 for a photo mounted in a cardboard frame with the ship's logo on it.

Chapter IX

LOOK OUT SCALE, HERE COMES: DINING AT SEA

1. Morning to Night
2. Selecting a Table and a Time
3. Drinking, Romancing, and Behaving Yourself
4. Special Occasions

TALK ABOUT fat city! Morning food, noon food, evening food, midnight food, mid-morning bouillon, afternoon tea, and in-between nibblies!

Let's get it straight right up front here: this is no time to begin a diet. This is no time to continue a diet. This is in fact no time even to recognize the existence of the *word* "diet."

If there's one single thing about cruising that appeals to everyone, it's the idea of all that wonderful food presented nonstop for seven or ten gluttonous days.

1. Morning to Night

All this glorious gorging gets started first thing in the morning. If you arise early, you'll find that the cooks have arisen even earlier to organize some kind of hunger appeteaser on deck to hold you until official breakfast hours begin.

Next comes breakfast in the dining room, where you can select from a menu every bit as long as the dinner menu: kippers, lox, bacon, bagels, muffins, fancy breads, sweet rolls, eggs cooked every way but Sunday, fruit-laden pancakes, butter-drenched waffles, even a steak if you like, toast, jellies, five or six kinds of juices, coffee, tea, milk, bloody marys, screwdrivers. You name it, someone will produce it.

Even as you eat, someone somewhere is preparing mid-morning bouillon to be presented about 10 a.m. so you should not starve before lunch. This intriguing custom stems from chilly transoceanic voyages where something warm mid-morning dispersed the chill. Some lines sailing in Alaskan waters serve hot mulled wine in mid-morning for just the same reason.

Then comes lunch, a four- or five-course event that can be as simple as a fresh fruit salad or as hearty as, say, turkey, mashed potatoes, gravy, cranberries, salad, biscuits, vegetables, and perhaps a couple of appetizers for starters. Dessert finale, of course.

On most ships, if you don't want to dine in the dining room for lunch you can roam up on deck, where you'll find a snackbar serving (still at no charge, of course) hamburgers, hot dogs, salads, perhaps lasagne or omelets. Some ships specialize in glamorous deck buffets with dozens of hot and cold selections elaborately presented outside so you don't miss a minute of sunshine.

That's it until dinner? Certainly not. Next comes another of the holdovers from the days of transoceanic voyages: afternoon tea. Not just tea, of course, but *tea,* including some kind of cake or cookies, sometimes even small sandwiches.

A few hours later and here comes dinner. Dinner is a major event on every ship, an event into which both crew and passengers throw themselves with fervor.

Many ships sponsor theme evenings at each or many of the dinners aboard. Waiters and busboys dress in costumes appropriate to whatever nationality's being saluted that night—Caribbean Night, America the Beautiful Night, French or Italian Night. On the menu you will find entree selections reflecting the night's theme—Kansas City beef on U.S. night, coq au vin on French night, conch chowder on Caribbean evenings, among six or eight other entree selections.

On some lines these theme evenings are carried out with all the pizzazz of a Cecil B. DeMille production. Crewmen gather somewhere before dessert and come marching into the room singing or accompanied by musicians. Often they carry flaming desserts high in the air, sometimes even balancing trays of liqueurs atop their heads while they dance around the room—Caribbean waiters are experts at that little trick.

What's more, you can have anything you want on the menu and as much as you want of it. If you're still hungry when you've finished the main course, just ask your waiter and he'll bring you another. Heaven for trenchermen!

If you do a little culinary adventuring and discover you don't like what you ordered, ask for something else. No one will frown at you, no one will be upset. Someone might ask you what was wrong with it, but they're only asking because they're trying to please all the people all the time. When they don't, they want to know why so they can correct the mistake.

Surely that's the end of the food barrage, you say. We can see you're a slow learner. Of course, that's not the end! A couple of hours down the evening comes the midnight buffet! Every ship has something served at midnight or thereabouts, although some have more sumptuous repasts than others. Some even go so far as to present something again at about 3 a.m., bringing their daily meal count to eight!

Some lines moderate their daily midnight presentations, saving their strength to produce the really big show, the grand finale event that features massive ice carvings, whole landscapes created from wax or lard, huge sides of beef, ham, poultry, breads baked into fish or animal shapes and presented in woven baskets also made of bread—all very elaborately decorated and presented. You'll probably take dozens of photographs that will floor the folks back home, those poor staring creatures.

Even if you're an early-to-bed, it's worth it to stay up for the extravaganza midnight buffet display. It's downright stupefying in beauty and sumptuousness, not even to mention tempting to the tastebuds.

What you'll want to know is that none of this costs you a cent! You paid all your bills when you booked the cruise and there's no more paying to be done. Everything from that dawn repast to the bouillon to the full-fledged dinners is free.

Those among us who are cooks will sooner or later wonder just what it takes to feed all these stuffees. If you're interested in some of those phenomenal statistics the chef is calculating even as you munch, here's a look at what the chef aboard the *Norway*—whose weekly market bill is $100,000—has on his shopping list each voyage:

Eggs	65,880
Ice cream	540 gallons
Hamburger, hot dog buns	9360
Bananas	2520 lbs.
Oranges	3600
Potatoes	14,700
Lettuce	2520 heads
Tomatoes	3000 lbs.
Onions	3000 lbs.
Carrots	1050 lbs.
Lobster	1800 lbs.
Shrimp	1650 lbs.
Bacon	1650 lbs.
Coffee	1155 lbs.

2. Selecting a Table and a Time

Now that you've come back from the refrigerator (we saw you sneaking off, salivating), it's time to consider the details of dining aboard a cruise ship.

Ships' dining rooms are not usually large enough to accommodate the entire passenger complement at one time. After all, how many 1000-person dining rooms have you ever seen?

DINING TIMES: To solve the problem, cruise lines have created a method of service known as "two seatings," sometimes also called sittings. That means that one group of passengers is assigned to dine at one time of the morning, afternoon, or evening, the remaining group entering the dining room about two hours later.

The earlier of the two times is called "first seating," the later event "second seating." On most ships, if you select first seating you'll have breakfast at 7 or 7:30 a.m., lunch at noon, and dinner at 6 or 6:30 p.m. Second-seating diners are usually served at 8:30 a.m., 1:30 p.m., and 8 or 8:30 p.m.

You don't have to worry about missing anything because the ship will see to it that all pre- and post-dinner entertainment is repeated for both groups of diners.

The best time to request a certain seating is when you book and/or pay for your tickets. Second seating is particularly popular and is generally completely booked well before the day of departure, so act accordingly.

SEATING ARRANGEMENTS: Yes, the little matter of dining companions. Wonderful new friends for the Christmas card list? Or a problem of such delicacy a U.N. ambassador would be boggled?

Let's dig right in here and discuss some of the possible seating arrangements you might encounter—or request.

Let it be known from the onset that all lines will try hard to accommodate requests, but most stop short of guaranteeing you any certain seating arrangement. Many reveal your table to you only at departure time when you pick up your ticket, some post the number of your table in your cabin.

Our advice is to request a certain kind of table and a certain seating when you book your ticket, no matter what the line's policy. It may not work, but then again it may, and what have you got to lose?

Honeymoon couples or couples whose jobs give them little time together may want to take this opportunity to fraternize at dinner only with each other. If that's your case, seek out a ship with tables for two and try very hard to secure one of those for yourself. If you want a table for two, it is wise to make that request as soon as possible, ideally when you book your ticket. Most ships have few, some no, tables for two, so the earlier you reserve one of those, the more likely your wish will be granted.

On some lines you can even ask to be seated with tablemates of a certain age bracket. Some grandmotherly types love to yak it up with the younger set, and vice versa, some prefer the dining company of those of a similar age.

The maxim in shipboard dining is "Ask!" You may not get what you want, but every effort will be put forth to make you happy.

Some lines now also feature smoking and nonsmoking sections in both dining rooms and cocktail lounges.

We've tried all kinds of table arrangements from tables for two up to tables for ten. Each has its own pleasures and drawbacks.

The drawback of a table for two is this: on board cruise ships, particularly very large ones, meals tend to be a friendship-forming time. If you dine alone you'll miss some of the fun of meeting others on board. On the positive side, you don't have to concern yourself with bad luck-of-the-draw that leaves you sharing a table with incompatible companions.

If you're traveling alone you'll probably enjoy being included in a larger table where you can get to know some other people aboard. A delightful Irish doctor we met on one cruise, however, sat at a table alone and informed us nicely but firmly that she preferred it that way. She was a pediatrician, so perhaps after a year full of nervous mothers her idea of a wonderful time was a plentitude of solitude. Yours may be too.

Next we come to tables for four. If you're traveling with another couple, tables for four are pleasant. If you're not, this kind of seating arrangement offers you the opportunity to meet two other people, usually a couple, with whom you may become friends. On the negative side of that coin, well, let's just hope you enjoy the company of that other couple.

Tables for six increase your chance of meeting dining companions whose friendship you will enjoy for your sojourn at sea, and perhaps for many years to come. Tables that size also decrease the possibility of boredom. With four or five personalities to choose from, surely one will be compatible.

Tables for eight always seem to end up as two tables for four, if for no other reason than it's difficult to talk over intervening diners.

Tables for ten are usually round, which means you can talk comfortably only with those on either side of you.

The best laid plans do not always work perfectly in this world. It is possible you'll find yourself with table companions whose conversation is absolutely stultifying to you. We once joined a table where the evening's conversation began with a discussion of appropriate cleaning compounds for grass stains and moved thrillingly on to a lively discussion of sump pumps.

If that happens to you, you need not endure. Just have a word with the maître d'hôtel, explain the situation as nicely and as courteously as possible, and ask to have your table assignment changed. Be nice about it but don't be shy. Dining room chiefs have dealt with this problem hundreds of times (at least) and will do all they can to settle you in with compatible dining companions. In fact, even as you're asking to have your table changed, someone else is probably doing likewise, making the switch just that much easier.

Understand, too, that much as the maître d'hôtel may want to make you happy, if the ship is packed and everyone else is pleased with his luck in dining companions, you may not get what you want. In that event, we have no solution to your problem. Look upon it as a challenge . . . or a cross to bear.

3. Drinking, Romancing, and Behaving Yourself

We know you already do all these things well. Still, when in Rome, let's discover how the Romans do things. Here are a few tips to make you feel more secure about things you might view a bit timidly and/or wonder what happens if. . . .

SEDUCTION SCENES: You might have seen romantic diner-pour-deux scenes on the "Love Boat," but don't count on participating in a candlelight, in-cabin dining experience on *your* love boat.

Dining in your cabin is possible on some luxury ships. Even on some not-so-luxury ships, passengers with suites or the most expensive accommodations aboard can sometimes have a meal served in their room. Less expensive craft, however, simply don't have the staff to offer that service successfully. Stewards are wonderful people, however. If you get a bad sunburn or twist your ankle or are otherwise too indisposed to go to the dining room for meals, they will see to it that you are fed and watered. They do that with such grace and ingenuity that you will want to take them home. (Sorry, they're not up for adoption.)

Some ships also offer snack service and/or basic beverage service in your cabin, often 24 hours a day.

SPECIAL DIETS: If you're on a special diet, by choice or by doctor's orders, don't be afraid your requirements will not be met on a cruise ship. These people can do anything.

They will in fact *do* anything, but they need a little advance notice so they can see to it that whatever you want is aboard in sufficient quantity to meet your needs.

On most ships you can request vegetarian meals, kosher meals, salt-free, sugar-free, fat-free—everything but calorie-free—meals. On the *QE2,* if you're paying top dollar for your accommodations you can even request some of the world's rarest edibles and, no surprise, they will be there on your table.

Tell your travel agent if you have special dietary needs or tell the line yourself, well in advance of sailing. Or both.

WINE AND THOU: People who like to have a cocktail before or with dinner will be happy to know that they need not change their habits on board a cruise ship. If you don't get dressed in time to have that drink in one of the lounges, just ask your waiter to bring you one, the same as you would in any restaurant.

If you like wine, you'll find extensive wine cellars on board many ships and at least a few wines aboard all ships. Cruise lines often display examples of the wines available in the ticketing area, so you can look over the selection even before you board the ship. You can purchase wine then too, and each night a gentleman will bring your wine to the table.

That gentleman is called the *sommelier* (pronounced "som-el-*yay*"). You will recognize him by the silver key or cup (it's called a *tastevin,* a wine taster) dangling from a heavy silver chain around his neck. He's in charge of the wine cellar and will take your wine order at the beginning of each meal and collect payment for it.

On all but one cruise line, Paquet Cruises, there is a charge for wine, just as there is a charge for cocktails. To emphasize its French connections, Paquet provides free table wine with dinner, but if you want a more expensive wine you pay for it.

Wine and liquor prices on ships are quite reasonable, however, generally less than you'd pay in a shoreside restaurant or bar. Figure $1.50 to $2 for a drink, another dollar or so for really fancy concoctions in special glasses.

Travel agents often send their clients a bottle of wine. If yours has done so, the sommelier will have a record of it and will bring the wine to you at dinner if it has not been sent directly to your cabin.

Yes, you tip the sommelier, about 15% of the cost of the wine, and you tip him when he serves it, not at the end of the voyage.

Some lines also have a worker who comes around after dinner with a cart full of after-dinner liqueurs. If you buy one of these, you pay him and tip him just as you would a bartender.

SAMPLING: To get an idea what treasures await, take a look at the sample menu we've reprinted here.

Just as ships have personalities, cooks aboard those ships have their specialties too. Lines born and bred in Scandinavia will naturally have a special affinity for fish prepared Scandinavian style, things like kippers, herring in cream sauce, cold fish dishes.

On Cunard's ships you'll find fish and chips with that sensational malt vinegar you just can't get in these parts (and without which fish and chips are pffft).

Paquet's chefs do marvelous things with sauces, and Greek vessels are

APPETIZER
Fresh Fruit in Cup with Kirschwasser
Smoked Sturgeon and Salmon with Onions and Capers
Swiss Cheese Salad—Melon Wedge with Prosciutto Ham
Chilled Celery and Carrot Sticks, Olives, Radishes

FROM THE TUREENS
Beef Consomme with Vegetables
Cream of Asparagus

FISH DISH
Golden Fried Fillet of Red Snapper with Sauce Remoulade
Salad "Doria" (Potato Salad with Cucumbers)

FARINACEOUS
Canneloni All'Etrusca (with Chicken Livers)

DINNER SELECTION
Broiled Sirloin Steak, Onion Rings, "Cafe de Paris" Butter
"Coq au Vin" (French Specialty)
Young Chicken, braised in Burgundy with Onions, Mushrooms and Bacon, flavored with Cognac

VEGETABLES
Glazed Baby Carrots, Parsley
Broccoli with Hollandaise Sauce

POTATOES
French Fried - Fluffy Mashed - Pilaw Rice
Baked Idaho Potato with Sour Cream and Chives or Bacon Bits

---

sure to feature those feta-topped Greek salads and black olives, lots of lamb concoctions.

Sitmar's pizza is renowned, as is its pasta, and Home Lines offers lots of unusual pastas too.

Norwegian Caribbean Lines has some great chocolate-chip cookies, and promises that they will soon be serving fresh Norwegian salmon aboard. Royal Caribbean Lines does wonderful things with lobster and poultry selections.

Carnival's Italian dining room staff produces some very good dinners, and we once had outstanding steaks aboard one of these ships.

After years of reviewing restaurants for newspapers and magazines, we've discovered two maxims: (1) you won't find meals prepared exactly the same way twice by any chef; and (2) you won't find two people who can

YOUR LOW CALORIE DISH
"The Executive Salad"
Cole Slaw on Crisp Lettuce, Chicory, Egg Wedges
Tuna Flakes, Cottage Cheese, Stuffed Peach,
Radishes and Tomatoes, Green Goddess Dressing

FROM THE GARDEN
Lettuce - Tossed Green - Tomatoes - Cucumbers

CHOICE OF DRESSINGS
Blue Cheese - French - Russian - Oil and Vinegar

THE FINALE
A Selection of International Cheeses from the Tray
Melba Toast - Rye Crisp - Pumpernickel - Dutch Rusks

SHERBET
Orange

DESSERTS
Surprise de Meringue with Assorted French Fruit and Pistachio Ice Cream
Cheese Cake - Key Lime Pie
Bavarois "Hawaii" - Fruit Jello
Vanilla and Chocolate Ice Cream
A Selection from our Pastry Cart

FRUITS
Fresh Fruit in Season from the Basket
Calimyrna Figs and Dates - Stemginger in Syrup

BEVERAGES
Coffee - Tea - Ovaltine - Sanka - Maxwell
Fresh Milk - Cold Chocolate

---

agree at any moment on the definition of "good." Food that didn't impress us might be just your style while what we found wonderful may be too gussied, too simple, too lean, too fat, too *something* to please your palate.

You'll often find that a kitchen does some things extremely well. After you've been aboard a day or two you'll be able to spot those "bests." Waiters can be good guides to what's cooking exquisitely today.

It would be simple-minded at best to say that the food on every cruise ship is outstanding. You get what you pay for in most things, and that's pretty generally true afloat as well as ashore. Ships that charge more have larger staffs and can afford to pay for the best in chefdom.

You'll soon discover the specific skills of the chef aboard your ship and learn to order around those skills. If he's a dessert demon, ease off on the rest of the dinner and wait for that creamy-rich chocolate cake or the brandy-touched mousse or the cream puff swans. If he's terrific with sauces, stick to sauce-y selections.

THINGS YOUR MOTHER NEVER TAUGHT YOU: Few of us were born with a silver-enough spoon in our mouths to be positive what's socially correct in sailing situations. Here we are, to the rescue.

Every ship has its Captain's Cocktail Party or Welcome Aboard Gala or something similarly named. On that night, you appear in the lounge at the appointed hour and are greeted in a reception line by several officers.

As you move through the line you'll be asked your name and be passed from person to person until you reach the chief hostess, who will introduce you to the captain. The captain will shake hands with you, perhaps make a small joke, and at that moment a photographer will pop out of the shadows and record your smiles on film. You can buy the photograph in a day or so at the photo shop.

Another crewman will step forward to offer you a complimentary drink and some hors d'oeuvres. Dance music plays and the atmosphere is everything you always dreamed a cruise would be.

Later you go on to dinner, but unless you've paid top dollar for your cabin or are a celebrity of sorts, it is unlikely you will be asked to dine with the captain. Depending on how gregarious the captain is, he may or may not even be present in the dining room for meals. Some captains are visible every night of the voyage while others show up only for the Captain's Dinner and perhaps one other evening.

If you are intent on dining with the captain, you might discuss the matter with the maître d'hôtel who may be able to arrange it, but no guarantees.

If you are asked to dine with the captain one evening during your voyage, consider it an honor as well as a delightful experience, perhaps even the highlight of your trip. Captains aboard these huge cruise ships all seem born with a marvelous, twinkly sense of humor. Perhaps that's not really so surprising. Think what it takes to accept with equanimity the responsibility for a thousand or so passengers and at least half that many personnel. He'd better have a sense of humor!

In any case, the captains we've met have been charming and not the least bit stuffy. One so loved the jokes of a Texas story-teller who dined with us that he dragged one of his colleagues up to the man's cabin one afternoon to have the story told over again. Another we know often sings the passengers awake with a morning song over the PA system!

So that invitees will feel a bit more comfortable at dinner with the captain, you'll usually receive a note asking you to meet with the top crew members and the captain in the lounge before dinner. Some small talk at that time helps break the ice for dinner conversation later. Top officers, and perhaps even the captain, may join you later to watch the show and share the evening's activities.

As for other socially acceptable things to do aboard ship: show up on time for meals. Your waiter won't censure you if you don't, but he's been working all day and is looking forward to his time off too. The later you show up, the longer his day lasts and the harder he has to work. Try to be in the dining room within 15 minutes of the appointed dining hour.

Nowhere is it written that you have to show up for every meal. If you can't face the thought of getting out of bed in time for breakfast, don't. There are no penalties for nonattendance.

If you'd like to have something that is not on the menu, ask for it. Within reasonable bounds, the staff is likely to be able to produce it at a moment's notice. If you want something quite complicated that's not on the menu, ask a day or so in advance.

If you try something you don't like, don't suffer in silence. Explain the problem to your waiter and he will do something to rectify it. You don't have to make a scene. Just explain the problem quietly and ask for another selection.

If you want seconds, don't fear that you'll suffer an Oliver Twistian fate. Just tell your waiter how wonderful it was and ask if you might try another helping.

On ships, as in many European dining rooms, you order your choices from the first several courses. Vegetables will all be listed on the menu but there's no need to choose among them. At the appropriate moment after your entree is served, a waiter will come around bearing the vegetables on a big silver platter. You can try all of them or none of them, or any combination in between.

4. Special Occasions

If you're celebrating a new marriage, the anniversary of an old one, a birthday, the day you met, or nothing at all, the ship will be happy to provide you with a cake and all the usual special-occasion salutes. Just let someone in the dining room know about your request a day or so before you'd like to have the cake and trimmings presented.

If you'd like to have some new friends up to your cabin for a cocktail party, once again let someone know a day or so in advance and hors d'oeuvres will be provided at the appointed time. Nice way to live, eh?

Chapter X

SMALL SAILORS: CHILDREN AT SEA

CAN YOU TAKE the kids? In a word, yes. Should you take the kids? Why not? Once you get them on the ship you'll hardly see them again until it's time to get off.

That last statement depends, as you might imagine, on what ship you take. As the cost of cruises has dropped, ship travel has become infinitely more attractive for families who never thought they could afford such a thing.

Indeed, in days of yore you couldn't afford it, but now you'll find more and more families sailing happily together, adults having a wonderful time and youngsters having, if it's possible, an even better time.

1. What Will It Cost?

Competition has spawned a flurry of special price breaks for couples sharing their cabins with the kids. Watch the newspaper ads each spring and you'll see a raft of special price breaks for parents traveling with children on summer holidays. Sometimes these breaks also occur on school holidays at Christmas or Easter, but that's not as common. On many ships there are special price deals for children, offering them a 50% reduction on the minimum fare aboard or a set price that's very low indeed.

At what age a child stops being a child and becomes an adult varies from line to line, ranging from 12 through about 17. However, even if your youngsters are old enough to be considered adults, they'll only pay the rate for a third or fourth passenger sharing a cabin. As you will see as you read the prices for each ship, that rate can be very, very economical indeed. Some cruise lines have even been known to offer deals in which the children can sail with you for free, so long as they share your cabin.

To make matters even better, cruise lines are thrilled to get families aboard their ships. Cruises had for so long been associated with high prices that family travel by ship has been virtually unknown outside the Rockefeller clan. Cruise lines found penetration of that market extremely difficult, so when they are now able to lure those families aboard, they are very pleased.

To prove it, your room steward will often be very accommodating to the needs of families. If the ship is not crowded and you ask nicely, you may very well get a separate stateroom nearby for the youngsters. Now doesn't that sound lovely—for both you and them?

2. Kids and Cabins

Even if that doesn't work out and you have to share a cabin with the youngsters, things won't be as bad as you might think. Ships are very large creatures so neither you nor the kids are likely to be spending much time in your cabin.

Admittedly, sharing the cabin with the kids doesn't do a great deal for romance, but it's not very much different than sharing a room in a hotel or resort with them. We guarantee that you'll get awfully clever awfully fast. (We aren't going to amplify that.)

Your cabin, unless you spring for a suite with separate sitting area and couch that becomes a bed, will probably feature upper and lower berths. You would do well not to scrimp too much on the cost of the cabin, for the lowest price will often buy you the tightest quarters. Opt for a larger inside room than a smaller outside one, for instance, or move up a bit in price category if the line or a travel agent can assure you there will be more room in the cabin. Also, older ships usually have much larger cabins for the money than the brand-new pared-down cruisers.

On ships that feature rooms very similar in size, it's safe to go for the lowest priced quarters, however. You won't buy anything but proximity to the main public areas when you pay the higher price, so you might as well tuck everyone away on a lower deck, save some money, and wear the kids out running up and down the stairs (you take the elevator and meet them).

There's no denying that quarters can get a bit tight, but you probably won't be spending too much time in them anyway. And as one cruise exec told us: "After you shut your eyes, it really doesn't matter what size the room is."

Consign the youngsters to the upper berths, unless there are compelling reasons not to do so. They'll love climbing the ladder up to bed each night, thus making even bedtime a terrific new experience. Well, you can bill it that way anyway. Good luck.

3. Keeping Them Busy

How wonderful a time all the family has depends on how the cruise line feels about children. Some ships simply don't have facilities for children and are not keen on having the little angels aboard. If so, they say so, flat out, in their brochure.

Most moderately priced cruise lines, however, go all out to welcome the kiddies and provide a round of entertainment for them that some *adults* envy!

We've met some terrific kids on board ships. You'll usually find them at the electronic games, where they'll gladly show you the benefits of youthful eye-hand coordination if you'll come up with a few quarters to keep the Pac-Man moving.

If you're lost, as you will surely be at first, just ask one of the youngsters to help you find your way. They know every corner of the ship by the time they've been on board for an hour, and will happily show you around the place.

If there's gossip aboard, the kids will know what it is. Crew members love the kids, tell them everything, and show them around, indeed spoil them to death at every opportunity.

In our descriptions of the ships we've tried to indicate ships with special facilities for children. Those facilities range from a small room with sandboxes and merry-go-round-like rides for children to the full-fledged children's center you'll find on Sitmar ships, where the youngsters even have a swimming pool designated just for them, a recreation room, the works!

In Sitmar's children's section of the ship, the recreation center for older youngsters is supplemented by a nursery for very young sailors. All of it is strictly off-limits for adults, a rule the youngsters adore.

Ships that cater to children show movies just for the youngsters and have counselors who oversee a full program of activities, sometimes both on board and on shore. Usually, however, you'll find children's counselors and a raft of planned children's activities only in the summer months when the line expects to see many more children aboard.

Games aboard ships include all kinds of board games, plus table tennis, shuffleboard, sometimes badminton or basketball. Kids love the evening Bingo games, and are often the "jockies" for the horse races.

Ships that feature special programs for children often organize those activities so they run simultaneously with adult programs, up to and including meals and post-dinner activities. Others see to the youngsters' needs only from early morning to about dinnertime. After that, you and they are on your own. Babysitters are available, but you pay for that service. Charges are quite reasonable, however, often about $2 an hour.

4. Kid Food

Ship food is well loved by children, who can eat their fill of hamburgers, hot dogs, and french fries on deck all day long, and need endure adult food only at dinner and sometimes not even then.

Home Lines' ships have an Italian ice-cream parlor for the youngsters and the greatest miniature disco afloat. Right next to the small dance floor and the video machines there's a nifty sitting area featuring a raised floor into which a hole has been cut so the kids can sit on the carpeted floor and dangle their feet down into the hole while they sip soft drinks.

You'll also discover that youngsters who consider jeans formal dress at home will take to dressing up for dinner like puppies take to water. One 5-year-old we met was so proud of his new suit and tie, his parents reported, that it was all they could do to keep him from wearing it all day long!

5. Ashore with the Small Fry

Special youth-oriented shore excursions are tailored just for children, with none of that boring shopping Mom and Dad want to do.

If you want to take the kids with you when you go ashore, be prepared to modify your walking and shopping to fit the energy and boredom level of children. There may be nothing worse in the world than dragging a squalling child around in the heat as you try desperately to find the right linen napkins for Aunt Millie. As you very well know from expeditions on your home turf, a bored child is given to crying, whining, racing off in all directions, and generally driving you crazy with disciplinary tactics or with worry.

On ships with lots of foreign crewmen or with visits to foreign ports, the youngsters will get a chance to learn a few words in another language either by design (classes) or by osmosis (chattering to the crew). You'll be amazed how rapidly the little ones begin rattling off foreign phrases *you* may have trouble wrapping your tongue around. If there are foreign children on board, as there often are, especially aboard ships that sail to a foreign country and permit debarkation there, you'll find the youngsters happily playing bilingually together in just a few hours. Amazing little devils.

As we mentioned, some lines even provide recreational activities for youngsters in port. Recreation directors, who are usually young and enthusiastic themselves, take the kids off on shore excursions designed to appeal to their interests: lots of swimming, roaming, and peeking and poking into places.

6. Is It Worth It?

Indeed, it's well worth it. It costs you little more, sometimes nothing more, than you'd be paying anyway.

Taking the kids along can make for a touching and rewarding vacation. You won't feel guilty about leaving them at home with a babysitter or the grandparents, and you'll often get a thrill out of watching their wonderment at meeting new kinds of people and experiences.

Watching children staring wide-eyed as they're hoisted up onto the shoulder of a gold-braided, snappily uniformed, smiling captain (who's thinking of his own toddlers at home) may be one of your most poignant cruise memories.

Chapter XI

ONE CAN BE FUN: SINGLES AT SEA

1. Will You Be Lonely?
2. Paying the Price
3. Delivery from Dining Traumas
4. Shipboard Friends . . . and Romances

BY NOW YOU HAVE absorbed the vision: romantic nights, action-packed days, fascinating ports of call, and no fretting travel details to distress you. But can you go it alone or will this turn out to be seven days of lonely Saturday nights? You haven't been listening carefully enough.

Forget Saturday nights and absorb this picture. You're on board a floating hotel with all the amenities of any major resort, but with one very special feature no landlocked resort can boast: no one can pack up and leave town.

1. Will You Be Lonely?

As a single person you have a captive audience of a thousand or so other passengers, among which you'll surely find a few who share your prejudices and your priorities.

What's more, cruise lines, well aware of the quantities of single people in the world, have dived into the world of matchmaking with all the fervor of a new escort service. One of the first announcements you'll hear aboard any ship is one telling you the time, place, and ambience of the singles' get-together. Hardly will the last mooring lines have been reeled in before the single travelers on board will be meeting somewhere to ID each other and get on the same tandem fun.

One cruise line, Royal Cruises, has even gone so far as to seek out good-looking unattached gentlemen with gregarious personalities. After careful screening, the gentlemen are treated to a free cruise in exchange for their services as a fourth at bridge and as dance and conversation partners for unattached women. How's *that* for working hard to keep singles from being all alone at sea?

It goes further than that, of course. All lines will work hard to see to it that, single as you may be, you are not alone unless you wish to be.

Now you may not think anyone would be alone by choice, but we once met a delightful Irish doctor who told us a couple of weeks of companionship strictly by *choice* was her idea of heaven. She stuck to it too, sitting happily alone at a table for two, conversing when she chose, but declining companionship just as frequently as she welcomed it. Now that's an independent spirit!

You can be just as independent, one of the joys of singlehood, or you can mix happily with others on board, meeting new friends among both crew and passengers.

2. Paying the Price

It's sad but true that single travelers must often pay a premium for what some consider a singular blessedness. Little by little these extra charges are easing a bit, particularly in slow season, but they do still exist.

There are, of course, sound economic reasons, from the cruise line's point of view, for the 150%, 175%, or 200% fares levied on single travelers. If you're living alone in a cabin for two in prime selling time, the line is automatically losing one full fare. No one stays in business by losing money.

Some ships, Home Lines' *Atlantic* is one, have cabins just for singles. These are a bit smaller than a double cabin naturally, but are quite comfortable for a single traveler.

On some lines you will pay more for these single cabins than you would if you were sharing a cabin for two. On other lines there is little or no price differential over the per-person, double-occupancy rate in that price category. On most ships, however, you will have to face a classic battle between budget and solitude. If you can afford privacy, you may find it worth the extra price. Or you may not. Many people enjoy having a roommate's companionship for the voyage, even if that companionship does not turn out to be a lifelong friendship.

If privacy is not vital to your enjoyment of the cruise, you can save some money by taking advantage of an offer made by nearly all cruise lines. Somewhere in the fine print of most ship brochures you'll find an offer by the line to team you up with one or more roommates with each of you paying half the rate for that cabin. If you don't see any mention of sharing arrangements, ask the line or a travel agent if the ship offers this kind of arrangement. That way both you and your roommate will pay the same price per person as a couple occupying those quarters.

Your roommate will be of the same sex and probably, but not definitely, in a similar age bracket. As with any grab-bag situation, you may or may not enjoy the company of your roommate. You will, however, have a companion for the first few ice-breaking hours, and that may be worth something to you.

If you don't like your newfound roomie, plan on spending plenty of time in the ship's public rooms because there's little or no chance that a room switch can be made.

If you really want to save money, some lines will offer you the opportunity to share a cabin for four with three other single travelers, each of you paying one-fourth of the total cost of the cabin. That kind of a deal can make passage quite reasonable, but has the usual drawbacks you'd expect in a cabin for four—less space, more chance for friction, crowded storage conditions.

We have known several adventuresome single travelers who have sailed off to Europe or Africa sharing a cabin way down in the recesses of the ship. They bought, quite inexpensively, a lifetime of memories. Everything has its price.

One, in fact, says she always books single space in a cabin for four, if she can, and has occasionally ended up alone in the cabin when the line failed to fill it. That pleasant offshoot can also happen when you book one of the share-a-cabin deals. It's all the luck of the game, however, and although it does often happen, particularly in slow seasons, there are no guarantees.

To make that kind of luck work for you, however, you must specify that you will book only on the per-person, double, basis. If the line takes your money under those conditions, it will try to find you a roommate, but if it fails to do so you won't be charged any additional fee for the cabin class you booked.

If you do book a shared cabin and find yourself with three roommates, ask your steward if there might be an empty cabin somewhere that you, or you and one of the others from your room, might occupy since no one is using it. Don't get demanding about this or you'll get nowhere. Do explain the crowded conditions or perhaps wave a bit of green about (or at least imply the appearance of some later) in compensation for his efforts. After all, if he manages to find an empty cabin for you he'll have to clean and care for two cabins instead of one.

A line need not accept your booking under these conditions, but many of them will do so, particularly during less busy seasons of the year. If they at first refuse, try presenting your case once again closer to the departure date when the line's chances of booking the cabin have become more remote. Don't bother to try any of these nifty plans at peak seasons like Christmas or New Year's, however.

Interestingly, because there are more single women travelers than men, single men have a greater chance of paying to share a single cabin and then finding they won't have to adjust to the presence of a roommate.

Singles can often save money by working with a travel agent who is very active in selling group cruises. Sometimes these groups are "affinity" groups, which means that they belong to the same garden club, church, or organization. Sometimes the group is just a loose coalition created by the travel agent who has booked a cluster of cabins in a certain price category for a specified cruise or cruises.

An organization called SingleWorld (tel. toll free 800/223-6490) offers guaranteed share rates for singles that can run as low as $500 for a week's cruise!

Many travel agents now send out regular newsletters and announcements of upcoming cruises you can join. It's often possible to save quite a bit of money over the regular cruise price by joining one of these groups. Unlike land tours, cruise tour groups need not spend much or any time together, so you don't have to worry about being stuck with a group of garden freaks when you wouldn't know an aphid from an asparagus.

3. Delivery from Dining Traumas

Any woman who has ever been single knows that one of life's worst moments can be the dinner hour when all the rest of the world seems to be couples. As if that isn't depressing enough, every one of us has met some haughty dining room host or hostess who has sneeringly led us to the table by the kitchen door where presumably we could depress only the chef with our single status. Sooner, rather than later, that sort of bad manners is disappearing, but the good news tonight is that you don't have to worry about anything like *that* on a cruise.

When you book your trip, simply tell your travel agent or the line that you want to be at a table for six or more, and explain that you'll be traveling by yourself. You'll find yourself welcomed in the dining room with the same quiet courtesy as everyone else aboard and shown to your table where introductions will begin. *Voilà!* Already you have met five potential companions.

If you'd prefer to sit in solitary splendor, you should have little trouble securing a place at a table for two. Most travelers like the experience of meeting new people on board, so tables for two may be available. On the opposite side of that coin, however, most ships have few tables for two, so the odds against your getting one increase.

Take a good look at the ship's deck plans too. Many of them indicate the kinds and locations of tables on board so you can select a table for two (in this case for one) that's near other larger tables, then join or not join in their fun.

You'll have to make your own decision about what you think of tables for four. You may find yourself the third party at a table with a couple. A fourth, probably also a single traveler, may be added to your table. Once again, if you make sure the ship's dining room staff knows you're traveling alone and don't particularly want to keep it that way, they'll make every effort to team you up with compatible companions.

Some lines, Carnival for one, will even make an effort to take your *age* preference in dining companions into consideration!

If you give your dining room companions a college try and find you aren't pleased with them, tell the maître d'hôtel or dining room captain your problem and ask for a change of companions. You are, after all, going to spend four or five hours a day with them. If it's humanely possible, the crew will try to accommodate you.

4. Shipboard Friends . . . and Romances

Once upon a time when one of us was single, that one took a weekend cruise, primarily, it must be admitted, to avoid a dateless weekend. What an avoidance! From the first dinner to debarkation it was a whirlwind weekend of laughter and dance that is remembered fondly to this day. On another occasion the voyage was a much longer but no less eventful one.

Perhaps the single most wonderful thing about a cruise ship is that you can wander into any of the piano bars, cocktail lounges, dining rooms, or decks, sit down and have a drink (or buy someone else one) without feeling like a lost gosling wandering into a den of foxes.

Everyone on board a ship is out to have a good time. You're all thrown together in a big unabandonable barrel, so you'll find everyone intent on making a great time of it. No one will draw any conclusions about a single man or woman in one of the ship's lounges. In fact it's very likely that the couple beside you or a fellow down the bar or a couple of women two tables away will strike up a conversation about the best buys in the next port.

We were charmed by two young women who sent us over a drink one evening as an ice breaker. No special reason, just for fun. They, like the other passengers, were in high spirits on that first night aboard and were anxious to talk about their impressions of this ship as compared to several others they had sailed. Happenings like that are the rule rather than the exception on a cruise.

Some travelers begin making acquaintances very early on in the cruise, that is to say, before the ship leaves the harbor. They do that, crew members tell us, by being among the first to answer the boat drill call.

You'll read more about boat drills in the Introduction, but for now you need only know that as the ship begins to leave the dock you'll be asked to don your lifejacket and get yourself to an assigned place on the ship where you will be instructed in safety procedures.

Get up to the assigned boat station early, experienced lookers tell us, and check out who's arriving. Fumble helplessly with the lifejacket in the immediate vicinity of someone interesting, and *voilà!* introductions.

If you prefer somewhat more organized introductions, the singles party we talked about earlier will be occurring either just after the ship leaves port or after dinner that first night out. See what we mean about the ship's crew wanting you to have a good time? If you're not already too busy with new friends, go to the party. At least you'll get a look at some of the options.

There's another way to get a look at some of the possibilities: ogle the crew. Every ship has many good-looking men and women aboard. What's more, the peripatetic nature of their seagoing career means that many of them are single. That almost always excludes the captain, so perhaps you should avoid shooting quite that high. On the other hand several captains have told us stories about marrying ladies they met aboard ship. That is, after all, where the captain spends almost all his time.

On most ships, officers are permitted—in some cases, encouraged—to mix with the passengers but to maintain basic discretion in their activities. Sometimes there is only moderate, if any, discouragement of crew-passenger romances. If you do make friends with a crew member, you may very well spend some time in the crew's own lounges. Crew members are very good party-ers and have an uncanny ability to cram ten friends into their tiny cabins for a party. You can be sure you'll have a good time.

We'd say it's up to the crew member, not you, to know and follow the ship's rules on fraternization with passengers. With so many more single men and women in the world and so many of them opting for a cruise vacation, it seems to us a bit counterproductive to bar the crew from friendships with passengers. But then we're not running a cruise line.

Certainly there are few more romantic atmospheres in which to pursue and be pursued: moonlight and roses, starlight and champagne, lazy days and dancing nights.

Good hunting!

Chapter XII

MAL DE MER: IT'S NOT THE SIZE OF THE SHIP IT'S THE MOTION OF THE OCEAN

1. Cures and Preventions
2. Is There a Doctor in the House?
3. Special Problems

IF YOU HAVE NEVER been to sea before (or only on troopships, and those don't count), your first question will be "Are cruises fun?" Your second question, delivered within seconds of the first, will, we predict, be "Will I get sick?"

Be encouraged by the news that modern ships are stabilized to a faretheewell with huge stablizers that shoot out like side fins and hold the ship steady in the water, keeping the roll to a minimum. In the ship's brochure are details describing the kind and amount of the ship's stabilizers. If you don't find that information, ask your travel agent to inquire.

Only a cock-eyed optimist would guarantee you won't suffer from that famous—and infamous—malady the French call *mal de mer*. Everybody is different and each inner ear reacts to motion in its own peculiar way. Some people can feel queasy in a Rolls Royce, then cross the Atlantic in a hurricane and love every blustery minute of it. Others ride rollercoasters and ferris wheels with never a moment's fear, but panic when terra firma becomes unfirma.

We can't tell you just how you'll react, but we can tell you that it doesn't really matter. There are ways to be sure you'll have a lovely cruise, no matter what your reaction to motion.

1. Cures and Preventions

Ask your physician for effective cures. There is a very new motion-sickness cure available which requires a small circle called Transderm V be attached to the skin behind your ear. This implantation, which doesn't hurt a bit, is an anti-motion-sickness drug that is time-released into your bloodstream. It isn't used for children, however, as it has not yet been determined to be safe for them. No one else need worry about it, however, particularly not pregnant women: the drug contained in Transderm V was first used in a medication called "twilight sleep" given to women prior to delivery of a baby. In a few cases, however, the drug may have a mild hallucinatory effect or produce confusion, but that's quite rare.

In any drugstore you can buy over-the-counter anti-motion-sickness drugs. Dramamine is the best known one, although there are now other brands as well. The drawback to these drugs is that the relaxant in them makes some people very drowsy. Better drowsy, however, than seasick, and you're not driving so why worry? Dramamine in fact has a similar history to Transderm V: its ingredients were first used to combat morning sickness.

What exactly causes seasickness nobody knows for certain. In general terms motion seems to affect the inner ear, which controls other parts of the body including your equilibrium. If that sensitive inner ear is disturbed by unfamiliar motion, you feel queasy.

If you have reason to suspect that you might be prone to motion sickness, try one of these preventatives. The key to the success of any of these remedies, doctors tell us, is to take it *before* sailing. Don't wait until you're feeling the butterflies to begin wondering how you should go about snaring them. You'll find plenty of anti-motion-sickness pills aboard any ship in the ship's drugstore and often in every lounge on board.

Once again, one of us is prone to this ailment and knows bitterly how miserable it can be. In a couple of all-too-memorable encounters with the *mal* of the *mer,* we've learned *absolutely* that you cannot drink your way to a cure. Whatever anyone tells you about a brandy or some champagne, don't.

On most cruises you won't find the water rough enough to cause you any problems. By far the majority of cruises in the Caribbean, Alaska, inland waterways, and along the Pacific coastline are operated, by design, in still waters.

It does occasionally happen, however, that the wind picks up and ruffles the waters, causing the ship to roll in the trough of the waves from side to side or to pitch forward and back. Pitch is easier to bear than roll. Transatlantic cruises are often rough too, particularly those that travel across the North Atlantic in early spring or late fall when the winds are brisk.

If you're suffering from seasickness, you may find some relief from its most immediate effects by getting yourself up on deck where you can see the horizon. People who get carsick if they read in a car but feel all right again if they look up at the horizon seem to do well with the up-on-deck cure. Believe us, you'll want to try anything without argument. We've found that the stabilizing effect of seeing the horizon often works so well that you are cured right at the start.

Yes, you say, but I can't stay up on deck all night. What happens when I go back inside? Well, chances are you'll feel queasy once again. Take a motion-sickness pill before you go up on deck and stay up there for a few hours after you start to feel better. Stay near the edge of the deck too.

Crew members often prescribe soda crackers and soup. Who knows where this old tradition started, but it seems to work for some sufferers.

It also often helps to take to your bunk and sleep it off. Cabins amidships and deep down in the ship have the least roll. If you're really worried, book one of these. Avoid quarters in the bow or as high up on the ship as the lifeboats.

If you're feeling horrible but hungry, don't try to make it to the dining room, where the roll may be worse and the sight and smell of food is . . . well, forget it. Explain your problem to the steward and ask him to bring some light meal to your cabin. He'll be glad to oblige.

There is this final consolation: you *will* get your sea legs after a bit (notice we're not saying how long "a bit" is) and begin to feel better on your own. Usually this only takes a day or two. By that time your body will have adjusted to the roll of the ship, so don't do anything to confuse it, for instance, don't try to eat at one meal enough to make up for all the meals you didn't eat. Dine lightly and give thanks.

One of the best antidotes to this sickness is to stay so busy you don't have time to think about it. That advice, we realize, is cold comfort when your stomach feels like Jello.

We don't think mal de mer will be a problem for you, but if you have doubts, ask your doctor about the behind-the-ear implant or take an anti-motion-sickness pill well before the ship sets sail.

Bon voyage!

2. Is There a Doctor in the House?

In a word, yes. Every large ship is required to have a doctor aboard, and some ships have a hospital nearly as big as one you might find in a small town!

On a recent visit to the *QE2,* we were amazed to be shown not only a handsomely decorated waiting room but a dentist's office, a complete pharmacy, 15 beds, a crew examining room, and a complete operating theater! Now *that* is prepared.

While there won't be such elaborate facilities on smaller cruise ships, there will be a doctor and a nurse on all but the tiniest inland cruisers. Even those will have someone on board with at least nurse's training. Those very small ships (100 or fewer passengers) also stop in port every evening and are rarely out of sight of land, so if you should need a doctor, the ship can get you to one quickly.

Ship's doctors are quite interesting people, as you might have guessed from watching "Love Boat." One we met had always dreamed of cruise-ship travel and spread the word around until he was finally selected to fill in for the ship's regular doctor during a vacation.

Ship's doctors are considered among the crew's top officers and will often be seen dining at the captain's table. That, of course, is the ideal way to meet the ship's doctor.

If, however, you must meet him or her by necessity, rest assured that you'll be getting top medical care. Most ship's doctors, however, say that about the most they ever see is a bad sunburn, a sprained something, or an occasional broken bone.

Speaking of sunburn, it's amazing how many people think they can take a pale epidermis that hasn't seen sun for months and stuff it right out there in the sunshine. They can—but they pay. In Caribbean or Mexican sunshine you will burn—and fast—so be smart and limit your sunbathing to 15 minutes the first day, adding an additional 15 minutes each day thereafter up to about an hour and a half on the seventh day.

Sunscreens are very effective products, and combined with a sensible sunning schedule can give you a nice tan that will look great back in your hometown (instead of a blotchy mess that flakes off behind you in little trails of peeling skin).

Handsome as the ship's doctor may be, meeting him when you're in major sunburn pain is not ideal. Be patient. Olympic-quality suntans are not acquired in a day.

If you're suffering from seasickness and don't seem to be improving as rapidly as you'd like, stop in to see the doctor. Doctors on board have regular hours which usually will be announced in the ship's newspaper and will always be posted at the infirmary.

Some ships charge a small amount, usually $10 or less for a visit to the doctor to have him sympathize with such things as sunburn or sea sickness. Others do not charge for that service. Like shoreside house calls, visits to your cabin and/or at night can cost about double that. Medication is sold to passengers at cost on some ships, and minor medication distributed free on most.

No one wants to think about this, much less talk about it, but if you should need major medical help, the ship's doctor has contingency plans to care for you until the ship reaches the next port where you can be taken to a hospital, should that be necessary. From there, if necessary, you can be flown home.

Ships maintain close radio contact with the home port and with nearby ports, so close, in fact, that EKG readings can be reported instantly to heart specialists. In really rare emergencies helicopters can remove passengers from large ships.

Naturally, such a calamity would incur awesome expenses, so you would do well to check your medical coverage to be sure that you're covered for care in another country. Travel agents and insurance companies, including special travel-oriented insurance companies, can explain what special travel insurance is available to help protect you if you have medical problems far from home.

3. Special Problems

If you have or have had an illness that could cause a problem during your cruise, speak to the ship's doctor early on in the voyage.

Those whose illnesses are so incapacitating as to require confinement to a wheelchair may or may not be welcomed on certain ships. If you or a companion must use a wheelchair, you must tell the line in advance so they can outline wheelchair size requirements aboard. Some chairs are simply too wide for the ship and won't be able to negotiate passageways or cabins.

Some ships have gone out of their way to provide facilities for those with special medical problems. One recently installed kidney dialysis equipment on board so that those requiring that kind of treatment periodically could still go sailing.

Wheelchair travelers should also take a very close look at the ship's deck plans and give some thought to the presence or absence of elevators and the access, or lack of it, to public rooms. Some ships simply are more accessible for wheelchair travelers than others. In general, more modern ships have wider passageways, more elevators, and more provisions for all kinds of handicapped travelers.

You should also examine the itinerary and check to see if the ship docks at each port or anchors offshore, taking passengers into port by tender. Generally, wheelchair travelers cannot negotiate the tender's accessways and must stay on the ship. Obviously, you'd be wiser to pick a ship that pulls into a dock in each port.

Wheelchair travelers must, by the way, be accompanied by someone who can push the chair around, since these days ships do not carry enough personnel to permit assigning a crewman specifically to you.

If you require any kind of special diet, you must let the line know in advance so they can plan and prepare it for you each day. A travel agent can make those arrangements for you too.

If you have special medication, take it with you. Do not, repeat, *do not* count on being able to fill your prescription at some port of call. For the most part you'll be visiting foreign countries ill-prepared to deal with filling your prescription. At best it will cost you time and money for long-distance calls to your doctor. At worse you won't get the prescription filled.

Avoid all those problems by being sure you have enough medication (even better, twice as much as you need), bottled and packed separately so that if you lose one you'll have a backup bottle. Naturally, we aren't talking aspirin here, just medication that you must take regularly.

Chapter XIII

SEA TALK: SOUNDING LIKE A SAILOR

1. Ahoy, Buoy, Get that Hand Off the Fantail
2. Ship Designations
3. Counting Stripes: Calling a Captain a Captain

GOODNESS KNOWS your mother said you sounded like one just before she washed your mouth out with soap, but that isn't exactly what we have in mind.

As you begin the first days of your seven years before the mast, you will hear people speaking in tongues, babbling on about "tendering"—no, they're not discussing an hour in the moonlight—or "heads," which have much to do with just the opposite. "All hands" is not one of those men your mother warned you about, and "abreast" is not what pops, er, instantly to mind.

If you hear some words that sound pretty risqué to you, it may just be some experienced swabbies talking sea talk. And it's nothing Mom would disapprove of!

Quite a separate language from the one the rest of us speak, nautical talk is comparatively easy to learn. Before long you'll discover that "port" is not only something you drink but somewhere you look.

To give you a clue to what everyone's talking about on board, we've compiled a list of the most common nautical terms, carefully excluding some of those that really will make you sound like a sailor.

You'll notice that throughout the book we haven't indulged in a great deal of sea talk, figuring that total immersion in companionways, bulkheads, and screws will come soon enough.

1. Ahoy, Buoy, Get that Hand Off the Fantail

abeam—at right angles to the keel, which runs from front to back down the center of the ship (see "keel"). Something may be said to be abeam of something else. Don't worry about this one; it's not very common anyway, and usually heard as a descriptive state about a ship or, sadly, about some bikini-clad lass as in "she's broad abeam."

aboard—on board, or on the ship.

about—most commonly used in the phrase "to come about," meaning to turn the ship around.

above board—decks located above the waterline. The expression "to be above board" about something stems from ship talk.

abreast—this is a reference to a ship pulling alongside another vessel or a dock.

aft—toward the rear, or more properly, the stern, of the ship.

aground—to run a ship up onto a sand bar where it becomes stuck until floated off by high tides, an extremely rare occurrence on cruise ships, so relax.

ahoy—a call from one captain or crewman to another to hail the vessel. On modern ships calls are made quite quietly on powerful radios so don't look forward to hearing the captain screaming across the bay.

alleyway—a narrow hallway, or more correctly, passageway, of a ship.

all hands—everyone working on a ship, most often heard as "all hands report to. . . ."

amidships—in the middle of the ship halfway between front and back, or if you're beginning to catch on, between bow and stern.

anchor ball—a black ball hoisted in the forward section of the ship to show that the vessel is anchored.

anchor off—an anchor, of course, is what is used to hold the ship in place in the ocean. To "anchor off" is to drop the anchor offshore but close in because the docks are filled with ships or the ship has too deep a draft to enter the harbor. If the ship anchors off, passengers get to shore on boats called tenders.

ashore—on shore. You "go ashore" when the ship pulls into port, but one would hope you are not still "ashore" when it leaves.

astern—toward the rear or stern of the ship, sometimes referring to something actually behind the ship or in its wake.

athwart—across the width of the ship.

ballast—weight that ships used to carry to keep on an even keel when empty, it also refers to any weight on board. Stones were often used in early sailing ships to keep them steady until cargo was taken on board.

bar—a sandbar, created by tidal conditions and the thing upon which you run aground.

barge—a ship with a flat bottom usually used as a cargo carrier.

beacon—a beam of light on shore that serves as a landmark and directional signal.

beam—the width of the ship at the widest point, usually right through the middle. Ships with wider beams are said to be broad of beam.

bearing—the way the ship is headed, a compass direction like northeast, southwest, etc., expressed in degrees.

below—on a deck lower than the main deck of the ship. To "go below" is to go to a lower deck, and sometimes refers to a crewman going off duty, as "I'm going below now."

bells—a now largely abandoned way of telling time, bells were once sounded at half-hour intervals with one bell at 4:30 a.m., two bells at 5 a.m., three bells at 5:30 a.m., and so on to eight bells at 8 a.m., when the count began again with a bell at 8:30 a.m., two bells at 9 a.m., etc., until 12:30 p.m., when the count began once again, ending with eight bells at 4 p.m. So the eight bells you may have heard mentioned was 8 a.m., noon, 4 p.m., 8 p.m., or midnight. It's really only six bells that matters anyway: that's cocktail time!

berth—bed, what you'll call the thing you sleep on in your cabin, if you're a nautical purist. It also refers to the "bed" the vessel sleeps in when it's in port, that is, the dock or place the vessel is docked.

bon voyage—a French term meaning "good voyage" or "good trip," pronounced "bawn voy-adge."

bow—the front or foremost part of the ship, pronounced to rhyme with cow.

bridge—where the captain and navigational officers control and operate the ship. It's located above the passenger areas of the ship and contains complex navigational equipment. Most ships offer daily or regularly scheduled visits to the bridge. Go, you'll love it.

bulkhead—walls inside the ship between cabins or public areas, or walls built to strengthen the ship; partitions. Walls of your cabin are not walls but bulkheads.

bunkers—where fuel is stored.

buoy—a warning float or a marker, usually pronounced "boo-eee" but sometimes boy.

cabin—if you can't figure this one out you're in trouble—it's your bedroom, also called a stateroom, although stateroom sometimes refers to accommodations larger than a cabin.

cable—heavy chains used to hold the ship's anchor.

cast off—to let go of the ship's lines in preparation for sailing.

charts—maps of the ocean showing depths, landmarks, sandbars.

class—years ago passengers traveled first class, cabin class, perhaps second, third, or tourist class on transoceanic voyages. Now almost all ships are one-class ships with the exception of the *Queen Elizabeth II,* which has two classes, first and "transatlantic."

colors—the national flag flown on the ship.

companionway—interior stairways connecting decks.

course—the route the ship takes. The course is plotted these days by computers but once was "reckoned" on the location of moon and stars by night, charts (or maps of the ocean) and landmarks by day.

crow's nest—once the tiny cage high on the mast where a crewman was stationed to look for land; now any lookout, including a bar or observation lounge, high on the ship.

davits—steel structures to which the ship's lifeboats are hooked and from which they and the ship's tenders are launched; pronounced "*da*-vits."

deck—each floor, or story, of the ship.

disembark, debark—to get off the ship, used interchangeably.

dock—a pier, wharf, or quay, a place to tie up the ship; also used as a verb, to dock, meaning to come into port.

draft—sometimes spelled draught, the amount of water a ship needs to sail without allowing the bottom of the ship to touch the ocean floor. It is figured from the lowest point of the ship underwater to the waterline. Ships with a "deep draft" cannot go into shallow ports without running aground, but ships with a "shallow draft" can negotiate shallow-water areas to visit some less frequented ports.

drill—any safety test or instruction session ordered by the captain. You will participate in a lifeboat drill as soon as you leave port; crewmen participate in their own fire drills, announced well ahead of time.

embark—to get on the ship, to board it.

fair wind—a tail wind, or wind blowing in the same direction as the ship is moving.

fantail—has nothing to do with feather dancers but refers instead to a part of the stern extending behind the stern post, an overhanging stern.

fathom—a measure used to determine water depth under the ship. One fathom is six feet. Depth is determined today by sophisticated sounding equipment.

flags—crewmen run up flags as signals to other ships if the ship is in distress or under certain other conditions, for instance, when a ship's pilot is on board. Flag codes are international and are recognized in every country in the world. On freighters flags may indicate what cargo is carried on board. Flags are not flown at sea except in emergencies. A flag of registry showing what country the ship is registered in appears at the stern of the ship. A ship's destination flag appears at the bow of the ship.

flag of convenience—refers to registration of a ship in a country simply because that country offers the vessel lower tax rates and other levies. Popular flags of convenience include Liberia and Panama.

fore, forward—referring to the front of the ship as opposed to the back or aft end.

free port—a port that is free from import taxes and hence can offer tax-free goods at a lower price. St. Thomas in the U.S. Virgin Islands is the most ballyhooed free port, but Freeport, Bahamas, Bermuda, and other islands also have tax breaks.

funnel—there is some debate about whether the smokestack at the top of the ship should be called a smokestack or a funnel. Either way, everyone will know what you mean.

galley—kitchen.

gangway—a bridge connecting the ship to the shore. After the ship docks, the crew will lower a gangway for you to walk ashore. When the ship leaves port the gangway is pulled back aboard. If you have not yet crossed the gangway and the ship's lines are being loosed, you had better go like gangbusters.

gross register tons—a size measurement by which ships are compared, although a somewhat controversial one. A gross register ton refers to 100 cubic feet of enclosed space on a ship.

hand—a crewman.

harbor master—the person in charge of harbor operations, ship dock assignments, etc.

hatchway—also known just as hatches, these are deck openings through which crewmen go to reach the "holds," which are places in which cargo and ship's supplies are stored.

head—toilet.

helm—the ship's steering equipment. To be "at the helm" is to be operating the ship, steering the course.

high seas—all the ocean beyond the territorial limits and waters not subject to the jurisdiction of any country.

hold—the ship's cargo area below decks. Steamer trunks used to be stored in the hold while passengers were on long transoceanic voyages.

hook—slang for the anchor. To drop the hook is to drop anchor.

house flag—the line's logo designating ownership of the ship; the ship's identification either on the funnel or on a flag.

hull—the outer structure of the ship, its "body."

Jacob's ladder—also simply called a ladder or accommodation ladder, and most often used by the pilot who comes aboard to advise the captain on port-departure maneuvers. It may also be used by passengers to board a tender.

Jones Act—this act, passed in 1886, prohibits foreign-registered ships from carrying passengers directly between U.S. ports, for instance between

New York and Miami, without a stop at a foreign port. That's also why you cannot get on the ship in Miami and get off, to stay off, in Puerto Rico, although you can do that in the Virgin Islands which is exempt from these regulations. U.S.–registered ships, however, are permitted to sail between American ports.

keel—the main structural member of a ship, running fore and aft along the bottom of the ship, the backbone of the ship to which all the crosswise parts are attached. Expressions like "keel over," meaning to turn bottom up or fall over, and "on an even keel," meaning to be stable or steady, stem from this word.

knot—the nautical equivalent of miles per hour. A knot is one nautical mile—6080.2 feet, about 1.15 land miles—per hour. A ship's speed is measured in knots, with most cruise ships capable of about 15 to 20 knots.

latitude—the distance north or south of the equator, expressed in degrees.

league—you've heard of *20,000 Leagues Under the Sea?* Well, multiply 20,000 times 3.45 nautical miles (that's how much a league is) and you'll find out how deep Jules Verne's 20,000 leagues was.

leeward—the sheltered side of an island or the direction toward which the wind is blowing. In nautical circles the word is pronounced "loo-erd," and is the opposite of windward.

let go—no, no, silly, not that. Lines, the ship's ropes, are "let go" as the ship prepares to sail.

lifeboats—small boats you will see rimming an open deck and used to carry passengers in an emergency. The location of your lifeboat station is posted in your cabin. You'll learn how to get there and what to do there at the lifeboat drill—mandatory attendance, no shirkers.

lines—massive ropes that are used to tie the ship up to cleats on shore.

log—a diary maintained by the captain and the ship's officers detailing the weather, ship's course, navigation details, and in the old days, some pretty interesting personal material.

longitude—the distance east or west measured by the angle that the meridian through a specified place makes with the Prime Meridian which runs through Greenwich, England. It's expressed in degrees, minutes, and seconds.

manifest—a list of the names of the ship's passengers, cargo, and crew.

master—used in reference as "the master," meaning the captain.

Mark Twain—a name taken by Mississippi River chronicler Samuel Clemens. It refers to a sounding or water measurement of two fathoms or 12 feet (see "fathoms").

moor—to hold a ship in place with cables at a pier or with an anchor. You do not "park" a boat, you moor it.

muster—a requested assembly of the passengers and/or crew. The phrase "to pass muster" stems from reviews of the troops or crew.

nautical mile—a nautical measurement of a mile, slightly longer than a land or statute mile (6080.2 feet as compared to a land mile of 5280 feet).

nautical timekeeping—at sea, as in the military, time is kept on a 24-hour basis beginning at 0001, which is 12:01 a.m., and moving along past 2 p.m. or 1400 hours, ending finally at midnight, 2400 hours.

navigable waters—water that is deep enough for the ship to pass through undamaged.

Old Man—slang meaning the captain. Like "skipper" it is less commonly heard on a cruise ship.

passageway—a hallway of the ship, usually a major thoroughfare through the vessel.

pilot—a specially trained and licensed captain who temporarily takes command of the ship to maneuver it into or out of harbor or in difficult waters. As you are sailing out of port, when the ship is safely underway, you may see the pilot climb down a Jacob's ladder and jump into a small craft called a pilot boat.

pitch—the forward-backward rise and fall of a ship in rough water, and the opposite of "roll," which refers to the sideward rolling motion of the ship. Roll is said to be more conducive to seasickness than pitch, a detail with which you will be little concerned if you are suffering from either pitch or roll or both.

port—the left side of the ship as you face forward, that is face the bow of the ship. You can remember which is port and which is starboard by remembering that both the word "port" and the word "left" have four letters.

quarters—crew living space.

quay—another word for dock or wharf. It's pronounced "key" and is an excellent word to use in the ship's Scrabble contest.

rail—railings running alongside the open decks of the ship to keep you from falling overboard and to provide you with something on which to lean as you gaze out to sea or into each other's eyes.

registry, country of registry—the country in which the ship's certificate of ownership is registered. The national flag of the ship's country of registry will fly from the stern of the vessel.

roll—a side-to-side motion of the ship in rough water, and the opposite of its forward-backward motion, called pitch.

running lights—colored lights required on all vessels, including small boats, at night so other ships can spot the craft and determine its size and course. Red lights appear on the port side of a vessel, green ones on the starboard side.

safety at sea laws—laws governing standards that must be met by ships embarking passengers in U.S. ports (see Chapter I).

screw—calm down, this is just another name for the ship's propeller.

scuppers—draining holes below the rails.

scuttle—a small opening or hatchway in the deck or side of the ship or valve in the bottom of a ship. Sailing ships were once scuttled by opening these valves, called sea cocks, or by putting holes in the bottom. Scuttle butt, referring to gossip, arose from scuttled butt, a cask of water around which people gathered and, of course, gossiped.

she—ships are called she, despite what feminists may think of the appellation. No one knows the derivation of this female reference, but theories relating to capriciousness, expense, and need for delicate handling are among the explanations you will hear. Our favorite is: ships are called "she" because her rigging is worth more than her hull. In more serious circles, it is believed to have stemmed from the grammatical gender of early French translations.

ship to shore—radio communication with land now frequently accomplished by using satellite telephone communications.

sister ships—ships built on the same design, or sometimes two ships owned and operated by the same line.

skipper—a slang word denoting the captain of the ship, although on cruise ships the captain is more often known as the master, or simply the captain.

sounding—measurements taken of water depth (see "fathoms").

stabilizers—retractable side pieces that extend into the water from the sides of the ship enabling it to sail more evenly in rough water.

starboard—the right side of the ship as you face the bow or forward end of the ship; the opposite of port.

stateroom—a bedroom or cabin, although sometimes used to mean accommodations grander than a cabin.

stern—the rear of the ship, the aft end.

stowaway—an unpaid passenger illegally on board.

swell—not as pleasant as it sounds. A swell is a big wave that rolls without breaking.

tender—nothing to do with romance, a tender is a launch used to ferry you ashore in ports at which the ship must anchor offshore. Usually quite a large boat, the tender has also spawned a verb form: to tender into or out of port.

under way—the ship that has "weighed anchor" and set sail is "under way."

wake—the track left by a vessel as it cuts through the water. Look for it at the stern of the boat, the white path behind the ship.

waterline—a line painted on the hull, or side, of the ship to indicate the level to which the water rises on the ship at various loads.

weigh anchor—to pull the anchor from the bottom and prepare to sail; also a command prior to sailing.

wharfinger—we know you're going to think we're making this up but we're not. Perhaps, however, somebody is putting us on. Either way, the term, which refers to the man in charge at a wharf, is alleged to have derived from early sailing days when the man in charge went out on the wharf and pointed his finger at the place an incoming vessel should dock, hence wharf-finger. Listen, do *you* know it's not true?

windward—on the side exposed to the wind, or in reference to the direction from which the wind is blowing. Waters are rougher on the windward side of land than they are on the leeward side.

the writer—no, it's not us, it's the purser's secretary.

yardarm—on old sailing vessels the yardarm was the tapering horizontal arm of a mast and was used to judge time passage by shadow and also to hang offenders as "Hang 'im from the yardarm, matey." When the sun is over the yardarm became a term for the time of the setting sun or . . . cocktail hour.

yaw—to steer wildly out of course in rough water, as in the ship "yawed."

2. Ship Designations

Just as people have Mr., Mrs., Ms., Master, or Mlle before their names, ships have titles too. Ships titles, however, are determined by the way the vessel is powered. Here is a list of ship prefaces:

H.M.S.	Her (or His) Majesty's Ship (British)
M.S.	Motor Ship
M.T.S.	Motor Turbine Ship
M.V.	Motor Vessel
T.S.S.	Turbine Steamship
S.S.	Steamship
U.S.S.	United States Ship

3. Counting Stripes: Calling a Captain a Captain

You will see some handsome, snappy-looking officers striding about the ship, so perhaps now is the time to discover who is who.

That gentleman with the most gold stripes or bars on his shoulder epaulet is the captain. Depending on the line, the captain may have one wide bar and three smaller ones or just four bars, plus a loop or diamond shape. He's in charge of everything, absolutely *everything,* but sorry, he cannot marry you anymore. He can, of course, be married *to* you—good luck!

Staff captains are the second in command and have four stripes on their epaulets. A chief officer has three bars, and a first officer, two bars.

Engineers in charge of the ship's engine room rank from chief with four stripes down through chief engineer junior with 3½ stripes, first engineer with three stripes, and second engineer with two. On many lines the engineer's epaulets also will have a propellor or something that looks like one.

A chief purser, as the word suggests, is in charge of the ship's purse, a kind of office manager overseeing money, information, safety deposit boxes, a good person to know. His or her insignia will be three bars, followed by 2½ for the first purser, two stripes for the second purser, and one stripe for junior purser. A leaf-like mark or a star shape may also appear on the epaulet of purser staff.

The chief radio officer will have three stripes, the first radio officer two. Each of those officers may have something suggesting radio waves on their epaulets.

The hotel manager for the ship is in charge of all the cabin services, and the food and beverage service as well. Hotel managers have four stripes. Working with them are food and beverage managers.

The chief of all the entertainment staff is the person known as the cruise director, responsible for all passenger entertainment on board and in ports of call. Cruise directors are the people you'll get to know best on the ship because you'll see the entertainment staff every day.

Electricians have three stripes for chief, 2½ for first, and two for second electrician, plus some electrical-looking wavy lines on their shoulder boards.

Your ship's doctor will have three or four stripes on the epaulet too.

Somewhere on board you will find a guide to officer identification. Ask the purser's staff where it is.

Chapter XIV

IS IT POSSIBLE A WEEK IS ONLY SEVEN DAYS?: HOME AGAIN

1. Packing Up
2. Customs
3. Getting Your Luggage and Getting Off

NO MATTER HOW LONG or how short the cruise, there comes that poignant moment you realize that when you wake in the morning it will be all over. Just as that first booming blast of the ship's great whistle thrilled you right to your toes, the final Farewell Banquet, sumptuous and fun that it was, was a sobering event.

Sure you're glad to be back home, but, oh, wasn't it wonderful when we went up on deck in the moonlight and watched the ship steaming through the water, its wake a gleaming diamond-tipped spray of foamy whiteness streaming out behind us? And remember the day we all hired that funny little taxi driver who kept calling you "boss" and saluting? And did you get Natalie and Dorothy's address? Wouldn't it be fun if we could stop to see them the next time we're near there?

Memories, already in the making even before the ship has pulled into port. Memories made in perhaps only a few days but made to last a lifetime.

Yes, a cruise *is* a wondrous experience, full of the wonder of nature and the wonder of man's ability to adapt to it and alter it—day after day of new foods, new friends, new experiences, new ideas.

There is something about the sea that is humbling, that can change you forever. Its vast, unending horizons put you in your place with crushing rapidity. Its ever-changing moods, frivolous as a coquette, are just as fascinating. You will return changed, unnoticeably perhaps but irrevocably.

Return, however, you must.

Let us deal with that bittersweet moment when you return once again to familiar places.

1. Packing Up

On your last night at sea, be it after 3 days or 30, you will dress casually for dinner on the premise that you have already packed your finest.

It would be a good idea at least to begin that packing on the final afternoon or evening aboard. In the wee hours of the morning your steward will pick up your luggage, which you'll leave outside your cabin door, and send it off to join everyone else's baggage at a central collection point. Crewmen will lug it off the ship when she docks.

Anything you haven't put outside your door for collection by the steward you'll have to carry off yourself. It is unlikely, if not downright out of the question, that you'll find anyone to help you. When the ship docks, cabin stewards are busy cleaning cabins for the next cruise so they can have some time off in port. Most other crewmen are working somewhere around the ship or are already off it, headed for a little well-earned relaxation.

When, ever the efficient soul, you put your suitcase outside the door for removal by the steward, remember to leave out the clothes you'll need to get off the ship in the morning! Silly as that may sound, tales are rife of organized, but not very bright, travelers racing about the ship in a towel, crying over packed—and now gone to the docks—luggage. You'll hear a couple of the more amusing stories from your cruise director at the debarkation talk. So keep out your toiletries kit and some clothes when you're packing up the night before arrival back in port.

If you discover, as you no doubt will, that you bought reams of stuff that won't fit in the suitcase, ask your cabin steward for help. These fellows can often roust out a carton and some string somewhere and you'll be in business.

Before you leave your cabin for the last time, look around carefully, under the beds and in the drawers. Items you have left behind will be kept for a month or so in the company's offices, but it's just another hassle to go pick them up or arrange for delivery. If you do find you've left something behind, however, write to the line.

In your cabin you'll find baggage tags and the necessary Customs declaration forms. If you don't find them, ask the cabin steward to bring you what you need.

Fill out the luggage tags and attach them to your baggage. Many ships color code your baggage, matching the colorful tags to colored stripes on the ground or colored signs. When you get off the ship you just locate your color area and look for your baggage in that section. Some use alphabetical designations.

If you've taken a hanging garment bag on board and don't find it piled up with the other luggage, don't panic. Crewmen often unsnap hanging bags and hang them from the bar of a trolley to help minimize wrinkling. Look around and see if there's one of those trolley-with-bar things set up somewhere in the luggage collection area.

If you have looked very carefully absolutely everywhere (including places it shouldn't be, like other color codes or letters) and still can't find your belongings, go back on board and explain the problem to the purser or to any visible crewman. Your belongings will turn up eventually and, in fact, will rarely be misplaced.

2. Customs

We've had a little fun with headlines in this book but we're being very serious at this point. Customs is not snicker material. In fact the very words "Customs officials" strike fear and dread in the hearts of the intrepid.

It need not be so, unless, of course, you're bringing back something you know the ladies and gentlemen of U.S. Customs Service will find disappointing at best, criminal at worst.

When you figure that many of these Customs officials have been rummaging through dirty laundry and poking into purses for years, it seems reasonable to assume that they know we all have a little larceny in our hearts. They really don't care much, we wouldn't think, about the $1.50 you spent over your quota, but they certainly do care if you're cheating the government out of hundreds of dollars of duty or bringing in some substances they'd much rather not see.

There is every indication, too, that by now they have a pretty good idea how to spot someone who's contemplating illegalities.

For most travelers, Customs clearance at the end of a cruise is marvelously simple, much easier than similar clearance at airports. It wouldn't hurt, however, to put your purchases on the top of your luggage or pack them separately. That way, if you are questioned by officials, you can point out what you bought without tearing up hours of packing. Keep your receipts too, if you feel there might be any question about the cost of your purchases.

In most cases you'll pick up your luggage, hand your declaration card to a Customs officer who will simply stack it with some others, and you'll go blithely off to your transportation. Sometimes there is a closer inspection of luggage, and a consequent delay, especially if you've visited a country known for the care and feeding of marijuana or cocaine fields (like Jamaica or Colombia) or a country famous for its precious gemstones (Columbia or Brazil).

Customs declarations must be filled out by every passenger, although couples can fill out one for both of them, and include any accompanying children in it too.

You can now make an oral declaration if you have not purchased more than $400 worth of items per person ($800 if you've visited the U.S. Virgin Islands), so there's no need to fill in the back of the form which suggests you should write down every straw basket or piñata you purchased.

Customs officers are most interested in expensive items like cameras, gemstones, expensive china or silver, and really don't care much about your simpler purchases unless they're concealing illegal substances or there are enough of those purchases for you to go into the import-export business.

On the matter of illegal substances: *don't.*

If you have purchased more than the $400 or $800 limit per person, you are required to declare in writing the amount of your purchases above the allotted maximum. Remember that *each* traveler gets that allotment, not just one of you, so you will declare only the amount that exceeds the total exemption.

Here are the basic exemptions on which you pay no duty: $400 worth of purchases per adult or child; a fifth of liquor per person over 21; any item made in the U.S. no matter where it is purchased; 100 cigars (but no Cuban ones); one carton of cigarettes per adult. If you are on a ship that has stopped in the U.S. Virgin Islands, your exemptions double to $800 per person, plus a gallon of liquor, five cartons of cigarettes, and 100 cigars for each person over 21.

Each day you are away, you can also send home duty free, as gifts, items valued at up to $50 ($100 in the U.S. Virgin Islands). A gift of that value can be sent by each person each day, but be sure to mark the package "unsolicited gift" and indicate the contents and value of the item on the outside of the package. Shops in the islands will know how to handle these gifts. Just remember to tell the kids they are absolutely *not* to open any packages until Christmas.

If you buy more than these allotted amounts, you pay 10% duty (5% from the U.S. Virgin Islands) on the excess above your exemption up to $1000, a higher percentage after that. Many people buy more than the allotted quota of liquor, finding it cheaper to buy in the islands even with the additional duties.

Other things you can bring in duty free are: original works of art, antiques at least 100 years old, any items made in U.S. territories like the U.S. Virgin Islands, American Samoa, or Guam.

In 1976 the United States put into effect a program called the Generalized System of Preferences (GSP) to help developing countries improve their lot through exports. Under that system (which is due to expire in 1985 but will likely be renewed) you may bring back duty-free products from more than 100 third-world nations. These products range from loose semiprecious stones to shell products, toys, binoculars, cameras, earthen tableware or stoneware, china figurines, wood or plastic furniture, furs, ivory, unset jade, music boxes, musical instruments, cultured or imitation pearls loose or temporarily strung without clasp, perfume, silver, electric shavers, ski equipment, unset stones except emeralds and diamonds, wood products.

If you're thinking about buying any of these in quantity, it would be wise to contact the U.S. Customs Service, 1301 Constitution Ave. NW, Washington, DC 20229 (tel. 202/566-8195). Ask for their booklets entitled "GSP & the Traveler" and "Customs Hints—Know Before You Go."

If you're thinking of buying ivory, skins, furs, or animal-related products, contact the U.S. Fish and Wildlife Service, Department of the Interior, C Street between 18 and 19th Streets NW, Washington, DC (tel. 202/343-1100).

If you're planning to stock up on Christmas presents and expensive purchases, it would be a good idea to do some comparison shopping at home before you leave on your cruise so you will know when a bargain really is a bargain.

If you are bringing any fruit, vegetables, plants, seeds, flowers, meats, or pets into the country, they must meet U.S. Department of Agriculture requirements for entry. You should contact the Department of Agriculture to find out what it takes to meet the requirements with any plants you are planning to bring back. Rules vary widely. If you can bear to pass up that stuff, *do*. You'll save yourself a lot of red tape.

Generally, Customs inspectors will just confiscate fruit and vegetable products, so don't bother bringing the remnants of your ship fruit basket off the ship. Those apples or oranges will cost you a lot more trouble and Customs inspections than they're worth.

Certain materials like Haitian goatskins and ivory and tortoise shell items have been banned at various times. Cruise directors may know what's legal to bring home these days, but one of the U.S. Customs Service booklets is the only really reliable guide.

Canadian Customs have been known to be particularly hard on

Canadians returning home from abroad. At last count, Canadians were permitted to bring home only $150 in goods purchased abroad, plus one liter of liquor for each person and one carton of cigarettes for each person over 16. For any amount over those quotas you are required to pay duty and taxes. If you are Canadian and planning to buy quite a lot of items on a trip, you should check details of duties and taxes with Customs officers to determine just what the duties, which can be as high as 25%, will be.

3. Getting Your Luggage and Getting Off

You would do well to attend the cruise director's little talk on the day or evening before the cruise ends. You will be briefed then on all the details of Customs clearance and baggage pickup, and given some good tips on car rental, bus transportation and transfers to airplanes.

Once again, get off the ship with only luggage you can easily carry yourself. You may have to walk some long corridors to get to the gangway, and from there it may be a bit of a distance to the luggage pickup area. There's no need to carry your baggage with you, so don't.

After the ship has docked and Customs inspectors have cleared the vessel, you will be permitted to debark. There will be announcements over the ship's public address system to guide you in your debarkation. You'll be asked to await the "all ashore" announcement in one of the ship's public rooms, and not to crowd the corridors. You would be wise to follow that advice. If you don't, you'll find yourself sitting on the floor with people stepping over you or standing up for perhaps an hour or more.

Figure that Customs clearance of a vessel will take at least an hour and more often two hours, and it might take you 15 minutes or so to pick up your luggage and go through Customs. Don't tell friends or relatives who are coming to pick you up to be at the ship the moment it docks. They'll just have to stand around and wait.

After you've turned in your Customs declaration card to the officer at the gate, you can hail a cab, find a bus or limousine service or your car, and head home. Some terminals have rental cars available right there. At others you'll need to call a rental-car company to pick you up or get to the company's office yourself. That information too will have been given to you by the cruise director at his debarkation talk.

Air/sea passenger arrangements and airport transfers also will be announced by the cruise director, so don't miss that talk.

Chapter XV

TAKING A SLOW BOAT: FREIGHTER TRAVEL

THE VERY FIRST THING you pack for a freighter trip is patience. You'll need it on these meandering trips that may not leave when they say they're going to leave, or go where they say they're going to go, or stop where they say they're going to stop, or get anywhere when they say they're going to get there.

That's no critical remark, just the facts. These are, after all, cargo ships first and passenger carriers second. When the captain has a chance to pick up some cargo, it gets picked up whether or not that means an extra two days in port or a stop at some unscheduled dock.

That devil-may-care capriciousness is just what appeals to many a starry-eyed freighter bum intent on steaming across the ocean for 25 or 50 or even 75 days. To go on one of these journeys you must have unlimited vacation time and be in no hurry to meet any schedules. That, of course, is the beauty of it all.

You get on the ship and never know just where you might end up next, although there will certainly be at least a rough itinerary.

If you have always wondered, sometimes longingly, what it must be like to sail a tramp steamer to veiled Casablanca or rough-and-ready Marseille or intrigue-fancying Venice, a freighter may be your kind of paradise.

Sadly, the era of the true tramp steamer is gone. True tramps just kind of hung around the oceans until they found cargo to transfer to another port. These days that kind of hanging around is too expensive, so the tramps are gone.

Nor will you find tramp-steamer conditions in this day and age. Most of these ships are small in passenger-carrying terms, but most offer excellent, if not downright luxurious quarters, both in public areas and in cabins.

Sadly, we haven't had the time to sail a freighter yet, but the dream of doing so lingers. We have read numerous reports and talked to several people who have sailed the freighters of the world to come up with some general information for you on what to expect and where to find out more about this kind of cruise travel.

We've read accounts, for instance, of freighter cabins that were, as one writer put it, "embarrassingly spacious—by no means can I tell friends that I roughed it across the Atlantic." Included in that cabin were two wood-framed beds, a six-foot couch, two lounge chairs, a coffee table, a large bureau, spacious closets, a sink and medicine cabinet, and an ocean view!

Cabin and dining room service is good and may even border on elegant, although the food is likely to be simple basic fare, nutritious and appealing but no nouvelle cuisine.

People say getting to know the officers and crew well is one of the most enjoyable parts of a freighter journey. Quite believable: just hearing about their unusual careers should fill many days of conversations.

And you won't find dancing girls and deck tennis, crafts classes or hula competitions aboard a freighter either, unless one of the other passengers becomes a teacher! On these vessels you are left pretty much to your own devices so you end up in marathon bridge or Scrabble games, trivia competitions, reading books, or just lying in the sun watching the ocean roll by.

Most freighters cannot carry more than 12 passengers plus officers and crew, so don't expect to find lots of other passengers aboard. Some freighters, Delta Line, for instance, carry up to as many as 100, but that's the exception rather than the rule.

We're going to tell you a little bit about Delta Lines, but don't get your hopes up: the company announced recently that it would cease its passenger operations at the completion of the 1984 cruise schedule. No more has been said about the cessation of passenger operations, however, and rumor has it that the company may rescind that decision. So who knows? We'll tell you about the line anyway.

Delta Line is among the best known of passenger-carrying cargo ships, but it's also the least like a true freighter operation. Delta operates on a predictable schedule with its three cargo craft, the *Santa Magdalena, Santa Mercedes,* and the *Santa Maria.* One of these liners steams out of Vancouver every three weeks headed for Tacoma, San Francisco, and Los Angeles, then on to South America. Each stops from 8 to 30 hours in port, calling regularly on Rio de Janeiro and Buenos Aires, perhaps at Belem at the mouth of the Amazon or in the Galapagos. Schedules and ports are subject to change without notice.

So organized are these ships that they offer shore excursions, which is indeed rare for a freighter. You can even elect to take an overnight trip to Iguassu Falls or Machú Picchú, then rejoin the ship at another port. Trips are usually 54 days long from Los Angeles, longer from ports farther north on the West Coast.

Cabins vary in size but are carpeted and adequately furnished. All cabins for two are outside quarters with large windows. Facilities aboard include a sports and sunbathing deck, heated swimming pool, putting green, darts, table tennis, and shuffleboard. There are some scheduled activities each day. Entertainers are on board, and there's a doctor too.

Fares aboard the vessels range from $2500 for a 28-day voyage from Philadelphia to Charleston, Miami, Caracas, Puerto Cabello, Balboa, Buenaventura, and Guayaquil, to $4225 for a 60-day voyage to African Ports from New Orleans or Houston, to $10,110 for a 63-day cruise from the West Coast to South America.

Other top names in freighter travel and information on how to reach them include:

Moore McCormack Lines (to South America or Africa from New York), Passenger Dept., 2 Broadway, New York, NY 10004 (tel. 212/09-8833).

Delta Lines (to the Caribbean, South America, and Africa from New York, New Orleans, Houston, Vancouver, Tacoma, San Francisco, and Los Angeles). Reservations for South America Service: One World Trade Center, Suite 3647, New York, NY 10048 (tel. 212/432-4700); Reservations for West African Service: International Trade Mart, P.O. Box 50250, New Orleans, LA 70150 (tel. 504/595-3355).

Polish Ocean Lines (from New York, Wilmington, and Baltimore to Europe), c/o McLean Kennedy Ltd., 410 St. Nicolas, Montréal, PQ H2Y 2P5 Canada (tel. 514/849-6111).

Prudential Lines (from New York to the Mediterranean), One World Trade Center, Suite 3701, New York, NY 10048 (tel. toll free 800/221-4118, or 212/524-8217).

Lykes Brothers (from Galveston, Houston, Pacific coastal cities, and New Orleans to Africa, the Mediterranean, and the Orient/Pacific), 300 Poydras St., New Orleans, LA 70130 (tel. 504/523-6611).

American President Lines (from Oakland to the Orient/Pacific or Southeast Asia), 1950 Franklin St., Oakland, CA 94612 (tel. 415/271-8148).

Ivaran Lines (from Baltimore or ports south to South America), c/o U.S. Navigation, One Edgewater Plaza, State Island, NY 10305 (tel. 212/442-8989).

Most passenger-carrying freighter operations carry no more than 12 passengers. If they take more passengers than that, the line must provide a doctor, more staff members, and additional lifesaving gear, so they solve the problem in the simplest of ways: they limit the passengers to 12.

That means, of course, that you'll probably need to book a freighter trip early to be sure you're included on this small list.

To find out what ship is going where, you can become a member of a freighter travel club or subscribe to one of several publications that outline freighter schedules. Among the freighter travel clubs in operation are **Freighter Travel Club of America**, P.O. Box 12693, Salem, OR 97309, or **Trav-L-Tips Freighter Travel Assn.**, 163-09 Depot Rd., Flushing, NY 11358.

Freighter Travel Club provides you with a monthly newsletter, *Freighter Travel News*, which contains accounts of freighter experiences, a few ads, and news about freighter travel.

Trav-L-Tips publishes a 32-page illustrated account of freighter and budget travel written by members who have been on freighter trips, and a supplementary *Budget Travel News* publication plus booking services. Price of membership is $25 a year, with occasional discount offers of $15 annual membership.

You can also write for a copy of a publication published annually each October that lists scheduled freighter tips. It's called *Ford's Freighter Travel Guide*, and you can get one for $6.95 by writing to the guide at P.O. Box 505, 22151 Clarendon St., Woodland Hills, CA 91365 (tel. 213/347-1677).

Official Airlines Guides also publishes a *World Wide Cruise and Shipline Guide*, published six times a year at a cost of $59. You can reach the company at 2000 Clearwater Dr., Oak Brook, IL 60521 (tel. toll free 800/323-3537, 800/942-1888 in Illinois).

Dress on freighters is much more casual than on scheduled cruise vessels. You will need sport and informal clothes with perhaps a few more elaborate outfits for port evenings.

Take lots of books, puzzles, crocheting, or whatever kind of amusements you prefer, for there will be few aboard. You may also have to bring your own liquor aboard some ships that do not provide it.

Bone up on ports before you go because there won't be any cruise director to help you find out where to go and what to see.

Don't wonder if you'll be invited to dine with the captain: you'll see him every night at dinner because you'll be eating with all the crew, usually early—about 8 a.m. for breakfast, noon for lunch, and 5 or 6 p.m. for dinner.

You'll have plenty of chances to learn foreign languages, so take advantage of your time with the crew to get them to teach you whatever language or, more likely, languages they speak.

Throw away your watch and calendar the first day aboard.

Tip about 5% of your cruise price distributed equally to your stateroom and dining room steward or stewardess on the last day of your trip, weekly on long trips.

Make sure all extra charges are clearly understood when you buy your ticket. There is usually no extra charge if a ship spends extra days in port or at sea.

Ask before you buy your ticket for a list of definite stopover ports and tentative dockings. Container ships spend less time in ports, so if you want to travel on land a bit, noncontainerized ships are a better idea.

Make sure you've gotten the definitive word on departure time from an officer of the ship *before* you go on a shore exploration trip. Then be back on time.

Pack a washable wardrobe that can be dunked in a sink and washed by hand. Some ships have washing machines, but don't count on it.

On freighter cruises you can expect to pay costs per day that range from just $18 to a high of about $60! That's less than half the per diem cost of a scheduled cruise, but as we've pointed out, there are plenty of differences.

The main one, once again, is the amount of time you can expect to travel: from a minimum of about 14 days to perhaps 150 or more. A trip from New York to India and return, for instance, lasts 90 days and costs $42 a day per person. Another trip departing from Tampa takes you to Holland and back in 30 days for about $29 a day. An around-the-world cruise from Los Angeles spends 132 days at sea for a cost of $35 per person per day!

Don't tell *us* you aren't tempted.

Chapter XVI

WHAT'S GOING WHERE: SHIP SCHEDULES

1. Caribbean/Bahamas
2. Alaska
3. Bermuda
4. Northeastern U.S. / Canada / Chesapeake Bay / Inland Waterways
5. Hawaii
6. Mexico
7. Transatlantic / Panama Canal / Pacific Ocean / Orient

FIRST, LET IT BE remembered that we are talking about floating ships here, not stationary hotels. These capricious floating resorts move, so all it takes for a cruise line to change its image, its market, and its appeal is to pull up anchor and move its ship or ships to another cruising ground.

As competition gets meaner and meaner in this growing part of the travel industry, you'll see ships changing their schedules and their ports of call more frequently. That's already happening.

We mention all this so you don't get angry at us when you find a ship you want to sail and then discover sailing plans have changed. We're working with the most up-to-date information available straight from the cruise lines themselves but no guarantees.

Many ships maintain a steady winter schedule in, for instance, San Juan to the Caribbean, moving in summer to Alaska. To get from San Juan to Alaska the ship makes what is called a "positioning cruise." Various segments of that cruise, say, San Juan to Acapulco or Los Angeles, Los Angeles to Vancouver, or San Francisco to Vancouver may be sold. The same holds true in reverse when the ship moves back to its winter schedule. We have referred to those cruises in listing. Lines or a travel agent will be able to supply you with the dates and details of positioning cruises.

To be sure exactly what's happening to "your" ship, check with the line or with a travel agent.

Okay, let's see what's going where.

1. Caribbean/Bahamas

FROM MIAMI: The following ships sail from Miami:

Carnival Cruise Lines

Carnivale: Every Friday, three-day cruises to Nassau; every Monday, four-day cruises to Freeport and Nassau.

Festivale: Every Saturday, year round, seven-day cruises to Nassau, San Juan, St. Thomas.

Mardi Gras: Year-round, Miami to Cozumél, Grand Cayman, Ocho Rios.

Chandris Cruise Lines

Britanis: Saturdays, December to June, two-day cruises to Nassau; Sundays, five-day cruises to Cancún, Cozumél, Key West.

Commodore Cruise Lines

Bohème: Saturdays, year-round, seven-day cruises to St. Petersburg, Port Antonio, Grand Cayman, Cozumél.

Caribe I: Saturdays, year-round, seven-day cruises to St. Thomas, San Juan, Puerto Plata.

Eastern Cruise Lines

Emerald Seas: Fridays, year round, on three-day cruises to Nassau and Bahamian Out Island; Mondays, year round, on four-day cruises to Freeport, Nassau, and Bahamian Out Island.

Norwegian Caribbean Lines

Norway: Saturdays, year round, to St. Thomas, Nassau, and Bahamian Out Island.

Skyward: Sundays, year-round, on seven-day cruises to Cancún, Cozumél, Key West, Bahamian Out Island.

Southward: Sundays, year round, on seven-day cruises to Puerto Plata, St. Thomas, San Juan, and Nassau.

Starward: Saturdays, year round, on seven-day cruises to Bahamian Out Island, Ocho Rios, Grand Cayman, Cozumél.

Sunward II: Fridays, year round, on three-day cruises to Nassau and Bahamian Out Island; Mondays, year round, on four-day cruises to Nassau, Bahamian Out Island, and Freeport.

Paquet Cruise Lines

Rhapsody: Sundays, in winter, on seven-day cruises to Ocho Rios, Grand Cayman, Playa del Carmen, Cozumél; May, transcanal cruise to Vancouver; summer in Alaska.

Dolphin: Mondays, year round, on four-day cruises to Nassau and Freeport; Fridays, year round, on three-day cruises to Nassau.

Royal Caribbean Cruise Lines

Nordic Prince: Year-round eight-day cruises to Nassau, San Juan, St. Thomas; or ten-day cruises to St. Thomas, Antigua, Barbados, Martinique, St. Croix.

Song of America: Sundays, year round, on seven-day cruises to Nassau, San Juan, St. Thomas.

Song of Norway: Saturdays, year round, on seven-day cruises to Grand Cayman, Montego Bay, and Cozumél.

Sun Viking: Saturdays, year round, on 7- or 14-day cruises to Ocho Rios, Curaçao, Caracas, Barbados; returning (seven days) from Barbados to Martinique, St. Maarten, San Juan, St. Thomas.

Scandinavian World Cruises

Scandinavian Sun: Daily cruises to Freeport.

FROM MONTEGO BAY: The following ship sails from Montego Bay, Jamaica:

American Canadian Lines

Caribbean Prince: From early January through mid-April, a 12-day circle-Jamaica cruise to Orange Bay, Savannah La Mar, Black River, Carlyle Bay, Port Royal, Kingston Market, Port Morant, Port Antonio, Port Maria, Ocho Rios, Discovery Bay, and back to Montego; positioning cruises at beginning and end of cruising season connect to Palm Beach and through Inland Waterway to Warren, R.I.

FROM NASSAU: The following ship sails from Nassau, Bahamas:

American Canadian Lines

New Shoreham II: Alternate Fridays, from late November to May, on 12-day cruises to Spanish Wells, South Palmetto Point, the Bluffs on Eleuthera, Governor's Harbour, Cape Eleuthera, Little Major's Spot, Exuma Sound, Sampson's Cay, Staniel Cay, Hall's Pond Cay, Highbourne Cay; first and last cruises of the season visit Spanish Wells, Lanyard Cay, Little Harbour, Hopetown, Green Turtle Cay, Treasure Cay, Man-O-War Cay, Marsh Harbour, Walker's Cay, and Freeport.

FROM NEW YORK: The following ships sail from New York:

Cunard Lines

Queen Elizabeth II: In mid-April and mid-November, on a ten-day cruise to San Juan, St. Thomas, St. Kitts, St. Maarten, Boston; in late June and late October, a three-day cruise to nowhere; late September, a five-day cruise to Bermuda; late November through early January, 13- and 14-day cruises to Port Everglades, Freeport, St. Thomas, Martinique, Barbados, St. Vincent, Caracas, Curaçao, Port Everglades, and via Norfolk to Port-au-Prince, Kingston, Curaçao, La Guaira, St. Thomas.

Home Lines

Oceanic: Saturdays to Bermuda and Nassau; one ten-day cruise in mid-April to Port Everglades, San Juan, St. Thomas, St. Maarten.

FROM PHILADELPHIA: The following ship sails from Philadelphia:

Cunard Lines

Queen Elizabeth II: In mid-May to Bermuda, St. Thomas, St. Maarten.

FROM PORT CANAVERAL: The following ships sail from Port Canaveral:

Premier Cruise Lines

Royale: Fridays, year round, on three-night cruises to Nassau and Andros Island; on Mondays, year round, on four-night cruises to Nassau and Andros Island.

Scandinavian World Cruises

Scandinavian Sea: Daily cruises to nowhere; occasionally two-day weekend cruises to Freeport.

FROM PORT EVERGLADES: The following ships sail from Port Everglades:

Home Lines

Atlantic: In February, 16-day cruises to Aruba, Cartagena, Cristóbal, Panama Canal, Balboa, Acapulco, Manzanillo, Puerto Vallarta, Cabo San Lucas, Los Angeles, and return; from October through March, to a number of Caribbean islands including San Juan, St. Thomas, St. Kitts, Nevis, St. Maarten; summer, New York to Bermuda.

Oceanic: Saturdays, January through April, on seven-day cruises to San Juan, St. Thomas, St. Maarten.

Royal Viking Lines

Royal Viking Sky: Four seven-day voyages in December and March to Puerto Plata, San Juan, St. Thomas, and Nassau; in mid-December, a 21-day trip to San Juan, St. Thomas, Martinique, St. Vincent, Barbados, Curaçao, Colombia, Panama Canal, Acapulco, Zihuatanejo, Puerto Vallarta; in March, a 17- or 22-day trip from Rio de Janeiro to Salvador, Recife, Fortaleza, St. Vincent, Barbados, Antigua, St. Thomas, Port Everglades.

Sitmar Cruises

Fairwind: Year round, 10- or 11-day cruises to St. Thomas, Antigua, Barbados, Martinique, St. Croix on 10-day itineraries; Grand Cayman, Montego Bay, Panama Canal (Gatun Lake only), San Blas Islands, Cartagena, and Nassau on some 11-day cruises, and Curaçao, Caracas, Martinique, St. Thomas, St. John, and Nassau on others.

Sun Lines

Stella Solaris: Mid-December to mid-March, cruises of various lengths from 10 to 34 days through the Caribbean islands; several voyages visit Caribbean islands, then make a double passage through the Panama Canal, with return stops at Montego Bay, Grand Cayman, Cozumél; 34-day cruise visits St. Thomas, Martinique, Barbados, Devil's Island, Belem, Salvador, Rio de Janeiro, Salvador, Recife, Fortaleza, Tobago, Fort-de-France, St. Thomas, and is available as a 17-day cruise; returns in summer to Mediterranean Sea cruising following transatlantic voyage.

FROM SAN JUAN: The following ships sail from San Juan:

Chandris Cruise Lines

Victoria: Mondays, year round, on seven-day cruises to St. Thomas, Martinique, St. Vincent, Caracas, Aruba; or to St. Maarten, Martinique, Barbados, Antigua, St. Thomas.

Costa Cruise Lines

Carla C: Saturdays, year round, on seven-day cruises to Curaçao, Caracas, St. Vincent, Guadeloupe, St. Thomas.

Daphne: Saturdays, from approximately December through April, on seven-day cruises to St. Maarten, Martinique, Barbados, St. Lucia, Antigua, Virgin Islands.

Cunard Lines

Cunard Countess: Saturdays, year round, on seven-day cruises to Tortola, St. Kitts, Nevis, Guadeloupe, St. Lucia, St. Maarten, St. Thomas, alternating weekly with seven-day cruises to La Guaira, St. Vincent, Barbados, Fort-de-France, St. Thomas.

Paquet Cruise Lines

Mermoz: From about mid-December to April, on ten-day cruises to St. Croix, Martinique, Trinidad, St. Lucia, Îles des Saintes, Antigua, St. John; and on 11-day cruises to St. Barthélemy, Martinique, Curaçao, Caracas, Barbados, Îles des Saintes, St. Thomas; in May, transatlantic to Mediterranean and summer cruising in Mediterranean.

P & O/Princess Cruise Lines

Sun Princess: Alternating Saturdays, October to mid-May, on seven-day cruises to Barbados, Grenadines, Martinique, St. Maarten, St. Thomas; or to Curaçao, Caracas, Grenadines, Martinique, St. Thomas; followed by transcanal cruise to Los Angeles; summers in Alaska.

Sun Lines

Stella Oceanis: Fridays, January through March, to St. Maarten, Dominica, St. Lucia, Barbados, Tobago, cruising Orinoco River, Ciudada Guayana, Bequia, St. Vincent, Martinique, Antigua, St. Kitts, St. Thomas; returning in summer to Mediterranean cruises.

FROM ST. CROIX: The following ship sails from St. Croix:

Sun Goddess Cruises

Sun Goddess I: Saturdays, October to May, on seven-day cruises to various Caribbean ports; followed by transatlantic voyage and summer in the Mediterranean Sea.

FROM ST. THOMAS: The following ship sails from St. Thomas:

Clipper Cruise Line

Newport Clipper: Sundays, November through May, on seven-day cruises to Tortola, Virgin Gorda, Jost Van Dyke, St. John.

FROM TAMPA/ST. PETERSBURG: The following ships sail from Tampa:

Bahama Cruise Line

Veracruz: Saturdays, approximately October to June on seven-day cruises to Playa del Carmen, Cozumél, Key West; summers in northeast.

Commodore Cruise Lines

Bohème: Saturdays, year-round, seven-day cruises St. Petersburg to Port Antonio, Grand Cayman, Cozumél.

Holland America Lines

Nieuw Amsterdam: Saturdays, mid-October through early May, on seven-day cruises to Playa del Carmen, Cozumél, Montego Bay, and Grand Cayman, except a 14-day cruise in late December to Montego Bay, Bonaire, Curaçao, San Blas Islands, Panama Canal, Cristobal, San Andres Island, Grand Cayman.

2. Alaska

FROM SAN FRANCISCO: The following ships sail from San Francisco:

Cunard/Norwegian American Cruises

Sagafjord: June through mid-August, 14-day cruises (final cruise is from Los Angeles) to Victoria, Alert Bay, Prince Rupert, Endicott Arm Fjord, Juneau, Columbia Glacier, Whittier, Yakutat Bay / Hubbard Glacier, Sitka, Vancouver.

Princess Cruises

Royal Princess: June through mid-September on 10-day cruises to Prince Rupert, Juneau, Skagway, Glacier Bay, Sitka, and Victoria.

Royal Viking Lines

Royal Viking Star: June through early September, 12-day cruises to Vancouver, Juneau, Skagway, Glacier Bay, Sitka, Victoria, occasional stop in Seattle.

Sitmar Cruises

Fairsky: June to September, 14-day cruises to Victoria, Prince Rupert, Juneau, Malaspina Glacier, Seward, Valdez, Columbia Glacier, Vancouver, with some cruises featuring Alert Bay, Lynn Canal, Haines, Skagway, La Perouse Glacier, Sitka, Astoria.

FROM VANCOUVER: The following ship sails from Vancouver:

P & O/Princess Cruises

Island Princess: Saturdays from June through mid-September to Prince Rupert, Juneau, Skagway, Glacier Bay, and Sitka.

FROM SEATTLE: The following ships sail from Seattle:

Exploration Cruise Lines

Pacific Northwest Explorer: In early May, an 11-day cruise to La Conner, Vancouver, Alert Bay, Ketchikan, Misty Fjord, Wrangell, Sitka, Tracy Arm, Juneau, Skagway, Haines, Glacier Bay, Petersburg, Ketchikan; cruising remainder of summer in same areas with departures on three-, four-, and seven-day trips from Juneau or Ketchikan.

Majestic Alaska Explorer: In early May, an 11-day cruise to Vancouver, Alert Bay, Ketchikan, Misty Fjord, Wrangell, Sitka, Tracy Arm, Juneau, Skagway, Haines, Glacier Bay, Petersburg, cruising remainder of summer in same areas with departures on three-, four-, seven-, or ten-day trips from Juneau or Ketchikan.

Great Rivers Explorer: In mid-June, an 11-day cruise to Vancouver, Alert Bay, Ketchikan, Misty Fjord, Wrangell, Sitka, Tracy Arm, Juneau, Skagway, Haines, Glacier Bay, Petersburg, Ketchikan; cruising remainder of summer in same areas with departures on three-, four-, seven-, or ten-day trips from Juneau or Ketchikan.

FROM VANCOUVER: The following ships sail from Vancouver:

Costa Cruises

Daphne: Fridays, approximately May through September, on seven-day cruises to Wrangell, Endicott Arm Fjord, Juneau, Skagway, Davidson and Rainbow Glaciers, Ketchikan.

Cunard Lines

Cunard Princess: Alternate Saturdays, June through mid-September, on 7- or 14-day cruises to Whittier, and return via Alert Bay, Ketchikan, Tracy Arm, Juneau, Skagway, Yakutat Bay/Hubbard Glacier, Prince William Sound, Columbia Glacier, College Fjord.

Cunard/Norwegian American Cruises

Nieuw Amsterdam: Tuesdays, mid-June through mid-September, on seven-day cruises to Ketchikan, Juneau, Glacier Bay, and Sitka.

Noordam: Saturdays, early June through mid-September, on seven-day cruises to Ketchikan, Juneau, Glacier Bay, Sitka.

Rotterdam: Thursdays, mid-June through early September, on seven-day cruises to Ketchikan, Juneau, Glacier Bay, Sitka.

Paquet Cruise Lines

Rhapsody: Thursdays, June through mid-September, on seven-day cruises to Juneau, Skagway, Lynn Canal, Glacier Bay, Ketchikan.

P & O/Princess Cruise Lines

Sun Princess: Wednesdays, June through mid-September, on seven-day cruises to Juneau, Skagway, Glacier Bay, Ketchikan, Misty Fjord.

Island Princess: Saturdays, June to September, on seven-day cruises to Juneau, Skagway, Glacier Bay, and Sitka.

Sundance Cruises

Sundancer: Fridays, mid-June through late September, on seven-day cruises to Juneau, Haines or Skagway, Tracy Arm, Ketchikan, Misty Fjord.

World Explorer Cruises

Universe: Sundays, July through early September, on 14-day cruises to Prince Rupert, Sitka, Glacier Bay, Skagway, Yakutat, Whittier, Columbia Glacier, Valdez, Juneau, Ketchikan.

3. Bermuda

FROM NEW YORK: The following ships sail from New York:

Bahama Lines

Bermuda Star: Saturdays, from June to October on seven-day cruises to St. George's and Hamilton.

Chandris

Britanis: Mondays from June to October on five-day cruises to Bermuda; Fridays on two-day cruises from New York and other East Coast cities to nowhere.

Home Lines

Atlantic: Saturdays from mid-April through mid-October on seven-day cruises to Bermuda.

Oceanic: Saturdays from mid-April through mid-November on seven-day cruises to Nassau and Bermuda.

4. Northeastern U.S./Canada/Chesapeake Bay/Inland Waterways

FROM BALTIMORE: The following ships sail from Baltimore:

American Cruise Lines

Independence: Saturdays, early May through June and early September through October, on seven-day cruises to Oxford, Crisfield, Yorktown, Cambridge, St. Michaels.

Savannah: Mid-April through mid-June and in October, on seven-day Chesapeake Bay cruises to Oxford, Crisfield, Yorktown, Cambridge, St. Michaels; with mid-April 14-day cruise including Charleston, Beaufort, Hilton Head, Savannah; return from Savannah on similar itinerary.

America: May to July, seven-day Chesapeake Bay cruises to Oxford, Crisfield, Yorktown, Cambridge, St. Michaels; a 14-day cruise in late April replaces some stops with Coinjock, Belhaven, Morehead City, Wrightsville Beach, Bucksport, Charleston, Beaufort, Hilton Head Island, Savannah.

Clipper Cruise Line

Newport Clipper: Mid-May to mid-June and late September to November, seven-day Chesapeake Bay cruises to Yorktown, Crisfield, Oxford, St. Michaels, Annapolis, with some itinerary alternations to include Chesapeake City, New York, Newport, Boston; a 14-day cruise in mid-October to Annapolis, Yorktown, Great Bridge, Belhaven, Morehead City, Wrightsville Beach, Bucksport, Charleston, Beaufort, Hilton Head Island, ending in Savannah.

FROM BOSTON: The following ship sails from Boston:

Clipper Cruise Line

Newport Clipper: Mid-June through late September, on seven-day New England cruises to Cape Cod Canal, Plymouth, Nantucket Island, Martha's Vineyard, Newport, New Bedford.

FROM FORT MYERS: The following ship sails from Fort Myers:

American Cruise Lines

America: November through March, on ten-day cruises to St. Lucie, Lake Okeechobee, Vero Beach, Port Canaveral, St. Augustine, Fernandina Beach, St. Simons, Hilton Head Island, to Savannah.

FROM HADDAM, CONNECTICUT: The following ships sail from Haddam:

American Cruise Lines

Savannah: Saturdays, mid-June through September, on seven-day cruises to Block Island, Nantucket, Martha's Vineyard, Newport; in

October, foliage cruises to Port Jefferson, Hudson River, West Point, New York, Oxford, St. Michaels, to Baltimore.

America: Saturdays, July through mid-October, on seven-day cruises to Block Island, Nantucket, Martha's Vineyard, Newport; in October, foliage cruises to Port Jefferson, Hudson River, West Point, New York, Oxford, St. Michaels, Baltimore.

American Eagle: Mid-June to mid-July and mid-August through late October, on seven-day cruises to Block Island, Nantucket, Martha's Vineyard, Newport, and on Hudson River foliage cruises.

FROM NEW ORLEANS: The following ships sail from New Orleans:

American Cruise Lines

Independence: Saturdays, mid-March to June, on seven-day cruises to Baton Rouge, Vicksburg, Natchez.

Savannah: Mid-December to mid-April, on seven-day Mississippi River cruises to Baton Rouge, Vicksburg, Natchez, or coastal cruises to Gulfport, Biloxi, Mobile, and Pensacola.

Delta Queen Steamboat Co.

Delta Queen: Year-round trips upriver from New Orleans: December through early May, on four- to seven-day cruises to Houmas House, Baton Rouge, Natchez, St. Francisville; May through August, on longer voyages farther upriver to Vicksburg, Memphis, Kentucky Lake, Evansville, Louisville, Madison, Cincinnati, Huntington, Marietta, Cincinnati, Wheeling, and Pittsburgh.

Mississippi Queen: Year-round cruises of varying lengths from 4 to 14 nights on routes similar to *Delta Queen.*

FROM NEW YORK: The following ships sail from New York:

Bahama Cruise Line

Veracruz: Saturdays, on seven-day cruises to Québec City, Saguenay Fjord, Halifax, Fall River through Cape Cod Canal, with occasional other ports including New Bedford, Sydney, Saguenay Fjord, Bonaventure Island, ending in Montréal, with bus return to New York; or vice versa, joining cruise by bus to Montréal.

Cunard Lines

Queen Elizabeth II: Mid-August, an eight-day cruise to Québec, Ingonish, Sydney.

Royal Viking Lines

Royal Viking Sea: August and September, two 14-day cruises to Nantucket, Charlottetown, Saguenay River, Montréal, Québec City, Perce Strait, Bar Harbor, Boston, Newport.

FROM PORTLAND, OREGON: The following ships sail from Portland:

Exploration Cruise Lines

Great Rivers Explorer: Late May through mid-June and late September through mid-October, six-night cruises to Columbia River, Astoria, Bonneville Dam, The Dalles, John Day Dam, McNary Dam, Snake River, Ice Harbor Dam, Lower Monumental Dam, Little Goose Dam, Lower Granite Dam, Lewiston, Sacajawea State Park, Kennewick, cruising Multnomah Falls.

Pacific Northwest Explorer: Mid-June to October, six-day cruises on same itinerary as *Great Rivers Explorer.*

FROM ROCKLAND, MAINE: The following ships sail from Rockland:

American Cruise Lines

Independence: Mid-July to early September, on seven-day cruises to Boothbay, Wiscasset, Bath, Bar Harbor.

American Eagle: Mid-July to mid-August, on seven-day cruises to Bar Harbor, Boothbay Harbor, Bath, Wiscasset.

FROM SAN FRANCISCO: The following ship sails from San Francisco:

Exploration Cruise Lines

Pacific Northwest Explorer: April through mid-June and October to December, on three-day cruises to Sausalito, San Joaquin River, Stockton, Sacramento River, Sacramento, Locke.

FROM SAVANNAH: The following ships sail from Savannah:

American Cruise Lines

Savannah: April to May and mid-November to mid-December, seven- and ten-day cruises to Charleston, Hilton Head Island, St. Simons Island, or 10-day cruises to St. Simons Island, Fernandina Beach, St. Augustine, Port Canaveral, Vero Beach, St. Lucie, Fort Myers.

America: Late November through March, on ten-day cruises to St. Simons Island, Fernandina Beach, St. Augustine, Port Canaveral, Vero Beach, St. Lucie, Fort Myers, returning on same route to Savannah; mid-April to June and in October, some 14-day positioning cruises to Baltimore via Beaufort, Charleston, Bucksport, Wrightsville, Morehead City, Belhaven, Coinjock, Great Bridge, Norfolk, Yorktown, Crisfield, Oxford, Annapolis, St. Michael's.

Clipper Cruise Line

Newport Clipper: Mid-April through mid-May and October through mid-December, to St. Simons Island, Beaufort, Charleston, Hilton Head; in December, a ten-day Inland Waterways cruise to Fort Lauderdale.

FROM WARREN, RHODE ISLAND: The following ships sail from Warren:

American Canadian Lines

New Shoreham II: Early June through early November, on 12-day cruises one-way to Tadoussac, Québec, via Narragansett Bay, Long Island Sound, Hudson River to Waterford, the Erie Canal to Little Falls, Oswego, Lake Ontario, the Thousand Islands, Prescott, Ontario, Montréal, Québec City, Saguenay River, and back to Montréal with bus return to Warren (reverse itinerary begins in Montréal); positioning cruise from Rhode Island to West Palm Beach (and vice versa in spring) via the Intracoastal Waterway with stops at Baltimore, Annapolis, Norfolk, Belhave, Wrights ville Beach, Georgetown, Charlestown, Beaufort, St. Simons Island, St. Augustine, Titusville, Jensen Beach; also four three-night sailings on the last weekends in June, July, August, and September to Newport, Martha's Vineyard, and Block Island.

Caribbean Prince: Mid-May through mid-November on either end of the season, two positioning cruises from West Palm Beach to Warren, R.I., through the Intracoastal Waterway, stopping at Norfolk, Baltimore, Charleston, Beaufort, St. Simons Island, St. Augustine, Titusville, Jensen Beach, and West Palm Beach (reverse in spring); followed by 12-day cruises from Warren to Long Island Sound, Hudson River to Troy, Little Falls, Oswego, Toronto, Niagara Falls, Welland Canal to Buffalo.

FROM DETROIT: The following ship sails from Detroit:

American Canadian Lines

Caribbean Prince: Mid-June to September, to Owen Sound via Alpena, Mackinac Island, North Channel, Algoma, Manitoulin Island, Georgia Bay to Owen Sound, with bus return to Detroit (or vice versa).

FROM WEST PALM BEACH: The following ships sail from West Palm Beach:

American Canadian Lines

Caribbean Prince: Early May, a 14-day positioning cruise to Jensen Beach, Titusville, St. Augustine, St. Simons Island, Beaufort, Charleston, Georgetown, Wrightsville Beach, Belhaven, Norfolk, Baltimore, Warren, R.I.

New Shoreham II: Late April, a 14-day positioning cruise to Jensen Beach, Titusville, St. Augustine, St. Simons Island, Beaufort, Charleston, Georgetown, Wrightsville Beach, Belhaven, Norfolk, Annapolis, Baltimore, Warren, R.I.

5. Hawaii

FROM HONOLULU: The following ships sail from Honolulu:

American Hawaii Cruises

Constitution: Saturdays, year round, to Hilo, Kona, Maui, Kauai, with an occasional seven-day trans-Pacific cruise in December to San Francisco and Los Angeles, returning to Honolulu.

Independence: Saturdays, year round, to Kaui, Hilo, Kona, and Maui, with an occasional July trans-Pacific cruise to San Francisco, returning to Honolulu.

6. Mexico

FROM LOS ANGELES: The following ships sail from Los Angeles:

Carnival Cruise Lines

Tropicale: Sundays, year round, on seven-day cruises to Puerto Vallarta, Mazatlán, Cabo San Lucas.

Cunard Lines

Cunard Princess: Alternate Saturdays, on seven-day cruises to Cabo San Lucas, Mazatlán, Puerto Vallarta, Manzanillo, Acapulco; returning alternate Sundays on seven-day cruises from Acapulco to Zihuatanejo, Puerto Vallarta, Mazatlán, Cabo San Lucas.

Eastern/Western Cruise Lines

Azure Seas: Mondays, year round, on four-day cruises to Enseñada; Fridays, year round, on three-day cruises to Enseñada.

P & O/Princess Cruise Lines

Pacific Princess: Alternate Saturdays, mid-September to June, on 7- or 14-day cruises (with occasional other-length voyages from San Francisco) to Cabo San Lucas, Mazatlán, Puerto Vallarta, Manzanillo, Acapulco; returning alternate Sundays on seven-day cruises from Acapulco to Ixtapa/Zihuatanejo, Puerto Vallarta, Mazatlán, Cabo San Lucas.

Island Princess: Alternate Saturdays from mid-September to June on 7- or 14-day cruises to Cabo San Lucas, Mazatlán, Puerto Vallarta, Manzanillo, Acapulco; returning via Ixtapa/Zihuatanejo, Puerto Vallarta, Mazatlán, Cabo San Lucas.

Sitmar Cruises

Fairsky: Late September to May, on 7- to 11-day cruises to Puerto Vallarta, Mazatlán, and Cabo San Lucas on seven-day voyages; to Guadalupe Island, Mazatlán, Acapulco, Zihuatanejo, Puerto Vallarta, and Cabo San Lucas on 10- and 11-day itineraries.

Fairsea: Late June to mid-September and through January on 7-, 10-, and 11-day cruises to Puerto Vallarta, Mazatlán, and Cabo San Lucas on shorter journeys; to Guadalupe Islands, Mazatlán, Acapulco, Zihuatanejo, Puerto Vallarta, and Cabo San Lucas on longer voyages.

FROM SAN DIEGO: The following ship sails from San Diego:

Princess Cruises

Pacific Princess: Saturdays from November to late April on seven-day cruises to Puerto Vallarta, Mazatlán and Cabo San Lucas; from May to November on Mediterranean cruises

FROM SAN FRANCISCO: The following ship sails from San Francisco:

Holland America Lines

Noordam: Alternate Saturdays, October through mid-May, on 7- or 14-day cruises to Cabo San Lucas, Puerto Vallarta, Ixtapa/Zihuatanejo, Acapulco, Puerto Vallarta, Mazatlán, Cabo San Lucas.

7. Transatlantic / Panama Canal / Pacific Ocean / Orient

Cunard Lines

Queen Elizabeth II: New York / Port Everglades / Los Angeles, about 89 days around the world, usually from mid-January; April through November, five-day transatlantic crossings New York–Southampton; early January, New York to Caribbean cruise to Port Everglades, Caracas, Curaçao, Panama Canal, Balboa, Acapulco, Los Angeles as segment of world cruise.

Cunard/Norwegian American Cruises

Sagafjord: Mid-January departure from Port Everglades on around-the-world cruise; several Caribbean sailings in late April from Port Everglades to St. Thomas, Santo Domingo, Cartagena, Cristóbal, through Panama Canal, Balboa, Acapulco, Mazatlán, Los Angeles on 17-day cruise.

Vistafjord: About January through March, 8- and 13-day cruises from Port Everglades to St. Croix, St. Barthélemny, St. Maarten, Cap-Haïtien; transatlantic crossing from Port Everglades to Europe, spending summer in Mediterranean.

Exploration Cruise Lines

Great Rivers Explorer: January to mid-April and November through December, from Balboa to Taboga, Pearl Islands, Contadora, Punta Alegre, through Panama Canal, Portobelo, San Blas Islands, to Colón.

Holland America Lines

Rotterdam: New York / Port Everglades 96 days around the world, from about January to April; April, on seven-day cruises from Port Everglades to St. Thomas, St. Maarten, Nassau; May through mid-June, trans–Panama Canal cruise to Vancouver; Thursdays, June through mid-September, seven-day cruises to Ketchikan, Juneau, Glacier Bay, Sitka.

P & O/Princess Cruise Lines

Sea Princess: Late January, Port Everglades 35-day cruise to Nassau, Montego Bay, Panama Canal, Balboa, Acapulco, San Francisco, Honolulu, Papeete, and Sydney; and continuing around the world, returning in summer to Mediterranean cruising.

Royal Princess: From September through mid-May 14- or 28-day Panama Canal cruises from Los Angeles to San Juan via Acapulco, Panama Canal, Columbia, Aruba, Martinique, St. Thomas, San Juan; returning from San Juan to Los Angeles via St. Thomas, Caracas, Curaçao, Panama Canal, Balboa, Acapulco, Cabo San Lucas.

Sun Princess: In May, 14-day cruise from San Juan to St. Thomas, Caracas, Curaçao, Panama Canal, Balboa, Acapulco, Cabo San Lucas, Los Angeles; reverse in October.

Royal Cruise Line

Royal Odyssey: From Miami to Acapulco in December on a nine-day cruise to Ocho Rios, Colombia, Panama Canal, Balboa, Costa Rica; several cruises in January and February for 11 days from Acapulco to Curaçao or reverse via Aruba, Cartagena, Panama Canal, Balboa, Costa Rica, Acapulco; from Acapulco to San Juan in February via Costa Rica, Panama Canal, Colombia, Aruba.

Royal Viking Lines

Royal Viking Sea: From New York (or Port Everglades) in late September and early November (with a Tahiti cruise in between) on 17- or 14- day cruise to Colombia, Panama Canal, Acapulco, Puerto Vallarta, Los Angeles, San Francisco; returning on same route except stops in Curaçao and St. Thomas; January through March, seven 14-day cruises from San Juan to Los Angeles through the Canal with approximately the same stops; followed by summer in British Isles and North Cape.

Royal Viking Sky: Mid-December, Port Everglades to San Juan, St. Thomas, Martinique, St. Vincent, Barbados, Curaçao, Colombia, Panama Canal, Acapulco, Zihuatanejo, Puerto Vallarta, Los Angels; continuing as around-the-world cruise.

Royal Viking Star: Late May, a 31-day cruise from Hong Kong to Shanghai, Dalian, Hsingang, Pusan, Nagasaki, Kobe, Yokohama, Honolulu, Lahaina, Los Angeles, San Francisco.

Sitmar Cruises

Fairsea: Late September to late December and February to mid-June, 7- or 14-day Los Angeles to Cabo San Lucas, and Acapulco for shorter journeys; continuing to Balboa, Panama Canal, San Blas Islands, Cartagena, Curaçao, St. Thomas, and San Juan for 14-day trips; returning same route.

World Explorer Cruises

Universe: Late April through late June, a 61-day cruise from San Francisco to Maui, Honolulu, Majuro, Saipan, Guam, Ponape, Honiara, Noumea, Suva, Tongatapu Island, Apip, Pago Pago, Rarotonga, Papeete, Bora Bora, Honolulu, Kauai, Vancouver.

American Cruise Lines

America/Independence/Savannah/American Eagle—

IN WINTER: Savannah–St. Simons Island–Fernandina Beach–Jacksonville Beach–St. Augustine–Port Canaveral–Vero Beach–Lake Okeechobee–Fort Myers and return same route.

IN SPRING: Baltimore–St. Michaels–Oxford–Cambridge–Yorktown–Crisfield–Annapolis–Baltimore

IN SUMMER AND FALL: Haddam, Conn.–Block Island–Martha's Vineyard–Nantucket–New Bedford–Newport–Haddam *Or:* Haddam–Boothbay–Rockland–Camden–Belfast–Castine–Bar Harbor–Haddam

American Canadian Line

New Shoreham II—

IN SUMMER: Warren, R.I.–Newport–Martha's Vineyard–Block Island–Warren *Or:* Warren–New York–Waterford–Oswego–Saguenay River–Prescott–Montreal–Quebec City–Tadoussac

IN WINTER: Nassau–Spanish Wells–South Palmetto Point–Eleuthera Bluffs–Governor's Harbour–Cape Eleuthera–Exuma Sound–Sampson's Cay–Staniel Cay–Hall's Pond Cay–Highbourne Cay–Nassau *Or:* Nassau–Spanish Wells–Lanyard Cay–Little Harbour–Hopetown–Green Turtle Cay–Treasure Cay–Man 'O War Cay–Marsh Harbour–Walker's Cay–Freeport–Nassau

Caribbean Prince—

IN WINTER: Montego Bay–Orange Bay–Savannah La Mar–Black River–Carlyle Bay–Port Royal–Kingston Market–Port Morant–Port Antonio–Port Maria–Ocho Rios–Discovery Bay–Montego Bay

IN SUMMER: Warren, R.I.–Hudson River–Toronto–Niagara Falls–Buffalo–Detroit–Alpena–Mackinac Island–North Channel–Algoma–Manitoulin Island–Georgian Bay–Owen Sound–Detroit and return same route

American Hawaii Lines

Constitution—Honolulu–Hilo–Kona–Maui–Kauai–Honolulu Occasionally trans-Pacific cruises from San Francisco and Los Angeles year-round

Independence—Honolulu–Kauai–Hilo–Kona–Maui–Honolulu Occasionally trans-Pacific cruises from San Francisco and Los Angeles year-round

Bahama Cruise Line

Bahama Star—

IN SUMMER: New York–Bermuda–New York

IN WINTER: New Orleans–Cozumel–Cancun–New Orleans

Veracruz—

IN SUMMER: New York–New Bedford–Cape Cod Canal–Sydney–Saguenay Fjord–Quebec City–Montreal and return same route; occasionally other stops

IN WINTER: Tampa–Playa del Carmen–Cozumel–Key West–Tampa

Carnival Cruise Lines

Carnivale—Miami–Nassau–Miami or Miami–Freeport–Nassau–Miami year-round

Festivale—Miami–Nassau–San Juan–St. Thomas–Miami year-round

Mardi Gras—Miami–Cozumel–Grand Cayman–Ocho Rios–Miami year-round

Tropicale—Los Angeles–Puerto Vallarta–Mazatlán–cruising by Cabo San Lucas–Los Angeles year-round

Chandris

Britanis—

IN WINTER: Miami–Nassau–Miami or Miami–Cozumel–Cancun–Key West–Miami

IN SUMMER: New York–Bermuda

Victoria—San Juan–St. Thomas–Martinique–Grenada–La Guaira (Caracas)–Curaçao–San Juan year-round

Clipper Cruise Lines

Newport Clipper—

IN SUMMER: Boston–Plymouth–Nantucket–Martha's Vineyard–Newport–New Bedford–Boston

IN SPRING AND FALL: Baltimore–Yorktown–Crisfield–Oxford–St. Michaels–Annapolis–Baltimore

IN WINTER: St. Thomas–Tortola–Virgin Gorda–Jost Van Dyke–St. John–St. Thomas

Commodore Cruise Line

Boheme (Commodore Cruise Line)—St. Petersburg–Port Antonio–Grand Cayman–St. Petersburg year-round

Carib I—Miami–St. Thomas–San Juan–Puerto Plata–Miami year-round

Costa Cruises

Carla Costa—San Juan–Curaçao–La Guaira (Caracas)–St. Vincent–Guadeloupe–St. Thomas–San Juan year-round

Daphne—

IN WINTER: San Juan–St. Maarten–Martinique–Barbados–St. Lucia–St. Thomas–San Juan

IN SUMMER: Vancouver–Wrangell–Endicott Arm Fjord–Juneau–Skagway–Davidson and Rainbow Glacier–Ketchikan–Vancouver

Cunard

Cunard Countess—San Juan–La Guaira (Caracas)–Grenada–Barbados–Fort de France–St. Thomas–San Juan or San Juan–Tortola, Nevis–St. Kitts–Guadeloupe–St. Lucia–St. Maarten–St. Thomas–San Juan year-round

Cunard Princess—

IN SUMMER: Vancouver–Alert Bay–Ketchikan–Tracy Arm–Juneau–Skagway–Haines–Glacier Bay–Petersburg–Ketchikan

IN WINTER: Los Angeles–cruising by Cabo San Lucas–Mazatlán–Puerto Vallarta–Manzanillo–Acapulco–Zihuatanejo–Puerto Vallarta–Mazatlán–cruising by Cabo San Lucas–Los Angeles

Queen Elizabeth II—

IN SUMMER: New York–England

IN WINTER: World cruise from New York, For Lauderdale and Los Angeles and some Fort Lauderdale–Caribbean cruises

IN SPRING/FALL: New York or Fort Lauderdale to various Caribbean islands

Cunard/Norwegian American Cruises

Sagafjord—

IN WINTER: Transcanal cruise from Los Angeles to Fort Lauderdale and return followed by world cruise

IN SPRING: Los Angeles–Fort Lauderdale and return and Los Angeles–New Orleans and return

IN SUMMER: San Francisco–Victoria–Alert Bay–Ketchikan–Endicott Arm–Juneau–Columbia Glacier–Whittier–Yakutat Bay–Hubbard Glacier–Sitka–Vancouver–San Francisco

IN FALL: San Francisco–Far East

Vistafjord—

IN WINTER: Fort Lauderdale–Santo Domingo–St. Vincent–Bridgetown–Antigua–Tortola–St. Thomas–San Juan–Fort Lauderdale

IN SPRING: Fort Lauderdale–Mediterranean

IN FALL: Fort Lauderdale–St. Croix–St. Maarten–Martinique–Devil's Island–Fortaleza–Salvador de Bahia–Rio de Janeiro and return

IN SUMMER: Mediterranean cruises

Delta Queen Steamboat Co.

Delta Queen—

IN SUMMER: New Orleans–various cities along the Mississippi and Ohio Rivers

IN WINTER: New Orleans–Houmas House–Baton Rouge–Natchez–St. Francisville–New Orleans

Mississippi Queen—

IN SUMMER: New Orleans–various cities along the Mississippi and Ohio Rivers

IN WINTER: New Orleans–Houmas House–Baton Rouge–Natchez–St. Francisville–New Orleans

Eastern/Western Cruises

Azure Seas—Los Angeles–Enseñada–San Diego–Los Angeles or Los Angeles–Enseñada–Los Angeles year-round

Emerald Seas—Miami–Nassau–Bahamian Private Island–Freeport or Miami–Nassau–Bahamian Private Island–Miami year-round

Exploration Cruise Lines

Pacific Northwest Explorer—

IN SPRING AND FALL: San Francisco–Sausalito–San Joaquin River–Stockton–Sacramento River–Sacramento–Locke–San Francisco

IN SUMMER: Portland–Columbia River–Astoria–Bonneville Dam–The Dalles–Snake River–through several dams–Lewiston–Kennewick–Multnomah Falls–Portland

IN WINTER: not in service

Great Rivers Explorer—

IN SPRING AND FALL: Portland–Columbia River–Astoria–Bonneville Dam–The Dalles–Snake River–through several dams–Lewiston–Kennewick–Multnomah Falls–Portland

IN WINTER: Balboa–Panama Canal–Colon

Majestic Alaska Explorer—

IN SUMMER: Ketchikan–Misty Fjord–Wrangell–Sitka–Tracy Arm–Juneau–Skagway–Haines–Glacier Bay–Petersburg–Ketchikan

IN WINTER: Cruises from Tahiti

Glacier Bay Explorer—

IN SUMMER: Ketchikan–Misty Fjord–Wrangell–Sitka–Tracy Arm–Juneau–Skagway–Haines–Glacier Bay–Petersburg–Ketchikan

IN WINTER: not in service

Home Lines

Oceanic—

IN SUMMER: New York–Bermuda–Nassau–New York

IN WINTER: Fort Lauderdale–San Juan–St. Thomas–St. Maarten; occasionally Antigua, St. Kitts

Atlantic—

IN SUMMER: New York–Bermuda–New York

IN WINTER: Fort Lauderdale–Caribbean on varying itineraries including San Juan, St. Thomas, Cozumel, Grand Cayman, Ocho Rios, San Andres Islands, Cristobal, St. Kitts, Nevis, St. Maarten, Curaçao

Norwegian Caribbean Lines

Norway—Miami–St. Thomas–Nassau–Private Bahamian Island–Miami year-round

Skyward—Miami–Cancun–Cozumel–Key West–Private Bahamian Island—Miami year-round

Southward—Miami–Puerto Plata–St. Thomas–San Juan–Miami year-round

Starward—Miami–Private Bahamian Island–Ocho Rios–Grand Cayman–Cozumel–Miami year-round

Sunward II—Miami–Nassau–Private Bahamian Island–Miami *Or* Miami–Nassau–Private Bahamian Island–Freeport–Miami year-round

Paquet Cruises

Dolphin—Miami–Nassau–Miami or Miami–Nassau–Freeport–Miami year-round

Mermoz—

IN WINTER: San Juan–St. Croix–Guadeloupe–Trinidad–St. Lucia–Iles des Saintes–Martinique–Iles des Saintes–St. Thomas–San Juan *Or* San Juan–St. Bart's–Guadeloupe–Curaçao–La Guaira (Caracas)–Barbados–Martinique–Antigua–St. John–San Juan

IN SUMMER: Mediterranean cruises

Rhapsody—

IN WINTER: Miami–Ocho Rios–Grand Cayman–Playa del Carmen–Cozumel–Miami

IN SUMMER: Vancouver–Juneau–Skagway–Glacier Bay–Ketchikan–Vancouver

Premier Cruise Line

Royale—Port Canaveral–Nassau–Andros (Bahamas)–Port Canaveral Or Port Canaveral–Nassau–Andros (Bahamas)–Port Canaveral year-round

P & O/Princess Cruises

Island Princess—

IN SUMMER: San Francisco–Vancouver–Prince Rupert–Juneau–Skagway–Glacier Bay–Sitka–Victoria–San Francisco

IN WINTER: Los Angeles–cruising by Cabo San Lucas–Mazatlán–Puerto Vallarta–Manzanillo–Acapulco–Zihuatanejo–Puerto Vallarta-Mazatlán–cruising by Cabo San Lucas–Los Angeles

Pacific Princess (Princess Lines)—

IN SPRING/SUMMER: Mediterranean cruises

IN FALL AND WINTER: San Diego–Puerto Vallarta–Mazatlán–Cabo San Lucas–San Diego

Royal Princess (Princess Lines)—

IN SUMMER: Vancouver–Juneau–Skagway–Glacier Bay–Sitka–Vancouver

IN WINTER: Los Angeles–Acapulco–Panama Canal–Cartagena–Aruba–Martinique–St. Thomas–San Juan, returning same route to Los Angeles

Sun Princess (Princess Lines)—

IN SUMMER: Vancouver–Juneau–Skagway–Glacier Bay–Misty Fjord–Vancouver

IN WINTER: San Juan–Barbados–Grenadines–Martinique–St. Maarten–St. Thomas–San Juan *Or* San Juan–Curaçao–La Guaira (Caracas)–Grenadines–Martinique–St. Thomas

Royal Cruise Line

Royal Odyssey—

IN WINTER: Miami–Ocho Rios–Cartagena–San Blas Islands–Panama

Canal–Balboa–Costa Rica–Acapulco *Or* Acapulco–Costa Rica–Panama Canal–Cartagena–Aruba–Curaçao and return same route

IN SUMMER: Mediterranean and Scandinavian cruises

Royal Viking Line

Royal Viking Sky—

IN FALL: New York–Nantucket–Cape Cod Canal–Charlottetown–St. Lawrence River–Saguenay River–Montreal–Quebec City–Bar Harbor–Boston–Newport

IN WINTER: Fort Lauderdale–St. Thomas–Curaçao–Cartagena–Cristobal–Panama Canal–Balboa–Acapulco–Zihuatanejo–Puerto Vallarta–Los Angeles–San Francisco and return

IN WINTER/SPRING: World cruise

IN SUMMER: Mediterranean and Scandinavian cruises

Royal Viking Star—

IN SUMMER: Vancouver–Juneau–Skagway–Glacier Bay–Sitka–Victoria

IN FALL: San Francisco–Far East

IN WINTER/SPRING: South Pacific and Orient cruises

Royal Caribbean Cruise Lines

Nordic Prince—Miami–St. Croix–Martinique–Barbados–Antigua–St. Thomas–Miami or reverse *Or* Miami–Nassau–San Juan–St. Thomas year-round

Song of America—Miami–Nassau–San Juan–St. Thomas–Miami year-round

Song of Norway—Miami–Grand Cayman–Montego Bay–Playa del Carmen–Cozumel–Miami year-round

Sun Viking—Miami–Ocho Rios–Curaçao–La Guaira (Caracas)–Barbados–Martinique–St. Martin–San Juan–St. Thomas–Miami year-round

Scandinavian World Cruises

Scandinavian Sun—Miami–Freeport–Miami year-round

Sea Goddess Cruises

Sea Goddess—

IN WINTER: St. Croix–The Baths–Gorda Sound–St. Maarten–St. Lucia–Mustique–Guadeloupe–Isles des Saintes–Guadeloupe–Antigue–St. Barthelemy

IN SUMMER: Mediterranean cruises

Sitmar Cruises

Fairsea—

IN SUMMER: Los Angeles–cruising by Guadalupe Island–Mazatlán–Acapulco–Zihuatanejo–Puerto Vallarta–Cabo San Lucas–Los Angeles

IN WINTER: Los Angeles–Cabo San Lucas–Acapulco–Balboa–Panama

Canal–San Blas Islands–Cartagena–Curaçao–St. Thomas–San Juan, returning same route

Fairsky—

IN SUMMER: San Francisco–Victoria–Johnstone Strait–Prince Rupert–Ketchikan–Juneau–Lynn Canal–Haines–Skagway–Glacier Bay–La Perouse Glacier–Sitka–Victoria–Astoria–San Francisco

IN WINTER: Los Angeles–cruising by Guadalupe Islands–Mazatlán–Acapulco–Zihuatanejo–Puerto Vallarta–Cabo San Lucas–Los Angeles

Fairwind—Fort Lauderdale–Grand Cayman–Montego Bay–Panama Canal transit–San Blas Islands–Cartagena–Nassau *Or* Fort Lauderdale–Curaçao–La Guaira (Caracas)–Martinique–St. Thomas–St. John–Nassau (some cruises stop in Antigua, Barbados)

Sun Lines

Stella Oceanis—

IN WINTER: San Juan–St. Maarten–Martinique–St. Lucia–Barbados–Tobago–Orinoco River–Ciudad Guayana–Bequia–St. Vincent–Guadeloupe–Antigua–St. Kitts–St. Thomas–San Juan

IN SUMMER: Mediterranean cruises

Stella Solaris—

IN WINTER: Fort Lauderdale–St. Thomas–St. Barthelemy–St. Maarten–St. Lucia–Barbados–Fortaleza–Salvador–Rio de Janeiro–Salvador–Fortaleza–Tobago–Martinique–St. Thomas–Fort Lauderdale

IN SUMMER: Mediterranean cruises

Sundance Cruises

Sun Dancer—

IN SUMMER: Vancouver–Juneau–Haines and/or Skagway–Tracy Arm–Ketchikan–Misty Fjord–Alert Bay–Vancouver

IN WINTER: Los Angeles–Puerto Vallarta–Mazatlán–Cabo San Lucas–Los Angeles

Westours/Holland America Cruises

Nieuw Amsterdam—

IN SUMMER: Vancouver–Ketchikan–Juneau–Glacier Bay–Sitka–Vancouver

IN WINTER: Tampa–Playa del Carmen–Cozumel–Montego Bay–Grand Cayman–Tampa

Noordam—

IN SUMMER: Vancouver–Ketchikan–Juneau–Glacier Bay–Sitka–Vancouver

IN WINTER: San Francisco–cruising by Cabo San Lucas–Puerto Vallarta-Zihuatanejo/Ixtapa–Acapulco–Puerto Vallarta–Mazatlán–Cabo San Lucas–San Francisco

Rotterdam—

IN SUMMER: Vancouver–Ketchikan–Juneau–Glacier Bay–Sitka–Vancouver

IN SPRING AND FALL: Fort Lauderdale–St. Maarten–St. Thomas–Nassau–Fort Lauderdale

IN WINTER: World cruise from New York, Fort Lauderdale and Los Angeles

World Explorer

Universe—

IN SUMMER: Vancouver-Prince Rupert-Sitka-Skagway-Yakutat-Columbia Glacier-Whittier-Valdez-Juneau-Glacier Bay-Ketchikan-Vancouver

IN WINTER: San Francisco-South Pacific-San Francisco

NOW, SAVE MONEY ON ALL YOUR TRAVELS!

Join Arthur Frommer's $25-A-Day Travel Club

Saving money while traveling is never a simple matter, which is why, over 22 years ago, the **$25-A-Day Travel Club** was formed. Actually, the idea came from readers of the Arthur Frommer Publications who felt that such an organization could bring financial benefits, continuing travel information, and a sense of community to economy-minded travelers all over the world.

In keeping with the money-saving concept, the annual membership fee is low—$15 (U.S. residents) or $18 (Canadian, Mexican, and foreign residents)—and is immediately exceeded by the value of your benefits which include:

(1) The latest edition of any TWO of the books listed on the following page.

(2) An annual subscription to an 8-page quarterly newspaper *The Wonderful World of Budget Travel* which keeps you up-to-date on fastbreaking developments in low-cost travel in all parts of the world—bringing you the kind of information you'd have to pay over $25 a year to obtain elsewhere. This consumer-conscious publication also includes the following columns:

Travelers' Directory—members all over the world who are willing to provide hospitality to other members as they pass through their home cities.

Share-a-Trip—requests from members for travel companions who can share costs and help avoid the burdensome single supplement.

Readers Ask . . . Readers Reply—travel questions from members to which other members reply with authentic firsthand information.

(3) A copy of *Arthur Frommer's Guide to New York.*

(4) Your personal membership card which entitles you to purchase through the Club all Arthur Frommer Publications for a third to a half off their regular retail prices during the term of your membership.

So why not join this hardy band of international budgeteers NOW and participate in its exchange of information and hospitality? Simply send $15 (U.S. residents) or $18 U.S. (Canadian, Mexican, and other foreign residents) along with your name and address to: $25-A-Day Travel Club, Inc., 1230 Avenue of the Americas, New York, NY 10020. Remember to specify which *two* of the books in section (1) above you wish to receive in your initial package of members' benefits. Or tear out this page, check off any two books on the opposite side and send it to us with your membership fee.